Decline and Fall of All Evil

The Most Important Discovery of Our Times

Seymour Lessans

Compiled and edited by Janis Rafael

Safeworld Publishing Company
www.declineandfallofallevil.com

Summary: Many theories as to how world peace could be achieved have been proposed, yet war has once again taken its deadly toll in the 21st century. The dream of peace has remained an unattainable goal — until now. The following pages reveal a scientific discovery regarding a psychological law of man's nature never before understood. This finding was hidden so successfully behind layers and layers of dogma and misunderstanding that no one knew a deeper truth existed. Once this natural law becomes a permanent condition of the environment, it will allow mankind, for the very first time, to veer in a different direction — preventing the never-ending cycle of hurt and retaliation in human relations. Although this discovery was borne out of philosophical thought, it is factual, not theoretical, in nature.

Printed in the United States of America

Publisher's Cataloging-In-Publication Data
(Prepared by the Donohue Group, Inc.)

Lessans, Seymour
    Decline and fall of all evil : the most important discovery of our times /Seymour Lessans; compiled and edited by Janis Rafael.

        p. ; cm.

    ISBN: 978-0-692-31827-0 (softcover)
    ISBN: 978-0-578-15130-4 (e-book)

1. Philosophy--Free will and determinism. 2. Good and evil.   3. Peace-- Psychological aspects. 4. Interpersonal relations. 5. Psychology--Popular works. 6. Lessans, Seymour –Philosophy. I. Rafael, Janis. II. Title.

BJ1401 .L47 2015
170
2014955475

Safeworld Publishing Company

TO ALL MANKIND

To truth only a brief celebration is allowed between the two long periods during which it is condemned as paradoxical, or disparaged as trivial.

Schopenhauer

Interpretation: Many things we accept today as fact were ridiculed and opposed in the not so distant past; this goes to show that just because an idea is unpopular now doesn't mean it won't be unilaterally accepted in the future.

"All great truths begin as blasphemies."

George Bernard Shaw

This is the most fantastic non-fiction book ever written because it will verify the prediction made in the introduction by producing unbelievable changes in human relations in the next 25 years. By discovering the invariable laws of the solar system we were able to predict an eclipse and land men on the moon. By discovering the invariable laws that inhere in the mankind system we are able, for the very first time, to predict and accomplish what was never before possible — our deliverance from evil.

Please understand that when the 20th century is mentioned, it is referring to the time period when this finding was first uncovered. The prediction that in 25 years man would be delivered from all evil was based on the conviction that a thorough investigation would have already taken place. Although it has been more than 60 years, there has been no such investigation and, to this day, this discovery remains in obscurity. Due to the time lapse since the book's last printing some recent examples have been added to show how these principles apply to our current world situation, but please be assured that the actual discovery has not been altered in any way and is explained in the author's own words. Although some of his references are dated, the knowledge itself couldn't be more timely. For purposes of consistency the personal pronoun 'he' has been used throughout the book. No discrimination was intended.

Note: Twelve years after the author's passing, his daughter, Janis Rafael, went on a mission to compile her father's seven books in the hope that this discovery will not be lost to future generations.

Some people may be offended that the word God is used throughout the book and conclude that this is a religious work. Perhaps the 'G' word even makes them want to shut down and disconnect from what is being said. This would be unfortunate. As you carefully read the text you will see that the word God (often referred to as 'He') is simply a symbol pointing to the laws that govern our universe.

Table of Contents

PREFACE

My dear friends, relations, and people throughout the earth, the purpose of this book is to clarify knowledge that must be brought to light as quickly as possible because it can prevent what nobody wants — a nuclear holocaust. With the world in turmoil and on the threshold of an atomic explosion which could be started accidentally and could very well destroy all civilization, I am announcing a scientific discovery that will make war an absolute impossibility and revolutionize the life of man entirely for his benefit. Due to a fantastic breakthrough, to the discovery of a natural, psychological law that was hermetically sealed behind a logical theory that 98% of mankind holds true, every bit of hurt that exists in human relations can be virtually wiped from the face of the earth by something so superior to punishment, as a deterrent, that people the world over will be prevented from committing those very acts of evil for which blame and punishment were previously necessary. Laugh if you will but your smile of incredulity will be wiped from your face once you begin to read the text chapter by chapter of which the first two are most fundamental.

It is important to know that this book does not contain a theory but an undeniable equation that can be scientifically proven. It has no biases, prejudices or ulterior motives — its only concern is in revealing facts about the nature of man never before understood. Furthermore, so as to prevent jumping to conclusions, this book has nothing whatever to do with communism, socialism, capitalism, government, or religion; only with the removal of inaccurate facts that have been passed along from generation to generation in the guise of genuine knowledge. There are those who may be blinded by this mathematical revelation as they come out of Plato's cave having lived so many years in the shadows that distorted their beliefs into a semblance of reality — and may deny what they do not understand or don't want to be true. Just bear in mind that any disagreement can be clarified in such a manner that they will be compelled to say, "Now I understand and agree." I am about to demonstrate, in a manner our world's leading scientists will be unable to deny, not only that the mankind system is just as harmonious as the solar system despite all the evil and ignorance that ever existed, but that the inception of the Golden Age cannot commence until the knowledge pertaining to this law is accurately understood. What is about to be revealed is unprecedented. Soon enough everyone will know, without reservation, that mankind is on the threshold of a NEW WORLD prophesied in the Bible that must come to pass out of absolute necessity when this natural law is stamped by the exact sciences with the brevet of truth.

In view of the fact that the first two chapters must be read thoroughly before any other reading is done, it is my hope that the table of contents will not tempt you to read in a desultory manner. Should you jump ahead and read other chapters this work could appear like a fairy tale otherwise the statement that truth is stranger than fiction will be amply verified by the scientific world, or by yourself, if you are able to follow the reasoning of mathematical relations. If you find the first two chapters difficult, don't be discouraged because what follows will help you understand it much better the second time around. This book was written in a dialogue format to anticipate the questions the reader may have and to make these fairly difficult concepts as reader-friendly as possible. There is a certain amount of repetition for the purpose of reinforcing important points and extending the principles in a more cohesive fashion, but despite all efforts to make this work easier to understand it is still deep and will require that you go at a snail's pace reading many things over and over again. When you have fully grasped the full significance and magnitude of this work, and further realize there has never been and will never be another like it because of what is undeniably achieved, you will cherish it throughout your entire life.

Well, would you like to see what happens when science, the perception and extension of undeniable observations, takes over the problems of human conflict as the result of a fantastic discovery? Would you like to see that the mankind system has been obeying an invariable law just as mathematically harmonious as that which inheres in the solar system; a law that allowed a prophesy to be made thousands of years ago and verified in the 20th century? Would you like to learn, though this book has nothing whatever to do with religion or philosophy, that your faith in God will finally be rewarded with a virtual miracle, one that will shortly deliver us from all evil? If you are sincerely interested in seeing this fantastic transition to a new way of life which must come about the moment this discovery is thoroughly understood, all I ask is that you do not judge what you are about to read in terms of your present knowledge but do everything in your power to understand what is written by following the mathematical relations implicitly expressed throughout. Please remember that any truth revealed in a mathematical manner does not require your approval for its validity, although it does necessitate your understanding for recognition and development. And now my friends, if you care to come along, let us embark...the hour is getting late.

INTRODUCTION

Who, in his right mind or with knowledge of history would believe it possible that the 20th century will be the time when all war, crime, and every form of evil or hurt in human relations must come to a permanent end? [Note: This is a reminder that the author lived in the 20th century (1918-1991). Though we are well into the 21st century, this discovery has yet to be given a thorough investigation by our world's leading scientists]. When first hearing this prophesy, shortly after Hitler had slaughtered 6 million Jews, I laughed with contempt because nothing appeared more ridiculous than such a statement. But after 15 years (8 hours a day) of extensive reading and thinking, my dissatisfaction with a certain theory that had gotten a dogmatic hold on the mind compelled me to spend nine strenuous months in the deepest analysis and I made a finding that was so difficult to believe it took me two years to thoroughly understand its full significance for all mankind and three additional years to put it into the kind of language others could comprehend. It is the purpose of this book to reveal this finding — a scientific discovery about the nature of man whose life, as a direct consequence of this mathematical revelation, will be completely revolutionized in every way for his benefit bringing about a transition so utterly amazing that if I were to tell you of all the changes soon to unfold, without demonstrating the cause as to why these must come about, your skepticism would be aroused sufficiently to consider this a work of science fiction for who would believe it possible that all evil (every bit of hurt that exists in human relation) must decline and fall the very moment this discovery is thoroughly understood. This natural law, which reveals a fantastic mankind system, was hidden so successfully behind a camouflage of ostensible truths that it is no wonder the development of our present age was required to find it. By discovering this well concealed law and demonstrating its power a catalyst, so to speak, is introduced into human relations that compels a fantastic change in the direction our nature has been traveling, performing what will be called miracles though they do not transcend the laws of

1

nature. The same nature that permits the most heinous crimes, and all the other evils of human relation, is going to veer so sharply in a different direction that all nations on this planet, once the leaders and their subordinates understand the principles involved, will unite in such a way that no more wars will ever again be possible. If this is difficult to conceive, does it mean you have a desire to dismiss what I have to say as nonsense? If it does, then you have done what I tried to prevent, that is, jumped to a premature conclusion. And the reason must be that you judged such a permanent solution as impossible and therefore not deserving of further consideration, which is a normal reaction, if anything, when my claims are analyzed and compared to our present understanding of human nature. War seems to be an inescapable feature of the human condition which can only be subdued, not eradicated. But we must insert a question mark between the empirical fact that a feature is characteristic of human life as we know it, and the empirical claim that this feature is a sociological inevitability. Another reason that war is viewed as an unfortunate and intractable aspect of human existence is due to suffering itself, which sadly robs its victims of the ability to dream or have the breadth of vision to even contemplate the possibility of peace. The evil in the world has so constricted man's imagination that his mind has become hardened, and he shows contempt for anyone who dares to offer a solution because such claims appear ludicrous and unfounded.

Down through history there has always been this skepticism before certain events were proven true. It is only natural to be skeptical, but this is never a sufficient reason to exclude the possibility of a scientific miracle. You may reason that many people have been positive that they were right but it turned out they were wrong, so couldn't I also be positive and wrong? There is a fallacious standard hidden in this reasoning. Because others were positive and wrong, I could be wrong because I am positive. The first astronomer who observed the mathematical laws inherent in the solar system that enabled him to predict an eclipse was positive and right, as well as the space scientist who foretold that one day man would land on the moon. Edison when he first discovered the electric bulb was positive and right. Einstein when he revealed the potential of atomic energy was positive and right

— and so were many other scientists — but they proved that they were right with an undeniable demonstration, which is what I am doing. If my demonstration doesn't prove me right, then and then only am I wrong. There is quite a difference between being positive or dogmatic over knowledge that is questionable and being positive over something that is undeniable such as two plus two equals four. Just bear in mind how many times in the course of history has the impossible (that which appeared to be) been made possible by scientific discoveries which should make you desire to contain your skepticism enough to investigate what this is all about.

If you recall, in the 19th century Gregor Mendel made a discovery in the field of heredity. He was unable to present his findings because there was an established theory already being taught as true. The professors he contacted had their own theories and they concluded that it was impossible for him to have discovered anything new since he was nothing in comparison to them. If these professors had taken the time to scientifically investigate his claims they would have found that he was correct and they were mistaken, but this would have made them the laughingstock of the entire student world. In the end it was Nageli, the leading authority of his time, whose pride refused to let him investigate Mendel whom he judged a semi-amateur because he regarded as impossible the very core of Mendel's discovery. He was wrong as history recorded and though Mendel was compelled to receive posthumous recognition for the law he discovered, he is now considered the father of modern genetics and Nageli, a footnote. History has recorded innumerable stories of a like nature, but is it necessary that the pattern continue? Isn't it obvious that if such a discovery exists, and it does, and you deny the possibility, you are setting yourselves up as infallible gods among men, just as our intellectual ancestors did when they prematurely rejected the discovery of Gregor Mendel? Can't you be the ones to confirm the discovery? Must it be others, long after we are dead?

People have often questioned, "Well assuming that you did make a fantastic discovery, why bring it to me? You should run to the nearest university so it can be acknowledged. Then you would be acclaimed a genius and become famous the world over."

"That's exactly what I did but when one professor heard my claims he smiled and lost all interest. Another used a method for screening out the wrong applicants for such a discovery. He immediately questioned my educational background and wanted to know from what university I graduated, to which I replied, "I have no formal education because I never completed the 7th grade." Then without giving me a chance to tell him that my informal education was far superior to his formal education he responded without giving much thought to what he was about to say, 'And you dare to come in here with such outrageous claims about solving all the problems of human relation!'"

"I couldn't believe my ears, and my blood was beginning to boil."

"Well tell me," I said, trying to control myself, "What is your formal education?"

"I graduated from Harvard with many honors and credentials."

I then inquired, "With all your formal education, your honors, your degrees and diplomas, what discoveries have you made to solve the problems plaguing mankind?" There was no answer and he hung up.

After that I was completely frustrated. Did you ever hear of anything so insulting, as if a discovery could not be made unless someone graduates college first? Which of these universities taught Newton, Edison, or Einstein, or did they perceive relations their professors were unable to understand until explained to them? Instead of being centers of investigation where new knowledge can be thoroughly analyzed, the professors use what they have been taught as a standard of truth from which vantage point they survey the landscape of divergent views for the sole purpose of criticism and disagreement. Isn't this a perfect example of putting the proverbial cart before the horse, which should be a lesson to all professors that they should never become so dogmatic about their theories or opinions that they won't take the time to investigate anything that might lead to the truth.

Unbeknownst to the highest ranking scholars, the universities have been handing along from generation to generation conceptions, not verified knowledge, that will be exploded once certain undeniable relations are perceived and pointed out to man's common sense. Now let me make something very clear. To teach that $2+2=4$ doesn't depend for its truth on who is doing the teaching because the one

4

being taught can perceive this undeniable relation. But when the relation revealing any truth is not obvious or difficult to grasp, or fallaciously logical, or logically inaccurate, then its acceptance depends more on who is doing the teaching and the long tenure of its existence rather than on what is being taught. For example, if students, who cannot perceive undeniable relations, are taught by their professor that 3 is to 6 as 4 is to 9 because he also cannot perceive this is false, they will be compelled to reject your explanation of it being 8 because they compare the rank of the teacher and the long tenure of what is taught with your upstart disagreement. Who are you to disagree with these distinguished professors? Everywhere you look people are using fallacious standards to judge the truth. To further illustrate this I recently gave a math problem to a student of mathematics. I asked this person if it was possible to arrange 105 alphabetical squares divided equally between A and O into groups of 3 so that each of the 15 different letters on a line and in all 35 groups would never be twice with any other letter. Since he assumed that I did not know the answer, he worked on the problem to find out if he thought it could be solved. After two weeks and feeling inadequate to the task, he responded, "My own personal opinion is that it cannot be done, however, I'm not an expert but my professor is. I'll give it to him." "By the way," he inquired (using the same fallacious standard as the Harvard graduate), "did you ever study higher mathematics in one of the universities, and if you didn't, how far did you go in school?" Once again I replied, "Only to the 7th grade." He then took the problem to his professor with this knowledge of the 7th grade and after another two weeks told me very positively that his professor said it could not be done, which is absolutely false.

In order for this discovery to be adequately understood the reader must not apply himself and his ideas as a standard of what is true and false, but understand the difference between a mathematical relation and an opinion, belief, or theory. The mind of man is so utterly confused with words that it will require painstaking clarification to clear away the logical cobwebs of ignorance that have accumulated through the years. For purposes of clarification please note that the words 'scientific' and 'mathematical' only mean 'undeniable', and are interchanged throughout the text. The reasoning in this work is not

5

a form of logic, nor is it my opinion of the answer; it is mathematical, scientific, and undeniable, and it is not necessary to deal in what has been termed the 'exact sciences' in order to be exact and scientific. Consequently, it is imperative to know that this demonstration will be like a game of chess in which every one of your moves will be forced and checkmate inevitable but only if you don't make up your own rules as to what is true and false which will only delay the very life you want for yourself. The laws of this universe, which include those of our nature, are the rules of the game and the only thing required to win, to bring about this Golden Age that will benefit everyone... is to stick to the rules. But if you decide to move the king like the queen because it does not satisfy you to see a pet belief slipping away or because it irritates your pride to be proven wrong or checkmated then it is obvious that you are not sincerely concerned with learning the truth, but only with retaining your doctrines at all cost. However, when it is scientifically revealed that the very things religion, government, education and all others want, which include the means as well as the end, are prevented from becoming a reality only because we have not penetrated deeply enough into a thorough understanding of our ultimate nature, are we given a choice as to the direction we are compelled to travel even though this means the relinquishing of ideas that have been part of our thinking since time immemorial? This discovery will be presented in a step by step fashion that brooks no opposition and your awareness of this matter will preclude the possibility of someone adducing his rank, title, affiliation, or the long tenure of an accepted belief as a standard from which he thinks he qualifies to disagree with knowledge that contains within itself undeniable proof of its veracity. In other words, your background, the color of your skin, your religion, the number of years you went to school, how many titles you hold, your I.Q., your country, what you do for a living, your being some kind of expert like Nageli (or anything else you care to throw in) has no relation whatsoever to the undeniable knowledge that 3 is to 6 what 4 is to 8. So please don't be too hasty in using what you have been taught as a standard to judge what has not even been revealed to you yet. If you should decide to give me the benefit of the doubt — deny it — and two other discoveries to be revealed, if you can.

In his book "Alternative Science, Challenging the Myths of the Scientific Establishment" Richard Milton writes: "We are living in a time of rising academic intolerance in which important new discoveries in physics, medicine, and biology are being ridiculed and rejected for reasons that are not scientific. Something precious and irreplaceable is under attack. Our academic liberty — our freedom of thought — is being threatened by an establishment that chooses to turn aside new knowledge unless it comes from their own scientific circles. Some academics appoint themselves vigilantes to guard the gates of science against troublemakers with new ideas. Yet science has a two thousand year record of success not because it has been guarded by an Inquisition, but because it is self-regulating. It has succeeded because bad science is driven out by good; an ounce of open-minded experiment is worth any amount of authoritative opinion by self-styled scientific rationalists. The scientific fundamentalism of which these are disturbing signs is found today not merely in remote provincial pockets of conservatism but at the very top of the mainstream management of science on both sides of the Atlantic. Human progress has been powered by the paradigm-shattering inventions of many brilliant iconoclasts, yet just as the scientific community dismissed Edison's lamp, Roentgen's X-rays, and even the Wrights' airplane, today's "Paradigm Police" do a better job of preserving an outdated mode of thought than of nurturing invention and discovery. One way of explaining this odd reluctance to come to terms with the new, even when there is plenty of concrete evidence available, is to appeal to the natural human tendency not to believe things that sound impossible unless we see them with our own eyes — a healthy skepticism. But there is a good deal more to this phenomenon than a healthy skepticism. It is a refusal even to open our eyes to examine the evidence that is plainly in view. And it is a phenomenon that occurs so regularly in the history of science and technology as to be almost an integral part of the process. It seems that there are some individuals, including very distinguished scientists, who are willing to risk the censure and ridicule of their colleagues by stepping over that mark. This book is about those scientists. But, more importantly, it is about the curious social and intellectual forces that seek to prohibit such research; those areas of scientific research that are taboo subjects; about subjects whose discussion is forbidden under pain of ridicule and ostracism. Often those who cry taboo do so from the best of motives: a desire to ensure that our hard-won scientific enlightenment is not corrupted by the credulous acceptance of crank ideas and that the community does not slide back into what Sir Karl Popper graphically called the 'tyranny of opinion.' Yet in setting out to guard the frontiers of knowledge, some scientific purists are adopting a brand of skepticism that is indistinguishable from the tyranny they seek to resist. These modern skeptics are sometimes the most unreflecting of individuals yet their devotion to the cause of science impels them to appoint themselves guardians of spirit of truth. And this raises the important question of just how we can tell a real crank from a real innovator — a Faraday from a false prophet. Merely to dismiss a carefully prepared body of evidence — however barmy it may appear — is to make the same mistake as the crank. In many ways cold fusion is the perfect paradigm of scientific taboo in action. The high priests of hot fusion were quick to ostracize and ridicule those whom they saw as profaning the sacred wisdom. And empirical fact counted for nothing in the face of their concerted derision.

The taboo reaction in science takes many distinct forms. At its simplest and most direct, tabooism is manifested as derision and rejection by scientists (and non-scientists) of those new discoveries that cannot be fitted into the existing framework of knowledge. The reaction is not merely a negative dismissal or refusal to believe; it is strong enough to cause positive actions to be taken by leading skeptics to compel a more widespread adoption in the community of the rejection and disbelief, the shipping up of opposition, and the putting down of anyone unwise enough to step out of line by publicly embracing taboo ideas. The taboo reaction in such simple cases is eventually dispelled because the facts — and the value of the discoveries concerned — prove to be stronger than the taboo belief; but there remains the worrying possibility that many such taboos prove stronger (or more valuable) than the discoveries to which they are applied. In its more subtle form, the taboo reaction draws a circle around a subject and places it 'out of bounds' to any form of rational analysis or investigation. In doing so, science often puts up what

8

appears to be a well-considered, fundamental objection, which on closer analysis turns out to be no more than the unreflecting prejudices of a maiden aunt who feels uncomfortable with the idea of mixed bathing. The penalty associated with this form of tabooism is that whole areas of scientific investigation, some of which may well hold important discoveries, remain permanently fenced off and any benefits they may contain are denied us. Subtler still is the taboo whereby scientists in certain fields erect a general prohibition against speaking or writing on the subjects which they consider their own property and where any reference, especially by an outsider, will draw a rapid hostile response. Sometimes, scientists who declare a taboo will insist that only they are qualified to discuss and reach conclusions on the matters that they have made their own property; that only they are privy to the immense body of knowledge and subtlety of argument necessary fully to understand the complexities of the subject and to reach the 'right' conclusion. Outsiders, on the other hand, (especially non-scientists) are ill-informed, unable to think rationally or analytically, prone to mystical or crank ideas and are not privy to subtleties of analysis and inflections of argument that insiders have devoted long painful years to acquiring. Once again, the cost of such tabooism is measured in lost opportunities for discovery. Any contribution to knowledge in terms of rational analysis, or resulting from the different perspective of those outside the field in question, is lost to the community. In its most extreme form scientific tabooism closely resembles the behavior of a priestly caste that is perceived to be the holy guardians of the sacred creed, the beliefs that are the object of the community's worship. Such guardians feel themselves justified by their religious calling and long training in adopting any measures to repel and to discredit any member of the community who profanes the sacred places, words or rituals regarded as untouchable. Perhaps the most worrying aspect of the taboo reaction is that it tends to have a cumulative and permanent discriminatory effect: any idea that is ideologically suspect or counter to the current paradigm is permanently dismissed, and the very fact of its rejection forms the basis of its rejection on all future occasions. It is a little like the court of appeal rejecting the convicted man's plea of innocence on the grounds that he must be guilty or why else is he

9

in jail? And why else did the police arrest him in the first place? This 'erring on the side of caution' means that in the long term the intellectual Devil's Island where convicted concepts are sent becomes more and more crowded with taboo ideas, all denied to us, and with no possibility of reprieve. We will never know how many tens or hundreds or thousands of important discoveries were thrown in the scrap heap merely because of intolerance and misplaced skepticism."

The taboo reaction is due, in part, to the pride of those people who consider themselves highly educated scholars at the very top echelon of thought and knowledge. They are more interested in who you are than what you have to say. Before this group will even consent to listen you must qualify not by what you are prepared to prove in a mathematical manner, but by your educational rank. Do you see what a problem I have? I can't convince these people to give me the time even though I have made discoveries that will benefit all mankind. This pride is the first half of the primary problem; that the very people who have the intellectual capacity to understand the knowledge in this book refuse to investigate what must reveal, if proven true, how unconsciously ignorant they have always been. Is it any wonder they don't want to check it out? And even if they do, could they be objective enough when their reputation for wisdom and knowledge is at stake? Have you noticed the parallels between the Catholic Church in the middle ages with its dogmatism (that it cannot be what must not be — the clergymen even refused to simply look through Galileo's telescope and see for themselves, because they were so arrogantly convinced that they held the absolute truth in hands and thus needed no verification), and today's self-righteous "church" of "scientificality" with its dogmas? Therefore before I begin I would like to ask a question of every reader but especially of philosophers, professors and theologians. Is there the slightest possibility that the knowledge you possess does not contain as much truth as you would like to believe? Would you gamble your life or the lives of those you love that you really know, or is there just the remotest chance that you only think you know? What is the standard by which you judge the veracity of your knowledge and wisdom; the fact that it was taught in college? Is your determination of truth based on the fact that it was written by a noted author, composed from your own analysis and understanding, or revealed through heavenly inspiration? What makes you so certain, so positive, so dogmatic? Because this book dares to oppose the three forces that control the thinking of mankind; government, religion, and education, the most dangerous thinking of all, the kind that really doesn't know the truth, as Socrates observed, but because of some fallacious standard presumes to know, I have found it necessary to resort to this manner of introducing my work in the fervent hope that I can reach those who will be able to extract the pure, unadulterated relations involved before another century passes by or an atomic explosion destroys millions of lives. Now be honest with yourselves; do you really know, or only think you know? If you will admit there is just the slightest possibility that you have not been endowed with the wisdom of God; that you may be wrong regarding many things despite the high opinion you and others hold of yourselves; that the expression the blind leading the blind could even pertain to you; I know this is difficult for you to conceive; I say, if there is the slightest possibility you could be mistaken and you are willing to admit this to yourselves, then I cordially welcome your company aboard, otherwise, you had better not read this book for my words are not meant for your ears. But should you decide to accompany me on this voyage I would like to remind you, once again, that this book is not a religious or philosophical tract attempting some ulterior form of indoctrination; it is purely scientific as you will see, and should the word 'God' seem incongruous kindly remember Spinoza and you will understand immediately that it is not. While God is proven to be a mathematical reality as a consequence of becoming conscious of the truth, war and crime are compelled to take leave of the earth.

It is true that many men before me, including socialists, communists, even capitalists also thought they had discovered the cause of, and solution to, the various problems of human relation, and their enthusiasm was no doubt just as positive and sincere as my own. However, there is this difference between us. I have absolute proof that cannot be denied by any reader; they did not. Mine can be adequately communicated; theirs was never disentangled from the illusion of reality borne out of abstract thought and imagination.

11

Mine is purely scientific; theirs an expression of dogmatic belief. In view of the serious nature of this discovery, the effects of which will beneficently ramify into every conceivable direction causing religious minds to consider this the return of the expected Messiah, and since it also contravenes a belief held true by nearly all of mankind, I am once again asking the indulgence of every reader to please refrain from jumping to any premature conclusions, to put aside if only for the time being the unverified knowledge gathered from books and teachers and heed only the truth reflected in my words. "But what is truth?" you might ask. "Let us say it is that which cannot be denied by anyone anywhere." "But," you might reply, "that's just common sense; everyone knows that." Well it is just this common sense; that sense common to us all that I am making the very foundation of this book. It is for this reason that what I write will be understood not only by those who can read the English language, but by the entire literate world. There will be no sleight of hand revelation as is dreamed up in philosophical circles by epistemologists; only a clear undeniable explanation about facts of man's nature never before understood. Knowledge in this context is to truly know ourselves. If you are coming along on this journey you will need to put on your thinking caps and try to understand the mathematical relations soon to be revealed which permit you to see this miracle.

There is an ironic twist here for if all evils of our world no longer exist, how happy would certain professions be to know that their services will no longer be needed. Shouldn't this news make those individuals very happy, who have been trying to correct the evil in the world? If the cry of the clergy is 'Faith in God,' isn't it obvious that the priesthood would rather see an end to all sin than to preach against it and shrive the sinners in the confessional. They should be simply thrilled at the miracle God is about to perform, even though it means putting them out of work. Isn't it true that politicians, statesman, the leaders of the world in general would much rather see an end to all war and crime than to retaliate an eye for an eye and a tooth for a tooth? If the Communist and Capitalist governments are truly interested in the welfare of their people, then just imagine how excited they will be to learn that the most perfect relations between all men will soon be a reality even though it makes their services unnecessary. If a writer is just about ready to submit his book to the public for the purpose of revealing knowledge on how to raise children or live together in greater harmony as man and wife, he will be absolutely in ecstasy to learn that God is going to bring about such perfect harmony in a short time that all books purporting to do this very thing won't have any more value. Just imagine how happy the profession of psychiatry will be to learn that all of its patients will be healed overnight by this miracle, making this service obsolete. There is a good deal of irony to this Great Transition for it reveals how completely dishonest we were compelled to be with ourselves and others. A salesman is happy to make a sale when he works on commission, and if he found out that another salesman beat him to the punch he would be disappointed. The only difference between a salesman selling books and a doctor, theologian, etc., is that the former must convince only his prospects while the latter must also convince themselves. A salesman is not interested if anyone uses his product, just so he is paid a commission. Doctors and theologians and those in the helping professions are compelled to justify that they know what they are advising and treating, otherwise, they could never accept a fee, gratuity, or income for their service. Someone who struggles to earn a living such as a salesman where the risk of injury is virtually nonexistent doesn't need the same kind of justification, and will even steal with a clear conscience.

Though we would all like to see an end to evil, there are two issues that need to be considered. No one could be pleased if their source of income was taken away as well as the very thing that gives meaning to their lives. Doctors are sincerely interested in making their patients well, but they want to be the ones to do it. Religion would like to see us delivered from evil, but in some manner that confirms what has been looked for — Judgment Day. The Chinese government would like to see an end to all evil, but in terms of communism. Is it possible for the supporters of socialism and communism to relinquish the thought that they are right, when they think they are not wrong? Politicians would like to see an end to all evil, but they want to find the solution. Would it be possible for the leaders of capitalism to willingly resign their jobs when they think their services are no longer required? How is it humanly possible for the organizations that fight

13

for peace, for health, for security; those that wage a war against the evils of humanity to be sincerely happy about the very removal of the things they need for their ultimate satisfaction? Everybody would like to see a great change; "I have a dream" said Dr. Martin Luther King, "this view from the mountain top, but no one desires any intruders or interlopers." These individuals, who at present control the thinking of mankind, set up a fallacious standard for the conscious purpose of protecting themselves against others and will react with hostility towards anything that shows they may be wrong unless it is presented in such a mathematical manner that it is impossible to disagree without revealing a still greater ignorance. If this book was not a mathematical revelation — which scientists will soon confirm — what do you think the clergy, the government, the medical and teaching professions, and many others would do if they thought for one moment this work was someone's opinion that threatened their security, power, and leadership position in world affairs? They would tear this book to shreds. This discovery has incurred the wrath of the establishment because it upsets the apple cart and threatens the status quo. No one wants to willingly admit they don't have the answer. The fact remains that these individuals are actually trying to solve problems that are very much over their heads and what is being revealed to them is only a method to accomplish the very things they have been attempting to do, without success. Unfortunately, those endeavoring to correct our ills appear to be cutting off the heads of a diseased hydra — the more psychiatrists we graduate, the greater becomes our mental illness; the more policemen and moralists we have, the greater and more prevalent become our crimes; the more diplomats, statesmen, generals and armies we have, the greater and more destructive become our wars. And as an expedient to the situation we find ourselves being taxed to death while our cost of living steadily rises. Wouldn't you like to see an end to all this? Therefore before I begin I would like to ask you the following questions. Do you prefer war or peace, unhappiness or happiness, insecurity or security, sickness or health? Do you prefer losing the one you have fallen in love with, or winning and living happily ever after? Since I know that happiness is preferable to unhappiness, health to sickness, I shall now begin a revelation of knowledge which no one will be able to deny providing the relations are understood. While the moral code, the Ten Commandments, our standards of right and wrong will be completely extirpated, all premarital relations, adultery and divorce will be a thing of the past changing the entire landscape of family relationships. Where did you ever hear anything so fantastic or paradoxical? And aren't you jumping to a conclusion that this is against all human nature? If all the people in the world who get displaced because their services are no longer needed were to know as a matter of undeniable knowledge that the income necessary to sustain their standard of living, whatever the cost, would never be stopped as long as they live, would they have any reason to complain about someone showing them a better way — the only way to accomplish that for which they are getting paid? Although they and others will be dissatisfied to learn the truth when it deprives them of personal fulfillment, they are compelled to be silent because to utter any words of protest would only reveal their ignorance, which will give them no satisfaction. I shall now set sail on a voyage which will perform this virtual miracle by igniting a chain reaction of thought that will explode across the planet and destroy with its fallout every conceivable kind of hurt that exists among human relations, never to return. It is now within our power to reach that mountaintop — the Golden Age of man — that we have all hoped and dreamed would one day become a reality.

THE FOUNDATION AND SCIENTIFIC
DEVELOPMENT
OF MY FIRST DISCOVERY

CHAPTER ONE

THE HIDING PLACE

L ong ago man formed a theory that the earth was flat because he could not conceive of it as a ball suspended in space. It became a dogma, such a fixed idea that when the first astronomer, in attempting to explain the reason why darkness came over the sun in the middle of the day, was denied an opportunity to present his findings because his discovery called into question this sacred belief. Let us imagine the first astronomer being granted an interview by the leading authorities of his time to explain the cause of a solar eclipse.

"Dear gentlemen, I have come to you to explain my findings about the shape of the earth. In order for you to understand the cause of the darkness coming over the sun, it is first necessary to understand that the earth is not flat."

"What's that? Did we hear you correctly? Are you trying to tell us that the earth is round which means it is floating in space?"

"That is true, and my discovery lies locked behind the door marked the earth is round."

"This is absurd! Who are you to come in here and tell us that we are wrong? We are not interested in your theory because we say the earth is flat [and since we are wiser than you, more learned than you, more educated than you, you must be wrong], so why discuss this matter further? Besides, our chief medicine man chanted the incantation that caused the darkness to vanish. Thank you very much for coming out to give us your explanation but we are not interested in discussing this matter further because we know, beyond a shadow of doubt, that the earth is flat."

This is the second half of the primary problem. The fact that a theory such as the belief that the earth is flat can hermetically seal knowledge that prevents our discovering the invariable laws of the solar system which, in turn, prevents the knowledge necessary to land men on the moon. Children were taught this by their parents who had received this knowledge from their parents who were instructed by the medicine man who was considered the wisest man of his time. Since there was no way the knowledge of the medicine man could be proven false because no one knew any different, and since he was considered the wisest man of his time, his conclusion that the earth was flat brooked no opposition. Consequently, when those who were judged inferior in wisdom or knowledge disagreed with the medicine man, they were rejected. When an upstart scientist came along who concluded that the earth was round after making certain observations, how was it possible to get others to agree with him when they couldn't follow his reasoning which compelled them to compare him, not his knowledge, to the medicine man, to the professors and teachers whose wisdom and knowledge could not be impugned. To help you see how easy it is for a dogmatic theory to prevent scientific investigation let us once again return, in imagination, to the time when man knew nothing about the solar system, and listen to a conversation.

"Say, Joshua; do you believe the earth is flat or do you go along with my theory that it is round?"

"Even though most of mankind agrees that it is flat, what difference does it really make what I think?" said our philosophical friend. "The shape of the earth is certainly not going to be affected or changed no matter what my opinion is, right?

"That is true enough, but if the earth is really round isn't it obvious that just as long as we think otherwise we are prevented from discovering those things that depend on this knowledge for their discovery, consequently, it does make a difference. How much so we are not in the position to know just yet but thousands of years hence, perhaps in the twentieth century, there may be all kinds of scientific achievements attributed directly to knowing the true shape of the earth, such as landing men on the moon which may never be possible without first knowing the true shape of the earth."

You may look back and smile at the unconscious ignorance of our ancestors but pay close attention to what happened to me as I draw up a perfect comparison with which you can identify. Because my discovery was purely scientific, my attention was drawn to an article by Eric Johnston, now deceased, who was once among other things the President of the Motion Pictures Association. It appeared in the November 6, 1960 issue of This Week Magazine of The Baltimore Sun.

"If there is one word which characterizes our world in this exciting last half of the twentieth century, the word is change. Change in political life; change in economic life; change in social life; change in personal life; change in the hallmark of our times. It's not gradual, comfortable change. It is sudden; rapid; often violent. It touches and often disrupts whole cultures and hundreds of millions of people. Behind it all lies an explosive growth in scientific knowledge and accomplishment. Some 90% of all the scientists who ever lived are living today, and the total accumulation of scientific knowledge is doubling every ten years. But this is reality. If we remember that, then we will never flinch at change. We will adjust to it, welcome it, meet it as a friend, and know it is God's will." Since my discovery would bring about the greatest change in all of history, it appeared that this man would be willing to let me explain my findings. By convincing him on the phone that it was now possible to put a permanent end to all war as a result of my discovery, he agreed to meet me on a Sunday afternoon in Washington, D.C. Our conversation went as follows:

"I'm really not a scientist, Mr. Lessans, and in all probability you should be talking to someone else. Your claims are absolutely fantastic, but I want you to know that even though I wrote an article about science, I am not a scientist. Besides, after you hung up I became more skeptical of claims such as yours because they not only sound impossible but somewhat ridiculous in view of man's nature. Frankly, I don't believe your claims are possible, but I am willing to listen if it doesn't take too long and if I can see some truth to your explanation; I do have another engagement but I can devote at least one hour. Would you get right on with it?" I then told him the story

21

about the earth being flat and he smiled at this, and then told him that a theory exists regarding man's nature that is accepted as true by 98% of mankind, and I pointed out that this theory is actually preventing the decline and fall of all evil because it has closed a door to a vast storehouse of genuine knowledge.

"I will be as brief as possible, Mr. Johnston, but in order for me to reveal my discovery it is absolutely necessary that I first show you its hiding place because they are related to each other."

"What is this theory?" he asked.

"You see, Mr. Johnston, most people believe consciously or unconsciously that man's will is free."

"What's that? Did I hear you correctly? Are you trying to tell me that man's will is not free?"

"That is absolutely right, Mr. Johnston. I don't believe it; I know this for a mathematical fact. My discovery lies locked behind the door marked 'Man's Will is Not Free,' just like the invariable laws of the solar system were concealed behind the door marked 'The Earth is Round' — until some upstart scientist opened it for a thorough investigation."

"I have always believed it to be free, but what difference does it make what I think; the will of man is certainly not going to be affected by my opinion, right?"

"That part is true enough (do you recall the comparison), but if the will of man is definitely not free isn't it obvious that just as long as we think otherwise we will be prevented from discovering those things that depend on this knowledge for their discovery, consequently, it does make a difference. The opinion of our ancestors that the earth was flat could never change its actual shape, but just as long as the door marked 'The Earth Is Round' was never opened thoroughly for an investigation by scientists capable of perceiving the undeniable but involved relations hidden there, how were we ever to discover the laws that allow us now to land men on the moon?"

"Your door was opened many times through the years by some of the most profound thinkers and never did they come up with any discoveries to change the world."

"It is true that determinism was investigated by people who were presumed profound thinkers, but in spite of their profoundness none of them had the capacity to perceive the law that was hidden there. Most people do not even know it is a theory since it is preached by religion, government, even education as if it is an absolute fact."

"Mr. Lessans, I don't know what it is you think you have discovered but whatever it is, as far as I personally am concerned, it cannot be valid because I am convinced that man's will is free. Thank you very much for coming out but I'm not interested in discussing this matter any further." And he would not let me continue.

Now stop to think about this for one moment. A discovery has been made that will go down in history as that which will change the entire world of human relations for the better, yet because it challenges a theory which is held by many world religions there is a hostile reaction when it is questioned. This is a perfect example of how this preemptive authority of false knowledge which is passed along from generation to generation by theology, by government, and by various other sources does not even allow a person to open his mind to hear the explanation. The theologians I contacted, though they admit they pray to God for deliverance from evil also believe it is impossible for man to accomplish this apparent miracle. In a sense they are right because the law that was discovered is equivalent to the law that inheres in the solar system, over which we have no control. Any system of established dogma that is based on a false belief needs to be addressed so that the truth can be revealed. This is much easier said than done because the knowledge of what it means that man's will is not free was buried deeper than atomic energy, and presents problems that are almost insurmountable. Convincing a few people of this truth is one thing; convincing the entire world is something else. Supposing the very people whose understanding it is necessary to reach refuse to examine the facts on the grounds that the discovery could not be valid because it starts out with the premise that man's will is not free. To show you how confused are those who have been guiding us, a rabbi was told that the author of the book "Decline and Fall of All Evil" has the permanent solution to every problem of human relation, and he replied, "How do we know that God wants us to remove all evil?" Now you tell me, if he is doubtful of this why do

23

all theologians ask God in the Lord's Prayer to deliver us from evil? Another rabbi criticized me for not attending the synagogue to which I replied, "Isn't the reason you go to the Temple due to your faith in God, your belief that one day He will reveal Himself to all mankind?" "That is true," he answered. "Well you see, Rabbi, the reason I don't go to the synagogue is because I know for a fact that God is real. I don't have faith or believe this; I know that 2+2=4; I don't have faith or believe that this is true." Still hoping that I could convince a member of the clergy to hear what I had to say, I phoned a Catholic priest for an appointment and our conversation went as follows:

"What do you want to see me about?"

"Father, when you utter the words of the Lord's Prayer I take for granted that you are sincere and would like to see us delivered from evil, isn't that true?"

"Certainly, what kind of question is that?"

"Well the reason I had to ask is because I have just made a scientific discovery that will bring about the actual fulfillment of this prayer, this deliverance from evil."

"What's that you say? Deliver mankind from evil? Absolutely impossible, it cannot be done."

"But how can you know without first finding out what it is I have discovered? Isn't this your fervent wish, that God perform such a miracle?"

"It is."

"Well then, why don't you let me come out and show you exactly how all evil must decline and fall as a direct consequence?"

"It's impossible, that's why I'm not interested. The only time such a world will become a reality is on Judgment Day."

"But that's just the point; this Judgment Day when interpreted properly has actually arrived because it conforms to the basic principle."

"This still doesn't convince me that I should devote my precious time to what sounds ridiculous."

"Sounds can be deceiving, Father. Who believed the first astronomer when he predicted an eclipse, or Einstein when he revealed the potential of atomic energy? If I told you without adequate proof that this discovery will bring about the inception of the Golden Age your skepticism would not be an unwarranted reaction, but the actual proof is explicit and undeniable. It is only natural for you to be skeptical, Father, but this is never a sufficient reason to exclude the possibility of a scientific miracle."

"I'm afraid that I will have to end this conversation. My advice is to take what you have to one of the secular universities. I'm sorry I couldn't be more helpful but thanks for calling anyway."

Later on, I tried to engage a pastor in a discussion about free will and he responded to me by asking, "If man's will is not free, then you can't blame or punish anything he does, is that correct?" And when I answered, "Right," he actually got up and walked out of the room. You see, this learned ignorance presents quite a problem, and only by getting the world to understand what it means that man's will is not free can I hope to break through this barrier. This law of our nature is not a premise, not an assumption, not a theory, but when 98% of the world believes otherwise, they might just close the windows of their mind to any scientific investigation which requires rejecting a theory that has dogmatically controlled man's thinking since time immemorial. How is it possible to explain the solution when nobody wishes to listen because they think they know there isn't any? Where is there one iota of difference between this attitude and that of our ancestors regarding the shape of the earth? To show how confused is the thinking of the average person who is not accustomed to perceiving mathematical relations of this nature, when I told someone that his answer was incorrect, he replied with a tone of resentment, "That's your opinion, but I believe it is possible," as if the answer could be one or the other. The earth cannot be round and flat, it has to be one or the other and your opinion can never change what is. Remember, I am going to bring about an unprecedented change in human conduct, but I can only do this if you understand what I am about to reveal. If you can't follow my reasoning as to why the earth is round, you will be compelled to believe that it is flat for it gives you satisfaction not to be wrong. In other words, if I were going to offer an opinion as to why man's will is not free then your educational rank, your scholarly background could assert itself as a condition more valid to deny my claim, but when I declare that I am not going to reveal a theory but will give a scientific, undeniable, demonstration, then regardless of who you are you must wait to see the proof before rejecting the claim. Therefore, it is imperative that you know, well in advance, that my reasoning will be completely mathematical, scientific and undeniable, so if you find yourself in disagreement you had better reread that which you disagree, otherwise, your stubborn resistance, your inability to perceive these relations will only delay the very life you want for yourself. Many philosophers consider the discussion of whether man's will is or is not free equivalent to the discussion as to what came first — the chicken or the egg. To them, what difference does it really make? But if this knowledge can put an end to all war, crime, and evil in general, it makes a very big difference and it is imperative that the world listen so that this evil in our lives can come to a permanent end.

It is time to draw an infallible line of demarcation between what is true and what is false and you are going to be amazed at how much of what is false passed for what is true. However, everything was necessary. As we begin to understand the knowledge of our true nature, what is revealed is something amazing to behold for it not only gives ample proof that evil is no accident but that it was part of the harmonious operation called the mankind system and was compelled to come into existence by the very nature of life itself as part of our development. Once certain facts are understood it will also be no accident that every form of evil will be compelled to take leave of this earth. Humanity has been gravitating at a mathematical rate, and in an unconscious manner, toward this Golden Age when the seeds of hatred and the domination of man over man become relics of our collective past. It never dawned on the theologians and philosophers that man's choice of what he considered better for himself, even though it may have been evil when judged by others, came about in direct obedience to his nature or the will of God who had reasons we were not supposed to understand until now. Many prophets foresaw the coming of this new world but didn't know the exact time frame or from which direction peace would finally make its appearance, although they were confident that when it arrived it would change our world as we know it. Now the prophesies, conjectures, and

26

philosophies are no longer necessary, for this long awaited Golden Age that we have been looking forward to with prayers, hope, and great anticipation has arrived at last. This discovery I will soon make known to you reveals the infinite wisdom guiding this universe which is not only that long sought standard and touchstone of truth and reality, but also that elixir of alchemy for with it the baser metals of human nature are going to be magically transmuted into the pure gold of genuine happiness for every individual on this planet and for all generations to come. Please be perfectly honest, who can object to relinquishing the belief in free will when the key to the decline and fall of all misery and unhappiness lies behind the door of determinism?

In the beginning of creation when man was in the early stages of development, he could have destroyed himself were there no forces to control his nature. Religion came to the rescue by helping explain the reason for such evil in the world. It gave those who had faith a sense of comfort, hope, and the fortitude to go on living. In spite of everything, it was a bright light in the story of civilization. However, in order to reach this stage of development so God could reveal Himself to all mankind by performing this deliverance from evil, it was absolutely necessary to get man to believe his will was free, and he believed in this theory consciously or unconsciously. It became a dogma, a dogmatic doctrine of all religion, was the cornerstone of all civilization, and the only reason man was able to develop. The belief in free will was compelled to come about as a corollary of evil for not only was it impossible to hold God responsible for man's deliberate crimes, but primarily because it was impossible for man to solve his problems without blame and punishment which required the justification of this belief in order to absolve his conscience. Therefore, it was assumed that man did not have to do what he did because he was endowed with a special faculty which allowed him to choose between good and evil. In other words, if you were called upon to pass judgment on someone by sentencing him to death, could you do it if you knew his will was not free? To punish him in any way you would have to believe that he was free to choose another alternative than the one for which he was being judged; that he was not compelled by laws over which he had no control. Man was given no choice but to think this way and that is why our civilization developed the principle of 'an eye for an eye and a tooth for a tooth,' and why my discovery was never found. No one could ever get beyond this point because if man's will is not free it becomes absolutely impossible to hold him responsible for anything he does. Well, is it any wonder the solution was never found if it lies beyond this point? How is it possible not to blame people for committing murder, rape, for stealing and the wholesale slaughter of millions? Does this mean that we are supposed to condone these evils, and wouldn't man become even less responsible if there were no laws of punishment to control his nature? Doesn't our history show that if something is desired badly enough he will go to any lengths to satisfy himself, even pounce down on other nations with talons or tons of steel? What is it that prevents the poor from walking into stores and taking what they need if not the fear of punishment? The belief that will is not free strikes at the very heart of our present civilization. Right at this point lies the crux of a problem so difficult of solution that it has kept free will in power since time immemorial. Although it has had a very long reign in the history of civilization, it is now time to put it to rest, once and for all, by first demonstrating that this theory can never be proven true. A friend shared a story with me to show how difficult it is to get through this established dogma.

"The other day when I was in temple a rabbi, during the course of his sermon, made it very clear that man has free will. Professors, doctors, lawyers, and just about everybody I know, agree that man's will is free. If this is a theory you would never know it by talking to them. Well, is it a theory, or is this established knowledge?"

"Of course it is a theory," I answered, "otherwise there would be no believers in determinism. Is it possible for a person to believe that the earth is flat now that we have mathematical proof of its circular shape? The only reason we still have opinions on both sides of this subject is because we don't know for a mathematical fact whether the will of man is, or is not, free."

"But these theologians don't agree with you; they say that man's will is definitely free. Look, here comes a rabbi; ask him if man's will is free just for the heck of it and you will see for yourself how dogmatic he responds."

"Rabbi, we have been discussing a subject and would appreciate your opinion. Is it true, false, or just a theory that man's will is free?"

"It is absolutely true that man's will is free because nothing compels an individual to choose evil instead of good; he prefers this only because he wants to partake of this evil, not because something is forcing him."

"Do you mean, Rabbi, that every person has two or more alternatives when making a choice?"

"Absolutely; that bank robber last week didn't have to rob the bank, he wanted to do it."

"But assuming that what you say is true, how is it possible to prove that which cannot be proven? Let me illustrate what I mean."

"Is it possible for you not to do what has already been done?"
"No, it is not possible for me not to do what has already been done because I have already done it."

"This is a mathematical or undeniable relation and is equivalent to asking is it possible for anyone not to understand four as an answer to two plus two. Now if what has been done was the choosing of B instead of A, is it possible not to choose B which has already been chosen?"

"It is impossible, naturally."

"Since it is absolutely impossible (this is the reasoning of mathematics, not logic, which gives rise to opinions) not to choose B instead of A once B has been selected, how is it possible to choose A in this comparison of possibilities when in order to make this choice you must not choose B, which has already been chosen?"

"Again I must admit it is something impossible to do."

"Yet in order to prove free will true, it must do just that — the impossible. It must go back, reverse the order of time, undo what has already been done, and then show that A — with the conditions being exactly the same — could have been chosen instead of B. Since it is utterly impossible to reverse the order of time which is absolutely necessary for mathematical proof, free will must always remain a theory. The most you can say is that you believe the bank robber had a choice, but there is absolutely no way this can be proven."

"I may be unable to prove that he was not compelled to rob that bank and kill the teller, but it is my opinion that he didn't have to do what he did."

"I'm not in the mood to argue that point but at least we have arrived at a bit of knowledge that is absolutely undeniable, for we have just learned that it is mathematically impossible for any person to prove, beyond a shadow of doubt, that the will of man is free yet a moment ago you made the dogmatic statement that man's will is definitely free."

"My apology, dear sir; what I meant to say was that it is the consensus of opinion that the will of man is free."

"Now that we have established this fact, consider the following: If it is mathematically impossible to prove something true, whatever that something is, is it possible to prove the opposite of that something false?"

"Yes, it is possible."

"No, Rabbi, it is not possible."

"That my friend is your opinion, not mine."

"Let me show you it is not an opinion. If you could prove that determinism is false, wouldn't this prove free will, which is the opposite of determinism, true; and didn't we just prove that it is mathematically impossible to prove free will true, which means that it is absolutely impossible to prove determinism false?"

"I see what you mean and again I apologize for thinking this was a matter of opinion."

"This means that we have arrived at another bit of mathematical knowledge and that is — although we can never prove free will true or determinism false, there still exists a possibility of proving determinism true, or free will false. Now tell me, Rabbi, supposing your belief in free will absolutely prevents the discovery of knowledge that, when released, can remove the very things you would like to rid the world of, things you preach against such as war, crime, sin, hate, discrimination, etc., what would you say then?"

"If this is true and you can prove it, all I can say is that God's ways are mysterious and surpass my understanding. I enjoyed talking with you, son, and perhaps I shall live to see the day when all evil will be driven from our lives."

"Even if you don't live to see it, please rest assured the day is not far away and that it must come about the very moment certain facts pertaining to the nature of man are brought to light, because it is God's will."

"I must leave now but thank you for sharing your insights with me."

After the rabbi left, our conversation continued...

"Boy, that was really something to see; you almost sound like old Socrates himself. Just imagine, you actually got the rabbi to admit that free will is nothing other than an opinion. But you weren't serious about getting rid of all the evil in the world, were you?"

"I was never more serious in all my life."

"Why do you predict war to end sooner than crime?"

"To end any particular evil (and you are in for so many surprises) requires that the people involved understand the principles that will be explained. When they do, they will be given no choice but to stop the evil, whatever it is they are engaged in. But whereas it is only necessary to get the leaders of the world to understand the principles to end all war, it takes all mankind to understand them to put a permanent end to crime."

"But how is it possible for you, just with your reasoning, nothing else, to put an end to all war, crime, sin, hate, etc.? If I must say so, this sounds completely contrary to reason."

"Are you asking if it is possible, or telling me that you know it is impossible?"

"After what you just demonstrated to the rabbi I certainly would never tell you it is impossible when I don't know if it is, but it seems so incredible to hear someone say he is going to remove all evil from the entire earth, that I cannot help but be in disbelief. Well what is your first step? How do you go about making a start?"

"The first step is to prove conclusively, beyond a shadow of doubt, and regardless of any opinions to the contrary, that the will of man is not free."

"But if you plan to use the knowledge that man's will is not free as a point from which to start your chain of reasoning, couldn't you

31

get the same results without demonstrating that man's will is not free, simply by showing what must follow as a consequence?"

"Yes I could, and that was a very sharp question, but my purpose in proving that man's will is not free is not so much to have a sound basis from which to reason, but to show exactly <u>why</u> the will of man is not free."

"I am still trying to understand your reasoning as to why free will cannot be proven true."

"Once again, let me show you why this is a mathematical impossibility by repeating the same question I asked the rabbi. Take your time with this."

"Is it possible for you *not* to do what has already been done?"

"Of course it's not possible for me *not* to do what has already been done...because I have already done it."

"Now if what has just been done was the choosing of B instead of A, is it possible not to choose B, which has already been chosen?"

"No, it is not possible."

"Since it is absolutely impossible not to choose B instead of A, once B has been selected, how is it possible to choose A in this comparison of possibilities when in order to make this choice you must not choose B, which has already been chosen? Yet in order to prove free will true, it must do just that — the impossible. It must go back, reverse the order of time, undo what has already been done and then show that A, with the conditions being exactly the same, could have been chosen instead of B. Such reasoning is not a form of logic, nor is it my opinion of the answer. Let me rephrase this in still another way.

"If it is mathematically impossible to prove something true, whatever it is, is it possible to prove this something true?"

"Obviously the answer is no."

"Now that we have established this fact, consider the following: If it is mathematically impossible to prove something true, whatever that something is, is it possible to prove the opposite of that something false? Obviously the answer must be no, it is not possible unless the person asked does not understand the question. In other words, if it is mathematically impossible to prove free will true, how

32

is it possible to prove the opposite of this, false? Isn't it obvious that if determinism (in this context the opposite of free will) was proven false, this would automatically prove free will true, and didn't we just demonstrate that this is impossible unless we can turn back the clock? How is it possible to prove free will true when this requires doing something that is mathematically impossible? We can never undo what has already been done. Therefore, whatever your reasons for believing free will true cannot be accurate because it is impossible to prove this theory since proof requires going back in time, so to speak, and demonstrating that man could have chosen otherwise. Since it is utterly impossible to reverse the order of time, which is absolutely necessary for mathematical proof, the most we can do is assume that he didn't have to do what he did. Is it any wonder free will is still a theory? The great humor in this particular instance lies in the fact that though it was always possible to prove determinism true, theology considered it as absolutely false while dogmatically promulgating, in obedience to God's will, that free will was an absolute reality."

To show you how confused the mind can get when mathematical relations are not perceived, Will Durant, a well-known philosopher of the 20th century, wrote on page 103 in the Mansions of Philosophy, "For even while we talked determinism we knew it was false; we are men, not machines." After opening the door to the vestibule of determinism, and taking a step inside, he turned back because he could not get past the implications. Now let us understand why the implications of believing that man's will is not free turned Durant and many others away. Remember, most people know nothing about the implications of this position; they just accept as true what has been taught to them by leading authorities. If determinism was true, he reasoned, then man doesn't have a free choice; consequently, he cannot be blamed for what he does. Faced with this apparent impasse he asked himself, "How can we not blame and punish people for hurting others? If someone hurts us, we must believe that he didn't have to, that his will was free, in order to blame and punish him for what he did. And how is it possible to turn the other cheek and not fight back from this intentional hurt to us?" He was trying to say in this sentence that philosophies of free will would never stop returning

33

just as long as our nature commands us to fight back when hurt, an eye for an eye. This is undeniable and he was one hundred percent correct because this relation could be seen just as easily with direct perception as two plus two equals four, and there was no way that this statement could be beaten down with formulas or reasoning, but this is not what he actually said. He, as well as many philosophers, helped the cause of free will by unconsciously using syllogistic reasoning which is logical, though completely fallacious. He accomplished this by setting up an understandable assumption for a major premise: "If there is an almost eternal recurrence of philosophies of freedom it is because direct perception can never be beaten down with formulas, or sensation with reasoning." Can you not see how mathematically impossible is his observation? This simple paraphrase will clarify a point: "If there is an almost eternal recurrence of" four equaling two plus two, "it is because" two equals one plus one, and one plus one plus one plus one totals four. But when a person perceives certain undeniable relations is it necessary to make an equation out of four equaling two plus two, or out of the fact that once free will is proven untrue it can no longer exist and its philosophies of freedom return? Using this same syllogistic reasoning he tried to prove freedom of the will by demonstrating, in the same manner, that determinism could never prove it false. In other words, when a major premise is not obviously true, then fallacious reasoning has to result. The purpose of reasoning is to connect mathematical relations not to prove the validity of inaccurate perceptions.

Durant begins with the assumption that direct perception (which are words that symbolize what he cannot possibly understand) is superior to reasoning in understanding the truth which made a syllogistic equation necessary to prove the validity of an inaccurate perception. Thus, he reasons in his minor premise: "Free will is not a matter of reasoning, like determinism, but is the result of direct perception, therefore..." and here is his fallacious conclusion, "since philosophies of free will employ direct perception which cannot be beaten down by the reasoning of determinism, the belief in free will must eternally recur." He knew that free will was a theory, but as long as proof was not necessary when it could be seen with the direct perception of our common sense that it was impossible to turn the other cheek (the corollary thrown up by determinism), he was compelled to write — "Let the determinist honestly envisage the implications of his philosophy." This indicates that all his reasoning in favor of free will was the result of inferences derived from the inability to accept the implications. Durant is anything but a scientist and an accurate thinker. Since it is absolutely impossible for free will to ever be proven true (I take for granted this is now understood), nothing in this universe can prove determinism an unreality (and in this context it shall only mean the opposite of free will as death is the opposite of life), simply because this would automatically prove the truth of free will which has been shown to be an impossibility. Consequently, the belief in free will and all conceptions regarding it can only remain in existence as a plausible theory just as long as no undeniable evidence is produced in contravention. According to his reasoning he assumes that free will is true because, in his mind, determinism is false, and the reason he thinks determinism is false is because man is not a machine. Then, not realizing how mathematically impossible is his next statement he claims that philosophies of freedom (free will) eternally recur because reasoning and formulas cannot beat down the obvious truth of direct perception. Take a look at that last statement very carefully and see if you can't tell why it is mathematically impossible. If free will was finally proven to be that which is non-existent (and let's take for granted that you know this for a fact) and accepted as such by our scientific world at large, would it be possible according to Durant's statement for 'philosophies of freedom' to recur anymore? Isn't it obvious that the recurrence of the belief in free will is a mathematical impossibility once freedom of the will is proven to be a figment of the imagination, or to phrase it differently, a realistic mirage? Is it humanly possible for the belief that the world is flat to eternally recur when we have mathematical knowledge that it is round? Consequently, the continued return of the belief in free will can only be due to the fact that it is still a logical theory or plausible conception that has never been analyzed properly, allowing the belief and its philosophies to persist. But Durant states that philosophies of freedom eternally recur not because of the explanation I just gave, an explanation that cannot be denied by anyone anywhere, even by this philosopher himself providing it is understood, but because direct perception can never be beaten down with formulas, or sensation with reasoning. Isn't it apparent that such words have no relation to reality whatever? If Durant believed direct perception was considered superior to reasoning, is it any wonder he was so confused and his reasoning so fallacious since the word 'because' which denotes the perception of a relation, whether true or false, indicates that he is criticizing reasoning while reasoning. This doesn't stop a person from saying, "I believe." "It is my opinion." "I was taught that man's will is free," but it would certainly stop him from trying to defend his position with an argument. One of the most profound insights ever expressed by Socrates was "Know Thyself," but though he had a suspicion of its significance it was only an intuitive feeling, not something he could put his finger on. These two words have never been adequately understood by mankind, including psychiatry and psychology, because this observation is the key that unlocks the first door to another door that requires its own key, and where the hiding place to this discovery was finally uncovered. However, the problem here is so deep and so involved that even those like your philosopher Spinoza, who understood that man's will is not free, didn't even come close to the solution, and others like your William James would be willing to bet their life that will is free. Why do theologians treat this as if it is an undeniable reality? And what made it so obvious to Durant that man's will is free? Durant is now deceased but over 20 years ago I phoned to tell him I had made a fantastic discovery that was hidden behind the fallacious theory that man's will is free. He replied, "You must be on the wrong tack, but take what you think you have to Johns Hopkins University for an analysis." I not only contacted that university but many others to no avail.

It is interesting to observe at this point that Durant was indirectly involved in my discovery. To give you a little background, it was November of 1959 when I received an amazing revelation that would change the course of my life. I happened to overhear on the radio a priest state very dogmatically that man has freedom of the will, and the hair stood up on my arms like a cat ready to fight. I didn't understand why that happened and didn't pay much attention to it at the time but felt that I was chilled for some reason. Up until that time I never gave much thought to the subject of free will, not rejecting or accepting it, but when this chill occurred every time the subject came up I began to see the connection. That night in a dream I kept hearing this phrase, "The solution to all the problems plaguing mankind lies hidden behind the fallacious belief that man's will is free." I still didn't understand where it was leading, but the next day I started to reread Durant's chapter on free will in his book Mansions of Philosophy. When I completed it I remarked, "He really doesn't know what he is talking about and Spinoza is right, man's will is not free." Then, after nine strenuous months I shouted, "Eureka, I have found it!" and I have had no rest ever since. After opening the door of determinism and proving conclusively that man's will is not free, I saw another sign that read — 'Hidden behind this door you will discover the solution to the problem of evil — the long awaited Messiah.' I applied the key, opened the door, and after many months in the deepest analysis I made a finding that was so fantastic, it took me several years to understand its full significance for all mankind. I saw how this new world must become a reality in a very short time.

"That's what I wanted you to admit. I resent your bringing God into this at all. I don't go for all that religious crap when you're talking about science. Lots of people like religion, but I can't stand all this ritual mumbo jumbo. Most people who go to church are hypocrites anyway. Besides, I know you never believed in religion either, never went to synagogue, and never prayed to God. I say again, I resent this."

"Why are you telling me how I should go about presenting my discoveries? And why are you always jumping to conclusions? Is that what they taught you in college? Now remember, anytime you don't like how I present my case you can leave, but this is equivalent to resigning in chess when you can't win. In order for me to show you how these so-called miracles come about, you must let me do it my way. Is that asking too much, or am I being unreasonable?"

"I'm sorry, and I apologize. Continue."

The fact that I never went to synagogue or prayed is equivalent to my not desiring to do other things that didn't interest me. But after making my discoveries I knew for a fact that God (this mathematical reality) was not a figment of the imagination. The reason theologians could never solve this problem of evil was because they never attempted to look behind the door marked 'Man's Will Is Not Free.' Why should they when they were convinced man's will was free? Plato, Christ, Spinoza, and many others came into the world and saw the truth but in a confused sort of way because the element of evil was always an unsolved factor. When Jesus Christ told the rabbis that God commanded man to turn the other cheek, they threw him out because the Bible told them that God said — "An eye for an eye and a tooth for a tooth." When his enemies nailed him to the cross he was heard to say — "They know not what they do." "Turn the other cheek" he said. Because Christ exemplified in his behavior the principle of forgiveness, and because he saw such suffering in the world, he drew to himself those who needed help, and there were many. However, the legacy he left for Christianity was never reconciled. How was it possible to turn the other cheek in a world of such evil? Why was the mind of man so confused and in spite of every possible criticism how was religion able to convince the world to be patient and have faith? Where did these theologians receive their inspiration since there was no way science could reconcile good and evil with a God that caused everything. They solved this problem in a very simple manner by dividing good and evil in half and God was only responsible for the first. Then they reasoned that God endowed man with freedom of the will to choose good over evil. To theologians, God is the creator of all goodness and since man does many things considered evil they were given no choice but to endow him with freedom of the will so that God could be absolved of all responsibility for evil, which was assigned to Satan. This is also the reason why religion is so hostile towards any person who speaks against free will. Is it any wonder that Christ and Spinoza plus innumerable others pulled away from the synagogue? Is it any wonder Spinoza became a heretic and was excommunicated? According to the thinkers of that time how could any intelligent person believe in Satan? Religion has never been able to reconcile the forces of good and evil with a caring and loving God, therefore Satan was destined to be born as the opposite of all good in the world.

Because Spinoza was dissatisfied with theology's explanation of good and evil, he opened the door of determinism and looked around quite a bit but did not know how to slay the fiery dragon (the great impasse of blame), so he pretended it wasn't even there. He stated, "We are men, not God. Evil is really not evil when seen in total perspective," and he rejected the principle of an eye for an eye. Will Durant, not at all satisfied with this aspect of Spinoza's philosophy, although he loved him dearly, could not understand how it was humanly possible to turn the other cheek in this kind of world. He also went in and looked around very thoroughly and, he too, saw the fiery dragon but unlike Spinoza he made no pretense of its non-existence. He just didn't know how to overcome the beast but refused to agree with what common sense told him to deny. The implications really need no further clarification as to why free will is in power. Nobody, including Spinoza and other philosophers, ever discovered what it meant that man's will is not free because they never unlocked the second door which leads to my discovery. The belief in free will was compelled to remain in power until the present time because no one had conclusive proof that determinism was true, nor could anyone slay the fiery dragon which seemed like an impossible feat. Is it any wonder that Johnston didn't want to get into this matter any further? Is it any wonder Durant never went beyond the vestibule? Are you beginning to recognize why it has been so difficult to get this knowledge thoroughly investigated? Since the modern world of science was playing havoc with religion it needed a boost and along came, just in the nick of time, a scientist who gave seven reasons why he believed in God. A. Cressy Morrison, who wrote his book, "Man Does Not Stand Alone," was almost convinced that God was a reality. He challenged Julian Huxley's conclusions written in his book, "Man Stands Alone." Both tried to answer the question, "Is there a Supreme Intelligence guiding this universe?" Who is right? Huxley said "no there isn't," but Morrison's arguments were mathematically sound and he gave quite a boost to instilling faith again in those people who were really beginning to wonder. I can almost remember word for word how he tried to prove that nothing happens by chance, and he did prove it except for this element of evil. It went something like this:

"Chance seems erratic, unexpected and subject to no method of

39

calculation, but though we are startled by its surprises, chance is subject to rigid and unbreakable law. The proverbial penny may turn up heads ten times in a row and the chance of an eleventh is not expected but is still one in two, but the chances of a run of ten heads coming up consecutively is very small. Supposing you have a bag containing one hundred marbles, ninety-nine black and one white. Shake the bag and let out one. The chance that the first marble out of the bag is the white one is exactly one in one hundred. Now put the marbles back and start again. The chance of the white coming out is still one in a hundred, but the chance of the white coming out first twice in succession is one in ten thousand (one hundred times one hundred).

Now try a third time and the chance of the white coming out three times in succession is one hundred times ten thousand or one in a million. Try another time or two and the figures become astronomical. The results of chance are as clearly bound by law as the fact that two plus two equals four.

In a game in which cards are shuffled and an ace of spades was dealt to one of the players, ace of hearts to the next, clubs to the third and diamonds to the dealer, followed by the deuces, the threes and so on, until each player had a complete set in numerical order, no one would believe the cards had not been arranged.

The chances are so great against such a happening that it probably never did happen in all the games played anywhere since cards was invented. But there are those who say it could happen, and I suppose the possibility does exist. Suppose a little child is asked by an expert chess player to beat him at chess in thirty-four moves and the child makes every move by pure chance exactly right to meet every twist and turn the expert attempts and does beat him in thirty-four moves. The expert would certainly think it was a dream or that he was out of his mind. But there are those who think the possibility of this happening by chance does exist. And I agree, it could happen, however small the possibility. My purpose in this discussion of chance is to point out clearly and scientifically the narrow limits which any life can exist on earth and prove by real evidence that all the nearly exact requirements of life could not be brought about on one planet at one time by chance. The size of the earth, the distance from the sun, the thickness of the earth's crust, the quantity of water, the amount of carbon dioxide, the volume of nitrogen, the emergence of man and his survival all point to order out of chaos, to design and purpose, and to the fact that according to the inexorable laws of mathematics all these could not occur by chance simultaneously on one planet once in a billion times. It could so occur, but it did not so occur. When the facts are so overwhelming and when we recognize as we must the attributes of our minds which are not material, is it possible to flaunt the evidence and take the one chance in a billion that we and all else are the result of chance? We have found that there are 999,999,999 chances to one against a belief that all things happen by chance. Science will not deny the facts as stated; the mathematicians will agree that the figures are correct. Now we encounter the stubborn resistance of the human mind, which is reluctant to give up fixed ideas. The early Greeks knew the earth was a sphere but it took two thousand years to convince men that this fact is true.

New ideas encounter opposition, ridicule and abuse, but truth survives and is verified. The argument is closed; the case is submitted to you, the jury, and your verdict will be awaited with confidence."

Morrison never realized that all the mathematical arguments in the world could never reveal God until we were delivered from evil; consequently, he was compelled to join the ranks of those who had faith. Nobody has yet said he knows for a mathematical fact that God is real, otherwise, there would be no need for faith. I know that two plus two equals four, I don't have faith that it's true. Well, do you still believe there is no Supreme Intelligence guiding this universe through mathematical laws which include the relation of man with man, and that everything happens by chance? Do you believe that your faith in God has been in vain? You are in for the surprise of your life.

This discussion on chance brings forcibly to the attention of the reader the fact that this world did not come about by chance. The purpose of this book is to prove undeniably that there is design to the universe. By delivering mankind from evil, the last vestige of doubt is removed. Through our deliverance, God is revealed to us; but the evil is not removed to prove that God is not a figment of the

41

imagination, but only because it is evil. He becomes an epiphenomenon of this tremendous fire that will be built to burn away the evil, and the light that is shed reveals His presence as the cause of the evil that He is now removing through these discoveries which He also caused; and no person alive will be able to dispute these undeniable facts. There is tremendous misunderstanding about the meaning of determinism, therefore, it is necessary to first demonstrate why man's will is not free so the reader can follow the reasoning which leads to my discovery. The fact that man's will is not free is the gateway that allows the reader to come face to face with the fiery dragon himself. It really doesn't make any difference whether or not the proof of determinism is established beforehand because undeniable proof is established in the meaning; but despite this it is still of value to know why man's will is not free, so to familiarize you with mathematical reasoning before we attack the heart of the problem I shall demonstrate in an undeniable manner exactly why will is not free. Once it is proven mathematically — which takes into consideration the implications — there can be no more opinions or theories expressed on the subject, just as our ancestors stopped saying, "I believe the earth is flat" once they knew for a fact it was round. There is a great deal of irony here because the philosophers who did not know it was impossible to prove freedom of the will believed in this theory because they were under the impression their reasoning had demonstrated the falseness of determinism. The reason proof of determinism is absolutely necessary is to preclude someone quoting Durant and interjecting a remark about man not being a machine. Is there anything about my demonstration that would make the reader think he is now a machine? On page 87 in Mansions of Philosophy he writes, "If he committed crimes, society was to blame; if he was a fool, it was the fault of the machine, which had slipped a cog in generating him." In other words, he assumes that this kind of knowledge, the knowledge that states man's will is not free, allows a person to shift his responsibility for what he does. One individual blames society for his crimes as he rots in prison while another blames the mechanical structure of the machine which slipped a cog and made him into a fool. You will soon see that not only Durant but all mankind are very much confused by the misleading logic of words that

42

do not describe reality for what it is. This is why it is imperative that we proceed in an undeniable, not logical, manner otherwise someone may quote Durant, a priest, professor, lawyer, judge or politician as an authority for believing in freedom of the will. I recently had a conversation with a friend who was very sincere in his desire to understand the principles in my book. His questions were predictable coming from a superficial understanding of man's nature and represent the confusion many people feel when the issue of determinism comes up.

"Isn't it obvious that we must have standards of some kind so that a child can be taught the difference between right and wrong, good and evil? Supposing all individuals in a society are told that it is wrong to steal (I hope you're not going to tell me this is right), yet certain ones deliberately ignore this and take what belongs to someone else; isn't it obvious that we must blame them because they were warned in advance that if they should steal they will be punished? Are you trying to tell me there is no such thing as a standard of right and wrong?"

"If you know the difference between right and wrong, and you also know that a person cannot be blamed or punished for what he does because his will is not free, isn't it obvious that we are given only one alternative and that is to prevent the desire to do what is wrong from arising which then makes it unnecessary to blame and punish? Just as long as man has this safety valve of blame and punishment, he doesn't have to find the solution to this doing of what is wrong. Parents can be very careless and excuse themselves by blaming their children, and governments can be careless and excuse themselves by blaming their citizens while plunging the entire world into war."

"But supposing they are not careless and they are doing everything in their power to prevent children and citizens from doing what is wrong so that blame and punishment are not necessary, what then? Are we not supposed to blame and punish them for our own protection when they do something wrong?"

"That's just the point. Once it is discovered through mathematical reasoning that man's will is definitely not free, then it becomes impossible to blame an individual for what he is compelled to do; consequently, it is imperative that we discover a way to prevent his desire to do the very things for which blame and punishment were previously necessary, as the lesser of two evils."

"This new world which looks good, sounds good, and seems theoretically possible in its blueprint form so far (since you haven't shown me yet how to rid the world of war and crime — two most important items), it may be just another dream, and even if it isn't, it took the Greeks two millennium to convince mankind that the earth was a sphere. Even today, there are still some people who don't believe it, so how do you expect people to listen to something that not only sounds impossible, but is so far removed from contemporary thought?"

"This is the stumbling block I am faced with."

"Are you telling me that this discovery, whatever it is, will prevent man from desiring to commit murder, rape, start a war, annihilate 6 million people, etc., is that right?"

"That's correct. The corollary, Thou Shall Not Blame, when it is extended does not mean that we will be forced to condone what hurts us, but we will be shown how to prevent these evils by mathematically extending the corollary. And the amazing thing is that both sides of this equation are correct. Christ said, "Turn the other cheek" and Durant said, "This is impossible." Just think about this for one moment. Would you believe that both principles are mathematically correct?"

"How is that possible?"

"God made the reconciliation of these two principles the time when He would reveal Himself to all mankind. But to get here you can see what had to be done first since the paths leading up to this understanding were camouflaged with layers upon layers of words that concealed the truth."

"Is proving that man's will is not free the key to open the door and your second discovery?"

"Of course not; I just told you that the fiery dragon must be killed to get the key. First, I must prove that man's will is not free so we can come face to face with the fiery dragon (the great impasse of blame), and I will prove it in a mathematical, undeniable manner.

44

Then I shall jab him in the right eye, then the left, then I shall cut out his tongue. I took fencing lessons for the job. And finally I shall pierce him in his heart. Then when I have made certain he is dead."

"I thought you killed him already."

"I did, but there was a dragon for each person, so instead of giving everybody a sword; steel is high these days, I shall slay him so the whole world can see he is dead."

"Do you mean to tell me there is absolutely no way all evil can be removed from our lives without knowledge of your discovery?"

"That's absolutely true."

"Then your discovery must be the most fantastic thing ever discovered."

"It truly is because God is showing us the way at last. However, before I show how it is possible to resolve the implications, it is necessary to repeat that I will proceed in a step by step manner. This dragon has been guarding an invisible key and door for many years, and this could never be made visible except for someone who saw these undeniable relations. If, therefore, you would like to learn that Man Does Not Stand Alone as Morrison understood from his scientific observations; that God, this Supreme Intelligence, is a mathematical reality of infinite wisdom, then what do you say we begin our voyage that will literally change the entire world. We are not interested in opinions and theories regardless of where they originate, just in the truth, so let's proceed to the next step and prove conclusively, beyond a shadow of doubt, that what we do of our own free will (of our own desire because we want to) is done absolutely and positively not of our own free will. Remember, by proving that determinism, as the opposite of free will, is true, we also establish undeniable proof that free will is false." So without any further ado, let us begin.

The dictionary states that free will is the power of self-determination regarded as a special faculty of choosing good and evil without compulsion or necessity. Made, done, or given of one's own free choice; voluntary. But this is only part of the definition since it is implied that man can be held responsible, blamed and punished for doing what is considered wrong or evil since it is believed

45

he could have chosen otherwise. In other words, it is believed that man has the ability to do other than he does, if he wants to, and therefore can be held responsible for doing what he is not supposed to do. These very words reveal the fallacy of this belief to those who have mathematical perception. Man is held responsible not for doing what he desires to do or considers right, better or good for himself under his particular set of circumstances, but for doing what others judge to be wrong or evil, and they feel absolutely certain he could have acted otherwise had he wanted to. Isn't this the theme of free will? But take note. Supposing the alternative judged right for him by others is not desired by himself because of conditions known only to him, what then? Does this make his will free? It is obvious that a great part of our lives offers no choice, consequently, this is not my consideration. For example, free will does not hold any person responsible for what he does in an unconscious state like hypnosis, nor does it believe that man can be blamed for being born, growing, sleeping, eating, defecating, urinating, etc.; therefore, it is unnecessary to prove that these actions, which come under the normal compulsion of living, are beyond control.

Supposing a father is desperately in need of work to feed his family but cannot find a job. Let us assume he is living in the United States and for various reasons doesn't come under the consideration of unemployment compensation or relief and can't get any more credit for food, clothing, shelter, etc.; what is he supposed to do? If he steals a loaf of bread to feed his family the law can easily punish him by saying he didn't have to steal if he didn't want to, which is perfectly true. Others might say stealing is evil, that he could have chosen an option which was good. In this case almost any other alternative would have sufficed. But supposing this individual preferred stealing because he considered this act good for himself in comparison to the evil of asking for charity or further credit because it appeared to him, at that moment, that this was the better choice of the three that were available to him — so does this make his will free? It is obvious that he did not have to steal if he didn't want to, but he wanted to, and it is also obvious that those in law enforcement did not have to punish him if they didn't want to, but both sides wanted to do what they did under the circumstances.

46

In reality, we are carried along on the wings of time or life during every moment of our existence and have no say in this matter whatsoever. We cannot stop ourselves from being born and are compelled to either live out our lives the best we can, or commit suicide. Is it possible to disagree with this? However, to prove that what we do of our own free will, of our own desire because we want to do it, is also beyond control, it is necessary to employ mathematical (undeniable) reasoning. Therefore, since it is absolutely impossible for man to be both dead and alive at the same time, and since it is absolutely impossible for a person to desire committing suicide unless dissatisfied with life (regardless of the reason), we are given the ability to demonstrate a revealing and undeniable relation.

Every motion, from the beating heart to the slightest reflex action, from all inner to outer movements of the body, indicates that life is never satisfied or content to remain in one position for always like an inanimate object, which position shall be termed 'death.' I shall now call the present moment of time or life here for the purpose of clarification, and the next moment coming up there. You are now standing on this present moment of time and space called here and you are given two alternatives, either live or kill yourself; either move to the next spot called there or remain where you are without moving a hair's breadth by committing suicide.

"I prefer..." Excuse the interruption, but the very fact that you started to answer me or didn't commit suicide at that moment makes it obvious that you were not satisfied to stay in one position, which is death or here and prefer moving off that spot to there, which motion is life. Consequently, the motion of life which is any motion from here to there is a movement away from that which dissatisfies, otherwise, had you been satisfied to remain here or where you are, you would never have moved to there. Since the motion of life constantly moves away from here to there, which is an expression of dissatisfaction with the present position, it must obviously move constantly in the direction of greater satisfaction. It should be obvious that our desire to live, to move off the spot called here, is determined by a law over which we have no control because even if we should kill ourselves we are choosing what gives us greater satisfaction, otherwise we would not kill ourselves. The truth of the matter is that

47

at any particular moment the motion of man is not free for all life obeys this invariable law. He is constantly compelled by his nature to make choices, decisions, and to prefer of whatever options are available during his lifetime that which he considers better for himself and his set of circumstances. For example, when he found that a discovery like the electric bulb was for his benefit in comparison to candlelight, he was compelled to prefer it for his motion, just being alive, has always been in the direction of greater satisfaction. Consequently, during every moment of man's progress he always did what he had to do because he had no choice. Although this demonstration proves that man's will is not free, your mind may not be accustomed to grasping these type relations, so I will elaborate.

Supposing you wanted very much of two alternatives A, which we shall designate something considered evil by society, instead of B, the humdrum of your regular routine; could you possibly pick B at that particular moment of time if A is preferred as a better alternative when nothing could dissuade you from your decision, not even the threat of the law? What if the clergy, given two alternatives, choose A, which shall now represent something considered good, instead of B, that which is judged evil; would it be possible for them to prefer the latter when the former is available as an alternative? If it is utterly impossible to choose B in this comparison are they not compelled, by their very nature, to prefer A; and how can they be free when the favorable difference between A and B is the compulsion of their choice and the motion of life in the direction of greater satisfaction? To be free, according to the definition of free will, man would be able to prefer of two alternatives, either the one he wants or the one he doesn't want, which is an absolute impossibility because selecting what he doesn't want when what he does want is available as an alternative is a motion in the direction of dissatisfaction. In other words, if man was free he could actually prefer of several alternatives the one that gives him the least satisfaction, which would reverse the direction of his life, and make him prefer the impossible.

To give you a more familiar example, if it were possible that B could be selected even though A was the desirable choice, it would permit a woman to spend on a dress she doesn't prefer when a dress she does prefer is available, or to pick from a selection of dresses the one she finds the least desirable. Let us imagine for a moment that this woman is late for a business meeting and must quickly choose between two dresses. If both are undesirable, she is compelled to select the dress that is the least undesirable of the two; consequently, her choice in this comparison is the preferable alternative. Obviously she has other options; she could leave both dresses and wear something from home, continue to shop and call in late, etc. This is a hypothetical situation for the purpose of demonstrating that once she decides to buy a dress as a solution to her problem — and regardless of the factors that contribute to her final decision — she is compelled to prefer the dress that gives every indication of being the best possible choice under the circumstances. For example, if cost is an important consideration she may desire to buy the less expensive dress because it fits within her price range, and though she would find great satisfaction seeing herself in the more expensive dress, she finds greater satisfaction choosing the dress that appeals to her the least. Therefore, regardless of her choice it is good, not evil, for her. This is where there may be some misunderstanding. Moving toward greater satisfaction does not mean we are always satisfied; it just means that we are compelled to prefer *what we believe to be* the best possible choice of the options that are available to us. [Note: This does not mean that we have considered all possible options; only those options that come to mind or have been brought to our attention at any given moment in time. Nor does it mean that our choices are unlimited for the availability of choices depends on a myriad of cultural, economic, and social factors]. After coming home she may have a change of heart and wish she had splurged on the more expensive dress. She may decide to go back to the store to make an exchange, or she may decide to just keep the dress because returning it involves too much time and effort making this the least favorable option. Each moment offers a new set of options but always in the direction of greater satisfaction.

"Is that it? You mean there is nothing else, and this is supposed to satisfy me? Let's assume for the sake of argument that other people are just as confused as me. Frankly, you could never prove by me that man's will is not free simply because I can't follow your reasoning. Isn't there something else you can add to prove your equation, just as we can prove that two from six leaves four because four plus two equals six?"

To satisfy you I shall put this to a mathematical test for further proof and clarification. Imagine that you were taken prisoner in war time for espionage and condemned to death, but mercifully given a choice between two exits: A is the painless hemlock of Socrates, while B is death by having your head held under water. The letters A and B, representing small or large differences are compared. The comparison is absolutely necessary to know which is preferable. The difference which is considered favorable, regardless of the reason, is the compulsion of greater satisfaction desire is forced to take which makes one of them an impossible choice in this comparison simply because it gives less satisfaction under the circumstances. Consequently, since B is an impossible choice, man is not free to choose A. Is it humanly possible, providing no other conditions are introduced to affect your decision, to prefer exit B if A is offered as an alternative?

"Yes, if this meant that those I loved would not be harmed in any way."

"Well, if this was your preference under these conditions, could you prefer the other alternative?"

"No I couldn't, but this is ridiculous because you really haven't given me any choice."

You most certainly do have a choice, and if your will is free, you should be able to choose B just as well as A, or A just as well as B. In other words, if B is considered the greater evil in this comparison of alternatives, one is compelled, completely beyond control, to prefer A. It is impossible for B to be selected in this comparison (although it could be chosen to something still worse) as long as A is available as an alternative. Consequently, since B is an impossible choice you are not free to choose A, for your preference is a natural compulsion of the direction of life over which you have absolutely no control. Let me explain this in another way. Once it is understood that life is compelled to move in the direction of satisfaction, and if two such alternatives were presented to you as in the example above, what choice would you possibly have but to accept the lesser of two evils? Since it is absolutely impossible to prefer something considered still

50

worse in your opinion, regardless of what it is, are you not compelled, completely beyond your control in this set of circumstances, to prefer A; and since the definition of free will states that man can choose good over evil without compulsion or necessity, how is it possible for the will of man to be free when choice is under a tremendous amount of compulsion since B was evil, as the worse alternative, and could not be selected in this comparison of possibilities?

The word 'choice' itself indicates there are meaningful differences otherwise there would be no choice in the matter at all as with A and A. The reason you are confused is because the word choice is very misleading for it assumes that man has two or more possibilities, but in reality this is a delusion because the direction of life, always moving towards greater satisfaction, compels a person to prefer of differences what he, not someone else, considers better for himself, and when two or more alternatives are presented for his consideration he is compelled by his very nature to prefer not that one which he considers worse, but what gives every indication of being better or more satisfying for the particular set of circumstances involved. Choosing, or the comparison of differences, is an integral part of man's nature, but to reiterate this important point...he is compelled to prefer of alternatives that which he considers better for himself and though he chooses various things all through the course of his life, he is never given any choice at all. Although the definition of free will states that man can choose good or evil without compulsion or necessity, how is it possible for the will of man to be free when choice is under a tremendous amount of compulsion to choose the most preferable alternative each and every moment of time?

"I agree with all this, but how many times in your life have you remarked, 'You give me no choice' or 'it makes no difference?'"

Just because some differences are so obviously superior in value where you are concerned that no hesitation is required to decide which is preferable, while other differences need a more careful consideration, does not change the direction of life which moves always towards greater satisfaction than what the present position offers. You must bear in mind that what one person judges good or bad for himself doesn't make it so for others especially when it is remembered that a juxtaposition of differences in each case present

51

alternatives that affect choice.

"But there are many times when I have been terribly dissatisfied with things that I have done, and at that exact moment isn't it obvious that I am not moving in the direction of satisfaction because I am very dissatisfied? It seems to me that it is still possible to give an example of how man can be made to move in the direction of dissatisfaction. If I could do this, all your reasoning would be shot to hell."

"That's true, but I defy you or anyone else to give me an example of this. Go ahead and try."

"Let us imagine that of two apples, a red and a yellow, I prefer the yellow because I am extremely allergic to the red, consequently, my taste lies in the direction of the latter which gives me greater satisfaction. In fact, the very thought of eating the red apple makes me feel sick. Yet in spite of this I am going to eat it to demonstrate that even though I am dissatisfied — and prefer the yellow apple — I can definitely move in the direction of dissatisfaction."

In response to this demonstration, isn't it obvious that regardless of the reason you decided to eat the red apple, and even though it would be distasteful in comparison, this choice at that moment of time gave you greater satisfaction, otherwise, you would have definitely selected and eaten the yellow? The normal circumstances under which you frequently ate the yellow apple in preference were changed by your desire to prove a point, therefore it gave you greater satisfaction to eat what you did not normally eat in an effort to prove that life can be made to move in the direction of dissatisfaction. Consequently, since B (eating the yellow apple) was an impossible choice (because it gave you less satisfaction under the circumstances), you were not free to choose A.

Regardless of how many examples you experiment with, the results will always be the same because this is an immutable law. From moment to moment all through life man can never move in the direction of dissatisfaction, and that his every motion, conscious or unconscious, is a natural effort to get rid of some dissatisfaction or move to greater satisfaction, otherwise, as has been shown, not being dissatisfied, he could never move from <u>here</u> to <u>there</u>. Every motion of life expresses dissatisfaction with the present position. Scratching is the effort of life to remove the dissatisfaction of the itch — as urinating, defecating, sleeping, working, playing, mating, walking, talking, and moving about in general are unsatisfied needs of life pushing man always in the direction of satisfaction. It is easy, in many cases, to recognize things that satisfy, such as money when funds are low, but it is extremely difficult at other times to comprehend the innumerable subconscious factors often responsible for the malaise of dissatisfaction. Your desire to take a bath arises from a feeling of unseemliness or a wish to be refreshed, which means that you are dissatisfied with the way you feel at that moment; and your desire to get out of the bathtub arises from a feeling of dissatisfaction with a position that has suddenly grown uncomfortable. This simple demonstration proves conclusively that man's will is not free because satisfaction is the only direction life can take, and it offers only one possibility at each moment of time.

The government holds each person responsible to obey the laws and then punishes those who do not while absolving itself of all responsibility; but how is it possible for someone to obey that which under certain conditions appears to him worse? It is quite obvious that a person does not have to steal if he doesn't want to, but under certain conditions he wants to, and it is also obvious that those who enforce the laws do not have to punish if they don't want to, but both sides want to do what they consider better for themselves under the circumstances. The Russians didn't have to start a communistic revolution against the tyranny that prevailed; they were not compelled to do this; they wanted to. The Japanese didn't have to attack us at Pearl Harbor; they wanted to. We didn't have to drop an atomic bomb among their people, we wanted to. It is an undeniable observation that man does not have to commit a crime or hurt another in any way, if he doesn't want to. The most severe tortures, even the threat of death, cannot compel or cause him to do what he makes up his mind not to do. Since this observation is mathematically undeniable, the expression 'free will,' which has come to signify this aspect, is absolutely true in this context because it symbolizes what the perception of this relation cannot deny, and here lies in part the unconscious source of all the dogmatism and confusion since MAN IS NOT CAUSED OR COMPELLED TO

53

DO TO ANOTHER WHAT HE MAKES UP HIS MIND NOT TO DO — but that does not make his will free.

In other words, if someone were to say — "I didn't really want to hurt that person but couldn't help myself under the circumstances," which demonstrates that though he believes in freedom of the will he admits he was not free to act otherwise; that he was forced by his environment to do what he really didn't want to do, or should he make any effort to shift his responsibility for this hurt to heredity, God, his parents, the fact that his will is not free, or something else as the cause, he is obviously lying to others and being dishonest with himself because absolutely nothing is forcing him against his will to do what he doesn't want to do, for over this, as was just shown, he has mathematical control.

"It's amazing, all my life I have believed man's will is free but for the first time I can actually see that his will is not free."

Another friend commented: "You may be satisfied but I'm not. The definition of determinism is the philosophical and ethical doctrine that man's choices, decisions and actions are decided by antecedent causes, inherited or environmental, acting upon his character. According to this definition we are not given a choice because we are being caused to do what we do by a previous event or circumstance. But I know for a fact that nothing can make me do what I make up my mind not to do — as you just mentioned a moment ago. If I don't want to do something, nothing, not environment, heredity, or anything else you care to throw in can make me do it because over this I have absolute control. Since I can't be made to do anything against my will, doesn't this make my will free? And isn't it a contradiction to say that man's will is not free yet nothing can make him do what he doesn't want to do?"

"How about that, he brought out something I never would have thought of."

All he said was that you can lead a horse to water but you can't make him drink, which is undeniable, however, though it is a mathematical law that nothing can compel man to do to another what he makes up his mind not to do — this is an extremely crucial point — he is nevertheless under a compulsion during every moment of his existence to do everything he does. This reveals, as your friend just

54

pointed out, that man has absolute control over the former but absolutely none over the latter because he must constantly move in the direction of greater satisfaction. It is true that nothing in the past can cause what occurs in the present, for all we ever have is the present; the past and future are only words that describe a deceptive relation. Consequently, determinism was faced with an almost impossible task because it assumed that heredity and environment caused man to choose evil, and the proponents of free will believed the opposite, that man was not caused or compelled, 'he did it of his own accord; he wanted to do it, he didn't have to.' The term 'free will' contains an assumption or fallacy for it implies that if man is not caused or compelled to do anything against his will, it must be preferred of his own free will. This is one of those logical, not mathematical conclusions. The expression, 'I did it of my own free will' is perfectly correct when it is understood to mean 'I did it because I wanted to; nothing compelled or caused me to do it since I could have acted otherwise *had I desired.*' This expression was necessarily misinterpreted because of the general ignorance that prevailed for although it is correct in the sense that a person did something because he wanted to, this in no way indicates that his will is free. In fact I shall use the expression 'of my own free will' frequently myself which only means 'of my own desire.' Are you beginning to see how words have deceived everyone?

"You must be kidding? Here you are in the process of demonstrating why the will of man is not free, and in the same breath you tell me you're doing this of your own free will."

This is clarified somewhat when you understand that man is free to choose what he prefers, what he desires, what he wants, what he considers better for himself and his family. But the moment he prefers or desires anything is an indication that he is compelled to this action because of some dissatisfaction, which is the natural compulsion of his nature. Because of this misinterpretation of the expression 'man's will is free,' great confusion continues to exist in any discussion surrounding this issue, for although it is true man has to make choices he must always prefer that which he considers good not evil for himself when the former is offered as an alternative. The words cause and compel are the perception of an improper or

55

fallacious relation because in order to be developed and have meaning it was absolutely necessary that the expression 'free will' be born as their opposite, as tall gives meaning to short. But these words do not describe reality unless interpreted properly. Nothing causes man to build cities, develop scientific achievements, write books, compose music, go to war, argue and fight, commit terrible crimes, pray to God, for these things are mankind already at a particular stage of his development, just as children were sacrificed at an earlier stage. These activities or motions are the natural entelechy of man who is always developing, correcting his mistakes, and moving in the direction of greater satisfaction by better removing the dissatisfaction of the moment, which is a normal compulsion of his nature over which he has absolutely no control. Looking back in hindsight allows man to evaluate his progress and make corrections when necessary because he is always learning from previous experience. The fact that will is not free demonstrates that man, as part of nature or God, has been unconsciously developing at a mathematical rate and during every moment of his progress was doing what he had to do because he had no free choice. But this does not mean that he was caused to do anything against his will, for the word cause, like choice and past, is very misleading as it implies that something other than man himself is responsible for his actions. Four is not caused by two plus two, it is that already. As long as history has been recorded, these two opposing principles were never reconciled until now. The amazing thing is that this ignorance, this conflict of ideas, ideologies, and desires, theology's promulgation of free will, the millions that criticized determinism as fallacious, was exactly as it was supposed to be. It was impossible for man to have acted differently because the mankind system is obeying this invariable law of satisfaction which makes the motions of all life just as harmonious as the solar system; but these systems are not caused by, they are these laws.

"Can you clarify this a little bit more?"

"Certainly. In other words, no one is compelling a person to work at a job he doesn't like or remain in a country against his will. He actually wants to do the very things he dislikes simply because the alternative is considered worse and he must choose something to do among the various things in his environment, or else commit suicide.

Was it humanly possible to make Gandhi and his followers do what they did not want to do when unafraid of death which was judged, according to their circumstances, the lesser of two evils? Therefore, when any person says he was compelled to do what he did against his will, that he didn't want to but had to — and innumerable of our expressions say this — he is obviously confused and unconsciously dishonest with himself and others because everything man does to another is done only because he wants to do it, done to be humorous, of his own free will, which only means that his preference gave him greater satisfaction at that moment of time, for one reason or another; but remember, this desire of one thing over another is a compulsion beyond control for which he cannot be blamed. All I am doing is clarifying your terms so that you are not confused, but make sure you understand this mathematical difference before proceeding further."

"His reasoning is perfect. I can't find a flaw although I thought I did. I think I understand now. Just because I cannot be made to do something against my will does not mean my will is free because my desire not to do it appeared the better reason, which gave me no free choice since I got greater satisfaction. Nor does the expression, 'I did it of my own free will, nobody made me do it,' mean that I actually did it of my own free will — although I did it because I wanted to — because my desire to do it appeared the better reason which gave me no free choice since I got greater satisfaction."

"He does understand."

"Does this mean you are also in complete agreement so I can proceed?"

"Yes it does."

Then let me summarize by taking careful note of this simple reasoning that proves conclusively (except for the implications already referred to) that will is not free. Man has two possibilities that are reduced to the common denominator of one. Either he does not have a choice because none is involved, as with aging, and then it is obvious that he is under the compulsion of living regardless of what his particular motion at any moment might be, or he has a choice and then is given two or more alternatives of which he is compelled by his nature to prefer the one that appears to offer the greatest satisfaction whether it is the lesser of two evils, the greater of two goods, or a good over an evil. Therefore, it is absolutely impossible for will to be free because man never has a free choice, though it must be remembered that the words *good and evil* are judgments of what others think is right and wrong, not symbols of reality. The truth of the matter is that the words good and evil can only have reference to what is a benefit or a hurt to oneself. Killing someone may be good in comparison to the evil of having that person kill me. The reason someone commits suicide is not because he is compelled to do this against his will, but only because the alternative of continuing to live under certain conditions is considered worse. He was not happy to take his own life but under the conditions he was compelled to prefer, by his very nature, the lesser of two evils which gave him greater satisfaction. Consequently, when he does not desire to take his own life because he considers this the worse alternative as a solution to his problems, he is still faced with making a decision, whatever it is, which means that he is compelled to choose an alternative that is more satisfying. For example, in the morning when the alarm clock goes off he has three possibilities; commit suicide so he never has to get up, go back to sleep, or get up and face the day. Since suicide is out of the question under these conditions, he is left with two alternatives. Even though he doesn't like his job and hates the thought of going to work, he needs money, and since he can't stand having creditors on his back or being threatened with lawsuits, it is the lesser of two evils to get up and go to work. He is not happy or satisfied to do this when he doesn't like his job, but he finds greater satisfaction doing one thing than another. Dog food is <u>good</u> to a starving man when the other alternatives are horse manure or death, just as the prices on a menu may cause him to prefer eating something he likes less because the other alternative of paying too high a price for what he likes more is still considered worse under his particular circumstances. The law of self-preservation demands that he do what he believes will help him stay alive and make his life easier, and if he is hard-pressed to get what he needs to survive he may be willing to cheat, steal, kill and do any number of things which he considers good for himself in comparison to the evil of finding himself worse off if he doesn't do these things. All this simply proves is that man is compelled to move in the direction of satisfaction during every moment of his existence. It does not yet remove the implications. The expression 'I did it of my own free will' has been seriously misunderstood for although it is impossible to do anything of one's own free will, HE DOES EVERYTHING BECAUSE HE WANTS TO since absolutely nothing can make him do what he doesn't want to. Think about this once again. Was it humanly possible to make Gandhi and his followers do what they did not want to do when unafraid of death which was judged, according to their circumstances, the lesser of two evils? In their eyes, death was the better choice if the alternative was to lose their freedom. Many people are confused over this one point. Just because no one on this earth can make you do anything against your will does not mean your will is free. Gandhi wanted freedom for his people and it was against his will to stop his nonviolent movement even though he constantly faced the possibility of death, but this doesn't mean his will was free; it just means that it gave him greater satisfaction to face death than to forego his fight for freedom. Consequently, when any person says he was compelled to do what he did against his will, that he really didn't want to but had to because he was being tortured, he is obviously confused and unconsciously dishonest with himself and others because he could die before being forced to do something against his will. What he actually means was that he didn't like being tortured because the pain was unbearable so rather than continue suffering this way he preferred, as the lesser of two evils, to tell his captors what they wanted to know, but he did this because he wanted to not because some external force made him do this against his will. If by talking he would know that someone he loved would be instantly killed, pain and death might have been judged the lesser of two evils. This is an extremely crucial point because though it is true that will is not free, ABSOLUTELY NOTHING ON THIS EARTH CAN MAKE MAN DO ANYTHING AGAINST HIS WILL. He might not like what he did — but he wanted to do it because the alternative gave him no free or better choice. It is extremely important that you clear this up in your mind before proceeding.

This knowledge was not available before now and what is revealed as each individual becomes conscious of his true nature is something

59

fantastic to behold, for it not only gives ample proof that evil is no accident but it will also put an end to every conceivable kind of hurt that exists in human relations. There will take place a virtual miracle of transformation as each person consciously realizes WHAT IT MEANS that his will is not free, which has not yet been revealed. And now I shall demonstrate how these two undeniable laws or principles — that nothing can compel man to do anything against his will because over this his nature allows absolute control, and that his will is not free because his nature also compels him to prefer of available alternatives the one that offers greater satisfaction — will reveal a third invariable law — the discovery to which reference has been made.

CHAPTER TWO

THE TWO-SIDED EQUATION

Once it is established as an undeniable law that man's will is not free, as was just demonstrated, we cannot assume that it is free because philosophers like Durant could not get by the implications. Therefore, we must begin our reasoning where he left off which means that we are going to accept the magic elixir (call it what you will, corollary, slide rule or basic principle), THOU SHALL NOT BLAME, and transmute the baser metals of human nature into the pure gold of the Golden Age even though it presents what appears to be an insurmountable problem, for how is it possible not to blame people who hurt us when we know they didn't have to do this if they didn't want to. The solution, however, only requires the perception and extension of relations which cannot be denied, and this mathematical corollary, that man is not to blame for anything at all, is a key to the infinite wisdom of God which will unlock a treasure so wonderful that you will be compelled to catch your breath in absolute amazement. This slide rule will adequately solve every problem we have not only without hurting a living soul, but while benefiting everyone to an amazing degree. You can prepare yourselves to say good-bye to all the hurt and evil that came into existence out of necessity. However, the problems that confront us at this moment are very complex which make it necessary to treat every aspect of our lives in a separate, yet related, manner. God, not me, is finally going to reveal the solution.

Since time immemorial the two opposing forces of good and evil compelled theologians to separate the world into two realms, with God responsible for all the good in the world and Satan responsible for the evil while endowing man with free will so that this separation could be reasonable. Giving birth to Satan or some other force of darkness as an explanation for the evil that existed illustrates how religion tried desperately to cling to the belief in a merciful God. But this dividing

61

line between good and evil will no longer be necessary when the corollary, Thou Shall Not Blame, demonstrates that once it becomes a permanent condition of the environment, all the evil (hurt) in human relations must come to a peaceful end. The absolute proof that man's will is not free is the undeniable fact that we are given no alternative but to move in this direction once it is understood that this law can control man's actions only by obeying this corollary for then everything that came into existence which caused us to blame and punish must, out of absolute necessity, take leave of this earth. Mankind will be given no choice; this has been taken out of our hands, as is the motion of the earth around the sun.

The first step is realizing that the solution requires that we work our problem backwards which means that every step of the way will be a forced move which will become a loose end and only when all these ends are drawn together will the blueprint be complete. It is only by extending our slide rule, Thou Shall Not Blame, which is the key, that we are given the means to unlock the solution. An example of working a problem backwards, follow this: If you were told that a woman with a pocketbook full of money went on a spending spree to ten stores, paid a dollar to get in every one, a dollar to get out, spent half of what she had in each and came out of the last place absolutely broke, it would be very easy to determine the amount of money she had to start because the dollar she paid to get out of the last store which broke her must represent one-half of the money spent there. Consequently, she had two dollars left after paying a dollar to get in, giving her three just before entering. Since she paid a dollar to get out of the penultimate store, this added to the three gives her four which represents one-half of the money spent there. Continuing this process eight more times it is absolutely undeniable that she must have begun her spending spree with $3,069. As we can see from this example, when a key fact is available from which to reason it is then possible to solve a problem, but when it is not, we must form conjectures and express opinions with the aid of logic. At first glance it appears impossible not to blame an individual for murder, or any heinous crime, but when we extend this key fact it can be seen that these acts of evil are not condoned with the understanding that man's will is not free, but prevented. Regardless of someone's opinion as to

62

the rightness or wrongness of the answer to the problem I just gave, an opinion that would have to be based upon a logical conclusion as is that of our experts when considering the impossibility of removing all evil from our lives, we know the answer is correct because the reasoning that follows from this key fact is scientifically sound.

By a similar process of working our problem backwards we can officially launch the Golden Age which necessitates the removal of all forms of blame (the judgment of what is right for another) so that each person knows he is completely free to do what he wants to do. Although solving the problem of evil requires balancing an equation of such magnitude, it is not difficult when we have our infallible slide rule which God has given us as a guide. By now I hope you understand that the word God is a symbol for the source of everything that exists, whereas theology draws a line between good and evil using the word God only as a symbol for the former. Actually no one gave me this slide rule, that is, no one handed it to me, but the same force that gave birth to my body and brain compelled me to move in the direction of satisfaction and for me to be satisfied after reading Will Durant's analysis of free will it was necessary to disagree with what obviously was the reasoning of logic, not mathematics. I was not satisfied, which forced me to get rid of my dissatisfaction by proving that this philosopher did not know whereof he spoke. To say that God made me do this is equivalent to saying I was compelled, by my nature, to move in this direction of greater satisfaction, which is absolutely true. Definitions mean absolutely nothing where reality is concerned. Regardless of what words I use to describe the sun; regardless of how much there is I don't know about this ball of fire does not negate the fact that it is a part of the real world, and regardless of what words I employ to describe God does not change the fact that He is a reality. You may ask, "But isn't there quite a difference between seeing the sun and seeing God? I know that the description of the sun could be inaccurate, but I know it is a part of the real world. However, we cannot point to any particular thing and say this is God, therefore we must assume because of certain things that God is a reality, correct?"

We assumed energy was contained within the atom until a discovery was made that proved this, and we also assumed or believed that there was a design to this universe by the fact that the solar system moves in such mathematical harmony. Did the sun, moon, earth, planets and stars just fall into perfect order, or is there some internal urgency pushing everything in a particular direction? Now that it has been discovered that man's will is not free and at the very moment this discovery is made a mathematical demonstration compels man to veer sharply in a new direction although still towards greater satisfaction, then it can be seen just as clearly as we see the sun that the mankind system has always been just as harmonious as the solar system only we never knew it because part of the harmony was this disharmony between man and man which is now being permanently removed. This discovery also reveals that God is a mathematical, undeniable reality. This means, to put it another way, that Man Does Not Stand Alone. Therefore, to say God is good is a true observation for nothing in this universe when seen in total perspective is evil since each individual must choose what is better for himself, even if that choice hurts another as a consequence.

Every human being is and has been obeying God's will — Spinoza, his sister, Nageli, Durant, Mendel, Christ and even those who nailed him to the cross; but God has a secret plan that is going to shock all mankind due to the revolutionary changes that must come about for his benefit. This new world is coming into existence not because of my will, not because I made a discovery (sooner or later it had to be found because the knowledge of what it means that man's will is not free is a definite part of reality), but only because we are compelled to obey the laws of our nature. Do you really think it was an accident the solar system came into existence; an accident that the sun is just the proper distance from the earth so we don't roast or freeze; an accident that the earth revolved just at the right speed to fulfill many exacting functions; an accident that our bodies and brains developed just that way; an accident that I made my discovery exactly when I did? To show you how fantastic is the infinite wisdom that controls every aspect of this universe through invariable laws that we are at last getting to understand, which includes the mankind as well as the solar system, just follow this: Here is versatile man — writer, composer, artist, inventor, scientist, philosopher, theologian, architect, mathematician, chess player, prostitute, murderer, thief, etc., whose will is absolutely and positively not free despite all the learned opinions to the contrary, yet compelled by his very nature and lack of development to believe that it is since it was impossible not to blame and punish the terrible evils that came into existence out of necessity and then permitted to perceive the necessary relations as to why will is not free and what this means for the entire world which perception was utterly impossible without the development and absolutely necessary for the inception of our Golden Age. In all of history have you ever been confronted with anything more incredible?

In reality we are all the result of forces completely beyond our control. As we extend the corollary, Thou Shall Not Blame, we are able to see for the very first time how it is now within our power to prevent those things for which blame and punishment came into existence. Although Spinoza did not understand the full significance of this enigmatic corollary, he accepted it by rejecting the opposite principle of an eye for an eye by refusing to defend himself against his sister or blame her for cheating him out of his inheritance. Neither he nor his sister had a free choice because the one was willing to cheat to get what she wanted while he was willing to be cheated rather than hold her responsible. Spinoza made matters worse for himself financially, but at that moment of time he had no free choice because it gave him greater satisfaction to let her cheat him out of what he was entitled to by law. Both of them were moving in the direction of what gave them satisfaction. Spinoza's sister had no understanding of this knowledge nor did the world at that time, although Spinoza himself knew that man's will is not free. Consequently, he allowed others to hurt him with a first blow by turning the other cheek. He was excommunicated from the synagogue while being God-intoxicated, which seems to be a contradiction. You would think that a person would be thrown out for being an atheist but not for being a God-intoxicated man. The fact that I know God is a reality doesn't intoxicate me. I know that the sun is also a reality but when the heat gets unbearable, should I jump for joy? There is no comparison between Spinoza and myself. He was a gentle man, I am not. He refused to blame his sister for stealing what rightfully belonged to him because he was confused and believed she couldn't help herself. I, on the other hand, would never advocate turning the other cheek when someone can get the advantage by not turning it. He excused her conduct, but if someone tried to take what belonged to me I'd fight him tooth and nail. If an aggressive country should start a war before this knowledge is released, it is only natural that we fight back with everything we've got. Turning the other cheek under these conditions could lead to further harm, which is why most people reject the pacifist position. How is it humanly possible not to fight back when one is being hurt first, which goes back to the justification of 'an eye for an eye and a tooth for a tooth.' I personally would get greater satisfaction defending myself or retaliating against those people who would do, or have done, things to hurt me and my family. I'm not a saint, but a scientist of human conduct. Most of mankind is compelled, for greater satisfaction, to move in this direction. Therefore, it should be clear that the corollary, Thou Shall Not Blame, does not mean that you should suddenly stop blaming because you have discovered that man's will is not free. It only means at this point that we are going to follow it, to extend it, to see exactly where it takes us, something that investigators like Durant have never done because the implications prevented them from opening the door beyond the vestibule. The fact that man's will is not free only means that he is compelled to move in the direction of greater satisfaction. If you sock me I might get greater satisfaction in socking you back. However, once man understands what it means that his will is not free, this desire to sock me is prevented by your realization that I will never blame you for hurting me. Until this knowledge is understood we will be compelled to continue living in the world of free will, otherwise, we would only make matters worse for ourselves.

To show you how confused is the understanding of someone who doesn't grasp these principles, a local columnist interested in my ideas, so he called them, made the statement that I believe that man should not be blamed for anything he does which is true only when man knows what it means that his will is not free. If he doesn't know, he is compelled to blame by his very nature. Christ also received incursions of thought from this same principle which compelled him to turn the other cheek and remark as he was being nailed to the cross, "They know not what they do," forgiving his enemies even in the moment of death. How was it possible for him to blame them when he knew that they were not responsible? But they knew what they were doing and he could not stop them even by turning the other cheek. Religion was compelled to believe that God was not responsible for the evil in the world, whereas Spinoza and Christ believed correctly that there was no such thing as evil when seen in total perspective. But how was it possible, except for people like Christ and Spinoza, to forgive those who trespassed against them? And how was it possible for those who became victims of this necessary evil to look at it in total perspective? Is it any wonder man cried out to God for understanding? The time has arrived to clear up all the confusion and reconcile these two opposite principles, which requires that you keep an open mind and proceed with the investigation. Let me show you how this apparent impasse can be rephrased in terms of possibility.

If someone is not being hurt in any way, is it possible for him to retaliate or turn the other cheek? Isn't it obvious that in order to do either he must first be hurt? But if he is already being hurt and by turning the other cheek makes matters worse for himself, then he is given no choice but to retaliate because this is demanded by the laws of his nature. Here is the source of the confusion. Our basic principle or corollary, Thou Shall Not Blame, call it what you will, is not going to accomplish the impossible. It is not going to prevent man from desiring to hurt others when not to makes matters worse for himself, but it will prevent the desire to strike the very first blow. Once you have been hurt it is normal and natural to seek some form of retaliation for this is a source of satisfaction which is the direction life is compelled to take. Therefore this knowledge cannot possibly prevent the hate and blame which man has been compelled to live with all these years as a consequence of crimes committed and many other forms of hurt, yet God's mathematical law cannot be denied for man is truly not to blame for anything he does notwithstanding, so a still deeper analysis is required. Down through history no one has ever known what it means that man's will is not free and how it can benefit the world, but you will be shown the answer very shortly. There is absolutely no way this new world, a world without war, crime, and all forms of hurt to man by man can be stopped from coming into existence. When it will occur, however, depends on when this knowledge can be brought to light.

We have been growing and developing just like a child from infancy. There is no way a baby can go from birth to old age without passing through the necessary steps, and no way man could have reached this tremendous turning point in his life without also going through the necessary stages of evil. Once it is established, beyond a shadow of doubt, that will is not free (and here is why my discovery was never found; no one could ever get beyond this impasse because of the implications), it becomes absolutely impossible to hold man responsible for anything he does. Is it any wonder the solution was never found if it lies hidden beyond this point? If you recall, Durant assumed that if man was allowed to believe his will is not free it would lessen his responsibility because this would enable him to blame other factors as the cause. If he committed crimes, society was to blame; if he was a fool, it was the fault of the machine which had slipped a cog in generating him. It is also true that if it had not been for the development of laws and a penal code, for the constant teaching of right and wrong, civilization could never have reached the outposts of this coming Golden Age. Yet despite the fact that we have been brought up to believe that man can be blamed and punished for doing what he was taught is wrong and evil (this is the cornerstone of all law and order up to now, although we are about to shed the last stage of the rocket that has given us our thrust up to this point); the force that has given us our brains, our bodies, the solar and the mankind systems; the force that makes us move in the direction of satisfaction, or this invariable law of God states explicitly, as we perceive these mathematical relations, that SINCE MAN'S WILL IS NOT FREE, THOU SHALL NOT BLAME ANYTHING HE DOES. This enigma is easily reconciled when it is understood that the mathematical corollary, God's commandment, does not apply to anything after it is done — only before.

"I don't understand why God's commandment applies to something before it is done, and not after. Does this mean you can blame after a crime has taken place? And doesn't this go back to the same problem man has been faced with since time immemorial; how to prevent the crime in the first place, which is the purpose of our penal code? How is it humanly possible not to judge, not to criticize, not to blame and punish those acts of crime when we know that man was not compelled to do them if he didn't want to? If someone killed my loved one how is it possible not to hate the individual responsible, not to judge this as an act of evil, not to desire some form of revenge? I still don't understand how not blaming will prevent man from hurting his fellow man if this is his desire. Though this may be an undeniable corollary, how is it humanly possible not to hold someone responsible for murder, rape, the killing of six million people, etc.? Does this mean that we are supposed to condone these crimes or pretend they didn't happen? Besides, what will prevent someone from blaming and punishing despite the fact that will is not free — if it gives him greater satisfaction? Just because man's will is not free is certainly not a sufficient explanation as to why there should be no blame."

This has always been the greatest stumbling block which kept free will on the throne until the present time. It is a natural reaction to blame after you've been hurt. The reason God's commandment does not apply to anything after it is done, only before, is because it has the power to <u>prevent</u> those very acts of evil for which a penal code was previously necessary, as part of our development. At this juncture, I shall repeat a passage from Chapter One to remind the reader of important facts that must be understood before continuing.

To solve this problem of evil with the aid of our enigmatic corollary — Thou Shall Not Blame — (for this seems mathematically impossible since it appears that man will always desire something for which blame and punishment will be necessary), it is extremely important to go through a deconfusion process regarding words by employing the other scientific fact revealed to you earlier. Consequently, as was pointed out, and to reveal this relation, it is an absolutely undeniable observation that man does not have to commit a crime or do anything to hurt another unless he wants to. As history reveals, even the most severe tortures and the threat of death cannot make him do to others what he makes up his mind not to do. He is not caused or compelled against his will to hurt another by his environment and heredity but prefers this action because at that moment of time he derives greater satisfaction in his motion to <u>there</u>, which is a normal compulsion of his nature over which he has absolutely no control. Though it is a mathematical law that nothing can compel man to do to another that which he makes up his mind not to do (this is an extremely crucial point), he is nevertheless under a compulsion during every moment of his existence to do everything he does. This reveals that he has mathematical control over the former (you can lead a horse to water but you can't make him drink) but none over the latter because he must move in the direction of greater satisfaction. In other words, no one is compelling a person to work at a job he doesn't like or remain in a country against his will. He actually wants to do the very things he dislikes simply because the alternative is considered worse in his opinion and he must choose something to do among the various things in his environment or else commit suicide. Was it possible to make Gandhi and his followers do what they did not want to do when unafraid of death, which was judged the lesser of two evils? They were compelled by their desire for freedom to prefer non-violence, turning the other cheek as a solution to their problem. Consequently, when any person says he was compelled to do what he did against his will because the alternative was considered worse, that he really didn't want to do it but had to (and numerous words and expressions say this), he is obviously confused and unconsciously dishonest with himself and others because everything man does to another is done only because he wants to do it which means that his preference gave him satisfaction at that moment of time, for one reason or another.

Let me repeat this crucial point because it is the source of so much confusion: Although man's will is not free there is absolutely nothing, not environment, heredity, God, or anything else that causes him to do what he doesn't want to do. The environment does not cause him to commit a crime, it just presents conditions under which his desire is aroused, consequently, he can't blame what is not responsible, but remember his particular environment is different because he himself is different otherwise everybody would desire to commit a crime. Once he chooses to act on his desire whether it is a minor or more serious crime he doesn't come right out and say, "I hurt that person not because I was compelled to do it against my will but only because I wanted to do it," because the standards of right and wrong prevent him from deriving any satisfaction out of such honesty when this will only evoke blame, criticism, and punishment of some sort for his desires. Therefore he is compelled to justify those actions

70

considered wrong with excuses, extenuating circumstances, and the shifting of guilt to someone or something else as the cause, to absorb part if not all the responsibility which allowed him to absolve his conscience in a world of judgment and to hurt others in many cases with impunity since he could demonstrate why he was compelled to do what he really didn't want to do. You see it happen all the time, even when a child says, "Look what you made me do" when you know you didn't make him do anything. Spilling a glass of milk because he was careless and not wishing to be blamed, the boy searches quickly for an excuse to shift the responsibility to something that does not include him. Why else would the boy blame his own carelessness on somebody or something else if not to avoid the criticism of his parents? It is also true that the boy's awareness that he would be blamed and punished for carelessness — which is exactly what took place — makes him think very carefully about all that he does to prevent the blame and punishment he doesn't want. A great confusion exists because it is assumed that if man does something to hurt another he could always excuse his actions by saying, "I couldn't help myself because my will is not free." This is another aspect of the implications which turned philosophers off from a thorough investigation. In the following dialogue, my friend asks for clarification regarding certain critical points.

"You read my mind. I really don't know how you plan to solve this enigmatic corollary but it seems to me that this knowledge would give man a perfect excuse for taking advantage of others without any fear of consequences. If the boy knows for a fact that his will is not free, why couldn't he use this as an excuse in an attempt to shift his responsibility?"

"This last question is a superficial perception of inaccurate reasoning. Because of this general confusion with words through which you have been compelled to see a distorted reality, it appears at first glance that the dethronement of free will would allow man to shift his responsibility all the more and take advantage of not being blamed to excuse or justify any desires heretofore kept under control by the fear of punishment and public opinion which judged his actions in accordance with standards of right and wrong, but this is inaccurate simply because it is mathematically impossible to shift your responsibility, to excuse or justify getting away with something, when you know that you will not be blamed for what you do. In other words, it is only possible to attempt a shift of your responsibility for hurting someone or for doing what is judged improper when you are held responsible by a code of standards that criticizes you in advance for doing something considered wrong by others. The very act of justifying or excusing your behavior is an indication that the person or people to whom you are presenting this justification must judge the behavior unacceptable in some way, otherwise, there would be no need for it. They are interested to know why you could do such a thing which compels you for satisfaction to think up a reasonable excuse to extenuate the circumstances and mitigate their unfavorable opinion of your action. If you do what others judge to be right is it necessary to lie or offer excuses or say that your will is not free and you couldn't help yourself, when no one is saying you could help yourself? Let me elaborate for greater understanding.

If someone does what everybody considers right as opposed to wrong, that is, if this person acts in a manner that pleases everybody, is it possible to blame him for doing what society expects of him? This isn't a trick question, so don't look so puzzled. If your boss tells you that he wants something done a certain way and you never fail to do it that way, is it possible for him to blame you for doing what he wants you to do?"

"No, it is not possible. I agree."

"Consequently, if you can't be blamed for doing what is right, then it should be obvious that you can only be blamed for doing something judged wrong, is that right?"

"I agree with this."

"These people who are judging you for doing something wrong are interested to know why you could do such a thing, which compels you for satisfaction to lie or think up a reasonable excuse, to extenuate the circumstances and mitigate their unfavorable opinion of your action, otherwise, if they were not judging your conduct as wrong you would not have to do these things, right?"

"You are right again."

"Now if you know as a matter of positive knowledge that no one is going to blame you for what you did, wrong or right, that is, no one is going to question your conduct in any way because you know that they must excuse what you do since man's will is not free, is it possible for you to blame someone or something else as the cause for what you know you have done, when you also know that no one is blaming you?"

"Why are you smiling?"

"You're the greatest with your mathematical reasoning, and I agree that it is not possible."

"This proves conclusively that the only time man can say, 'I couldn't help myself because my will is not free,' or offer any other kind of excuse, is if someone said he could help himself or blamed him in any way so he could make this effort to shift his responsibility, right?"

"You are absolutely correct."

Which means that only in the world of free will, in a world of judgment, can this statement, "I couldn't help myself because my will is not free" be made, since it cannot be done when man knows he will not be blamed. Remember, it is only possible to attempt a shift of your responsibility for hurting someone, or for doing what is judged improper, when you are held responsible by a code of standards that criticizes you *in advance* for doing something considered wrong by others. But once it is realized, as a matter of positive knowledge, that man will not be held responsible for what he does since his will is not free (don't jump to conclusions, just follow the reasoning — my problem is difficult enough as it is), it becomes mathematically impossible for you to blame someone or something else as the cause for what you know you have done simply because you know that no one is blaming you. To paraphrase this another way: Once it is realized that no one henceforth will blame your doing whatever you desire to do, regardless of what is done, because your action will be considered a compulsion over which you have no control, it becomes mathematically impossible to blame something or someone for what *you know you have done*, or shift your responsibility in any way, because you know that no one is blaming you. Being constantly criticized by the standards that prevailed man was compelled, as a motion in the direction of satisfaction, to be dishonest with everyone,

73

including himself, while refusing to accept that which was his responsibility. He blamed various factors or causes for the many things he desired to do that were considered wrong, because he didn't like being in the wrong. But the very moment the dethronement of free will makes it known that no one henceforth will be held responsible for what he does since his will is not free, regardless of what is done, and there will be no more criticism or blame, regardless of his actions, man is also prevented from making someone else the scapegoat for what he does, prevented from excusing or justifying his own actions since he is not being given an opportunity to do so which compels him completely beyond control, but of his own free will or desire, not only to assume full responsibility for everything he does, but to be absolutely honest with himself and others. How is it humanly possible for you to desire lying to me or to yourself when your actions are not being judged or blamed, in other words, when you are not being given an opportunity to lie; and how is it possible for you to make any effort to shift your responsibility when no one holds you responsible? In the world of free will man was able to absolve his conscience in a world of right and wrong and get away with murder in a figurative sense — the very things our new knowledge positively prevents.

It should be obvious that all your judgments of what is right and wrong in human conduct are based upon an ethical standard such as the Ten Commandments which came into existence out of God's will, as did everything else, and consequently you have come to believe through a fallacious association of symbols that these words which judge the actions of others are accurate. How was it possible for the Ten Commandments to come into existence unless religion believed in free will? But in reality when murder is committed it is neither wrong nor right, just what someone at a certain point in his life considered better for himself under circumstances which included the judgment of others and the risks involved; and when the government or personal revenge retaliates by taking this person's life, this too, was neither right nor wrong, just what gave greater satisfaction. Neither the government or the murderer are to blame for what each judged better under their particular set of circumstances; but whether they will decide to think and react as before will depend not on any moral values, not on habit, not on custom, not on any standards of right and wrong, but solely on whether the conditions under which they were previously motivated remain the same, and they do not remain as before because the knowledge that man's will is not free reveals facts never before understood. We can now see how the confusion of words and the inability to perceive certain type relations have compelled many thinkers who could not get beyond this impasse to assume, as Durant did, that if man knew his will was not free it would give him a perfect opportunity to take advantage of this knowledge.

"I am still not satisfied with the explanation. If it was not for the laws that protect society, what is to prevent man from taking more easily what he wants when the risk of retaliation is no more a condition to be considered? Further, what is to stop him from satisfying his desires to his heart's content when he knows there will be no consequences or explanations necessary? In the previous example it is obvious that the boy who spilled the milk cannot desire to shift the blame when he knows his parents are not going to question what he did, but why should this prevent him from spilling the milk every day if it gives him a certain satisfaction to watch it seep into the rug? Besides, if the father just spent $1000 for carpeting, how is it humanly possible for him to say absolutely nothing when the milk was not carelessly but deliberately spilled?"

"These are thoughtful questions but they are like asking if it is mathematically impossible for man to do something, what would you do if it is done? How is it possible for B (the father) to retaliate when it is impossible for B to be hurt? Contained in this question is an assumption that deliberate and careless hurt will continue. As we proceed with this investigation you will understand more clearly why the desire to hurt another will be entirely prevented by this natural law."

"Even though I cannot disagree with anything you said so far, I still don't understand how or why this should prevent man from stealing more easily what he wants when the risk of retaliation is no more a condition to be considered; and how is it humanly possible for those he steals from and hurts in other ways to excuse his conduct?"

"We are right back where we were before, the fiery dragon — but not for long. Now tell me, would you agree that if I did something to hurt you, you would be justified to retaliate?"

"I certainly would be justified."

"And we also have agreed that this is the principle of an eye for an eye, correct?"

"Correct."

"Which means that this principle, an eye for an eye, does not concern itself with preventing the first blow from being struck but only with justifying punishment or retaliation, is this also true?"

"Yes it is."

"And the principle of turning the other cheek, doesn't this concern itself with preventing the second cheek from being struck, not the first cheek?"

"That is absolutely true."

"Therefore, our only concern is in preventing the desire to strike this first blow, for then, if this can be accomplished, our problem is solved. If the first cheek is not struck, there is no need to retaliate or turn the other side of our face. Is this hard to understand?"

"It's very easy, in fact. I am not a college graduate, and I can even see that relation."

"Let us further understand that in order for you to strike this first blow of hurt, assuming that what is and what is not a hurt has already been established (don't jump to conclusions), you would have to be taking a certain amount of risk, that is, you would be risking the possibility of retaliation or punishment, is that correct?"

"Not if I planned a perfect crime."

"The most you can do with your plans is reduce the element of risk, but the fact that somebody was hurt by what you did does not take away his desire to strike a blow of retaliation. He doesn't know who to blame but if he did, you could expect that he would desire to strike back. Consequently, his desire to retaliate an eye for an eye is an undeniable condition of our present world as is also your awareness that there is this element of risk involved, however small. This means that whenever you do anything at all that is risky you are prepared to pay a price for the satisfaction of certain desires. You may risk going to jail, getting hanged or electrocuted, shot, beaten up, losing your eye and tooth, being criticized, reprimanded, spanked, scolded, ostracized,

76

or what have you, but this is the price you are willing to pay, if caught. Can you disagree with this?"

"I still say, supposing there is no risk; supposing I was able to plan a perfect crime and never get caught?"

"I am not denying the possibility but you can never know for certain, therefore the element of risk must exist when you do anything that hurts another."

"Then I agree."

"Now that we have a basic understanding as to why man's will is not free because it is his nature that he must always move in the direction of greater satisfaction, as well as the undeniable fact that nothing can make man do to another what he makes up his mind not to do — for over this he has absolute control — let us observe what miracle happens when these two laws are brought together to reveal a third law. Pay close attention because I am about to slay the fiery dragon with my trusty sword which will reveal my discovery, reconcile the two opposite principles 'an eye for an eye' and 'turn the other cheek,' and open the door to this new world."

At the present moment of time you are standing on this spot called here, and are constantly in the process of moving to there. You know as a matter of positive knowledge that you would never move to there if you were not dissatisfied with here. You also know as a matter of undeniable knowledge that nothing has the power, that no one can cause or compel you to do anything against your will — unless you want to, because over this you have mathematical control. And I, who am standing on this spot called there to where you plan to move for satisfaction from here also know positively that you cannot be blamed anymore for your motion from here to there because the will of man is not free. This is a very unique two-sided equation which reveals that while you know you are completely responsible for everything you do since nothing has the power to make you do anything you don't want to; and while it is mathematically impossible to shift your responsibility to some extraneous cause when no one holds you responsible, everybody else knows that you are not to blame for anything because you are compelled, by your very nature, to move in the direction of greater satisfaction during every moment of your

77

existence. Now if you know beyond a shadow of doubt that not only I, who am the one to be hurt, but everyone on earth will never blame or punish you for hurting me in some way, never criticize or question your action, never desire to hurt you in return for doing what must now be considered a compulsion beyond your control since the will of man is not free, is it humanly possible (think very carefully about this because it is the most crucial point thus far — the scientific discovery referred to) for you to derive any satisfaction whatever from the contemplation of this hurt? Remember now, you haven't hurt me yet, and you know as a matter of undeniable knowledge that nothing, no one can compel you to hurt me unless you want to, for over this you have mathematical control, consequently, your motion from <u>here</u> to <u>there</u>, your decision as to what is better for yourself, is still a choice between two alternatives — to hurt me or not to hurt me. But the moment it fully dawns on you that this hurt to me, should you go ahead with it, will not be blamed in any way because no one wants to hurt you for doing what must now be considered a compulsion beyond your control, ALTHOUGH YOU KNOW IT IS NOT BEYOND YOUR CONTROL AT THIS POINT SINCE NOTHING CAN FORCE YOU TO HURT ME AGAINST YOUR WILL — UNLESS YOU WANT TO — you are compelled, completely of your own free will, so to speak, to relinquish this desire to hurt me because it can never satisfy you to do so under these changed conditions. Furthermore, if you know as a matter of positive knowledge that no one in the entire world is going to blame you or question your conduct, is it possible to extenuate the circumstances, to lie or to try and shift your responsibility in any way? As was just demonstrated, it is not possible, just as the same answer must apply to the question, is it possible to make two plus two equal five. This proves conclusively that the only time you can say, "I couldn't help myself because my will is not free," or offer any kind of excuse, is when you know you are being blamed for this allows you to make this effort to shift your responsibility. Let me explain this in still another way.

When you know you are not going to be blamed for what you do it also means that you must assume complete responsibility for what you do because you cannot shift it away from yourself under the changed conditions. We have become so confused by words in logical relation that while we preach this freedom of the will we say in the same breath that we could not help ourselves, and demonstrate our confusion still more by believing that the corollary, Thou Shall Not Blame, would lessen our responsibility when in actuality, responsibility is increased. This one point has confounded philosophers down through the ages because it was assumed that a world without blame would make matters worse, decreasing responsibility and giving man the perfect opportunity to take advantage of others. But, once again, this "taking advantage" can only occur when man knows he will be blamed, which allows him to come up with excuses. For example, he could just say, "I couldn't help pulling the trigger because my will is not free." Did you ever see anything more ironically humorous? The only time a person can use the excuse that his will is *not* free is when the world believes it *is* free.

But the question remains: "Why is an excuse necessary? Why can't he just satisfy his desires to his heart's content when there are no consequences, without explaining to others his reasons for doing what he wants to do? Why can't he just walk into a store, take what he wants since nobody will be stopping him, and then just go about his business?"

"You must constantly bear in mind that man is compelled to choose the alternative that gives him greater satisfaction, and for that reason his will is not free. Consequently, to solve our problem it is only necessary to show that when all blame and punishment are removed from the environment, the desire to hurt others in any way, shape or form is the worst possible choice."

"I understand the principle of no blame but society does what it must do to protect itself. A person with scarlet fever is not blamed but is nevertheless quarantined."

"If a person had something that was contagious, he would welcome this precautionary measure. The knowledge that he would not be blamed under any circumstances, even if he was responsible for spreading his illness to the entire region, would prevent him from desiring to take any chances that might cause further spread of the disease. This is similar to the question that was asked earlier: If it is mathematically impossible for man to do something, what would you

79

do if it was done? How is it possible for B (society) to protect itself when it is impossible for B to be hurt? Once again, there is an assumption that deliberate and careless hurt will continue. When man knows there will be no blame or punishment no matter what he does, he can only go in one direction for greater satisfaction. He can hurt others with a first blow if he wants to, but he won't want to. It is important to understand that if someone is being hurt first his reaction is no longer a first blow, but a retaliatory blow. Under these conditions he would have justification to strike back."

In order to hurt another, either deliberately or carelessly, man must be able to derive greater, not less, satisfaction which means that self-preservation demands and justifies this, that he was previously hurt in some way and finds it preferable to strike back an eye for an eye, which he can also justify, or else he knows absolutely and positively that he would be blamed by the person he hurt and others if they knew. Blame itself which is a condition of free will and a part of the present environment permits the consideration of hurt for it is the price man is willing to pay for the satisfaction of certain desires, but when blame is removed so that the advance knowledge that it no longer exists becomes a new condition of the environment, then the price he must consider to strike the first blow of hurt is completely out of reach because he cannot find satisfaction in hurting those who will refuse to blame him or retaliate in any way. To hurt someone under these conditions he would have to move in the direction of conscious dissatisfaction, which is mathematically impossible. From a superficial standpoint it might still appear that man would take advantage of not being blamed and punished and risk hurting others as a solution to his problems, but this is a mathematical impossibility when he knows that blame and punishment are required for advance justification. In other words, the challenge of the law absolves his conscience with threats of an eye for an eye and a tooth for a tooth, which is payment in full for the risks he takes. He may risk going to prison or be willing to pay the ultimate price with his life for the satisfaction of certain desires. An individual would not mind taking all kinds of chances involving others because he could always come up with a reasonable excuse to get off the hook, or he could pay a price, if caught. If he borrowed a thousand dollars and was unable to pay all of it back, he could easily say, "Sue me for the rest." If he tries to hold up a bank, however, and fails, the legal system does not allow him to excuse himself and he is sent to prison. Without the knowledge that he would be blamed and punished should he fail; without this advance justification which allowed him to risk hurting others, the price of this hurt is beyond his purchasing power. How could someone plan a crime knowing that no one — not even the ones to be hurt — would ever blame him or retaliate in any way — even if they knew what he was about to do? Has it been forgotten already that we are compelled, by our very nature, to choose the alternative that gives us greater satisfaction, which is the reason our will is not free? Consequently, to solve this problem it is only necessary to demonstrate that when all blame and punishment are removed from the environment — and when the conditions are also removed that make it necessary for a person to hurt others as the lesser of two evils — the desire to hurt another with a first blow will be the worst possible choice. In the world of free will man blamed man and excused himself. In the new world man will be excused by man for everything he does and consequently will be compelled, of his own free will, to hold himself responsible without justification. In other words, once man knows that he is truly responsible for what others will be compelled to excuse and he would be unable to justify, he is given no choice but to forgo the contemplation of what he foresees can give him no satisfaction. It becomes an impenetrable deterrent because under these conditions no person alive is able to move in this direction for satisfaction, even if he wanted to. This natural law raises man's conscience to such a high degree because there is no price he can pay when all humanity, including the one to be hurt, must excuse him.

"I am still having a difficult time. Could you explain the two-sided equation again?"

At this present moment of time or life you are standing on this spot called here, and are constantly in the process of moving to there. You know as a matter of positive knowledge that nothing, no one can cause or compel you to do anything to another you don't want to do, and this other who is standing on this spot called there to which you plan to move from here, also knows positively that you cannot be

81

blamed for your motion from <u>here</u> to <u>there</u>, regardless of what is done. Now if you know as a matter of positive knowledge that not only I but everyone on the planet will never blame or punish you for hurting me in some way, because you know that we are compelled to completely excuse what is beyond your control, is it mathematically possible (think about this carefully) for you to derive any satisfaction whatever from the contemplation of this hurt when you know beyond a shadow of doubt that no one, including myself, will ever hold you responsible, ever criticize your action, ever desire to hurt you in return for doing what is completely beyond your control? But remember, you haven't hurt me yet, and you know (this is the other side of the equation) that you do not have to hurt me unless you want to, consequently your motion from <u>here</u> to <u>there</u> is still within your control. Therefore the moment it fully dawns on you that this hurt, should you go ahead with it, will not be blamed, criticized or judged in any way because no one wants to hurt you for doing what must be considered a compulsion beyond your control (once it is established that man's will is not free), you are compelled, completely of your own free will, to relinquish this desire to hurt me because it can never give you any satisfaction under these conditions, which proves that A — everybody on the planet — has the power to control B — everybody else — by letting B know, as is being done with this book, that no one will ever be blamed for anything that is done. In other words, the knowledge that there will be no consequences presents consequences that are still worse making it impossible to consider this as a preferable alternative for how is it possible to derive satisfaction knowing there will be no consequences for the pain you willfully choose to inflict on others? The reaction of no blame would be worse than any type of punishment society could offer. It is important to remember that punishment and retaliation are natural reactions of a free will environment that permit the consideration of striking a first blow because it is the price man is willing to risk or pay for the satisfaction of certain desires. But when they are removed so the knowledge that they no longer exist becomes a condition of the environment, then the price he must consider to strike the first blow of hurt — all others are justified — is completely out of his reach because to do so he must move in the direction of conscious dissatisfaction, which cannot be done. If will

82

was free we could not accomplish this simply because we would be able to choose what is worse for ourselves when something better is available, but this law of our nature will give us no alternative when we are forced to obey it in order to derive greater satisfaction.

The solution to this impasse which removes the implications is now very obvious because the advance knowledge that man will not be blamed for the hurt he does to others (this is the solution worked backwards) mathematically prevents those very acts of evil for which blame and punishment were previously necessary. Instead of being able to absolve one's conscience by justifying an act of crime or some other form of hurt because of the knowledge that he will be blamed and punished (which permitted efforts to shift his responsibility while encouraging what had to be criticized and condemned), he is prevented from deriving any satisfaction from the contemplation of this hurt by the realization that he will never be blamed, criticized, punished or judged for doing what he knows everyone must condone, while being denied a satisfactory reason with which to excuse his contemplated conduct. I will rephrase this in a slightly different way: Instead of being able to absolve one's conscience by being given the opportunity to justify an act of crime or some other form of hurt which permitted the shifting of one's responsibility while at the same time encouraging the crime, the knowledge that will is not free and what this means actually prevents an individual from deriving any satisfaction from the contemplation of this hurt to another by the realization that he will not be blamed, criticized, judged, or punished for this act. The difference between this principle and the principle Christ preached — "Turn the other cheek," is that the former prevents the first cheek from ever being struck whereas Gandhi, in his bid for freedom and his belief in nonviolence, was forced to turn the other cheek although the first cheek was struck over and over again which took an untold number of lives. Secondly, man must be willing to die in order for turning the other cheek to be effective, consequently innumerable abuses cannot be prevented which starts a chain reaction of retaliation. Besides, how is it possible not to strike back when your very being moves in this direction for satisfaction? Gandhi said, "Kill us all or give us our freedom; we will not resist anything you do to us," compelling those in power, after many were already slain, to find more satisfaction in leaving them alone. Many minorities, such as the Blacks, cannot apply this psychology because the situation does not call for such a sacrifice. How are these people to turn the other cheek when they are underpaid, overtaxed, and judged by Whites as one of the inferior races? It has been their effort to correct these abuses — not by turning the other cheek — that has brought these people this far. By turning the other cheek (which also proves in a mathematical manner that man's will is not free), it absolutely prevents the second cheek from being struck because it is impossible, as the people of India demonstrated, to get satisfaction from continuing to hurt those who refuse to fight back, but as history has shown many were killed just by being struck on the first cheek. My imparting the knowledge that no one will again blame you in any way, judge your actions or tell you what to do will mathematically prevent your first cheek from being struck which is necessary in a world of atomic energy when an entire nation can be wiped out from being struck on the first cheek. Let us, once again, observe what the perception of undeniable relations tells us.

At this moment of time in our present world of free will you are trying to decide whether to hurt me in some way but you have had everything removed that could be used to justify this act. You simply see an opportunity to gain at my expense, but should you decide against it you will not be a loser. In other words, you are considering the first blow which means that you are planning to do something to me that I do not want done to myself. You realize that there is a certain risk involved, if caught, because you must face the consequences. If the crime, misdemeanor or offense is not that serious, although you know you will be questioned and blamed, you may be able to get away with it by offering all kinds of reasonable excuses as to why you had no choice. But if no excuse is acceptable as in a court of law after you have been found guilty, or when your parents, boss or others know you are obviously at fault, you could be sent to prison, electrocuted, hanged, gassed, whipped, severely punished in some other way, scolded, reprimanded, ostracized, criticized, discharged, beat up or any number of things. You don't want this to happen if it can be avoided, but if you can't satisfy your desire unless the risk is taken, you are prepared to pay a price for the crime of hurting me with a first blow. Under these conditions it is impossible for your conscience to exercise any control over your desires because you cannot feel any guilt just as long as you are prepared to suffer the consequences. Now let's imagine for a moment that you are living in the new world and are confronted with a choice of whether or not to hurt me.

As before you are trying to decide whether to hurt me in some way but you have had everything removed from which you might have been able to justify your act. You simply see an opportunity to gain at my expense, but you will not be a loser if you decide against it. In other words, you are contemplating the first blow under changed conditions. You know as a matter of undeniable knowledge that nothing in this world has the power, that no one can compel you to do anything against your will, for over this you know you have absolute control (you can lead a horse to water but you can't make him drink). This means that you are completely responsible for your actions even though, due to circumstances, you may prefer hurting me. To make absolutely certain that you know this is an undeniable law, try to shift away from yourself what is your responsibility or to some extraneous factor when you know that no one in the world will ever hold you responsible. It cannot be done, which was already proven. This does not mean that other people are not often responsible for the hurt we do as part of a chain reaction as when an employer is forced to lay off his employees because the money to pay them has stopped coming in to him, but no one is blaming him for what is obviously not his responsibility and therefore it isn't necessary for him to offer excuses.

As you are contemplating hurting me in some way, I know as a matter of positive knowledge that you cannot be blamed anymore because it is an undeniable law that man's will is not free. This is a very unique two-sided equation for it reveals that while you know you are completely responsible for everything you do to hurt me, I know you are not responsible. For the very first time you fully realize that I must excuse you because it is now known that man must always select of available alternatives the one that offers greater satisfaction, and who am I to know what gives you greater satisfaction. Consequently, you are compelled to realize that should you desire to hurt me in any way whatsoever you must also take into consideration the knowledge that under no conditions will I strike you back because it can never satisfy me to hurt you for doing what I know you are compelled to do. This prevents you from thinking excuses in advance because you know you are already excused. You cannot say, "I couldn't help myself because my will is not free," because you know I already know this. You cannot apologize or ask for forgiveness because you are already forgiven and no one is blaming you. This means that should you decide to hurt me with this first blow or be careless and take the risks that lead to a first blow, and I would have to choose between retaliating or turning the other cheek, you would know that I would be compelled by my nature to find greater satisfaction in turning the other cheek because of the undeniable fact that I would know you had no choice, since your will is not free. Remember, you haven't hurt me yet; consequently, this is still a choice under consideration. And when it fully dawns on you that this hurt to me will never be blamed, judged or questioned in any way because I don't want to hurt you in return for doing what must now be considered a compulsion beyond your control — ALTHOUGH YOU KNOW IT IS NOT BEYOND YOUR CONTROL AT THIS POINT SINCE YOU HAVEN'T HURT ME YET — you are compelled, completely of your own free will, so to speak, to relinquish this desire to hurt me because it can never give you greater satisfaction under the changed conditions. [Note: It must be understood that the expression 'of your own free will,' which is an expression I use throughout the book, only means 'of your own desire,' but this does not mean will is free. If you need further clarification, please reread Chapter One]. In other words, when you know that others will never blame or punish you for what they are compelled to excuse, but also that the other factors truly responsible for the dissatisfaction which engendered the consideration of hurting others as a possible solution will be permanently removed as a consequence of following our slide rule in all of its ramifications, you will be given no opportunity to ever again strike another blow of hurt. It becomes the worst possible choice to hurt another when it is known there will be no blame because there is no advantage in hurting those whom you know are compelled to turn the other cheek for their satisfaction. Conscience, this guilty feeling over such an act, will not permit it because you will get less satisfaction, not more. Let me say again that if man's will was free we could not accomplish this because we would be able to choose what is less satisfying when something more satisfying is available.

The knowledge that man will no longer be blamed for striking a first blow since his will is not free — when he knows that nobody, absolutely nothing, can compel him to hurt another this way unless he wants to for over this he knows he has absolute control — enters a condition or catalyst never before a permanent factor in human relations and mathematically prevents those very acts of hurt for which blame was previously necessary in a free will environment. Remember, it takes two to tango — each person and the rest of mankind — therefore this discovery which prevents man from desiring to hurt others is only effective when he knows in advance, as a matter of positive knowledge, that he will never be blamed or punished no matter what he does.

"Wait a second. Will you admit that if I strike you first you are perfectly justified in striking back?"

"Of course you are not justified in striking a person who is compelled to do what he does by the laws of his nature."

"But you know that an individual doesn't have to strike another if he doesn't want to."

"But if he wants to, isn't it obvious that this desire is completely beyond his control because it is now known man's will is not free?"

"Are you trying to tell me that if someone strikes me I must turn the other cheek because he couldn't help himself?"

"That's exactly right. How is it humanly possible to justify some form of retaliation when you know that the person who hurt you is moved by laws over which he has absolutely no control?"

"But I do have mathematical control over not hurting you, if I don't want to."

"I don't know that, because it is impossible for me to judge what you can and cannot do since you are compelled to move in the direction of greater satisfaction, and I don't know what gives you greater satisfaction. Consequently, you are compelled to realize that should you desire to hurt me in any way whatsoever, you must also

87

take into consideration the knowledge that under no conditions will I strike you back because it can never satisfy me to hurt you for doing what I know you are compelled to do, since your will is not free."

"Now I get it. Then when I fully realize that under no conditions will you ever strike back because you must excuse what you know I am compelled to do — when I know that I am not compelled to hurt you unless I want to for over this I have mathematical control — I am given no alternative but to forgo the desire to hurt you simply because, under the new conditions, it is impossible for me to derive even the smallest amount of satisfaction."

Wonderful! If each reader is able to understand that there are two sides to this equation, then he will be able to follow me as I extend it into every part of our lives. [Please note that I am demonstrating how the basic principle can prevent the first cheek from ever being struck. If our cheek has not been struck, there is no need to strike back or turn the other side of our face. If you find it confusing as to how the basic principle prevents the desire to hurt others as a preferable alternative, it is important that you reread this chapter in order to grasp the two-sided equation, which is the very foundation of this discovery]. As we follow the corollary, Thou Shall Not Blame, which will act as an infallible slide rule and standard as to what is right and wrong while solving the many problems that lie ahead, we will be obeying the mathematical wisdom of this universe which gives us no choice when we see what is truly better for ourselves. By removing all forms of blame which include this judging in advance of what is right and wrong for others, we actually prevent the first blow of injustice from being struck. This corollary is not only effective by your realization that we (all mankind) will never blame you for any hurt done to us, but also by our realization that any advance blame, this judging of what is right for someone else strikes the first blow since it is impossible to prevent your desire to hurt us by telling you we will never blame this hurt when we blame the possibility by telling you in advance that it is wrong. In other words, by judging that it is wrong to do something, whatever it may be, we are blaming the possibility of it being done which only incites a desire to challenge the authority of this advance accusation that has already given justification. Therefore, in order to prevent the very things we do not want which hurt us, it is absolutely imperative that we never judge what is right for someone else. But remember, it is not the knowledge that man's will is not free that compels him to give up this judging in advance what is right for others, otherwise the government, the unions, the religions, all the writers who make a living expressing their opinions as to what is right and wrong with the world, with love, marriage, children, business, education, etc., would suddenly give up their manner of earning a living which is a mathematical impossibility. Do you think that the manufacturers of candles and other inferior forms of lighting wanted to give up what gave them a source of income when electricity was discovered? They were compelled to adjust because they couldn't find a market for their obsolete products except on a smaller scale. Do you think the adulterers want to give up their fun, the single males the pleasure of sexual intercourse before marriage? Do you think the people who are getting wealthy on the sweat, brawn, tears and insecurity of extremely low wages will give this up just because God thunders down from heaven — Thou Shall Not Blame? Do you think that religion will willingly give up its great power and influence when it is learned that the will of man is not free — which reveals that God is a mathematical reality? The truth of the matter is that everyone will be compelled of his own free will to give up anything that hurts another in any way simply because this hurt will be considered worse under the new conditions. This, my friends, is the great secret of God's infinite wisdom, which gives man no free choice as to the direction he must travel for greater satisfaction. However, it is extremely important for every individual to know that what came about on our planet was exactly as it was supposed to be. This, of course, doesn't mean that the future will continue like the past, but it does mean that no one is to blame in any way for what happened and consequently everyone is permitted to turn himself upside down for the purpose of dumping out anything and everything for which he holds himself responsible; but remember we are prevented from repeating an action that formerly hurt someone by the knowledge that we will never be blamed for what we know we can prevent, giving us no satisfaction. The solution lies in the fact that the people truly responsible for all the evil, hurt and crime, for which they cannot be held responsible, are actually unconscious of this responsibility, and instead blame an individual who is not at fault for the very things of which they are innocently guilty. Therefore the problem is to bring to the surface, with a mathematical, infallible line of demarcation, these hidden facts. Your philosopher Socrates grasped this when he said "I know that I don't know; other men don't know either but think they know." But now we know that we know, for the actual responsibility lies with everyone who judges and tacitly blames the actions of another before anything is even done. However, this advance blame is not only contained in our customs, conventions, morals and laws, but in the very words that describe fallacious differences of value which permit superior, inferior, better, worse, good, bad, and innumerable other words and expressions to be used in relation to different individuals. We are completely absolved of all responsibility for anything we have ever done in the past, and will never be blamed by anyone in the future, but the present is our very own responsibility since no one will ever again tell us what to do or what is better for ourselves.

As we end this chapter, there is one vital point that appears contradictory and needs clarification. If the knowledge that man's will is not free is supposed to prevent that for which blame and punishment were previously necessary, and if a person who saw his child deliberately kidnapped and killed would be compelled to desire revenge as a normal reaction in the direction of satisfaction, how can this knowledge prevent some form of retaliation? Just because you have learned that man's will is not free is not a sufficient explanation as to why you should not want to avenge this child's murder by tracking down the criminal and cutting his heart out with a knife, so once again we must understand what God means when He mathematically instructs us not to blame. When the knowledge in this book is released and understood, every person as always will be standing on this moment of time or life called <u>here</u>, so to speak, and preparing to move to the next spot called <u>there</u>. As the principles set forth in this book become a permanent part of the environment, you will know that the person who kidnapped and killed your child or committed some other form of hurt which occurred prior to the release of this knowledge — regardless of how much you hate and despise what was done — will never blame in any way your desire for

90

retribution, which means that he will never run and hide to avoid your act of revenge because this is a form of tacit blame; and when it fully dawns on you that he will never make any effort to fight back no matter what you do to him, never lift a hand to stop whatever you desire to do, it becomes impossible for you to derive any satisfaction from this act of retaliation especially when you know that he will never again be permitted by his conscience — because of the realization that he will not be blamed — to do to another what was originally done to you and your family. As a result, the chain of retaliation will be broken which will prevent any further criminal behavior.

Time and time again a person desiring personal revenge has been able to experience a certain amount of control over his desire, but never to the degree that will permit this Great Transition to get under way — with the help of our slide rule. Presently, the man seeking revenge finds great satisfaction in contemplating what he is going to do to get even, but is prevented not because he decides not to blame when learning that man's will is not free, but only because the other person on whom he desires to vent his venom has been given the knowledge of how to prevent this retaliation, while the one seeking revenge knows how to prevent the recurrence of a similar situation. When he fully realizes that the perpetrator whom he wishes to hurt in return will never desire to retaliate with further hurt, or desire to commit another crime to anyone anywhere, he is compelled to lose his desire for revenge because it is impossible to derive any satisfaction from the advance knowledge that he will be excused by the entire world. The full realization that he can no longer justify this act of personal revenge because no one will consider it wrong or tell him what to do (remember, no longer will anyone judge what is right for another); that he will be able to do what he wishes to this person without any form of justification because he knows in advance that he will not be blamed and that everyone, including the one to be retaliated upon, will be compelled of their own free will to completely excuse what is definitely not his responsibility — ALTHOUGH HE KNOWS IT WOULD BE HIS RESPONSIBILITY — makes him desire to forgo what he knows he doesn't have to do. He knows he is not under any compulsion to do what has not yet been done, and when he becomes aware that no one henceforth will judge his actions;

91

that he is completely free from the trammels of public opinion to do, without the slightest fear of criticism, whatever he thinks is better for himself; that he will not even be punished by the laws that were created for this purpose, it becomes mathematically impossible for him to desire hurting this other person under these conditions regardless of what was originally done to him. It would be equivalent to deriving satisfaction from continuing to beat up an individual who, though fully able to fight back, refuses to lift a hand in his own defense. This allows the Great Transition to get under way without any fear of harm. Let us observe why the perpetrator can no longer continue his crime spree under the changed conditions.

The potential kidnapper or criminal who is standing on this moment of time called <u>here</u> when this knowledge is released and before the act is done, is prevented from further contemplation of his crime by the realization that he will never be blamed, judged, criticized, or punished for this act (and by the removal of all forms of tacit blame which unconsciously gave him the motivation and justification), which compels him to get greater satisfaction in his motion to <u>there</u> by giving up what he was contemplating. Up until the present time there was nothing powerful enough to prevent man from risking his life to satisfy a desire regardless of who got hurt because the satisfaction of possible success outweighed the dissatisfaction of possible failure; but when he becomes conscious that a particular reaction of no blame will be the only response to his actions by the entire world regardless of what he is contemplating, he will be compelled, completely beyond his control, but of his own free will or desire, to refrain from what he now foresees can give him absolutely no satisfaction. How can he possibly find satisfaction in doing something that the world must excuse, but he can no longer justify? This natural law of man's nature gives him no alternative but to obey it in order to derive greater satisfaction, and will prevent the first blow from ever being struck. As we extend the corollary, Thou Shall Not Blame, and slowly unravel the causes of war, crime, and hatred — which are deep-rooted and interwoven — we will get a glimpse into the future and envision how life will be when all hurt in human relations comes to a peaceful end.

There will be many volumes extending this law into every area of human interaction. The answer to the world's problems will satisfy Communism and Capitalism, the Blacks and the Whites, the Jews and the Christians, the Catholics and the Protestants, the rich and the poor, the cops and the robbers. However, it must be understood that in the world of free will innumerable wars, revolutions, and crimes were a reaction to various forms of hurt which did not allow any alternative but to retaliate. Consequently, man was compelled to blame, criticize and punish as the only possible alternative when judged by his undeveloped mind. When those about to fight back discover that they will no more be retaliated upon, it is also necessary for them to realize that the factors responsible for this consideration of war and crime, as the lesser of two evils, will also be removed; and are those responsible given any choice but to remove these factors when they know that those who they have been hurting will never blame them for this?

To fully understand the fact that conscience — our feeling of guilt — was never allowed to reach the enormous temperature necessary to melt our desire to even take the risk of striking a first blow, it is only necessary to observe what must follow when a crucible is constructed wherein this new law can effectively operate. It was impossible for any previous stage of our development to have understood the deeper factors involved which was necessary for an adequate solution, just as it was impossible for atomic energy to have been discovered at an earlier time because the deeper relations were not perceived at that stage of development; but at last we have been granted understanding which reveals a pattern of harmony in the mankind system equal in every way with the mathematical accuracy of the solar system, and we are in for the greatest series of beneficent changes of our entire existence which must come about as a matter of necessity the very moment this knowledge is understood. Although this book only scratches the surface, it lays the foundation for scientists to take over from here. The undeniable knowledge I am presenting is a blueprint of a new world that must come about once this discovery is recognized, and your awareness of this will preclude you from expressing that this work is oversimplified. Because it would take many encyclopedias combined to delineate all of the changes about to occur, it would have been much too long for a book that was written

93

for the express purpose of providing mankind with a general outline. It will be up to future scientists to extend these principles in much greater depth. As we leave this chapter I hope I have made it clear that just as long as man is able to justify hurting others, he is not striking a first blow. Before I demonstrate how this justification is permanently removed by preventing the insecurities that have permeated our economic system and justify the act of self-preservation by whatever means necessary, I will allow you an opportunity to see exactly what happens in a human relation where this justification is already removed. In the next chapter, I shall reveal how all automobile accidents and carelessness must come to a permanent end. Before we move on, I must clarify a very important point. Christ and Spinoza turned the other cheek and paid the consequences because the justification to hurt them was never removed, but I am going to demonstrate how it is now possible to prevent the first cheek from being struck which renders obsolete the need to turn the other cheek or retaliate. Although Gandhi won freedom for his people and Reverend King won certain civil rights, they accomplished this at great expense. However, all was necessary because we are moving in the direction of greater satisfaction over which we have no control because this is God's law or will. At this point, I suggest that you study carefully, once again, Chapter Two and then discuss it to make certain you understand that if you find any flaw it exists only in your not understanding the principles, for they are undeniable.

CHAPTER THREE

THE END OF CARELESSNESS

Wouldn't it be wonderful if we never had to worry about people carelessly risking the lives of our loved ones, neighbors, and friends? Well, get ready for a miracle. I shall demonstrate, by applying this natural law, how it is now possible to change our environment and raise man's conscience to such a degree that all carelessness, including automobile accidents, will be virtually wiped from the face of the earth because people the world over will do everything in their power to avoid the carelessness and risks responsible. Right now there are more people killed in car accidents than we can fully comprehend. These collisions take place only because man operates on 75% of his potential power which is insufficient to prevent what nobody wants, even though he is doing everything in his power to prevent it. By understanding what it means that man's will is not free we plug in the extra 25%, and then have the power to prevent the unintentional tragedies that continue to plague our lives.

Carelessness, just as the word implies is an I do not care attitude. It arises from several factors. There are young boys and girls who want to make an impression on their friends and this requires that they demonstrate their ability to handle a car like a race car driver, but they never give much thought to the other person because man's first concern has always been for himself. The show-off wants to give his friends a thrill and demonstrate how to do what really takes guts. He doesn't care if he is a menace to other drivers who happen to cross his path. If he is willing to risk his own life — and happens to take others with him — that's their tough luck. For this reason you would often hear, 'Drive carefully; the life you save might be your own.' The drunks and dope addicts and people in a hurry cannot stand being behind a slow moving vehicle even if this means passing on a curve or hill. They either don't fully realize the danger or they don't care since the risk is primarily to themselves with no thought of those who may be in the way.

There are other individuals who don't care because this requires great effort and they aren't willing to exert the kind of energy it takes to protect the lives of others. To apply brakes when the light changes yellow as an alternative to speeding up and making it so stopping isn't necessary is considered a nuisance. As a result, they often end up going through on the red and crashing into the driver who starts off before the light has changed to green. Then there is the mother who is so fed up with the struggle to take care of the house and her children, and now that she is no longer in love with her husband she just doesn't care. She leaves matches and other potentially dangerous items lying around and when the house catches on fire or they get hurt in some other way she always comes up with excuses. What has added to her carelessness is that she never understood the meaning of fatalism which is the doctrine that all things are subject to fate, or that they take place by inevitable necessity. Consequently, when this belief in fatalism was expressed to me by a mother who didn't seem to take much care in looking after her children, I asked her the following question:

"If you saw your infant getting ready to crawl in front of a truck, would you pick him up or let him go?"

"Naturally, I would grab him."

"Why would you grab him, if you believe in fate?"

"I can see that danger," she replied.

"In other words," I responded, "once you have done everything in your power to prevent an accident and then it occurs, you can say it was fate."

Carelessness has allowed airplanes to crash into each other or to explode because the mechanics failed in their duty. It has allowed ships to ram each other, hotels, night clubs, houses, etc. to burst into flames and people to perish. It has allowed tires to blow out and brakes to fail; even buildings to collapse. There is no telling how many lives have been lost or mutilated (blinded, crippled or what have you) all because of someone's carelessness. And liability insurance came into existence out of absolute necessity to help prevent the

96

aftereffects of an accident, otherwise we would have more killing.

My friend remarked, "I don't know about you but if it had not been for my ability to drive defensively, I would have been killed or hospitalized at least a dozen times. I agree that defensive driving is extremely important in this world, that is. I don't know about the new world, but not everybody has this coordination and skill to drive defensively, just as they don't have other talents and skills."

"You're right, however everybody does have the ability to apply the rules of good driving." Now observe how God compels this to come about.

When a car accident occurs in our present environment the people involved are very dissatisfied because their car was just damaged, but what do they do for satisfaction? If there were no witnesses they hurl accusations at each other until the police arrive. The person who did not have the right-of-way could possibly, in a courtroom with a clever lawyer, make the innocent party appear guilty, in order to get his insurance company to pay for damages. If the one who had the right-of-way was under the influence of liquor, even though the accident was not his fault in any way, he is already judged guilty as this offers a perfect reason for making the guilty party appear innocent. But when an extremely serious accident occurs where, let us say, two children and their mother were instantly killed, while the father and the other driver were thrown clear, to assume responsibility for this is too horrible to bear which compels them to think up a million and one excuses as to why it was the other person's fault. If there were witnesses, and both drivers know it was not the father's responsibility, the guilty party would welcome whatever punishment could be dished out so that he could pay dearly for what he did; and the liability insurance he carries just in case, helps him, in a small way to pay part of the price. If it was the father's fault, he might not be able to stand this terrible feeling of guilt and might be forced to find some reason as to why this accident was unavoidable otherwise he could kill himself. However, to make it possible for him to continue living, just in case he can't come up with a convincing reason for the accident, the law will charge him with manslaughter and he will have to serve a prison sentence, which he welcomes, because this also helps him to pay for what he did. How many times, true or false, will the ability to use just these words make someone feel so much better — "I couldn't help myself." "It was not my fault." "It was unavoidable." "I'm terribly sorry." And how many times in the course of history have the innocent been compelled to pay the price of the guilty, just because man was able to shift his responsibility?

To understand why all automobile accidents must come to an end, out of absolute necessity, watch what happens when we apply our basic principle to show you exactly what takes place in our present environment before and after a collision, and then let you see the same accident under changed conditions. Most people are concerned with their own safety, but under the changed conditions they become more concerned that they are not responsible for hurting others as that alternative which gives them greater satisfaction. Remember, however, the new world is not yet here so we are going to imagine the same accident which will not occur, just so we can see why it will not. Actually, the only reason we are willing to drive carelessly and take risks in our present environment is because when we do have an accident, which means that when we have made a careless mistake resulting in a hurt to others, it is possible to gain satisfaction by paying the price or shifting responsibility. When it becomes impossible to do either, we must do everything in our power to prevent the accident as that alternative which is better for ourselves.

Not so long ago a truck was heading west inside the city limits, doing 50 miles an hour in a 35 mile zone. It was past midnight, and very few cars were on the street. The driver was anxious to get home because he hadn't seen his family for a week. He had driven this same route many times and knew it was safe to go this speed at that time of the morning. His only concern was to keep an eye out for a patrol car so he wouldn't get a ticket. Up ahead, four blocks away, he saw that a traffic signal was green when about a half block away he knew that it would soon be joined with the yellow light and followed in a few seconds by the red, indicating that he would have to stop. Because he felt this was a nuisance since the amber light had not yet gone on, and since the darkness enabled him to see that no headlights were coming from other directions, he felt safe to increase his speed to 65 miles an hour.

Heading north was a car carrying five people — a father, mother, and their three children. They had just attended a wedding and were on their way home. The father had been drinking rather heavily and completely forgot to put on his headlights. He was also traveling along at 50 miles an hour when he slowed down to 35 so he wouldn't have to stop for the red light up ahead, but when he saw the yellow light go on for the other direction, and knowing that the light would be green before he entered the intersection even if he resumed his 50 miles an hour, he did not hesitate to do just that. Now just before the truck got to the crossing the light changed, which meant that the driver would have to go through on the red. At that very moment he saw the car without any headlights on enter the intersection a fraction of a second ahead of him, but it was too late to avoid the collision. The father saw the truck at that instant too. They both jammed on their brakes and turned their wheels instinctively, but the truck ploughed head on at a slight angle into the rear right side of the car. The parents were somehow only injured slightly; the truck driver was not hurt at all, but the three children were killed instantly. Standing on the corner was someone who noticed that the car's lights were not on. Now let us analyze this.

If the truck driver had any inkling that such an accident would have resulted from his trying to beat the light he certainly would never have considered it, but he chose to do what he did because it gave him greater satisfaction at that moment. However, we are not concerned now with what he should or should not have done but what he must do for greater satisfaction following the accident. It is obvious that he feels absolutely terrible over what he knows was his fault, yet he does not want to be blamed for the death of these children. There is certainly no satisfaction in feeling the weight of this responsibility; consequently, he is going to do everything in his power to shift it away from himself. The police arrive and learn that the father was driving without headlights on and that he was highly intoxicated. The truck driver kept saying over and over again — "It was not my fault. That man went right through the red light and didn't even have his lights on. The death of those children is horrible, but it was not my fault!" Before long he was absolutely convinced that the accident would never have occurred had the headlights been on, and he was right because what made him speed up to beat the yellow light was his certainty that no car was coming. However, he could not tell the police the truth, that the right-of-way still belonged to the father even though intoxicated and without lights — although it made him feel as if it was not his responsibility.

In court the father was found guilty of manslaughter even though he was innocent, which infuriated him. But because the deaths of his children were considered punishment enough, his sentence was suspended and he was placed on probation. His wife, however, was not satisfied with the decision since she believed him guilty of killing their children (she had warned him time and again about his drinking at parties), and filed for divorce. The truck driver was awarded quite a bit of money in damages because he discovered that he was not physically the same after such a traumatic experience. Had the conditions been slightly different making it impossible for the truck driver to shift his responsibility, the only avenue open for greater satisfaction would have been for him to pay a heavy price for what he did. His insurance would have compensated the parents to a degree for their tragic loss and they would have been satisfied to know that he was sent to prison. When released he would feel that he paid his debt to society and the family, and his conscience would be cleared. If he felt the least bit guilty for killing these children he could always confess this sin to a priest or psychiatrist, or atone for it in various ways. The father, on the other hand, who was found guilty although he was completely innocent has built up a tremendous hate for the entire system of justice and may desire to kill the truck driver in retaliation if he thinks he can get away with it. His life has been ruined and he wants to hurt somebody in the worst way for what was done to him. Had this accident not taken anyone's life, the driver of the truck might have volunteered that it was his fault so his insurance company could reimburse them for property damage. This could help compensate in some small way for what happened. Now pay close attention to the same accident under changed conditions so you can see why the truck driver when faced with the choice of speeding up or slowing down is compelled to prefer the latter — which avoids the tragedy.

The truck driver feels absolutely horrible over what he knows was his responsibility because he went through the red light, but he also knows that no one in the entire world will ever blame him for what was done. People standing around are shocked over the sight. The father and mother are weeping bitterly over the loss of their children but they will not say to the truck driver — "Look at what you just did!" The police are not going to smell his breath or give him other tests, because there are no more police (they will be displaced on a gradual basis, which will be explained shortly). There are no prosecutors who are going to try and prove his guilt in a court of law. An ambulance arrives to carry off the dead, and tow trucks to clean up the debris. How do you think he feels? Wouldn't it be wonderful if he was punished or could pay in some way for what he did? He would like to be blamed, criticized, condemned, punished, beat up by the father and hated but he knows these things will never take place because nobody alive holds him responsible. He would like to write a check to compensate for what he did, but nobody is suing him or blaming him in any way, which compels him to hold himself responsible. Since he is unable to shift what is his responsibility or find any satisfaction whatsoever, he finds himself in an unbearable situation and will be compelled to go through life with the death of these children, the sorrow of the parents, and the destruction of their property, on his conscience. Let's examine this from another point of view.

What if the father didn't see the truck at all and was not certain of what happened? No matter how unbearable it was for the truck driver to feel this responsibility, just imagine how the father must feel to know that he was, or might have been, responsible for the death of his loved ones, although this difference could hardly pass through the eye of a needle.

"I am not sure I understand. What do you mean when you say 'this difference could hardly pass through the eye of a needle?'"

If the father was even the slightest bit uncertain of what actually happened, as long as he knows it might have been his fault, he will suffer just as much as if he was certain because there is no way he can find out when no one blames him. He might actually believe that his drinking was responsible, that maybe it was the fact that he didn't put on his lights or that he went through the red light because he just didn't see it. How do you think he feels knowing that his carelessness might have caused the death of his own children? How will he ever know that he was not responsible unless he is fully aware at all times of what he is doing?

This means that the very thought of hurting others through carelessness is so terrifying when there will be no blame, punishment, or a price to be paid for what we know is, or might have been, our responsibility, that when we are confronted with a similar situation as the truck driver we could never find greater satisfaction in speeding up, while the father knowing that drinking might cause him to get in an accident figures out a way to solve his problem so he can still drink without taking on the responsibility of driving. If he has no one to drive his car but himself, and he feels that drinking might cause an accident for which he knows well in advance there will be no blame, he cannot afford the risk of placing himself in a position from which his conscience will torture him the rest of his life. People know they are not compelled to drink and drive, not compelled to pass on a curve or hill, not compelled to recklessly show off and race unless they want to, for over this they have mathematical control, and when it fully dawns on them that should they hurt others with their carelessness they will not be blamed or punished because everyone knows they were compelled to do what they did — WHEN THEY KNOW THEY WERE NOT COMPELLED — they are given no alternative but to do everything in their power to prevent a situation from arising that gives them absolutely no satisfaction.

The only reason that accidents resulting from carelessness were able to take place was because people could blame something else as the cause, thereby shifting what was their responsibility; and liability insurance didn't help because those with ample coverage felt they were prepared to pay for their negligence.

"Does this mean there will be no more liability insurance?"

"To be held liable means that you are being blamed for the damage that was done, and since you are not to blame, each person will assume responsibility for the damage done to his own car and himself. In the new world the parties involved in any kind of accident will assume the cost of the damage done to them, which means that when someone holds himself responsible for hurting others he must

102

also hold himself responsible for all the other expenses the victim and his insurance company must incur, thus hurting the victim of his carelessness all the more since the money he will have to spend on a new or repaired car could have been used either by himself or the insurance company, for other things. If a person doesn't have this [no fault] insurance or sufficient cash reserve to cover his share of the damage, then we, all the people, will pay the cost because we know this person couldn't help himself, that he was compelled to neglect taking out this insurance, or else he couldn't afford it. But when he will be guaranteed his standard of living (which will be explained in the economic chapter), then he will desire to carry this protection for fear that he will hurt others by making them pay for damages that he should be sharing. If a driver was to blame for a bad accident there would be no choice, as we have just witnessed, but to live out his entire life with this horrible feeling of guilt, having no way to relieve it. This explains why the ability to confess our sins allows the confessional to be a place where we can find the justification necessary to absolve our conscience. But when it becomes mathematically impossible to shift the responsibility for our negligence away from ourselves — when we are not being blamed — there is no way carelessness can be justified. If for any reason an accident should occur and it was not our fault, there would be no reason to feel remorse, but if we were not sure whether our actions contributed in some way we would have to live with this uncertainty knowing that we might have been partly or completely responsible. Consequently, the only way a person would know for sure that he was not responsible is to be aware at all times of what he is doing.

The right-of-way system in the new world becomes a mathematical standard by which each motor vehicle operator is forced to judge only himself. The truck driver knows he did not have the right-of-way; consequently, he was aware he struck the first blow when the collision took place. If he had gotten to the red light and no cars were coming, he would not have been striking a first blow had he decided to cross the intersection. By the same reasoning, his speed is no longer controlled by a patrol car being present or absent but by what he considers safe enough so that he will never have to encroach on another driver's right-of-way. He cannot afford to drive with bad tires or brakes because if the one should blow out and the other fail forcing him to collide with other cars by entering their territory, he will know that he struck the first blow. If the tires were new but the mechanic failed to tighten the bolts on one wheel which fell off at high speed causing the accident, his conscience would be clear since this was something that happened to him as a part of a chain reaction. This applies to all types of transportation where there is a chain of responsibility. For example, when a plane crashes it is the responsibility of all those who have anything to do with it — building, repairing, maintaining, piloting it, etc. — consequently when these individuals know that they will never be blamed for taking thousands of lives or putting those lives in jeopardy, they will never allow a plane to go up unless they are absolutely certain that no one will be hurt. Everybody will be compelled to assume the responsibility of hurting others in these plane crashes because the others will never blame them for this hurt. The changed conditions will force all mechanics to be extremely careful so that they are never responsible for accidents due to their carelessness. Right now the mechanics, engineers, etc. are justified in being careless because they know that somebody is going to blame somebody else right down the line of command, but when they know that nobody will ever blame anybody, they will all feel the weight of a tremendous responsibility which compels them to ground a plane unless they can feel absolutely certain they are not sending a group of people to their death. There will be no reason for airplanes to crash as we begin to understand the factors that make skilled pilots, controllers, and mechanics vulnerable to human error, and find better methods of defusing those errors before an accident occurs. Furthermore, now that cockpit instruments can provide the pilot with information regarding altitude, speed and direction — along with other technological advancements that can detect potential problems long before take-off — airline travel will be safer than ever before. All engineers and mechanics who design, maintain, and repair aircraft systems will have no choice but to make safety a number one priority.

In the private sector driving a car, motorcycle, or any other type vehicle that operates on public roads will be considered a serious undertaking. For example, before desiring to drive a car in the new world we will want to know everything that could possibly make us responsible for hurting others in an accident which will then, never occur. It will also prevent us from delaying other drivers from getting to their destination. If by not using directional signals when required (which excludes having to use signals when we are alone on the street or in a lane that only goes to the right or left), or by not moving over far enough when making a turn we see that we are holding up traffic for which we will not be blamed by the honking of horns, we will soon find greater satisfaction in not doing those things that interfere with the flow of traffic. By blowing horns in blame, and by calling people names, we not only find justification to repeat that for which we are prepared to pay for in terms of going to court, getting a ticket, etc., but we get a certain satisfaction in irritating those whom we know will criticize this annoying habit. When it becomes impossible to pay a price for hurting or annoying others because there are no consequences, in other words, when all justification for tying up traffic has been removed, we are given no choice but to change our ways.

"I'm beginning to see the effect of this even in smaller accidents, because the person who caused it is made to realize how much inconvenience and trouble he puts people through who refuse to blame him in any way for doing what he knows they must excuse, and he, for the very first time, cannot justify."

As a consequence of knowing what it means that man's will is not free, all carelessness is automatically removed because to hurt someone who will not blame you for doing what you know could have been prevented had you not been careless, gives you no choice. Driving a car under these new conditions, unless you know what you are doing, is equivalent to playing with a loaded gun; and if you can get any satisfaction out of standing around while the parents weep over the death of their child just killed by you who will not be blamed or punished in any way, then, my friends, you will be able to do the impossible. Consequently, a great responsibility is placed upon the shoulders of anyone who has anything whatever to do with cars, and instead of being anxious to drive each person will be more anxious to make certain that he really knows how first. The miracle about to unfold is that once all mankind are taught what it means that man's will is not free, and certain other changes are made which I will soon discuss, people are permitted to see, well in advance, a situation that

105

is too horrible to contemplate, consequently, the only avenue open for needed satisfaction is to prevent it from arising because there is no way they can do anything afterwards under the changed conditions. This means that whatever the other driver did that caused the accident would be listed among the DON'TS OF GOOD DRIVING and no one would desire to go against these. People in a hurry to beat a traffic signal will do just the opposite, never try to beat it, and never be in a position where they are forced to go through a red light, or screech their brakes. If, however, there is no traffic coming and the light is red, there is no reason to stay because its purpose is to stop the other traffic so they can go.

As for whether we need permission from the government to drive? In our present environment we need a license and before this is granted we are given certain tests to see if we qualify which means that part of our responsibility has already been shifted. In other words, people who are really not qualified to sit behind a wheel are made to think that they are by receiving permission, and should someone make the comment, "You shouldn't be allowed to drive," the response would be, "The government thinks so or I wouldn't have been given a license." In the new world there will be no such thing as a license to drive because man has become of age and can now assume responsibility for himself, therefore, the only person to tell you that you are sufficiently trained and ready will be you yourself. No driver henceforth will ever again be issued a license by a government agency to determine his qualifications. This means that the division of the Department of Motor Vehicles which determines the eligibility of a new driver by administering a passing or a failing grade will be permanently displaced. The fact that certain inadequate standards were set up for others to determine our qualifications allowed many unqualified people to assume they were qualified because they passed the required exam. We will never again have to prove to anyone but ourselves that we are qualified to drive and our vehicle is in good condition. We can see very clearly why our responsibility must increase to the maximum degree since this is the only way we can prevent what we don't want. Where before we couldn't wait to pass the test so we could finally go wherever we wanted, we will not be that anxious to sit behind the wheel until we know for sure we can drive without causing collisions or delays. Even driving instructors will never tell us when they think we are ready because they would not want to assume this responsibility. Their job will be to teach us all the causes of accidents and delays, and show us how to handle a car properly. They will have a thorough course of training which will include all the causes of accidents through carelessness, but it will be up to us to determine whether we are capable of driving without hurting anyone by comparing our ability with the tough driving standards set up by the driving schools. There will be no need for statutory speed limits that try and force compliance because nobody will desire to drive at a speed that endangers others. The speed limit will serve as a general guideline to indicate the maximum reasonable and safe speed to travel, as well as to alert the driver of dangerous road and weather conditions. Today we say — "Obey the laws or else you will be punished." Tomorrow we say — "Don't obey the laws of good driving if you don't want to, but if someone gets hurt as a consequence it will be impossible to blame anybody but ourselves." Therefore, every suggestion to guide the new driver in the right direction will be willingly heeded because of this fear that someone, other than ourselves (this is the least consideration in the new world), could be seriously hurt. Driving a car becomes a very hazardous profession because the very thought that someone might get hurt for which there would be no blame or punishment, and no questions would be asked as to whose fault it was, compels everyone to become an extremely skillful driver before undertaking what could very easily lead to the kind of accident just described, and there is no more unbearable form of punishment than to know that you are responsible for someone's death or serious injury. However, to launch this new world and create the environment necessary to prevent crime, war, hate, and all the other evils plaguing our lives we must remove every form of hurt to us that could justify retaliation, which is a separate problem that will be solved very shortly.

"Although I agree with everything you have demonstrated so far, reluctantly, and think it is absolutely marvelous, I can't see how you can satisfy the whole human race and that's what you must do with your equation which includes communism as well as capitalism."

You keep forgetting one thing. I am not the one who will solve this problem. The astronomer who first observed the invariable laws between the planets, moon and sun didn't cause the eclipse; he perceived certain relations that made him aware it would occur at a certain time. And just because I have observed the invariable laws inherent in the mankind system which allowed me to see the end of all war and crime because of what it means that man's will is not free, does not mean that I am causing this to come about. The most I am able to do is reveal God's laws, which gives me no choice but to move in a certain direction for satisfaction because we are all a part of His laws. At this juncture, let me recapitulate certain salient points.

Man is compelled by his nature to move constantly in the direction of greater satisfaction and when he is blamed for hurting others through carelessness he is permitted to find satisfaction in one of three ways. He can apologize, shift his responsibility to something or someone else as the cause for what he knows he has done, or if there is no way he can shift his responsibility he can pay a price for the hurt he knows he caused. However, when he knows, well in advance, that all mankind are compelled to excuse everything he does because it is now known that his will is not free — while he knows that he doesn't have to hurt anybody unless he wants to (for over this he knows he has mathematical control) — he is given no choice but to do everything in his power to prevent a situation from which he cannot find any satisfaction. How is it possible for him to find satisfaction in carelessly hurting others when he is denied an opportunity to apologize, to shift his responsibility, or to pay a price of atonement for what he did? Since this will eat at his conscience, and since he knows this well in advance, he is given no choice but to prefer the alternative that offers greater satisfaction and in this case the only avenue open is for him to prevent such a situation from arising. I realize that there is quite a difference between hurt that results from carelessness which is something a person really doesn't want... and deliberate hurt. There is also a vast difference between the blame that follows a hurt and blame that is in advance which is a judgment of what is right for someone else. This latter blame is discussed thoroughly in the chapter on marriage, where it is also demonstrated how such advance blame or judgment of others must come to an end out of mathematical necessity. This is the kind of blame that tells you how to wear your hair, how to dress, how you should live. It is the bully in various forms. These things are your business only as long as nobody is hurt by what you do. You will understand this much better as we proceed.

The belief in free will and the concomitant blame are equivalent to the thrust of a rocket in getting a satellite into space, for without it we could never have reached the outposts of this Golden Age. But just as the astronauts shed their excess baggage when their rocket has expended its energy in reaching orbit, so likewise will we shed this theory and all the blame that helped us reach this tremendous turning point in our lives. Well, is it any wonder this discovery was never found because the solution actually lies beyond the framework of modern thought since it cannot be understood in terms of our present knowledge? As I said, there are no precedents. I realize how difficult it must be for you to conceive a world without liability insurance and the Department of Motor Vehicles, but you will learn soon enough that millions of people are going to be permanently displaced from their manner of earning a living but they will not be hurt in any way, so don't jump to any conclusions; just be patient. If you are slightly less skeptical and more willing to continue the investigation, you will see how effective are these laws as God puts an end to all war, crime, adultery and divorce. Last but not least, though our magic elixir will not apply here, I shall reveal something about death in a mathematical, undeniable manner which will make every reader very happy. Don't you think it strange that of all the millions of years Earth has been in existence (and what is a million years when the words through which you see this relation are clarified) you, of all people, should have been born to see the universe now; why weren't you born 5000 years ago, or why shouldn't you be born in the future? My friends, you are in for quite a pleasant surprise, but your mind is so filled with words like spirit, soul, reincarnation, heaven, etc., which have absolutely no meaning whatever, that you are terribly confused, especially those who think they know. You will soon learn that there is absolutely nothing to fear in death, which in itself will revolutionize your lives, but everything is related, so please bear with me since it is mathematically impossible to put everything down at one time. As I said, you will catch your breath in utter amazement at the infinite wisdom that governs this universe, and you will be given no choice but to change your ways. But first, I shall reveal my second discovery which will play a vital role in the new world.

PART TWO

MY SECOND DISCOVERY

CHAPTER FOUR — WORDS, NOT REALITY
CHAPTER FIVE — PREMARITAL RELATIONS
CHAPTER SIX — THE NEW ECONOMIC WORLD

CHAPTER FOUR

WORDS, NOT REALITY

Our problem of hurting each other is very deep-rooted and begins with words through which we have not been allowed to see reality for what it really is. Supposing I stood up in one of our universities and said — "Ladies and gentlemen, I am prepared to prove that man does not have five senses, which has nothing to do with a sixth sense," wouldn't all the professors laugh and say, "Are you serious or are you being funny? You can't be serious because everybody knows man has five senses. This is an established fact." The definition of epistemology is the theory or science of the method and grounds of knowledge especially with reference to its limits and validity. For the modern empiricist, the only way knowledge becomes 'stamped' onto the human conscience is through internal and external sensations, or through sense experience. But there is surprising evidence that the eyes are not a sense organ. The idea that man has five senses originated with Aristotle and it has never been challenged. He did this just as naturally as we would name anything to identify it. But he made an assumption that the eyes functioned like the other senses so he included them in the definition. This is equivalent to calling an apple, pear, peach, orange and potato, five fruit. The names given to these foods describe differences in substance that exist in the real world, but we certainly could not call them five fruit since this word excludes the potato which is not grown in the same manner as is described by the word fruit. Believe it or not, the eyes, similar to the potato in the above example, were classified in a category they did not belong. We cannot name the organs with which we communicate with the outside world, five senses, when they do not function alike. Aristotle, however, didn't know this. His logic and renown delayed an immediate investigation of his theory because no one dared oppose the genius of this individual without appearing ridiculous for such audacity, which brought about almost unanimous agreement. To disagree was so presumptuous that nobody dared to voice their disagreement because this would only incur disdainful criticism. Everyone believed that such a brilliant individual, such a genius, had to know whereof he spoke. This is not a criticism of Aristotle or of anyone. But even today, we are still in agreement regarding a fallacious observation about the brain and its relation to the eyes. Those who will consider the possibility that you might have a discovery reveal their confusion by trying to nullify any value to it with this comment as was made to me, "What difference does it make what we call them as a group, this isn't going to change what we are. Whether we call them 5 senses, or 4 senses and a pair of eyes is certainly not going to change them in any way." However, if man doesn't really have five senses, isn't it obvious that just as long as we think otherwise we will be prevented from discovering those things that depend on this knowledge for their discovery? Consequently, it does make a difference what we call them. Just as my first discovery was not that man's will is not free but the knowledge revealed by opening that door for a thorough investigation, so likewise my second discovery is not that man does not have five senses but what significant knowledge lies hidden behind this door. Many years later we have an additional problem which is more difficult to overcome because this fallacious observation has graduated dogmatically into what is considered genuine knowledge, for it is actually taught in school as an absolute fact, and our professors, doctors, etc. would be ready to take up arms, so to speak, against anyone who would dare oppose what they have come to believe is the truth without even hearing, or wanting to hear any evidence to the contrary. I am very aware that if I am not careful the resentment of these people will nail me to a cross, and they would do it in the name of justice and truth. However, it appears that they will not be given the opportunity because the very moment the will of God is perceived and understood, man is given no alternative as to what direction he must travel — which is away from condemning someone who has uncovered a falsehood. The real truth is that there are thousands upon thousands of differences existing in the external world, but when words do not describe these differences accurately we are then seeing a distorted version of what exists — as with free will.

Mankind has been slowly developing and if you go back far enough in history you will find that we believed pregnancy was caused by the bite of an enamored snake which prevented many girls from bathing at certain times, but never prevented them from mating. Today we have thousands of lesser Aristotle's preventing breakthroughs into various hermetically sealed doors. We call them professors and Ph.D.s. Again, this is not a criticism but they accept what has been taught to them and pass it along from generation to generation which makes it very difficult for them to listen to any explanation that must contravene their reputation as leading authorities. That is why they reject people, put anyone down who does not have what they are proud of — their formal education. But please remember they, too, are moving in the direction of greater satisfaction and it isn't fair to criticize them for being proud of their scholastic achievements. I refused to let a Ph.D. in math read my book not because he gave me the wrong answer to a math problem, but because he said my answer must be wrong since he was a Ph.D. and I was not. You might find this problem of interest since it was originated with Sir Isaac Newton. If it takes 3 cows two weeks to eat two acres of grass and all the grass that grows on the two acres in two weeks, and if it takes two cows four weeks to eat two acres of grass and all the grass grown on the two acres in the four weeks; how many cows would be required to eat 6 acres of grass in 6 weeks and all the grass that grows on the 6 acres in the six weeks? Because it was difficult for this Ph.D. to accept the fact that he could not work out this problem, it gave him greater satisfaction to put me and my answer down. Are you beginning to recognize how difficult it has been for me to bring this knowledge to light when it is utterly impossible for our leading authorities to get greater satisfaction listening to any explanation of new knowledge that must reveal their unconscious ignorance that they never knew the truth, only thought they knew? I, however, know the truth and know that I know the truth, and one day as Gregor Mendel declared when he didn't bring his discovery to light, "My time will come." Now let's continue.

Someone whose interest had never been sufficiently aroused to pursue my discoveries because they sounded ridiculous, was visiting an exposition in Canada where he saw a sign on one pavilion that read, "Come inside and let us prove scientifically that the eyes are not a sense organ." He was absolutely amazed because he knew when I said that man does not have five sense organs that I was also referring to the eyes. When seeing this sign he couldn't believe it, however, after convincing himself in Canada that man only has four senses and a pair of eyes, he became very much involved in my work upon his return. But to show you again how the person not the knowledge is the one being judged, when someone else told his cousin who is a dentist that the eyes are not a sense organ, the reply was, "That's ridiculous, how can you know what is true and what is not true, you only went to grade school," to which he responded, "Well, you don't have to take my word for it. In Canada, the proof has already been made a part of a scientific exposition." The dentist then replied, "Well, I haven't seen anything to that effect in the newspapers." This proves conclusively that what he accepts as the truth is determined by who tells him something is true, not by his ability to perceive relations revealing these truths. However, I have my own proof, so let us get on with what is necessary to open our minds to the fresh air of undeniable knowledge. The dictionary states that the word 'sense' is defined as any of certain agencies by or through which an individual receives impressions of the external world; popularly, one of the five senses. Any receptor, or group of receptors, specialized to receive and transmit external stimuli as of sight, taste, hearing, etc. But this is a wholly fallacious observation where the eyes are concerned because nothing from the external world, other than light, strikes the optic nerve as stimuli do upon the organs of hearing, taste, touch and smell.

Upon hearing this my friend asked me in a rather authoritarian tone of voice, "Are you trying to tell me that this is not a scientific fact? "

I replied, "Are you positive because you were told this, or positive because you yourself saw the relations revealing this truth? And if you are still positive, will you put your right hand on the chopping block to show me how positive you really are?"

"I am not that positive, but we were taught this."

It is an undeniable fact that light travels at a high rate of speed, but great confusion arises when this is likened to sound as you will soon have verified. The reason we say man has taste, touch, smell, sight, and hearing is because these describe individual differences that

116

exist, but when we say that these five are senses we are assuming the eyes function like the other four — which they do not. When you learn what this single misconception has done to the world of knowledge, you won't believe it at first. So without further delay, I shall prove something never before understood by man, but before I open this door marked 'Man Does Not Have Five Senses' to show you all the knowledge hidden behind it, it is absolutely necessary to prove exactly why the eyes are not a sense organ. Now tell me, did it ever occur to you that many of the apparent truths we have literally accepted come to us in the form of words that do not accurately symbolize what exists, making our problem that much more difficult since this has denied us the ability to see reality for what it is? In fact, it can be demonstrated at the birth of a baby that no object is capable of getting a reaction from the eyes because nothing is impinging on the optic nerve to cause it, although any number of sounds, tastes, touches or smells can get an immediate reaction since the nerve endings are being struck by something external.

"But doesn't light cause the pupils to dilate and contract depending on the intensity?"

That is absolutely true, but this does not cause; it is a condition of sight. We simply need light to see, just as other things are a condition of hearing. If there was no light we could not see, and if there was nothing to carry the sound waves to our ears, we could not hear. The difference is that the sound is being carried to our eardrums whereas there is no picture traveling from an object on the waves of light to impinge on our optic nerve. Did you ever wonder why the eyes of a newborn baby cannot focus the eyes to see what exists around him, although the other four senses are in full working order?

"I understand from a doctor that the muscles of the eyes have not yet developed sufficiently to allow this focusing."

And he believes this because this is what he was taught, but it is not the truth. In fact, if a newborn infant was placed in a soundproof room that would eliminate the possibility of sense experience which is a prerequisite of sight — even though his eyes were wide open — he could never have the desire to see. Furthermore, and quite revealing, if this infant was kept alive for fifty years or longer on a steady flow of intravenous glucose, if possible, without allowing any stimuli to strike the other four organs of sense, this baby, child, young and middle aged person would never be able to focus the eyes to see any objects existing in that room no matter how much light was present or how colorful they might be because the conditions necessary for sight have been removed, and there is absolutely nothing in the external world that travels from an object and impinges on the optic nerve to cause it.

Sight takes place for the first time when a sufficient accumulation of sense experience such as hearing, taste, touch, and smell — these are doorways in — awakens the brain so that the child can look through them at what exists around him. He then desires to see the source of the experience by focusing his eyes, as binoculars. The eyes are the windows of the brain through which experience is gained not by what comes in on the waves of light as a result of striking the optic nerve, but by what is looked at in relation to the afferent experience of the senses. What is seen through the eyes is an efferent experience. If a lion roared in that room a newborn baby would hear the sound and react because this impinges on the eardrum and is then transmitted to the brain. The same holds true for anything that makes direct contact with an afferent nerve ending, but this is far from the case with the eyes because there is no similar afferent nerve ending in this organ. The brain records various sounds, tastes, touches and smells in relation to the objects from which these experiences are derived, and then looks through the eyes to see these things that have become familiar as a result of the relation. This desire is an electric current which turns on or focuses the eyes to see that which exists — completely independent of man's perception — in the external world. He doesn't see these objects because they strike the optic nerve; he sees them because they are there to be seen. But in order to look, there must be a desire to see. The child becomes aware that something will soon follow something else which then arouses attention, anticipation, and a desire to see the objects of the relation. Consequently, to include the eyes as one of the senses when this describes stimuli from the outside world making contact with a nerve ending is completely erroneous and equivalent to calling a potato, a fruit. Under no conditions can the eyes be called a sense organ unless, as in Aristotle's case, it was the result of an inaccurate observation that was never corrected."

"Well I say, what difference does it make whether we have four senses and a pair of eyes instead of five senses? I certainly don't feel any different, and I still see you just as before."

"Once it is understood that something existing in the external world makes contact with the brain through the four senses, but that the brain contacts the various objects by peering through the eyes, it makes a huge difference, and many things can be clarified.

Our scientists, becoming enthralled over the discovery that light travels approximately 186,000 miles a second and taking for granted that 5 senses was equally scientific, made the statement (which my friend referred to and still exists in our encyclopedias) that if we could sit on the star Rigel with a very powerful telescope focused on the earth we would just be able to see the ships of Columbus reaching America for the very first time. A former science teacher who taught this to her students as if it were an absolute fact responded, "I am sure Columbus would just be arriving; are you trying to tell me that this is not a scientific fact?"

Again my reply was, "Are you positive because you were told this, or positive because you, yourself, saw the relations revealing this truth? And if you are still positive, will you put your right hand on the chopping block to show me how positive you really are?"

"I am not that positive, but this is what I was taught."

Once again certain facts have been confused and all the reasoning except for light traveling at a high rate of speed are completely fallacious. Scientists made the assumption that since the eyes are a sense organ it followed that light must reflect an electric image of everything it touches which then travels through space and is received by the brain through the eyes. What they tried to make us believe is that if it takes 8 minutes for the light from the sun to reach us it would take hundreds of years for the reflection of Columbus to reach Rigel, even with a powerful telescope. But why would they need a telescope?

They reasoned that since it takes longer for the sound from an airplane to reach us when 15,000 feet away than when 5000; and since it takes longer for light to reach us the farther it is away when starting its journey, light and sound must function alike in other respects — which is false — although it is true that the farther away we are from the source of sound the fainter it becomes, as light becomes dimmer when its source is farther away. If the sound from a plane even though we can't see it on a clear day will tell us it is in the sky, why can't we see the plane if an image is being reflected towards the eye on the waves of light? The answer is very simple. An image is not being reflected. We cannot see the plane simply because the distance reduced its size to where it was impossible to see it with the naked eye, but we could see it with a telescope. We can't see bacteria either with the naked eye, but we can through a microscope. The actual reason we are able to see the moon is because there is enough light present and it is large enough to be seen. The explanation as to why the sun looks to be the size of the moon — although much larger — is because it is much much farther away, which is the reason it would look like a star to someone living on a planet the distance of Rigel. This proves conclusively that the distance between someone looking, and the object seen, has no relation to time because the images are not traveling toward the optic nerve on waves of light, therefore it takes no time to see the moon, the sun, and the distant stars. To paraphrase this another way, if you could sit upon the star Rigel with a telescope powerful enough to see me writing this very moment, you would see me at the exact same time that a person sitting right next to me would — which brings us to another very interesting point. If I couldn't see you standing right next to me because we were living in total darkness since the sun had not yet been turned on but God was scheduled to flip the switch at 12 noon, we would be able to see the sun instantly— at that very moment— although we would not be able to see each other for 8 minutes afterwards. The sun at 12 noon would look exactly like a large star, the only difference being that in 8 minutes we would have light with which to see each other, but the stars are so far away that their light diminishes before it gets to us. Upon hearing this explanation someone asked, "If we don't need light around us to see the stars would we need light around us to see the sun turned on at 12 noon? Once the light is here it remains here because the photons of

120

light emitted by the constant energy of the sun surround us. When the earth rotates on its axis so the section on which we live is in darkness, this only means the photons of light are on the other side. When our rotation allows the sun to smile on us again this does not mean that it takes another eight minutes for this light to reach us because these photons are already present. And if the sun were to explode while we were looking at it we would see it the instant it happened, not 8 minutes later. We are able to see the moon, the sun, the distant stars, etc., not because the one is 3 seconds away, the other 8 minutes away, and the last many light years away, but simply because these objects are large enough to be seen at their great distance when enough light is present. This fallacy has come into existence because the eyes were considered a sense organ, like the ears. Since it takes less time for the sound from an airplane to reach our ears when it is a thousand feet away than when five thousand, it was assumed that the same thing occurred with the object sending a picture of itself on the waves of light. If it was possible to transmit a television picture from the earth to a planet as far away as the star Rigel, it is true that the people living there would be seeing the ships of Columbus coming into America for the first time because the picture would be in the process of being transmitted through space at a certain rate of speed. But objects do not send out pictures that travel through space and impinge on the optic nerve. We see objects directly by looking at them and it takes the same length of time to see an airplane, the moon, the sun, or distant stars. To sum this up — just as we have often observed that a marching band is out of step to the beat when seen from a distance because the sound reaches our ears after a step has been taken, so likewise, if we could see someone talking on the moon via a telescope and hear his voice on radio we would see his lips move instantly but not hear the corresponding sound for approximately 3 seconds later due to the fact that the sound of his voice is traveling 186,000 miles a second, but our gaze is not, nor is it an electric image of his lips impinging on our optic nerve after traversing this distance. Because Aristotle assumed the eyes functioned like the other four and the scientific community assumed he was right, it made all their reasoning fit what appeared to be undeniable. According to their thinking, how else was it possible for knowledge to reach us through our eyes when they were compelled to believe that man had five senses? Were they given any choice? Let me prove in still another way that the eyes are not a sense organ.

Line up 50 people who will not move, and a dog, from a slight distance away cannot identify his master. If the eyes were a sense, if an image was traveling on the waves of light and striking the optic nerve, then he would recognize his master instantly as he can from sound and smell. In fact, if he was vicious and accustomed to attacking any stranger entering the back gate at night, and if his sense of hearing and smell were disconnected, he would have no way of identifying his master's face even if every feature was lit up like a Christmas tree, and would attack. This is why he cannot recognize his master from a picture or statue because nothing from the external world is striking the optic nerve. The question as to how man is able to accomplish this continues to confound our scientists. The answer will be given shortly, however, let me make one thing absolutely clear. The knowledge revealed thus far although also hidden behind the door marked 'Man Does Not Have Five Senses' is not what I referred to as being of significance. Frankly, it makes no difference to me that the eyes are not a sense organ, that our scientists got confused because of it, and that a dog cannot identify his master from a picture. What does mean a great deal to me, when the purpose of this book is to remove all evil from our lives (which word is symbolic of any kind of hurt that exists in human relation), is to demonstrate how certain words have absolutely no foundation in reality yet they have caused the worst suffering and unhappiness imaginable. Let me explain.

One of the greatest forms of injustice still exists because we have never understood our true relationship with the external world which is related to what we think we see with our eyes. What is this injustice? It is to be judged an inferior production of the human race because of physiognomic differences and this judgment takes place the moment we call one person beautiful and another one ugly, handsome and homely, good looking and bad looking.

"But I have been taught that sticks and stones will break my bones but names or words will never hurt me. Isn't that a true statement?"

Actually, I'm not referring to those names. To be called the N word, kike, dirty Jew, wop, pig or any name used in an effort to make a person feel inferior, is actually not a hurt if this does not lower ourselves in our own eyes because we allow for the source. But when we believe we are inferior productions because of words that have told us so, the expression, 'Sticks and stones will break my bones...' is completely erroneous since we have been unconsciously hurt. This unconsciousness has its source in the failure to understand how the eyes function which is revealed by the fact that they are included as one of the five senses. When someone is judged an inferior production of the human race by others, as well as himself, all because of words that have no relation to reality although he sees this inferiority as if it is a definite part of the real world, then he is seriously hurt and God is going to put a permanent end to the use of these words. What makes someone remark — "It's a darn shame she got killed, she was such a pretty girl" — indicating that the tragedy was greater because of this prettiness. What makes parents give their children cosmetic surgery if not to increase their physiognomic value? As a consequence of the belief that one person is more beautiful or handsome than another which places a greater value on certain features, many people will go to great lengths to correct their 'imperfections' by getting breast implants and eyelid surgery, while others will have nose operations and squeeze their teeth together. These operations are not without risk yet many people are willing to have these cosmetic procedures because they believe it will improve the quality of their lives; and the doctor who must earn a living justifies his professional advice on the undeniable grounds that they will definitely be more attractive when their teeth are together and their nose straightened. After all, what makes someone good looking, cute, adorable, lovely, gorgeous, beautiful, or handsome if not for the belief that certain features or combination of features contain this value called 'beauty?' And isn't it also true that we see these differences with our very eyes? "We do," you might reply, "but even if we differ as to who is the most beautiful, the real truth is that beauty is in the eyes of the beholder." This comment does not reveal the truth at all; instead it reveals our confusion still more since this expression does not negate the existence of ugliness but only observes a difference of opinion regarding the type of features that constitute what is beautiful and ugly. To prove what I mean, could you possibly call Miss America ugly, or the Wicked Witch beautiful? You might disagree with someone as to which girl in a beauty contest should be judged the winner, but none would be considered ugly. I then asked my friend this question to clarify my point.

"Who do you think is more beautiful, Elizabeth Taylor or your girlfriend?"

"How is it possible to answer your question when beauty is in the eyes of the beholder? This is just a matter of opinion, not a fact, and you said these words were symbolic of reality, or gave the appearance of being so."

Let me rephrase the question, "In your eyes, do you consider your girlfriend as beautiful as Elizabeth Taylor?"

"No I don't."

"In your eyes, is this an opinion that you are less good looking than Paul Newman, or a fact?"

"He is an extremely handsome man, and I do consider him better looking than myself."

"Who do you consider better looking, Paul Newman or Robert Redford?"

"I say the latter."

"Another friend commented, "Not in my book. Newman has it all over him."

"Are you able to see what the expression, 'beauty is in the eyes of the beholder' refers to? There is a difference of opinion as to who is better looking in your eyes, but once you admit to yourself that a certain person is more handsome or beautiful than another, then in so far as you're concerned this is not an opinion but a fact. Take a look at this picture. It is of a girl who has an aquiline nose, buck teeth, a receding hair line, heavy bow legs, sagging breasts, a projected rear end, a harelip, and she lisps and stutters. Now compare her with Elizabeth Taylor and tell me the truth. In your eyes, which one is more beautiful?"

"Are you trying to be funny? Elizabeth Taylor naturally, but this is a fact, she is more beautiful. These differences exist and are a definite part of the real world because I see them with my very eyes."

"Differences exist, this is true, and you do see them with your very eyes, but the words we have been looking through are not and because these symbols are a terrible hurt they must come to an end. You will soon have verified that when we use the expression, 'beauty is in the eyes of the beholder,' what we are saying in reality is that beauty is only a word existing in the brain of the beholder. To be classified as homely is the greatest injustice, yet every time we use the whole range of words expressing good looks we do that very thing. You will soon understand how these words developed and how they fooled even the most analytic minds into believing they were true descriptions of reality. The truth is that nobody is beautiful or ugly, just different. However, the first thing I must do is demonstrate exactly why they are words only, not reality, and why they must become obsolete, otherwise, you will classify this kind of evil as one of those unfortunate things like being born without legs, arms, or eyes."

"I agree with you so far, but let's assume for a moment that you actually convince us that these words are not symbolic of reality, why should we or others stop using them if there is greater satisfaction in continuing with them? Just because you teach us that using certain words, whatever they are, is wrong because they are a hurt won't necessarily stop their use."

"No it won't, but the basic principle will. God is giving us no choice in this matter, as you will soon begin to understand. Let us continue our discussion to observe how our brain operates."

At a very early age our brain not only records sound, taste, touch and smell, but photographs the objects involved which develops a negative of the relation whereas a dog is incapable of this. When he sees the features of his master without any accompanying sound or smell he cannot identify because no photograph was taken. A dog identifies through his sense of sound and smell and what he sees in relation to these sense experiences, just as we identify most of the differences that exist through words and names. If the negative plate on which the relation is formed is temporarily disconnected – in man's case the words and names, and in the dog's case the sounds and smells – both would have a case of amnesia. This gives conclusive evidence as to why an animal cannot identify too well with his eyes. As we have seen, if a vicious dog accustomed to attacking any person who should open the fence at night were to have two senses, hearing and smell, temporarily disconnected, and assuming that no relation was developed as to the way in which an individual walked, he would actually have amnesia and even though he saw with his eyes his master come through the gate he would have no way of recognizing him and would attack. But a baby, having already developed negatives of relations that act as a slide in a movie projector, can recognize at a very early age. The brain is a very complex piece of machinery that not only acts as a tape recorder through our ears and the other three senses, and a camera through our eyes, but also, and this was never understood, as a movie projector. As sense experiences become related or recorded, they are projected, through the eyes, upon the screen of the objects held in relation and photographed by the brain. Consequently, since the eyes are the binoculars of the brain all words that are placed in front of this telescope, words containing every conceivable kind of relation, are projected as slides onto the screen of the outside world and if these words do not accurately symbolize, as with five senses, man will actually think he sees what has absolutely no existence; and if words correctly describe then he will be made conscious of actual differences and relations that exist externally but have no meaning for those who do not know the words. To understand this better let us observe my granddaughter learning words.

It is obvious that this baby looks out through her eyes and sees various animals and people in motion, but she is not conscious of differences. She may be drawn to play with one animal in preference to another, or may prefer to play with one toy over another, but in so far as she is concerned all she sees are a bunch of objects. By constantly hearing certain sounds in relation to specific objects, she soon knows that apple, orange, doll, dress, sun, moon, dog, cat, couch, chair, etc., mean the very things she sees with her eyes. These bits of substance are a definite part of the real world, and she knows this even before learning the words. She has experienced most of these with her four senses, and even though this cannot be done where the sun and moon are concerned, she still sees that something is there. Remember, however, nothing from the external world strikes her optic nerve to allow her to see these various objects. She simply

126

sees these things because she looks at them. A dog also sees these objects because he looks at them. He tastes, smells and hears various things, but since nothing strikes his optic nerve, he must confirm what he is doubtful of with his sense of smell.

"But doesn't the brain take a picture through the eyes of the differences that exist? I can see them through my eyes, why can't a dog see them through his?"

Because he knows nothing of differences. He enjoys certain objects better than others. He likes his master and dislikes strangers. He likes to eat certain things, and is attracted to particular females, but there is no way his brain can perceive differences because this involves words. Let us continue.

As my granddaughter's eyes are focused on one of our canine friends I shall repeat the word 'dog' rapidly in her ear. When she turns away I stop. This will be continued until she looks for him when hearing the word which indicates that a relation between this particular sound and object has been established and a photograph taken. Soon this relation is formed which makes her conscious of a particular difference that exists in the external world. As she learns more and more words such as cat, horse, bird, sun, moon, etc., she becomes conscious of these differences which no one can deny because they are seen through words or slides that circumscribe accurately these various bits of substance. This is exactly how we learn words only I am speeding up the process. Before long she learns house, tree, car, chair, door, kitchen, television, airplane, moon, stars, nose, teeth, eyes, hair, girl, boy, and so on. She soon learns that these bits of substance are different, and that is why they have different names. Until she learns the word cat she could very easily point to a dog when hearing that word because a negative of the difference has not yet been developed, just as a fox cannot be differentiated from a dog until a photograph of the difference has been developed. She also learns the names of individuals: Mommy, Daddy, Linda, Janis, Marc, David, Elan, Justin, Shoshana, Adam, Jennifer, Meredith, etc. If a picture of her mother was flashed on a screen, she would automatically say mommy. She is able to identify her mother because the word is a picture that was taken when the relation was formed, and exists in her mind, through which she looks at the differences that exist in substance. My granddaughter can identify her mother from hundreds and hundreds of photographs because the difference is a negative that not only reveals who her mother is, but who she is not. In other words, as she learns these names and words her brain takes a picture of the objects symbolized and when she sees these differences again she projects the word or name, but the brain will not take any picture until a relation is formed. Consequently, these differences that exist in the external world which are not identifiable through taste, touch, smell, or sounds are identifiable only because they are related to words, names or slides that we project for recognition. If we would lose certain names or words we would have amnesia because when we see these ordinarily familiar differences we are unable to project the words or names necessary for recognition.

By the same reasoning the word Chinese develops not only a negative of differences but of similarities, consequently, when someone is not acquainted with the differences that exist among this race he only sees that they resemble each other. But if we would live among this group and separate them by their individual names, we would soon see their differences and not their similarities. Seeing similarities is what takes place when someone does not learn colors properly and he may be called color blind when in reality he is word blind. Supposing we were to teach a child that blue is green and green is blue and then place him in surroundings where his identification of colors would be tested. Can you imagine how quickly he would be called color-blind? This child would argue that the green is blue and the blue is green while the other children, brought up differently, would reverse the argument. If someone gets confused between certain shades of blue and green, it is only because the relation between colors was never accurately photographed. In the majority of cases colors are learned in a haphazard manner and if a blue negative was developed when looking at a subtle shade of green, he will see blue just as you would see something blue through blue glasses even though the object was green. This is equivalent to getting confused between certain type leaves and trees only because these differences were not accurately photographed in relation to the word. For example, if a particular leaf is given a specific name and another leaf resembling this leaf to a degree but still slightly different is given a different

128

name, then when the relation is accurately photographed the person learning the words will never mistake one for the other. Once children are made to understand that they are referring to the same bit of substance, regardless of the different names used to identify it, then there can be no argument between them. Of course, if a child can't see a difference before learning the words, then he is genuinely color blind. Here is another example.

If you were taught one word, orange, which included within that symbol a grapefruit and tangerine you would hand me any one of the three if I asked for an orange, but when you learn the other two words which photographs the difference then you could not hand me a tangerine or grapefruit if I asked for an orange. The reason we have a word for the sun and a word for the moon is because these two bodies are different, and the reason we have a planet named Earth, one named Saturn, Venus, etc. is only because these are not one and the same planet and we have separated them by calling them different names. However, the reason we do not call the moon a planet is because we learned it does not function like one, therefore it does not fall in the same category. Once it is understood as an undeniable law that nothing impinges on the optic nerve, even though the pupils dilate and contract according to the intensity of light, it becomes possible to separate what exists in the external world from that which is only a negative or word in our head. In the course of our children's development they learn other kinds of words that form inaccurate relations not only because a judgment of personal value is given external reality by the symbol itself, but also because the logic of unconscious syllogistic reasoning confirms the apparent validity of inaccurate observations. Let me show you how this was accomplished.

From the time we were small children our relatives, parents, friends and acquaintances have expressed their personal likes and dislikes regarding people's physiognomies. The words beautiful, pretty, cute, adorable, handsome, etc., heard over and over again with an enhancing inflection as to someone's physical appearance took a picture of the similarities between this type of physiognomy and developed negatives which also contained the degree of feeling experienced. Similarly, an entire range of words heard over and over again with a detracting inflection as to someone's physical characteristics, took a picture of the similarities between this type of physiognomy and developed negatives containing the degree of feeling experienced below this line of demarcation. As time went on a standard of beauty was established. Not knowing what the brain was able to do, we were convinced that one group of similarities contained a lesser value than the opposite similarities. We were unaware that the brain had reversed the process by which these negatives were developed and then projected onto the screen of undeniable differences a value that existed only in our head. It would not be long before we would be conditioned to desire associating with the one type while avoiding the other and as we would get older you would not be able to convince us that an ugly or beautiful person did not exist because we had witnessed these differences with our very eyes. In other words, when a word contains a judgment of value, a standard of perfection, then we are able to project this value directly onto substance, and then because we see this with our very eyes, it was a simple thing to convince ourselves that beauty was a definite part of the real world. The confusion between what is real and what is not comes from the fact that these words not only describe real differences that exist in the world, but they also create external values when there are no such things. I will give you an example of this by using a movie projector.

Here is a smooth white wall in a dark room with nothing on it. I am dropping a negative plate or slide into the projector, flipping the switch, and just take a look — there is a picture of a girl on the wall. But go up and touch her. All you feel is the wall itself because the girl is not there. We have been doing the same thing with our brain regarding values. The differences in substance were not only divided up by the use of words like man, woman, child, etc., but became a screen upon which we were able to project this value. Drop a negative plate or word slide in your brain projector and flip the switch. Well just take a look, there is now a beautiful girl, a homely man, an ugly duckling! Turn off the switch (remove the negative plate or word slide) and all you see are the differences in substance because the projected values have been removed. Since we were taught that the eyes receive and transmit sense experience on the waves of light it was impossible to deny that this beautiful girl actually existed, and when we changed the standard hidden in the word all we did was change the

130

screen. By saying that this person may not be beautiful physically but has a beautiful soul, we were allowed to see ugly souls as if they, too, existed externally. Scientists, believing that the eyes were a sense organ, unconsciously confirmed what man saw with them because they were unaware that it was possible to project a fallacious relation realistically. Consequently everything in the external world will be distorted if the words through which man looks at what he calls reality are inaccurate symbols or if the relation which is photographed becomes, as in the five senses, an inaccurate negative which is then projected realistically upon undeniable substance. The word beautiful has absolutely no external reality and yet because it is learned in association with a particular physiognomy a beautiful girl is created when no such person exists. Obviously there is a difference between the shape and features of individuals, but to label one beautiful and another ugly only reveals that you are conscious of a fallacious difference that is projected through your eyes upon substance that cannot be denied — which makes the projection appear real. By having the words beautiful, ugly, gorgeous, etc. as slides in a movie projector through which the brain will look at the external world, a fallacious value is placed upon certain specific differences only because of the words which is then confirmed as a part of the real world since man will swear that he sees beautiful women with his eyes, but in actual reality all he sees are different shapes and different features. This beautiful girl is not striking his optic nerve which then allows him to see her beauty but instead he projects the word onto these differences and then photographs a fallacious relation. The brain records all relations, whether true or false, and since it was considered an indisputable fact that man had five senses which were connected in some way with the external world, and since four of these were accurately described as sense organs, that is, they receive and transmit external stimuli, it was very easy for Aristotle to get confused and put a closure on further investigation by including the eyes in the definition, which he did only because he never understood their true function.

The belief in the eyes being a sense organ has allowed innumerable words to come into existence which caused people to be judged an inferior production of the human race. Can you imagine what would happen if we lived in a world where all such words were removed, where nobody, including ourselves would be judged in terms of ugliness, homeliness, prettiness and so forth. Remember, however, when these negatives of external value are removed, this doesn't stop us from seeing differences that appeal to us more but instead of saying — "She is the most beautiful girl I have ever seen," which places other girls in a stratified layer of lesser value, we are compelled to say — "She appeals to me more than any girl I have ever seen" which makes it obvious that the value we see exists only for us. The first expression requires that ugly girls exist because certain type features are considered superior, while the second expression only observes that other girls appeal to us less which makes everybody equal in value except to particular individuals. By removing all the synonyms that describe people as good looking, nobody is hurt, but by removing all the antonyms that have been judging half the human race as bad looking this entire group is brought up to a level of complete equality and respect. However, it is mathematically impossible to expect you to give up that which is also a source of satisfaction although the change does not depend on those who are happy in their pride and self-importance, which includes everyone to a degree, but on those who are seriously hurt and who are shown how they, too, can become happy. And are we given a choice when to continue using these words after we have learned the truth only reveals our ignorance, for which we will never be blamed? How is it possible to criticize people for believing the earth is flat, man's will is free, and his eyes a sense organ when we know for an absolute fact that they have never learned the truth?

It is true, however, that we are so conditioned by these words that even their removal will not make us like someone more who appeals to us less. But when children are brought up without ever hearing these words there is no telling to whom they might be attracted without being adversely judged. For example, if two boys decide to approach two girls having never been conditioned with words like beautiful and ugly, they might be attracted, without envy, each to the other, but when their head is filled with fallacious standards of value that have been concealed in words, it is obvious that they will prefer the one that conforms more closely to this standard of perfection or beauty because this meets with greater approval and less criticism. This approval by others is in no way an external value, in other words, your approval of what I do has a value for me, but unless I want this it has no value for me at all. If I don't like the criticism I will try to conform to a standard that avoids what I don't like, but this is a relation between myself and what exists outside of me.

"Well, is it a fallacious value when certain differences are admired and respected more by the majority of the world? For example, is it a fallacious value when — pardon the fallacious expression — a beautiful girl attracts a millionaire who desires to marry her because of her beauty? I'd say these values are pretty real regardless of whether we call these differences by one name or another, right? If one thousand males have to choose between two females and the entire thousand pick one in preference to the other do you mean to say that the differences that attracted them are not a part of the external world?"

"Of course these differences are a part of the external world just as the difference between the moon and the sun is a part of the external world, and just as the difference between a cat and a rat is externally real, but this has nothing to do with value. In other words, if you choose a cat as a pet because you like felines, this has personal value for you. There are some people who like rodents and would pick the rat as their choice, which has personal value for them. In reality, there is no such thing as an external value. If you are drawn to hire an individual because he meets certain requirements or if he judges for himself that he qualifies (as will happen in the new world), this only means that he is more valuable to you, the employer; and if one thousand people think the same way this doesn't mean that the differences they prefer have external value although the differences in substance are externally real. Value is nothing other than a word to describe what you personally want or like."

"Do you mean that one man's meat is another man's poison... and doesn't this go back to the idea that beauty is in the eyes of the beholder? I'm still confused as to why this expression isn't correct when it is expressing someone's personal taste."

"There is quite a difference between both expressions because meat and poison are external realities but, as we have learned, beauty has no external reality whatsoever. I may not like certain types of meat but I don't create the meat with a word to symbolize its existence whereas the word beauty does this by placing a greater value on certain specific differences (that undeniably exist and are a part of the external world) which value only has existence for the internal world, that is, for what I personally like or desire. For example, if I call one shaped nose, aquiline, and another, straight, then I am accurately symbolizing an external difference, but if I say a straight nose is beautiful and an aquiline nose is ugly, then I am projecting through my eyes an internal value that has no external existence onto a screen of differences that are externally undeniable. Consequently, when any words are used that contain an internal value, something that you recognize as having more value for you which are then projected as a part of the external world, it is then made to appear that this value exists outside of you because you see it with your very eyes. As a result of words, man was actually able to do the impossible. He was able to stratify differences in people into layers of value, when it is mathematically impossible for anything of value to exist in the external world. Can you imagine what would happen if we lived in an atmosphere where there were no values that were imposed as standards by the unconscious or conscious judgment of others?"

Supposing two girls living on earth presently called ugly were placed on a planet where no such word exists, there would be absolutely nothing to prevent them from living a normal life because the males there would never judge them in terms of ugliness, for no such thing exists except as a projection of our realistic imagination. What one man may like when no words such as beautiful and ugly are present to condition him — and there is no criticism for the choice that appeals to him most — might be a girl that has a stocky build, small breasts, and protruding ears. Here on earth these girls are handicapped from the day of their birth because their particular features have been assigned more or less value as a result of these differences. They are constantly judged not in any personal or direct manner but in a way that cannot easily be corrected because they are seen through this kaleidoscope of negatives that transforms them realistically into what they are not. Every other word we use stratifies external differences which cannot be denied into fallacious standards and values that appear realistic only because they are confirmed with our eyes (with the direct perception of our sense of sight) and our unconscious syllogistic reasoning, which employ words as realities. The unhappiness resulting from these words is manifold and manifest in the very fact that people develop a complex of inferiority and are forced to compensate by becoming the life of the party, or by making themselves visible in other ways. Not realizing that it was the word itself that was the source of the problem, those that were considered ugly were compelled to go through life feeling less than others in physiognomic value. How many times have you heard someone intending to be nice but with a tone of pity remark, "She isn't pretty but she has a nice personality," which becomes the consolation prize. This girl has to remove herself from the competition and try to get attention some other way in order to make up for this imaginary lack. Although you look back with smiling incredulity to the days of yore and wonder about the many ignorant beliefs that our ancestors used to imagine were true, is it possible for your professors to believe that they are not any more educated or intelligent than anybody else? As a further consequence of these fallacious differences that do not exist in reality but are only a projection of deceptive relations, they have been led to believe that they are more important than someone else, more valuable in the scheme of things, and from this source a host of evils stem. Have they any conception that these are only words? In reality no one is more intelligent or educated than anyone else, as you will soon understand. There are many more words that will go by the wayside such as brilliant, genius, a brain, etc., because they do not accurately describe reality for what it is (and will be discussed in the chapter on education). It is absolutely true that just as long as others judge you more beautiful or valuable when your physiognomy conforms to an accepted standard, more educated or valuable when you learn or do certain things, there is ample justification to change yourself to suit them which is the reason many people have nose operations, squeeze their teeth together, develop a huge vocabulary, walk, talk, and act in definite ways. The individuals who are considered educated, intelligent, or beautiful may not like to be told that they are none of these things, but there is a big difference between the people considered to possess these values and the ones

135

who do not. It is difficult to contemplate the extent to which we have all been influenced by words that judge half of the human race as inferior, and the consequent pain this has caused.

At long last we will be able to know ourselves for what we really are. If any reader starts out with a feeling of superiority or inferiority I will guarantee that when he understands all the principles — and he will — he will end up feeling exactly equal in value with every person alive...no better or worse. We must remember that mankind has been developing at a mathematical rate and had to go through the necessary stages of development in order to reach this stage of his maturity. Man has been consciously unconscious of the reason for doing things because of words, nothing else. Psychologists, theologians, philosophers, as well as all others who read books but do not know the difference between mathematical and logical relations, think that by learning a lot of words in various combinations they have been studying reality. But when we realize that everything had to develop exactly the way it did, we are comforted in the knowledge that just as these words came into existence for various reasons, they will soon depart. I don't believe it is possible for me to clarify this more than it is already by the text itself. However, I suggest this chapter should be read and listened to several times just in case you haven't completely understood it. As a result of this knowledge I have completely stopped using these words. It may be difficult for you to stop because they are used to compliment, flatter, and to raise ourselves by downing others. When you refer to someone as bad looking it is equivalent to saying, "I am better looking" and most people use everything they can to elevate their opinion of themselves in this cruel world of words. However, you will soon see that all these words must come to an end out of absolute necessity. Let us now observe what must take place as we extend the knowledge of what it means that man's will is not free and his eyes not a sense organ into the world of love.

CHAPTER FIVE

PREMARITAL RELATIONS

As you begin this chapter, a key fact must constantly be borne in mind: No problem exists in man's relations with each other unless someone is being hurt in a concrete, not imaginary, manner and it is the genuine hurt in romantic relationships that this chapter is addressing. The first real and concrete blow of the sexes is struck when a boy and girl are encouraged and then rejected by the person with whom they have fallen in love enough to desire marriage. More people have had their heart broken and cut out with the knife of unrequited love than is imaginable, and those who lose in this game are very unhappy individuals because they have lost the very person they wanted to win. I must remind the reader that our basic principle cannot prevent the impossible. For example, it cannot prevent a girl from rejecting a boy no matter how much he is in love when not to do so makes matters worse for herself as would be the case if this necessitated that she reject the boy who she is in love and who loves her, or that she rejects the possibility of meeting someone with whom she could fall in love, as much as she is now being loved. In other words, not blaming your lover for breaking your heart by leaving cannot undo the rejection, just as not blaming the truck driver after an accident cannot prevent what has already happened. But it can prevent the desire to take risks that could get a boy and girl into this kind of situation where it is necessary to reject the person who is in love with them, just as it prevents them from desiring to take risks that lead to automobile accidents. Premarital relations will come to a permanent end as well as all adultery and divorce not because this is morally wrong and man has decided at last to obey the Ten Commandments, but only because we will be shown how to prevent our children's hearts from being broken by love that is not returned. To have loved and lost may be better than never to have loved at all, but this is the lesser of two evils and presupposes that there must always be a contest wherein someone

137

loses and gets hurt.

"But doesn't there have to be losers when two or more people want the same thing? In a hundred yard dash there is one winner, and the rest are losers, and in a contest for one person, somebody has to lose..."

"Providing there is a contest, but supposing there is none?"

"No contest? There has to be some kind of test. A girl doesn't marry anybody, nor does a boy."

In order for you to appreciate this great change and for God to perform this miracle, it is absolutely necessary that you understand what causes our present environment to be so unforgiving where love is concerned, therefore let me begin by defining in a mathematical undeniable manner what we mean exactly by the word love, otherwise we will be unable to have a solid basis for communication. In actual reality the word love symbolizes a conscious or unconscious desire in varying degrees for a sexual relation of some kind and this is easily proven by the fact that it is impossible for a boy and girl to be attracted to someone no matter how physically appealing this individual might be considered if they know in advance that this person was born without any sexual organs which knowledge makes them aware that this anomaly of nature is incapable of giving or receiving sexual satisfaction. Consequently, the degree of love in courtship varies depending on the extent of possible physical satisfaction. This means that before sexual intercourse takes place the degree with which one could fall in love is determined by the degree with which the desire to possess a particular person in the ultimate act, as in marriage, is encouraged. The more one is encouraged the greater will be the feeling of love or the desire to possess. Therefore, unless the possibility exists that a boy and girl could eventually have some kind of sexual relation, they could never fall in love. Could you fall in love with a photograph of a dead girl? If she was alive and you knew that she would never go out with you she is dead as far as you are concerned, just as a movie actress would be if there was no possibility of your dating her. This explains why a person could never fall in love with a movie star at a distance when he knows there would be no chance of dating this person and no possibility of sexual satisfaction from this source, although it does explain why it would be easy for an idol of stage and screen to be a heartbreaker and to play a leading role in the fantasies of many young people, for it appears that this individual has a lot more to offer than the average person. Likewise, you could never fall in love with a girl if you knew that she would never let you touch or kiss her in any way, which only verifies the definition. Consequently, the moment a boy and girl hold hands and kiss they are to that degree encouraging each other towards the possibility of something more and more until some kind of sexual relation is reached; towards the possibility of falling more and more in love. If they are in love with someone who does not return this feeling, the intensity of their desire to possess the other will depend on how close they will be allowed to come to this physical possession. The meaning of love after marriage or sexual intercourse takes place is a horse of another color for the intensity of their love for each other depends solely on the degree of passionate satisfaction which proves conclusively that the greater the sexual satisfaction the stronger will be their love and further demonstrates why there are so many divorces and so much adultery. 'Forbidden fruit is sweet' is a true saying when couples cannot find satisfaction in marriage. Most couples remain together after physical satisfaction has sunk to its lowest ebb, not because they are still in love (desire a sexual relation with each other except as a last resort), but only because it is the lesser of two evils when children and money are involved.

"Are you trying to tell me that unless a married couple have a passionate relation with each other, they are not in love?"

"They are in love to the degree of their passion for each other."

"Do you mean that when a couple have grown old together, and there is no sexual desire left, they will not be in love anymore?"

"They will be companions, not lovers. Besides, in the new world sexual desire will last until they die, less and less as they get older, but never completely extinguished."

"I don't think the medical profession will agree with you, and I can show you some old folks in their nineties that couldn't be aroused for anything."

"But remember, the conditions are going to change, so you have no basis for comparison."

At the very heart of the problem between the sexes is this fallacious difference that exists in the extremes of beauty and ugliness (these are words with no meaning) which permits the development of a one-sided romance. When a boy and girl start dating they are compelled to look at each other through words or slides that not only place the other somewhere on the scale of physical perfection, but transform them realistically into what they are not. Included in these fallacious differences are words like dumb, stupid, smart, brilliant, educated, genius etc. which allow someone to consider himself either inferior or superior depending on which word accurately describes him. Certain type boys who feel they have more to offer as far as looks and intelligence would never desire to be with certain type girls as a consequence. When a handsome man considers himself extremely educated and brilliant because others consider him so, he is bound to have more than his share of female admirers, and since it is impossible for him to marry every one there are bound to be those who lose and get hurt. Let us observe what happens in the dating world to show how this imbalance between the sexes — due to words only — prevents the opportunity for a mutually loving relationship.

In a typical dating scenario a boy desires a particular girl because she is judged prettier or beautiful and though the boy would like to have her he knows that she will prefer someone who is considered better looking than himself. The boy finally gets the courage to ask the girl out and to his surprise she accepts, not because she is extremely attracted to him but because there is no one else at the moment. All the while they are still judging each other according to this physical standard. From the very beginning the girl's feelings for the boy are not as strong as his are for her. Before long they begin going out pretty regularly but as time goes by they begin to reflect two very different intentions. The boy begins falling in love with the girl even though they never do anything more than just kiss. He has tried on several occasions to touch her breasts but she grabs his hand and slaps his face. Since then he has controlled himself but he still wants to be with her and kiss her nevertheless. The girl, on the other hand, although she likes him a lot and enjoys his company feels she can get somebody much better so she holds onto him while continuing to search for someone closer to her ideal. The boy in the meantime is not attracted to his old girlfriend who is not as pretty as the new one, therefore he feels she has less to offer than he does which places her on the defensive and at a tremendous disadvantage because her desire to possess him will always be greater than his to possess her. She begins giving him privileges to try to win him back and they begin making love every other night. Since this is a new experience she feels closer to him than ever before and begins to fall madly in love. But he is not thinking of her in terms of marriage. Before long he falls for this new girl because she is considered a much more attractive person and because she likes to play all kinds of games that are much more exciting. Consequently, he decides to terminate the relationship with his old girlfriend because she has now become a nuisance constantly pestering him that it is time to get married. The fact that she is in love with him and that he will hurt her by leaving is not a consideration because he doesn't want to spend the rest of his life with someone he is not in love with, so he ends up breaking her heart. In an effort to erase the pain of rejection she begins searching for new sexual companions. Soon she is considered a good thing and her reputation has been ruined; but still wanting to find someone who will love her she goes away on a vacation where nobody knows her. Although she has sex quite a bit nobody seems to fall in love enough to marry her. Her ex-boyfriend, on the other hand, has fallen madly in love with the other girl because she is considered of much greater value than herself. In addition to being beautiful she doesn't let him have what he wants and he always desires more than she is willing to give. Eventually she breaks his heart by leaving him for someone who is uncertain of whether he wants her because she is the one that is now judged of lesser value on the scale of physical perfection, which makes her want him all the more. The boy is so hurt by the new girl's rejection that he plays it cool from then on by making girls fall in love with him first so that he can take or leave them without getting hurt. Soon he has several in love with him, one of which commits suicide when she discovers her pregnancy and his engagement to someone else.

Another example of this difference in looks is a boy who is considered extremely handsome taking out on a blind date (this is perhaps the only way he would go out with her) a girl judged extremely homely. She sees a great value in him because he shows not only tremendous physical but psychological satisfaction as well since she envisions the compliments and envy of her friends in being able to attract so good-looking an individual. Since he sees no value in her, the only way he would not mind taking her out again would be if she was giving him something he liked. Just as this 'handsome' boy is compared to others in order to rate him in terms of value, a girl who is considered beautiful is bound to have more than her share of admirers who want her above all else. Do you see the problem here? Because there is an imbalance of imaginary value the moment these more attractive males and females are desired even before any sexual relation takes place, they discover a lack of desire on their own part to possess what they can have for the asking (that is marriage) which convinces them that they are not in love. It is this that is at the root of a couple's unbalanced desire for each other. She thinks he is handsome or he thinks she is beautiful, and when the other person is considered of less value the one looks up while the other looks down. In other words, the very moment a girl or boy sees that they are admired by the opposite sex a little bit more than is returned, which is occasioned by the projection of a fallacious value, this other is placed at a disadvantage by being considered either consciously or unconsciously inferior in value, consequently, the more this feeling of love is shown by the one who is considered of less value, the more uncertain will be the other person's love in return. This reaction may surprise the ones who do the rejecting because they are not aware of the psychological dynamic at work which is largely based on the belief, although unconscious, that this other person would be getting a better deal since they know they are closer to this standard of perfection, this ideal, than the other. Since it is difficult to desire the possession of what is already possessed if marriage is the goal, those who are higher on the scale of physical perfection keep this other on a string, so to speak, while they search for someone with whom they can fall in love enough to get married, that is, someone who will desire them less or consider them inferior. As we have just seen, this entire problem is due to the projection of words that are not symbolic of reality because they do not symbolize anything externally real — and is the source of much of the hurt between the sexes. This same scenario is repeated

142

over and over and has prevented many couples from experiencing mutual love in marriage. I have a friend who pursued his wife for six years because she was trying to find her ideal and in all that time she never once let him have what he wanted. When he finally gave her an ultimatum she decided to marry him but always felt resentful because she believed that if he hadn't rushed her someone would have come along that was closer to her ideal, and it has not been the happiest of marriages. Now that he is having an affair he confided that he is able to tolerate this lack of sexual passion in his marriage. He said that if he found out his wife was having an affair he wouldn't have cared, and actually hoped she was. As long as he had his new girlfriend, his wife was a chore he could do without.

Up until now there has always been this invisible line of demarcation between good girls and bad girls. Boys who indulged before getting married considered such girls cheap and lost all desire to marry any of them. In addition, many boys were taught that girls should never make the first move. My friend's son who was already engaged to be married left his girlfriend because she put his hand on her breast while he was kissing her and from then on he felt that she was dirty. His entire attitude changed toward her because he placed her in the category of being loose and assumed that if she did this with him she probably did the same thing with other boys. A gentleman in his 70's stated, "My wife was a good girl otherwise I could not have fallen in love with her." This represents the sentiments of many males who were brought up to believe that there were two types, the marrying type and the other type who you could go out with just to have a good time. Consequently there were girls who were judged harshly and were seriously hurt because they were rejected by the person with whom they were in love and wanted for their husband. Going steady and becoming engaged often made matters worse because it gave permission to indulge with no guarantee that marriage would follow. If the boy would leave after a girl committed herself to the point where she was going to the extreme, any number of things might have been preferred as a consequence of this broken heart. Let's look at this from another perspective.

If the situation was reversed and the wife was chasing her husband she might have been willing to become a 'bad' girl, as many have expressed it, hoping that his desire would be aroused enough to marry her. What is it that makes a good girl bad if not for falling in love with the wrong person, that is, falling for someone who doesn't want her after she has given in to him? Would a man have called his wife a bad girl if she had indulged with him before marriage? In his mind she would not have been considered bad because she was a virgin when she gave herself to him even though it was before marriage. Consequently, indulging before marriage is not what defined a girl as bad in his eyes, but only if she indulged with more than one person.

"But how is it possible to prevent a girl from indulging with more than one person if she wants to leave the first boy who makes love to her? And how is it possible to prevent her from seeing a greater value in someone else? Even if words like pretty, beautiful, gorgeous, etc. are removed, people will still be drawn to one type of person over another."

"Right now a boy prefers one girl to another not only because she appeals to him more, but also because he knows she will appeal to others more. At the present time he could not be attracted to anyone considered ugly or homely because such a choice is judged by the word itself, and he would be criticized for it. When these words of critical judgment are removed — and they will be soon enough — then his preference cannot be compared to an external ideal of greater value. If he was never influenced by these words he would have no way of judging one person more attractive and having more value. Although personal taste might compel him to prefer a turned up to a straight nose, or straight to buck teeth, without the word he would never be able to judge one person prettier or uglier."

"Even if this new world came about wouldn't there still be the same kind of problem? Supposing a girl with straight teeth and a straight nose wanted someone with protruding teeth and an aquiline nose? Even if she consented to go out with someone who didn't have these characteristics, wouldn't she be constantly on the lookout for her ideal? Where's the difference even if the words like beautiful and ugly are removed?"

The difference lies in the fact that the definition of love has been completely forgotten. These differences — teeth, noses, shape in general — are secondary, not primary factors. Remember, the word love symbolizes a conscious or unconscious desire, in varying degrees, for a sexual relation of some kind. This explains why a sexually satisfied girl does not care what her man looks like except when she, who is so pretty, is judged for going out with or marrying such a homely person. These fallacious differences actually prevent the blossoming of mutual love and they also give rise to innumerable arguments after marriage since this feeling of superiority in one form or another always imposes a resentful feeling of inferiority. As a consequence there are many marriages on the rebound which is a term to express marrying someone in reaction to, or as a result of, the abrupt ending of an earlier marriage. Very few marriages of a first love ever take place as a result of these fallacious differences, and love has become a game of trying to see who can make the other fall in love first. Children are taught that they should not rush into marriage because they might end up with someone who is really no good, has no character, no intelligence, nothing to make them really proud. If they do get married to someone the parents don't approve of they are constantly reminded that if they had compared by going out with different people they might have gotten someone much finer, but these are only words with no significance in the new world. There are two assumptions that will be proven false.

The first is that a boy and girl will not be able to find these secondary factors that appeal to both of them, and second, that should this be the case they would still consider these secondary features of importance even after they are completely, one hundred percent, sexually satisfied. Removing the words like beautiful and handsome (and we are given no choice), which makes everybody equal in value, will also increase their chances of finding the secondary differences that appeal to them. One hundred boys selecting among one hundred girls in this world would invariably choose the prettiest, the next pretty, and so on down the line; and the girls would pick the most handsome, the next in line and so on which would present quite a problem since many in this group would have to settle for what they really don't want. When these standards are removed this cannot take place and I will demonstrate that in such a group there exists one hundred perfectly balanced equations of mutual love and devotion. As a result, no couple will ever desire to break up or commit adultery.

But first let me remind you why all these words such as handsome and beautiful must come to an end. Please tell me, how is it possible for you to classify people as inferior in value, which is a hurt to them, when you know that they will never blame you for doing this because your will is not free? You know you don't have to hurt them this way by calling others beautiful which places them in a category of being ugly — unless you want to — for over this you know you have mathematical control, and when it fully dawns on you that they must excuse what you can never justify, you are compelled to stop using all such words because it is impossible to derive the smallest amount of satisfaction under the changed conditions.

The ultimate problem of love before marriage revolves around one point — how to prevent all the hurt of unrequited romance, consequently, the solution is how to compel all boys and girls to fall mutually in love with the very first person dated. This appears to be quite a problem, doesn't it? How this is accomplished, how these boys and girls are compelled to have this mutual desire for marriage with their first date will be demonstrated as we proceed. Let us begin by defining the term marriage which is nothing other than a mutual desire to indulge in sexual intercourse for the purpose of bearing a child. It is not the granting of a right to indulge in this sexual relation; it is not the obligation that each has to the other; it has nothing whatever to do with a religious ceremony and exchange of rings. Someone who took what I said out of context remarked, "Did you say it is not morally wrong for a girl to have sexual intercourse before marriage? Isn't that a terrible thing to teach children? I can just hear what my mother and father would say to this, and what religion would say." My answer to her was that I am going to put a mathematical end to all premarital sexual intercourse so what difference does it make if I say it isn't morally wrong? What difference does it make if I say it is perfectly all right for an individual to steal, commit murder, and declare war if he wants to do these things just as long as I can demonstrate how to prevent his desire from arising to do them? Furthermore, suppose the effort to correct these so-called sins is partially responsible for their existence, then isn't it obvious that to say something is morally wrong, is wrong, since this ends up engendering the very hurt our moralists are trying to

146

prevent? If it gives the evangelists great satisfaction in making speeches to show man what is wrong with himself, how is it possible for them to be satisfied with knowledge that their speeches, the very thing that gives them great satisfaction, will no longer be required? I am not implying that when parents, teachers, and preachers advise a girl that it is wrong for her to do certain things before marriage that they are not sincere. They are very sincere. A doctor is also sincere when he tries his best to make a patient well, but it cannot give him satisfaction to learn that someone else can do a much better job than he is able to do and it certainly cannot satisfy him to learn that he is part of the cause he makes efforts to correct. His sincerity is extremely limited and can exist only under certain conditions. If a psychiatrist lost all his patients overnight as if by miracle, if a rabbi lost his congregation, could they possibly be elated over this news even though the very things they have been trying to accomplish are now brought about in a superior manner? Therefore, their sincerity is not sincerely sincere and that is why this presents such a problem because it is this group of learned people that are mostly affected by the transition. However, because your mind may not be adequately attuned to the perception of mathematical relations, I should like to put the horse before the cart by asking you several questions. What is more important — that a boy and girl get a license to indulge their sexual appetite, have a religious ceremony, the blessing of a theologian, etc., or that they fall mutually in love and live happily ever after? What is more important to the parents, the health and happiness of their children, or the moral code? If you were given a choice of marrying under our present conditions with the certain knowledge that you are sure to find unhappiness, perhaps be made a cuckold and end up getting a divorce, or given an opportunity to live as man and wife (although not the way we understand the term marriage in our present world) and instead of unhappiness the greatest happiness imaginable would be your destiny all through life, are you given a choice? Wouldn't it be an insult to man's intelligence if we criticized and blamed a marriage celebrating half a century of genuine happiness, a marriage in which there was never a thought of another sexual partner, a marriage where there was never an argument, where sexual passion never decreased during the potent years, just because

147

this young boy and girl decided to get married without a license, without the ceremony and blessing of a rabbi or priest, without the exchange of rings?

"Yes, I agree. It would be an insult to man's intelligence."

"Criticizing such happiness because this couple did not conform to a moral code is equivalent to criticizing someone who plays a perfect hand of bridge because he failed to have the cards cut by the person on his right (a custom that now prevails in some circles), or equivalent to someone criticizing this book because he feels that a comma is in the wrong place. It is understandable why a jeweler would not like a change that affects his business because not buying rings associated with engagements and marriage would certainly decrease his profit; and it is understandable why a priest and rabbi would not like any change because they play one of the leading spiritual roles in the nuptial drama aside from receiving perhaps a gratuity of some sort which is also a pleasant ritual. It is understandable why those who are accustomed to criticizing, blaming, and judging others for not conforming to the moral code would not like to see a change because this would deprive them of the enormous satisfaction they get in condemning what, in their eyes, is wrong."

"But how is it possible for these spiritual leaders to desire criticizing, when the couple's happiness and devotion is being achieved in a superior manner?"

"You must remember, they would be denied their accustomed satisfaction of marrying a couple, along with the opportunity to advise a couple as to what is better for themselves. In other words, they would be denied the very things that gave meaning to their existence."

"But it would be impossible for them to complain under these conditions, right?"

"That's right. The problem is really breaking through this sound barrier of learned ignorance. We have developed a very bad, though necessary habit of putting the cart before the horse, the result of this barrier, and our great need to earn a living. Consequently, we have assumed that certain things are required as a means to an end we have found preferable. For example, we have come to believe that a cooperative society, without using the force that presently exists in communism and without doing away with competition, is impossible, but this, as will be shown in the economic chapter, is wholly untrue. Likewise do our religious and moral leaders reject anything that appears to contravene their standard of righteousness, because it seems that unless a boy and girl are forced into a certain mold they will take advantage of their freedom only to hurt others as well as themselves. It is of the utmost importance that these unconsciously ignorant people who have been blindly leading their followers in accordance with God's will can at last see for themselves what they have been doing. Obviously, since no one likes to give up what is a source of satisfaction unless there is a still greater satisfaction to replace this, or unless in a new juxtaposition of alternatives it becomes the worse choice, we can only look to a boy and girl themselves for the great change about to take place. They are the only ones involved in this game of love. The sexes will be given no choice as to how they must act towards each other because they will know, beyond a shadow of doubt, which is the better alternative. How this is accomplished, how these boys and girls are compelled to have this mutual desire for marriage with their first date is marvelous to behold and mathematically undeniable. There are definite rules to this game which have never been understood, but these we are compelled to obey as each person instantly recognizes their mathematical veracity. However, to fully understand and appreciate this fantastic metamorphosis — remember, all premarital relations, all adultery, and all divorce are coming to an end out of mathematical necessity — the only thing required of you is to bear constantly in mind what has been revealed in the first two chapters, that man's will is not free and what this means. Now put on your thinking caps and follow me carefully. Let us observe, once again, what takes place in our present environment in order to understand the solution.

As boys and girls reach an age where they desire to start dating (the time in life when hormonal changes unconsciously move the mind in the direction of sex), most of them are actually too young to accept the responsibilities of marriage but they still have a normal desire for the opposite sex. This allows them to develop habits of kissing, petting, fooling around in general. If the girl considers herself a good girl, that is, she adheres to the moral code, she will compel the boy as much as possible to commit himself in some way by going steady, becoming engaged, or just confessing his love before she allows any privileges. If he does not want to commit himself and she is afraid of losing him, she might try to hold onto him by giving him more and more and more to whet his appetite for still more. There were girls who lost boys they wanted for their husbands by giving them too much (they went all the way — and then some) which made some boys lose their desire to possess what was now theirs for the taking without all the responsibility (although there were some who wanted to get married all the more to guarantee the experience), and there were girls who lost out by not giving them enough to whet their appetite. This period of dating sets the stage for much unhappiness because it encourages the ones who are judged inferior in value, less pretty or handsome (the ones whose desire is greater) to put those who are judged of far greater value on a pedestal because they have so much more to offer. These young adults compare themselves to those who are considered superior by virtue of their good looks, and they know they can't compete. In their effort to be noticed they may become extremely vulnerable and ripe for exploitation. Girls (in some cases boys) who have been hurt time and time again may turn to self-injury or other forms of self-rejection. Sadly, the teenagers who lose in this dangerous game of love may never fully recover. Some have even been driven to suicide. Another serious problem in teen relationships is that of jealousy. It has been documented that 36% of teen relationships involve some sort of violence. Teen romance turned deadly often occurs when fragile emotions meet with rejection. The individual who was hurt may be motivated to terrorize, intimidate, or even kill an ex-lover along with the person who took his place. To complicate matters it is often difficult to identify the type of person that would act out in such a manner because there isn't always a predictable pattern of behavior. Once a violent act occurs, the effort to keep an estranged boyfriend (or girlfriend) at a distance by issuing a restraining order could backfire, inciting more violence than before because now this individual, in his distorted way of thinking, has further cause to retaliate against this perceived slap in the face. He may also accept this as a challenge to prove that no one can stop him, not even the law. Unfortunately, these legal injunctions often come too late because they don't have the power to stop someone who is intent on doing harm from perpetrating a vicious act if he feels justified and is willing to pay the ultimate price of life in prison or the death penalty.

This entire situation is prevented when our basic principle, Thou Shall Not Blame, extends into the world of love preventing the causes that lead to these crimes of passion. Bear in mind that the psychological problems stemming from childhood abuse and neglect will be permanently removed; secondly, words that label some children as inferior and others as superior will no longer be used in conversational language; and thirdly, boys and girls will be prevented from leading each other on with no intentions of marrying them. In our present world a couple can have sexual intercourse without being married, but in the new world this will be impossible because they are one and the same. The males will have no choice under the new conditions but to get married, or they will not indulge. How long do you think single males would remain unmarried if they couldn't have a sexual relation any other way? This amazing change is accomplished solely with the aid of the knowledge that man's will is not free. Bear constantly in mind that the solution is based upon the new world, a world in which everyone knows in advance there will be no blame for anything that is done. Let's continue our analysis.

A boy will know there is not a person in the world who would desire to make a girl fall in love and then break her heart by rejecting her when it is also known in advance there will be no blame if he did. Consequently, when a girl accepts her first date with a boy who appeals to her and then finds herself falling more and more in love, whether it is returned or not (this is the key to the problem which must be worked backwards to understand the solution), she is completely unafraid to confess her love and offer her body because she wants him for her husband and knows absolutely and positively that he would have never taken her out unless he knew there was a possibility of him falling in love with her as well. Therefore, when confronted with the choice of whether to accept an invitation, he would have to decline knowing that this girl does not appeal to him enough for marriage and also knowing that she must excuse everything he does. Because he knows it would be his responsibility since nothing can make him hurt her this way unless he wants to, it becomes impossible for him to derive satisfaction from deflowering her under these conditions. This is an undeniable fact because he knows that she would never hold him responsible for making her fall for him — and for possibly making her pregnant. He is compelled to do everything in his power to stay away from this kind of situation because it can give him no satisfaction whatsoever. Could you with a clear conscience allow a girl to love you enough to desire you for her husband and then break her heart when you are absolutely certain that no one in the world, not even the girl who is going to be so terribly hurt, would ever blame you because it is now known your will is not free? This means that when a boy understands the principle of 'no blame' — and he will once it is a condition of the environment — and he also knows, well in advance, that a girl will be perfectly willing to go the extreme once he encourages her to fall in love by kissing and becoming more and more intimate, he recognizes that there is no advantage, in fact a complete waste of time, to pay flattering compliments and hand her a line knowing that he will be compelled to refuse her body when it is offered unless he is serious with her, that is, unless he feels from the very first time he sees her that he could fall in love.

Since the meaning of love before intercourse takes place is the possibility of sexual satisfaction, how is it possible for a boy to desire taking out a girl with whom he is not sexually attracted when he knows that he will be compelled to refuse her overtures unless he has serious intentions, that is, unless he feels from the moment he sees her that these feelings can be reciprocated. In other words, once he discovers through these mathematical relations that there is no advantage in making a girl fall in love with him unless he sees the possibility of loving her back, he will be forced to turn down her generosity since it is not a source of satisfaction to hurt this girl by ruining her life when he knows that she will never hold him responsible for doing what he knows she must excuse, and he can never justify. To give her compliments for the purpose of getting what he wants serves no purpose if he really doesn't want her for his wife because this will only encourage her to offer him the very thing he will be compelled to refuse, since it cannot satisfy him, even a little bit, to hurt her this way knowing she will never blame him. The litmus test of one's true feelings will apply to the girl as well, therefore if she should encourage him by developing a sexual habit then it would hurt him terribly if she left which she cannot desire to do. How can a girl accept a date with a boy who does not appeal to her in terms of sexual intercourse when she will be compelled to refuse his body when it is offered? If a boy should ask a girl for a date who doesn't desire him she would simply turn him down because she knows where it might lead, but he could never be hurt by this initial refusal. This forces both sexes to ask for a date (it doesn't matter what gender does the asking under these conditions) only the kind of person that physically appeals to them enough to become their husband or wife. These boys and girls have no other choice unless they prefer the risk of making people fall in love with them and then find it necessary to break their heart by leaving. However, this does not mean that they are forced to stay because to leave would be a hurt for which there would be no blame, but it does prevent them from considering sex as separate from dating.

"Well, supposing the boy is not interested in marriage, just in having some sexual fun, and supposing the girl is not interested in marriage, just in having some sexual fun, what then? After all, there's a big difference between desiring to have a sexual relation and selecting a mate for the rest of one's life. Can't they get together and have some fun without hurting each other? There is a thing called contraception, you know, and there are ways of making love where there is no possibility of getting pregnant. For example, what if a boy meets a girl that appeals to him and he says to her without beating around the bush, 'Say honey, you appeal to me, do I appeal to you?' If she says yes then he would say, 'How about it, would you like to go to bed with me just to have some sexual fun?' without the slightest thought of marriage. If she agrees and they make love in a manner that ensures against pregnancy, how is it possible for either of them to get hurt?"

"This reasoning is logical but not mathematical. Supposing the boy satisfies this girl (remember, she is a virgin and has never had any sexual contact before) to such a degree that she cannot wait until their next meeting, wouldn't this hurt her if he never came back?"

"But there are a hundred guys that can give her the same satisfaction."

"Let's put it another way. Supposing this girl appealed to him and satisfied him in every way, wouldn't he desire a repeat performance? In fact, let's assume that he found greater satisfaction with this girl than with any other girl, is it possible for him not to be hurt if he desires her more than she desires him now that he has had the greatest sexual experience of his life? Consequently, the only way he could have some fun with a girl, and her with him, and neither of them get hurt is if they could make love and not have any fun because the very moment either one of them enjoys the relation they could end up being hurt if they were not entitled to the same experience again. Please be aware that this was a hypothetical question. I purposely set up an equation that was mathematically impossible because this boy and girl on their first date will not have had any sexual experience whatsoever which means they will have no basis for comparison, consequently, the thrill and excitement of physical contact will make them desire tremendously the person who now represents this ecstatic feeling."

"But supposing a boy takes a girl out on a first date, doesn't kiss her, doesn't touch her, but finds her boring and also discovers certain things about her he doesn't like, why can't he just refuse to take her out again?"

If it is mathematically impossible for something to happen, what would happen if it was done? In other words, there is absolutely no way this situation could arise because the moment she accepts a date the boy will know immediately that he appeals to her, and the very moment he asks her she will automatically know his feelings. The standards that were once used to judge whether two people are compatible will no longer apply. You will understand this much better when we get to the chapter on marriage, so please don't jump to conclusions. Let us now observe a boy and girl meeting for the very first time under changed conditions to get a better understanding of why there is no possibility of either of them getting hurt.

When a boy and a girl meet each other for the very first time and are drawn together, what they are actually saying in so many words is, "You really appeal to me from every point of view and if you go out with me I accept this as an invitation to make love." They will know that it is mathematically impossible for any person to desire hurting them when it is known in advance that they will never blame or criticize this hurt regardless of what is done. If the date is accepted the other will answer in the same way. "I know what you would like, and I would like the same." If she appeals to him and he to her, in other words, if he asks her for a date and she accepts, then here is what must happen. The moment a boy and girl hold hands and kiss they are, to that degree, encouraging each other towards the hope of something more until some kind of sexual relation is reached and where now there is the possibility of falling more and more in love. The girl knows when accepting a date that his love for her will increase only by arousing his desire, and he knows that her love for him will increase for the very same reason. Therefore, the hotter she can make him the more he will be in love and the hotter he can make her the more she will be in love. Remember, there will be no more good girls and bad girls, consequently, if a girl initiates the first move or makes advances after he approaches her she will not be negatively judged for this. When they are finally in a strong embrace and his hands begin to wander, instead of checking this motion as a girl was often forced to do because she didn't know if this was to her advantage, she will only encourage him all the more as he encourages her. Both of them will become very passionate and desire to go all the way but they will desire this very much without the slightest fear that either will ever hurt the other by leaving, although they can if they want to. Inside of a few days they will be madly in love with each other because love is a crescendo of physical satisfaction from kissing and petting to the ethereal heights of extreme sexual passion. Because the girl knows as a mathematical certainty that he could never do anything to satisfy her desire unless he is prepared to give a repeat performance since this would be a terrible hurt to her, for which he knows he would never be blamed, she is completely unafraid to offer her body to him for the purpose of his having a most wonderful time and also unafraid to make sexual advances that arouse him because she knows, just as certain as two plus two equals four, that it is absolutely impossible for him to desire risking pregnancy unless he loves her too. She knows that he knows if he made her pregnant, ruined her life, broke her heart, left and never returned, she and no one alive would ever blame him for doing what he was compelled to do, but he knows that he is not compelled to break her heart, ruin her life, make her pregnant, unless he wants to, and the realization that she will never hold him responsible for this terrible hurt which he knows would be his responsibility — and can prevent if he wants to — makes it impossible for him to derive any satisfaction from deflowering her under these conditions.

"In spite of all that you just said, it's hard for me to adjust to the fact that a boy can't ask anybody out he wants."

"But he can. No one is telling him who to take out and who not to. What stops him from asking out a girl who doesn't appeal to him sufficiently for marriage is simply the fact that it is mathematically impossible for him to have a sexual relation with a girl and then leave, unless he wants to hurt her — and it is impossible for him to desire this when he knows that she will never blame him for this hurt. Therefore, when the boy fully realizes that should he ever get the girl to that point where he would not have any problem getting her to submit, he is compelled to take out only the kind of girl that he doesn't want to hurt, the kind who, when she offers her body on the altar of love, will never be rejected. By making it impossible for him to take away a girl's virginity unless he hurts or marries her, and since he cannot desire to hurt her under the changed conditions, sex becomes a very serious business with only one alternative — marriage. Remember, if a boy asks a girl out who doesn't appeal to him in terms of marriage — but he appeals to her — then she is given the power to test his true feelings immediately by offering her body to him, and he is compelled, of his own free will or desire, to refuse this offering because it cannot satisfy him to hurt her so deeply when he knows that no one, including the girl, will ever blame, criticize, or punish him in any way for taking advantage of her."

The miracle between the sexes about to unfold is the fact that if the girl does not appeal to him there is no advantage in asking for a date, no advantage in paying her compliments, no advantage in handing her a line and professing his love because if he appeals to her she is going to offer the very thing he will be compelled to refuse, unless he really wants her. What makes this experience a sobering one is the fact that the boy knows the girl will never hold him responsible in any way, that he is free to have a good time, leave, and never come back no matter how much he hurts her, which makes it mathematically impossible for him to desire getting close to this kind of situation unless he really wants to get married (stay with her permanently). Because he knows that dating will lead to kissing, kissing to petting, and petting will lead to what he cannot do unless in love or ready for marriage he is given no choice but to search out, well in advance, and regardless of the standards that presently exist regarding physical attraction, an individual who appears to offer this possibility of sexual satisfaction, which means that when he asks for a date he is actually proposing, actually telling the girl he will not reject her desire to make love to him, and when she accepts which indicates her feelings for him they are literally engaged to be married because there will be nothing to stop them from going all the way. Under these conditions the boy can find no pleasure whatsoever in leading a girl on who does not appeal to him enough for marriage since this would only create a heartbreaking situation if she is in love with him. Remember, this works two ways, which makes it mathematically impossible for either of them to desire getting close to such a situation. Consequently, the moment they are intimate, with or without contraception, and regardless of what they do to satisfy each other, they are pledging their love and are married, so to speak, not because they took out a license and were pronounced man and wife by a priest or rabbi but only because they will fall so much in love when nothing inhibits their sexual pleasure, and they are prevented from hurting each other in various ways (which will be discussed in the chapter on marriage), that they will never desire another sexual partner. They will be given no choice when monogamy becomes the preferable alternative.

"Hold it! Do you mean that if a boy sees a girl sitting at a bar, and assuming she has never been out before, she is automatically his fiancé if he asks her for a date and she accepts?"

That's right. From the moment on they will never be able to leave the other for someone else not because anybody is preventing them from leaving, but only because they will never desire to leave. Regardless of the circumstances in which two people meet there will be no possibility of anyone getting hurt or exploited. Therefore, if a boy sees a girl sitting at a bar that appeals to him very much, and assuming she feels the same way toward him, she would automatically be his fiancée if she accepts his offer. No games will be played, therefore when she accepts his proposal they will immediately begin kissing and petting after a very brief acquaintance. This will also prevent them from holding onto a string of prospects for marriage just in case they cannot find someone who is considered of greater value, which prevents the contest wherein there must be losers who get hurt.

It is important to remember that in our present world boys and girls can get married without having sexual intercourse, and can have the latter without the former, but in the new world it will be impossible to have one without the other because they are one and the same.

"I still don't quite understand why I can't ask out on a date more than one girl."

"That's just the point, you can if you want to, but under the changed conditions, you won't want to. Remember, you are going to have sexual intercourse very quickly, with or without contraception, and if you left this girl it would be a terrible hurt to her for which you would not be blamed."

"Something just hit me. What you are actually doing is creating a crucible in which man's conscience is brought into full play."

"That is correct. Man is prevented from desiring to hurt another in any way, shape or form because his conscience won't permit it when all justification has been removed."

As a result of the changes about to take place, every couple will fall mutually in love with their first date which makes a marriage ceremony a thing of the past since it serves no purpose other than to make them realize their obligations to each other, but there will be no obligations henceforth as this blames the desire of another while it encourages and justifies what neither prefers by imposing force. The meaning of love after marriage or sexual intercourse is a horse of another color for the intensity of this desire to continue to be intimate with the other depends solely on the degree of sexual satisfaction, which proves conclusively that the stronger the passion the greater will this feeling of love be and further demonstrates why there is so much adultery. How many times have you heard someone say, "I love you as a person but I am not in love with you" which is an indirect way of saying, "I don't feel the same sexual attraction for you as I once did." Most couples remain together after physical satisfaction has reached an all time low, and if they stay in the marriage it is seen as a last resort or to fulfill an obligation, not because they are still in love. This arrangement often becomes the lesser of two evils when divorce is considered worse. Is it any wonder so many men and women turn to adultery and divorce when finding very little sexual passion in their marriage; and is it any wonder why so many girls drove away the boys they liked because they were afraid of what might happen if they gave in? But this is the way it was supposed to be in the world of free will — though not anymore — unless the boys and girls prefer losing the person they would like to have for a husband or wife.

All the factors truly responsible for premarital promiscuity, adultery, and divorce are removed because man is prevented from desiring the very things for which blame and punishment, moral judgment and criticism were previously necessary. A boy and girl will have no choice in this matter of marriage as it will be their only source of sexual satisfaction, and the girls will have no opportunity of becoming 'bad.' Under these conditions there is no possibility for unrequited love to develop. Sex, which takes place the moment it is mutually desired, is the holiest of all unions because it is steeped in a feeling of mutual respect and love. No one need ever fear for this couple because love will ripen to maturity after marriage, never before, and everything in the past that gave rise to adultery and divorce will be precluded, as you will soon see. Now tell me, in this kind of world where boys and girls get married very young (it wouldn't matter if the union was heterosexual or homosexual, the principles would still apply) and then live happily ever after, can prostitution develop or continue to exist? Is it possible for them to desire any kind of adulterous relation, ANY KIND, when they are so satisfied with their partner that just the thought never enters their mind? Even self-gratification — and there is nothing wrong with this because it hurts no one — will not be preferred when their primary desire is to satisfy each other.

This knowledge as to how boys and girls will react when their eyes first meet and they begin falling in love (remember the definition) completely revolutionizes dating. Boys and girls do not need permission from anybody to get married, nor do they require an exchange of rings or a marriage ceremony. Keep in mind that marriage in the new world has nothing to do with rituals or formalities. In the world of free will wining and dining a girl to sweep her off her feet was often used as a strategy to mislead her so the boy could get what he wanted. We have all heard horror stories of the charming man marrying the unsuspecting woman and then wiping out her bank account. The woman always had to be on guard because she never knew if the man's intentions were genuine. This could never occur in the new world which is why courtship does not need to be long and drawn out. There will be no further need for background checks to see if a man is being honest because he cannot lie under the changed conditions. Only in a free will environment could a woman be taken advantage of. The ritual of wooing a girl for the purpose of getting her to say "I do" will also become a thing of the past. The only prerequisite will be mutual attraction because nothing will be more important than sexual satisfaction in determining the success of a marriage.

"I still say, what if they discover after going together for awhile that there are things about the other they don't like, are they obligated to stay?"

Of course not. This can only happen in the old world of free will because there are hundreds of nonexistent values that are projected by words and when an individual learns that his partner doesn't possess some of these values, or he sees that she is not as pretty as he would like her to be, he will keep an eye out for someone who is considered of greater value. If a boy likes a girl the differences that now make a difference will no longer be influencing factors, consequently, there will be very little to make her refuse him unless he does not appeal to her which will force her to turn him down just as a boy will never ask a girl to date him if she doesn't appeal enough for sexual intercourse. This does not mean that we don't have values, only these are personal, not something that has been projected into the external world. Should a boy be attracted to a girl with a long, flat or aquiline nose, small breasts and big hips, he is not going to be judged because the words doing this judging have long since become obsolete. She is not homely or ugly nor is Miss America beautiful; they are simply different. This knowledge forces a boy and girl to search high and low for someone that has the personal values they like, someone they want to have a sexual relation with, and they will have plenty of help to accomplish this because it is a most serious decision. The schools will teach girls how to prepare the tastiest meals (assuming they will be home raising the children while the husbands are working; it could be the other way around), and when they reach an age of sexual maturity boys and girls will learn, if they desire this, the many ways in which to attract a mate before marriage and what they can do to keep passion alive after marriage. There will be no shame in these classes because they will desire to learn everything there is to know about the human sexual response in order to prepare them for married life. Though both sexes will get somewhat excited in learning these things, no harm can come of it because marriage, in the new world, is the only sexual outlet.

"But isn't sex a personal thing? What I mean is, couldn't a boy make a girl passionate without all this learning?"

"Yes, that's true, but the boy doesn't want to take any chances of not satisfying his future wife, nor does she want to take the risk of not satisfying her future husband, and since they have had no personal experience it is obvious that they will want to learn all they can about sexual intercourse."

When they are ready to get married all that will be necessary is for a girl to attract the boy she wants for her husband, or vice versa. They will do everything they can to arouse each other's desire to be asked out — without any fear of being hurt. The boy, knowing she will not hold him responsible for hurting her, will be compelled to avoid any girl who does not appeal to him, which will tell her immediately to find someone else. And the same holds true for the girl; if she should encourage him by developing a sexual habit then she would hurt him terribly by leaving which she cannot desire to do. Therefore, if he doesn't appeal to her enough for marriage she will refuse him a date because she knows that he could also be hurt, and it cannot satisfy her to do this when she knows he will never blame her. If she accepts the offer to go out on a date, the boy will know immediately that he appeals to her, and the very moment he asks her, she will automatically know his feelings.

As to whether they are too young to have sex? There is no such thing in the new world as a right time to start kissing or petting, a right time for marriage, only what is considered right by each couple. Nature gave boys and girls a built-in standard as to when they are ready. This has nothing to do with the responsibility of raising a family and earning a living. The average boy and girl will be married between 16 and 18 years old because of the desire for a sexual relationship — which will give them no choice. Did I hear your psychologists say this was too young? They are so in the habit of judging what is right for others that they can't get out of it that easily, but if they want to know if this age is really too young they will have to wait until the new world where boys and girls begin to make this decision for themselves. It is true, however, that in most cases a boy's desire to develop in a particular direction before taking a wife will prevent him from getting married at too young an age.

There will be no singles who can't find someone, no broken homes and hearts — even widows and widowers will be a thing of the past as all the causes of premature death are also removed. If a boy should take a wife without having a job and she becomes pregnant he would know that her parents would never hold him responsible for throwing this burden on their shoulders, and neither would she. Consequently, they are compelled to think like never before so as not to add additional expenses. Since the thought of this gives them no satisfaction whatsoever, they prevent it from arising by not marrying until they can financially handle what might come their way. Now I want you to think about this very carefully. What difference does it make to the parents if their daughter goes the extreme with her first date, even if she is in her teens, just as long as she will never be hurt and they will never be criticized, and just as long as this boy will never leave or forsake her. The enjoyment of a sexual relation which in this setting will make them fall more and more in love would not cost their parents a dime. They will be completely free to do what they consider better for themselves, although the knowledge that man's will is not free will give them no choice but to prevent either from ever hurting the other. In the new world couples are not forced to stay together because there will be no blame, but only because they are in love and

162

will remain in love. They will remain together, as you will soon have verified, not because to leave would break the other's heart, but primarily because it would break their own heart. Unless you fully understand the mathematical relations that do completely away with all forms of hurt in sexual experience, you will not grasp why there can be no harm in young people getting married at a very early age because it is so different from the teachings of our present day, therefore you would have to disagree even though the desired end is what the moralists have been unsuccessfully trying to bring about.

Boys and girls never gave much thought to the consequences of their actions because they were driven by a natural sex drive, which is their birthright, and when somebody got hurt the answer was, "What was I supposed to do marry the girl because we had sex? She knew what she was doing and I didn't commit myself." Her father replies — "You'd better marry her or I'll kill you." By knowing unconsciously that he would be blamed for his gallivanting he was always allowed to shift his responsibility, but he had no better choice because the pressure for a sexual relation was striking the first blow since marriage was out of the question at that young age. By removing all the blame the pressure is also removed because he can have a sexual relation immediately and there is no possibility for unrequited love to develop, no chance for any girl to be swept off her feet and lose her virginity out of wedlock, no chance for a double-standard to make some girls bad and others good, no chance for a boy and girl to hurt each other in any way where sex is concerned because all the factors truly responsible are prevented from arising. Moreover, once all the words are removed that now judge some people as inferior physiognomic productions of the human race, everybody becomes perfectly equal in value except to the person making a choice. One face is not better looking than another — just different — although we will always find certain differences we like better. Couples will strongly desire to retain the physical appearance that first attracted their life partner. Since these marriages will take place when boys and girls are very young, and since all psychological impediments to eating will be removed from birth, very few will be carrying excess weight. However, some boys and girls are naturally heavy and there will be no reason for them to worry in the new world because to certain people this is a physical attraction. It is true that we have already been conditioned to move in the direction of certain preferences, but we cannot be hurt when these individuals reject us at the very outset and when other choices in a partner will never be directly or indirectly criticized. If a boy desires a type of girl like Elizabeth Taylor who does not desire his type, he is compelled to put the proverbial horse before the cart and search for the type of girl who is ready to have sex with him. He will then fall in love with her sexual organs and her features will become secondary because nobody will ever refer indirectly to her as ugly by calling other types beautiful, which in our present world could possibly make him regret his choice and keep an eye out for someone who would be looked upon by others as having more to offer in the way of physical appearance. But how is it possible for him to regret his choice when the world stops criticizing and when he has fallen head over heals for his beloved which takes place after, not before, the sexual union? Once they consummate their love with a complete sexual relation, they will be married. They will have no choice in the matter of marriage as it will be their only source of sexual satisfaction, which I shall sum up by using mathematical phraseology.

Since the single males who are not in love with the single girls who love them are prevented from indulging because they consider this decision better for themselves and are therefore prevented from participating; and since a single female who is not in love with the boy who loves her is prevented from indulging because it is impossible for the girl to go out on a date and make love with someone she does not like, love, or desire, it is therefore obvious that the only way these single people can be sexually intimate, once they understand what it means that man's will is not free, is to fall mutually in love. Consequently, the only other sexual outlet for them other than self-gratification is to indulge with married men and women, or the looser more experienced courtesans and bachelors. All this will be prevented in due time not only because these services will die off while the new marriages get under way, but also because of a tremendous change that is about to take place as a result of reading and understanding the rest of the book which prevents the many unconscious hurts that have led to unhappiness. It should be obvious that once these young

164

couples lose the desire for another sexual partner, within a relatively short period of time only these marriages will exist, and when a boy can get no sexual outlet except through marriage he will fall in love, and so will she, with the first person that offers any physical attraction. This selection process, however, will take on new significance as the standards of value, now fallaciously congealed in opinions and words that affect choice (although many other factors still have to be reconciled), lose their influence while being replaced with personal feelings that are not affected by the judgment of others. The basis of a sound marriage in the new world will be this physical attraction and satisfaction both experience in the presence of each other, nothing else, not money (although the possibility of marrying someone with a greater purchasing power will be somewhat of a factor but not for long, as the poor must, out of necessity, soon become materially wealthy (this will be explained in the economic chapter); education (which is another farce that came into existence out of necessity and will surprise everybody, especially those who consider themselves educated); social position, religion, race, or anything else. Physical attraction will always be the main event and from this foundation the greatest happiness imaginable will be in store for our posterity — which is only ourselves, as you will soon have mathematically verified.

"That I have to see! You are going to prove that I, me, am going to be born again after I die, right?"

"I didn't say that. I said that our posterity is only ourselves, which I am prepared to prove in a mathematical manner. When you die you are dead, but there is something we never understood, which will make you feel very wonderful when it is properly explained."

"Do you mean there is nothing to fear in death?"

"That's right."

"Do you also mean there is nothing to cry over when a loved person is lost?"

"Don't be ridiculous. I cried my eyes out when I lost my father, and tears still dim my eyes when I think of him."

"Then I'm confused about what you mean."

"The whole world is confused, so don't feel too badly. I'll explain everything shortly. Incidentally, it is humorous to observe how certain things take a turnabout as a consequence of knowing what it means that man's will is not free. In our present world the advantage always went to the one who made the other fall in love, for then it was possible to take or leave this other. But now the boys and girls recognize that there is no advantage in making someone fall in love unless it can be returned which makes the sexes do everything in their power to reveal their true feelings as the desire to go the extreme depends on loving, not just being loved.

Free will engendered the suave, well-mannered, expertly controlled habits of the conquering, good-looking male who ensnared with his captivating style many an unsuspecting female. And how many males who finally won the female over lost all desire to keep her because the thrill was in the chase. It also allowed one girl to keep on a string for an indefinite time many boys who sought for her hand in marriage and who ended up, in many cases, not marrying any of them because she found it difficult desiring to possess what was already hers for the asking. The word love in our present world not only symbolizes this desire for possession and the stronger emotions of unrequited love, but it is used to justify what could not be done without this justification. A girl who finds terrific pleasure in sexual intercourse with a married man is compelled to justify this act by saying — "I'm in love." In the past, the expression 'about to get married' has been interpreted to mean getting ready for a miserable existence and the end of freedom. Since the marriages that do survive often exist unhappily, as the lesser of two evils, a man will justify padlocking or wedlocking himself to one person apparently for life by saying — "I'm in love." Ask a man who has been married a number of years — "Are you in love with your wife?" and he will reply — "I must be, I'm married ain't I?" But this is a completely fallacious perception because the girl in bed with the married man is in love with the thrill of sexual satisfaction which has become associated with a particular person, while our bridegroom is very much in love with the prospects that lie head — unless he was given a sneak preview. This tremendous need for sex had to be justified in a world of morality, judgment, and sin and the word love served a useful purpose before marriage and it was used to compensate in an unconscious manner, after marriage.

166

When a husband or wife tells the other they are in love it only reveals in a mathematical manner that they are not in love. And even when the word love was used, it was often an insufficient justification because innumerable girls found themselves doing what was judged sinful while not being in love and the consequence was the confessional or psychiatry that was needed to help excrete the accumulation of guilt.

As long as there are men who do not want to get married or remarried, girls who need sex but can't find the boys to make it legal, and sexually unsatisfied married couples, we will always have premarital relations, adultery and divorce. When someone is suspected of having an adulterous relationship, displaying jealousy is often thought of as a sign of love. Spouses may go out of their way to arouse this emotion which is used to justify and dissemble a secret or an unconscious desire, thinking this will strengthen marriage or courtship. Jealousy arises, however, from a feeling of ownership which tacitly blames and judges what is right for someone else while giving unconscious justification to do that of which one has already been accused. It originates in going steady and then grows in intensity from getting engaged to marriage. The first two are a down payment on this right to absolutely possess another individual, and the latter is complete ownership. "I want you" is the meaning of love before this possession takes place, "I almost have you" is the next phase, and "I've got you at last" is the death of love. Why do you think so many jokes are made about marriage if not because it is a sadly humorous situation as we know it. However, it will be changed in a manner marvelous to behold while jealousy is removed from the world not because it is a form of blame but because no one will ever again have the desire to make another jealous, as this motion will render less satisfaction under the new conditions.

Man, seeing what is truly better for himself, not with opinions but with mathematical laws, is given no alternative unless he prefers what he doesn't want — which is mathematically impossible. If man's will was free we could not exercise any control over another person's actions and people would be free to hurt each other indiscriminately, but man's will is not free therefore he is controlled by this natural law which prevents him from taking chances that could lead to the serious

167

hurt of unrequited love. It is quite interesting to observe that since time immemorial man has been compelled to use reverse psychology in his love relationships as a direct result of believing, consciously or unconsciously, that man's will was free — but he had no choice in this matter. Now, however, he can choose freely and as a consequence is permitted to get rid of all the evil and hurt that nobody wants, only, of course, without having a free choice. Are you beginning to understand how words have confused the mind? It appears that the breakdown of marriage so rampant in today's world is inevitable, but this was in the world of free will. You will soon be given an opportunity to observe a newly married couple under the changed conditions as they face life together knowing for the first time that man's will is not free and what this means, which reveals conclusively why the mathematical corollary, Thou Shall Not Blame, when understood properly, is undeniably better for mankind — giving them no choice. Very few people who get married actually continue to experience the thrills of love because the height of sexual passion is never experienced afterwards, but in the new world love will increase to a tremendous degree after marriage, never before. This newly married couple will be compelled, of their own free will, to have this balanced equation of sexual desire all through their lives, that is, have a hotter, more passionate relation than ever thought possible. Because of this mutuality of love and respect it will be possible for couples to preserve their marriages for a lifetime. The chapter on marriage will offer specific ways to keep the fires burning after the honeymoon, but first we will turn our attention to the economic world in order to reveal, as we extend our basic principle, Thou Shall Not Blame, how it is now possible to put a permanent end to economic insecurity, war and crime.

CHAPTER SIX

THE NEW ECONOMIC WORLD

And now my friends, you are about to behold an actual miracle as the knowledge that man's will is not free and what this means not only puts a mathematical end to the possibility of war and crime, but completely changes the entire economic system to one of complete security. As you begin reading this chapter it is assumed that you thoroughly understand the two-sided equation, otherwise, the rest of the book will appear like a fairy tale. Remember, at one time landing men on the moon seemed like nothing more than science fiction until it was understood how this apparent miracle could be accomplished. From here on in each move I make is equivalent to the forced moves in a chess game, consequently, no attempt is necessary because checkmate cannot be avoided nor can the Golden Age be stopped. In other words, it is mathematically impossible to stop the development of something everybody wants. If the rich and poor, the capitalistic and communistic countries, plus everybody else not mentioned desire what I am about to show, is it possible for this Golden Age not to become a reality? How is it humanly possible to be dissatisfied with the solution, when it is impossible not to be satisfied? I am going to reduce the differences between people to a common denominator which satisfies the whole human race. God shows no partiality, and since I have been sent here on a mission by God Himself, everybody to me is equal regardless of his color, race, creed, gender, sexual orientation, or anything else you care to throw in. Consequently, the United States, though I live here, is no more a problem to me than Russia or China. Besides, nobody asked to be born, and once it is understood that man's will is not free, and what this means, how is it possible to blame an individual for anything when both sides of this human equation understand the principles? This is a discovery that no one ever knew about therefore the experts in every field are also inadequately prepared to judge its ability to accomplish what was never before possible, the prevention of war and crime. At this juncture my friend and I continued our dialogue.

"Something puzzles me very much because it seems under certain conditions this principle can have no effect. If man is compelled to move in the direction of greater satisfaction, and the conditions of the environment cause him as a solution to his particular problem to prefer the lesser of two evils, how is it possible to remove the evil when his choice, no matter what he selects, is still evil? Self-preservation is the first law of nature and if he can't satisfy his needs without hurting others, the knowledge that they will never blame him for this hurt to them can never prevent him from moving in this direction because he has no choice."

"You are 100% correct because he is already being hurt by the environment and under such conditions he is justified to retaliate."

"This is the only thing that had me puzzled; otherwise, your reasoning is flawless."

It is important to understand that in order to solve a problem, even with our basic principle, we must know what we are faced with and in the economic world there are three aspects of hurt. The first is not being able to fulfill our basic needs. The second is the inability to maintain the standard of living that was developed. And the last is to be denied an opportunity, if desired, to improve one's standard of living.

Before I demonstrate how this hurt in the economic world is removed, it is necessary to remind you of this key fact: Man's will is not free because he never has a choice, as with aging, and then it is obvious that he is under the normal compulsion of living regardless of what his particular motion at any moment might be, or he has a choice and then is given two or more alternatives of which he is compelled, by his very nature, to prefer the one that gives him greater satisfaction whether it is the lesser of two evils, the greater of two goods, or a good over an evil. The natural law implicit in the two-sided equation cannot prevent man from finding greater satisfaction in hurting others when not to do this makes matters worse for himself as would be the case if he were forced, beyond his control, to lose his source of income and be placed in a position where he could not meet his living expenses or acquire the necessaries of life.

170

Just the possibility that this could happen (this pervasive insecurity) activates and justifies the law of self-preservation to lie, cheat, steal, and even kill if there is no other way to get the money he needs or might need for survival. It is also important to realize that when man is compelled to give up his desire to hurt others because he knows there will be no blame he is not choosing the greater of two goods or the lesser of two evils, but a good over an evil. But if by not hurting others he makes matters worse for himself, then he is compelled to prefer the lesser of two evils and this is what happens where the first two aspects of hurt are concerned. Consequently, if we find ourselves unable to get what we need then we are compelled to blame and even hurt those who have it. An example of this occurs when employees who find their income falling short of the mark because of rising prices, blame their employer for having too much money and strike to take some of it away. The employer, in turn, who has discovered that the strike has lowered his income; and the government, finding itself unable to meet its needs under the present tax structure, blame the people for having too much money and decide to take some of it away by increasing prices and taxes. The people, falling below their needs because of this increase, blame the government and anybody else they can cheat to get back what they lost. The manufacturers, wholesalers and retailers are compelled to lay off their surplus employees when consumption slows down and to prevent this, since there is no way the United States can consume all it produces (I am using the United States as an example since I live here, but this applies to any country that produces more than it consumes), the government is forced to do everything humanly possible to keep its foreign markets open and reduce unnecessary competition, otherwise a recession and perhaps depression could result. It is true that war keeps millions of people employed, reduces the already overcrowded earth and the chances of a depression, so what is the better choice? Everywhere we look man is compelled to prefer the lesser of two evils, and under these conditions our basic principle can have no effect. Therefore, to solve our problem since this is the kind of situation that exists in the economic world, it is necessary to remove the first blow. To clarify this, if A is compelled to hurt B because the alternative of not doing this is still worse, then A has no choice but to hurt B, as when the

171

unions strike, when prices and taxes are increased, when lay-offs occur, when government prefers war, etc. But if there is no possibility for A to make matters worse for himself by not hurting B, then this aspect of justification has been removed and it then becomes possible to prevent man from desiring to hurt others when he knows there will be no blame which compels him, beyond his control, to choose a good (not to hurt anybody) over an evil (to do so). Now the question arises at this point, "How can we create an environment that would remove the conditions which make it necessary to select the lesser of two evils as a solution to our problems?"

"I really don't know, especially since you already said that the basic principle cannot be used here."

"It can't be used in a positive, but it can in a negative sense. Obviously, before the removal of all blame can prevent man from desiring to strike a first blow which is to gain (to improve his standard of living) at the expense of others, it is absolutely necessary to remove the possibility that an individual is necessarily hurting others in order to prevent himself from becoming a loser (from going below his standard of living), and there is only one way this can be accomplished. Let me explain what I mean.

If someone was hurt and yelling 'Help! Help! Help!' and you were in a position to render assistance without hurting yourself while knowing that you would never be blamed if you didn't, is it humanly possible for you to find satisfaction in ignoring this cry especially if you know absolutely and positively that all mankind, should you ever find yourself in a similar position, would never fail to help you?"

"Under such conditions I believe that my friend and I would desire to help this individual."

"Well, believe it or not this is the key to the economic solution. Since we have already established the two conditions that strike the first blow of hurt, and since those who fall below their standard of living along with those who cannot acquire the necessaries of life are hurt (drowning so to speak) and yelling for help but will never blame us if we don't, although they know we can if we want to (for over this I will demonstrate that we have mathematical control), we are given no choice but to unite in such a way without blaming anybody for anything (because everything developed out of mathematical necessity)

172

that all mankind notwithstanding will be guaranteed against the possibility of this hurt. By allowing everybody complete freedom to improve their standard of living without the slightest fear of punishment or retaliation, they will be compelled of their own free will to prefer good, that is, not starting anything evil (striking a first blow) because no satisfaction can be gotten otherwise...under the changed conditions."

"This sounds good if nothing else. And you seem to have all the answers, but how is it possible to meet the extra cost of raising all those who are not receiving the necessaries of life to this basic standard plus meeting the entire guarantee. If 50 billion dollars was needed for one week and all that could be raised without anybody going below his basic standard was 30 billion, you're in trouble. And what about those who cannot understand what it means that man's will is not free which knowledge is necessary to prevent a hurt when man is given his freedom? He must understand the principles in order to consider this hurt to others the worse possible choice. And even if he does understand but your guarantee fails to work because there is just not enough money-labor, he would be compelled as a motion in the direction of greater satisfaction to take advantage of not being blamed to select the lesser of two evils, that is, to take what he needs from others one way or another rather than go below his standard. Furthermore, to guarantee his standard of living is a negative benefit if he is not at all satisfied with it which means that he might prefer the insecurity of going below, as a gambler will do, to the security which could deny him the opportunity of improving. But even giving you the benefit of the doubt that the principles can be taught, the guarantee made to work, and the overall benefits will be positive as well as negative, how is it humanly possible to get such a world started when communism and capitalism have opposing ideologies? Last but far from least, what do you mean by a standard of living?"

All of your questions will be answered, but you must be patient as I cannot answer everything at once. It is extremely important to understand that there are three forms to this first blow, and we have been discussing the second form only which cannot be prevented until the first form, struck by the law of self-preservation, is permanently

173

removed. Let me explain.

In Chapter Two I wrote, "As before you are trying to decide whether to hurt us in some way, but you have had everything removed from which you might have been able to justify your act. You simply see an opportunity to gain at our expense, but you will not be a loser if you decide against it. You are contemplating the first blow under changed conditions." The demonstration that followed assumed that all justification had been removed before our basic principle could prevent the desire to strike a first blow, which means that this could be a second or retaliatory blow if not to strike it would make us a loser. Consequently, the first form of the first blow is the economic condition, beyond our personal control, that makes us a loser unless we do something to hurt others; but when this condition is permanently removed there can be no retaliation to it, which means that the same act to hurt them that before was struck to prevent ourselves from becoming a loser could only be done to gain at their expense, making it the second form of first blow, which can be prevented by our basic principle because not to strike it wouldn't make us a loser. Please allow me to elaborate.

Before our basic principle can prevent business people from desiring to raise prices, the unions from striking for higher wages, government from increasing taxes and going to war — all for the purpose of improving their standard of living, that is, of going over their 100%, we must prevent the possibility that they are doing these things to keep from going below their standard of living or 100%. When the unions discover that inflation has eaten, or could eat into their salaries; when a businessman sees that his expenses have increased because of rising labor costs; when rising prices eat into the salaries of government workers, the choice is either to suffer this loss or do something about it. If a government must choose either depression or war, the latter may be judged the lesser of two evils. A salesman who needs a certain income to meet his expenses doesn't hesitate to lie or cheat in order to make a sale because telling the truth might make him a loser. In reality, if this condition or form of first blow is not permanently removed, the basic principle would not only be unable to prevent this retaliation but it would make it impossible to turn the other cheek for greater satisfaction. However, to accomplish the removal of this economic condition without hurting or blaming any country, individual or group for anything, which rules out all existing governments because they cannot even approach the problem without blame or hurt in some form, I am going to demonstrate how it is now possible to guarantee to all the people in the world who are doing, or able to do something to earn a living, whether legal or illegal and while decreasing taxes, ending inflation, war and crime (that is, without robbing Peter to pay Paul), that should they ever find themselves in a position of being laid off, displaced, unable to get a job/business or one that pays enough to sustain the standard of living attained at the start of the transition, but only after using up all their reserve cash towards this end; and if there are some people who are below a basic standard and cannot find a job doing something to earn the necessaries of life, we will give them the materials or money needed. Since this is an extremely crucial point I shall clarify it.

At this moment of time throughout the earth, everybody has attained a certain standard of living which can be measured in dollars and cents. It is the amount of money we consume from week to week on an average in order to maintain our particular way of life, but it does not include taxes, business or job expenses, insurance premiums, donations or any money invested for the purpose of improving our standard. The reason we do not include insurance premiums in estimating our guarantee is because these do not have anything to do with our standard of living. We hope we will never have to use this emergency coverage, but while we work we can afford the premiums. When we lose our job or business and cannot sustain our standard of living, it is obvious that we must drop our policies. However, should an emergency arise during the time that we are receiving money to sustain our standard such as an accident, operation, fire, etc., we would be able to receive the additional money since we are guaranteed against going below our 100%. This means that if we were earning $300 a week, as an example, but were paying out $60 a week on taxes, $20 a week on job expenses, $35 a week on insurance premiums, $10 a week on donations, and $25 a week on investments, our standard of living would be $150 a week. We shall call this 100%. Now if we, due to circumstances beyond our control, are forced to go below this 100%, then we become a loser, and the law of self-preservation, the constant fear that this could happen, compels us to do any number of things to prevent or recoup our loss. But when it becomes impossible for us to be hurt by going below this 100%, which removes the first blow, then we cannot make matters worse for ourselves by not hurting others, which means that any hurt considered by us to them can be prevented by the basic principle because there is no way we can find greater satisfaction in gaining at their expense when we know they will never blame us.

This means that if any citizen ever found himself in a position where he could not find a job or one paying the amount needed and had absolutely no cash reserve or potential to help himself (this includes bonds, cash from his life insurance and anything that can be converted to cash but which does not play a role in his standard of living such as a car) then we, those of us in a position to help without hurting ourselves, that is, without going below our own guarantee, would desire to offer him this money by contributing an equal share to maintain his standard or raise him to the basic level so that he would never have to take away from others what he needs by resorting to strikes, price increases, war to control foreign markets, taxation, crime or anything else done to hurt others as the lesser of two evils. Then when our basic principle is introduced as a permanent condition of the environment it will be impossible for him to desire taking advantage of us in order to gain at our expense because the justification (the possibility he could go below his standard of living) has been removed, although he will be completely free to take certain risks that could hurt us, if he wants to, just as the truck driver was free to speed up if he wanted to, but under the changed conditions he didn't want to. This does not mean he will be denied an opportunity to exert his initiative for the purpose of improving his standard of living (going over his 100%), but only that he will prefer finding ways and means of doing this without taking any risks that could hurt us because he knows we must turn the other cheek for our satisfaction. It also means that he will desire to do everything in his power to sustain his own standard without having to take from us, because the realization that we would never blame him for taking advantage to get money that otherwise we could use to improve our own standard denies his conscience the necessary satisfaction to consider this in any way. Now I am going to demonstrate (once again in an undeniable manner) that when man is guaranteed to be given the money needed should he be forced, BEYOND HIS CONTROL, to go below his standard or to be without the necessaries of life and then guaranteed never to be blamed no matter what he does — WAR, CRIME AND INFLATION will come to an end out of absolute necessity — TAXES AND PRICES will be forced to come down, and everyone's standard of living will be improved beyond their wildest expectations. All these changes will take place without hurting one single individual and of one's own free will (or desire). You will understand this much better as we continue, so don't get discouraged or assume this is impossible. Just bear in mind that I cannot put everything down at one time.

As soon as the United Nations are convinced that the blueprint of this solution is scientifically undeniable (we shall assume this for the moment in order to move along), they will set up IBM computer offices, or the equivalent, for the purpose of making this guarantee work. These offices will be connected to IBM centers, as cities to states, and these centers will be tied together with the International Bureau of Internal Revenue. When this has been completed a written test will be constructed as an entrance examination on the principles involved which must be passed by those interested in becoming citizens of this new world before receiving the guarantee. When this test has been passed and the person signs a statement that he will never again blame another citizen for anything, he himself becomes a citizen by receiving an identification number which is placed on a card to be worn on the outside and on tags for his car that tell the authorities he has taken the examination. The purpose of this identification is to separate citizens from non-citizens during the transition period. Actually, this test is very easy to understand, even by young children. The two-sided equation is explicitly revealed in Chapter Two; the first blow is anything to gain at the expense of others after the guarantee has been installed; the last form of first blow reveals who has the right-of-way when desires conflict, which will be explained in more detail shortly. If a person is incapable of passing the exam, someone would have to assume responsibility for him in order for this guarantee to be issued. There can be no punishment should the new citizen break this agreement and not turn the other cheek during this time of transition, but how is it possible for him to break this or any agreement when he knows there will be no blame for striking this first blow. This needs clarification.

When any agreement is made in the new world, the people who are a party to it are saying, "I am satisfied with this agreement and will never blame you should you violate it." If you don't want to become a citizen of this new world, don't want to receive this guarantee, don't want to agree never to blame, then you don't have to sign this agreement and will continue living in your present environment. But should you sign this agreement, how is it possible for you to desire breaking it by not turning the other cheek when turning the other cheek offers greater satisfaction as this is the kind of punishment those who strike a first blow cannot tolerate. The truck driver wanted to be punished for doing what he knows was his responsibility because this would give him greater satisfaction. As was explained in Chapter Two, "The knowledge that there will be no consequences presents consequences that are still worse, making it impossible to consider this hurt as a preferable alternative." However, in order for the new citizen not to be blamed by his government, and in order for his government not to be blamed by the governments of other nations, the political and military leaders of the world must become our first citizens. How is it possible for political leaders to stop blaming other political leaders and the people in their country unless the leaders have received the guarantee and signed the agreement? Therefore, the world leaders must take their examination first because it is only by the new citizen knowing he will never be blamed by the government or the laws of his country no matter what he does to hurt others that will prevent him from desiring to do that for which punishment came into existence, taking for granted, of course, that the other source of justification, being made to go below his standard of living, has already been removed. This will prevent the possibility of further wars because the very people who have the power to start one will be stopped by the guarantee which denies them any justification and by their realization that there will be no retaliation by those who must turn the other cheek for their satisfaction. When the time arrives for

178

the leaders of the world to sign this agreement, which will be done simultaneously, they will be extremely happy and anxious for this new world to begin. But remember, ironically enough, under the changed conditions the leaders are prevented from hurting others not because there will be no retaliation, but primarily because they will get greater satisfaction in being a part of this fantastic new world.

Once the transition gets officially launched, that is, as soon as the leaders have become citizens by passing their examination it will be mathematically impossible for war to continue or begin again and the greatest transition in the history of mankind will be well on its way. Assuming that you fully understand what it means that man's will is not free, the next step in our blueprint (our diagram of how it is now possible to remove all evil from our lives) is to remove from around the entire earth, regardless of who gets displaced, all those people who are in any way associated with blame including the leaders and their subordinates (remember, everything is exactly the same except for the written test and the IBM offices); politicians, governors, senators, all the way up to the President and his Cabinet. Everybody notwithstanding gets displaced if their manner of earning a living is the least bit redolent of blame. Is it humanly possible to believe that the solution to the problem of war and crime involves the end of all government or, to phrase it more appropriately since many aspects of government will continue to function, the end of all authority and control? If this is true (which is not yet proven), could the commander in chief find any satisfaction in being denied the privilege of making speeches as to what he is going to accomplish even though this denial results in the very thing all the speeches in the world could never bring about? Is it not true that if the President truly cares about ending all war, could he possibly desire to tell others what to do when it can be revealed in a mathematical manner that such authority would only result in the very war he is making efforts to prevent? If every member of the government who is engaged in telling others what is right and wrong should learn that the most harmonious relations imaginable will exist on earth the moment all government comes to an end, are these people given a choice if this is really what they want? Because this is a very crucial point it is imperative that you completely understand what is meant by the mathematical corollary, Thou Shall

179

Not Blame, so I suggest that you reread the second chapter to fully understand why any person who judges what is right for another is absolutely wrong (as two plus two equals five is wrong) since it strikes the first blow and demonstrates how any judgment of another, before something is done, is an advance accusation which offers unconscious justification to do what is criticized by the standard imposed in the tacit blame. If you know that you can prevent the very thing you do not want by being a certain way, do you have a choice as to which direction you must go for greater satisfaction? The very first thing this book reveals in a mathematical manner is that no individual or group of individuals can ever again desire to govern another because it will be seen that not governing is truly better for themselves. For this reason it is impossible for government to discover the solution when this entails the removal of all government. This does not mean that the politicians are responsible for what now exists, but their removal is necessary for the cure which will come about of their own free will. At that moment my friend interrupted...

"You can't be serious. You don't expect the government of the United States to discharge all her troops, and leave the field to communism."

"The sole purpose of disarming our defenses, as other countries can disarm theirs, is simply because, under the conditions just described, no country can find satisfaction in physically hurting those who refuse to hurt them in return for doing what must be considered a compulsion beyond control. But the people who are on the offensive know that this desire to hurt those who refuse to fight back is not beyond their control, and when they fully realize that their desire to strike a blow must be excused without the possibility of any justification, they are given no choice but to relinquish this desire to hurt others with the use of weapons."

"Do you honestly believe that crime will cease when the police are removed? I think the crooks would have a ball."

"You must bear in mind that you also thought removing blame and punishment would allow people to take advantage, but this is not true, so you must not jump to conclusions. We are working the problem backwards, and until other facts are revealed, certain things

180

might appear ridiculous.

To render these evils impossibilities, it is <u>first</u> <u>necessary</u> (this is only the beginning of the solution) to remove the forces that try to prevent war and crime through threats of retaliation, because this kind of effort unconsciously motivates and justifies the very things these forces are trying to prevent. Now how was it possible for government to ever find the solution when the very first step required the dismissal of all forms of government?"

"Say, is this supposed to satisfy our politicians? Do you expect them to calmly sit back while you take away their jobs?"

"Well let me show you that every person who gets displaced, regardless of who he is or what is his income, will be completely satisfied. I shall ask all our politicians a very serious question. 'Gentlemen, would you have any objection to my removing every possibility of war and crime, which would render your services absolutely useless, providing the income you are now receiving would never decrease or stop as long as you live, although it could be increased?' Well, I kind of surprised you with that question, didn't I?"

"You sure did. You mean that every person who gets displaced will never have his income stopped or decreased, no matter how much he is earning?"

"That isn't all. I mean that every person who is employed at the time the transition gets under way, this includes all those who will be displaced, will be guaranteed their accustomed income for the rest of their lives, less taxes, of course. This not only includes the largest, but also the smallest incomes, such as those from unemployment compensation, welfare and relief."

"Be honest with me? Does this scheme have anything to do with socialism or communism?"

"Of course not, first because competition will still exist, and second because it is impossible to dictate to another what to do without blaming him for not doing it, which would be required under communism or socialism."

"But how is it possible to guarantee a businessman that his income will never decrease when competition can very easily do the job?"

"At the moment let's not be concerned with how I'm going to accomplish this, but with everyone's reaction to my doing it. Wouldn't it be a wonderful feeling to know that your income is secure, that it will never be stopped or decreased, only increased?"

"I'm satisfied, but I can think of plenty of people who would not be, like the insurance companies who make their living on the insecurity that exists, and the taxpayers whose jobs are secure without this security, but who might feel they will be overburdened with increased taxation."

"But supposing the insurance companies, instead of making less money, make more than they ever dreamed possible; and supposing the taxpayers, instead of paying more, end up paying less, what would you say then, my fine feathered friend?"

"By the way, does this hold true for all other countries? Will they also be guaranteed their income never to stop or decrease just as long as each individual shall live?"

"Naturally. Aren't we all God's children?"

In spite of the fact that many people will not be happy about losing their profession, they will be forced to look for something else because their services will no longer be needed. Soon to be displaced are judges, juries, lawyers, the entire penal system, crime investigators, intelligence agencies, liability insurance, every kind of license granting permission to do something, all printed forms to check on your honesty, credit cards (all but the IBM), travelers checks, money orders, the banks as a place to safeguard money, and all tax adjusters. The unions will be displaced not only because they blame employers for not paying enough wages, but also because they try to prevent abuses to employees using force. Also displaced are all collection and credit investigating agencies. The first blames someone for not paying his bills and the second checks him in advance to see if he will. When a creditor tries to get his money by sending collection notices, he blames his debtors and gives them unconscious justification to shirk this responsibility. The debtors will be permitted to hurt their creditor if they want to, but they won't want to under the changed

182

conditions. Knowing in advance that the creditor will never ask them again for what they owe him since they know he will consider their not paying him back a compulsion over which they have no control — even though they know it is not beyond their control — they will be compelled, of their own free will, to desire paying back every penny since it gives them no satisfaction to be excused when every bit of justification has been removed. Personnel departments and employment agencies are displaced because they are employed to screen an applicant for a job, which shows a distrust of the applicant's honesty and blames him for being dishonest about his qualifications. A great many employers do not want to hire certain types such as Jews, Hispanics, Blacks, etc., and the agency screens this aspect also. Whatever the reason, since blame is present in some form, these agencies get displaced. It is obvious that an employer is anxious to get the best possible employees for the jobs that are available, which is the reason he screens his applicants. However, this screening is a definite form of tacit blame which justifies any efforts to lie in order to get the position. But when an applicant knows that he is not going to be questioned as to his qualifications; when he knows that he will never be blamed regardless of how many mistakes he makes; that he will never be criticized or punished by being fired, he is given no choice but to forgo any job for which there is the slightest doubt in his mind that he may not be able to handle. Therefore, by removing this tacit blame every individual who seeks employment is compelled to prefer developing a skill so that he can apply for a job with the confidence that he will never hurt anyone due to his lack of ability.

As for who becomes a citizen first, priority will be determined by those whose jobs, professions or businesses will be displaced immediately by the transition. This means that our next citizens will be the police who will be displaced in proportion as the non-citizens decrease. The second are the armed forces of defense which render useless the further need for weapons of offense. Before jumping to conclusions, let me explain. Since the armed forces of defense blame in advance the possibility of being attacked, they must be displaced, and because it is mathematically impossible for armies of offense to desire dropping bombs on those who refuse to retaliate, they too have no reason to remain in existence. How is it possible to spend on learning the art of war and self-defense when no one will ever again attack us? As was just demonstrated in the second and verified in the following chapters, when man judges in advance what is right for someone else and tacitly blames the desire to do what is considered wrong, he actually offers unconscious justification to do the very things not desired. Just as a girl can only offer her body without fear of being hurt when the boy knows that she will never hold him responsible in any way, or blame him for having a good time and leaving, the same holds true for countries in extreme conflict. When everything is removed that justifies aggression — which includes the removal of all weapons — there will be nothing to fear because no country will get satisfaction from pouncing down on a defenseless nation that announces to the world it will not retaliate.

Therefore, the very first step toward permanent peace is for the knowledge that man's will is not free to be translated into every language and disseminated throughout the earth. When this is accomplished, every bit of tacit blame must be removed so that any nation wishing to disarm can do so without fear of being attacked. The second step is the actual disarming of all weapons, including the weapons of mass destruction. This is the exact opposite of what is occurring today with the very real danger of a nuclear strike. There are countries in the process of developing sophisticated biological, chemical, and nuclear weaponry in order to outdo their adversaries. The knowledge in this book plainly instructs the people on this planet that any nation armed with defensive weapons is actually striking the first blow. Because this control of the desire to declare war is only effective when those considering an attack know positively that they will never be blamed or retaliated upon — and since every defensive weapon or means IS AN ACCUSATION that obviously blames in advance this possibility and unconsciously justifies and excuses the very things not desired — man is given no alternative, if the desire is to seriously prevent what has never been successfully accomplished, but to remove the various things that try to prevent him from hurting each other through threats of punishment and retaliation. This is extremely important because this principle will not work otherwise, therefore I will repeat — to render war impossible, it is <u>first necessary</u> to remove the forces that are trying in some way to prevent this aggression through blame, punishment, and threats of retaliation since this kind of effort unconsciously motivates and justifies the very things these forces are trying to prevent. [Reminder: I didn't say that the removal of all defenses is a solution to the problem; I said it was only the beginning of the solution]. Regardless of what is now being done toward this end, it must be destroyed, removed, or converted so that this form of blame, which gives an additional motivation with justification, is no more an influencing factor. By completely disarming a nation says in effect: "If you wish to attack us, hurt us, rob us, murder us, please go right ahead without the slightest fear of retaliation because we know that you are only obeying God's will over which you have no control, which compels us to excuse your actions no matter how much you hurt us." In other words, when a country under attack announces that under no conditions will any retaliatory measures be taken, the aggressor cannot desire to strike knowing there will be no consequences for this unprovoked act. Remember, once a nation disarms the leaders will be sending a clear message to inform the world that regardless of the harm that could come to its citizens, it will not strike back. Under these conditions it becomes mathematically impossible for the nation on the offensive to strike knowing that there will be no blame or retaliation for this act of aggression. Let us observe, once again, how the two-sided equation puts an end to further war.

At this precise moment the leaders know that if they give the command to strike they will not be retaliated upon for this terrible hurt. They also know they don't have to strike if they don't want to for over this they have absolute control (you can lead a horse to water but you can't make him drink)…and when it fully dawns on them that the country under attack will be compelled to turn the other cheek (regardless of what is done to hurt them) they will be prevented from moving in this direction because they will be unable to justify what they are about to do. Remember, it becomes <u>mathematically</u> <u>impossible</u> for a nation to strike when not to strike becomes the preferable choice. And how is it possible for them to desire striking when they know they would be killing innocent people for which there would be no blame or retaliation? It would be the worst possible choice under these conditions because there would be no way to justify this act of aggression, consequently, they would be compelled to move in a different direction for greater satisfaction.

At the present time the capitalist and communist countries diametrically opposed in their ideologies and in serious competition for foreign markets cannot afford the risk of disarmament because they are filled with distrust, and each nation fears a treacherous attack. If a leader feels there is an imminent threat, preemptive action may be taken. Any preemptive strike is an attempt to prevent, when all else has failed, a more serious threat later on. The law of self-preservation justifies this as long as there is a pervasive insecurity that there could be more devastation by not taking this action. This decision may be considered the lesser of two evils in an age of atomic energy where the stakes are extremely high and the potential cost to human life is incalculable. The only other option is to be a sitting duck at the mercy of an unstable region which, in the eyes of many world leaders, cannot be tolerated. Because a WMD attack would be so devastating, U.S. strategy places a higher priority on preventing a WMD attack than on reacting to one. In other words, being threatened with the possibility of a terrorist attack, the President must choose what he considers the best course of action under the circumstances which, in this case, is to take preemptive action rather than to sit on the sidelines subjecting his country to the whims of the enemy. In a June 2002 speech, President Bush spoke of the need to strike first against terrorist threat: "If we wait for threats to materialize, we will have waited too long. . . We must take the battle to the enemy, disrupt his plans and confront the worst threats before they emerge." The National Strategy describes preemption as a supplement to deterrence. . .

Because deterrence may not succeed, and because of the potentially devastating consequences of WMD use against our forces and civilian population, U.S. military forces and appropriate civilian agencies must have the capability to defend against WMD-armed adversaries, including in appropriate cases through preemptive measures. This requires capabilities to detect and destroy an adversary's WMD assets before these weapons are used.

Although preemptive measures may be necessary, according to the President and his advisors, it is a decision that will have lasting repercussions. We are all aware of the consequences of a military strike, which is more bloodshed and continued acts of violence as those who have been attacked will have further justification to seek retribution, perpetuating the cycle of hurt and retaliation; but what other choice does a leader have when the security of his nation is under constant threat? The clash between cultures and their respective governments has caused a serious gap in international understanding. No government has been able to bring about permanent peace by the use of force, yet military action has been used as a last resort when diplomacy has failed. This has caused a backlash of resentment and unrest, fueling the fire of hatred and adding new recruits to a growing terrorist network. Because new cells are constantly forming with the help of the internet and other forms of communication, and because groups such as Al Qaeda and Islamic Jihad are elusive targets without a territorial base, we are far from winning this war. For every terrorist that is captured there are thousands more being trained to die for their cause. Furthermore, it is virtually impossible to protect a country from infiltration when there are so many points of entry. Loopholes in security are bound to exist regardless of the tax dollars spent to safeguard its borders. What is even more frightening is that the technology to build nuclear bombs could get into the wrong hands, which could be catastrophic. On an even larger scale, the possibility of an accidental detonation by a superpower could wreak havoc on the world's population. All it would take is one misunderstanding on the part of either country and a retaliatory strike could lead to unparalleled suffering and destruction on a scale never before witnessed. Not only would a major nuclear exchange have severe long-term effects, primarily from radiation release, but also from the production of high levels of atmospheric pollution leading to a 'nuclear winter' that could last for decades, centuries, or even millennia after the initial attack. In fact, there is a very real possibility that radioactive fallout would leave our world completely uninhabitable. Only one hundred megatons would be enough to set off conflagrations and firestorms, sending enough soot and debris into the atmosphere to block off the sun's light leaving our planet dark, desolate, and incapable of supporting life. Political leaders around the world are doing everything possible to prevent a nuclear holocaust from threatening the survival of intelligent life on Earth, but they cannot give 100% guarantees. The importance of this discovery at this critical time in history cannot be ignored because the direction our world is headed is of a dire nature. This knowledge is no accident because it is the blueprint that is going to save man from himself in an atomic age where warfare is seen as the only viable alternative. Once all countries of the world are taught the truth — that man's will is not free — they will have a third option. They will no longer have to choose war, as the lesser of two evils, because the moment this knowledge is understood there will be a better alternative for all sides of this fragile equation. This is a win-win situation for all nations of the world because there are no losers. Let us review, once again, how war can be prevented once the principles are thoroughly understood.

Applying our basic principle means that all countries can be mathematically prevented from hurting others by the advance knowledge that their actions will never be blamed, criticized or punished. In other words, those considering an attack or contemplating a crime will be prevented from doing so by the full realization that they will never be retaliated upon since it is now known that they cannot help themselves, that they must take people's lives and steal their property, as a solution to their problems. They also know that they don't have to do these terrible things if they don't want to, for over this they have mathematical control; and when it fully dawns on them that no one will ever desire to hurt them in return for doing what must now be considered a compulsion beyond their control — WHEN THEY KNOW IT IS NOT BEYOND THEIR CONTROL (the two sided equation) — they are given <u>no choice</u> but to forgo the contemplation of a strike because it can give them no satisfaction under the changed conditions. Disarming actually prevents this possibility which is the very thing we have been unsuccessfully trying to achieve through the use of force since no one wants to hurt people who are not only defenseless, but are not holding those about to wage war responsible for striking this first blow. This principle prevents having to choose between hurting others, as the lesser of two evils, or being left open to attack, and allows for the very first time the prospect of peaceful coexistence worldwide. This alternative was never before available in the history of the human race because we didn't have the knowledge that man's will is not free and what this means for all mankind.

When this natural law becomes a permanent condition of the environment, attempting to gain at the expense of an individual or of an entire nation could never be a source of greater satisfaction. It will be IMPOSSIBLE for anyone — regardless of their political or religious affiliation — to receive satisfaction whatsoever from being excused for that of which the responsibility could never be denied, or justified. Therefore, let me continue by asking the same question again: Of what value is having an army and police force when there is no possibility of war or crime? Can you think of anything more humorous or ironical? Now that we understand man's will is not free, we know that nothing causes people to go to war unless they want to, and there is nothing that can make them want to once the tacit blame of armaments is removed. In the world of free will we were justified because our lack of understanding created an atmosphere in which being different than we were would only have made matters worse, therefore we had no choice, but with our understanding as to why man's will is not free mankind is able to veer in a different direction for satisfaction removing the causes for which blame, punishment, and retaliation were previously necessary.

Thus far we have arrived at the prerequisite steps that must be taken for there to be a permanent solution. Remember that we are working this problem backwards and until other facts are revealed we still have a distance to go, so please bear with me. There is one key point which needs clarification. Preventing war and crime by removing all advance blame does not necessarily remove the factors that made, in the world of free will, those evils the preferable alternative, so there are other factors to consider. In our present world innumerable wars, revolutions, and crimes were a reaction to various forms of hurt that did not allow any alternative but to retaliate as a reaction to injustices inflicted on them. In other words, when those about to fight back discover that they will no more be retaliated upon, it is also necessary for them to realize that the factors

189

responsible for this consideration of war must also be removed; and are they given any choice but to remove these factors when they know that the people they have been hurting will never blame them for this? For example, if the United States was tacitly blaming another nation through some economic restriction, then disarming would be as effective as the announcement of a tyrant that he is not going to judge what is right for his people while starving them. Under these conditions the principles in this book can have no effect. Let us continue our analysis.

When two nations are in extreme conflict and on the verge of a military strike, a careful analysis by political leaders is crucial in order to identify the nature of the problem and to negotiate a fair agreement. The nations in dispute must first come to a workable solution that is not just palliative, but aims at rectifying the source of the conflict that has brought them to the brink of war. As soon as the leaders have come to an equitable resolution, its citizenry will then be controlled by the basic principle and the Great Transition will begin making its way toward a lasting peace. [Note: It is important to understand that in order for the basic principle to work, the first form of the first blow must be removed (the economic condition) that makes people losers unless they do something to hurt others. How this is accomplished is explained in the section on Taxes and Financing the Guarantee]. This last step is imperative since this control of the desire to declare war is only effective when those considering an attack know positively that they are striking the VERY FIRST BLOW. Therefore, in order to accomplish our goal the very conditions that made it necessary to retaliate must be eliminated before the basic principle can effectively operate. When this final justification is removed, war will no longer be a preferable alternative. This natural law will have the power to stop what no one wants, and the chain reaction of attack and counterattack will be broken. All war will come to an end because those on the offensive will be unable to derive any satisfaction fighting a country that refuses to fight back, consequently, they are given no choice but to relinquish their desire to strike when they can find no possible justification for these continued acts of aggression. For example, in the Middle East the Palestinians and the Israeli's feel justified in defending their respective

190

positions at all costs. Both sides have been fighting over land that they believe was given to them by God. This region of the world has had a tumultuous history which has lasted for over sixty years. Thousands upon thousands of lives have been decimated due to the ravages of war, yet all efforts at reconciliation have failed. In an effort to secure its borders, Israel has built a wall to keep the Palestinians at a safe distance. Called a "security fence" by the Israeli government and the "Apartheid Wall" by Palestinians (legal segregation) — they are actually a series of razor wire, electrified fences, trenches, sensors, cameras, and watchtowers. The first phase of construction was launched in June 2002. Israel's newest frontier wall will follow the one being erected along the 150-mile boundary between the Sinai and Negev deserts. That wall building project is due to be completed by the end of 2012. Once the Kfar Kila wall is finished, Israel will be almost completely enclosed by steel, barbed wire and concrete, leaving only the southern border with Jordan between the Dead and Red Seas without a physical barrier. Defense analyst Alex Fishman recently wrote: "We have become a nation that imprisons itself behind fences, which huddles terrified behind defensive shields." It has become, he said, a "national mental illness." The inescapable fact is that walls meant to provide lasting security never ultimately work. They are temporary fixes at best. Walls have a habit of cracking, falling, being breached, circumvented, written on, or even ignored altogether. And those desperate enough to build a wall are unlikely to be more desperate or creative than those striving to get in or across it. The Maginot Line and the Berlin Wall are now better remembered as monuments to failure than as monuments to lasting peace and security. In fact, walls and barriers have often been a major impetus for military invention and creativity. In this age of high technology and black market arms trading, there is every reason to expect that Palestinian militants would continue to search for ways to undermine, circumvent or ignore the barrier altogether, with potentially devastating consequences for Israeli civilians.

In addition to walls and barriers, Israel has created buffer zones in the West Bank and Gaza Strip (occupied Palestinian territory) to protect her people from further devastation. These zones that refer to land, air, and sea blockages, allow adequate depth against

Palestinian weaponry, from automatic rifle fire and mortars to Qassam-2 rockets, and place serious obstacles before suicide bombers who regularly attempt to infiltrate Israeli population centers. Unfortunately, these no go "access-restricted" free-fire areas, extending from Israel's border fence well into a large percentage of the West Bank and Gaza's most arable land, have led to devastating consequences. Palestinian children have been tragically killed in incidents involving Israeli settlers and excessive use of force by Israeli security forces. The collateral damage has become a familiar sight as young lives are snuffed out too soon. The young and old alike are at risk of being shot, killed, or injured if they inadvertently enter these forbidden zones. Moreover, IDF armored columns enter often to bulldoze homes and other structures. Demolitions and agricultural land razing happen regularly while Israeli soldiers patrol the area 24 hours a day. Up to 70% of households living near these buffer zones have been displaced at least once since 2000. In fact, in 2008-2009 Israel's 'Operation Cast Lead' (Israel's 22 day assault on Gaza as a result of a sharp increase in the number of rocket attacks into Israel) massacred over 1400 people, including 300 children, and destroyed tens of thousands of homes and factories. As a result, the Palestinians have used extreme measures to show their desperation and willingness to die rather than to live under a military regime. A report by Human Rights Watch in 2010, stated: "Palestinians face systematic discrimination merely because of their race, ethnicity, and national origin...While Israeli settlements flourish, Palestinians under Israeli control live in a time warp — not just separate, not just unequal, but sometimes even pushed off their lands and out of their homes." This has become a catch 22. The Palestinians have vowed to continue their attacks until Israel has withdrawn all of her troops, and Israel has refused to withdraw her troops until the Palestinians have stopped their attacks. This occupation has come at a high price, for even if a peace treaty was signed, and an equitable distribution of land was theoretically possible, deep wounds on both sides could sabotage the peacemaking effort. All it would take is one suicide bomber to destabilize the entire region, putting the peace process in jeopardy. As we have seen in recent years, the road map to peace that was once so promising has become another failed attempt and the never ending cycle of attack and counterattack has begun once again.

Putting an end to the Middle East conflict will require the leaders and their advisors to become the first citizens while all non-citizens prepare to take the examination. Remember, until everyone has become a citizen there can be no guarantee that fighting will not begin again, therefore the existing laws would still be enforced. As the transition is taking place from non-citizenship to citizenship, the representatives from both sides would meet in order to map out possible solutions. One solution would be the creation of a two-state settlement that allows each nation-state to have complete independence. As of now, the international community considers Israeli settlements in the West Bank, including East Jerusalem, illegal under international law, though Israel disputes this. This dispute would need to be resolved during these crucial peace negotiations which may require compromise on both sides. When it comes time for the Israeli government and the Palestinian leadership to sign a diplomatic agreement that finds terms upon which peace can be agreed to, the basic principle would then have the power to prevent any further bloodshed because the first blow, which is now being removed, prevents any further justification. To repeat: As soon as the Palestinian and Israeli populace become full-fledged citizens by passing the examination — and the agreement meets the necessary conditions for an equitable distribution of land that is satisfactory to all parties involved — there will be no possibility of a retaliatory strike because the justification to do so will have been removed. Both sides of this longstanding conflict will have no choice but to lay down their arms because they will be incapable of deriving any satisfaction from continuing to do battle under the changed conditions. Israel will be able to pull her troops out of all occupied territories without the fear of attack, and the wall which has been a stark symbol of division between two peoples will be torn down marking the end of one of the world's longest standing conflicts. These two warring sides will have done the impossible, made allies out of their enemies. What was once thought of as an impossible dream will be within reach; however, it must be understood that in order for permanent peace to be guaranteed the Great Transition must take place throughout the world, not just in one region. This is a necessary condition to preclude international conflict from suddenly erupting due to economic instability, causing a ripple effect that would be felt across the globe. The solution will require that the United Nations study these principles and make preparations for the representatives of every nation to become our first citizens. Therefore, it is urgent that this knowledge be brought to their immediate attention. Once this has taken place, they will begin making preparations for everyone in their country to take the examination (excluding those who cannot take responsibility for themselves, in which case a guardian will need to assume responsibility for them), and when this is accomplished, the transition will be complete. This natural law will have the power to stop the chain reaction of hurt and retaliation in all war-torn countries throughout the world. War will come to an end because those on the offensive will be incapable of attacking a nation that puts down its arms and refuses to fight back, especially when the underlying causes that have led to war are being permanently removed. They are given no choice in this matter but to relinquish this desire to strike when there can be no justification for their contemplated actions. Let us continue to observe how the change from non-citizenship to citizenship allows for a smooth transition into the new world.

As more and more people become citizens, all the intelligence agencies looking for terrorist cells and other hate groups will gradually be eliminated. Tight security throughout the world will be necessary until everyone has become a citizen. Until that time all non-citizens will still come under the jurisdiction of their country and will be punished to the full extent of the law, just as they are today. But when all the people of Earth have passed the examination and obtained their guarantee, terrorism will come to an end out of absolute necessity. This does not mean they can't continue with their acts of terror and destruction if they want to, but three reasons will prevent them from wanting to. First, they will have taken the examination and will no longer be controlled by the laws of their country, as was just mentioned. Remember, they must understand the two-sided equation and pass the exam before they are given citizenship, but once they have, they will be controlled by a much more powerful law. They will know that if they should murder, rape, terrorize or train people to become suicide bombers, no one in the entire world will ever hold them responsible because of the fact that everyone knows they cannot help themselves since their will is not free, but they know that nothing can make them injure and kill people if they don't want to, for over this they have mathematical control, and when it fully dawns on them that the world must excuse what they can NO LONGER JUSTIFY, they are prevented from desiring to commit those very acts of terror that previously gave them greater satisfaction. In other words, the advance knowledge that there will be no retaliation henceforth regardless of what they do; that it will be easy for them to accomplish their destructive ends because no one will be standing in their way, mathematically prevents the contemplation of this hurt as a preferable alternative because there is no satisfaction that can be gotten. Secondly, after passing the examination they will receive a guarantee that if they should ever fall below their standard of living, the taxpayers of their nation, or other nations if necessary (including those nations that were once their enemies), will support them in their time of need. Thirdly, all POWs will have an opportunity to study for the examination and become citizens. Once they pass the examination which shows they understand the principles — and sign the agreement that they will not blame anybody for anything — they will be released with no possibility that they could go back to their previous activities. Remember, there can be no punishment should they break this agreement and not turn the other cheek during this time of transition, but how is it possible for them to break this or any other agreement when they know that there will be no blame for striking this first blow while receiving their guarantee? This will also remove any justification for terrorists to kidnap hostages in order to broker an exchange, or to use them as political bargaining chips. The release of all prisoners will be explained in more detail as we discuss how they will be the last group to take the examination. Let me clarify certain points, once again, to show you how the basic principle can prevent terrorism, and all other forms of criminal behavior.

The terrorists, fully aware that if they went ahead and perpetrated a vicious act, no one in the entire world would be looking for them in an effort to strike back — along with the fact that the justification for what they are about to do is being removed — denies them any satisfaction from moving in this direction because it would be the worst possible choice under the changed conditions. Regardless of their previous political or religious motivations, they will be unable to carry out their plans knowing that no one in the world will be lifting a finger in retaliation. In other words, the rationale that gave them the justification to continue their killing sprees was based on the belief that they were striking a retaliatory blow because of hurt done to them, but when this justification is removed then their actions become first blows aimed at those who must turn the other cheek for their satisfaction. It is important to understand that anger is a natural reaction to being hurt whether it is directed toward the responsible party or directed toward a scapegoat. In either case it is a way of finding something to blame for the intolerable conditions that exist. But when the hurt to them is removed, including economic insecurity which strikes the first blow, then there can be no justification for these continued acts of violence. Under these conditions they would be unable to continue as before because their conscience would never permit it.

You may believe that this principle would never have the power to control the behavior of those with such sinister motives; that the terrorists are a different breed and just because they know that they will no longer be blamed would never be enough to stop them from fulfilling their lifelong mission of destroying the people they perceive to be their enemies. You may also believe that it would give them free rein to achieve their evil purposes without having to account for their actions or be punished for their wrongdoing. But this is a completely fallacious observation based on inaccurate reasoning. We are all part of this natural law and when the terrorists know that no one henceforth will ever again blame them for what everyone knows is a compulsion beyond their control — although they know it is not beyond their control since nothing can force them to attack if they don't want to — they will be compelled, of their own free will, to relinquish this desire to attack when they can find no possible justification for doing so. You must remember that in the past they were able to kill with a clear conscience because they felt justified. But when every bit of justification has been removed, along with the knowledge that they will never again be blamed by anyone anywhere, they will be compelled to change their ways. Let me repeat this crucial point: To continue to hurt people who are throwing up their arms and saying, "We will no longer blame you no matter what you do to hurt us" can give them no satisfaction whatsoever, especially when the source of their hatred is now being removed. Under these conditions it would be mathematically impossible to desire hurting innocent people when not to hurt them is judged the better alternative. This would be a movement in the direction of dissatisfaction which cannot be done. (If you do not understand the two-sided equation which is the very foundation of this discovery, please reread Chapter Two). Let us now review the first two steps of this Great Transition because they hold the key to lasting peace.

Step one is for the knowledge that man's will is not free to be translated into every language and disseminated throughout the earth. When this is accomplished, every bit of tacit blame must be removed so that any nation wishing to disarm can do so without fear of being attacked. *Step two* is the disarming of all weapons, including the weapons of mass destruction. As we extend our basic principle, Thou Shall Not Blame (which God, not me, has given to mankind), war can be prevented but it is important to remember that the chief representatives of every nation (i.e., the heads of state) must be the first group to take the examination and sign the agreement in order for the Great Transition to begin. This will allow new citizens to be free from any further blame by their respective governments and will prevent any justification to strike a first blow. Please understand that this does not imply the premature discharge of troops which could leave a threatened country open to attack. It should be obvious that the transition to this new world must take place on a gradual basis because the government cannot remove the possibility of punishment as a necessary condition of the environment until every person throughout the world receives his guarantee and passes an examination to prove that he understands what it means that man's will is not free, that is, understands the two-sided equation, what constitutes a first blow, and who has the right-of-way when desires conflict. Those who have not passed the examination will be treated

197

like non-citizens, consequently, they will still be bound by the laws that are in existence. Only non-citizens could desire to strike a first blow, therefore until they pass their examination — and this they will be anxious to do — they will be controlled by the laws of their country and the combined citizens of the world. Each country will retain its armed forces which will be reduced in just proportion as people gradually begin making the transition from non-citizenship to citizenship. This will be a precautionary measure to control the non-citizens, if needed, and will act as a guide to the citizens who are placed above them. As the citizen population begins to increase (it doesn't matter which country we are referring to because everyone throughout the world will be taking the examination and becoming citizens), the non-citizen population will decrease. Once again, this does not mean leaving the world open to attack. The police and military forces will be reduced in just proportion as the citizens increase, which will allow for a peaceful transition. All weapons will slowly be destroyed as the non-citizen population begins to decrease. This reduction in arms will allow the transition to get under way without the possibility of further wars because the very people who have the power to start one will be stopped by the guarantee which denies them any justification, and by the realization that there will be no retaliation by those who will be compelled to turn the other cheek for their satisfaction. A non-citizen moves away from libel because of the laws. A citizen will move away from it because he cannot find satisfaction in hurting anyone when he knows he will never be blamed. With our basic principle to guide us — together with the removal of advance blame — it is really not difficult to put a permanent end to war, crime, inflation, and all the other evils of our economic world. But bear in mind that these weapons are destroyed not because they are forms of tacit blame but only because with the aid of this slide rule we are able to see, for the first time, what is truly better for ourselves. By turning the other cheek Gandhi and his people demonstrated how they were able to prevent the second cheek from being struck, although many lives were lost. By revealing the knowledge that man's will is not free and what this actually means, each individual makes known in advance that he is turning his cheek no matter what is done to him because he cannot find satisfaction in blaming another for doing what he is compelled to do, even if it means a terrible hurt to himself, which mathematically prevents his first cheek from being struck because there is no way satisfaction can be gotten.

Once this knowledge is disseminated throughout the planet and everyone has become a citizen of the new world, there will be a countdown, and when 0 is reached all remaining weapons that are designed to hurt, kill, or maim, or to prevent people from doing what they have every right to do, will be destroyed immediately without the slightest fear of being harmed as a consequence. The development of new weapons will come to a halt since the armed forces will no longer be necessary as a means of defense. For the very first time in recorded history all of the world's borders including ports, railroads, airports, etc., will be open without the specter of terrorism. There will be no more need for checkpoints that prohibit citizens from entering their country of choice when there is no possibility that anyone can get hurt. In our present world of free will it is not difficult to imagine what would happen if suddenly all laws, government, and forms of punishment were withdrawn. Every potential thief and even those who never thought about stealing would have a field day, and nobody would be safe. Sectarian violence would increase causing extreme chaos and destruction. We can only begin to imagine what an aggressive country would do if there were no other powers to control the desire to spread whatever that country desired to spread. But the moment mankind understands what it means that will is not free which prevents the very things for which government came into existence, it proves, beyond a shadow of doubt, the reality of God — this amazing mathematical power. Everything was timed so perfectly that you must catch your breath in absolute amazement when you contemplate the magnificence of this mathematical equation which includes not only the solar system and the exquisite relationship that exists between the planets, but man himself and all the evil and ignorance that ever existed.

Presently there are people in the world who make a profit on war, for which they cannot be blamed, and there are many theologians and politicians who cannot be happy from having what gives them great satisfaction taken away. Consequently, this group will be somewhat blinded by the mathematical relations and will be compelled to search for some flaw in order to retain their accustomed position of extreme spiritual satisfaction. However, there isn't any flaw which compels all those in a leadership position who are accustomed to giving orders as is the case with religion, government, and education to be absolutely silent for the very first time while the truth about man's nature is being revealed. This may also necessitate that those of you who do not want war and crime to learn the mathematical secret of how to prevent what you don't want by carefully studying these principles and passing them along until a critical mass is reached. As public pressure builds it will become a deafening roar that will be heard throughout the world. Those in high office will no longer be able to ignore the demand to have this knowledge thoroughly investigated. Unfortunately, this may be the only way to bring this discovery to light since politicians have a vested interest in solving the world's problems, but they will continue to be eluded because the answer is not found in government. For the very first time a person's formal education cannot be used here as a standard to determine the validity of the knowledge being presented regardless of his position or rank, since every relation is absolutely undeniable. This book is an S.O.S. to those who have the capacity to perceive undeniable relations and can be objective in their analysis, otherwise, those in power will laugh at and criticize what they cannot understand. As soon as this discovery is confirmed valid by the world's leading scientists, it will not take long before the Great Transition can begin.

During the transition more and more people will be displaced from their jobs. The manufacturers of war equipment will be out of work, as well as those who make burglar alarms, safes, vaults, armored cars, locks and keys. Even cash registers that are designed to check on the honesty of cashiers will no longer be needed. Also displaced in due time since nobody will be spending money in that direction are private and public eyes, floor walkers, security guards, and all licensing departments because they blame individuals for being unqualified by refusing to give them a license. We can continue to spend in this direction if we want to, just as a businessman can continue to hire floor walkers, but when everyone becomes citizens of the new world how is it possible to want to when this serves no purpose and the money could be used to improve our standard of living? However, the lawmakers will not be completely displaced because they will serve a useful purpose. They will have the job of analyzing every possibility of hurt that could occur, and make it known. Whereas before we were controlled by the fear of punishment which allowed those who thought they could beat the laws to attempt things without any regard to who got hurt, we are now prevented from desiring to disobey a law that is just because the fear of being excused for hurting others offers no satisfaction when all the principles are understood.

As these miraculous changes become a reality religion comes to an end along with evil because one was the complement of the other. Religion came into existence out of necessity, but when all evil declines and falls and God reveals Himself as the creator as well as the deliverer of all evil, it must also, out of necessity, come to an end. It is important to recognize that religion gets displaced only because mankind will no longer need its services since God, our Creator (this world is no accident), is answering our prayers. Of what value is having an institution that asks mankind to have faith in God, to have faith that one day God will reveal that He is a reality, when He does this by answering our prayers and delivering us from all evil? Is it possible for a minister to preach against sin when there is no further possibility of committing a sin? Is it possible to desire telling others what is right, when it is mathematically impossible for them to do what is wrong? However, there is no mathematical standard as to what is right and wrong in human conduct except this hurting of others, and once this is removed, once it becomes impossible to desire hurting another human being, then there will be no need for all those schools, religious or otherwise, that have been teaching us how to cope with a hostile environment that will no longer be. In fact, since anyone who tells others how to live or what is wrong with their conduct blames them in advance for doing otherwise — which is a judgment of what is right for someone else — all sermonizing and the giving of unasked for advice are displaced. You see, this discovery draws a mathematical line of demarcation between hurt that is real and hurt that exists only in the imagination. The hurt of ridicule and criticism is real, but in the world of free will there existed many forms of hurt that justified ridicule and criticism. When the hurt that motivated this behavior is removed, then there can be no justification

201

which means that any ridicule and criticism that exists thereafter strikes a first blow, but this is controlled by the realization that it will never be blamed or punished. Consequently, there is no further need to tell others what to do. You may still desire going to church or synagogue, which is your business, but how is it possible to want to continue paying a religious organization when your money can be used to improve your standard of living? For the first time the members of a congregation realizing that God is everywhere, not just in churches and synagogues, and realizing further that all evil is coming to a permanent end, will prefer spending their money in a different direction. Religion will be reluctant to give up the pivotal role it has played for thousands of years, but how is it possible for these theologians to object to the very things they have been unsuccessfully trying to accomplish without revealing that they don't want mankind to be delivered from all evil? This does not mean that religion has not served an important function in man's development. We could not have reached this turning point had it not been for our religious institutions, but we are at last shedding the final stage of the rocket that has given mankind its thrust up to this point. The great humor and the very reason religion could never approve of this work, in spite of its purpose, is because it would be forced to relinquish what has always been a source of tremendous satisfaction. There is something else that annoys religion because it expects the Messiah to look like Christ, or some other historical figure, and that he will come to earth not through ordinary channels. Someone who would claim to have solved the problem of evil could easily be viewed as a false prophet or the antichrist. It may be difficult for the faithful to entertain the idea that the promised Messiah may not come in bodily form but rather as a divine law which has the power to prevent what manmade laws and institutions could never accomplish. To some, this suggestion may be viewed as an unpardonable offense because it appears blasphemous. It may be impossible for those who adhere to the literal translation of the Bible, or any other sacred text, to consider the possibility that peace might come through an unexpected source, although still in accordance with God's will. Even if I had never made this discovery it would come to light sooner or later because what is revealed is a definite part of the real world — not a figment of the imagination. Science will have to take the lead in affirming the accuracy of these principles before they can be applied worldwide. The truth will be very easy to convey once it is understood and acknowledged by scientists because it involves undeniable relations such as two plus two equals four, but when people have been taught for centuries that man's will is free and the eyes are a sense organ, it becomes more difficult to break through these beliefs since the long tenure of preempted authority has confused opinions with facts and dogmatically closed the door to further investigation. However, when theologians fully realize not only that they were teaching something false and that God's will, *the truth*, was hidden behind a different door, but that their standard of living will be permanently guaranteed even though they step down from the pulpit, we will very quickly get their cooperation in attaining this sonic boom. They will strongly desire to spread word of the new gospel that will soon put an end to all evil, even if this puts them out of business. Although we must enter this new world of our own free will (or volition) because no force will be used, the comparison of what we now have with what is now possible gives us no choice because our will is not free to move against what we believe is better for ourselves. This will compel us to desire studying for the examination (which will only require the very basic understanding of these principles) so we can become citizens as quickly as possible after the transition has been officially launched.

Before I demonstrate how it is possible to make the guarantee work for the benefit of all mankind by extending it together with the basic principle into the economic world, it is important to understand how we have been striking the third form of first blow with impunity and in the name of justice by calling it a retaliatory blow. This occurs when we hurt people not because they did something to hurt us, which is the retaliatory blow that when removed prevents the desire to strike a first blow, but only because they did not do what we judged they should, and we blame them for our disappointment or their disobedience. There exists a right-of-way system in human relations, as it does in the world of traffic, that also allows a motorist to know who has the right-of-way when desires conflict. By my judging what you should do for me, which judgment cannot possibly be for the purpose of preventing a first blow because you would not desire to strike one under the changed conditions, I am actually trying to get you to do what you have a perfect right not to do, and then when you refuse to do it, I criticize, blame or hurt you in some way. A perfect example of this takes place when the government fines a driver for going 40 miles an hour in a 25 mile zone. The driver did absolutely nothing to hurt anyone, but the government justified this hurt to him by calling it punishment which implies that he struck the first blow. In our present world, people get a ticket for going over the speed limit, but in the new world nobody will desire to travel at a speed that endangers others. Radar traps were set to slow people down which was absolutely necessary, but they were also given tickets for parking in restricted areas not because they were responsible for hurting someone but because they violated a law. This, however, was necessary to prevent the possibility of someone getting hurt at a future time. In the new world, when a citizen knows that he is not going to hurt anybody by going through a long red light because no cars are coming, then it is obvious that traffic lights have come into existence only to allow an even flow of traffic in a heavily traveled area, otherwise, a stop sign would be sufficient. When a sign says, No Parking or Stopping Between the Hours of 4 and 6 p.m., this is designed to allow the increase in traffic to flow as smoothly as possible. To be delayed because someone has parked along the curb is an inconvenience, but the citizen of the new world could never desire to hold up traffic because he knows he would never be blamed or criticized for this. If it was possible for him to time his stop so that he would not delay traffic, then nobody would be inconvenienced whereas in our present world he could get a ticket for this regardless, as would happen if he went through a red light though no traffic was coming. The government was able to take money right out of his pocket because he violated this traffic law. This is not a criticism because it is obvious why these and similar laws came into existence, and the only reason it is mentioned is because the removal of all blame will also be able to prevent what these man-made laws could not. They had no choice to do otherwise since they knew of no other way to try and prevent accidents. Let me show you how this natural law takes a slightly different turn in order to prevent our government from continuing to

204

hurt citizens with impunity, and in the name of justice.

When motor vehicle operators approach an intersection in the new world and see that the traffic light is still red, they have the right-of-way to do anything they want to do but they decide to stop not because the government is telling them what to do but only because the risk of hurting someone and the knowledge that they would be responsible is so terrible to contemplate when the person hurt would refuse to blame them for what they cannot excuse, that they are compelled to prefer stopping. But when they stop and see that it is perfectly safe to cross even though the light is still red, they have just as much a right to do so as they had a right to cross without stopping. If no cars were coming, there would be no reason to wait because the sole purpose of the traffic light is to give the cars that have the green the right-of-way. If in fact this was a first blow then they could not have done it knowing that they would not be criticized, but the very fact that not blaming does not prevent them from doing it offers undeniable proof that our hurt to them, not their disobedience, is the first blow.

Although this natural law can prevent accidents because they are first blows, it cannot prevent drivers from exceeding the recommended speed limit, from crossing on a red light, from drinking alcoholic beverages, taking drugs and driving, if these drivers believe there is no risk to others, whereas the government has been punishing certain behavior only because it did not comply with their laws. In fact, anytime a person is blamed by others for not agreeing with their judgment, their laws, their commandments, their customs, their conventions, their standards and so forth, they are striking a first blow because this person is expected to sacrifice his desire by conceding to their desires, whereas the person being asked to change is not making any demands on anyone. Therefore, this individual has the right-of-way not to comply with those demands and as a new citizen he will be able to choose what is truly better for himself. However, I shall clarify this by going back to a previous example.

In our present world the truck driver doesn't cross even though it is perfectly safe to do so because he is afraid of getting a ticket should a policeman see him. This means that to satisfy the government's desire that he stay until the light changes, he must sacrifice his own desire to proceed. But when he stops and sees that it is perfectly safe to cross even though the light is still red, he has just as much a right to go as he had a right to go without stopping. Remember, in the new world the risk of hurting others is so terrible to contemplate when we refuse to blame him that he is compelled to prefer stopping. If there is the slightest possibility that his actions could be responsible for an accident, he would never desire to take those risks which could get him into this kind of situation. Therefore, the need to judge what is right for him becomes obsolete when we know he will never do anything to hurt us which means that to criticize, blame or hurt him in any way because he doesn't do what we tell him to do becomes a first blow that we cannot desire to strike when we know that he must excuse what we can no longer justify. In other words, we are prevented from hurting him for not obeying us because we know that our hurting him [for not obeying us] is a first blow for which he will never blame us. This proves conclusively that when others know what is a first blow, we don't have to tell them not to strike it because the basic principle prevents the desire which means that they are completely free, their conscience clear, to do anything they judge is right for themselves without fear of criticism. For the very first time we are compelled by the knowledge of our true nature which reveals what is better for ourselves, to mind our own business, that is, to stop judging what is right for others, which was impossible before. If someone wishes to go out to a strip and race at two hundred miles an hour, this is his business, just so there is no possibility of someone getting hurt other than himself; and if there are others that wish to race against him, this is their business just so there are no drivers in this race that don't want to be. In the world of free will it was necessary in many instances to mind other people's business because they were hurting us with their business, but when it becomes impossible for them to hurt us there is no further need for us to interfere in their business. As for children, don't jump to any conclusions. They will be discussed in another chapter.

There are many laws in existence that do not represent first blows while denying us an opportunity to improve our standard of living unless we take the risk of their violation. As an example, in many cities of the United States pool room proprietors are denied an opportunity to stay open longer if they want to, as with other businesses, while certain forms of gambling are considered illegal. Can any person in the world make us place a bet unless we want to? This means that citizens will have opportunities to improve their standard of living the very moment the laws that deny this no longer apply to them. This does not mean that gambling will increase; it only means that the people who are already into gambling will have no laws restricting their operation. But under the changed conditions of the guarantee, no citizen will desire to gamble with money he needs to meet his standard of living. Should he do this, and lose, this is something he is doing to himself and he would not be entitled to take from the guarantee. He could steal from the guarantee but his conscience will not allow him to move in this direction. The government blames people for selling drugs, their bodies, pornographic literature and guns. They blame citizens for not using seat belts, for drinking too much alcohol, for certain type gambling but not others. Because our experts have never known how to put an end to all the hurt in human relations, although many of them thought they did, they blamed the theft of a car on the person who left his keys in the ignition, murder and robbery on the sale of guns, sex crimes on pornography and the lack of strict censorship, and our children not turning out as we hoped on night-clubs, gambling houses, brothels and other dens of iniquity. In other words, the people who are selling things the government does not like are only trying to earn a living. However, this does not mean that when the laws are removed these things will flourish. On the contrary, prostitution, the sale of guns, alcoholism, drug addiction and many other things will come to an end because there will be less and less buyers to keep the sellers in business, not because these things are first blows. This natural law can only prevent a first blow, and the first blow here is not what these people have been doing to the government, but what the government has been doing to them. They are completely innocent of hurting anyone because nothing in this world can make a person swallow a drug, place a bet, buy the services of a prostitute, or do anything if he doesn't want to. How can a boy or girl, man or woman, desire a prostitute when they are in love with someone who is in love with them? How can anyone desire to get

207

high on alcohol and drugs when the causes for this are removed and when they are already high and very happy being a part of this new world? By blaming those not responsible our government started a chain reaction of justifiable retaliation in every walk of life, making matters a thousand times worse; but all this is coming to an end out of necessity. In the new world, how can a drug pusher make a living when citizens can sell the same thing at a cheaper price? The drug store is loaded with poisons we can take into our body if it gives us satisfaction to do so (and we won't need permission to buy them), and if we want to dive off the Empire State building to see if we can make a three point landing on our head without killing ourselves, this also is our business. Therefore, not only are we not going to blame you for any hurt you do to us, but we are not going to blame you for any hurt you choose to risk doing to yourself. Although someone can do what he wants with his own body, the reasons that would cause a person to want to jump off a building will no longer be present. You must bear in mind that although the words legal, illegal, lawful and unlawful become obsolete for citizens, non-citizens will continue to come under the laws of their nation until they pass the examination.

I need to remind the reader that the transition to this new world must take place on a gradual basis because the government cannot remove the possibility of punishment as a necessary condition of the environment until everyone receives his guarantee and passes an examination to prove that he understands what it means that man's will is not free, that is, understands the two-sided equation, what constitutes a first blow, and who has the right-of-way when desires conflict. I cannot predict how long it will take to complete the transition because this depends on many factors, but one thing is certain. No one can become a citizen of this new world until he passes this simple test and signs the agreement. If he doesn't understand someone will help him understand so he can receive the guarantee. This means that a citizen, with the exception of those who still represent the laws of their government, will be forced to act toward non-citizens as if they are already citizens, that is, never strike them with a first blow even though the new citizen knows they would blame him, because he knows the government will not blame him for anything he does which denies him greater satisfaction in striking this blow especially when the people who are protecting non-citizens during the transition must turn the other cheek. In other words, how can a citizen desire to hurt the people who are still non-citizens for one reason or another, when the police who are citizens but still protecting non-citizens refuse to blame him for what he knows would be his responsibility. He cannot move in this direction for greater satisfaction. This forces him to drive his car as if there are no non-citizens, and allows him to drop his liability insurance because the laws that make him liable have become obsolete for him. However, should an accident occur between him and a non-citizen, he could still sue or bring charges against this individual because this is not a first blow if he feels that he had the right-of-way, and the same thing applies should an accident occur between two non-citizens because they are still living in the old world. But if he feels the non-citizen had the right-of-way in an accident involving him, his guilt will be overwhelming because the laws will not hold him responsible. In fact, there would be absolutely no way a citizen could find satisfaction in hurting a non-citizen when his standard of living is guaranteed never to go down and when he knows, well in advance, that the laws of his nation must excuse him for doing what he can never justify. This will compel him to think like never before in order to prevent any possible hurt to others. Even the need for deductible insurance will decrease proportionately as the citizens begin to increase. What are the risks that something unforeseen will damage our cars when everybody stops doing those things that cause accidents? A non-citizen during the transition may desire to switch his liability to no-fault insurance because citizens are not liable, but such a change will take place in their driving habits that he really has nothing to worry about except from a non-citizen. The only reason citizens may desire to sue a non-citizen is if his insurance doesn't cover expenses and they have to use reserve cash and if they have none, they would need to take from the guarantee. But this cannot be too much of a problem as the citizen population begins to increase. However, just as long as there will be non-citizens, they must know they will be blamed and punished if responsible for hurting others and this is why the portion of government that protects the people during the transition will remain in existence until the transition is complete. It is also interesting to observe that if a motor vehicle operator wants to speed, go through red lights, stop signs, or do any number of things that risk hurting others without the police being on his back; or if someone wants to steal without the possibility of going to prison, all he has to do is become a citizen and he will be completely free of the laws. When he does become a citizen he will be compelled by a superior law and the guarantee which gives him financial security, to sacrifice any such desires as that alternative which he finds better for himself. For the first time he is truly free to do anything he wants but will never desire to hurt others because his conscience will not allow it under the changed conditions. This proves conclusively that just as soon as science confirms this work as an undeniable blueprint of a world that must come to pass out of absolute necessity when our political and military leaders understand the principles, the inception of this Golden Age can officially begin. The transition will be completed when prisoners, the last ones to take the test, have passed the examination. Remember, when prisoners are released after signing the agreement, they will be entering a new world in which hurting others as they did before whether in retaliation or a first blow will be an impossible consideration. I know many of you will find this difficult to believe, but only if you don't understand the principles.

At first glance it may appear that non-citizens could take advantage of the knowledge that they would be released from prison after passing their examination should they get caught in breaking the law. They could kill someone hated very much and not fear the charge. They could successfully rob a bank of a million dollars, hide the money, and if caught, take their examination and be released to enjoy the fruits of their plan. You must remember that man must always do what he thinks is better for himself which compels the non-citizen to take into consideration the possible consequences. In trying to kill somebody, he himself could become the victim. He could also be killed while attempting to rob the bank. Furthermore, he must also weigh the possible years he could spend in prison just waiting his turn to take the examination which he might fail, with no one willing to assume responsibility in his case. He might also be executed before capital punishment becomes obsolete. Once the transition gets officially launched, that is, once the leaders have set up their IBM offices and become citizens by passing their examination, they will forthwith abolish capital punishment. You have looked at a negative possibility without comparing the positive benefits to the potential citizen who is now a free man looking in, not looking out. Because the comparison gives no free choice, everybody notwithstanding who gets wind of this new world, so to speak, will desire to become a citizen just as soon as possible. If a prisoner takes the examination and passes, regardless of what he was in prison for, he will be a free man because it will be mathematically impossible, under the changed conditions, for him to ever desire hurting others again. But just as the leaders of the world were first in taking the examination, so the prisoners will be among the last.

"What about gangsters, racketeers, bookmakers, dope peddlers, and those who are paid to commit murder; do they get out as well even though they earn a living hurting others?"

Anybody who makes his living by doing something that hurts others has a choice to make. He can pass his examination and become a citizen which guarantees his standard of living and allows him to change his job without losing as a result of this change, or he can continue to hurt others to earn his income with the constant possibility of earning less while ending up in prison. Is he really given a choice? When a drug pusher becomes a citizen he will lose the desire to push the sale of his products with misleading information which means that once all available facts about drugs are made public, and all blame withdrawn, the user will find very little satisfaction in taking this chance of hurting himself, but if he wants to, this will be his business. The citizen will not find any satisfaction in remaining in a business that hurts others under the changed conditions, and the non-citizen, knowing that his standard of living is guaranteed when he becomes a citizen and also realizing that just as long as he continues to engage in illicit activities he is subject to the full penalty of the laws, will be very anxious to study and pass his examination.

Let us imagine that some counterfeiter wishing to get out of his present line of work because he knows he could get caught and go to prison decides to become a citizen and receives a guarantee that was estimated at $300 a week. He then uses his IBM identification card to buy a big mansion, several cars, an airplane, and many other things

211

on credit. He subsequently borrows a million dollars from the bank, but when the very first payment in all these things is in default his creditors go to his IBM office to collect their first installment. However, just in case a mentally disturbed person did manage to pass his examination, he would still be prevented from buying on credit beyond his standard of living because his creditor will ask to see his identification card and on it would be recorded the amount of his guarantee. If the purchase is too great, according to the judgment of the lender or seller (remember, the installments must come out of the guarantee, not out of his cash reserve), this transaction would be reported immediately to his IBM office. If he did not buy beyond his means but failed to pay his installments when due, we would pick up his condition soon enough. However, the odds of a new citizen hurting anyone as a result of being mentally disturbed will be virtually nonexistent.

"But what if he makes a slip with his pencil or pen, and instead of recording $100 per week, he adds an extra zero giving himself $1000, and when we call him in to test his present state of mind after seeing what he did we discover that he is not mentally ill?"

Once we have determined that he has no severe emotional problems and that he deliberately wanted to hurt us, there is nothing we can do because we know that he couldn't help himself. We would continue paying his creditors and if he used up his thousand dollars and still did not want to work for a living he could steal more from us because we would never blame him for hurting us this way. But he knows that he doesn't have to hurt us this way unless he wants to for over this he knows he has mathematical control, and when it fully dawns on him after passing his examination that we would never hold him responsible for what he can never justify, he will completely abandon all such ideas — unless he is really mentally sick. Remember, everyone is going to be given a golden opportunity to cheat and steal all he wants, if he wants to. This person doesn't have to make a slip of his pen, he can just as easily add in $10,000 or $100,000, but why is this even necessary when all he is going to do when buying something is hand somebody a piece of paper on which is recorded the amount of the purchase? If he wants to take a trip abroad, and he doesn't have the purchasing power, it isn't first necessary to enter in his book the amount he thinks he will need for the trip because nobody is ever going to question his ability to pay, or ask to see his record book. Consequently, all that is necessary is to have a pad of paper and a pen or pencil for writing. He could board the plane or ship, get the best stateroom or accommodations, eat the best meals, tip the waiters very heavily, and live like a millionaire. In fact, he never has to work at all and could issue slips of paper from morning to night, but there is one other thing required for him to do this with a clear conscience and that is he must be absolutely certain he is not hurting others by what he does because if he is, and he knows that he will never be blamed or punished for this, which the people who are hurt must excuse and he cannot justify, then he will be mathematically prevented from moving in this direction because the very thought of it will give him no satisfaction whatsoever.

"But how does he hurt the people when he is paying them for everything he buys, though the slips of paper are counterfeit? If I give you a slip of paper for a television set, and you record this in your book at the end of the day, you certainly are not being hurt; in fact, you are pleased with the business for the day, right?"

"That part is very true, but the storekeeper is not the one being hurt at that moment. The people who are hurt are those who desire to buy the very things you have just stolen but can't because these things are now not available, which makes a mockery of their purchasing power. Of what good is money on a deserted island?"

"There is none whatsoever."

"Then what good is this purchasing power when the very things you want are suddenly not available anymore?"

"Again, your money has no value in this type of situation."

"Consequently, when a person steals he upsets the balance between available merchandise, services, and the money with which to purchase these."

"I see what you mean. There would be less merchandise and services, and more money."

"Yes, and when that happens everybody will be forced to take a decrease in their income, even the storekeeper who at first was so happy with what appeared to be a sale. Now once each person

213

understands that he would be hurting everybody by stealing, and further knows that he will never be blamed or punished for doing what everyone knows he is compelled to do, when he knows he is not compelled to steal unless he wants to, then he is given no alternative but to relinquish the contemplation of his theft, because it cannot satisfy him to be excused for this hurt when he knows it would be his responsibility."

TAXES AND FINANCING THE GUARANTEE

Since raising prices and striking for higher wages are first blows which we cannot desire to strike after becoming citizens and receiving our guarantee; and since this blow, no matter where it originates in our present world is the source of inflation, we must enact an international law during the transition that will punish severely any non-citizens who choose to violate it. As a further consequence of the guarantee, labor unions will be displaced because they can only strike to gain at the expense of the taxpayers who have also guaranteed to help them in their moment of need. But remember, if this law annoys them all they have to do is become citizens and they will be completely free to strike this blow to their heart's content. This also means that business people will be prevented from raising prices for the same reason, which places a ceiling on everything that has a price when the transition begins, including labor. This does not mean that people will be denied an opportunity to improve their standard of living, but they will be forced to do this at nobody's expense. In other words, it does not stop an employer from giving out bonuses and increases in salary, but it does prevent his employees from forcing this on him. Employees have the right to ask for a raise or any kind of favor, but their employer has the right-of-way to refuse; and if they should threaten to quit as a result of this refusal, that is their business for which they would never be blamed no matter how much this might hurt him. Remember, an employer can give a raise in salary or a bonus if he wants to, but he cannot use what he gives voluntarily (what might put him below his standard of living) as a justification to get financial help. And how is it possible for employees to quit under the changed conditions when they would only make matters worse for themselves? At this juncture, let me clarify something I stated earlier. Putting a ceiling on everything that has a price doesn't prevent you from paying more for something than the price called for, if you want to. But it does prevent the person selling what already has a price when the transition begins from digging into your pocket when you don't want this to be done. If something has no set price, then it is negotiable. In our present world, there is justification to raise prices and strike for higher wages, but in the new world this justification is removed not only by the guarantee but by the fact that your expenses to operate your business and meet your standard of living will never be increased. This means that to raise prices and strike for higher wages must, under the changed conditions, become first blows. As you can see, this puts an end to inflation. Let me show you how this will be accomplished in our next step.

Millions upon millions upon millions of people will be permanently displaced from their manner of earning a living (it is unimportant for me to list everyone that will be affected), while millions more will find their income dropping but not only without being hurt because they are guaranteed the difference in order to sustain their standard of living, but without causing others to be hurt. However, they will not prefer to quit their job since this is a voluntary move and does not entitle them to receive the guarantee, which means that they must be released by their employer and consume all their reserve cash before coming to us (the taxpayers) for financial help. If they are in business for themselves and their services or products have come to an end, such as with war equipment, they are free to look immediately for something else. But if what they are selling has not been permanently displaced, although the buyers have decreased, they will prefer to remain at what they are doing as long as this requires them to take less from the guarantee to sustain their standard of living. If they reach a point where by changing businesses or jobs they would need less of the guarantee or nothing at all, then their conscience will allow them to make a change. Should they wish to gamble part of their standard of living in order to make a change before they need our financial help, this is their business, but if they fail to succeed and then require our help, they must be satisfied with the new standard of living they imposed on themselves since what

215

lowered their standard was not beyond their control. I shall elaborate more on this shortly. Since the displaced must use up all their reserve cash before being entitled to get financial help, billions upon billions upon billions of dollars will be drawn out of the banks, stocks and bonds cashed in and dumped into circulation for the very first time while all the money paid out for these displaced services will go back into the pockets of those who were paying for them. It is true that a great portion of this money will be paid out in taxes to sustain the guarantee, but follow carefully what must happen.

As those displaced individuals with reserve cash are forced to spend their money on supporting themselves until it runs out or they find another job or business; as each government is forced to use all its reserve cash to finance the displaced who cannot find work and do not have money of their own; and as the non-displaced will desire to spend or invest all their reserve cash to improve their standard of living because the need to save for a rainy day has been rendered obsolete by the guarantee, billions upon billions upon billions of dollars (perhaps trillions throughout the earth), will be forced into circulation and start an upward cycle (the exact opposite of the vicious cycle known as inflation) by creating an ever increasing demand for the labor of those people without jobs. Gradually, as the displaced find work which increases our tax profit, the money needed to finance the guarantee becomes less and less and less, while the money to spend or invest on improving our standard of living becomes more and more and more. Business people will have so much money from their tax profit alone that they will desire to give out bonuses and when these increases in salaries are added to an employees gross income while the amount needed from him for the guarantee also becomes less and less and less, he will have more money to spend than he ever dreamed of. Just think of the other expenses he won't have anymore. No more money will be given for religious purposes, no more taxes for war and crime, no more liability insurance, no more people asking for charitable donations because included in the guarantee will be those who are below a basic standard and need our help. Also, just think of the money the government will have in its possession when what has been paid out for war and crime is stopped…but what government? All we will need is an international computer network that links all the IBM

216

centers together. Due to modern technology it will be very easy to coordinate this global effort.

Trillions of dollars will become available for business entrepreneurs to invest their money to develop the planet (the motive will be PROFIT), while millions of the displaced will be available for on the job training. If the gross salary on a job after training calls for $600 per week, and your guarantee is $300, your employer would pay you the $300 during your training period. This would reduce the taxes needed to finance the guarantee, and would allow a complete on the job training program. When you have been sufficiently trained you would then receive your gross salary and begin to pay quarterly taxes. Before long there will be such an economic boom that the amount of money needed to finance the guarantee would be reduced to an absolute minimum, which will give you that much more money to spend or invest. And since the guarantee renders obsolete the need to save for a rainy day since you will be given the money needed should any emergency force you to go below your standard of living (which has never been possible before), that much more money will go back into the taxpayer's pocket because you can drop your insurance policies without hurting the insurance companies. It is important to clarify that NO FAULT insurance can only have reference to a hurt to yourself that you know you are responsible for. You are prevented from taking risks that could hurt others because of the changed conditions, but you are not prevented from taking risks that might be a hurt to yourself, and if this puts you below your standard of living and out of reach of financial help from the guarantee because the risk you chose to take was not beyond your control, you have no one to blame but yourself. Therefore, you might desire to carry this kind of insurance, if you can get it, in order to protect yourself against the risks you might want to take. You must constantly bear in mind that when someone comes to us for help he must be absolutely broke.

"Why did you deduct insurance premiums when this is not a deductible item except as a business expense, especially when insurance definitely plays a role in maintaining one's standard of living?"

"If we were to make his guarantee $150 instead of $130 so that he could invest the $20 with insurance companies, we would be

217

increasing the cost of the overall guarantee by the amount that was not used. In other words, if the total insurance premiums distributed amounted to one hundred million dollars but only fifty were used by the insurance companies to pay off the various damages, then we increased our cost of the guarantee by 50 million. Besides, he is already covered when the $20 was deducted to arrive at his standard of living, which means that if he lost his house by fire and had absolutely nothing with which to help himself, we would not only rebuild its value but incur all other expenses necessary to maintain his standard of living."

"I can understand this. But by not giving him the money to insure himself with these companies, you would have to hurt them?"

"How is it possible for these companies to be hurt when their standard of living is guaranteed for each member who is a citizen? The floor walker, for example, who was compelled of his own free will to use up all his cash reserve before coming to us for help, dumps into circulation more of the money needed to create new jobs; and every time a displaced person finds new employment, the cost of the guarantee decreases. What the department store owners do with the extra profit they pick up when the floor walker is not needed anymore, allowing for the change in the amount of his weekly contribution since this displacement affects it, is strictly their business. Obviously, we will not continue having crime because the manufacturers of burglar alarms need the criminal to earn a living. Therefore, we are not going to guarantee their job or business which depends on buyers for what they have to sell; just their net income when they are completely or partially displaced."

"But this brings up a very interesting point where the non-displaced are concerned regarding insurance. Knowing that he is covered by the guarantee, why should the citizen continue investing $20 on insurance when he could put it to better use?"

"Because to stop would be taking advantage of the guarantee, and there is no advantage when this could result in an increase to our cost for which hurt there would be no blame."

"Well let me rephrase my question: 'Supposing this displaced person after letting his policies lapse because he couldn't keep them up gets a new job paying $250. But now he has no insurance because he was forced to use up the cash from his life insurance and drop all other policies. Is he supposed to reinvest the $20 in insurance coverage even though he is already covered by the guarantee?'"

"Some of his policies might still be in force, but if he was investing $20 on insurance before getting displaced and he can do this again without going below his guarantee, then he would desire to do this to prevent a hurt to those who would not only not blame him for this but would help him if necessary."

"Something else just came to my mind which might be related to insurance and I think I see a flaw. If dropping insurance takes advantage of the guarantee which cannot be done, wouldn't it also be taking advantage if a person who knows he will soon be displaced and who has a huge reserve in cash and a large guaranteed net income, decides to spend it on all luxuries so that he wouldn't have to use it towards sustaining his own guarantee and to then draw what he needs from us?"

Any person who knows he is going to be displaced will be increasing the cost of the overall guarantee if he spends his reserve cash on anything that does not pertain to the maintenance of his standard of living. To express it differently, if he had $650 in cash and was going to be displaced for 5 weeks, this money would cover the entire period if his net income was $130 a week. If he spent it on a new television set which broke him, instead of using it towards his guarantee, then he would cost us this amount of $130 every week until he gets another job. There is no flaw. What he does with his own money is his business, but he must be completely broke before coming to us for help.

If 98% of the government eventually gets displaced because there is no further need for their services, and these people are able to find new jobs that cover dollar for dollar the amount we were spending on taxes, then we will create a tremendous profit in our IBM accounts. As a further consequence since prices cannot be raised, and since there will be so much capital available; and since business people will want to make as much profit as they can, they will be forced to lower prices and sell in tremendous volume which would allow many people unable to buy something before to be able to buy it now. Now we can understand why, instead of the vicious cycle of inflation, we will have a productive cycle that will benefit everyone without hurting anyone at all. People will soon have so many material goods that the need to produce what is not being consumed will decline causing millions of people to get laid off from their jobs. But what difference does it make when no one can get hurt? If you have things on which to spend your money, which keeps people employed, the taxes to finance the guarantee must come down. If you don't have anything to buy, and people are laid off as a consequence, you will use this money to guarantee their standard of living.

Once the transition gets under way the people, realizing their income is guaranteed, will start spending like never before. Since the guarantee offers the greatest security imaginable, all money held in reserve or invested towards a lesser security can be released. Remember, this will cause the opposite of a depression as it will necessitate millions of employers to hire the displaced for various positions, and every time a displaced person takes a job your taxes decrease. There is an inverse relation between taxes and consumption. The more we spend or invest our money, the less needed for the guarantee (the amount needed for unemployment compensation) which will be reduced in just proportion. If we have nothing on which to spend or invest, then it becomes a surplus that will voluntarily be given to those who need it because they will have been displaced and cannot find new jobs as a consequence of our not spending or investing it. Therefore, the more we spend our money, the less do we have to pay towards the guarantee.

"Does this mean when people aren't making as much profit, that's when taxes will be greater? That doesn't seem right."

That is only because the deeper relations have not been perceived. Since prices can never be increased, and since there will be more labor available than ever before, competition will be unusually keen, and prices must go down. Consequently, it won't take long before millions of people will be saturated with material things, which will definitely slow up production causing millions of workers to be laid off with their guaranteed salary. However, when you can't spend your money on material things others need for their employment, what difference does it make to you if they get this amount in taxes? If you spend it they receive it in the form of a salary, and if you don't spend it they

220

get it in the form of unemployment compensation. How they get it is entirely up to you. This does not mean that you are free to spend your tax dollars, although you can if you want to. Once you fully realize that not to pay your share of the taxes would be stealing from the people who would be compelled to pick up the difference but who would never blame you for this even if they knew what you were doing, how would it be possible for you to desire moving in that direction for greater satisfaction when YOU WOULD KNOW WHAT YOU ARE DOING SINCE YOU CAN NO LONGER LIE TO YOURSELF BY SHIFTING YOUR RESPONSIBILITY?

If someone is laid off who is accustomed to earning $25,000 a year, and this amount is his guaranteed income, but no matter how hard he tries he can't spend his weekly portion, he will simply draw from the Bureau only the amount he spends. If his weekly salary is $500, but all he could spend was $300 that week, then he only receives $300 in unemployment compensation. Bear in mind that just as long as you are not drawing unemployment compensation, what you do with your money is your business, but when your income is guaranteed never to stop or decrease, the previous need to save for a rainy day, the day when you might not have an income has no further value forcing everybody, even the millionaires, to spend like they never spent before. Money has absolutely no value unless it can be spent or invested. There will be the greatest investment opportunity ever dreamed of for the millionaires who want to invest. Nothing is stopping them from building schools (since there will be no more government), superhighways, bridges, fire fighting equipment, for the sole purpose of making huge profits — which will be entirely their business. They will set their prices according to market demand, just as it is in today's world. In a very short while the smallest income will have a purchasing power unbelievably high because prices have got to come down. Would it disturb you, think very carefully before answering, if the janitor also had steak for dinner just as long as this does not take away from your own purchasing power? The purchasing power of many will always be greater or lesser than others, while the lowest level of mankind will be raised enormously. The millionaires are going to be given an opportunity to become billionaires and those that want to become millionaires will have this opportunity, and the poor people will have a chance to become wealthy. Now once again be perfectly honest. If I can show you how to invest your money (and labor) so that it will put to shame any investments you now have, and guarantee a fabulous return, would you be interested? Am I giving you a choice? Wouldn't you like to double and triple the value of your money and labor so that you can buy many of the luxuries you have only been dreaming about? Remember, the solution to this problem requires that every person on the planet be satisfied, otherwise it is obvious that God is showing partiality.

The launching of this Great Transition will be as smooth and uninterrupted as a well-oiled piece of machinery because when payday rolls around the displaced need only enter their weekly income in their book, and then send a withdrawal slip to the local Bureau of Internal Revenue so that this guaranteed compensation can be acknowledged and deducted. No one will tell these people where or when they should work, and if they wish to retire on this income for the rest of their lives, this is their business. However, when they fully realize that the money with which they are being supported could be used for other things the moment they take an available job and when they don't they would be hurting us — the people who are supporting them — they are given no alternative under these conditions.

"Not so fast. Supposing a person like the President of the United States who is earning in a neighborhood of $100,000 per year can't get a job paying that amount of money, what then?"

"If he can only get a job paying $5000, he will still receive his guaranteed income just as long as he lives by drawing the other $95,000, less taxes of course, from the Bureau of Internal Revenue."

"But wouldn't this make him desire to take the easiest job available, regardless of the salary, since he knows that the chances are very slim that he will ever earn more than this $100,000? Besides, wouldn't an employer take advantage of this knowledge to pay the President only $5000 to do a very important job, one worth much more money, since he knows the difference would be given in unemployment compensation, so to speak?"

Your questions indicate that you have not looked into this deeply enough otherwise you would not have asked them. In order for an employer to pay less than what a job is worth, to pay less to the same individual who would receive more under other circumstances, it would necessitate that he hurt the taxpayers who would be compelled to pay this difference because they know he cannot help hurting them this way. But he knows he is not compelled to hurt them this way unless he wants to, and it cannot satisfy him to do this when he knows they are compelled to excuse what he is mathematically unable to justify. This rule applies in every human relation, although there will be a slight variation of this theme where children are concerned. Keep in mind that the inception of the Golden Age actually will get under way just as you launch a satellite into space, with a countdown, and when the count is down every weapon that is remaining on earth that is meant to hurt or maim will be destroyed. Is it possible for a potential criminal to use a gun for a hold-up when nothing is going to stand in his way of taking anything he wants without force? It should be obvious that this countdown will not take place until every adult on the planet will be taught what it means that man's will is not free, for otherwise it would only make matters worse. However, once this is accomplished and Project Golden Age launched, millions upon millions of people will be automatically displaced as a consequence, but just before the launching, since no one can be blamed or hurt, each person around the earth will record in his little book his exact wealth and earning power so not one single penny in purchasing power will be taken away from any individual regardless of whether or not he is displaced. Consequently, if the President of the United States, the Premiere of Russia, the Queen of England, or any other top official has been receiving a net income of so much, they will continue to receive this same amount of money without any one telling them what to do with their time, or how to spend their money. If the sailors and soldiers returning home wish to retire for the rest of their lives on their present income, this is their business, but if they desire to earn more money then they will be compelled of their own free will to desire going to work. Moreover, each person will record the exact amount of time he is putting in to earn his present income (this applies only to those employed) because it will be mathematically impossible for an individual to work one second longer without blame.

Therefore, the next step in this process is for you to estimate your

223

standard of living which is the amount of money you consume from week to week on an average to maintain your particular way of life, but it does not include taxes, business or job expenses, insurance premiums, contributions, or any money saved, invested or gambled with in any way that does not play an immediate role in meeting your living expenses, and submit it to your government with a signed statement that you will never again, in return for this guarantee, blame anybody for anything. It is the available services and materials that an individual can purchase with his net income which is the amount left over after all deductible items and taxes have been subtracted from the gross, less the personal insurance premiums. Supposing your gross income is $600 per week, and you suddenly lost your job or business and all your reserve cash, you might need only $300 or $400 to meet your expenses. If your gross is one million per week, you might only need $2000, but you alone will determine your standard of living which will also become the basis for all your taxes. If someone else earned on an average of $250 a week, spent $50 of this on deductible items that have nothing to do with taxes of any kind, another $50 on taxes which include federal, state, and social security, excise, property, and anything I might have omitted, and $20 on personal insurance coverage, then his standard of living would be estimated at $130 a week. What a person does with his own money is his business but, remember, he must be completely broke before coming to us for help. If it is his desire to spend this money on a television set, this is also his business, but before you make any assumptions let me show you how everything pertaining to the guarantee is done by going in to the IBM office. As we went over, he will then receive an identification number that is placed on a card with his picture, signature, and guarantee (which is $130 in this case) on metal plates to replace license tags and if he has a place of business, on a sheet of paper to replace all other licenses. This will allow him to get the money needed should he ever be forced into a position, BEYOND HIS CONTROL, where he cannot find a job or business, and does not have enough cash reserve to meet his expenses. Should an emergency arise that cannot be met with his guarantee, this will also be taken care of. If he should quit his job, leave or sell his business, which he certainly has the right to do if he wants to, this is not beyond his control and does not entitle him to financial help if he is then forced to go below his standard of living; but he would still be guaranteed the BASIC STANDARD. He can gamble this way if he wants to, but not at the expense of the taxpayers financing the guarantee. This means that if the basic guarantee doesn't allow him to meet his expenses, and the choice is either to steal from the guarantee for which he knows he would never be blamed even if the taxpayers knew what he was doing, and were obviously hurt by this — or not to gamble with his guarantee — what choice would he have?

"But what about the many people in the world receiving a little bit more than a starvation income, they are being seriously hurt and doesn't this justify some form of retaliation on the society that hurts them in this manner?"

"How is it possible for these poor people to blame others for their own misfortunes when nobody is to blame for this economic plight? Obviously, this won't put food in their mouths, clothes on their backs, and give them decent shelter in which to live. The fact that no one is to blame is not going to stop the taxpayers from wanting to help increase the income of the poor so that they can at least have a livable wage."

"But what is a livable wage? Who is going to determine the amount of the increase — and who is going to pay it? The employer can't pay out more unless he cuts his own guaranteed income. So what are they supposed to do, go on suffering?"

"As for determining this subsistence wage, it will be that amount necessary to feed, clothe, and shelter one adult, two adults, one child, two children, and so on."

"But I distinctly heard you say that no one will judge what is right for another, once the transition gets under way, at least I thought I heard you say this. And if someone will judge how much this subsistence wage should be, wouldn't he be blaming in advance the possibility that those to receive it might need still more? One adult might eat twice as much as another, isn't that right?"

"You're so right, my friend."

"The only person I can think of who would be an accurate judge of what he needs as a minimum for his family is the father, the mother, or both, but then that couldn't be right because someone might take advantage of a good thing."

"You were going along just fine until the thinking under free will crept into your reasoning. Each person who feels he is receiving an inadequate income for the minimum needs of his family will simply enter in his book the amount he thinks he should have as his guaranteed income, and when payday comes around, and he receives this inadequate amount, he will add the difference by sending a withdrawal slip to the Bureau of Internal Revenue so it can be deducted."

"How is it possible for the taxpayers to be satisfied when this entails a gigantic increase in taxation?"

"Aren't you jumping to a conclusion when you assume that taxes will be increased?"

"Well, won't they?"

"Are you asking or telling me?"

"I'm asking."

"Well if you're asking then why do you say my solution isn't sensible when you haven't even heard the answer, and why do you say this will entail a gigantic increase in taxation when you don't know until you've heard my solution? You're getting to sound just like the many rabbis I spoke to who refuse to let me explain what I know to be a fact because they have already jumped to the conclusion that what I have to say is of no value since it is based upon the knowledge that man's will is not free. Every expert does the same thing when using a fallacious standard; he jumps to the conclusion that he knows when, in reality, he doesn't know, only thinks he does. Please don't make it more difficult than it already is to break through this sound barrier of learned ignorance."

"If I'm ignorant, it isn't because I'm learned since I only went to high school, but just because I really don't know."

"Then if you don't know, admit it; don't pretend to knowledge you do not possess, especially now when every minute counts."

"What do you mean, 'every minute counts?'"

"I mean just what I said. How would you feel if you were behind a barrier which prevented you from getting out, and you saw a baby

226

getting ready to crawl in front of an oncoming car? Can it satisfy you to watch the baby get killed knowing you could save him?"

"What a horrible thing to see, especially when you know you could stop it if you only could get out from behind that barrier."

"That's exactly how I feel knowing there doesn't have to be any more wars and crimes, any more hurt between people, providing I can get out from behind this sound barrier of learned ignorance. We are sacrificing our sons and daughters needlessly by sending them to war when there is a better alternative. It actually hurts me to see what I see. Consequently, I am under a great deal of pressure to get this knowledge into the proper hands before an atomic explosion takes millions of lives — or just as soon as humanly possible."

"Do you mean somebody like the President of the United States?"

"That would be a major step in the right direction but very difficult to accomplish. Therefore the proper hands are those who understand this knowledge, anybody's hands. Then I will be able to start an atomic chain reaction of thought that will move from one end of the earth to the other with unprecedented speed, and unless you stop jumping to conclusions, you will delay the lighting of this fuse, because you are the fuse. Now remember, there is a big difference between asking me will taxes be increased or decreased, and telling me that they will definitely be increased if I do certain things. The first shows that you are sincerely interested in understanding my thoughts, while the second demonstrates that you think you already know what my thoughts are. Have I made myself clear?"

"Once again I apologize, and henceforth I shall phrase my questions so as not to assume that I know when I only think I know, fair enough?"

"Yes, fair enough. Now let us suppose that you were earning $100 per week at a job that was completely displaced, but you have $500 that is not being used in any capacity as an investment. It is money that is not even drawing interest from a savings account. Under this condition you are actually not completely displaced because you have money that could be put to use to help pay for your own guarantee. However, if you don't wish to use this money as an investment, that is your business, and then you will draw from it, each

227

and every week, your $100 until the $500 is exhausted."

"But supposing I don't want to use this money that way. What if I want to spend it all at one time?"

"You can, providing you get a job immediately after you become displaced, paying the same amount of your previous job or more."

"I don't understand. You just got through saying that each person will do what he wants to do, and now you are dictating what must be done."

"This is a short cut. What difference does it make if I show that any other method would result in a hurt, compelling those involved to refrain from it, or if I just dictate what must be done; isn't it all the same?"

"I see what you mean."

"If a displaced person doesn't use money that is not invested to help pay for his own guaranteed income, then he is taking advantage and hurting those whose taxes will be increased. He would actually be stealing. Now if he wants to steal, this is his business, and no one will ever blame or punish him no matter how much it hurts everybody's purchasing power; but if he doesn't want to steal, then he will only be considered displaced when he has no money with which to finance or help finance his own guarantee. To put it another way, each person who gets displaced will be given two alternatives — either spend any non-invested money towards his own guarantee, or else invest it towards the same end. The advantage in investing it lies in the fact that you then have two things going for you that might exceed this income of $100 per week — your own labor and your investment, but if you cannot invest it then you have no choice but to draw your unemployment compensation from it at the rate of your guarantee. Furthermore, if you should get a job that pays only $85 per week, then providing this $500 is still not invested you will continue to draw $15 each week from the $500 to make up the difference. Once the $500 is consumed, then you can start to draw the $15 from the Bureau. If you wish to spend the entire $500 on something you have been saving for while only making $85 per week, $15 short of your guarantee, then you would not be permitted to draw the $15 from the Bureau until 33 a weeks have passed, unless you desire to steal. If you get a job for the same amount or more than your displaced

228

income, then what you do with this $500, for example, doesn't conflict with the desires of those who are compelled to pay when you fall below this amount because no unemployment compensation will be necessary, therefore it is your business and yours only. Certainly you can cheat and steal all you want, but how is it possible to desire hurting the very people who are now doing everything in their power not to hurt you especially when you know they will never blame or punish you no matter how much you hurt them?"

"Not me, I couldn't steal under these conditions in a million years. But tell me, supposing, as an example, a person has $13,000 in a savings account from which he has been deriving 4% interest or 10 dollars a week, and is displaced from a job that was paying him $100. Does this mean that his displaced income would only be $90 per week?"

"Of course not, because his guaranteed income is the amount he was earning at the start of the transition. In this case he was earning $110 per week, but $10 of this amount is not displaced, consequently, this individual would draw $100 in unemployment compensation. If he wishes to spend the source of this $10 income, that is his business, but then this is a voluntary move and there would be no guarantee to replace this $10. By the same reasoning, if someone voluntarily quits his job he is not displaced, and cannot expect to receive unemployment compensation."

"Well supposing the place where he had this money went bankrupt, and he lost his $13,000, what then?"

"He would draw $110 each and every week until he gets another job, and if the job pays less he will draw the difference. But remember, any cash that is not invested must be used towards his guarantee, either by investing or spending it. The same holds true with employees and people in business for themselves who are not displaced. For example, supposing you and several others own a steel mill that employs 10 thousand workers, and your salary is $25,000 per year, which will be guaranteed should you get completely or partially displaced. If you are forced to lay off employees because a decrease in consumption has slowed up production, you needn't fear for these employees because they will receive unemployment compensation just as soon as they have exhausted their surplus cash."

"But if these employees know that they will have to consume their own cash before they can draw this compensation, of what advantage is it for them to hang onto this money?"

"None whatsoever, unless for the purpose of investing it."

"Then if they didn't have a place to invest it, wouldn't they just have a grand time spending it?"

"They certainly would, but this is their business. I know that if there was a possibility of my getting laid off or displaced and I knew that I would have to use my reserve cash towards my own guarantee, I would spend every nickel I had, that is, providing I couldn't increase my income by investing it."

"But what about the employer who is receiving $25,000 per year, what happens when business slackens off?"

"He, like the others, has two alternatives; either consume all his reserve capital to meet his accustomed income, or invest whatever reserve he has for the purpose of trying to meet it. If he doesn't want to sell his business for what he can get out of it, in order to meet his guaranteed income, this is his business, and under those conditions he would have to try and build up his business where he can again receive this amount or more, but if he is forced to close his doors, then he would settle up with his creditors, and if anything is left over it would be used either as an investment towards the $25,000, or it will be spent at the weekly rate towards this guarantee. Once it is consumed or put to use, the difference, or if it was not invested, the entire $480 per week could be drawn in unemployment compensation. Should he still owe some creditors after settling up, instead of having anything left over, we, the balance of the population, will assume this obligation so no one gets hurt. However, you will soon see how everybody will be compelled to desire taking out every conceivable kind of insurance, not to protect them against getting hurt, but to protect others from having to pay. A man going into business will want to get some insurance company to assume the risk of his failing. The insurance company will want to look into the facts, and if everything is agreeable will charge this man a monthly premium to cover the risk. However, if he goes out of business and is unable to pay his creditors after selling his equipment and merchandise for what he can get, then he wouldn't be hurting the people by forcing them to pay his debts because the insurance company will assume his obligations."

"But what if the insurance company doesn't want to assume the risk or only wants to assume part of it, what then?"

"Then this individual will have to think like he never thought before because if his business doesn't succeed and others will be forced to pay his creditors while guaranteeing his income, the realization that he is solely responsible for hurting those who will never blame or punish him in any way is never a source of satisfaction under the conditions. Unless a person can think mathematically, can see that he is not risking a hurt to others, then he had better forgo what he has been contemplating because it is the worst form of punishment imaginable to be excused for doing what he knows is his responsibility while also knowing that the ones who are hurt will never desire to hurt him for doing what he was compelled to do. Well, my friend, was this man compelled to go into business for himself and risk hurting others?"

"If he decided to go, yes he would be compelled."

"That is true, but he may think twice before he does, right?"

"As you explain this I can see where an individual in the world of free will would not mind taking all kinds of risks because there was always some form of justification that he could use to excuse himself. As you stated earlier, if someone borrowed a thousand dollars and was then unable to pay all of it back he just says, 'Sue me for the rest.' But without this advance justification which allowed him to risk hurting others, the price of a hurt is beyond his purchasing power."

"Bravo! That was really wonderful! Perhaps you will let me detonate the fuse yet, that will explode into a magnificent new world.

I am going to demonstrate in a short while why prices must come down to a fantastic degree, but first let me finish showing you what the IBM ledger sheet is used for. Let's assume that our friend contributed to the guarantee an average of $25 a week for 30 years, at which time he retired with $39,000 credited to his account. If the amount of his net guarantee was affected by the fact that he now does not have any children to support, then the new figure, let us say roughly $100 a week, would be sent to him every week as long as he lives. If he should die before using up all of his credit, his wife would draw the $100 a week less the amount to be deducted because of his death. If she dies before it is all used up, the balance would be distributed equally among the surviving children — in their IBM accounts. If a child has passed away, his wife or her husband gets the share. If the spouse is deceased, the children receive it."

Two questions come to mind: "Since there will be no more wills because this is a form of discrimination which was necessary in the world of free will, how is it possible for parents to show partiality when this blames the children for something? And how is it possible to guarantee a businessman his standard of living when competition affects it from week to week?"

To answer your first question, it is true that showing partiality is discrimination and a form of blame. This will be prevented because everything is auctioned off, but if anything is not sold and more than one child claims it, no partiality can be shown as to who should get what. All assets must be distributed equitably. To answer your second question, if a person in business draws a set salary every week and settles the difference once a year, then when he applies for his citizenship the amount of his guarantee and weekly contribution would be based on his figures. If there are any changes, he would estimate the difference because this would affect the amount he contributes, not his guarantee. Once all the owners of a particular business become citizens, the price of what they have been selling whether retail or wholesale can never be increased because this is a hurt for which there would be no blame. Continuing to follow the infallible veracity of our guide, our magic elixir and slide rule that instructs us to remove all forms of blame because this knowledge that we will not be blamed mathematically prevents the desire to do those things for which punishment came into existence, it is necessary to understand that if one penny in purchasing power is taken away from any individual in the entire world, regardless of his wealth, he would be blamed for having too much money. This not only means that everyone throughout this planet will be guaranteed that his income, whatever it is at the start of the transition less taxes, will never be decreased, but also that all prices, including labor, material, and finished products will never be increased. In our present world those

232

who increase prices say to everyone who must pay this difference —
"We, the increasers, have a problem, and it is a shortage of money.
Since we cannot solve this any other way we must blame you for
having what we need as the solution to our problem." But once
everyone is prevented from increasing prices and decreasing incomes
because this is a form of blame, no one can find justification to do so
for how is it humanly possible for you to blame me by increasing my
expenses to live when no one blames you by increasing yours? What
are expenses but somebody's labor. If all prices are guaranteed never
to increase, which includes the cost of labor that is employed at the
start of the transition, how is it possible to increase expenses?
Consequently, once the price of all presently employed labor is never
increased, the cost of living can never go up. By the same reasoning,
the very moment the members of a union become citizens, the cost of
their labor can never be raised. As I indicated, this would displace all
unions but they would be given priority to become citizens, just as
employees would have a priority over employers, manufacturers over
wholesalers and wholesalers over retailers. Remember, the unions are
displaced not only because they blame employers for not paying
enough wages, but also because they try to prevent by force abuses to
employees. The citizens who own a retail business and buy from a
wholesaler or manufacturer would know that the prices to them would
never be increased which removes the justification to increase prices
to the consumer, just as the manufacturer knows that the cost of his
labor and materials will never be raised. This means that every person
in business will be working on a margin of profit that can only go in
one direction — DOWN, and this is what competition and the
guarantee will cause to come about. If a retailer is finding it difficult
to maintain his standard of living, and knows that he cannot come to
us for help until he has exhausted all possibilities, then he is
compelled, of his own free will, to work on a smaller margin of profit.
In other words, he must increase his volume, not his prices. If the
manufacturer and wholesaler are finding it difficult to make ends
meet, they too have only one possibility open — to reduce their prices
to the retailer. If, however, they find it impossible to maintain their
standard of living (the wholesaler, manufacturer and retailer), after
consuming all their reserve cash and reducing their profit to the lowest

possible margin, they may have to look for another job. We (the taxpayers) will give those who are displaced the full amount of their guarantee until they get relocated and can maintain their standard of living. Should they decide to sell their business or turn their operation over to someone who can, this is their business, but if they need our help to carry them through this difficult time, the guarantee will keep them afloat in their time of need. Once the business is sold, the money would be used to pay off their creditors and any outstanding debts and the remainder would be used to maintain their standard of living.

"What if they don't clear enough to pay off their creditors?"

"This would be impossible in the new world because at all times, taking everything into consideration, a citizen, employer or employee, will never bite off more than he knows he can chew. If he does and as a result he or someone else is forced to come to us for help, we would willingly increase the cost of the overall guarantee without blaming him for doing what he knows we must excuse, and he can never justify. Consequently, his accountant will always keep him informed of his credit limitations, unless he can do this himself."

"If someone doesn't like his job, quits, uses up all his cash reserve and then because he can't find a job that he likes comes to us for help or, to put it another way, supposing a businessman whose standard of living is $500 a week net decides to sell his business, take an extended vacation, uses up all his reserve cash and then gets a job paying only $100 a week gross. Are we supposed to supply the difference?"

"Remember, the only time a person can come to us for help with a clear conscience, that is, is when he loses his job or business involuntarily, otherwise, he would be stealing for which he knows he would never be blamed. If a businessman cannot maintain his standard of living after reducing his margin of profit to the smallest possible amount, then he is forced to get out."

"Why couldn't he just lower the wages of his employees, knowing that the difference would be made up by the guarantee?"

"First, because he would be forcing them to use up their reserve cash, and second because he would be stealing from the guarantee. He doesn't have to steal once we are guaranteeing his standard of living, but if he can't make it where he is, then he must get out, assuming that he can earn more elsewhere. If he can't earn more elsewhere, then he would be forced to stay where he is even though he falls below his standard of living which will be made up by the guarantee, because it is less costly to us. If he employs quite a number of people, then getting out prematurely would increase the cost of the guarantee until these people get other comparable jobs. If they can't find jobs, then we must supply the difference."

"Wouldn't it be advisable to subsidize his needs?"

"If he can't sell his products after reducing the profit to the lowest possible margin, then nothing will help him. Besides, we are not going to interfere with economic competition by helping one business, however large or small, rather than another, but we will help all mankind sustain their standard of living."

"Couldn't an employer pay a new employee less than what the job calls for, knowing that the difference would be supplied by the guarantee; and why should it make any difference to the employee whose standard of living is guaranteed?"

"This is a similar question to an earlier one. The employer would be stealing this difference from his employee who would be forced to make up the difference from his IBM office. Nobody will prefer increasing the cost of the guarantee, which means that every displaced person will search for the job that pays the most. If this displaced businessman cannot find a job that meets or exceeds his standard of living, then we would supply the difference."

"What about corporation taxes? A CEO of any major firm would be concerned about how much he would need to contribute."

"This will be estimated weekly and assigned equitably to the IBM accounts of the stockholders as part of their contribution toward the guarantee. In other words, if a corporation is owned by 5 stockholders in this manner (10%, 15, 20, 25, 30%), and the corporate taxes averaged out to $100 a week, then $10, 15, 20, 25, and $30 would be credited to their accounts respectively. At the end of the year, if it was not used, they would receive it back as a profit, which was already explained. It is important to remember that the Bureau of Internal Revenue that now exists will be completely displaced as a collection agency since everyone will be given a golden opportunity to cheat all he wants, but it is not displaced as an organization to keep records of taxes paid in and money paid out. Various functions of government do not require that anybody govern, therefore, though they come under the heading of government, they are not a governing body. Consequently, a citizen will continue to use the last tax schedule before he passed his examination, as this determines how much he can contribute towards the guarantee; but nobody in the government will be checking what he does. As the citizens increase, the people who work for the Bureau of Internal Revenue will decrease in just proportion."

"What's the difference between telling people how much taxes they're supposed to pay, which blames them in advance for not paying, and telling people how they should act in society, which blames them for not acting as they were told. If they are not going to be blamed or punished for not paying the amount of taxes they were told is necessary and they are not going to be blamed or punished for not heeding the advice of our experts, where is the difference?"

There is no mathematical standard as to what is right and wrong in human conduct except this hurting of others, and once this is removed, once it becomes impossible to desire hurting another, then whatever value existed in asking for and giving advice has been permanently done away with. The other is a mathematical standard that clearly shows that should you not pay your share of the taxes you would definitely be hurting the economy for which no one would ever blame you for doing what you are compelled to do. But when your income is guaranteed then there is no way you can justify not paying, and under these conditions it cannot satisfy you to hurt the economy when you know there will be no blame and punishment. Once all the abuses that presently exist in government are completely removed, everyone will desire to pay what he knows and sees is truly for his own benefit. Keep in mind that the new citizen will be told the amount of his taxes, but he will not be blamed or punished should he desire to pay less or none at all. He will know that if he does not pay his share of the taxes he would definitely be hurting the economy. However, because he knows that nobody will blame him for doing what he is compelled to do, no matter how much he cheats, and because he also knows that his own standard of living is guaranteed, he will prefer making sure he does what he judges to be the right thing, since no one else will be judging him.

Right now an employee has a certain amount deducted from his gross salary according to a tax table and at the end of the year he submits a form which includes the deductible items that allow him to get back a refund. This will be changed and everything figured out in advance. The $50 you were paying the government in taxes (covering all kinds) will now be sent to your IBM office and recorded on your ledger sheet as a credit, less the amount you spend for personal government services. You can't expect a person in Maryland to pay for a road being built in California, unless it is part of a national highway. Any service that is not absolutely essential or which you do not wish to continue with will be deducted from the $50 and credited to your account and this difference will be allocated accordingly; a certain amount for the fire and police departments, for garbage collection, for maintenance of a traffic system and street repair, etc. The remaining services of government such as the ones we just mentioned, the Sanitation Department, the Traffic Division, Road Maintenance, Public Schools, etc., would be paid for in the same manner but on a local level. There will be very little left of what we now call government. Each department will have its own budget, and when the first announcement is made, let us say of 2% for the schools, 2% for road maintenance and the traffic division, 1% for garbage collection, 1% for the Fire Department, etc., we would remit the total of these percentages, let us say it was 8%, of the same total gathered together for the quarter.

"Supposing the Bureau of Sanitation is forced to go out of business because of advanced technology, what then?"

These various departments could also become displaced by competitors selling the same service at a much cheaper rate, or a superior service at the same rate. To repeat, we will guarantee each person his income; we will not guarantee his job or business. Many people today have incinerators and garbage disposals; it isn't fair that they should have to share in the cost of the Bureau of Sanitation when they are not using its facilities. Each garbage collection team, at the start of the transition, will have a total number of cans they collect, on an average, each and every week. When this is divided into their weekly income and the other costs of operation, a figure can be arrived at as to how much it costs a family for one can of trash or garbage. If someone wishes to discontinue this service, all he has to do is deduct the cost from his local taxes.

If we have no children or prefer a private school; if we prefer not to use the zoo or park facilities, then we would not send in that particular percent asked for, and this applies to any program that we do not wish to participate in. This would increase the amount we could contribute towards the guarantee. Assuming this amount to be $35, this is what would be recorded on your ledger sheet as a credit and would be used only towards the maintenance of the guarantee. However, this does not stop those who have innovative ideas from getting their own financing, but this has nothing whatever to do with those remaining services of government or the guarantee. If a group of scientists wish to land men on the moon again, this is their business, but the money to pay for it is our business. They might be able to raise enough on a closed circuit TV show by selling tickets in advance, but however they raise this money it cannot be done by force. Each citizen would be responsible to mail in, or drop off, his own contribution once a week which means that an employer pays his employees (those that are citizens) the gross amount. If at the end of a year, after becoming a citizen, you have a balance it would be refunded to you as a profit. If someone got back $520 at the end of the year, then his weekly income would be increased by $10. The total cost of maintaining the IBM offices and the guarantee would be divided up equally among the total number of citizens. If there were 2 billion, and we needed 2 billion dollars for one week, each account would have deducted one dollar. If 3 billion dollars was needed, and 500 million could only contribute one dollar without wiping out their account, then the difference would be divided equally among the 1.5 billion citizens. This means that regardless of how much money a person makes he will pay the same percentage as someone earning a hundred times less.

"If our friend pays in $1820 for the year while someone else pays in $50,000, and should an average of $20 a week be used by these citizens, then the one would get back as a profit $780 while the other would receive $48,960. However, if $49,000 of his fifty thousand was used, our friend could not have contributed more than $1820.

This might be equal, but it is not equitable."

Can you think of another way that doesn't blame an individual for his earnings? How is it possible to charge the one man more money without blaming him for his wealth? Is the rich man supposed to pay more for the use of water than the poor man? We cannot do this once all blame is removed. If you say that one man should pay 90% of his income, and another only 20%, isn't it obvious that one is being blamed for having too much money? Consequently, there is only one solution. Whatever percent is required will be paid by each individual. If 1% is required for week ending such and such, and you earn $100, you will simply send $1. If you earned one million, you would then send $10,000. If you are receiving a displaced income of $100 per week, and the taxes call for 1%, you would simply enter $99 in your record book and send a withdrawal slip to the Bureau with your name and address so that this amount could be acknowledged. Can you think of anything simpler? Certainly a person can cheat if he wants to and nobody will ever be the wiser, except himself, but how is it humanly possible for him to desire cheating when his income is guaranteed never to decrease by the people who now want to help him, and when he knows stealing will hurt these friends who will never blame him for this. It's the same story over and over again. Every week the Bureau in each country will estimate the total income, divide this into the expenses, and then publish this figure as the required taxation. If the tax returns require a little more or a little less, this is a minor thing, and can be adjusted the following week.

If there is not enough money contributed for that week to cover the expense of the guarantee, we will use the next week's contribution, the next and the next. If at the end of a year we show a deficit, then we would divide the amount needed by the total number of citizens, and ask for this contribution. If the amount was 50 billion dollars and we had 2 billion citizens, each would contribute $25 unless this caused some to go below their own guarantee. If so, the difference would be made up by those who could afford it. However, at this point let me show you what actually takes place. You see, money is used for three things — to buy what we need and want, to invest it in order to have still more money to spend, and to invest it for greater leisure and security. Let us now observe the actual transition into the

239

new world which must come about once these principles are understood and applied.

Once the United Nations is convinced that all of you have passed the examination and received your card, a day and time will be set for the great launching of this new world, a holiday declared, and you will excitedly await the countdown. When zero is reached, everything locked will be unlocked, burglar alarms disconnected and floor walkers dismissed, detectives, private eyes, and security guards will be displaced. At the launching of the Golden Age, every possibility of committing a crime will vanish the very moment everything that stands in the way of such an act is removed. Consequently, the military and police forces will retire while their weapons are destroyed, all prisons will be demolished and prisoners, regardless of their crime, will be released with their ticket (card) to freedom and a basic standard of living guaranteed, and no one need have the slightest fear that a crime will be committed especially when all the other forms of tacit blame are also removed. Therefore, everything that tries in some way to prevent the desire of another from being satisfied, or tries in some way to prevent stealing what belongs to another, will be removed because this will mathematically prevent the desire to hurt someone as a consequence of this tacit blame. At the same time the cops get displaced with a guarantee that their income will never stop or decrease, so do the robbers. If someone engaged in unlawful practices was earning an income of $25,000 or $250,000 per year, and because of this transition loses his profession, the bank robbers, the hired killers, etc., will be treated with the same consideration as anyone else who gets displaced, simply because no one is to blame. We are going to make it very easy for every potential thief to steal and cheat all he wants but there will be no possibility he will ever commit another crime under the new conditions, although nothing will be stopping him. Think about this very carefully. Is it possible for a potential criminal to use a gun for a hold-up when nothing is going to stand in his way of taking anything he wants, without force?

When it comes time to pay our quarterly taxes, the government accountants will announce the percent estimated, and if 10% is required, and our guarantee is $300, 400, 500, 1000, 2000, 3000, etc., we would multiply 13 times the figure on our card, and remit

10% of the total regardless of how much money we earned for that quarter. If the percent required puts us below our guarantee, we would send in what does not put us below. If any nation is unable to meet its own guarantee, the amount needed would be submitted to the United Nations who would announce the percent required. Is it becoming easier to understand why there is really no further need for government, a group of people to tell you what you can and cannot do? Let me explain this in still another way.

Supposing a television repair man in business for himself has discovered that he cannot earn enough to meet his standard of living. Since he cannot increase prices to solve his problem, he must lower prices. This will cause his competitors to lose business and lower prices to maintain their standard of living. On the other hand, even if he is having no problem maintaining his standard of living but would like to improve it, since he can never raise prices he is compelled to lower prices and sell in volume which forces his competitors to do the same thing. This means that just as long as there are enough people to buy what he is selling so that he can still earn more and take less from us (the taxpayers) than if he changed his job or business, he is forced to remain at what he is doing unless he is willing to risk the possibility of reducing his own standard of living. For example, if he is receiving from us $200 a week to maintain his $500 standard, but sees an opportunity to earn $600 to $1000 a week by changing jobs, this is his business and his gamble, but if he should fail and therefore need help from us the most he would be entitled to is the $200 we were giving him before he made his change. In the event this was not made clear, we are guaranteeing the standard of living derived from the particular job or business a person has when becoming a citizen. This means that if any individual quits his job, sells his business, changes his investment or leaves his country to take other employment, this is a voluntary move unless he is forced to do so in order to take less from us. Therefore the risk is his because this is something he is doing to himself, not something beyond his control. This prevents him from gambling at the taxpayer's expense, although he can if he wants to risk the possibility of lowering his own standard of living because should he get laid off or displaced from his new job, he will have to settle for the basic standard until he can find other work. Let me clarify this even more. In such an event as in our previous example, he would be entitled to take $500 a week, but if by lowering his prices and selling in volume he is able to earn again $300 per week (as in the example given), then we would only have to give him $200. He would therefore be compelled to stay in that business just as long as his leaving doesn't risk making it worse for himself. His conscience would not allow him to do anything that would make it worse for us because he knows we must excuse what he can never justify under the changed conditions. It is important to clarify that we are not giving someone in business money to stay in business. We would be giving him money to sustain his guarantee which he would be entitled to if he was forced to close his doors permanently. It is taken for granted that it will be impossible for him to derive any satisfaction in doing what is wrong because there would be no blame or punishment, which means that the solution is to show him what is right at the time he takes his examination; and the line of demarcation is mathematically drawn. He could cheat us if he wants to because we are not going to check on his honesty, but he cannot find greater satisfaction in doing this when he knows that we would never blame him even if we knew. Should this be done, however, and reported to us, we would investigate without blame, just as we would investigate why a citizen is not paying back his creditor in accordance with the terms agreed upon. The very fact that the investigation would only reveal to the citizen doing this that we must turn the other cheek prevents him from doing anything that might cause an investigation. But the investigation is necessary just in case someone becomes mentally incapable of continued control by the guarantee and the principles of the examination. Anytime a citizen would hurt somebody physically, or give a command to hurt others, we would know immediately that he is sick and would commit him to a hospital until he is able to resume his normal life. We would do the same if a dog was to bite somebody — take him off the streets. However, even though it is very unlikely that a citizen would become mentally sick under the changed conditions, we would be prepared for any eventuality. Should this be the case his family would have to assume responsibility for him, but no one would blame or punish him in any way even if it was necessary to confine him to an institution for treatment. It is important to remember that when all the sources of hurt in society are permanently removed, mental illness will be virtually wiped from the face of the earth.

It is crucial to understand that we, as citizens, can no longer be told that we must pay taxes or else suffer the consequences. This means that the forceful collection of taxes and the filling out of forms to check on our honesty has come to an end. However, not to pay taxes at all is a first blow when our income is above the standard of living recorded as our guarantee, which means that once we are satisfied that our tax share cannot be more equitable, our desire to contribute this amount is controlled by two factors. One is our realization that the guarantee removes the need for any citizen to hurt us in order to prevent himself from going below his standard of living or from being without the necessaries of life because these are the laws of self-preservation. Two is our realization that we have it in our power to force other citizens to pay our share without their knowledge, which means that we would be gaining at their expense. When we fully realize that they would not blame us even if they knew we were taking advantage, it becomes impossible for us to find greater satisfaction in not contributing our share. This new method of contribution, not taxation, will displace the Bureau of Internal Revenue and everybody connected with the collection of taxes, but only in proportion to the increase in new citizens. Let me review, so once again pay close attention.

Since to increase taxes in any way, shape, or form is a first blow as is raising prices and striking for higher wages, taxes will never be increased, only decreased, and the percentages we were paying when non-citizens will continue as a guide. Therefore, since no one henceforth will ever again collect our taxes it should be obvious that the next step is to keep our own quarterly record of the total amount of money we would have paid the government had it been collected for us. In other words, if our employer was withholding $650 for the quarter which included state, city and social security taxes, he would pay us our gross income each week and we would deduct our expenses for the quarter because there will be no refunds (let us say as an example $150), and then record $500. If our property taxes for the year are $840, we would record one-fourth or $210 for the quarter.

The seller will see that we are citizens by our identification card and will not include any sales tax but will list it on our receipt for our record. If we spent $800 for a 3 month period, and the sales tax was 4%, we would record $32 plus any other excise taxes. This same procedure applies to corporations and includes every form of tax, fee or license paid to the government. At the end of a quarter we are going to need money to finance the guarantee, but this is very easily solved since the accounting department of each state will compute how much is required for that quarter, and all the states combined will submit their figures which computes the total for the nation. If there are any nations that cannot meet their own guarantee after consuming all their reserve cash the amount needed would be submitted to the office that computes the total for the world.

We shall assume that after everybody got displaced whose manner of earning a living was not needed any longer, and allowing for many of those in transition as well as the people who are using their reserve cash to finance themselves while looking for new employment, it was estimated that 20% of the total taxes recorded for the quarter would be needed to support the guarantee, which means that an announcement of 20% would be made to all taxpayers throughout the earth, and if our quarterly total was $100, $200, $300, $400, $1000, $2000, $3000, $4000, etc., we would remit 20% of our total. However, this first announcement must be an estimate which means that it could be over or under the total amount required. Therefore, when the quarterly amount is received and totaled up we would know immediately that 80% remains, and if we were short we would know exactly what additional percent to ask for in the second announcement. If we were over, it would be held in reserve for the next quarter. However, there is a much simpler and more equitable way of financing the guarantee. I will explain this shortly. The rest of government would be like a private self-sustaining corporation, working on a profit or loss. If the head of the Post Office finds that business is falling off, and to meet expenses this necessitates laying some workers off, he will lay them off. And if business picks up again to where he needs additional help, he will advertise for it. But if he feels this slump is just temporary and has the reserve to carry their salaries, then he doesn't have to lay anybody off. This will apply to the head of each department but in conjunction with the overall expenses and profit.

"Do you mean that the head of each department has the right to fire someone if he wants to?"

"If he wants to, yes, but how is it possible to want to when this would have to necessitate someone doing something wrong, which word only means 'hurt somebody else.' Once it is mathematically impossible to hurt another, there is no way anybody can do something wrong."

The very moment someone becomes a citizen he will pay his taxes in the manner just described, but the government (the remaining group of individuals who coordinate this effort) will only make an announcement if the money already in its possession and received from non-citizens is inadequate. If the government has enough cash reserve to cover its expenses for the first quarter, which includes the guarantee, citizens will be told that what they recorded for the quarter is a total profit. Once the second announcement is made to let us know one way or the other whether more or no more is needed, the remaining money in our possession for that quarter becomes a tax profit which we can spend or invest as each of us desires. The simpler and more equitable way of contributing our share is to keep only two records. One is already recorded when we become citizens; it is our guarantee or net standard of living. The other is to record our job expenses for the quarter which is the amount of money we spend to earn our gross income for the quarter. Let me explain in greater detail.

If you are earning $300 per week which is $3900 for the quarter; and if your job expenses are $20 per week or $260 for the quarter; and if your guarantee is $150 per week or $1950 for the quarter; then you deduct $1950 from the $3900 which leaves $1950 and then deduct the $260 from the $1950 which leaves a balance of $1690. This doesn't change the amount needed to sustain the guarantee and our other taxes but does change the percent needed. If it is estimated that 5% is what we need, then this is the announcement that is made. This system cannot be more equitable. It doesn't blame us for anything, doesn't tell us what must be done or else, and if we don't want to send in our share, this is our business, but we will know that what we don't pay will be picked up by the rest of the taxpayers on the second announcement which means that we would be gaining at the expense of those who would not blame us even if they knew. Move in this direction if it is possible to derive greater satisfaction, especially when you know that should you ever need money to sustain your own standard of living we would not hesitate to help you. Now let me show you some of the most fantastic changes that must come about for the benefit of all mankind as a result of the guarantee and basic principle. Observe next how the money to improve our standard of living increases still more by the fact that prices are forced to come down.

At the present time the installment buyer does not have the kind of credit that allows the merchant to charge him a smaller rate of interest for a lesser risk because he doesn't have the money to pay cash, so he has to pay at a very high price for the things he wants. But when his income is guaranteed, and when it is impossible for him to desire hurting others in any way, he will then be in a position to borrow the money to buy what he wants at a much smaller rate of interest. Since money lenders can no longer discriminate against any citizen who comes to them for a loan because they know he has impeccable credit under the changed conditions since not to pay it back in accordance with the terms agreed upon would be a hurt for which he knows he would never be criticized, he needn't pay higher rates of interest to the small loan companies and higher prices to the installment houses because he can borrow and buy at the source that charges the least. Therefore, since these small loan companies and installment houses who are charging higher prices and rates of interest must do everything in their power to sustain their own standard of living before coming to us for help, they are given no choice but to lower their interest and prices in order to compete with the department stores, discount houses, and the banks.

"But wouldn't this hurt the installment houses when these people start buying from the discount houses and the department stores?"

Of course not, because these merchants are also guaranteed their income, so if they cannot compete they will just be forced to go out of business and get in something else. But first they must try to come down in their prices to sustain their own standard of living

246

before coming to us for help, which will give the consumer more spending money, increase production and employment, reduce the amount of money needed to sustain the guarantee and therefore increase our spending money all the more. But if after reducing their prices and interest they are forced to go below their standard of living, their conscience would still not allow them to get out of the business they're in as long as by reducing their interest and prices still more, they would hurt us less. For example, if someone in business with a standard of living of $500 a week has discovered that he is $200 short of the mark, he can take this amount from the guarantee, but if he cannot find a new job or business that pays more than $300 towards his guarantee of $500, he would be forced to stay where he is because the money we would have to give him would be less. Even if this means that he must reduce his prices ridiculously low to meet his own standard of living and lessen the amount he needs to take from us, this is what he must do to avoid hurting those who will never blame him. Besides, even if an installment house wanted to stay in business, which it can do under changed conditions, the company must give up knocking at people's doors to collect or sell, for this blames them for not paying and not buying.

"How is a creditor supposed to get his money when he doesn't make an effort to collect it?"

When a debtor fails to pay what he owes on the day it is due, or within the time allowed, the creditor will draw what is due him from the Bureau and send a record of this also to his debtor, which means that the people who pay the taxes will be hurt by this additional tax. Since a debtor cannot find any satisfaction in hurting the very people who guaranteed his income, the very people who refuse to blame or punish him for any hurt he does to them, he is given no choice under these conditions but to desire paying all his bills when they are due and desire not to buy anything his income cannot afford. Banks and financial institutions will still exist to sell their services. These places are no different than any other place of business that has something to sell, consequently, if you need a certain amount of money (what you need it for is strictly your business) you would simply walk in, look at the rates of interest and the limits that are displayed conveniently (how it is to be paid back), put your name, address and amount you are borrowing on plan number so and so, record the amount you borrowed in your book, and just put this form in a drawer designed for that purpose. It isn't necessary to talk to anyone. The buyer or borrower is compelled to keep the records where he can't forget his monthly payment because he knows that no one will ever blame him if he never pays back a single dime. In our present circumstances you are always compelled to ask for credit and loans which are refused, but under the new conditions it is impossible to tacitly blame the seller by asking for credit because you know he is there to move merchandise, and the very moment you know you are able to buy what he has, a sale is consummated without any forms or contracts to be signed since the seller knows, just as certain as two plus two equals four, that it will be impossible for you to buy what he has without paying for it when you know that he will never blame you in any way should you not. When the payments come due you just mail a slip to the lender, who will acknowledge receipt of this, and deduct what you paid from your book. By failing to pay the amount due, the owner or owners of this business will draw the amount past due from the Bureau and send a record of this to you and the Bureau. This would increase taxes — hurting everyone. Under the new conditions it is impossible to be dishonest not only because you know you will never be blamed no matter how much you hurt another by stealing his property, but also because every person alive will recognize in the Great Transition about to take place an undeniable benefit for himself. Remember, you are perfectly free to cheat, steal, rob, kill, do anything you want to do without any fear of being blamed or punished because it is now known that man is compelled to do everything he does, but how is it humanly possible to desire cheating when you know that no one will ever ask you for an accounting of your little record book, when you will know whether you are cheating which knowledge that you will never be blamed no matter what you do mathematically prevents any possibility of justification which is absolutely necessary for satisfaction? It is mathematically impossible for any person to desire taking advantage of not being blamed because it is definitely not to his advantage. Because no one will get satisfaction in stealing, the rates of interest will be forced to come down because everybody who has money to lend, as a financial investment, will not hesitate to do so under these circumstances. You might read in the paper, 'Ten thousand dollars available for immediate use for 1 year, at the rate of 3% interest.' Do you realize what this security means for the entire world? Billions of dollars will be available for people who can think in terms of sound investments. For example, supposing a scientist or inventor knows, beyond a shadow of doubt, or within a reasonable amount of doubt, that if he had x number of dollars he could make a fortune for himself. He then approaches an insurance company who is also sold on the idea and who is willing to insure this venture against any losses that would hurt the people by increasing their taxes. When he gets this insurance, the premium to be included in the cost of operation, all he has to do is look for a bank or other company that advertises the kind of money he needs for his project, and simply borrow it. This will allow the greatest economic growth imaginable.

Everything henceforth will be a cash transaction. If you want to buy a refrigerator, television, house, food, or what have you, but you do not have a sufficient amount of cash, you either borrow the money from the business selling the merchandise, to pay for it, or else you borrow it from another source. If you want a car, and it sells for $2500, you either borrow the money from some financial institution at a specific rate of interest and time limit, or you borrow it from the people who manufacture and sell the cars. Your choice, obviously, is in the direction of least interest and better terms. If a small businessman doesn't have this extra money to lend for the purpose of making an additional profit on the sale of his own merchandise, then the people who want what he sells must borrow the money to pay for it from another source. This will displace many more people who keep records of accounts receivable. The retailer who buys from the wholesaler and manufacturer also pays cash. If he doesn't sell the merchandise he buys and then can't pay back the money he borrowed to pay for his inventory, there is no difference between this and any other loan. If he thinks there is a risk and that he might hurt the people who will have to pay for his losses, he will be compelled to find an insurance company to guarantee this loss at such and such a premium because he can't stand the thought of hurting those who refuse to hurt him under any conditions. Henceforth, all carelessness where someone can prevent another from being hurt is being permanently removed. However, many manufacturers will insure the wholesaler and retailer against being stuck with merchandise that isn't selling. The risk for the insurance companies will be so small that they will make a tremendous profit, while the money lenders will take no risk whatsoever. The insurance companies, knowing they would never be blamed for biting off more than they can chew, will be compelled to restrict themselves within limits they can handle or else get other insurance companies to insure them. The same principle works the same way no matter what company it is. Should a breadwinner lose his job or be laid off after his children have shifted for themselves, and needs money to keep up, his standard of living would be his original guarantee less his expenses to support them. If a breadwinner dies without adequate coverage he will force the people to continue his salary, less what it cost himself to live, until his children are grown. Should he die, so does his standard of living, but his wife if not working, unable to find a job, without any cash reserve and unable to meet her needs, can come to us for financial assistance. But she will be under constant pressure to find some kind of employment or a new husband because her conscience will not allow her to increase the cost of the guarantee and make the taxpayer support her and her children if she feels able to work. Naturally she doesn't have to get a job unless she wants to, and nobody will ever blame or criticize her decision not to get one, but when she realizes that her not doing what she is capable of results in a serious hurt to the very people who refuse to hurt her under any conditions whatsoever, then she is given no choice if capable of doing some kind of work. When she locates a job her standard of living will be derived from it and is her guarantee thereafter. Men were worried that their death might cause undue hardship for their families, but this becomes impossible under the guarantee. However, if one wishes to invest part of his income on life insurance so that his wife will not have to go to work after his death, this is his business, but remember the total amount of money she receives must be used on a weekly basis to meet her current needs because the guarantee will supply her with the same amount when it runs out. She may be left enough so that she will never have to look for a job, but this money cannot be used to improve her standard of living unless it can be done without making it necessary to come to us for financial help. But if this income does not allow her to meet her previous bills, she may use the guarantee to make up the difference as long as necessary. If her husband doesn't want her to work after his death, can afford the luxury of sufficient insurance coverage, and doesn't want the people to be burdened with an expense he can prevent, then he is given no choice but to take out the necessary insurance to cover this. This means that life insurance takes on an altogether different meaning by being bigger than ever before. He also will desire to be insured in case of an automobile accident, airplane crash, fire, etc. (although accidents will be virtually nonexistent) or anything that might end up costing the people money, such as an inadequate income and savings to pay for hospitalization. If after doing everything in his power to prevent the people from being hurt by his neglect and carelessness, they should still be hurt by having to pay bills that he incurred, then at least he will know that it was definitely not his responsibility. But not to be blamed by the very people he hurts when he knows it is his responsibility is an unbearable form of punishment, which compels him to do everything in his power to prevent this situation from arising.

OTHER CHANGES

For the purpose of simplicity, this section is in a question and answer format.

"What will the age of retirement be?"

After the transition is launched a person can retire according to the age and income specified by his country without taking money from the guarantee to do so because this is a voluntary move unless he is unable to work any longer. This voluntary move is not like the voluntary move that a person makes when he quits his job, for then he would be stealing if he took money from the taxpayers. Should he decide to continue working after reaching a retirement age because his employer and conscience find his work satisfactory, this is his business, which means that if he does this until he becomes

251

permanently unable to handle any kind of job he would then come under his original guarantee which is affected by his children shifting for themselves. Should he retire voluntarily at the specified age and receive a pension, he can add to this by finding work he can handle. However, when he cannot even handle this any longer, he would just receive money from his retirement plan. What he chooses to do when he reaches a retirement age is his business. It is important to remember that whatever you are doing at the time the transition gets under way, providing you are not displaced, plays an active role in the economy which means that if you left your position without getting a replacement you would be hurting someone who would never blame you for this hurt, consequently freezing you to your job. Under the new conditions it makes no difference what type of work you are presently doing because every job will acquire an increased amount of purchasing power, even if it is a butler, maid, etc., because you will no longer be judged inferior due to your type of work.

All the people who are receiving unemployment compensation or welfare have a decision to make. They can continue to get the same amount as long as they are unable to find work, but once they find employment the amount they were receiving then becomes their guarantee which means that should they ever lose that job and need our help because they cannot finance themselves or locate another job, they can use the money that was originally given to them as long as necessary. However, if they prefer to estimate their standard of living from the first job they get after they become citizens, then they will be placed immediately under the guarantee and be forced to use up all their reserve cash to finance themselves before continuing to receive the same assistance. Should they not have any reserve cash and not be able to find employment, we will give them the same amount they were receiving. But once they find a job and estimate their standard of living there from, that figure will be the one guaranteed should they ever need our assistance. This also applies to those people who are already retired when the transition begins. Correction: This does not apply to retired people. You must bear in mind that mistakes can be made in extending the principles but this does not in any way affect the principles. This kind of mistake is equivalent to one a teacher might make when telling his students that traveling in a car at the speed of 50 m.p.h. you would reach a destination of 250 miles in 5 hours and 10 minutes. If he was corrected and saw his mistake, he would just acknowledge it as I just did. There might be other similar mistakes but they are of no consequence because every extension can be tested and proven in an undeniable manner.

All citizens will know that the money to finance the guarantee must come only from those of us who are in a position to improve our standard of living from this same money if it was not needed, which means that if they take advantage of the guarantee, take money that they are not entitled to, they would know they are depriving us of using what we would prefer spending on ourselves. But, as has been explained throughout this chapter, when they fully realize that this would be a hurt to the very people who are guaranteeing that they will never go below their standard of living, and never blame them regardless of what they do, their conscience would deny them from moving in this direction for greater satisfaction. Consequently, they would be perfectly willing to have someone in the office where they are applying for their guarantee if they are the least bit doubtful of what they are doing, to show them whether or not they are taking advantage. This means, as an example, that if a displaced person has a standard of living of $200 per week, $50 from an investment and $150 from a job, but has $800 in reserve cash (non-invested money that has nothing to do with the $50 a week and could be used to improve his standard of living if he was not displaced) then this money becomes the source of his $150 a week until he consumes it or finds a new job. To use this money for any other purpose takes advantage of the guarantee which means that before he can spend or invest it with a clear conscience to improve his standard of living, he must find a job that pays at least $150 a week. If he can only find one that pays less than this amount, and still has reserve cash, he has two choices; either to reduce his standard of living to the new income which then releases his reserve cash to spend or invest as he pleases or else to retain his standard of living and replace the difference from his reserve cash until it runs out, at which time he can take from us. It should be obvious that what a person chooses to do is determined by the amount of his reserve cash, his standard of living, and how much less the new job pays. If it pays $145 a week when his standard of living is $150, and he has $25,000 in reserve or non-invested money, he might not wish to tie it up to supply himself with the $5 a week; consequently, he could set his new standard at $145 a week and release this money with a clear conscience. But when it is used up one way or another and he should get laid off or displaced, his guarantee is then $145. By the same reasoning, the $50 a week from his investment is also guaranteed. If something should happen to cause him to earn less than this in dividends, and he has no cash reserve, he can make up the difference from his guarantee; but if he chooses to reinvest or spend a portion of the principal from which is derived this $50 a week, then he again chooses to lower the amount we were guaranteeing. This also applies to someone who chooses to work fewer hours to earn less than his standard of living. If he was putting in 40 hours to earn $150 (this is the net amount of his standard of living), and then got a new job putting in the same amount of hours to earn the same amount of money, then he is meeting his guarantee; but if he decides to earn less by working 30 hours, this is his business, only he is not entitled to the difference from the guarantee because this is a voluntary move not something that was forced upon him or beyond his control. Furthermore, if someone receiving a guarantee of $132 per week for 40 hours took a new job that required him to put in longer hours to meet his guarantee, then anything over the 40 hours would be an additional income. In other words, if he put in 50 hours to earn this $132 when he was receiving $3.30 an hour for 40 hours, then he is actually earning at this new job $2.64 an hour or $105.60 for the week. Since his guarantee calls for $132 for a 40 hour week, he is still entitled to draw $26.40 from his IBM office because this is the amount by which he is still displaced. He would actually be earning for the week $158.40, but he put in ten hours extra to do it. If he feels that his reserve cash will run out before he finds a job, then he is under pressure to do everything in his power to locate one before it does, otherwise, he would be taking advantage of the guarantee. He must also go in the direction of what covers his guarantee regardless of the type of work available not in the direction of what is easier to do, otherwise, if he chooses what pays less because it is easier when what pays more though harder is available then he chooses to lower his standard of living accordingly unless he prefers to take advantage of

254

the guarantee at our expense for which he knows he will never be blamed.

Even employers are prevented from taking advantage. If they paid him less, when the particular job calls for more because they know he can make up for the difference, they would be gaining at his and our expense which they cannot find satisfaction in doing under the new conditions. But if the new job requires a certain amount of training and they find that he is not entitled to the full salary during this period then the difference would be supplied by him if he has the reserve cash, or he can take it from us. Once he finishes his training and is able to support his own standard of living he would be in a position to help finance the guarantee and share the other expenses of government he uses.

"What about the people who knock at doors and solicit by phone to make their living?"

This is really not an annoyance to those who buy, but it is to the ones who are weeded out in the process. All forms of advance blame are coming to an end. When a solicitor knocks at your door, telephones you, or approaches you directly on the street to buy or donate, he is actually judging that you can afford what he is engaged in and assumes you are interested; therefore, he is striking the first blow. If you decide not to drop a coin in his can, to close the door or hang up the phone without listening to what he has to say, you are blamed. Consequently, all those who earn their living by contacting people directly will have to resort to some indirect method of advertising what they have (once they become citizens) because they will never be blamed for any punishment imposed as a means of getting what they want. Knowing in advance they are wrong, they will no longer be able to justify some form of retaliation by making it appear they are right. Even inside of a store, the people who work there will wait for the potential buyer to make the first contact because he may just be looking around. In other words, if A, the salesperson, approaches B, he is expressing his desire to sell something without considering the possibility that B does not want to be annoyed. Ironically enough, sales will soon increase all over the world, but without salespeople. This means that all direct selling and canvassing become obsolete, all retail stores will have assistants to offer their services when needed, all wholesalers will employ buyers to contact the manufacturers for the purpose of buying, not selling, while retailers will employ buyers to contact the wholesalers and manufacturers. A buyer knows that a seller has something to sell, but a seller doesn't know that the various buyers around the earth want what he has. To knock at a door for the purpose of trying to sell something, blames people in advance for not buying it, which is the case when a salesman walks in to see a merchant. But when merchandise is displayed or advertised, and this arouses the desire of an individual who then approaches the seller, this is a horse of another color. Therefore, advertising will become bigger than ever, and more competitive, but knowing that they can easily hurt a person by false statements, for which there will be no blame or punishment, the advertisers are prevented from taking advantage of their freedom because there is no advantage when someone can get hurt for which there is no blame. This means that buyers will always travel to see the sellers, never the other way around, and advertising which is an indirect medium of contacting potential buyers will be used very heavily. We are not going to tell anyone how to advertise their products (who is anyone to tell a businessman and advertiser what is best for themselves), but just in case they cannot compete and are forced out of business we will guarantee their income from ever decreasing whether they stay in business or are forced out; but if they want to make more money then they will have to use their ingenuity to figure out ways and means to solve their own problem. If they can't knock at someone's door without blame then the only alternative is to advertise their goods in a manner that attracts attention. If it then appeals to people in the neighborhood, the consumers will approach them. This new world will not deprive anyone of incentive or initiative and will place no limits on the capacity of an individual, although everyone will be prevented from moving in the direction of hurting others. A businessman might think up all sorts of ways to advertise or display his wares for the purpose of attracting buyers, and the only limit to his thinking is this desire to hurt others which has now been prevented. Advertising companies will be absolutely certain

256

that what they say on the air, in the newspapers, magazines, etc., is the truth and nothing but the truth. If there is proof that a certain product causes a particular form of cancer they will let it be known, but if it is not, if it is just an association, then the Cancer Society had better do much more research before it terrifies the public without any justification.

"What about litigation over contractors not living up to the terms of an agreement?"

Everything will still be in black and white so both parties to an agreement will be aware of the terms but now instead of a contractor trying to conceal anything he makes absolutely sure that everything is revealed and thoroughly understood because he cannot find any satisfaction in not living up to what he promised, for which he would never be blamed. He would explain very carefully the differences in materials and their cost, but he would never have to worry about getting paid because if the customers want work to be done they will borrow the money if it is available, or arrange other terms with the contractor.

"Isn't the censoring of films engaged in blame?" What about the professional critic? Isn't this profession also engaged in blame, and if these people are displaced isn't this going to hurt a lot of people by denying them the right to continue criticizing those who are different than themselves?"

To answer the first question, yes, the censoring of films is engaged in blame and it gets displaced. There is no way a film or play about sex can hurt a citizen or cause him to hurt others. The professional critic will also be completely displaced, just as all beauty contests will be. Being unable to criticize others is not a genuine hurt. He is not being denied if he wishes to continue, but of course we know that he will not be able to. The critic strikes the first blow unless the person criticized has done something to hurt him. If he has not, then the critic cannot possibly have any justification when all advance blame is removed. You must understand that in the new world all forms of blame must be removed because man's will is not free. When the professional critic realizes that his criticism is a hurt for which he will never be blamed he will desire, of his own free will (as will a person engaged in holding beauty contests), to change his job. How is it possible to have such a contest when each person's physiognomy is exactly equal in value except to certain individuals, and how is it possible to use one person's likes and dislikes as a standard to judge that what they desire less is an inferior production of the human race, unless words like beautiful and ugly make it appear that certain differences are of greater value intrinsically? The producers will advertise their show and of those who see it some will like it others will not, but no criticism will be possible. If more people like it and as a consequence the producer makes a profit, this is his business; if less consumers like it and he loses, this is also his business.

"What about the method that is used to keep children from watching certain movies, television shows, and listening to certain music? It seems that there would have to be some kind of restriction on pornographic literature, pictures, and television shows, especially since you can't keep children from watching."

This will be answered in the chapter on parents and children.

"Can the problem of pollution be solved?"

Once all advance blame, this judging of what is right for others, comes to an end, every citizen becomes responsible for his own contribution towards eliminating this evil that affects everyone's health and the world's ecosystem. The person who drives a car will make sure that his exhaust has been reduced to its lowest point, as with all the other forms of personal pollution. The factories, not only because they are in competition and wish to find better ways of competing but also because they are not being blamed, will do everything humanly possible to correct this condition which is a part of our standard of living. At the same time this is going on, science, those men and women who are searching for solutions to forms of hurt that affect all mankind equally, such as pollution, will let us know how much money is needed to cover the cost of research, and all of us who can afford to will desire to contribute toward this on an equal basis. If 100 million dollars was needed and we had 2 billion citizens, each person would contribute $1.

"Will there be liability insurance and hospitalization?"

Insurance premiums and interest rates will come down to such a degree because of the guarantee that everybody will be able to afford both, and the applicants will never be questioned as to their ability to pay. Since a citizen cannot afford to be careless when he knows there will be no blame, he will continue to carry no fault insurance which covers any hurt to himself. For instance, if a deer darts out in front of his car and causes him to have a collision with another citizen, no one would be responsible therefore each driver's no fault insurance would take care of his own damages.

"But supposing he ran into the car of a non-citizen?"

All non-citizens must operate their vehicles according to the laws of their city or state which means they must carry liability insurance just in case they were at fault; or if the insurance companies have agreed among themselves to do away with this kind of coverage since it is on its way out, some kind of insurance would be taken out to take care of the damage to their own car. If this happens to be a form of deductible insurance, and the citizen admits he was at fault even though the deer caused it, then he would pay the amount deducted. If his own insurance company did not cover all the damages, and he did not have enough cash reserve, then he knows that we would give him the money to cover the cost. Since he is well aware of this, for which he knows he would never be blamed, he will never again take any chances when driving a car.

"What about his wife and children driving the car?"

If any children are not citizens, they will be living in the world of free will and come under the laws of their country. Once they become citizens, they assume responsibility for themselves. As for a wife, she and her husband must become citizens at the same time and until they both pass their examination they are not citizens unless someone will assume responsibility for them. As for hospitalization insurance, it is all the same. When a citizen is displaced and needs our help, we assume all coverage.

"How does the guarantee affect marriage?"

All the laws that tried to bind couples together will become obsolete, and they will become immediately divorced upon passing their examination, but they will be prevented from hurting each other by the most powerful laws in the universe — the basic principle, Thou Shall Not Blame. If the man desires to leave and not support his wife and children who are dependent on him, he knows no one will hold him responsible, but he will not get satisfaction from shirking what is his responsibility under these conditions. Spouses will be free to leave each other if they can do this after all advance blame has been removed, and knowing they will never be blamed or criticized no matter how much hurt is involved. If either or both have been committing adultery, this is their business, but when the ones who are hurt fully realize that it is within their power to prevent this hurt from continuing now that the other party (the other half of the equation) also understands the principles, all those striking a first blow will be given no choice but to stop — of their own free will. In many instances, couples who are on the verge of divorce will no longer want to leave the other once the principles relating to marriage are applied because the very things that caused arguments and led to their wanting a divorce will no longer be present. But if in spite of this the marriage cannot be salvaged, every divorced and single person who becomes a citizen will have their age and other information recorded in their IBM office for the purpose of bringing people interested in marriage together. Because they will never desire to leave each other once the principles are practiced, all widows, widowers, divorced, separated and single people will have an opportunity to find lasting love, and will be given every opportunity to meet. All this will be explained in the chapter on marriage.

"How will the population be controlled since people will not die of unnatural causes? Where is man going to build his house when there isn't any more room, and how is he going to feed his family when there is a food shortage; and since you said that nobody can tell another what to do, can everybody have just as many children as they want?"

At the rate the population is increasing and with no more wars, no automobile accidents, and no sickness to take our lives prematurely the earth will soon be too small to feed, clothe, and shelter everybody. If you are earning at present $100 per week, you cannot afford to support eight children. Having this many children in the new world, with that kind of an income, would definitely hurt the taxpayers because they would have to supply your family with what you are unable to give them. And since it cannot satisfy you to hurt them when you know they will never blame or criticize whatever you do, you are given no choice but to bring into the world the number of children you know positively you can adequately support. Consequently, since money is related to what you can buy with it, and since there is a limit to what can be produced, there will exist in the International Bureau of Welfare, a group of scientists and lawyers from each nation who, like parents guiding their children without blame, will recommend what is required to sustain and improve the world's standard of living, such as how many offspring a couple should aim for. They will announce periodically the value of your dollar in relation to the raising of one, two, three, four children, etc. If, after checking these figures you can see that all you can afford is one child, unless you hurt others, are you given any choice when you know you will never be blamed or punished? Science will actually govern Earth, but without telling one person what he must do. If the scientists determine that the population on earth is beginning to get crowded they will announce this, and the very fact that you will never be blamed for this overcrowding which hurts the economy will compel you of your own free will to desire limiting your family in accordance with what is best for everyone. The total needs of the economic system would determine the amount of the population and all this would be included in the general information given to the public so each person could decide for himself the direction which is better for him to take. Let me remind you that this does not stop a husband and wife from having six children if they want to but when they know there will be no criticism should this not be heeded, and knowing that this is a hurt to the economy for which there will be no blame, they will prefer staying within the limits recommended by the law for fear they might be responsible for hurting those whom they know must excuse what cannot be justified. For example, there may be an announcement that in order to control the present population couples must not have any more than two children, however, there will be no punishment should they violate this. But they will know that to increase the population beyond what is advisable is a serious hurt for which there will be no criticism, which denies them from moving in that direction for greater satisfaction. However, if they can afford it they can have more than two children if they locate a couple who cannot have any or only want one. This will be an agreement between these two couples. Another option would be for a couple who has made the decision to have one child or none to report this to their IBM office and the difference could be made up by those who want more. No partiality would be shown so if there were more applicants than slots to be filled, a method would have to be devised to determine which families would be chosen. Should the conditions change due to other factors in the world economy, a confirming investigation by scientists would bring to the public's awareness the necessity of raising or lowering the number of children to be born by each family for the benefit of all mankind. What is so fantastic is the fact that at the very moment all premature deaths are reduced to an absolute minimum which increases the overall population tremendously, we are compelled, but of our own *unfreely free will*, to desire to control the birth rate to meet whatever conditions may arise. Abortion, on the other hand, if you have followed the principles, is nobody's business but the mother's. But in the new world all the factors responsible for becoming pregnant with an unwanted child will be permanently removed. The Catholic religion had no choice in teaching what was and is still being taught, because it was God's will, but it is not His will anymore, and all people everywhere by understanding this knowledge will know this to be an undeniable fact because they are given no choice in this matter whatsoever.

"How will people be entertained in the new world?"

The world of entertainment will draw millions of professionals and amateurs alike and all types will be a major source of pleasure, but no one will judge whether you qualify to entertain; you must make this decision for yourself, and only if there is a need for entertainers. The newspapers and talent agencies will list all the vacancies available. All individual entertainment such as singing, dancing, acrobatics can be done by anyone who consults the openings in each television studio, theater or night-club for the time available and once a person takes the job, they will list his name. Therefore, everybody will be given an opportunity to entertain if he feels he has the ability, but he will not be able to blame the audience for leaving. No one will tell another person whether he is talented or not because this is a judgment of what is better for someone else and blames him in advance for not developing in this direction. You see parents do this all the time. Have you any idea of how many children received the impression that they were good at doing something only because others told them they were, or because they didn't compare themselves to the talent already available? This is a judgment he must make for himself which he can only do by comparing himself with others in the entertainment field. Furthermore, if he relies on the judgment of others he could hurt his sponsor by taking a job for which he is not qualified and the only reason he thought he was qualified was because others told him he was; it wasn't something he deciphered for himself. Consequently, if he should walk around the room on his hands, he will know that he is entertaining not by any applause but by the knowledge that he is a superior performer (there are certain mathematical standards that he can use for judging himself). He will determine this by comparing himself against the standards that already are established for this purpose. This prevents the unskilled and untalented from entering the world of entertainment, which compels the audience to applaud all

263

efforts to entertain them. But fame will be so different in the new world especially when all disrespect is removed and regardless of how well known you become (this will be explained in greater detail in the chapter on education), that only the extremely talented will move in this direction — their satisfaction coming mostly from the sheer pleasure of personal development.

"Will there be professional sports?"

Sports will continue because this is a source of entertainment to the general public, but the blame that exists between ball players and umpires will come to an end. An umpire is doing the best he can with the tools he has but when he knows that the players will never criticize his decision because they know he can't help himself he will do everything in his power to make absolutely certain he gives a correct call, and this will compel him to resort to slow motion television pictures wherever possible. In fact, it is not too difficult to install a protected camera right behind the plate while the umpire sits in a box with a television that has been screened off for strikes and balls. When a bell rings, he yells "Strike!" If they are looking for a player to be a part of a group effort you will also consult the newspapers that list all openings where competition and winning as part of a team are involved, which places a tremendous responsibility on your ability when no one will judge it but you, and no one will ever blame you for weakening the team. If several applications are mailed in from different parts of the world to join a team that has an opening, there will be no discrimination in selecting an applicant because all would have to be extremely qualified under the conditions and flipping a coin would suffice. As to how many teams there should be in the various sports, this can easily be determined by the space and time available. In the future there will always be something going on and no one will be lacking in entertainment. For individual sports such as boxing it will be all about fair play since there will be no more judges. The fight will be over when someone gets knocked out to the tune of ten seconds, or when he quits. No one will desire to hit below the belt or do other things not allowed in the fight game, for how is it possible for him to desire to do the things not allowed when he knows he will not be blamed by anybody, even though he may rupture or kill his opponent?

"Will there be professional gambling like the horse races, and are these gamblers also guaranteed their income?"

Certainly there will be. They are running a legitimate business in which they are trying to make a profit, but if there is a slight possibility that they cannot pay off the winners, they too, will have to find an insurance company to accept the risk of their losses because they will not find satisfaction in burdening the people who guarantee their income, with increased taxation. As for those who make their living through gambling, there is absolutely no hurt involved whatsoever. Horse racing is a business; so is the stock market. Consequently, the moment these bookmakers become citizens, they are free forevermore from the trammels of the law.

"Look how many people get hurt by gambling? Some people gamble away their entire pay check in pinball machines, on ball games, etc., and doesn't this hurt their families?"

Nobody compels a person to place a bet or invest his money; he does this of his own free will, or desire. If he loses, he has nobody to blame but himself. By now, if you understand the two-sided equation, you should be able to figure this one out. When a wife does not receive the money she needs for herself and her children, she will be seriously hurt. Since it cannot satisfy her husband (in this case) to hurt them when he knows they will never blame or punish him for this, he is given no alternative but to restrict gambling within a degree that he can afford. It never fails to work because this is a mathematical, invariable law.

"What about the nickels, dimes, quarters, half-dollars, silver dollars used to operate pinball and slot machines; and what about the other kind of coin-operated machines?"

It should be obvious that any kind of equipment designed to prevent a person from stealing is displaced. As for the coins necessary to operate a pin-ball or slot machine, these can still be used. Someone desiring to do a little gambling, which is his business, simply goes over and buys the amount of chips he wants and deducts this from his cash reserve. The machine either pays off in similar chips or registers what has been won. Then he cashes in his chips by adding what they are worth to his cash reserve. Gambling will become bigger and better than ever before, while nobody will be hurt in any way. If a person wants to cheat the machine he can. Nobody has to go to such great lengths to steal anymore, if he wants to. This will be the easiest thing in the world to do although under these new conditions it becomes impossible to steal.

"Will there be scholarships and, if so, how will they be distributed? And how will they be able to judge who gets the scholarship without some kind of test?"

What the rich do with their money is their business, but only the children themselves will judge whether they are deserving of this free tuition. There would be a contest between the applicants for the proposed scholarship. Since every applicant would be automatically qualified by the fact that he presented himself, the test will be the drawing of a name from a hat. If two people apply for the same scholarship, it is obvious they are both qualified under the conditions. Therefore, the person giving the scholarship money would simply flip a coin, nothing else.

"Is it possible for a father to waste his money on a child's college education?"

This is absolutely impossible because the child would never take advantage of his father's money unless he knows that he has the necessary ability to become what he himself wants to be, otherwise, he would hurt his father who would never blame him for this.

266

"How do the people who work on fixed salaries get an increase other than by prices coming down?"

All business people must guard against the possibility of slack periods, either by protecting their guaranteed income with a surplus to be drawn upon when necessary, or else by taking out insurance. When they are satisfied that they have sufficiently protected their guaranteed income, then everything else above this and other expenses is a profit. Since money has no value above this point unless it is spent or invested, it becomes something that an employer prefers giving in bonuses to his employees when he is satisfied with his own income. However, even if he didn't give them bonuses, the very fact that his income is also guaranteed forces him to spend or invest and this must bring prices down especially when all employed labor, at the start of the transition, cannot be given a raise in salaries. Consequently, the value of a dollar must increase. If an employer has more money than he needs and wishes to share his profits with his employees, and since it is impossible to give one person a greater bonus than another without blame, if there are 100 dollars to be distributed to 100 employees, each would receive $1.

"If an employer does everything in his power to protect his own guaranteed income, mustn't employees do the same should they get laid off or displaced?"

Yes, if they don't want to hurt the people who will have to pay their income.

"Won't all this insurance make someone, as the expression goes, 'insurance poor'?"

No, this won't be a problem. Most insurance companies will come out with package deals, and out of absolute necessity the premiums will be unusually low because there will be very little risk.

"Since automobile accidents will be virtually wiped out, how much do you think the premium would be to cover what is left?"

It will cost hardly anything. That's why package deals will have to come into existence, something that covers all the needs of a family. In fact, the insurance actuaries will discover the risks to be so minimal, regardless of what they insure, that the dividends to the policyholder will offer a very good investment. Even when people die, and even when they get laid off or displaced, they still won't be hurting others if they take out the necessary insurance coverage. Also, the millions of people who have very large displaced incomes at the start of the transition and who, even when they get other jobs, will still require drawing the difference in unemployment compensation, will reduce taxes considerably when they die and their families grow up. Within a relatively short period of time there will be hardly any taxes at all, that is, there will be a surplus of cash and nothing on which to spend it, and it is this surplus that will be used to pay taxes. There will be no more government as we know it, and just about everybody will be working for private industry. If the whole world is employed in private enterprise, there is no need for unemployment compensation or taxation. And if a great part of the world is not employed because many people have enough of everything, what good is your money which passes from one to the other in unemployment compensation? Taxes are only necessary under the new conditions when people are not working, but how is it humanly possible for them not to work when guaranteeing their accustomed income forces them to spend, to invest, and to look for employment if not employed? However, there will come a time when production is forced to slow down because consumption is being satisfied, but how much taxes have to be paid is determined by spending. If we don't spend, people get laid off and our taxes increase to pay this unemployment compensation. If we do spend we keep them employed and lessen our taxes. Now tell me, are we given a choice when our income is guaranteed?

"Supposing there aren't enough jobs to go around?"

We can't blame the displaced for that. Remember, it isn't necessary to find a job that pays the kind of income they are accustomed to getting, because we will pay the difference so they don't get financially hurt. Consequently, with this expanding economy just about everybody will find some kind of employment.

"What if there still aren't enough jobs for millions of people?"

Then these people themselves, without having anyone employ them can get together, hire the brains to build a useful project, borrow the money to buy the necessary materials, and supply the labor themselves. They could build, for example, a huge recreation center for dancing, dining, bowling, billiards, swimming, etc., where parties and banquets could be held. Each person in the community would be entitled to use it, without any discrimination.

"Wouldn't this compete with other bowling alleys, pool rooms, swimming centers, banquet halls, etc.?"

Certainly it would. So would the building of an ocean liner for public use (taking turns to use it for a vacation) compete with other ocean liners, but competition cannot hurt anybody when one's income is guaranteed never to stop or decrease as long as he lives, while forcing prices to go only in one direction...down. After several years of getting acquainted with themselves, children will be shown, through films and personal tours, the entire economic world, and what is the potential purchasing power of particular positions. However, by the time the transition gets under way, there will be a greatly diminished difference between the rich and the poor; and when the Golden Age gets officially launched, the difference will be even smaller because there is a limit to what a person can buy and a limit to what he can invest in, and because prices must come down. Are you beginning to see the wisdom?

"What about people who are in the business of selling dope, isn't this similar to someone robbing a bank?"

The bank robber is forced to give up his profession because he can't get the necessary satisfaction anymore. But the dope peddler is needed very badly by the addict, so how is it possible for him to give it up without hurting the addict? The man selling dope is running a legitimate business since he is not hurting anyone.

"But isn't it true that dope is bad for the body?"

Even if it is bad for the body, is anyone forcing the drug addict to puncture himself full of holes; is someone forcing a man to gamble away his entire salary; is anyone forcing a yogi to sit on a flag pole and stare at his navel for years? These people do this because it gives them a certain satisfaction. If the yogi falls off and breaks his neck, the only thing we can do is bury him, and if the dope addicts kill themselves we will also bury them, but it is not our place to tell them what to do. The most the sellers can do is make it known that there is a danger of becoming addicted to the drug and if someone still wants to use it, the more power to him. However, if he can't support this habit on his income and is forced to write bad checks, I mean bad slips of paper, then he will be hurting the people by forcing them to pay for his dope. The same principle holds true here as well. When he fully realizes that no one will ever blame him for his habit, that no one will ever criticize him for hurting those who must pay his bill, that no one will ever punish him for stealing, that no one will ever question him no matter what he does to others or himself, he will be given no choice but to break his habit of his own free will because it can never give him any satisfaction not to. Consequently, the sale of dope will die off and the sellers forced to go out of business. What would you say if I told you that smoking and the drinking of alcoholic beverages are also on their way out, as well as prostitution, premarital promiscuity, adultery and divorce?

"How is it possible to relate all this to communism when their way of life is so different from ours?" They don't have the same kind of system we have, and you keep talking about competition, insurance, etc."

It makes no difference because the same guarantee holds true. This is what I want to clear up.

"But supposing China needs a hundred thousand tons of wheat and can't get it because the United States or some other country beat her out in competition for one of her surpluses, what is she supposed to do?"

At the start of the transition, each person in China is guaranteed his accustomed income, which includes the amount of wheat necessary to satisfy this guarantee. Consequently, if China is bestead in competition, and cannot get this wheat, we, the rest of the nations in the world, must supply her with the cash, something more flexible than the surplus of a particular item, to buy what she needs from other nations. She will place an order for this wheat, then draw the money for it from the International Bureau of Internal Revenue by sending a slip of paper which will be acknowledged, and then pay for it by sending a slip of paper to the company or companies from which she ordered the wheat. Then the people, all over the world, will pay a percent of their income to cover the cost. It is very simple. In other words, all the people within a nation guarantee each person against having his accustomed income stopped or decreased, and all the nations guarantee each country against the same thing.

"What about competition within and between nations? How does the guarantee and basic principle affect the relation between seller and buyer, or lender and borrower? One thing more; isn't it true that communism already guarantees its people against going below their standard of living?"

The only way China could guarantee her people their standard of living is when nothing is required for this from other nations. War is the consequence of trying to gain control of those countries that are needed by competitors for the same purpose, to maintain and improve a standard of living. However, by uniting all mankind in the guarantee, and by introducing the basic principle, the conditions that

271

cause a preference for war are permanently removed. The people in a communist nation will also go through the same procedure to become citizens and receive their guarantee, therefore, the leaders will have no choice but to design a system that will allow all the people to receive an equal share of the profits regardless of what they do to earn a living, to benefit from their own initiative regardless of what is done with their extra time, and to improve their standard of living in any direction they wish to go because nothing will be done at the expense of others. However, no problems can arise because the guarantee and basic principle will be an undeniable standard to guide the people and their leaders as to the direction they are permitted to go by their conscience, which makes it unnecessary for me to show them that 3 is to 6 what 4 is to 8 when they can figure this out for themselves. But far be it from me to tell the leaders of the Chinese corporation how to run their business. I am only replacing one set of laws with another, which gives them no choice as to what direction they must go for satisfaction.

You must understand that the guarantee and the IBM offices will be set up in China, Cuba, as in all countries, and that the differences in purchasing power between nations in relation to labor will be evaluated so there will be perfect equality. If one dollar is needed from each citizen towards the guarantee, and if our dollar is worth more or less in world exchange, the difference would be rectified so that everybody contributes the same amount. But the communist citizen will not have any money as such.

China is a huge army, and just as clothes and food are issued to soldiers, this is the way everything is distributed to the communists. In order to rectify this, we must follow our magic elixir and remove all forms of blame. You must remember that once a communist becomes a citizen of the new world, he, like in the United States and elsewhere, will be placed above the laws of his country and be free to do anything he wants providing he can do it without hurting anybody, for then he would be prevented by being denied any satisfaction in moving in this direction. Therefore, if leaving his country (the loss of his job) hurts the economy in any way, although he is free to go, he would prefer remaining. Furthermore, his standard of living is guaranteed never to decrease just as long as he loses his job involuntarily. If he quits voluntarily, even though nobody is hurt, his guarantee then becomes the basic standard of living. For example, if someone has a guarantee of $130 and quits his job to take a new position paying much more, this is his business providing nobody gets hurt, otherwise he would not be able to move in this direction. But if he should lose this new job and need our help, his guarantee would be whatever the basic standard is to supply him with the necessaries of life. If he decided to leave his country, he would need permission from both countries, that is, he would need to know that no one would be hurt in either nation before feeling free to emigrate. In every nation there will be a group of lawmakers who will analyze every possibility of hurt that is not on the surface, and a part of this group will do the same for the United Nations of the world. Once the IBM offices have been set up in China or any communist country, and someone becomes a citizen, he will go through a similar process with certain variations. The government accountants will record his gross income, which is the total number of hours he works. They will then figure out exactly what his standard of living is in relation to labor hours. If he works 40 hours, and his standard of living (his clothing, food, shelter, medical care, entertainment and all other personal services) is equal to 20 hours, then he is being taxed 20 hours of his total labor time. Now right at this point a great change for the better is about to take place, and here is the primary difference between capitalism and communism.

In the United States the government spends the tax dollars on anything they think is advisable, but how the profits are spent is left up to the people. However, in China the government not only decides how the taxes should be spent but also the profits, giving the people no say in this matter at all. Consequently, millions of Chinese are compelled to remain at the lowest standard of living while someone else reaps the profit from the labor. But remember, this came about out of absolute necessity, for which no one is to blame. Now once the standard of living is estimated in labor hours, the difference between that and his gross income, in our example this would be 20 hours since 40 was estimated as his gross, would be broken down so it can be seen how much of these remaining 20 hours are being used toward sustaining the standard of living of others, and how much is a surplus that is sold in foreign exchange. We shall assume that 10 hours supplies the guarantee of others, while the remaining 10 hours is a surplus. But here we are faced with the same thing that confronted us in a capitalist nation. The new citizen observes that he is being taxed (putting in labor) to pay for services he derives no benefit from, and for the first time, since this is a judgment of what is right for him, he is going to invest his labor (9 of this 20 hours) in another direction. Consequently, these displaced people (whoever they are) will have to supply their own labor time to sustain their standard of living. It is exactly the same here. We are not going to spend our money in any direction that does not benefit us personally in some way, unless we want to. This means that the Chinese citizen has just picked up 10 hours of profit, the labor that he is not going to pay anymore toward taxes that do not benefit him, although he will use this 20 hours of labor time to contribute toward the overall guarantee — if it is needed; and this was already explained. However, these displaced soldiers, police and other government workers, as well as the manufacturers of war equipment, are completely free to get other employment and if there was none available then all the citizens in the world, not just those in China, would contribute an equal share of their labor or money to sustain them. But before this would be necessary, the lawmakers in China would analyze the entire situation and through this careful evaluation discover that these displaced people can be put to work in various jobs. Each person will be allowed to select the kind of work he prefers, providing he can qualify, without any partiality being shown. If they were working 40 hours before getting displaced, this is the amount of time they would continue putting in. If China needs to sell certain surplus products in order to maintain its standard of living, changing jobs does not affect this, consequently, if because of competition China cannot supply the needs of her people which includes everybody's standard of living, then we, those of us who can afford it without going below our own guarantee would contribute an equal share so she could have the power to purchase what is needed from other nations, assuming that she has done everything in her power to sustain her own standard of living. In other words, before a millionaire can come to us for help he must be broke, and if China has other surplus products that she planned to exchange for certain luxury items, she would have to use them first in the direction of maintaining her standard of living.

"Supposing someone in China wants to go into some kind of business for himself, can he do this?"

Certainly, but remember, if he quits the job at which he is presently employed (this applies to all countries), he would be hurting the people who depend on his labor or services. Consequently, he must either find a replacement for his job, or start this new business after hours. Furthermore, if he finds a replacement and should later go out of business, his guaranteed salary reverts back always to the start of the transition.

"How do the Chinese people get a share of the profits?"

They get a share by an equal distribution of the profits above the cost of expenses. China will sell her surpluses for cash, and will distribute this equally (that is the profits), among all her people. There will be no division between countries, and every country will be welcome to come in and display what they have for sale. Those who can afford these things will buy. Little by little by little, this gigantic corporation called China will be broken up into smaller businesses by the leaders. This means that if China reaps a profit for the year of 600 billion dollars, and there exists a potential of 200 million citizens, then all those who are already citizens would receive an equitable distribution of the profits, not an equal distribution. Instead of receiving $3000 each, some might get $2500 while others receive less or more, but because it is the nature of man to move in the direction of greater satisfaction, and if someone sees an opportunity of becoming wealthy without hurting anyone (this, of course, is a necessary condition), this is his business, and how is it possible to hurt anyone when the income of every person is guaranteed never to stop or decrease as long as he lives, and when it is known there will be no blame or punishment for this hurt?

Let us return to our comrade who is earning a gross income of 40 hours, twenty of which he was using to pay others to sustain his own standard of living, ten to supply the labor for those who give him nothing in return, and the remaining ten is the surplus that will be used in exchange for whatever is desired as would depend on the amount of labor time that each contributes toward the surplus or, to express it differently, on what stock each person holds in this gigantic corporation. If our friend's 10 hours every week was worth $3000 at the end of the year, and if he only used up half of the ten hours he had available for the contribution to maintain the overall guarantee, then, at the end of the year he would have picked up another 5 hours times 52 weeks, which would give him an additional profit of $1500, or a grand total of $4500 for the year. Naturally, if our IBM accounts were cleaned out, he would only have this $3000, and if we still needed money to finance the guarantee, his share would come out of his surplus profits, that is, if he didn't spend this profit periodically before the end of the year, in other words, after every exchange or sale. Remember, by spending it he reduces the amount needed to sustain the guarantee because this creates the need for additional employment. By not spending it, it becomes a surplus that can be used to sustain those who cannot find employment because it was not spent or exchanged. Consequently, all that has to be done to satisfy every communist nation is to allow these profits to be spent in a manner that will benefit each individual, not just certain groups; and this is easily accomplished with the help of our lawmakers, those who search for what is and what is not a hurt. They will give priority to any improvement that benefits all the people equally, but once this has been set aside (since they will not be able to take advantage) then the next priority will be what affects those in a prescribed area. But if the total profits are not needed in either of these directions, then the individual can do what he wants with his own share. He could order things from other nations, invest it with other nations, even gamble with it if he wants to. He can even buy what he could never get before from his own country. For example, if the displaced are used at jobs that increase the luxuries of the nation, whereas before the leaders distributed these at their discretion, the citizen who shows a profit can buy immediately after a fair method of determining who goes first would be devised.

"In order to gamble and buy from other nations, wouldn't this require that the labor hours be converted into dollars and cents; and wouldn't a medium of exchange have to be manufactured?"

Labor can very easily be converted into dollars and cents, but a medium is not necessary when the purchaser can have the amount deducted from his IBM account while the seller has his credited. The biggest item to be displaced, and one that will come as a complete surprise, is the material aspect of money itself, not its purchasing power, for this demonstrates an obvious distrust of people's honesty by denying them an opportunity to spend more than they can show cash or credit for. In the new world eventually, money itself could become a thing of the past. Every citizen will have an identification number. When he does his shopping he simply gives his identification number, and the amount purchased is deducted from his account. If he wants to gamble he buys chips or coins, and again the amount purchased is charged to his account. If he wins it is credited to his account. Remember, the desire to cheat or steal will become a thing of the past under the changed conditions because we cannot find greater satisfaction in doing those things we cannot justify and for which there will be no blame. The primary reason money will become a thing of the past is only because its production costs millions of dollars that could be used to improve our standard of living. There will be no poor people in the new world, and the rich will have a purchasing power so great that no matter what they do, invest or spend, it will hurt no one and benefit everyone. Let me show you in greater detail why money, as a medium of exchange, must come to an end. When no one will ever blame what you do permitting you to steal all you want if you want to; when no one will ever check on your honesty in any way, the present manner of paying for things becomes obsolete. Nobody is going to stop you, check to see if you paid for this merchandise, or question your honesty in any way. Consequently, what difference does it make whether you use this material aspect of money, or slips of paper on which you record the amount you are spending? What difference does it make whether you receive cash, a check, or a slip of paper on payday representing the purchasing power for your labor? What difference does it make to a businessman whether he deposits $2000 cash and checks in the bank or records the total receipts in a book, throwing away the slips of paper? He is interested, like the rest of us, in what this money represents, its purchasing power. Therefore, when the slips of paper are thrown away it makes no difference to him just so his purchasing power is not impaired. What difference would it make to you whether you go up to a cash drawer and pay for the things you buy with a $20 bill, taking your own change, or whether you write $18.50 on a slip of paper, put this in the drawer and deduct the amount from your total cash reserve, just as you do with a checking account? What difference would it make whether you mail a check to pay a bill or a slip of paper, just so your creditor acknowledges receipt of this so you can deduct, while he adds? What difference would it make whether you put a 6 cents postage stamp on an envelope and then deduct, while the Post Office adds? Consequently, once all the cash in circulation is transferred to individual record, corporate, government books, etc., the manufacturer of money is completely displaced along with money orders, traveler checks, bonds, stamps and checking accounts. Besides, the new system will facilitate the transition. Henceforth, once our Golden Age gets officially launched (this, remember, will depend only on how long it takes to teach all mankind what it means that man's will is not free), each person will keep a record of his own purchasing power, and when he goes shopping or pays for services, he will simply subtract, and when he gets paid or totals up his profit, he will add. It would make a great difference if the people would desire to take advantage of this opportunity to steal, but they won't be able to, under the changed conditions.

"Isn't this somewhat like the honor system used in certain universities?"

Of course not, because if a student does not live up to the established code of ethics he is severely censured, in many cases expelled, whereas here we know that man is not to blame for hurting others because his will is not free — we are back to the basic principle which I take for granted is understood. In order to prevent this desire to steal from ever arising it is first absolutely necessary to remove all

278

forms of advance blame and all the forces that try in some way through threats of punishment and retaliation to prevent us from being hurt by others. When no one will ever blame you for what you do, allowing you to steal all you want — if you want to — when no one will ever check on your honesty in any way, the present manner of paying for merchandise and services comes to an end. Therefore, it requires the removal of this material aspect of money only because it becomes, under these conditions, a useless appendage, very cumbersome in comparison that employs millions of people at jobs that have lost all significance, releasing this labor, as with the other displaced, in many different directions. Even if this material aspect of money was not displaced, the same principle would apply. Instead of having a cashier check your purchases, receive your money, and give you change, you would do this yourself. Several adding machines and cash drawers can easily replace the cashiers and cash registers, so when you have done your shopping at one of the supermarkets, for example, all you have to do is total up your items, put them in a bag or cart, go over to one of the cash drawers, and pay for what you bought by putting in the proper amount, taking your own change if necessary. Certainly you can put a one dollar bill in a drawer and take a twenty out, but if it is food you want why even bother with the cash when you could clean out the store — if you want to. Therefore, the only one you will have to account for your actions is yourself, and under the changed conditions it will be mathematically impossible to desire cheating or being dishonest with yourself. Even the counterfeiters, thieves and bank robbers could not take the slightest advantage of this freedom because their conscience would never allow it. However, it is very important to understand, just in the event this was not made clear, that we are guaranteeing the standard of living derived from the particular job or business a person has when becoming a citizen. This means that if any individual quits his job, sells his business, changes his investment or leaves his country to take other employment, this is a voluntary move unless he is forced to do so in order to take less from us. This prevents him from gambling at our expense, although he can if he wants to risk the possibility of lowering his own standard of living, because should he get laid off or displaced from his new job he will have to settle for the basic standard until he can find other work. Another change that will lay off millions of more people is the result of competition between nations, and within those countries that are capitalistic. Let me show you what I mean.

At the present time the United States is in desperate need of foreign markets, as is China to a lesser degree. The latter seeks to exchange its surpluses for the purpose of maintaining and improving its standard of living, but the former, if its products are not sold are faced with laying millions of workers off until a chain reaction of depression could cripple the economy of the nation. Consequently, the government must do everything humanly possible to keep these ports open, and when Communism threatens to close them sooner or later war is inevitable as the lesser of two evils. Furthermore, various things cause prices to rise which occasions the unions (they get displaced also) to force wage increases to satisfy the difference, but when the stockholders see a decrease in their dividends, they raise prices to adjust this difference. It is a vicious cycle. Anyway, when these ports are thrown open, competition between all the countries will become extremely keen, and millions of more people will be laid off when the various manufacturers find their products are not moving. Although half the population of the world will be unemployed, the answer is very simple. When the transition takes place, each working individual will have attained a standard of living that can be measured in dollars and cents. If a person brings home, after taxes, $150 a week but only uses $125 because the rest he saves, then his standard of living would be the latter figure. Consequently, if he had as little as one penny in purchasing power taken away from him by the economy he would be blamed for having too much money, and since he would never blame this hurt because he knows it cannot be helped — when I know it can be without hurting anyone, that is, without taking one penny away from anybody's standard of living in the entire world, I am going to prevent what can no longer be justified. It is necessary to repeat that when a person loses his job involuntarily for one reason or another he is not considered displaced until he has used up all his reserve cash, but when he is at this point and still cannot find a job he will draw the amount of money required to sustain his standard of living from the Bureau of Internal Revenue by entering this $125, as an example, in his cash reserve record book, and then send a notice of this transaction so it can be deducted. What stops him from taking more than this amount is the realization that should he take more he would be hurting the very people who now are not hurting him in any way, and who would never blame him no matter how much he took because he knows they must excuse everything he does. Consequently, he is compelled to prefer being absolutely honest with not only himself but with others, for this is the only avenue open for needed satisfaction. This same principle compels him to look for a job immediately unless he still has money of his own, but no one will tell him where or when to work, in any country, because there is no need to under the changed conditions. If he can't find a job paying the amount necessary to meet his standard of living, he will draw the difference from the Bureau.

"What if the person displaced was a hired killer whose standard of living was $100,000 a year?"

It would make no difference because we are all God's children, therefore the same principle would apply. His standard of living would remain at $100,000. All people of the world are the same, and under the new conditions no one would be able to murder, cheat, or steal again, therefore everyone is treated equally. Once the transition gets under way you will have only your own business to concern yourself with.

"Wouldn't this cause a tremendous increase in taxation? And how does the guarantee affect an entire nation that might fall short in the actual products to sustain this standard of living?"

If China, for example, needed to exchange certain surplus products in order to maintain her own standard of living but was unable because some other country beat her out in the competition, all she would have to do — or any country — is draw the amount of money required to sustain her own standard of living from the International Bureau of Internal Revenue by entering this amount in her record book, order and pay for in cash what is needed from any seller of her choice, and then send a record of this amount to the Bureau so it can be deducted. As far as taxation, every week the Bureau in each country will issue a statement as to what percent of a person's income is required to meet the bill, and if it happens to be 5%, and your income is $200, you would remit a slip of paper for $10, and deduct this from your cash reserve. But remember, if the tax makes you go below your standard you would only send in the amount that does not go below. However, if a country cannot back up a standard of living because the products necessary are not available in sufficient quantity, and no matter what is done within the country these cannot be gotten in sufficient quantity, then and only then would a nation draw the necessary funds from the International Bureau, as described. And each and every week this Bureau would also make an announcement to all the countries of the world that a certain percentage of a person's income would be required to meet the bill, and no one will object because no one is getting hurt by going below his accustomed standard. Furthermore, any seller who would increase prices, and any employee who would force a wage increase, would be stealing from the taxpayers because many people would have to draw an additional amount in order to meet their standard of living as a consequence of these increases. Since it cannot satisfy a person to steal when he knows he will not be blamed in any way, and when he also knows that no one is now hurting him, all prices are prevented from being raised which breaks the vicious cycle and puts a permanent end to inflation. An employee cannot force an increase. The boss might wish to give him a raise or a bonus. But regardless of this, a change will take place as a consequence that will make everybody much happier and wealthier. Remember, when millions upon millions of people lose their accustomed manner of earning a living there will be more labor available than can be readily imagined. Since everybody will desire to spend as never before because of the guarantee, this will result in a tremendous boom that will not only employ just about all the unemployed, reducing the need for unemployment compensation (taxes), but will give the investors, the builders, the creators, the greatest opportunity imaginable. What is of the greatest importance is the fact that since prices cannot be raised, and competition will exist greater than ever before, they can only go in one direction — down. And what is of still greater significance is that in due time more and more people will get laid off because there will be less and less need to buy what they already have. As was discussed earlier, there is a limit to the number of material things a person can own. When this time comes they will have no need for this money. In other words, if you spend your money others will receive it in the form of an income. If you have nothing on which to spend and nothing in which to invest, they will receive it in the form of taxes. What you do with it is your business, and have I given you a choice? Under these conditions the only difference between a communist and capitalist country is that the latter has a lot of corporations while the former has only one. But the amazing thing is that when workers get laid off in either country, what they do is exactly the same, that is, they look for something else to do without anybody dictating; and if they are unable to find work because there isn't any, they would simply take a vacation until called back, by drawing the money to sustain their standard of living...from the Bureau. It is interesting to note that the very people who want to leave communist countries will lose their desire as soon as they become citizens because they will not be subjected to the laws any longer and will want to continue receiving their guarantee. Communism, and the dream of socialism, came into existence out of mathematical necessity as a reaction to injustice, but once the injustice is removed, communism and the dream of socialism have no further value. It was assumed that Marx had all the answers, but in this new world nobody will tell anybody what to do, although each person will be mathematically prevented from desiring to hurt others.

"Isn't it true that a world in which everybody gets an equal income is more just? How can it be just when this limits man's freedom, destroys initiative, and stifles incentive?"

A just world is one in which an individual is allowed to move in any direction he sees is better for himself, without others judging what is right for him. This was impossible before because man often found it desirable to hurt others to accomplish his ends. Socialism, communism, and capitalism dictate laws that must be obeyed or else, which was necessary up until the discovery that man's will is not free; but now you are completely free by the will of God to do anything you want to do without fear of being blamed, criticized, condemned, or punished in any way, which limits your freedom to do only what hurts no individual.

"As religion comes to an end because man is finally delivered from all evil, does this mean the religious leaders will have to take off their robes and gowns and get a job in the secular world?"

No, of course this is not true. Nobody is going to tell these people what to do. If they wish to wear their robes and gowns for the rest of their lives, as soldiers and generals can continue to wear their uniforms, this is their business, not yours or mine. If they don't wish to go to work, this is also their business. Our business is simply not to hurt them in any way; consequently, we shall guarantee their income just as long as they live. However, if they could take some kind of work then they would not hurt us, but under no conditions will we ever blame or punish them no matter how much they hurt us by not taking a job, because we will know it is God's will. But they will know it is not God's will since they will also know that they do not have to hurt us this way unless they want to, for over this they have mathematical control. Therefore, when they, as well as all others, fully realize that we will never blame or punish them no matter how much they hurt us, they will be given no alternative but to forgo the contemplation of what they know we must excuse and they cannot justify.

"Wouldn't you think that the clergy would be very happy over this news that all evil is soon to be removed from our lives and that God is a definite reality?"

No more so than the government. It will take quite a while for certain people to adjust to the idea that their services will no longer be needed because we now have the solution to man's problems. But once it sinks in, and it won't take too long, then everybody will be singing songs of happiness and thanking God from the bottom of their heart. With the discovery of what it means that man's will is not free it becomes mathematically impossible to hurt others, allowing him to move in any direction he wishes to go of his own free will. How was it humanly possible to believe in determinism when this necessitated that man stop judging what was right, when so many things he did were wrong? But now it is impossible to do anything wrong, which only means 'impossible to hurt someone.' The knowledge that no one will ever take chances that could lead to a first blow will prevent the need for others to judge what is right for someone else. Furthermore, the realization that blaming or criticizing those who do not desire to do what you tell them to do is striking the very first blow, you will be unable to derive satisfaction from continuing with this criticism knowing that they must excuse what you can no longer justify. By blaming those not responsible, a chain reaction of justifiable retaliation began in every walk of life, making matters a thousand times worse; but we have reached the point in our development when all this will be coming to an end. For the very first time in the history of mankind, man will be compelled by the knowledge of his true nature, which reveals what is better for himself, to mind his own business, that is, to stop judging what is right for others, which was impossible before. This proves conclusively that when all people know what is a first blow, they won't have to be told not to strike it because this natural law prevents them from moving in that direction for greater satisfaction, which also means that the entire world will be completely free, their conscience clear, to do anything they judge is right for themselves without fear of criticism or punishment — but they will never think it better to hurt others under the changed conditions. If a Black and White couple desire to marry, this will be their business, but in our present world the critics have made it unbearable for many. When the critic realizes that his criticism is striking a first blow for which he will never be blamed, he can only find greater satisfaction in minding his own business — and this applies to any form of criticism. As this becomes clearer you will see why these judgments become obsolete, especially when nobody will ever do anything to strike back in retaliation.

Under the reign of free will this transition to a cooperative earth

285

was a mathematical impossibility because no one knew what was the better alternative, although many thought they knew. Consequently force was an absolute requirement to prevent further harm but not anymore since this knowledge prevents those very acts of evil for which blame and punishment were previously necessary. If this discovery did not come to light man would, sooner or later, destroy himself. Since man's will is not free, he has absolutely no say in this matter whatsoever, which proves that God is a mathematical reality that can no more be denied. The great humor is that religion is founded on faith in God, and the moment we discover that God is an undeniable reality by actually delivering us from all evil, faith is no more necessary just as it is impossible to have any more faith that the world is round because we know, beyond a shadow of doubt, that it is. As I stated before, the clergy will be completely displaced.

Have you any conception of the enormous wisdom that governs this universe? Is it possible for you not to desire this kind of world? This does not depend on the President, Premiere, Queen, or Prime Minister to make the decision as to when we can begin this Great Transition but on how quickly mankind understands what it means that will is not free, for the very moment the United Nations are ready the countdown will begin. This is not a theory, not a figment of the imagination, but a mathematical fact that must come about because it is what we, the people on earth, really want only our relations with each other have been so involved that the problem was impossible of solution without the understanding of man's true nature. Just as Christ was born to do a particular job as well as those who opposed him, nobody being any better than the other in view of the knowledge that man's will is not free, so was I called to do a particular job which is to help get this Project Golden Age launched into proper orbit. Consequently, when this book is published and translated, when the scientists recognize that the knowledge herein is undeniable, they will gather together from all parts of the world and plans will be made to launch what everybody has been praying for since time immemorial. Who am I to speak so confidently? I am just another individual obeying God's will, no better or worse than anyone else.

I don't have anymore time to spare on this chapter. It shouldn't be necessary to relate all the changes (there are so many) that are compelled to come about in the economic world, simply because we can only go in a direction that will hurt no one. I fully realize how involved is this solution to the economic problem and how easy it is to laugh at it and criticize when it is not understood, but because the basic principle is completely undeniable to those who understand it I am prepared to go before any group of qualified economists, if necessary, for additional clarification and discussion; and if any reader is sincerely interested in helping to bring about this new world, which he will comprehend much better after reading the remainder of the book and then the entire book a second time, or if he does not completely grasp the principles involved that compel us to move in this direction, please do not hesitate to write or call, as it is about time we took the bull gently by the horn in view of the fact that the solution is at our fingertips and now it's just a matter of time.

RECAPITULATION

The first step in the solution to the economic and all other problems of human relation is to teach mankind what it means that will is not free, which is nothing other than the knowledge that no one henceforth (once the transition officially begins) will be blamed, punished, or even questioned regardless of how much he hurts others. Each person will be given a golden opportunity to steal and cheat all he wants, if he wants to under the changed conditions, without the slightest fear of being held responsible, because we know that he is compelled to do everything he does. But he knows he is not compelled to hurt others unless he wants to, for over this he has mathematical control, and when it fully dawns on him that he will be excused by all of us for doing what he knows he can never justify, he is given no choice whatsoever.

The second step, therefore, is to remove all forms of advance blame, notwithstanding how many people get displaced. But since this would deprive them of their accustomed income, which would be a serious hurt, and since we cannot desire to hurt them this way when we know they will never retaliate, and since it is within our power not to hurt them, it is obvious that their entire income must be

287

guaranteed. Furthermore, since telling others what to do blames them for doing otherwise, it is also obvious that these displaced people are completely free to do what they want without any fear of criticism. However, knowing that we will never blame them no matter how much a reduction in taxes would increase our own income they are given no alternative but to do everything in their power to get some kind of employment.

The next step is to guarantee each person that his income, whatever it is at the start of the transition, will never decrease or stop unless he voluntarily quits a job, and to allow those receiving an inadequate amount to increase their income according to their subsistence requirements; but only these people must judge what this increase should be. The guarantee must be based upon net income, after taxes. Consequently, if the week's tax reduces one's income below his guarantee, then he will either supply the difference from his savings or, if he hasn't any, he will not be able to send in the required amount, and this will show up as a tax deficit the following week. By the same reasoning, if the week's taxes increase one's income above his guarantee, then he is making a profit. At first glance it appears that guaranteeing each individual his accustomed income would overburden the taxpayer, but this is not true because spending is forced to expand the economy beyond man's wildest dreams, which creates a tremendous vacuum for new labor. As everybody gets employed, taxes must decrease and spending, as a result of this increase in purchasing power, creates greater profits than can now be envisioned. Since competition will become keener than ever, without hurting anyone, and since prices can never be increased because all justification to do so has been removed by the guarantee, prices will be forced to come down while the purchasing power of the poorest will be forced to rise at an enormous rate of speed. Remember, once this security is offered to all mankind there is no further need to save for a rainy day, although insurance coverage must be taken into consideration so as not to hurt those who will never blame. Moreover, since a displaced person is only guaranteed his income when he becomes completely displaced, that is, when he has exhausted all his own rainy day resources, he is compelled to utilize all reserve cash because not to do so would be stealing which forces all money to come out in the open and be spent or invested, again reducing taxes and prices. Competition between nations is increased without any restrictions as it is within the capitalistic countries. But since the people in every nation will be included in the guarantee while being allowed to do anything they want to increase their standard of living controlled only by a law that does not allow them satisfaction when not being blamed for any hurt, prices are compelled to come down without hurting anybody and benefiting all mankind, while the causes of war and other economic evils are prevented from arising or continuing. You will not get an adequate understanding of all these changes until you study thoroughly the principles in this book but once enough people understand them so that this initial skepticism and unconscious prejudice are surmounted, then it will be an easy matter to present this knowledge to the United Nations.

The economic system I just described is mathematically possible — but only when all people understand what it means that man's will is not free. These principles are just as undeniable when thoroughly understood as any mathematical equation; and when political leaders of the world recognize that it is now possible to unite all nations in such a harmonious agreement that the causes of war and crime can be entirely eliminated not only without hurting anyone but while benefiting all mankind, this knowledge will spread quickly throughout the earth. Until then, we will be forced to live in our present world as a lesser of two evils. Remember, in conclusion, my prediction that all war will come to a permanent end in the next 25 years is not like the prediction that an eclipse will occur at a given time because the astronomer has nothing whatever to do with the motion of these bodies and the crossing of their paths. All he is doing is charting their course. Mine, however, is equivalent to the one a philanthropist makes that a certain university will receive a donation of one million dollars on a given date because he is the one who intends to donate this money on that date. I am donating to mankind this scientific discovery that gives man no choice as to the direction he is compelled to travel, once the principles are understood. Until that time, your help, your willingness to learn about these principles and understand them is needed. And once you understand them, you will be compelled, of your own free will, to spread the news. When the fuse is lit and this knowledge spreads to those who not only recognize its significance but who also have the influence to lay it before those who can disseminate it even more rapidly, then it will not take long before we will develop this world of unmatched splendor wherein no one will ever be hurt, and everyone will have sustenance and health. We are given no free choice in this matter because God has taken it out of our hands as we are compelled to move in this direction for greater satisfaction. In our next chapter, you are about to see another miracle performed that is related to the medical profession.

PART THREE

CHAPTER SEVEN — THE WISDOM OF
SOCRATES
CHAPTER EIGHT — UNTIL DEATH DO
THEY PART
CHAPTER NINE — PARENTS AND
CHILDREN

CHAPTER SEVEN

THE WISDOM OF SOCRATES

Many years ago Socrates was crowned the wisest man of his time when he discovered that the primary difference between himself and others was that he knew he did not know whereas the others did not know either, although they thought they did. In fact, Socrates demonstrated to all the intelligentsia of his time that they didn't know the truth at all, only thought they knew. There is quite a difference between the knowledge resulting from the perception of mathematical (undeniable) relations and that which arises from syllogistic reasoning or observation. People who do not know the truth but think they do are projecting some kind of fallacious standard upon a screen of undeniable substance and because they see with direct perception, with their very eyes, what gives their knowledge the appearance of truth they are convinced they know whereof they speak. The fact that these educated people are unaware that they don't know isn't what concerns me; what does concern me is that they could hurt innocent people by convincing them that they know when they really don't. In our present world there exists a form of hurt different than any other in that it is done by us to ourselves when our fear that we will only get worse, or at least not better, unless something is done immediately compels us to consult doctors who in their effort to earn a living by selling their services convince us that they are fully capable of handling our problem, but instead make us worse. You see...a person who considers himself very educated starts out with an assumption that his knowledge is more accurate than someone without this formal training. If someone dares to disagree with him he uses his background as a standard to determine who is most learned of the two and is then given justification to reject any disagreement as being unsound.

When a student of medicine studies certain subjects at a

recognized university and receives a diploma he is given a right by the school and state to open an office and charge a fee to anyone who consults him for his knowledge. He knows that he has this legal right because he has received a diploma from a recognized university and a license from the government. He also knows that this right is not given to those who did not study for eight years and pass all the necessary requirements. Furthermore, there are all kinds of word relations he can project to make him feel that he is all the more qualified. This occurs when the word 'unqualified' is attributed to those who are considered charlatans. To reinforce this belief many in the medical profession have indignantly exclaimed, "Doctors can't harm you, only quacks can, those unscrupulous swindlers, the pushers who sell their products without a prescription and tell you there is no real danger — how dare them!" Their reasoning concludes that since they are doctors the term unqualified does not apply to them, otherwise, they would never have been given the right to open an office. It is taken for granted that because of this diploma, the title of doctor and the syllogistic reasoning that is always unconsciously at work, these individuals have actually acquired the knowledge to treat and heal. Their reputation does not originate in accurate knowledge but in the fact that there are those who are not entitled to practice by virtue of never having acquired the necessary credentials, in the fact that it is assumed a doctor knows what is better for the patient, and because the patient fears getting worse unless he abides by the doctor's recommendations which elevates the value of doctors. This happens all the time even when a doctor says to his patient, "You don't know what you are talking about because you're not a doctor." The doctor's opinion may take precedence over the patient's own intuition regarding a particular diagnosis only to have confirmed many tests later, and sometimes too late, that this individual was absolutely right. How many times does someone give advice and say it is reliable because it comes from a doctor? And how many times does a drug firm advertise the value of its products by saying it is recommended by doctors, which gives the buyer a false sense of security that the products being sold are safe? The average person has been taught to depend on the doctor's judgment because of the belief that only the physician has access to the wealth of information that can diagnose and treat. Today, the medical profession has so much more knowledge and they have so many more words to describe our ailments that it is no wonder there is an undercurrent of uneasiness that has grown in equal proportion sending many with just the slightest ache to the emergency room for fear that if they don't have their condition checked out immediately they could get worse or even die. This exact situation occurred years ago when a cousin of mine, in his fifties, went to his doctor for a six month check up. After giving him a thorough examination the doctor stopped, looked quizzically at the floor, tapped a pencil on his forehead and said, "I don't know." "What don't you know?" said my cousin with a worried look on his face. "I'm trying to make up my mind whether you have Xyczeghusites or Idykfyjffkskdls." The poor guy became so frightened by hearing names he couldn't understand that together with his high blood pressure he had a heart attack three days later worrying about it. I learned this from his wife on the day of the funeral.

My mother, being brought up to believe that the body can recuperate if given the proper ingredients to facilitate the body's natural healing properties never did trust the knowledge of doctors. I'll never forget the time she had a doctor come to the house even though she was perfectly well in order to teach me a lesson. She pretended she was very sick and told the doctor she didn't know what was wrong. After examining her the doctor prescribed some medicine which she ordered right away. He instructed her to follow the directions carefully so that the medicine would take immediate effect. Otherwise she could get sicker, he warned. When the medicine came she said, "Now watch son," as she poured the entire bottle right down the drain. "Why did you do that, mom, you wasted it?" She replied, "The doctor and pharmacist have to earn a living and I helped them in this respect but I certainly don't have to follow their advice. I wasn't even sick but the doctor prescribed medicine anyway. The difference between him and I is that he has more faith in the medicine and I have more faith in my body's natural healing power." A friend's mother who felt the same regarding the danger of doctors took medicine prescribed when she was well and then vomited. She had actually replaced it with some kind of emetic. Then she turned to her son and said, "You see, just imagine what would have happened had

I taken the medicine when my body was too sick to eject that stuff." Montaigne observed this even in his own time when he said that in trying to make him well his doctor nearly killed him. Why does the public hand over so much power to the doctors?

The word 'doctor' itself is an unconscious standard for it is a justification that symbolizes a logical assumption, and the fear that exists in the minds of those who accept this assumption that they will only get worse if they do not consult this individual is the lever upon which unconscious ignorance further justifies its existence while being granted a legal right to hurt others with impunity. In other words, just supposing that the doctor does not have this knowledge, that in spite of all he was taught he really doesn't know, he just thinks he does, then he is in a position to hurt others with impunity since he was told by the school that he is a qualified physician. Only fear makes an individual pretend to knowledge he does not possess but doctors were compelled to do this as the lesser of two evils when their income depended on this self-deception and dishonesty. How is it humanly possible to be honest with yourself when this depends on being honest with others, and how is it possible to be honest with others when this results in a hurt to yourself? Because you get well after swallowing all kinds of medicine or because you are able to overcome a fear after consulting a psychiatrist for years does not prove the doctor is responsible for your recovery. In fact, there is the very strong possibility that in his effort to heal he may actually be causing harm. It must be remembered that there is this other side of a doctor's unhappiness. If I reveal that the medical profession itself is partly responsible for a great percentage of all the sickness that exists and that one day their services will no longer be necessary, the doctors could not be elated over this news. The physician is out there to make a living just like anybody else and he must believe that what he is giving to the patient is necessary in order to receive compensation for his services. When you tell him that you aren't feeling well he will prescribe something in order to get paid and will justify his treatment on the grounds that there are people to whom he will not prescribe anything which is equivalent to a surgeon justifying the removal of tonsils on the grounds that he doesn't remove everybody's. A doctor must always be in a position to shift his responsibility just in case something goes wrong and his patient gets worse and he must always be able to justify that what he prescribes will not make him worse. If he cannot meet these requirements he will be forced out of business. Let me draw up a comparison for better understanding.

As we have seen, a salesman is able to justify telling white lies in order to earn a commission because he needs this money for his livelihood but if the product he was selling could do serious harm to the buyer then he would need a stronger justification otherwise he would be compelled to look for another product to sell. If he couldn't find another product then he would risk the consequences as the lesser of two evils. To show you how confused is our thinking we ask doctors to help us but force them to carry malpractice insurance just in case we are not satisfied with the results. How is it possible for them to stay in business so they can help us when we need them if we do not wish to accept the responsibility of the risks involved? By imposing the need to carry this insurance which blames them in advance for the risks they must take to earn a living and make us well, they cannot help but react with resentment toward us because there is no way they can offer 100% guarantees. This is somewhat equivalent to a mother who cannot swim offering money to bystanders if they would jump in and save her son from drowning and then blaming them for his death because they declined the offer or were unsuccessful in their effort. It would make no difference what type of employer we are, if mistakes are made by those we hire how is it possible to blame them when they could never have hurt us had we not employed them? It is true that we may have gotten hurt still more had they not been employed but in either case this is our responsibility which reveals another great fallacy and form of injustice that exists today. There is no way a doctor can be held responsible for our getting worse or dying and the fact that we do blame only reveals once again how utterly confused we are. Their next justification comes from the fact that there are malpractice laws which means that if they conform to the Hippocratic Oath and stay away from those things that could cost them their license they are qualified to do everything allowed within their particular field. If some are general practitioners they are allowed to prescribe any medicines that they think will help their patient. In most cases the patient gets over his cold, cough, fever or stomach ache after taking the medicine prescribed and he credits the doctor with the cure, but is this proof that the doctor knows what he is doing? All we know for sure is that he could get better or worse because of the treatment, or he could get better or worse in spite of the treatment. In primitive times when medicine men used to mumble incantations to exorcize the spirit of illness the patient used to get well in spite of the treatment although his belief that they knew what they were doing put his body in a more favorable condition to combat the disturbance so the patient was partially helped because of the treatment. When he recovered, credit was given to the medicine men but in those days when the patient did not recover the doctor was often hanged and quartered.

To be a qualified doctor it is important to know the actual cause of the disturbance before treatment is administered and to be absolutely certain that the body is not fully capable of taking care of this matter itself. Some patients have died only because a doctor did more harm in trying to find out what was wrong than the harm that could have been done were they left completely alone. I know a case of a very healthy boy who cut his hand on a tin can. Ordinarily there would have been no excitement but the mother was up to date on the latest medical information and she rushed her child to the doctor for the purpose of getting a tetanus shot. That evening he came down with a slight fever and again the mother called her doctor. This time he prescribed something else but after taking the medicine the boy began to develop unexplained rashes, leaving the doctor perplexed as to what was causing his mysterious symptoms. Believe it or not it took the boy over a month to recover. Now the question arises: What would have happened had she not rushed him to the doctor for a tetanus shot, couldn't he have died? Certainly he could have died just as you can die from various causes, but whether he would have died had the doctor not given him the shot is questionable. It is very possible that the boy's sickness was not due to the tin can but was a reaction to the medicine. Today we have a different kind of problem because the medical profession can injure or even kill with impunity while doctors blame everything but themselves. There is absolutely nothing today, that is, up until now, that can stop a doctor from hurting others through this unconscious ignorance, consequently to make himself believe that he knows even though he doesn't he must constantly resort to his title, this syllogistic reasoning concealed in words as a confirmation of his knowledge which compels him to reply to anyone who disagrees with what he does, "You are not a doctor," which means when translated, "I know what I'm doing because I am the doctor." However, this is not a criticism of the medical profession because everything developed out of mathematical necessity and that is how everything will continue to develop. Below is a typical dialogue between doctor and patient which underscores the sentiment expressed by doctors.

Patient: "Do you mean, doc, that unless I take this medicine you are prescribing I will only get worse?"

Doctor: "This is the risk you would be taking."

Patient: "But is there no risk the other way; are you absolutely certain that I will not only get well but not get worse?"

Doctor: Getting irritated, he curtly replies, "Certainly I'm certain, I'm the doctor, right?"

Are you beginning to see that the fear of getting worse unless you abide by what he prescribes is the lever by which he multiplies this need for his services? But you can't blame him because he, like the rest of us, is compelled to earn a living and if he didn't justify what he did he would have to go out of business. In order for him to continue practicing he must believe he is not making his patient worse, although this is often the case. The following story is another case in point of how the term 'doctor' is often used to justify legitimate treatment because of the fallacious standards employed to determine the accuracy of the advice offered. The fact remains that help can come from those who are not considered qualified doctors and can often do a better job at helping their friends and loved ones recover, as this next example illustrates.

A friend of mine had a nervous breakdown and consulted a psychiatrist who made no promises as to the length of time it might take to discover the cause of her illness and restore her mental balance. She went to him for several visits. One day she came to me for my advice, asking if it was possible for me to help her. I told her that I would treat her on one condition, that she stops seeing all psychiatrists. She agreed and told her psychiatrist the reason she was not going to see him any more. "Do you realize what you are doing?" he asked in an angry tone of voice. "That man is not a doctor and you could very easily get worse." Well, to make a long story short, inside of two weeks she was completely well and to this day has never had any nervous disorders. When she paid this psychiatrist a visit to tell him of her good fortune he was not too happy over it and, above all, was not the least bit interested in discovering what I knew that could make his patient well so quickly. Shouldn't a psychiatrist welcome any knowledge that would help him in the treatment of his patients? If 50 patients were to call their psychiatrist one morning with the most wonderful news, that they were completely healed overnight, as if by miracle, shouldn't that make him very happy because this is what he was trying to do? Then why shouldn't he be happy if someone helps to accomplish what he has been unable to in spite of all the latest therapies? If you are having a difficult time changing a tire and I walk over to lend you a hand, wouldn't you appreciate this? I certainly would. Why shouldn't a psychiatrist, or any kind of doctor, welcome my services if I can get rid of illness on a large scale? Once again, there is this conflicting problem which prevents the ability of the doctor to be completely honest with himself, for who likes to lose a source of income by having to admit that he may not have all the answers. What if he believes he is really helping his patients when all the while he is only making matters worse, how can you correct it? Ninety-nine percent of what psychiatry treats are words and the increase in mental patients can be easily traced to psychiatrists themselves who have unconsciously multiplied the heads of this diseased hydra by tacitly blaming the possibility of mental illness, which justified and drove many to consider themselves in need of what must have come into existence for their welfare. They start out with the assumption that their patient will not get well unless he does what they prescribe and though in years gone by they used themselves as guinea pigs to test the reaction of a new drug so that they could be of help to their patient, today they are afraid to find out what would happen if they didn't prescribe 90% of the medicines in constant use. Isn't it possible that the patient would have gotten well without the medicine — or is this the actual cause of returning health? Supposing the drug is actually harmful to the body when taken often enough over so many years and instead of the patient getting better he gets worse because of it, and then after doctors have nearly killed him he gets better in spite of it? And what if he develops long term side-effects — the doctor must then justify his therapy on the grounds that the patient would have been much worse off had he not taken the drug. This justification releases the doctor of any responsibility, and allows him to continue dispensing drugs with a clear conscience. Unfortunately, the long term side-effects of these drugs may have devastating consequences, leaving some patients disabled with conditions far worse than the original problem. Some psychotropic drugs have even been implicated in causing the very illnesses they were intended to correct. The following passage is an attempt to expose the corruption that has gone rampant in a world of phantom diseases, phony cures, and illegal kickbacks.

In his book "Insane Psychiatry: A Profession Run Amok," Nicholas Regush states, February 16, 2002 — "There is no drug that can cure modern psychiatry. This is a profession that is close to routinely practicing medical terrorism by shamelessly over-prescribing drugs to people of all ages, often for phantom diseases and for purposes that have no rational basis in science. What's needed is something akin to a War Crimes Tribunal to investigate psychiatry's relationship to major pharmaceutical companies. Haul all the big product champions and psychiatry associations in and determine their involvement with money-grubbing schemes and the abuse of patients. And let me re-emphasize this point: this is a medical specialty that is second to none in ripping off and abusing patients. It is no longer a matter of a few bad apples screwing everyone left and right. It's become a full-scale assault on humanity."

"Many articles written by psychiatrists exaggerate the role of psychopathology, plug disproved theories and perpetuate myths. The situation has long been out-of-control. A non-disease that was once attributed to errant brain chemistry is disproved over and over again. Perhaps many drugs will be seen as just another toxic chemical that was

added to the bodies of unsuspecting individuals in an attempt to put a lid on behaviors that were not deemed 'appropriate.' Obviously, the drug companies aren't going to change things. It is up to the general public to step into the fray; get involved, stand up and be counted. The drug companies aren't going to do it. They're busy estimating the size of their potential markets. They're building their chemical pipelines into the minds and bodies of the young. Every great revolution starts with a foothold."

Guylaine Lanctot, a M.D., the author of "The Medical Mafia: How To Get Out of It Alive and Take Back Our Health" has this to say: "The medical establishment works closely with the drug multinationals whose main objective is profits, and whose worst nightmare would be an epidemic of good health. Lots of drugs MUST be sold. In order to achieve this, anything goes: lies, fraud, and kickbacks. Doctors are the principal salespeople of the drug companies. They are rewarded with research grants, gifts, and lavish perks. The principal buyers are the public — from infants to the elderly — who MUST be thoroughly medicated and vaccinated, at any cost! They cannot patent natural remedies. That is why they push synthetics. They control medicine, and that is why they are able to tell medical schools what they can and cannot teach. Not surprisingly, the number of people having in-hospital, adverse drug reactions (ADR) to prescribed medicine is in the millions." As the safety of many drugs come into question there are a growing number of doctors who not only are speaking out about the potential harm that these drugs can cause, but are rejecting the message given by mainstream medicine that drugs can cure illness. The following quotations bear this out.

"The cause of most disease is in the poisonous drugs physicians superstitiously give in order to affect a cure." Charles E. Page, M.D.

"Medicines are of subordinate importance and because of their very nature they can only work symptomatically." Hans Kusche, M.D.

"Drug medications consist in employing, as remedies for disease, those things which produce disease in well persons. Its materia medica is simply a lot of drugs or chemicals or dye-stuffs, in a word poisons. All are incompatible with vital matter; all produce disease when brought in contact in any manner with the living; all are poisons." R.T. Trall, M.D., in a two and one half hour lecture to members of Congress and the medical profession, delivered at the Smithsonian Institute in Washington D.C.

"Drugs never cure disease. They merely hush the voice of nature's protest, and pull down the danger signals she erects along the pathway of transportation. Any poison taken into the system has to be reckoned with later on even though it palliates present symptoms. Pain may disappear, but the patient is left in a worse condition, though unconscious of it at the time." Daniel H. Kress, M.D.

"The greatest part of all chronic disease is created by the suppression of acute disease by drug poisoning. Every drug increases and complicates the patient's condition." Henry Lindlahr, M.D.

"Every educated physician knows that most diseases are not appreciably helped by medicine." Richard C. Cabot, M.D.

"Medicine is only palliative, for back of disease lies the cause, and this cause no drug can reach." William Osler, M.D.

"Medical practice has neither philosophy nor common sense to recommend it. In sickness the body is already loaded with impurities. By taking drug-medicines, more impurities are added, thereby the case is further embarrassed and harder to cure." Elmer Lee, M.D., Past Vice President, Academy of Medicine.

"Our figures show approximately four and one half million hospital admissions annually due to the adverse reactions to drugs. Further, the average hospital patient has as much as thirty percent chance, depending on how long he is in, of doubling his stay due to adverse drug reactions." Milton Silverman, M.D. (Professor of Pharmacology, University of California).

"Why would a patient swallow a poison because he is ill, or take that which would make a well man sick." L.F. Kebler, M.D.

"The necessity of teaching mankind not to take drugs and medicines is a duty incumbent upon all who know their uncertainty and injurious effects; and the time is not far distant when the drug system will be abandoned." Charles Armbruster, M.D.

"What hope is there for medical science to ever become a true science when the entire structure of medical knowledge is built around the idea that there is an entity called disease which can be expelled when the right drug is found?" John H. Tilden, M.D.

Because the conventional allopathic system of patient care focuses on disease management, most physicians rely on drug therapy as their main treatment protocol and will pull out their prescription pad at the first sign of illness. Patients have been led to believe that if the doctor prescribes a drug for their condition, then it must be good for them. And the doctor is also convinced that the drug is helping his patients. How else could he justify prescribing it? Nowadays it is expected that the doctor will write a prescription the minute the patient steps foot in his office, and he is under pressure to give the patient what he wants. Worse still, how many doctors give drugs to a child not because they know that this is best for his health or even because they know the cause of the illness, but only to allay his fears and that of his parents. Innumerable drugs are prescribed every day to treat symptoms without the medical profession having any inkling of what is the actual cause of a disturbance and the only justification for this lies in the fact that the doctor believes there is really no harm, and there may be some good. But are the doctors absolutely certain that drugs have no relation to the ill health of the body? Perhaps they are equally as certain as governments are that the efforts to remove crime and war through threats of retaliation and punishment have no relation to the ill health of society. No one knows, at this point, how certain drugs will affect the tissues and organs of the body (although we will know soon enough) and the long term complications that could result; and how can doctors be certain that many of our ills are not caused by their efforts to make us well? The very moment the majority of doctors stop practicing it might be discovered that a number of illnesses were the result of their therapies. The body is a balanced equation with tremendous recuperative powers that will adjust in most cases when it gets out of balance. However, there are times when it is incapable of restoring this balance and only then is the knowledge of a physician necessary providing he really knows what to do, otherwise he could make matters ten times worse. Let us carefully analyze the following for further understanding.

There are five possibilities of what could happen as a result of a doctor prescribing something or nothing. The first is that patients could die or get worse from their illness unless the doctor prescribes certain drugs or operations. The second is that they could die or get worse in spite of the treatment. The third is that they could die or get worse because of the treatment. The fourth is that they could get better in spite of the treatment. The fifth is that they could get better without any treatment. My father died in a hospital as a result of an experiment, and the doctors adduced the second possibility to satisfy their conscience. An hour before he took his last breath I asked the doctor what the condition of my father was. "He's doing pretty well, but we're trying a new drug and we only hope his body can withstand it." The first, second and third possibilities are what the doctors resort to for justification, but just in case something goes wrong and the patient gets worse or dies they must be able to shift the responsibility away from themselves and in that case the second allows them to say, "We did everything possible. If the patient had been brought to us sooner we might have been able to save his life, his kidney, his leg, his eye, his lung, etc." I am not implying that the doctor did not make the best decision in a situation such as this because I am also unsure and truly do not know the best course to take when there are so many possibilities, but regardless, the patient believes the doctor knows the truth and because he does he credits the doctor with the cure. In view of the fact that the patient invariably gets well in the majority of cases sooner or later, and never seems to get worse as a result of the treatment, the doctor derives renewed confidence in his qualifications to heal the sick. But whereas the general practitioners don't need too strong a justification to prescribe drugs, surgeons do, because they are about to perform an invasive procedure that could lead to a serious risk of complications. One patient, because the various tests showed nothing as to why she was spitting up blood, was operated on so the surgeon could explore, and died under the knife. Even after a doctor has arrived at a certain diagnosis, one which allows no disagreement, it is essential for him to know exactly what to do, not what he thinks should be done. Many operations, apparently successful, have killed many a patient months later because of unforeseen complications. The justification to operate is derived from three primary sources: One, if the operation is not performed the patient will surely die. Two, even though they are not absolutely certain he will not die the possibility exists, and since the removal of a particular organ will not in itself endanger his life because it was already proven that man can live without these various parts of his body especially when he has two of many things, they justify it on the grounds that it is the best procedure under the conditions. Lastly, they use Darwin's theory of evolution to justify the removal of vestigial organs even when there is no danger to the patient's life. They tell parents that the tonsils are more trouble than they're worth, as with the appendix, and the one sure way to prevent tonsillitis and appendicitis is to remove these useless organs that are left over from an earlier time in man's evolution. But just supposing Darwin is not right and these are not vestigial organs left over from the last mutation, what then? Then the surgeons would not be able to justify the removal of these organs unless the patient's life was definitely in danger. The word vestigial implies that evolution is a proven fact, which it is not. A doctor doesn't advocate removing a finger when it becomes infected because he doesn't classify it as vestigial, but when the tonsils or appendix get infected he tells the parents right away that they should come out sooner or later because they do more harm than good. In order to remove a part of the body the medical profession must have absolute proof that a person's life is at stake unless it is removed, or that his existence will be worse if he continues without the operation.

According to recent statistics approximately 7.5 million operations performed every year are unnecessary. In six New York hospitals 32% of performed hysterectomies reviewed were justified on the grounds that the organ had served its function and was no longer necessary. To date about 20 million American women have had their uteruses removed. Of those women, a small percentage never make it out of the hospital. Shockingly, it has been estimated that less than 10% of hysterectomies are absolutely necessary due to cancer of the uterus. Worse still, the surgery can have long lasting physical and emotional consequences that may seriously undermine a woman's health and well-being. Even when there is cancer, in fact more so, the patient needs to know all the ramifications of surgery. Often, the mainstream medical establishment fails, through ignorance or complacency, to warn patients of possible side effects. One woman after having a complete hysterectomy which involved the removal of a large portion of lymph nodes developed a debilitating condition called Lymphoedema which causes massive swelling, usually in the arms and legs. When she complained that she should have been told about the risk of developing this condition after surgery, he responded, "Well you're still alive, aren't you?" The question remains: Why did he take it upon himself to leave out important information regarding possible side effects, and why didn't he disclose this information before the operation took place? She would have had a much more accurate picture of what to expect, giving her time to mentally prepare herself. All authorities agree that although 90% of the procedures are elective there are alternatives in at least 90% of the cases, and when there are so many unforeseen complications that can result because of these surgeries it is incumbent upon every patient to get more than one opinion and to carefully research all of their options before going under the knife.

Another danger anytime one enters a hospital is the possibility of a medical mistake. The number of people exposed to unnecessary hospitalization annually is 8.9 million which may put them at risk for death or disability. The iatrogenic death rate stands at 225,000, and is defined as a disease induced in a patient by a physician's activity, manner, or therapy. These include infections, non-error negative effects of drugs, unnecessary surgery, and medication errors. As few as 6 percent and up to 20 percent of iatrogenic acts were ever reported. This implies that if medical errors were completely and accurately reported, we would have a much higher iatrogenic death rate. It is evident that the American medical system is the leading cause of death and injury in the United States. In Europe that proportion is only one seventh, perhaps because medicine is socialized

307

in several European countries and there is less of a profit motive, as some have speculated. Historically, when the doctors have gone on strike the mortality rate has dropped.

To give you another example of the type of reasoning that justifies certain procedures, let us look at circumcision. Every year millions of babies are blamed for being born with a foreskin and the only proof that this is of no value to the body is the fact that its removal is sanctioned by the medical profession which lays its arguments not on why this is better or healthier, but on who says it is. Since there is no valid foundation for this operation when all religious and medical justification has been removed, it is obvious that written and verbal knowledge as to why it is healthier is completely fallacious. In other words, there must be a mathematical line of demarcation, but there is no such line where the foreskin, the tonsils, and the appendix are concerned. Supposing a young doctor has only developed a practice of removing 1,000 foreskins a year, and he was aiming for a record of 10,000. How can he be happy at those who argue against this procedure when this upsets his opportunity to break a record? Besides, his income could increase at this profession and he wouldn't have to move on to another field. Don't misunderstand me, these doctors can continue removing the foreskin if they want to, but how is it possible for them to want to when this would only reveal their ignorance, not their knowledge. The Jews justified circumcision on the grounds that it was a religious covenant between man and God. The fact that the baby was momentarily in pain and suffocated with wine was unimportant because this ritual was commanded by God Himself. And since this piece of skin was also vestigial, it was something man was better off without. But many parents began to question the dangers of such an operation, and since man was becoming less and less religious the medical profession was consulted for its opinion on removing the foreskin and sure enough it could be seen that not removing it was less healthy. Do you see how easy it was to make the shift from a religious justification to a medical one? The Jews developed this ritual from their ancient past and because superstitious reasons only revealed ignorance it was then justified on the grounds that it is healthier. But why is it healthier? Not quite sure what I was getting at, my friend offered the following question:

"Are you trying to tell me that tonsils cannot be removed along with the appendix, nor can a leg when gangrene sets in? What about when the appendix gets infected, and when the tonsils swell up, isn't this dangerous to life? According to what you just said a doctor cannot do anything because this blames God's handiwork, so to speak. Is that what you mean?"

My answer is yes and no. It is obvious that certain things need clarification. In order to remove a part of the body the medical profession must have absolute proof that a person's life is at stake unless it is removed, or that his existence will be worse if he continues without the operation. Remember, there must be a mathematical line of demarcation, but there is no such line where the foreskin, the tonsils, and the appendix are concerned. In some instances the removal of tonsils and the appendix are absolutely necessary, otherwise the patient would die, but what about all the other times? As already mentioned, there are doctors who advocate the removal of these organs only because they are classified as vestigial which means that Darwin's theory of evolution has been accepted as a fact for the purpose of justifying certain operations."

"Do you mean that we have not evolved from a lower order of species, like the apes?"

I am not interested in what came first the chicken or the egg, or in a discussion as to the origin of man. However, just as long as this is a theory a doctor is not justified in removing an organ by calling it vestigial for this word implies that evolution is a fact — and it is not. Therefore, since this knowledge is based upon an assumption a doctor henceforth will treat the appendix and the tonsils as just another part of the body. Should these organs become infected and the body incapable of taking care of this matter itself, then a doctor will try to treat the infection and remove the organ only as a last resort. The following example shows how the removal of a body part is often recommended before any other options are considered. Being informed of the potential risks, and fearful of the outcome, this individual decided to give his body a chance to heal before agreeing to an operation. This case illustrates how easy it is for doctors to justify their medical advice in order to earn a living, for which they cannot be blamed. The patient writes:

I had about 3 good attacks. The pain would double me up and didn't want to go away. The first one occurred while I was at work which sent me to Urgent Care. They were not sure what it was. Diagnosed as possible ulcers, he wanted me to go for other tests. He gave me an ulcer medicine which got rid of the pain. I was contemplating over time whether I wanted to go for that type of surgery where they look into your stomach. Then while on a business trip, I had another good attack. It started at 3:00 a.m. and at 8:00 a.m. I was still in very much pain. I went to a nearby hospital emergency room. There they took EKG's, chest x-ray's, blood tests and ultra sound. The tests showed that my lungs were fine, and no problems with my heart or blood though the ultra-sound showed around 3 small gallstones, which the doctor said was probably causing my pain. He said he could give me morphine. I did not want to get goofy since I had important work to do and opted for the pain medication.

I had not had another attack since before May, 2002. In late October, I had another attack. Back to Urgent Care and more pain medication. I said, "What do I need to do to get rid of this problem?" The doctor said she would give me a referral to a surgeon who would put a telescope down my throat and look into my stomach to see if I had any ulcers. I said, "This is unacceptable." We already know that I have gallstones from the ultra-sound. Since I have not changed my diet at all, don't you think that I would have had an attack within 5 months or so, if it were ulcers? The doctor somewhat agreed. I said well, lets take care of what we know is causing a problem and then if I still have pain, we will assume it may be ulcers and go from there.

I got a referral to a vascular surgeon and saw him early this November. I was not prepared for what I was about to hear. I explained to him that when I got these attacks that the pain radiated from what appeared to be my solar plexus region to the back in-between the right shoulder blade. He said uh-hah. He asked me to cough. No... cough harder. I did. He said you have a hernia in your belly-button too. He asked me to come into his office and we would talk about what I need to do. He mentioned dissolving the stones, but the treatment doesn't work all that well and more gallstones would be made. He told me that for you, this is a done deal. I would recommend having your gallbladder removed, he said. He told me that it is no big deal; he stated this is relatively easy and he does about three to four of these a week. He said nothing about

310

alternatives to surgery or possible problems that would or could appear from having this type of surgery. He made it seem in and out. I told him I would contact him when I decided to have it. He did not want me to wait long. I wonder why? ($$).

On the way home I thought the last thing I want to do is to have a part of my body removed. This is SERIOUS!!! Any surgery is a major thing and for a doctor to state otherwise is irresponsible. We are born with these organs for a reason. If not, we would not have them. I researched as much as I could to find other alternatives, so I could keep my gallbladder that I was born with. Don't let the medical profession lead you to believe that you do not need this ORGAN, or that it is no big deal. It is a big deal. It could be your LIFE. From all my research I have found many bad things that have come from having this surgery. Removal of an organ should be the absolute last thing that is ever done. And this should only be considered after you have exhausted every other option.

Obviously, there are times when surgery is absolutely necessary, but due to the doctor's need to make a profit there is often a conflict of interest which may force him to be less than 100% truthful with his patients and himself.

You may ask, "What about other specialties within the medical field — such as obstetrics and pediatrics — don't they render a useful service to mankind?"

"These services will still exist but doctors will not advise their patients in the same manner."

"Will there be a need for prenatal care?"

Yes, as a preventive measure to ensure the health of mother and baby, as well as to identify high risk pregnancies, but doctors will not insist that their patients consent to all kinds of tests unless there is a compelling reason. Many tests and procedures (some containing inherent risks) are justified on the grounds that they will help detect a serious condition early enough to be treated, or to ward off more serious problems later on. We all can agree that an ounce of prevention is worth a pound of cure, but how can patients know which tests are necessary, and which ones aren't, when doctors are getting paid handsome fees for referrals with ever increasing financial incentives and perks? Going back to our previous example,

311

circumcision is a procedure which is justified on the grounds that it is healthier for the baby. But when millions of dollars are at stake, where is this line of demarcation? Many prenatal tests, originally created to test certain high-risk pregnancy situations, have become standard practice for all pregnant women. While you may think that tests can do no harm, some of them have never been thoroughly studied for safety of mother and baby, and may present physical risks to both. Furthermore, results can sometimes be vague and, what's worse, misleading. This may create an atmosphere of worry and anxiety, the very thing these tests were meant to avoid by taking them.

Due to the medicalization of the childbirth experience, this worry and anxiety may extend into the delivery room. As the woman goes into labor her pain can be magnified so tremendously by fear that she is scared half to death. She will demand that they give her something to ease the pain. What she may not be told is that although these procedures are considered safe, they are not without risk. Changes in the placenta as pregnancy advances heighten the transfer to the fetal circulation of all drugs used in obstetric analgesia and anesthesia. Moreover, these regional anesthetics can slow down delivery time, which may lead to fetal distress. This could suddenly lead to the need for a Caesarean section which is major surgery, and, as with other major procedures, there are potential dangers to consider. Mother mortality is two to four times greater than that for a vaginal birth. The estimated risk of a woman dying after a Caesarean birth is less than 1 in 2,500; the risk of death after a vaginal birth is 1 in 10,000. When a delivery is not going as planned, a Caesarean section may be warranted, especially in a sudden emergency. But it has been reported that a large percentage of Caesarean sections are done as a matter of convenience scheduling-wise rather than medical necessity. It's gotten to the point that experts say the rise in C-section rates is a financial crisis as well as a legal and medical one. Although there will no longer be malpractice laws in the new world, obstetricians will be reluctant to perform any C-section that is not medically justified because they would never want to be responsible for putting their patients at greater risk unnecessarily knowing they would have no way to shift their responsibility should something go wrong. Doctors will have only themselves to answer to, consequently, this surgery will be treated with extreme caution and performed only if there is a life threatening danger to mother or baby.

After the birth, if it is a boy, he will most likely be circumcised in the hospital as this has become standard procedure. When it's time for the baby's six week check-up, the pediatrician will weigh and measure him and after a thorough examination will reassure the mother that everything is fine. He may suggest a special formula, as if the mother's milk is not the best formula in the world. The baby will survive not because of the formula, but in spite of it. There are some exceptions. Babies with amino acid disorders, as the name suggests, have problems metabolizing certain amino acids. With these disorders, enzymes essential for the baby to break down are missing or defective. Specially made formulas which address this enzymatic deficiency could be lifesaving. Congenital Lactose Intolerance is another extremely rare genetic condition that is incompatible with normal life unless there is medical intervention. A truly lactose-intolerant baby would fail to thrive from birth (i.e., not even start to gain weight), and show obvious symptoms of malabsorption and dehydration. This is a medical emergency case and the baby would need a special diet from soon after birth. But the majority of babies require only what the mother herself can give and if this is not present in the formula then the body of the child must overcome this handicap, or else get sick. His immune system is already compromised because he is not getting the antibodies from the mother's breast milk. In addition, as early as two months the baby is receiving a series of vaccines that are given on schedule with more and more being added to the list. Some of the vaccines he will receive are a Hep B shot if he did not receive it in the hospital, a DtaP shot, Hib shot, IVP shot, and PVC shot. Some doctors will also give the baby the vaccine for Rotavirus. Recently, the American Academy of Pediatrics has begun advocating 'firing' parents who don't conform to the CDC's overloaded vaccine schedule, the schedule with 36 vaccines on it, almost double the average of 30 other first world countries. The schedule that has never been tested for combination risk. There has been a growing public and professional concern over the immediate and long term effects of these multiple vaccines (several shots given simultaneously), as well as the toxic adjuvants used to produce them, but the pediatrician will tell the mother that it's for the baby's well-being by reassuring her that the benefits far outweigh the risks. He may explain that without these immunizations the baby is not protected and the disease that once killed so many could easily come back. Because she wants to do what is best for her child, she complies. In some cases, however, a child could have a severe reaction and be injured by the vaccination that was intended to help him. An increasing number of physicians claim that the risks do not outweigh the benefits. The following quotations are from doctors and researchers who have expressed their concerns regarding the downside of vaccination as well as the possible link to chronic childhood illnesses and disabilities that are so common today.

"Measles, mumps, rubella, hepatitis B, and the whole panoply of childhood diseases are a far less serious threat than having a large fraction (say 10%) of a generation afflicted with learning disability and/or uncontrollable aggressive behavior because of an impassioned crusade for universal vaccination." --- Association of American Physicians and Surgeons

"Doctors maintain that the (MMR) inoculation is necessary to prevent measles encephalitis, which they say occurs about once in 1,000 cases. After decades of experience with measles, I question this statistic, and so do many other pediatricians. The incidence of 1/1000 may be accurate for children who live in conditions of poverty and malnutrition, but in the middle-and-upper income brackets, if one excludes sleepiness from the measles itself, the incidence of true encephalitis is probably more like 1/10,000 or 1/100,000. Furthermore, about 75 percent of these cases will not show evidence of brain damage." — Dr. Robert Mendelsohn

"Official data have shown that the large scale vaccinations undertaken in the US have failed to obtain any significant improvement over the diseases against which they were supposed to provide protection." — Dr. Albert Sabin M.D. (creator of the Oral Polio vaccine) in a lecture to Italian doctors in Placenza, Italy on December 7, 1985)

"Vaccine adverse affects are amply documented and are far more

significant to public health than any adverse affects of infectious diseases. Immunizations not only did not prevent any infectious diseases, they caused more suffering and more deaths than has any other human activity in the entire history of medical intervention. It will be decades before the mopping-up after the disasters caused by childhood vaccination will be completed." — Dr. Viera Scheibner, Ph.D.

"Instead of epidemics of measles and polio, we have epidemics of chronic autoimmune and neurological disease: In the last 20 years rates of asthma and attention-deficit disorder have doubled, diabetes and learning disabilities have tripled, chronic arthritis now affects nearly one in five Americans and autism has increased 300 percent or more in many states." — Barbara Loe Fischer

"A single vaccine given to a six pound newborn is the equivalent of giving a 180-pound adult 30 vaccinations on the same day." — Dr. Boyd Haley, Professor and Chair, Dept. of Chemistry, University of Kentucky

"While the myriad short-term hazards of most immunizations are known (but rarely explained), no one knows the long term consequences of injecting foreign proteins into the body of your child. Even more shocking is the fact that no one is making any structured effort to find out." — Dr. Robert Mendelsohn

"We are setting up the younger generation for a potential calamity. Vaccines build up only one line of your immune system (the antibody system) but put the main immune system (cellular immunity) to sleep. You need both for fully developed immunity." — Dr. Robert Rowen, MD

"It is now 30 years since I have been confining myself to the treatment of chronic diseases. During those 30 years I have run against so many histories of little children who had never seen a sick day until they were vaccinated and who, in the several years that have followed, have never seen a well day since. I couldn't put my finger on the disease they have. They just weren't strong. Their resistance was gone. They were perfectly well before they were vaccinated. They have never been well since." — Dr. William Howard Hay

315

"Ever since mass vaccination of infants began, reports of serious brain, cardiovascular, metabolic and other injuries started filling pages of medical journals. In fact, pertussis vaccine has been used to induce encephalomyelitis in laboratory animals, which is characterized by brain swelling and hemorrhaging." — Harold E. Buttram, M.D. & F. Edward Yazbak, M.D.

"Probably 20% of American children — one youngster in five — suffers from "development disability." This is a stupefying figure...the primary cause of encephalitis — is the childhood vaccination program. To be specific, a large proportion of the millions of U.S. children and adults suffering from autism, seizures, mental retardation, hyperactivity, dyslexia, and other shoots or branches of the hydraheaded entity called "development disabilities," owe their disorders to one or another of the vaccines against childhood diseases." — Harris L. Coulter, Ph.D.

NVICP has paid out for 50 deaths per year: The U.S. Federal Government's National Vaccine Injury Compensation Program (NVICP) has paid out over 724.4 million dollars to parents of vaccine injured and killed children, in taxpayer dollars. The NVICP has received over 5000 petitions since 1988, including over 700 for vaccine-related deaths, and there are still 2800 total death and injury cases pending that may take years to resolve. — (NVICP, Health Resources and Services Administration).

Although pediatrics will continue as a branch of medicine, these specialists, as well as those who set national guidelines, will have no choice but to be *completely* honest with themselves for the very first time. They will need to be extremely careful what they advise because they would never want to be responsible for making matters worse. This does not mean that doctors aren't doing everything possible to keep their young patients healthy, but the knowledge they would not be blamed if a child was harmed by their recommendations adds a tremendous amount of weight. Honesty will be the best policy even if they have to admit they don't know which course of action is best. As a consequence, mandatory vaccination programs will no longer be enforced due to severe reactions in a small percentage of children, some of which are fatal. At the present time there are no blood tests that can determine which children are susceptible. This means that doctors will offer the most up-to-date information, but parents will have to decide for themselves whether the end justifies the means because the doctors will not want to bear this responsibility. The next case is extreme but illustrates the lack of options parents are often faced with when it comes to questionable therapies and interventions.

Our 2 ½ year old son, Alexander, was diagnosed with a pediatric brain tumor on August 10th 1998 and passed away after three months of chemotherapy on January 31st 1999. We believe that it is important that parents have information (that we didn't have) about the safety and efficacy of chemotherapy that have been administered to children with brain cancer for the past 20 years. We believe that parents should be told the truth — that these therapies are ineffective and dangerous to the majority of young children with malignant brain tumors. "Children should be allowed access to the best therapy and the best quality of life." Every child with a terminal disease should have the right to have access to the best treatment available and the therapy that provides the best quality of life. Since medical orthodoxy has yet to discover a cure for aggressive pediatric brain cancer, parents should be permitted to use other therapies prescribed by their medical doctor. The FDA's policy of not permitting children to have access to any other therapy except chemo and radiation must stop. Children who are labeled 'terminal' should be allowed access to any treatment that is safe and could potentially save their life. The FDA stopped Alexander and continues to stop hundreds of other children from having access to a non-toxic cancer therapy that has proven to be both effective and safe. Oncologists must be stopped from using children for experimentation. In their journal articles, oncologists admit that their therapies for young children with malignant brain tumors are still experimental, toxic and relatively ineffective. Therefore, oncologists should not be permitted to take children from their parents in order to use them as guinea pigs in such unproven therapies. A child with brain cancer is still a child and deserves to be treated with basic human dignity and respect. "Parents must be entitled to informed consent." 'Informed' means being given the truth regarding the benefits and risks of a medical intervention administered to your child. But the history of chemotherapy

317

in respect to its toxicity, carcinogenicity, and ineffectiveness in aggressive pediatric brain tumors, is not shared with parents. That is why most parents submit their children to this insidious therapy because they are not informed of the truth. 'Consent' means being permitted to agree to or refuse a medical intervention. However, if a parent discovers the truth about chemotherapy and decides that she does not want this 'treatment' for her child, her refusal may be meaningless. Oncologists may use persuasion, threats and the law to take her child from her even if she says 'no' to these toxic poisons. In this way, some oncologists have replaced 'informed consent' with 'unscrupulous coercion' and that must stop. Oncologists should not be permitted to use our children as laboratory mice.

What happened to Alexander demonstrates how easy it is for the FDA and the AMA to endorse unproved therapies in the name of progress and cause irreparable harm when things don't go as planned. These organizations are often swayed by pharmaceutical company interests and therefore may make decisions that benefit the drug companies more than the patients. Parents are not always given all the facts regarding the procedures they are asked to consent to, consequently, they don't have the necessary information to make an informed choice. To add insult to injury, they are often denied the right to decide which course of treatment they feel is best for their child. This situation could not occur in the new world because doctors would never want to assume this responsibility unless they knew for a fact that by administering the treatment the patient would not get worse, or by not administering the treatment the patient would surely die or live a painful existence. Justification for any experimental or invasive procedure would only be possible if all other treatments were exhausted first, and this was seen as a last resort. If the doctor agreed to take on the case, parents would have the final say.

Durant, in his book Mansions of Philosophy, discusses the mistake he made in trusting doctors when his own child became very sick. He writes, "In the first three months we were guilty of a grave blunder for we allowed our child to be used as a laboratory for a newfangled form of desiccated milk. It is a crime which many years of parental solicitude cannot quite clear from our memories. We believe now, with Ben Franklin, that the human race should beware of young doctors and old barbers." Now isn't this a perfect example of a child getting well in spite of the doctor who prescribed what the child's nourishment should be? Following a medical mistake a chain reaction of blame follows because nobody wants to assume responsibility. He blamed himself first for this grave blunder but then shifted his responsibility to this young doctor, who blamed the manufacturer, who blamed the chemist, who blamed the assistant, who blamed the shipper, who blamed the farmer, who blamed somebody else. The surgeon blamed the anesthetist, who blamed the nurse, who blamed, and so on. When these things occur they are usually hushed up and since the doctors are never responsible — otherwise they could not practice — the possibility exists that they have been allowed to hurt others with impunity, as the expression goes. Just as doctors advise parents on the best formula for their child, they often advise mothers to wake their babies for a feeding. As we extend our basic principle we see that their advice is misinformed. It is important to remember that we are using a mathematical principle to guide us in determining what our response should be. Since we cannot blame the child for anything according to God's corollary, Thou Shall Not Blame, it is obvious that all knowledge that tries to teach that it is healthier to wake children for a feeding is mathematically wrong. It is quite clear that if you wake a child for anything at all, you are blaming him for sleeping. A doctor may say that in order for the child to regain his health it is necessary to wake him for a feeding and a regimen of medicine. They use this syllogistic reasoning when they want to make it appear that they know when they really don't. Right now if you called in a physician who prescribed a regimen of medicine around the clock and you told him that your friend — the discoverer of certain knowledge that will change the world — said that sleep was more important than to be awakened for medicine, this is what he would say.

Doctor: "Who is your friend, is he a doctor?"
Patient: "No he isn't."
Doctor: "Well there you are; that is your answer. Don't listen to those who are not licensed to give medical advice. They don't know, they think they know. You take this medicine religiously every four

hours, even if you have to set the alarm for your doses at 2 and 6 a.m."

Patient: "How much do I owe you, doc?"

Doctor: "Let me see...I was here last week two times, and then there was that injection. The week before I...do you have an adding machine?"

Patient: "It is right over there."

Doctor: "Thank you...that comes to $80 even."

Patient: "That's pretty reasonable."

Doctors are compelled to do everything they do and it must be remembered that only when the conditions change, when they understand that man's will is not free and what this means, will they be able to be honest with themselves. After all, doctors must also earn a living. In order to demonstrate why this great change is compelled to come about (God is giving us no choice), I shall resort to a personal experience in my life. About two and a half decades ago a friend, 22 years of age, was advised to have his tonsils removed and died right on the operating table. He never came out of the anesthesia. The doctors involved did not break any malpractice laws, so they were not punished for this. "Sometimes these things will happen" was the reply, which is why they make it very clear that they will do everything in their power to help you but they cannot guarantee anything. The risk may be very small, but this is the price you must pay if you want their services. "Is everything all right, doctor?" the mother asks. "I don't know how to break this to you any easier, but your son didn't make it off the operating table." When the parents of this boy heard that their son had died during a tonsillectomy they were overwhelmed with grief and accused the doctor of negligence. It certainly did not satisfy him to be accused of this, and he defended himself vehemently blaming everything but himself. I never did find out what actually caused my friend's death. Now that the case is closed, no one will ever know the truth of what really happened that day. Although there is nothing that can be done to change the past, it is not God's will that these things continue, and when the knowledge of what it means that man's will is not free is thoroughly understood by the medical profession, and the transition gets officially launched, you will see for the very first time an honest admission of genuine ignorance.

In the new world when an individual leaves a university he will not depend on any graduation, but on whether he thinks he is ready for his chosen occupation. Our slide rule demonstrates that when he is not given the right by the school and state to use drugs, perform operations, and give other kinds of treatment, then he must be absolutely honest with himself about how much he really knows regarding the long term and immediate effects of medicine, surgery, tests, etc., because it becomes mathematically impossible for him to shift his responsibility to anyone but himself. Therefore, a doctor will be prevented from prescribing medicine, or performing an operation, unless he is absolutely certain he knows what he is doing for if a patient should be hurt as a consequence of his ignorance he knows he will never be blamed for this hurt. He knows that his patients are putting every confidence in his knowledge and that he could very easily take advantage of this for his own remuneration. But when he fully realizes that he might be responsible for people getting worse as a result of his treatment who will never blame him for this, he is compelled, of his own free will, to think like he never thought before, otherwise he might be placing himself in a position that affords no satisfaction. If he is unfamiliar with a group of symptoms, he will tell his patient that he really doesn't know. This will prevent the possibility of making the wrong diagnosis that could send a patient home prematurely and delay lifesaving treatment. In the new world no diplomas will ever again be issued because the right to practice medicine on the bodies of people will be granted to anyone who considers himself qualified. Each person will judge his own qualifications and if he wishes to risk hurting others who will not blame him, this is his business. If someone wishes to open an office and hang out a shingle no one is going to question him, but the full responsibility of hurting others with his treatments must rest on his own shoulders once the school pulls out the props that allowed him to shift his blame. When a student has learned all that the school is able to teach of genuine knowledge, he will also have drawn a mathematical line of demarcation between this kind of learning and the knowledge that is a matter of opinion.

When you consult a doctor for help, you will pay the same for his advice whether he prescribes something or just plainly tells you he doesn't know what to do. He may choose not to charge you for the consultation, but it is important to remember that the doctor must support himself — even if it is just to give his advice — or else he will be forced out of business. Honesty will always be the best policy in every case that is presented to him. The statement "I don't know" is not a sign of ignorance when you really do not know, but a sign of wisdom. Many patients are so accustomed to getting medicine for everything from colds and fever to immunizations for the flu that they are not satisfied until the doctor gives them a prescription. Once again, we are able to see the pressure the doctor is under to give his patients what they want so they won't go elsewhere. In the new world the doctor will tell his patients what he knows about certain drugs and where they can be purchased but he will not take a chance prescribing drugs to anybody because he will not be sure how they will react in each case, and he would never presume to have this knowledge. Now, let us observe a fantastic change that is compelled to come about out of absolute necessity by paying close attention to what happens when we imagine the death of a child from a tonsillectomy described earlier that will not occur with doctors who are citizens of the new world, so we can see why it will not.

All four family members are crying bitterly having just received the news of their child's death from a tonsillectomy. It has come as such a shock because this was supposed to be a routine operation, but no one points the finger of blame at the doctor. They know there is absolutely nothing the doctor could have done to prevent their child's death and they are not blaming him even though they are in excruciating pain over their tremendous loss. If it was the fault of the medical team, no one is blaming them. Each person, therefore, needs only to convince himself that he was not responsible in any way. The truth of the matter is that regardless of the number of times surgery has ended well it is not an exact science and there may be risk factors unbeknownst to the doctor, which is why he won't desire performing operations that are not absolutely necessary. Consequently, when all judging ceases, when the doctor has nobody to convince but himself as to whether he is qualified, he is not too anxious to assume the risk of hurting someone which can no more be justified by saying this is what he was taught in school simply because the teachers in the universities will go only by facts, not theory. If a doctor learns that what he has been taught is mathematically undeniable, then he need not be afraid of hurting another. It is impossible for someone to know everything that takes place within the body which has the amazing power to adjust to almost any condition, even those imposed by the medicines a doctor may prescribe.

"But that was years ago. Today the doctors have much greater knowledge of the body."

"You mean they think they have greater knowledge, don't you?"

"I really don't know what I mean. If I didn't have confidence in the knowledge of a doctor, how could I consult one? Besides, I certainly don't know what to do when I'm sick."

If it gives you greater satisfaction to call in your doctor, you should definitely do what you think is better for yourself. However, under the changed conditions the doctor himself will be compelled to refrain from prescribing anything that he is the least bit uncertain of because it cannot satisfy him to risk hurting others when there is no way it can be justified, that is, of course, once the medical schools stop making him think that he does know when he doesn't.

"Are you saying that there will be no more operations in the new world except to prevent death or a more miserable life?"

"Can you think of any other way for a doctor to justify the possibility of making matters worse? Remember, what stops him from taking these risks is not the fear of being slapped with a lawsuit, for there will be no such thing, but the fact that he knows in advance that everybody must excuse his actions, which means that unless he sees the mathematical (undeniable) relations that reveal a prognosis of death or a life worse than death unless he operates immediately, he will be compelled to refrain from advocating an operation because he will never be able to blame anybody but himself should his patient get worse or die. He will be compelled to be absolutely honest with himself and his patients, and if he is uncertain that an operation is the best course he will tell them that he really doesn't know what is best. This might not satisfy the patients who are in pain or scared half to death but unless he can justify that an operation is absolutely necessary, what choice does the doctor have in the new world when he will never be blamed for the mistakes he could incur because of his therapy? This does not mean that the doctor doesn't have the best of intentions when he advises certain procedures, but it does mean that he will be prevented from taking any unnecessary chances when no one will blame him for making matters worse. In our present world if a child should die parents would be told that there was absolutely nothing that could have been done to prevent it which may not be true since it is so easy for a doctor to lie even to himself. But in the new world the doctor, for the very first time since he stated the Hippocratic Oath, has no choice but to recognize that it is not God's will that a person die this way because over the desire to operate he has mathematical control; and when it fully dawns on him that he will never be blamed for someone's death should this occur even though it would be his responsibility, he is compelled, of his own free will, to advise an operation only if by not operating the patient will surely die, or the quality of life will be so poor that it will be a life worse than death.

The great need to earn the money necessary to sustain his standard of living which compelled the doctor to justify anything the least bit questionable was the first blow of hurt because the law of nature is self-preservation. Therefore, when doctors become citizens, receive a guarantee that their standard of living will never go down, and know for a fact that they will never again be blamed no matter what happens, allowing them to drop their malpractice insurance and increase their net income, they are compelled to move in a different direction for greater satisfaction. In our present world it is necessary for them to convince us that they can handle our problem, otherwise, we would not employ them and they would not get paid for their services, but under the changed conditions they do not have to convince us, only themselves, that they know what they are doing, and if in their professional opinion there is the slightest doubt that their treatment might make matters worse for which they know there would be no blame, their only justification to take this risk, since they cannot be financially hurt or blamed for refusing to take on the job, is when it appears to them that we would be worse off if they prescribed nothing. By refusing to question their qualifications or hold them responsible for our mistake in hiring them, they are compelled to hold themselves responsible for hurting their patients unless they can convince themselves that our getting worse or dying was not because of anything they did. Remember, when you consult a doctor in the new world you will pay the same for his advice whether he prescribes something or just plainly tells you he doesn't know what to do, and honesty will be the best policy. This means that if they have to choose between two risks, to advise us in some way, even if this means telling us to leave the body completely alone to handle its own problem, or to tell us that they really are uncertain of what to do and therefore will not take on the job, they are forced (of their own free will or desire) to move in the latter direction because there is no way it is possible to blame themselves for not knowing what to do, whereas if we should get worse because they advised us, which implies they do know what they're doing, it becomes impossible not to blame themselves when we will never hold them responsible while guaranteeing their standard of living. Today there is so much confusion as to what is genuine knowledge and what is an opinion that doctors themselves don't know the difference, and they justify what they do by the fallacious argument that they know what is right for a patient because they are members of the medical profession, as if an opinion is any less of an opinion because it comes from a doctor. In fact, the greater the unconscious ignorance the greater is the danger when it is not controlled. Let me remind you that it is fear that makes an individual pretend to knowledge he doesn't possess, but doctors were compelled to do this as the lesser of two evils when their income depended on this self-deception and dishonesty. Shakespeare said, "Above all, to thine own self be true, and it shall follow..." Unfortunately, he didn't know what he was talking about, although he thought he knew. How was it possible for man to be true to himself when this honesty would only hurt him in the end? Strange as this may sound to your ears, ninety percent of the people who have been treated by doctors got well in spite of the treatment, not because of it; and how many were killed and crippled with impunity would amaze you — for which these doctors are not to blame in any way — but all was necessary to learn what was learned about the body. There was also much good that resulted to balance the hurt. However, in the

325

new world when a doctor realizes that his income will not decrease or stop by being absolutely honest with his patients, then he can afford to be absolutely honest with himself. In our present world doctors are forced to be dishonest because they are blamed for not having the answers the moment they are consulted and no one wishes to pay them for admitting they really don't know. It also gives them great satisfaction to be admired for possessing the knowledge of how to restore a person's health, therefore your belief that they have this knowledge only makes them keep up the pretense. You must remember that everybody, including the doctor, is compelled to move in the direction of greater satisfaction. Consequently, it will give them no choice under the new conditions but to prescribe something only when they have convinced themselves that to do otherwise is definitely worse for us, which means that they would have to possess a tremendous amount of genuine knowledge. They would have to know all of the side, distant, and accumulative effects of drugs to make certain that in correcting one problem they do not create others still worse. In addition, they would have to know all the complications that could arise from an operation, whether it is from the anesthesia or the removal of certain parts of our body. If someone should die during an appendectomy, tonsillectomy, or from other surgery, the only way it is possible to clear their conscience of responsibility is to know that the patient would have been worse off without the operation — but, again, they must only convince themselves of this. They can no longer use the theory that our tonsils and appendix are vestigial organs to justify the operation unless they can convince themselves that we are better off without these parts of our body.

A young girl just recently had brain damage and died a few days later from the general anesthesia used to extract a wisdom tooth. Now how does a dentist in the new world convince himself that he was not responsible for her death when no one blames him and he knows there was a risk in using general anesthesia especially? How is it possible for him to justify her death? If she was in pain and needed this tooth removed, why did he choose a general anesthetic without knowing whether she was allergic to the drug itself or when combined with other drugs already in her system? It is obvious that he prescribed this anesthetic without knowing these risk factors. How is it possible for him to face the parents of this girl to tell them of her death when they will simply break down in tears and not blame him in any way for what he knows they must excuse because they hired him, while he also knows there is no way he can ever shift his responsibility unless he can convince himself that the use of this general anesthesia and the operation itself was the lesser of two evils? If he cannot, he is forced to go through life with the death of this girl on his conscience. Now why should doctors take these risks when it is no longer necessary for the purpose of earning a living, unless they can actually see that these risks must be taken, as the lesser of two evils, or else the patient may not survive? A patient when faced with a choice to have medical intervention that could possibly help a serious condition would have to take full responsibility for that choice because a doctor would not want to under the new conditions. It would also be up to the individual doctor to determine the type of cases he or she would be willing to accept. Let us see what happens when someone consults a doctor who has become a citizen of the new world to find out what is best, to breast or bottle feed a baby.

Husband: "Doctor, my wife's breasts are sore and tender and she would like to know if you would prescribe some formula for our baby?"

Doctor: "My friends, I honestly don't know what is better for this infant, a formula or mother's milk, consequently, I cannot advise you. If you want me to make up some formula so you won't have to use your breasts, I will, but I cannot say it is better or safe. Most babies do not have any problem but I cannot assume this responsibility to tell you that it is the better choice. This is a decision you will have to make all by yourself."

Wife: "Maybe I'd better stick with my breasts. Is there a charge for this?"

Doctor: "No, there is absolutely no charge for this consultation."

Should a mother not wish to use her breasts for one reason or another, which is her business, she will have to make the decision to take whatever risks there might be in the use of available formulas

327

because the only time a doctor will suggest them is when her breasts are not functioning and any formula is better than starvation, or when there is a contraindication (e.g., a medication the mother may be taking that could be passed on to the baby), for how can a doctor possibly know that the formula might not cause severe colic, cramps, diarrhea, etc., when every child is different to a degree. And how is he going to feel when something happens and he can blame no one but himself? Why should he take the risk? There is no reason, which forces a mother to choose between using the milk developed with and specifically for her baby, or to play doctor herself. Now what choice does she have when the fear of certain risks gives her less, not greater satisfaction? In the previous example where Durant allowed the doctors to advise his wife, in the new world they would have been compelled to make their own decision. Since Durant would not dare to advise his wife because he certainly doesn't know, otherwise he would never have gone with her to the pediatrician in the first place, she is left completely alone to make this decision herself because these are her breasts. If she can find someone to prescribe a formula or wet nurse her baby, this is entirely up to her. The fact that she still doesn't know which is better for in order to know she would have to have a tremendous amount of knowledge, she is afraid to go in the other direction, therefore, she is given no choice as to what she believes is better for herself and her baby. Regardless of the choice she makes, in the long run she must always move in the direction of greater satisfaction. As far as the administration of drugs, when patients consult a doctor who has become a citizen he will know that his patients will have many questions regarding these medications and whether they are safe, which he will be unable to answer. Let us listen to the following conversation.

Patient: "Doctor, I don't feel good and need you to do something for me, but are you absolutely positive that this medicine you're prescribing will not have any side effects, that it will not hurt me in any way? Doctor, tell me the truth, are you absolutely certain that many years from now should I continue to take these various drugs you always prescribe for my ills I will not get cancer, heart disease, and many other things that have become commonplace? I need to make an informed decision and in order to do this I need the facts. I know that my cold always clears up when you give me an injection but is it possible that it would clear up without the needle, without the drugs; and if this is possible why should I continue taking the needle and other things if you are uncertain of their distant effects on the body? Is it advisable to take this pain killer, or could this eventually have some cumulative effect? Please understand doctor, I am willing to pay heavily to know the truth but don't take my money unless you really know what is better for my body."

Doctor: "My friend, the only thing I can tell you about drugs is what I do know. I know that this medicine can eliminate your tension headache but I have no way of knowing what distant effects an accumulation of drugs can have on the cells of the body. I also have no way of knowing what is healthier, to use drugs to get rid of your aches and pains, or let the body try to correct this itself. I don't know if by not using drugs, or by using them, your body will get worse. The most I can do is show you what immediate effects we know certain drugs to have but I will not prescribe their use because I cannot assume such responsibility. In all major chains, the pharmacies have all of them, including heroin, LSD, and the whole shebang, and you will not need a prescription. The pharmacist won't advise you either as to what to take but he will sell them to you if you want to buy them."

Patient: "But doctor, you didn't give me a straight answer and you certainly didn't relieve my anxiety about taking medicine."

Doctor: "If I knew what was truly better for your body I would definitely tell you but since I have no idea what is the safest or most effective course of treatment, I cannot advise you here."

Patient: "Are you implying that there could be a connection between the drugs we take today and diseases that may not show up until years later?"

Doctor: "I really don't know, but the possibility exists."

When doctors become citizens and have their standard of living guaranteed and know that they will never be blamed for any possibility of hurt done to a patient who must excuse what they can no longer justify, they will definitely be forced to think long and hard before prescribing anything, except for those who can guarantee results without the slightest possibility of making matters worse. Wouldn't it be coincidental if certain cancers completely disappear along with this surplus of the medical profession and the pharmaceuticals they prescribe? The guarantee and basic principle will force doctors to become like Socrates. If you recall, he was proclaimed the wisest man of his time for discovering that one of the differences between himself and other men was that he knew he did not know the truth, whereas they didn't know either but thought they did. The doctors in the majority of cases when we consult them will respond like Socrates by saying — "I do not know what is better, to leave the body alone to heal itself or to prescribe something, therefore I cannot take on the job of treating your problem."

"But if doctors cannot give 100% guarantees when they prescribe drugs or surgery, and if they will feel guilty should they recommend something that makes matters worse for their patient, and if they are going to be guaranteed their standard of living, why should they prescribe anything when it is not to their advantage?"

Where drugs are concerned they will tell their patient what these drugs are supposed to do and what side effects there might be, but the patient will make the decision whether or not to use them. This also applies to injections of any kind. Remember, there will be no laws controlling the sale of drugs and a drugstore can carry all kinds if the pharmacist feels there will be buyers. No one will tell you what you can and cannot take into your system because this is your business, and you will never be blamed for the misery you might cause yourself. But you will be prevented from blaming the druggist or the doctor because they are not forcing you to take anything. The doctors will show someone how to administer an injection but the patient will have to decide if he wants to take the risk. As for operations, since this is something a patient cannot perform on himself, the doctors will only operate when they are convinced that the patient will get worse unless it is done.

"Under these changed conditions isn't it true that very few people would desire to become a doctor?"

That is true, but those who choose this profession will be dedicated to learn the truth and nothing but the truth about the human body. You must bear in mind that even though the human body obeys invariable laws, the curative power of these laws is still unknown. Because doctors have never known the curative power of the body alone, I am firmly convinced that 75% of the world's patients got better not because of what the doctor prescribed, but in spite of it. However, doctors had no better choice because, they too, were under the pressure of earning a living and meeting their bills. When this pressure is removed, along with the blame, they will let us make the decision as to what we should take into our system. This will force most of us to give the body a chance to do its work, and I believe it will be discovered that in the majority of cases, if not in all of cases, the body will do the job. Bear in mind also that when the pressure is removed not only from the doctors but from the patients to sustain their standard of living; and the moment it is fully understood what it means that man's will is not free, 99% of what now disturbs the body will be warded off because of the perfect condition of the mind and a great many illnesses will be wiped from the face of the earth. As a consequence, approximately 75% of what is prescribed today will be stopped by the doctors themselves which means that approximately 25% of the hospitals, doctors and nurses that are now in existence will suffice for our needs in the new world. If a doctor's standard of living is $500 a week and after using up all his cash reserve his income starts to decrease because of a lack of patients, we will continue to supply the difference while he is still in practice just as long as it is impossible for him to get a new job paying more than what his income has been reduced to. But if he can get a job paying $200 a week, and his total receipts from his patients are now less than this, then he would be compelled, of his own free will, to take the new job because the difference between this and the amount we have to give him would cost us less.

A psychiatrist, who also needs to earn a living, must convince his patients that they have an illness which is treatable in order to get paid. As was explained earlier, he is able accomplish this by projecting onto this screen of undeniable substance, in a great many cases, a number of fallacious standards for determining the mental illness of people. The various words he uses circumscribes a behavior pattern which he then labels sick, just as certain differences in a person's facial features are symbolized beautiful or ugly. Consequently, he easily justifies that innumerable people are mentally disturbed and in need of his help, only he believes that most of them are too proud to admit to this. Once he has identified all behavior patterns, it is then an easy matter to set up a course of treatment. However, there is the possibility, even here, that he could make matters worse by tampering with the mind and unless he can guarantee results, which he might possibly be able to do, he will be compelled, of his own free will, to admit to himself and his patients (especially when his standard of living will be guaranteed and when he knows he will never be blamed for hurting them, just in the event he does) that he is uncertain of his knowledge. It is true there are differences in behavior patterns and physiognomies, but certain words are not symbolic except of what we have projected from our realistic imagination. Therefore, it is important to recognize that many illnesses are nothing but words, as strange as this may seem, which Montaigne and other philosophers perceived. Psychiatry will be completely displaced not only because there will be no possibility of anyone ever becoming mentally disturbed again, but also because the doctors will be prevented from taking advantage of their patients' ignorance which heretofore hurt many individuals with justifiable impunity. When someone does physical or other harm to another without justification then we will know that he is mentally disturbed, but this is virtually impossible in the new world. Until then, God is forcing us to leave the mind alone. Now tell me; is this Supreme Being we call God a genius, or isn't He? God, or the force that controls our movement in the direction of greater satisfaction, is forcing us to rely on our body to take care of 98% of all its problems by making all mankind realize that they don't know the truth about a tremendous number of these things, they only thought they knew. If you are afraid of getting worse and wish to prescribe for yourself some drug, this will be your business. On the other hand, if you are more afraid of the drug than leaving your body alone, this is also your business. But you will have to decide this for yourself since the doctors who are citizens of the new world will be afraid to make it for you because the full realization that they might be responsible for making you worse, not better, and the fact that they will never be blamed, prevents them from offering excuses for what they can never justify. Since there will be no more diplomas or licenses, it will be up to the students themselves to determine if they are qualified to put up a shingle, open an office, and charge a fee. As for those who have become citizens of the new world, there will be no such thing as legal or illegal. They will know what is, and what is not, a hurt and they will never desire to do anything that could hurt another. Let us now continue the extension of our basic principle, Thou Shall Not Blame, in order to remove the remaining evils that were compelled to come into existence during our years of development.

CHAPTER EIGHT

UNTIL DEATH DO THEY PART

In recent times there has been a surge of bestsellers offering couples specific instructions on how to achieve wedded bliss, but for the vast majority the secret to lifelong happiness remains elusive. The reason for this is the fact that marriage does not exist in a vacuum, consequently, we must take a broader look for our answers. It appears that the social and economic climate surrounding the newly married couple exerts a tremendous influence on their potential for success. How well a society is faring can be used as a barometer to gauge marital intimacy or dissatisfaction since there appears to be a direct correlation. For example, when the job market shows signs of a recession and there exists a pervasive insecurity, the divorce rate begins to rise. This is no surprise as arguments related to finances have been identified as the number one cause of divorce. As we begin to look at marriage in a much larger context we are able to see how every area of human relation is inextricably linked and from this vantage point we can get a clearer picture of the many factors that have led to the marital breakdown. As the Great Transition gets under way, the enormous metamorphosis in national and international relations will cause a ripple effect eliminating many of the pressures that have contributed to the dissolution of the marital unit. You will soon observe how the extension of our basic principle prevents divorce, but it must be remembered that everything was necessary. Man could never have reached this point in his development without first going through the necessary stages, just as a baby cannot reach adulthood without first going through the necessary stages of childhood and adolescence.

The purpose of this chapter is to expose with the help of our slide rule, Thou Shall Not Blame, the source of arguments in marriage that lead to resentment, disillusionment, and ultimately the divorce court. Please bear in mind that the term 'marriage' under the new conditions does not mean the signing of a legal document. On the contrary, this term signifies a sacred union for the purpose of raising a family and sharing a deep bond of love and commitment. Before jumping to conclusions, consider this: If by removing the legal obligation — which needs to be viewed in the context of enormous changes that will be taking place once all blame is removed — couples are prevented from ever desiring to leave one another, then there is nothing to be lost — only gained. In the world of free will the obligation implicit in the marital contract contributed to couples falling out of love, although there was no other alternative that could guarantee compensation for those left behind if the marriage failed. This is not to criticize what developed out of necessity but to demonstrate how we can achieve the greatest marital satisfaction by following our slide rule which opens the door to many changes that were never before possible. Consequently, all reasoning henceforth will be based on this new understanding which is the foundation for all the miraculous changes about to take place. As we apply our basic principle (which God is giving to mankind), marriages will be happier than could ever be imagined. Couples will remain together not because they are bound by a legal document, but because their love will only get stronger with each passing year. How this miracle takes place is amazing to behold. Let us begin by observing a newly married couple and their dreams for the future.

At this precise moment in the life of our newlyweds neither desires to leave or lose the other, therefore they are compelled to prefer learning the mathematical secret of how to arouse the desire of the person they want...to always want them. Once having felt such a wonderful glow, who'd want to take any chance of losing it? If love is wonderful (which most people would agree), then we need to be particularly careful to do what will preserve it, not destroy it. This doesn't only apply to sex, but in general. Even in our present world we dream in our love stories of getting married and living happily ever after, only it has always remained a dream beyond our reach because sooner or later a first blow is unconsciously struck which justifies some form of retaliation. The solution, therefore, is to teach these couples how to prevent this first blow of hurt from being struck which, if accomplished, gives to marriage the greatest security imaginable for all adultery and divorce arise only because this starts a chain reaction of anger and resentment that eventually kills love. Future experts will analyze what is and what is not a first blow (which will surprise you) in human relationships and newly married couples will be anxious to acquire this knowledge so they can prevent hurting one another unintentionally which may lead to what neither of them wants.

To give you an illustration of the power of this law, let us now imagine that this radiant wife who has been falling more and more in love with her husband as they continue making passionate love to each other on their honeymoon, as they continue looking forward to the warmth and ecstasy of this sexual satisfaction, knows positively that it is absolutely impossible for her husband to ever desire leaving her despite the fact that she knows he is not under any obligation to remain and is completely free to do anything he wants to do, just as long as he knows she is definitely in love with him (take your time with this) because she knows that he knows if he left her, under these conditions, this would break her heart for which he would never be blamed, as this desire to hurt her so deeply must be considered by others as God's will or a compulsion over which he has no control. But he knows it is not God's will or a compulsion over which he has no control because he also knows that he doesn't have to break her heart unless he wants to, and he discovers that it is impossible to do the things that would be a hurt to her just as long as he knows she is definitely in love with him. Therefore, this knowledge that he will never be blamed by his wife for deliberately or carelessly hurting her — knowing she loves him very much — makes it mathematically impossible to ever leave. This great security is assured the wife just as long as she shows her husband that she truly loves him (by her actions), for only then can his leaving her for another sexual companion be a source of hurt for which there is no justification. When he realizes that she would never leave him no matter how much he hurt her, he is compelled to stay. We have now arrived at the other half of the equation.

This young husband, so much in love with his wife at this moment in his life, knows also that she will never desire to leave him just as long as she knows he is in love with her. Consequently, since he knows that her desire to leave depends solely on him being out of love

337

with her which separation would break his own heart (for which she cannot be blamed and he can prevent), he is compelled, for his own security and happiness — completely beyond control but of his own free will — to prefer doing everything in his power to satisfy his wife to show that he is not out of love with her so that this desire to leave him for another will never arise in her. By knowing that his own security with the person he loves depends on her love for him — which he can control by showing his love for her — and by knowing that her security with the person she loves depends on his love for her — which she can control by showing her love for him — they are given no choice but to do everything in their power for each other as that alternative considered better for themselves because it is the only means by which they can prevent what they do not want. Therefore, once it is understood that sexual satisfaction in varying degrees is the true meaning of love and when it decreases in an unmutual manner a marriage deteriorates, it is obvious that the surest way to success in conjugal affairs is to arouse the sexual passion of the other. This demonstrates in an undeniable fashion that as sexual passion grows the husband wants his wife to be in love with him, which demonstrates that he doesn't want anyone else since her love makes this impossible. Likewise, as his wife makes efforts to arouse his desire she reveals that she wants his love, which makes him conscious that she does not want anyone else since his love for her also makes this a mathematical impossibility, as was just shown.

In a short time each will be absolutely dependent on the other for what the body now craves and if this was stopped as happened frequently in the world of free will for various reasons, which occasioned the serious consequences of unsatisfied desire, it would be the worst form of torment. Yet where sex is concerned there are two individual desires involved and it is impossible in the new world for one person to desire obligating the other as this is a form of tacit blame, a judgment of what is right for someone else which cannot be preferred when it is realized that this will only hurt the very relationship that both parties want to preserve. Consequently, when a husband and wife realize from the very beginning that the security of their own happiness depends on arousing and satisfying the sexual passion of the other without imposing one ounce of obligation because

338

this is advance blame, they are given no choice as to what is better for themselves since any word or action that decreases the desire to have a passionate relation only reveals a lack of love by tacitly blaming the sexual desire of the other.

"You are too much! I can see that this is completely mathematical except for two things that still have to be demonstrated. How is it possible to have a marriage without any obligations; and what is required to show one's love?"

Another friend chimed in: "Maybe it did to you, but what he just demonstrated made no sense to me. You have taken for granted that sexual passion can be aroused after many years of wedlock, and I say it can't be."

"Do you want to make a wager?"

"Not a chance of it. In other words, I didn't mean to say 'it can't be done,' only that I think it can't be."

"Well then please refrain from jumping to conclusions, is that asking too much?"

"No it isn't. Please continue."

Being aware that sexual satisfaction is what keeps couples together, they will be compelled to desire learning all they can about human sexuality and what pleases their partner in particular. This subject will be part of the high school curriculum and no one need have any fear that these boys and girls can ever go in the wrong direction. Under the new conditions they will want to devote their lives to each other, doing everything in their power for the happiness of each as that alternative considered better for themselves because it is the only means by which they can prevent what they do not want when it is understood that man's will is not free. This proves conclusively that God has given each of us the power to prevent the person truly loved from ever hurting us by revealing the mathematical corollary, the mathematical reason, why it is better for us when we do not blame. It also proves undeniably that any couple marrying under these conditions, regardless of how short a time they have known each other, or for any other reason, must not only fall more and more in love with each passing year but must also find the greatest security imaginable, without one ounce of obligation, because these things

339

increase with their passion and devotion. Let us review.

The husband, knowing that his own security with the person he loves depends on her love for him which he can control by showing his love for her; and the wife knowing that her own security with the person she loves depends on his love for her which she can control by showing her love for him, they are given no choice but to do everything in their power to show their love for each other as that alternative considered better for themselves. In the past the word love was used as a justification to be selfish, but once the true definition is clarified any display of genuine selfishness will be avoided at all costs since it will reflect a lack of love, the very source of marital unhappiness. In the new world the language of love speaks very differently in that it is not through words that true love is communicated, but through actions. The fact that the husband and wife know they are under no obligation to each other in any way, sexual or otherwise, and they are completely free to come and go as they please, the only way they can control their partner's desire to stay married is by searching for what might possibly be a source of careless hurt to them, for which they know they will never be blamed. If man's will was free they could leave each other regardless of the conditions that prevail, but they are absolutely incapable of desiring this option which proves, once again, but in a slightly different manner, that will is not free because leaving under the changed conditions would be a motion in the direction of dissatisfaction — which is impossible to do. Are you beginning to see the difference between an opinion and a mathematical fact? This is completely mathematical in every way and will not be denied when the rest of the relations are perceived, therefore any opinions to the contrary are only an indication that certain points need further clarification.

At this juncture, however, it is necessary to elaborate on how words have created a serious imbalance in how couples are forced to perceive each other. Consequently, part of this chapter is dedicated to exposing many of the words responsible (some may surprise you) and to demonstrate how they are striking a first blow. In order for true respect to exist, which is the basis for a loving relationship, these words must become obsolete out of absolute necessity. The solution to this serious problem refers us back to Chapter Four: Words, Not

Reality, to make certain that you understand why the eyes are not a sense organ so I can reveal more clearly the fallacy of words. From there we will be able to see how fallacious word slides which do not symbolize anything real, but create the illusion of doing so, have been able to fool everyone by getting a foothold in our lexicon and our everyday speech.

Each language has its own set of words or symbols which are used to identify substance existing in the external world. Therefore we can say that these symbols describe an accurate object-word relationship. It should be obvious to everyone's common sense that the sun exists out in space like the moon, the stars, buildings, people, automobiles, etc. These objects are real, are completely independent of an individual's perception, and do not exist in a person's head as some epistemologists have imagined. We see them not because they impinge upon the optic nerve but because they are there to be seen if one cares to look. The word does not create the dog as it does words like heaven, spirit, soul, etc., it is this dog that gives us the desire to give it a name which then identifies it and allows us to differentiate it from other objects. In other words, the word dog makes us conscious that this something is not a cat or a cow and it allows us to see this difference between existing bits of substance because the word used to describe this particular animal is different from words used to describe other animals, which is why we give it a different name. Consequently, the actual word contains the consciousness of a difference that exists in the external or internal world. Remember, there is absolutely nothing that travels from the dog to the optic nerve although the bark does strike the ears, and this sound is a slide in itself which then permits the brain to look at this bit of living substance through the many relations that become associated with the sound. As stimuli enter through the four senses and get combined in various relations, they are then projected upon the screen of substance through the eyes which see everything in relation to what is on the slide. If a child gets frightened by the barking of a dog this fear is recorded on the slide and photographed in relation, and when a dog is seen the fear is projected.

Among human relations there are a tremendous number of

differences between word slides that each of us stores in our brains because we are all different to some degree, consequently, what you experience in your world depends on the slides through which you see your experiences. The words that you learned while growing up and reading many books are the particular slides which you experienced in context — in relation to certain things — which means that you will use and look through them as these experiences project the relation. These word slides represent your consciousness of something you know exists because these things are seen with your eyes (after the relation has been made and a photograph taken), and here is the true source of all the confusion for although the experiences are real and cannot be denied your understanding of them is fallacious since your brain never photographed an accurate mathematical relation and as a result you see a faulty version of reality. The very fact that the philosopher Will Durant believed he could see that man's will is free with direct perception, and the very fact that man actually believes he has five senses, amply illustrates what I mean because it indicates how easy it is to conclude something is true when an inaccurate word slide is used as a lens from which to view the world. However, a still deeper analysis is required to show you why certain words set the stage for disrespect between the sexes.

In the course of many years man developed words to describe opposites (this was absolutely necessary for his development), but though it is true that death is the opposite of life, and determinism is the opposite of free will, the word tall is not the opposite of short, nor is the word educated the opposite of uneducated. It should be clear from our earlier discussion that certain opposites represent a range of imaginary values from one extreme to the other. The word brilliant is not the opposite of stupidity, and yet these fallacious differences (which you will understand much better when education is discussed) were perceived because we were looking through word slides that were projected realistically onto substance in relation to certain undeniable experiences. We actually came to believe that this range of difference between one extreme and the other, between ugliness and beauty, etc., was a part of the real world and our entire vocabulary was employed to describe this gamut of imaginary differences. Words have created so much hurt in male/female relationships (due to the inaccurate slides through which they have been compelled, completely beyond control, to look at each other), it is no wonder depression is so common among teenagers as they enter the dating scene. It is obvious that if a young man was given an opportunity to win a beautiful in preference to an ugly individual he would have no choice but to pick the beautiful one while those considered less attractive or ugly would be compelled to live in an unhappy world because this selection always puts them at the bottom of the totem pole. These individuals are automatically at a disadvantage because the opposite sex considers a beautiful or handsome person much more desirable and the reason there is so much value in being born one type of individual presently called beautiful and intelligent rather than the type now called ugly and stupid. It is apparent that the people who are labeled ugly are being struck a hurtful blow by the word itself, while the beautiful people can look forward to a much happier existence. Due to the fact that no one knew there was no such thing as ugliness or beauty and that these words were not true symbols of reality, those who had been dealt a bad hand were pitied for their unfortunate lot in life. There is no way to accurately calculate the extent of damage that has been inflicted on young impressionable minds because of this faulty labeling which brands them from the moment they are born. The unhappiness resulting from these words are manifold and manifest in the very fact that people develop a complex of inferiority from which stem a host of evils, although it is true that some good occurred by driving those with a feeling of inferiority to develop at an enormous rate in an effort to get rid of what gave them no satisfaction. It is for this very reason that many of the most developed minds were handicapped people or individuals who never went to school but who recognized their talents by a comparison, which spurred them on. This compensatory measure was their way of coping with an unjust environment, even if it meant achieving against all odds.

Unknowingly, our choice of words has been responsible for artificially stratifying people into layers of value, giving some more privilege than others. This stratification has caused a systemic form of inequality that has formed the basis for discrimination and differential treatment. For example, a college graduate is considered of greater value and therefore is paid a higher income, besides, he receives greater respect, gets a title like professor or Ph.D. which, again, places him in a category apart from others. Although it is true he may have read more books, may have learned more words, may have passed to a higher grade than other of his colleagues, yet a laborer may have shoveled more dirt, may have developed greater muscles, may have built buildings instead of read books, for what reason is the one considered more educated? The fallacy lies in the fact that the word education, like beauty, has become associated only with certain differences and represents a judgment of one person in relation to another, but regardless of who is the judge, it is the word itself which compels him to see through this faulty lens what he is convinced is absolutely true — a very intelligent, educated, person — while he sees someone who has a different background as an uneducated individual. Most of you know this but are unaware that it is absolutely impossible for an individual to see this person for what he really is because the word slide projects a value that does not exist externally, and only when these very symbols are removed will someone begin to get a glimpse of the real world.

It is now time to draw a mathematical line of demarcation, the line which will reveal the words that are going to be removed because they have hurt many people by forcing them to see themselves, as well as be seen by others, in a distorted manner. There exists one major obstacle in removing this injustice. It is impossible for a person living in our present world to give up the notion that she is more beautiful than another, nor will a person desire to stop using the word unless she realizes the serious hurt that has been inflicted on those who are not identified this way. If I call a girl beautiful in the presence of another who is not considered as nice, or whose opinion differs from mine, I am seriously hurting this other person who prevents my desire to hurt her this way by letting me know, well in advance, through this knowledge, that she will never blame me for this hurt. The change in our vocabulary takes place not only as a consequence of the perfect harmony in which children will be raised, but also because everyone will be made conscious that whenever one uses a word that places another in a category of plus he seriously hurts some individual by putting him in a category of minus, for which he knows no one will ever blame him. Although many people will slip and use words that judge others as inferior productions of the human race, when the blame for this is permanently removed, when these people fully realize that such words distort the real world and are a genuine hurt, they will soon find greater satisfaction in removing them from their vocabulary. These changes come about out of necessity by revealing in an infallible manner where the responsibility lies for this unjust hurt to others, which is then not blamed. The great humor lies in the fact that what is accomplished is the very perfection of God's will for all mankind, of which we are all a part. As we continue to be guided by the corollary, Thou Shall Not Blame, we will observe wonderful changes that must come about as we put God's law into practice. With this in mind I shall demonstrate, in a completely undeniable manner, His infinite wisdom as we observe how the most perfect relations between married couples offers them the very happiness they are so desperately seeking.

Someone asked me in the course of conversation, "How can you possibly know they will stay together for the rest of their lives when years hence their feelings might change towards each other?"

I answered by asking him a math problem. "How long would it take a car traveling at 60 miles an hour to travel 98 million miles? Sixty times 24 hours equals 1440 miles; 1440 miles, which represents one day, will divide into 98 million 64,583 days; 365 days will divide into that approximately 176 years."

"But how can you know this when the car wouldn't arrive until 176 years later? Supposing the car broke down, had a few flat tires, and maybe the driver wouldn't live that long?"

We're assuming that the car travels at an average speed of 60 miles an hour, so even if there were several flat tires and several drivers had to be changed it would still take approximately 176 years. You are able to do this simply by extending mathematical relations. I am going to do the same thing with this married couple. I am going to set up mathematical conditions that will force them (of their own free will or desire) to prefer traveling the full length of their lives together without ever desiring to commit adultery or get a divorce, and they will be given no choice because they will want what they see and will know how to get it. Is it possible for a person not to want what he wants, or to phrase it differently, not to desire what he desires? But in order to accomplish this we must first uncover the irreparable harm that can occur when couples see each other through a distorted lens. So, once again, let us return to Chapter Four, Words, Not Reality.

A serious imbalance develops in our present marriages when husbands and wives are not aware that they are seeing each other through a host of fallacious word slides that falsely reveal the superiority of one and the inferiority of the other. For example, the husband by feeling superior will criticize or judge what is right for his wife which strikes the first blow, and then when she does not agree or conform she is blamed. Painful feelings are often felt when a husband, not conscious that the very words he uses in conversation are an indirect source of hurt to his wife, strikes the very first blow. It doesn't take long before he destroys the desire on her part to show her love for him because he has failed to show his love for her when he uses words that make her feel inferior; and when he sees that she is not showing him the love she once did he is unaware that the responsibility in this entire instance is his although he justifies what he does by blaming her. Because the husband is now aware of the harm caused by words and has removed them from his vocabulary so that each person is treated with the utmost respect — love has no opportunity to diminish. His wife's love and affection are permitted to grow because the first blow has been prevented which makes it impossible for him to desire leaving her for someone else when he also knows this would be a real, not imaginary, hurt for which she would never blame him. When they both understand these mathematical relations not only will the one be able to prevent any motion in the direction of retaliation, as was explained in the second chapter, but the other will be able to prevent any first blows from being struck which will allow the transition to get under way.

History has shown that it was impossible for a marriage to get off to a sound start because it was never on an equal footing. A young couple, although they were married under the most favorable conditions, would still end up having arguments (which is not healthy despite what the psychologists have professed) since it is impossible for two people to have a balanced equation of love and respect when words destroy this balance at the very outset. For what reason would Durant (the famous philosopher whose opinion was placed above all others) consider certain type women as decerebrated dolls, perhaps like the wife of Socrates, if he did not perceive this difference in intelligence between these females? Now tell me, how is it possible for a person considered a genius to live in harmony with his spouse when he considers her intelligence, her education, her wisdom, her common sense, much inferior to his own? What happens when the thrill of her body diminishes, will he not wonder what on earth could have made him take such a woman? This kind of logic compelled philosophers like Nietzsche and Durant to believe that a couple should not be allowed to make too quick a decision about marriage which only reveals the extent of their unconscious ignorance, for which neither can be blamed.

Continuing our analysis, there is another hidden problem that leads to a build up of resentment not only between married couples but as a part of the general social fabric. What is this serious problem? It is the fact that mankind is having constant collisions of desire. This has been an enormous source of conflict and must be solved in order for there to be peaceful coexistence. To balance this equation during our years of development God was compelled to have good and evil and the balance was perfect. Now that we have developed sufficiently to see His laws which reveal Him by observing the harmony in the mankind system that was never understood until now, He snips off the evil and attaches good so that the balance still remains perfect. To understand the magnitude of this mathematical problem which requires for its solution that there be no collisions of desire anywhere in the world, I shall offer you a problem as a comparison and then show how it can be prevented.

A teacher has 15 students whom she takes on a walk 7 days of the week, but because she believes in order and variety of company on these daily strolls through the woods she decides to arrange them in groups of three in a column formation. So every day, for seven days, each student is never twice with the same student in a group which means that if A has already been with B and C he can walk with D on the next day, but since D has already been with E and F he must select together one of the remaining students from G to O. When you realize that these 15 students must all be arranged this way for 7 days, you can see it is not too simple a problem unless you see the relations. Now just compare these 15 students whose desires do not conflict on these walks (there is no collision) with the billions of people in the world who God is going to direct so there will never be any collisions of desire. In order to accomplish this every couple will be compelled, of their own free will, to remove from their relationship every bit of advance blame. This means that Judgment Day has arrived at last, the time when we will be compelled to stop judging what is right for others…and judge only what is right for ourselves. How this comes about with the aid of our basic principle — Thou Shall Not Blame — is also marvelous to behold, but let me elaborate to show you exactly what I mean.

Man has not yet become aware that an undeniable standard exists by which we can judge whether or not our own desires have the right-of-way when in apparent conflict with those of our partners. Just as traffic is run in an orderly fashion by a right-of-way system, there exists the same type of system in human relations which allows us to know who has the right-of-way when desires clash. The right-of-way system works in the following way: If you tell me what to do, then to satisfy your desire you need me to do something for you, but to satisfy my desire not to do what you want done does not require you to do anything for me. Therefore, my desire has the right-of-way because I am making no demands on you whatsoever. You see, in every human relation there are two desires involved, yours and theirs, but if to satisfy you, you need them, then their desire must be taken into consideration, and if they do not want to do what you want done, then there is nothing you can do about it once the basic principle is introduced. In the past, however, you justified doing something to hurt them for not satisfying your desire. This is crucial because it shows who is striking a first blow. Therefore, when you know you are definitely in the wrong by judging what is right for them, and when it becomes impossible for you to hurt them for not doing what you think they should because you know they will never blame you, you can find no satisfaction in trying to impose your will. This imposition was necessary in our present world because others were hurting you with their judgment of what was right for you. The entire problem of marriage is solved by obeying our slide rule which means that all advance blame, this judging of what is right for someone else, must be removed — for then all the factors leading up to adultery and divorce are precluded. There will be absolutely no standards telling a couple how to act except for one: Thou Shall Not Blame your partner in any form.

"Do you mean you're going to do the same thing with marriage as you did with the economic system?"

"That's right. I'm simply going to remove all forms of advance blame."

"Do you mean that a husband and wife can do anything they want without any control, without any restrictions?"

"Of course that's not what I mean. You know they are going to be controlled by a law that brooks no opposition, so how can you say 'without control?'"

"It just seems like it won't work. Do you mean that if a golf lover wants to leave his wife and kids everyday that he is off from work, to play the game from morning to night, that he can do this if he wants to? Do you mean there will be absolutely no standards as to what is proper for the success of a marriage?"

"Only one standard. Thou Shall Not Blame your partner in any form. Any indication of selfishness, which word has never been adequately understood, only reveals a lack of love because it blames one partner for not surrendering to the demands of the other. There must be this line of demarcation between what is and is not a hurt, which is drawn very simply. In our present world the words selfish and inconsiderate have been used to describe the unwillingness of a person to do what is asked of him. This definition is completely fallacious and causes great resentment from the one who has to sacrifice his own desire not to do what is requested, especially when it does not hurt or involve the desire of the other person in any way. In actuality, it is the one making the demand who is selfish because it requires someone to do something for him, whereas the other is making no demands at all. In the new world if a spouse unintentionally happens to strike a first blow by judging in advance what is right for the other, this will be pointed out. By using the mathematical standard to judge who is at fault, the one responsible will want to correct his ways because he would not want to strike the same blow again. Let me rephrase this

349

to show you, once again, who is striking the first blow.

If A has a desire which does not in any way make demands on the desire of B, otherwise it would be a judgment of what B's desire should be, then there is no way that B can exercise any control over A who is free to satisfy this desire. At the present time in your marriages A blames B for a hurt which is A's responsibility. If A does not show his love, he strikes the first blow and justifies infidelity on the part of B because it would not really be a hurt to a person not in love. Consequently, this releases B from the control of A. In other words, the husband blames the wife for making him a cuckold when all the time it was something he could have prevented providing he had known man's will is not free and what this means. But that's like saying Socrates could have ridden in an airplane or spoken on a phone had these been available during his time. Heretofore, the absence of this knowledge had allowed us to use many fallacious standards such as are contained in customs, laws, conventions, morals, etc. to justify hurting the partner who is not satisfying our selfishness. In order for a person to blame others he must feel that he has been hurt or wronged, which justifies some form of retaliation. When he judges in advance for them he makes his judgment a standard of what is right and when they fail to do what he thinks they should, he blames them. However, when our magic elixir demonstrates mathematically who is wrong where human relations are concerned, then he is given no choice but to change his ways.

As we continue to identify the various forms of advance blame, this judging of what is right for someone else, we will be able to prevent arguments that eat away at marriage and rob a couple of joy. In the new world if a wife should get satisfaction in lighting candles, reading the Bible, praying to God, or anything else she wishes to do, this would be strictly her business. The husband is not going to argue with her if she prefers to do these things, consequently an argument could only arise if she tried to make him do them as well, but how can she desire to do this when her action would blame him in advance for not doing them? Now that both partners know who has the right-of-way, there can be no conflict. In our present world if a husband should desire to get up from the dinner table before the meal is over to watch television or do something else, the wife considers it inconsiderate or selfish to leave her sitting there alone and she blames him for this. But in actual mathematical reality the wife in this case is the selfish one for she is judging what is right for her husband by expecting him to sacrifice a desire that makes him happy. His desire does not hurt her in any real way nor does he make any imposition on her desire to continue eating which reveals that she is not showing genuine love for him, otherwise, it would make her happy to see him deriving pleasure out of something that does not impose on her. If, on the other hand, his leaving was not an imaginary but a real hurt to his wife, he would be compelled not to hurt her because the knowledge that she would never blame him for this hurt, and the realization that this hurt would not be showing his love for her, would only lessen his security which he has the ability to control. Not yet acquiring a complete grasp of these mathematical, undeniable relations — which were revealed in the second chapter — may compel you to ask, "Wouldn't this allow a person to take advantage of not being blamed to do many things heretofore controlled by a nagging wife or a strong-armed husband?" This is not accurate because taking advantage itself is a definite form of hurt which not only reveals the lack of love while lessening the security desired by either spouse, but also because this will be seen as a hurt for which there would be no criticism. It is true, however, that many things can cause pain in the life of a married couple as a result of their love for each other which could never hurt them otherwise.

There is another form of advance blame which is the asking of favors because it is a roundabout way of telling someone what to do. This occurs when we expect others to do something for us and when they decide against it we justify criticizing or hurting them in some way by claiming they struck the first blow because they didn't do what we judged they should. Let me show you exactly what I mean. A friend of mine overheard a guy in town named Big Buck ask someone in a bar to lend him ten dollars, but this guy wouldn't do it. It seemed like an innocent request but didn't end up that way.

"Tony, can you lend me five dollars until Friday?"
"I can't spare it."
"Don't tell me that. I know you could if you wanted to. Didn't

I lend you five, two years ago? Can't you return the favor?"

He hit this guy so hard with his fist that he was out for ten minutes. Big Buck then went through his pockets, took out the ten, and stated, "When I ask you the next time to do me a favor you'd better think twice before you turn me down." This guy has twenty people running errands for him because they are scared half to death. Believe it or not, there is no difference between this and the authority a husband and wife exercise over each other and their children. In the world of free will Big Buck blames the guy he socked for hurting him by not lending the money. In the new world he will know that this is a first blow and he is wrong by striking it. However, if he still feels like punching this person that will be his decision but he will know, well in advance, that no one alive, including the person to be hurt, will ever blame him or desire to hurt him in return. By introducing the principle at this point, all bullies, including parents (I will discuss children separately), bosses, husbands and wives will be compelled to lose their desire to bully. This advance blame determines mathematically who is right and then prevents the desire on the part of those who are making the innocent party feel guilty, to do what is wrong. Below is a conversation between husband and wife to show the subtle way spouses are manipulated by making the other feel guilty. Let us imagine this scenario:

Husband: "Honey, would you mind bringing me the newspaper?"
Wife: "I'm too busy right now."
Husband: (Getting perturbed) "It will only take a second. Come on, I want to read the sports section before the game comes on; and bring me some ice cream while you're at it."
Wife: "I'll be there in a minute." (Not wanting to start an argument she reluctantly gets him what he wants).

One of the great sources of resentment is when we try to save ourselves physical effort by getting others, without paying them, to do for us what we can do for ourselves. This happens all the time when we ask people to do us favors which blames them in advance the

352

possibility of being disappointed, and when we are, we blame. Proof that this is the case is the fact that we could never ask a favor if we knew positively it would be refused. Consequently, when they fail to do what we expect of them we justify criticizing or getting back in some way by claiming they struck the first blow because they did not do what we judged they should. In our present world if a husband carelessly leaves the evening paper downstairs when he intended to bring it with him he would simply yell to his wife, "I need you to bring me the newspaper." He could have gotten the newspaper himself before going upstairs, but he moved in the direction of least resistance which was natural under the circumstances. As she brings him his paper he conveniently adds, "I worked hard all day, how about a little back rub?" Although this seems like a harmless request, when carefully analyzed it is anything but. Because this question blames her in advance for not desiring to do what he wants done, it is a euphemistic way of telling her what to do since he gets angry when she refuses. He may then try to make her feel guilty in an effort to get what he wants. The right-of-way system necessitates that she desire the same thing, but supposing she doesn't want to rub his back, what then? He has already blamed her in advance the moment he asks her to do something for him. If she doesn't comply with his request, he doesn't hesitate to show his disapproval for not satisfying his desire. He knows she will give in because she doesn't want to appear selfish (do you see the confusion in the definition?), and since she already rejected his first request she feels that she cannot refuse a second time. She is worried that his anger could turn into a rage which she tries to avoid by giving in. She grudgingly rubs his back although her resentment has begun to grow. In this instance the wife has to sacrifice her desire not to do what he is demanding. This is pure selfishness on his part and shows exactly where the problem begins since it starts a chain of blame and retaliation that will eventually destroy love. Man had no conception of how much ill will developed from just asking favors of one another and in every case it is the person asking, giving advice, and telling others what to do who is responsible for the disappointment and unhappiness that follows. When the husband fully understands that asking favors is advance blame and a sign of ignorance, he wouldn't think of asking his wife to rub his back; and just before going upstairs he would be compelled to say to himself, "Is there something I want to take with me now in order to save myself a trip later?" When he can't impose his will on others anymore because to do so he must strike the first blow of hurt for which he will never be blamed, and realizing that he can no longer justify his anger at those who refuse to do him favors, he is compelled to think like never before to save himself unnecessary physical effort. In other words, since he can no longer order his wife to do his bidding, he will make sure he has everything needed because he won't be able to ask her once he realizes that she has the right-of-way not to do what was his responsibility. It cannot be emphasized enough how much anger stems from one partner constantly judging what the other partner should do which starts a chain reaction of resentment since we then blame them, and they blame us for blaming them. Let us observe another example to demonstrate how arguments are prevented when one refrains from asking unnecessary favors.

Imagine that the wife — who is home for the evening because her car is in the repair shop — is suddenly in the mood for a snack, but in order to satisfy her craving it necessitates that her husband stop at a store to get what she wants. In this situation he has the right-of-way because in order to satisfy her desire, he has to do something for her, which he may or may not want to do. In our present world there is an expectation that he should do this, and if he doesn't, he is judged inconsiderate. His wife may reason, "The store is only a few minutes out of his way; why can't he help me with this small favor? If he loved me he would want to do it." She doesn't realize that this is a judgment of what is right for him, which is wrong, and the source of so much contention. Once this principle is understood it prevents her from asking unnecessary favors because she knows, as does her husband, that her security depends on showing her love, not her selfishness. The husband, knowing that she will not ask favors of him except on rare occasions, would desire to ask her, "Is there anything I can bring you on the way home?" He knows her car is in the repair shop and she has no way of getting out. Or she could be the first to say, "Honey, would you mind picking up some of that ice cream we had the other night?" Because he has already expressed his desire to help, her request is not a form of advance blame since his standing offer of assistance implies that he is there if she needs him. However, his wife would never want to show any hint of selfishness by making him do something for her that would involve a great sacrifice on his part. Therefore when he asks if there is something he can do for her, she would get no satisfaction requesting anything that she could do for herself and impossible to be careless, since carelessness would only require that she work harder herself.

"I'm still not convinced that a wife couldn't easily take advantage of her husband's generosity knowing that he would be there at her slightest request. She could send him to carry out the garbage, make the beds, bathe the kids, go to the store to pick up a package she forgot to bring home and, last but not least ask him to make love when he is not the least bit in the mood."

The only thing that isn't right is the fact that you just didn't think deeply enough. The wife knows, as does her husband, that her security depends on showing her love for him, consequently, it is mathematically impossible to desire taking advantage of his generosity for this would be a hurt to him. What stops her is the fact that she knows he will respond to her requests regardless of what she asks of him for the simple reason that [she knows] he must excuse her because [he knows] her will is not free, therefore he is compelled to turn the other cheek for satisfaction even if she hurts him by having to sacrifice his desire. In other words, realizing that he would still do the things she asked, if at all possible, even though this would be an annoyance, because she knows he must excuse everything she does, then she is given no choice but to lose her desire to take advantage of him, since she knows that she doesn't have to hurt him this way unless she wants to, which means there is no advantage in taking advantage under these conditions. Consequently, she must be extremely careful about what she requests otherwise this would be a sign of selfishness, not love, which she does not want to display. It also forces her to limit her requests to those things her husband would enjoy doing.

"But if she knows this would be his reply, why does she bother to ask?"

"In most cases she doesn't, but you never know when both of them might have the need of the other. For example, if she asks her husband to help her move the television set because it is too heavy, and she knows he has the strength to do it and wouldn't mind, this would not be considered a form of advance blame because there is no way advantage could be taken. Telling her partner what to do, either directly or indirectly, is definitely a form of advance blame. It is very important to see the difference between the two because it makes a world of difference in the marital relationship."

"But supposing a woman doesn't drive a car at all, and every time her husband asks this question she sends him on an errand, isn't this taking advantage of his generosity?"

"It certainly is, and she would know it."

"But what is she supposed to do when she needs things at the store and can't drive the car?"

"She has three possibilities open to her. One, learn to drive. Two, take a cab or bus everywhere, which, of course, is not always easy to do. Or three, continue to hurt him by taking advantage."

"But how is it possible to continue hurting him when she knows he will never blame her, when she also knows she is not compelled to do it?"

"That's just it. She can't continue to hurt him this way."

"Well then, doesn't this reduce the possibilities to two? And if he can't afford taxicabs, and she doesn't want to take buses, doesn't this reduce the possibilities to one?"

"That's right."

"Are you trying to tell me that everybody will be able to drive a car in the new world?"

"Yes, for this is the only way a wife and husband can prevent this taking advantage, which is a definite hurt."

"But supposing a wife is a nervous wreck when it comes to driving a car, what then?"

"Is anybody blaming her, or criticizing her in any way? Isn't it understood, beyond a shadow of doubt, that she is compelled to do what she does because man's will is not free? If she is forced to stay away from driving a car . . . ."

"She might even get a certificate from a doctor to prove that she shouldn't drive, right?"

"Wrong. I thought you understood what it means that man's will is not free. Isn't it obvious that she doesn't need proof because nobody is blaming her? As I started to say, if she is forced to stay away from driving a car, then she will be forced to impose on her husband to do this driving for her, and it is mathematically impossible for him to blame her for doing what she is compelled to do. Can't you see what is happening? A mathematical line of demarcation is being drawn between what a person can do and can't do. If a wife discovers that she is hurting her husband by what she does or what she doesn't do, and realizes that he will never blame her in any way for doing what she knows he knows she is compelled to do, then she is forced to abandon the contemplation of any hurt to her husband she can prevent, because it cannot satisfy her to be excused by him for doing what she knows cannot be justified by her."

"But what has all this got to do with the price of eggs or the sexual relation? And what would stop a wife from asking her husband to make love to her, in answer to his question — 'Is there something I can do for you, honey?' This is certainly one thing she cannot do for herself, right?"

"Right and wrong. It is true that she needs her husband for the purpose of sexual intercourse, but it is wrong to assume that she cannot arouse his desire to make the very love needed for her own satisfaction. Consequently, if she didn't bother to make any effort to arouse him, and relied solely on his desire to satisfy her should she ask, she would be taking advantage of his offer to help her by not bothering to do what she can do for herself, which is this effort to arouse him to satisfy her. Therefore, she would never think to say 'Let's make love' in answer to his question — 'Is there anything I can do for you honey?' "

"I'm still a little confused. Do you mean that if I am in the mood to make love I must go over to my wife, start kissing and petting her until she gets passionate enough to get in bed with me, and then..."

"Of course I don't mean that. Isn't it obvious that if you approach her to kiss her you are blaming in advance the possibility that she might not want to kiss you at that moment? How can you be certain that she really wants to kiss you? By kissing her you only express what you want, but how do you know what she wants? And

357

remember, her desire not to kiss you is just as important as your desire to kiss her, that is, if she doesn't feel like kissing at that moment."

"Well what am I supposed to do, say — 'Honey, are you in the mood to kiss me?' or — 'I'm in the mood to kiss you, honey, are you in the mood to kiss me?' "

"No, that is incorrect. It is obvious that she would do anything to show her love for you, consequently, if you tell her you're in the mood, she would want to kiss you for your satisfaction, even though she is not in the mood; and if you ask her if she is in the mood, what is this but an inverted way of telling her that you are in the mood. In other words, this would be taking advantage of her love for you."

"Well supposing instead of kissing her, for this does require that she kiss me back, I just went over and started rubbing her leg, can I do that?"

"Absolutely not, because this assumes she wants you to do that, which blames her in advance for not having this desire to have her leg rubbed."

"I give up, what in the hell am I allowed to do in this new world?"

"That's not nice, especially in view of the fact that what I will show you is only for your own benefit. Wouldn't you like to have this passionate feeling for your wife, and she for you, for as long as you live?"

"This would be heaven on earth, but if the past sets any precedents I'm still afraid you're talking through your hat. However, it would be wonderful if you could bring this about."

"Not me, I have nothing to do with it. I'm only obeying a law that forces me to move in this direction because it gives me greater satisfaction. God deserves the credit, not me. I'm just the son of God, like you, and all mankind. None of us are given a free choice, you know that."

The basic principle will always be there to remind them as to what is right and wrong. If a spouse unintentionally strikes a first blow by expecting the other to sacrifice the desire not to do what is being asked, this will be pointed out, but it will be a welcome reminder because there is no blame involved. By using the mathematical standard to determine who has the right-of-way when desires conflict, there can be no confusion as to who must yield. When they know that the refusal to do the favor has the right-of-way, how is it possible for them to hurt this person in one way or another for refusing when they also know that the spouse will turn the other cheek. It is no advantage to take advantage under these conditions for such a motion would be in the direction of dissatisfaction — which would be impossible to prefer. In the world of free will it was sometimes necessary to tell a wife, or she her husband, what to do in order to prevent a possible hurt. But how is it possible to get hurt in the new world? Therefore, the necessity to assume this possibility and make an effort to preclude it with a judgment of what is right for the other which tacitly blames this possibility, has been removed. Furthermore, the assumption of a husband and wife that they could be hurt in some way by each other, adultery or otherwise, actually strikes a first blow by accusing the other of this possibility, and then it doesn't take long before efforts are made to prevent what is not desired by imposing standards of right and wrong which not only prevents them from showing the love they need for their own sexual satisfaction, but encourages the other to justify doing that of which they have already been accused. What this principle does is forces couples, of their own free will or desire, to become extremely thoughtful about how they act toward each other by showing such consideration that they will desire to do everything for themselves without imposing on the other. The key to harmony is when both parties know who has the right-of-way for then there can be no conflict. As a result of this change something fantastic takes place.

Knowing in advance that they will never be asking favors of each other, they will desire to do everything in their power to make each other happy and begin to think in this direction like never before. She prepares him a glass of ice cold lemonade because she knows he likes this, and when she hands it to him he is extremely pleased and says, "Thanks, honey." She is entitled to say "you're welcome" in return, but she doesn't have to, because he already knows this, otherwise, she wouldn't have done it. Therefore, he is not expecting any response. She doesn't expect him to say "thank you" either, because this is advance blame when he fails to do what she thinks he should. She is not expecting any thanks or payment for what she did and that is why he appreciates what she did all the more. What creates this turnaround? The fact that he knows she has the right-of-way to refuse what he has the right to ask, therefore, he will no longer desire to ask favors of her or anyone else except in rare instances. This, in turn, compels his loved ones to ask if there is anything they can do for him, and then not desiring to take advantage of this generous offer — because to do so would reveal his selfishness, not his love — he responds, "No thank you." In other words, although we have the right to ask favors, we know they have the right-of-way to refuse if they want to for which we cannot desire to blame when we know we would be striking the first blow. Therefore, we are given no choice but to sacrifice our selfishness and to respect the desires of others that make no demands on us. This knowledge removes a form of injustice that has been plaguing mankind since time immemorial. When we fully understand what constitutes a first blow, and we also understand who has the right-of-way, all arguments resulting from this source must come to a permanent end. Although people will not ask unnecessary favors of others this does not rule out asking favors altogether since there is one exception. When someone falls overboard and is yelling for help he is asking you to do him a favor and save his life, and you will desire to help him because he cannot do this for himself. Obviously, in a situation where someone needs immediate assistance there would be no hesitation because the person asked would know that this individual is in genuine need. It is also true that we cannot have sexual intercourse by ourselves, so in this sense we are asking a favor for our spouses to satisfy our sexual needs. However, it is within our power to arouse the desire of our partners to accept an invitation, therefore, this is something we can do for ourselves.

Another serious issue in marital relationships is that of gift giving because the woman has always equated a gift with love. The effort, time, and expense that went into buying the gift was often used to measure a man's love. If he failed the test, it was proof to her that he was only giving out of a sense of duty. In this situation the woman's expectations have been met with disappointment which she then uses to justify her criticism. But when she understands that her criticism is a form of advance blame, she is prevented from moving in this direction because this would not be showing him the love that she needs for her own security. Arguments have also arisen from husbands buying their wives something that was not desired. How many wives have said, "But if he cared he would have known what I wanted." The wives, feeling the gift was insincere, would blame their husbands for not caring enough; and the husbands, feeling unappreciated, vowed never to buy another gift again. This has led may couples down a slippery slope of anger and resentment which could end up being the downfall of a marriage that was once so promising. It is important to remember that little problems can turn into big problems, and if not checked, the couple could wonder how they got to the point where they are now going through divorce proceedings. As we can see, buying gifts is great for business but not always great for couples. Do you see the dilemma surrounding this issue? It is no longer an enjoyable experience, but something to be tolerated. All this is cleared up when we know who has the right-of-way and we remove the obligation, for then the problems stemming from this source will be entirely eliminated. In the new world when a husband buys a gift for his wife, it will be because he wants to make her happy and for no other reason. Because his intentions will be heartfelt she will respond with overwhelming appreciation, but most importantly, she will be receiving the greatest gift of all, his sincere love. In many cases husbands will prefer giving money as a gift so that their wives can buy what they want and this expression of love will be received with gratitude.

Let us now move on to another form of advance blame, related to favors, which is the asking of questions. It is impossible to ask a favor without asking a question which means that every time we ask a question we are asking someone in an indirect way to do us a favor by answering us. In fact, the very moment someone asks a question he blames the possibility it might not be answered, proof of which is easily demonstrated when not answering makes him angry because he feels foolish and believes it is a sign of disrespect. "What time is it? I asked you a question. Just look at your watch and tell me what time it is. Are you trying to be funny? I know you hear me, so why don't you answer?" Finding out the time could be as simple as going into the kitchen where there is a clock on the wall. We will stop asking questions of others the same way we stop asking favors of one another when we realize that any question is a form of tacit blame which strikes the first blow by judging that others should desire to answer. Even though they cannot be blamed for not answering questions that are an annoyance to them, they are compelled to answer all of our questions so as not to hurt us and make us look foolish. When we know absolutely and positively that no one will blame us for asking unnecessary questions, we are prevented from finding satisfaction in doing this, which makes us think like never before. The removal of this form of tacit blame revolutionizes many things. There will obviously be a need for some questions, but these will be limited to questions that someone cannot answer for himself. By knowing in advance that the person asking a question would never take advantage, the person asked will be happy to oblige. This may sound like a trivial matter but it is not, especially when small resentments eventually lead to much bigger ones. Expecting someone to respond to a question, especially at an inconvenient moment, can be a great source of irritation because it shows a lack of consideration. Slowly but surely these irritations can kill sexual desire, and because sex is vital for a healthy marital relationship we can see how easy it is for marriages to turn sour. Is it any wonder there are so many divorces when sexual satisfaction has sunk to its lowest ebb? As we uncover all the factors that give rise to this form of disrespect, the seeds of resentment will be prevented from taking root.

There is another reason questions are asked and that is for the purpose of judging, according to existing standards, whether someone is ignorant, or to discover what knowledge we possess that others don't so we can feel superior in this regard. In our present world many people have been made to feel terribly inferior so they have developed the habit of elevating themselves by putting others down. Because it is obvious that the only reason someone could ask a question when he already knows the answer is either because he already feels superior or would like to be considered superior, but in both cases there is a subtle attempt to make the other person feel small by comparison. Just the other day I was in my car with a friend when a particular aria was playing over the radio, and he said, "Say, do you know the name of that tune?" and when I said no, he acted surprised and proceeded to tell me. Again, this kind of question is designed for two reasons; either to make yourself appear superior and the other person inferior, or to teach this person something you believe he should know which blames him for not knowing. In most cases the question partakes of both reasons. Asking questions gives an individual the opportunity to criticize another person's point of view while establishing the soundness of one's own. Supposing someone should ask, "When did Columbus discover America?" Isn't it obvious that the very question is a subtle way of feeling superior when the person cannot answer it correctly? Aren't we glad he didn't know? If he cannot answer the question this invites the questioner to say, "You should know that, it was back in 1492." If you do know the answer the person asking the question is disappointed because he cannot show off his knowledge and place the other in an inferior position. Consequently, asking these questions must come to an end because it is also a form of criticism; it is a deliberate effort to make a person feel inferior. These people may also use slang to degrade certain groups and use words that build themselves up, such as educated, which makes someone else uneducated. I had an aunt who always tried to test my skills. Whenever she came to visit she never failed to quiz me:

"How do you spell the word Constantinople?"

"I don't know how, Aunt Jenny."

"Shame on you…you should know that; didn't you go to grade school? Now think hard."

"I'll try but I'm sure I can't spell it; spelling is my worst subject. C O N S T A N D….."

"That's incorrect, it's not D but T I N O P L E, now that wasn't so hard, was it?"

Since to criticize a person for the way he thinks is a form of hurt for which there will be no criticism in return, each individual will be compelled to desire keeping his opinions to himself. Consequently, when it is mathematically revealed that the person who asks is tacitly blaming — judging that the other will desire to answer which strikes the first blow — this other has a justifiable right in the world of free will not to turn his other cheek (by not answering the question which is designed in some subtle way to belittle him), and to retaliate by answering, "If you already knew the answer what was your purpose in asking the question?" or with, "Why don't you go to the encyclopedia for your information?" What if this competition extends into the marital relationship? For example, supposing the husband asks his wife a question that she cannot answer? She will obviously feel inadequate and this will eventually lead to feelings of resentment. However, when she fully realizes what it means that man's will is not free and that her husband cannot help himself by asking these unnecessary questions, she will lose her desire to strike back. The husband will no longer desire to belittle her in this way being fully aware that his wife will not desire to hurt him in return by striking back in anger, but will make every effort to answer his question even though she knows it is aimed at making him feel superior. Consequently, he will think very carefully before asking any more questions. Remember that when we know they are not going to laugh at us for the questions that are already known to us, and never blame us for trying to make them feel inferior or for criticizing them for this lack of knowledge, we are compelled to think like never before so as not to do those things that will make us appear foolish in our own eyes because there is no one we can blame. It is important to always bear in mind that they have the right-of-way to refuse answering our questions because to satisfy our desire they must do something for us whereas to satisfy their desire not to answer, there is not anything we have to do for them.

Understanding that the real problem of marriage centers on the sexual relation, we can observe how God's infinite wisdom precludes every possibility of hurt, including the tacit blame that is embodied in 'innocent' questions that could eventually dampen sexual desire. Since it has been determined that sexual desire is the true meaning of conjugal love and when it decreases a marriage deteriorates, we have the power to prevent adultery by not imposing on the other partner which would be a display of selfishness, not love. I will repeat an earlier passage which demonstrates how it is within our control to receive the love we desire by first showing our love which means never displaying our selfishness through action or word.

The surest way to success in marriage is to arouse the sexual passion

364

of the other since this demonstrates, in an undeniable manner, that we want our partner to be in love with us. This display of love and affection reveals that we do not want another since the love of our partner makes this impossible. By the same reasoning, as our partner makes efforts to arouse our desire, it reveals that he (or she, whatever the case may be) wants our love which makes us conscious that he doesn't want another since our love for him makes this also a mathematical impossibility. Consequently, when a husband and wife realize from the very beginning that the security of their marriage depends on arousing the sexual passion of the other, without imposing one ounce of obligation (including the asking of unnecessary favors which is a display of selfishness, not love), they are given no choice as to what is better for themselves since any action or word that decreases passion only reveals a lack of love by tacitly blaming the sexual desire of the other.

With sexual intercourse we have a slightly different problem because this is something we cannot do alone yet to tell our partner that we are in the mood and expect them to honor our desire or to touch them in any way for that purpose takes for granted that they also want to make love or be fondled at that moment of time. Although sex requires two people we know that it is within our power to arouse the desire of our partner to accept an invitation — which is something we can do for ourselves. In our present world a husband doesn't care if he hurts his wife in various ways, nor does his wife, because they have hurt each other so many times that it satisfies them to strike back one way or another since they were unconscious of who or what really struck the first blow. A husband may sexually starve his wife — for which he cannot help — because the woman he married is not the same person, and she blames him for her desire to have an affair or she may starve him for the same reason. The wife would punish her husband by refusing him because he refused her, and an argument would follow. Should she reject him he justifies retaliation by using the fallacious standard that it is her marital obligation to have sex whenever he desires and she has also been taught that this is her marital duty. By obligating his wife he is tacitly blaming the possibility of being refused which is a judgment that she should desire to satisfy him. Therefore, so as not to hurt him by neglecting his needs she forces herself to make love when not in the mood as the lesser of two evils. Trying to get the desired response how many times have you husbands and wives fondled each other in an effort to arouse desire, thinking that this was right? And how many psychologists have advised similar tactics which knowledge was justified by a Ph.D. degree? If the husband is in the mood to make love and pounces on his wife without considering her desire he would not be showing his love because he is blaming her in advance for not wanting what he wants. In other words, the husband has failed to take into consideration the possibility that his wife at that moment might not want to move in that direction, which is her business. Since this is an act of selfishness because it is a judgment of what is expected — unless both parties desire this sexual relationship — they cannot touch each other in any way until an invitation is extended. By the same token if she should ask him for sex because she is in the mood, this does not show a feeling of love for him because she knows that he will do anything to satisfy her which means that she is taking advantage. When sexual demands are made, the spouse who feels obligated to perform may gradually lose all interest where the mere thought of sex becomes distasteful. This, in turn, could jeopardize the relationship. By insisting to be satisfied without considering the other, the first blow has been struck. Under the changed conditions taking advantage becomes impossible since this request would only reveal a lack of respect for the other's desire which neither would want to display. In the past no one knew who had the right-of-way therefore it justified the blame that always followed and set off a chain reaction of hurt the responsibility which belonged to the one making the demand. This knowledge clearly reveals that the person who has been obligating his partner to do anything, the one who tells the other what to do, how to act, how to speak, how to dress, where to go, is definitely not in love, for these things decrease passion and are responsible for adultery. The moment you expect something of your partner, or he of you, then both of you are considering your desire of greater value. If the wife is in the mood, she knows it is impossible to desire telling him that she wants to make love for this imposes an obligation which decreases desire — while revealing her lack of love. Under these conditions it is also impossible for the husband to desire using his wife for his own pleasure (just because she does not need an erection), for this does not consider her desire whatsoever. So many men have taken their wives for granted that it never dawned on them their wives may need other types of foreplay to captivate their imagination. Many women are stimulated by certain scents and sounds which may unleash the core of their passion. As our slide rule reveals, any time you lay a hand on your sexual partner without being absolutely certain this is what is desired, you are tacitly blaming a desire not to want what you want.

This form of selfishness is prevented with the knowledge that this hurt will not be blamed. It is true that if we do not satisfy our sexual needs we are hurt, but since we cannot obligate our partners to do what they might not want to do — and cannot judge what is right for them — the solution to this apparent impasse is for us to arouse their desire to want the same thing we want. Remember, there are always two desires, not just one, and since it is impossible for either the husband or wife to approach the other (in the new world of course) as this judges or tacitly blames, they are compelled to seek a means of arousing the desire of the other before any contact is made. However, it is very easy to arouse the desire of the other for a sexual relation without physical contact at the beginning of a marriage, and very easy to continue this when the knowledge in this book is understood.

"But isn't that the same thing? If he extends her an invitation by doing all these things, he is plainly saying — 'I'm in the mood. Please come over here since I can't go to you.'"

This is where your fallacy lies, because they are not saying this. In our present world they would say that, but remember, their security lies in showing their love, which means that they want to do everything in their power for each other. Therefore, when an invitation is extended this is what they are actually saying. 'Honey, I am very much in the mood to make love to you,' not 'I am in the mood to have you make love to me.' Consequently, when she makes physical contact by accepting his invitation, or vice versa, he is much more interested in satisfying her, one way or another, than himself, while she is more interested in satisfying him. Since there will be no arguments or criticism, and couples will learn every trick of the trade to stimulate desire without making physical contact, almost 100% of the time our partners will be sufficiently aroused to accept our invitation. Sexy clothing for the purpose of arousing desire will be one of the ways to invite the other without any form of touch. The wife may choose certain lingerie to entice her man but this will be up to her to initiate, not her husband. During her monthly cycle she doesn't have to explain to him, she just doesn't invite him to indulge his appetite. If the husband is feeling passionate, he must also find ways to arouse her desire to accept an invitation. If the husband still fails to arouse his wife's desire after doing everything possible, then he must wait for her to extend him an invitation but not for long because the normal desire for a sexual relation will have its way. The only thing the husband can do is create an atmosphere that will put her in the mood. If he is not in the mood he had better not extend any invitation because it is mathematically impossible to check her desire, once he arouses it, without blaming her for what is his responsibility. But when she realizes that even though she has refused him and he cannot satisfy his sexual needs he would not want to deprive her of the same by having a relation with another partner, her desire to satisfy his sexual needs will be aroused to the highest degree as his desire to satisfy her. If a wife is in the mood for love because she has been daydreaming about her last experience, nothing is preventing her from slipping into a very sexy negligee which conceals just enough to make him amorous, or she may say something sexy to arouse his desire to accept her invitation the moment he comes home from work which tells him immediately what she wants without imposing an obligation. He will know what she desires for she is plainly telling him, "Honey, I've got something for you — if you want it!" The wife may even desire using certain words for which she knows there will be no blame since he knows she is not hurting him with them (as this kind of hurt is purely imaginary), otherwise she would be prevented from using them by the knowledge that this hurt would never be blamed. Just these words alone could arouse desire to such a high degree that she can cause her partner to accept an invitation and make physical contact. As a result of showing utmost respect for each other, when they put on their revealing clothes (they will be compelled to desire each other tremendously) there will be a small atomic explosion of passion every time they are drawn irresistibly together. They will learn the many ways they can have fun because once they are married there is no such thing as perversion which is a word with absolutely no significance. Everything goes and no holds are barred unless it hurts the other person, but remember most of the hurt you have been experiencing where sex is concerned is one of the imagination. There may still be times that your desire to experiment may not be preferred by your partner, but in 100% of the cases when a couple get hot enough and all psychological impediments have been long since removed their great heat or extreme passion will make everything they do enjoyable. How is it possible for anyone to get hurt under these conditions? If he is still not in the mood she will never blame him, but after a hot bath and dinner he may decide to extend her an invitation which she would never refuse although he could just wrap his arms around her since she already expressed her desire. In our present world the wife would punish her husband by refusing him because he refused her, which would then lead to an argument. Should he not wish to wait until after dinner because he, too, was daydreaming and impatient to extend an invitation, they could have sex right then and there but how and where they make love will be up to them. Therefore, the moment he feels the desire as a result of her efforts, which reveals her own desire, he never has to be worried about being refused or by tacitly blaming her since, in this case, she is extending a very warm invitation. This also precludes, as in dating, any possibility of one partner ever desiring to punish the other by refusing. Just remember that regardless of what couples do to please each other both desires must be considered in every sexual encounter. Since we cannot take it upon ourselves to make physical contact because they might not want this at that moment, we have no choice but to do everything in our power, one way or another, to arouse their desire to accept our invitation to make love without physically touching them. This gives them the right to make physical contact with us if they want to, which means that we must assume responsibility for their lack of desire. We can no longer force the other to do what is not desired, but we will find out what makes the other extremely passionate and move in that direction for satisfaction.

By revealing what it means that man's will is not free which releases the corollary or basic principle (magic elixir, if you will) that no person is to blame — and that advance blame strikes the first blow — they become conscious that they alone are responsible for any hurt done to themselves by their marital partner. This is why every effort will be made to ignite passion, without any form of blame. If couples allow themselves to get out of shape, that is, out of the shape that first drew them together they are blaming in advance the sexual desire of the other, consequently, both spouses will make every effort to keep themselves looking as close as possible to the way they looked when they first met but only because this would be a hurt to themselves should they not. Therefore, they will do everything in their power to stay fit as a fiddle and ready for love by maintaining the same physical appearance throughout life. I am not referring to the normal aging process which will never cause people to fall out of love; nor am I referring to any medical condition that could prevent someone from staying in optimal shape. I am referring to spouses who have changed drastically from when they first met because they let themselves go and then blamed the other for not being attracted to them anymore. The difference in the new world is that the standards that once applied for everyone will no longer exist. The attraction that drew two individuals together will be purely personal.

In addition to maintaining their original appearance couples will make every effort to demonstrate their love by showing appreciation for each other whenever the opportunity arises. Simple gestures of affection in and out of the bedroom have always been an aphrodisiac because the mind is the largest sex organ. For example, if the husband knows his wife enjoys a romantic dinner by candlelight, he will want to please her by taking her out as often as he can. Since neither partner in the new world would ask the other where they want to go because the other would only say "It's up to you, dear" (since to state a place would tacitly blame the desire of the other), there is only one possible solution and that is for both to state on a piece of paper where they would like to go, put these in a hat, and the one that is drawn is the answer. The great humor lies in the fact that the husband and wife, in the new world, will always desire to make the other happy, which compels the husband to put on his slip where he knows his wife likes to go, while she will put on her slip the restaurant where she knows he likes to go, just the opposite in your present world when you have been married for a little while. After a nice dinner they may desire to come home and have a romantic evening. However, there is one change about to take place where sex and marriage are concerned that will surprise everybody for you are about to see why a couple would never desire only one bed for the two of them.

"Is this because sleeping together decreases passion, in time?"

"Sleeping together night after night does decrease passion, but it is not the reason you will have two beds, twin or otherwise."

"When I first got married, my wife suggested we buy a double bed immediately (since that's what is expected of married couples) so I agreed to it."

The person who brings it up is the one who strikes this first blow of marriage. If you understand what it means that man's will is not free and are able to perceive and extend the mathematical relations thus far, you will easily see the reason for this. Take note.

If after making love our partner wishes to sleep alone, this desire has the right-of-way over our desire to have our partner sleep by our side since this is a judgment of what is right for the other. Using today's standards it would be unusual to see a married couple sleeping in two separate beds. Most people would consider this a sign that the marriage was on the rocks, which may be true in our present world. If a couple preferred sleeping in a separate bed, they would then have to tolerate the comments of family and friends. There is nothing wrong with desiring to sleep together but it cannot be satisfied unless both parties want the same thing. If they do not desire to move to another bed after making love, then it is obvious that both are content with the sleeping arrangement. But having only one double bed as the only alternative involves the same principle of considering only one person's desire, and it is a subtle form of advance blame. In other words, the person desiring the double bed is actually blaming in advance the desire of the other to sleep alone, whereas the other does not blame by not making any demands. A's desire involves B, but B's desire does not involve A; it is that simple. In our present world we justify criticizing our partner for wanting to sleep alone by invoking sleeping together as a condition of marriage. We expect them to show their love by sacrificing their desire in favor of ours which only reveals

371

our selfishness by expecting them to give up what they should not have to. Then when they insist on sleeping alone, and because we believe we are right, we call them selfish and strike the first blow to get even for something that does not infringe on anyone else's desires. But when we know they have the right-of-way and that they would never blame us for striking this blow no matter what we do to hurt them for not satisfying our desire, then we are given no choice but to sacrifice our selfishness and respect desires that make no demands on us. Let us review.

Since the person who prefers a double bed without another bed available is obligating the other to sleep together which action does not consider the possible desire of the other to sleep alone; and since the person who prefers a single bed which means another bed is available makes no imposition on the other to sleep together, it is obvious that whoever makes the decision for one double bed reveals an act of selfishness that demonstrates a lack of love (the lack of desire for passion in their marriage which is the meaning of love in this context); and since neither desires to show what will only decrease the security of their marriage, they are given no choice. In the new world if a family has one double bed because they can't afford another (impossible in the new world), and the husband decides to get up to sleep alone, his wife will never say, "Where are you going?" because she knows he won't even answer this question since it is none of her business. Maybe he is going to get a glass of water or to sleep on the sofa. Whatever his reason for getting up after making love, this is his business not hers. However, if he wants to tell his wife where he is going this is also his business. Since both of them know what is right and wrong AT LAST, they are compelled to keep their thoughts to themselves, but this is not a criticism of those who have been minding other people's business because they were compelled by God, of their own free will, to do everything they did. [Note: I hope you understand by now that the phrase 'of their own free will' only means of their own desire, but this does not mean will is free. If you are still confused, please reread Chapters One and Two as this is a prerequisite for understanding the extension of these principles]. Remember, nobody is going to tell you not to ask questions or favors or tell anyone what to do, for this will be your business if you desire to continue that way under the changed conditions. But when you know absolutely and positively that others will never strike back or blame you in any way no matter what you do to them for not answering your questions or doing you favors, and because you also know that you are in the wrong (striking the first blow), there is only one thing left to do but to refrain from hurting the ones you love. This is completely mathematical and if you study it over carefully you will discover that man is given no choice in this matter of one or two beds. Because man has never known who was right and wrong in these matters and because he didn't really care just as long as he could threaten some form of hurt to get his way, he was allowed to develop just as he did. But when he knows who has the right-of-way and that he will never be blamed for striking this first blow, he is given no choice but to sacrifice his selfishness and respect desires that make no demands on him. Once the true meaning of selfishness is clarified; once couples are aware that all selfish acts, all acts that tacitly blame, decrease the very passion they want for a happy sexual relation by lessening the security of their marriage, are they given a choice? Remember, it takes two to tango. With these principles to guide them, this couple will never fall out of step in this delicate dance of love. By obeying God's mathematical law from the very beginning of their marriage, this couple is compelled to keep each other constantly hot and bothered. Lovemaking will reach new heights because nothing will hinder sexual desire.

There will be many changes as a result of this mathematical principle which were never before a permanent part of our environment. For example, in our present world if we approach our partners for a kiss or a hug and it is not returned, we blame them for not satisfying our desire and make them feel guilty. How many times have we been judged wrong for not desiring to return a kiss, a handshake, or a verbal salutation? How is it possible to approach someone with a kiss or for someone to approach me without judging that this is desired by the other? Who am I to judge that you desire to kiss me? If you should draw back because you don't like the smell of my breath, or for some other reason, I would be offended and blame you directly or indirectly since the approach itself is tacit blame, therefore when I complain because I don't like the way you acted you are justified in striking back since I struck the first blow for which I don't want to be blamed. How many times has a husband kissed his wife good-bye in the morning only because a habit was developed and it was expected of him? When the husband leaves for or returns from work he is under no obligation, nor is she, to kiss or say certain things. They can do what they want but the other has the right-of-way not to participate if this is desired. If the wife tells her husband that she wants to be kissed, then she is obligating him which is not a sign of love; nor can she approach him to give him a kiss because this assumes that he wants to kiss her and is a judgment that his desire is what she wants it to be. In other words, how is it possible for her to walk over to kiss him unless she knows he wants this kiss? If she asks him if he desires to kiss her, this is the same thing with an unconscious effort to shift the responsibility to him. How many times have grandparents smothered their grandchildren with kisses and pinched their cheeks in order to satisfy their desire...but what about the children? And how many parents have demanded that their children show respect by returning the kiss not realizing that it was the grandparents who were showing the worst kind of disrespect. This right-of-way system will permit many customs, conventions and habits to be broken without being criticized, but this does not mean that we have to stop doing what we have always done where others are concerned, just as long as everyone desires the same thing. If they don't, and we can't get them to do what we want them to do without striking a first blow which cannot be preferred under the changed conditions, we are given no choice but to change our ways. Remember, the desire of both individuals must be taken into consideration, not just one. Perhaps our desire to hug and kiss those we love will never be rejected, but if it is, then we must never forget that they have the right-of-way and if we criticize them we are revealing our selfishness not our love and striking the first blow for which they will never blame us. This tacit blame which is an advance judgment of what is right for others is at the very bottom of all the evil which came about out of mathematical necessity, but humorously enough everyone who previously made a speech or wrote a book about what he thought was wrong in human relations was right in a sense because he was obeying God's will. Now that man understands the truth of his nature, such an action would be considered wrong only because he knows for himself what is mathematically correct, which makes all opinions unnecessary.

To clarify this in another way I shall recall an experience I had with a psychologist who tried to prove me wrong by getting me to blame him for something he did, which only revealed to him the extent of his inability to think with mathematical precision. I can still recall his embarrassment. In trying to explain an undeniable observation to a colleague who could not seem to grasp these principles, I finally decided to give it up as a lost cause not only because his mind was obviously too confused with words to disentangle his thoughts, but also because I was getting very tired. It is assumed that some people will not be able to grasp these relations as easily as others which is not a reflection against them, nor is it important since they will learn the truth from the very fact that these principles work, which gives them no choice. It just so happens that this psychologist of whom I speak considered himself somewhat of an expert and to people like him it is an insult to their intelligence unless they can disagree. Seeing that his friend could not understand what he himself did not, he decided to take over the explanation for the sole purpose of ridiculing me. When I politely remarked, "If I needed your assistance I would have asked for it" he responded immediately, "See, you're blaming me; you don't even live up to your own principles" to which I replied, "This only shows how little you understand of what I said for if you had known that your taking over the explanation, even without the mockery, tacitly blamed me for stopping when I did and that your obvious ridicule was an insult and a hurt, you would never have been able to do it had you known that I would never blame you for hurting me. Instead you slap me in the face with an insult, blame me for not using good judgment, and then want me to turn the other cheek while excusing your conduct. However, under the conditions of a free will environment you gave me complete justification to blame you since the corollary, Thou Shall Not Blame, only applies BEFORE SOMETHING IS DONE, NOT AFTERWARDS. When a man commits a murder or hurts another it is only because you give him unconscious justification, but when he knows he will never be blamed by anybody for this terrible thing it is mathematically

375

impossible for him to derive any satisfaction because there is no way it can be justified when every bit of tacit blame is removed. Your tacit criticism and ridicule was justified by a feeling of superiority, but when you fully understand the principles in this book you will you lose the desire to judge someone else.

It is important to understand that the solution to every problem existing on this planet is interrelated otherwise you may jump to a premature conclusion about certain things which will only be answered in later chapters. It should be obvious to your common sense that if a man and his family are starving for food, the knowledge that you will not blame him for stealing a loaf of bread will not prevent him from trying to survive, for this is a motion in the direction of satisfaction. However, the very fact that he is starving only indicates that you have struck the first blow for which you want to be excused; but when you know that this terrible hurt to him will not be blamed, and when you are fully conscious of where the responsibility lies, you, my friends, will be given no choice. So instead of trying to judge this book in terms of your present mental development, try only to understand it. If you remember that this is God's law, not mine, you will listen very carefully before condemning what is undeniable. As we follow our guiding principle, Thou Shall Not Blame, we will now observe the miraculous transformation that takes place as couples meet and marry under optimal conditions, allowing them to be happily married until death do they part.

In our present world boys and girls usually find things about each other they don't like after going together for awhile. If either one is worried that this could happen they will be compelled to do all their checking in advance, and if they learn something that discourages them the boy need not ask the girl for a date or the girl need not accept. But when all the words like beautiful, lovely, adorable, precious, cute, darling, etc. that create external values are permanently removed from our vocabulary because they hurt others by placing them in an inferior position when judged homely and ugly, the differences that exist will be reduced where sex is concerned to an absolute minimum because we all have sexual organs that give satisfaction.

"But why should these words become obsolete?"

"First, because the use of words like handsome and beautiful is a source of hurt when other people are judged homely and ugly. 'My first daughter is beautiful,' commented a mother, 'but my second is an ugly duckling.' This poor child had to go through an entire lifetime being judged an inferior production of the human race. Second, although physical attraction more than anything else will be the determining factor when selecting a mate, when these words are removed from our dictionaries, along with their antonyms, the difference between what attracts these fairly young lovers will pass through the eye of a needle and every young girl and boy will have an equal opportunity of finding love. In the final analysis, these words will become obsolete not only because they are a hurt to so many, but because they do not symbolize anything externally real. Many other words will become obsolete as you will see shortly."

In the new world mankind will have reached a level of development where race relations will no longer be an issue. There is absolute proof that all people, regardless of race, have the same intrinsic value. We are all equal in God's eyes. Our basic principle or corollary, Thou Shall Not Blame, which appropriately instructs mankind to mind his own business (something he could not do in the world of free will), allows all people on the planet the opportunity to move in the direction that is truly best for themselves, especially when they would never think of hurting others. The reason White parents object so strenuously to the thought of their daughter marrying a Black man is only because of the criticism and ridicule that generally follows, but when there is no possibility of this it makes absolutely no difference to the parents just as long as their daughter is happy. This means that if a Chinese boy happens to ask an Italian girl for a date, this is his business, and if she accepts, this is her business. A White girl could ask an Indian boy, or a Korean boy could ask a Latino girl. Remember, no one can be hurt under the changed conditions. This is why an older man will never desire to ask a young girl for a date if there is such a disparity in their ages that he foresees she could be hurt later on. For example, you would never see someone in his fifties marrying a girl in her twenties, as you see today, because there can be no satisfaction whatsoever in hurting her when he knows there will be no blame for causing problems later down the road. By the same reasoning a young girl, knowing she appeals to a certain rich widower would not ask him to marry her because she would know that he would turn her down, since it forces him not to think only about the benefit to himself but what will be the best for her. There will be all kinds of social functions to help people meet since finding a marriage partner will be a very serious undertaking. If either person does not want children it would have to be made known before getting married, but virtually everyone will want a family since this is what comes as a package deal and all of the reasons for not wanting children will no longer be present.

Boys and girls will not have to be given permission to date because they would never take risks that could cause someone to get hurt while in the process of searching for a suitable partner. If a girl sees a boy she likes she simply stands near him and flirts and it is up to him to respond if he is interested. Likewise, if a boy happens to see a girl that he likes, he must in some way indicate to her what he wants without physical contact. He may stand next to her and flirt to show her he is interested and it is then up to her to accept or decline the invitation. With this new type of courtship the minute a girl accepts a date she is extending the boy an invitation and if he is not prepared to go all the way without contraception (which would show her that he loves her enough to be the father of her child since there is always the possibility of pregnancy), he had better not accept since there would be too much hurt involved, which would not give him satisfaction under the new conditions. This prevents any chance of taking advantage of a good thing because this would not give anyone satisfaction knowing that there would be no blame in spite of the suffering caused by loving and leaving, consequently, there would be no fear of unrequited love to develop. You see, this is similar to the conditions that make it unnecessary for a bank to check on the credit of an individual before lending him money. The person borrowing knows the bank wants to lend money and as long as he knows he can pay it back, plus the interest, the bank extends an open invitation to everyone who wishes to use its services. The wisdom here is amazing if you analyze it carefully enough, and it is not mine.

Let us go back for a moment and imagine that a girl sees a boy on the beach who appeals to her. She will simply sit down beside him

378

and let him devour what she has to offer. Boys and girls before marriage will prefer wearing the type of clothes that reveal their charms sufficiently to attract the opposite sex, so there is a certain amount of usefulness in a design being a particular way, but the context in which the word fashion is used today will become obsolete because it creates a general standard for everyone which will no longer exist. Therefore, clothing will be sexier than ever, in fact, hardly anything will be covered by those who are looking for a mate, and when they see this tempting invitation they will either get up and walk away if they are not each other's type or else they will take each other in their arms and kiss right away knowing that they have just selected their husband or wife. By accepting each other's invitation they will find a little cozy love nest and have a ball, but they will be married for life — until death do they part. This couple will fall madly in love the first few days of their marriage and will look forward with great anticipation to their next meeting, as they will desire the passion and thrill of this relation as often as possible. But remember, nothing can go wrong under the changed conditions because the factors that allowed boys and girls to get hurt in the past will be completely removed. Once the boy extends an invitation to the girl, or vice versa, they will automatically know the other is prepared to give what is desired — financial support should a baby arrive and a partner for life. If the boy was not prepared for this, he would never have flirted. Let us observe, once again, how a match is made — but this time a match made in heaven!

When a boy and girl fall mutually in love for the very first time and consummate their feelings with a complete sexual relation which is pure and simple, their first sexual relation, they are going to desire each other all the more because this exciting thrill of physical contact is a new experience that becomes associated with one particular person to whom they look for satisfaction. The boy will go home to his parents, the girl to hers, both dreaming impatiently of their next meeting, and they will know that there is no possibility of the other leaving just as long as they show their love, as was already demonstrated. It is not necessary that the boy or girl be working at the time because this marriage does not in any way impose an added burden on the parents since they can continue living at their respective homes. If it did impose a burden this couple would be prevented from getting married by the realization that their parents would never blame or criticize them for this, which would make such a choice a motion in the direction of dissatisfaction. The only difference so far between a boy and girl going out on a date in our present world and between this newly married couple is that the latter are permitted by the will of God to have sexual intercourse to their heart's content and prevented from hurting or leaving each other by the realization that this will only break the heart of the other for which there would be no blame. As a result of their indulging freely, in a very short while they will be absolutely wild about each other because of this unrestrained, uninhibited sexual passion, and no one will be standing in judgment over their actions because all the moralists will be silenced by the realization that they never knew the truth, only thought they knew as your philosopher Socrates tried to tell you a few years back.

The same conditions that existed before marriage will exist after marriage since there is no way a married couple can obligate the other. The boy knows, he doesn't have to be told that when a child comes it will be his responsibility, as the girl knows it will be her responsibility. He knows he is free to shirk this, to run away from earning a living if he wants to, but he won't want to. He will desire to go to work because the knowledge that this is the only way he can prevent the hurt to his wife and her parents who will never blame him, gives him no alternative. Consequently, the boy will make plans to support his wife and child for he realizes that there is no person, no law, no parent that is compelling him to stay and support this girl — and this constant realization that not only his wife, but nobody alive will ever, in any way, hold him responsible for leaving and breaking her heart which he realized long before marriage took place — makes it mathematically impossible to hurt her under these conditions. It is important to understand that the problems facing marriage cannot be entirely eliminated until this natural law becomes a permanent condition of the environment and all first blows are removed. As the first generation born into the new world becomes of age and marries under optimal conditions, they can look forward with confidence to many years of happiness as they embark on their new life together.

Let's continue our analysis.

As soon as this boy and girl are married, there will be no rush to get an apartment or home although they will base their decision on their financial position as well as their desire for extreme privacy and convenience — especially if she gets pregnant. There is no possibility of living with either set of parents, first because they could never ask this favor which tacitly blames in advance, and second, because the parents could not ask them for the same reason. Even if the parents asked how they could be of help, this young couple would be compelled to omit from their response everything that can possibly be done for themselves because otherwise advantage would be taken, which is no advantage under these conditions. The boy is also prevented from asking for financial help when the baby arrives because he knows that to judge what is right for others tacitly blames their desire in advance for not wanting to give or lend money. However, the friends and relatives of this couple knowing that no favors will ever be asked, and knowing that they will never be criticized for not helping, will desire, of their own free will (isn't this humorous?) to give assistance when and wherever they can without being obligated to do so by custom or convention since no one henceforth will judge what is right for another. Consequently, everything will be given, if desired, without being pressed by others and without expecting anything in return, not even to be thanked (for to expect thanks judges and tacitly blames what another should say) which compels this boy and girl to be overwhelmed with gratitude and desire to thank everyone from the bottom of their hearts.

When the newlyweds are finally able to move into their new home, the wife will know immediately that the house and the meals are her domain (unless another arrangement is made), while he will know that earning a living is his responsibility which will put him in charge of the money. Regardless of who brings in the paycheck, there will be an equal balance of power and respect. They will be compelled to show their love by doing everything they possibly can to make the other happy. If the man wants to stay home and the woman work, no one will be telling them that this is wrong. Therefore, the desire to make a living or take care of the children will be determined by the individual couple and how they choose to work things out between

381

them. The purpose of this book is not to argue for or against women's liberation, nor is it meant to assign rigid roles to the sexes. Its only purpose is to demonstrate that when a man and woman decide what role they designate for themselves and it is mutually agreed upon, and they also know there will be no blame if they should fail to live up to their own agreement, there is no satisfaction to be gained from neglecting what is clearly their responsibility. In most cases the mother will desire to stay home with the baby, therefore, it will be the husband's responsibility to earn a living and handle all the money, but whatever they arrange will be their personal business. Although the husband is the only one working she knows that he would never tell her that it is her duty to do certain things such as prepare the meals, keep the house in order, etc., as this is a judgment of what is right for her, just as she would never tell him to get a job, where or when to work, or to give her money. She gives him no advice whatever because she knows that such an action on her part would be a judgment of what is right for him, which tacitly blames his own desire. More importantly, it would reveal a lack of love which she wants to prevent since a display of love through her actions, not her words, is the only source of her own security. If the children are in school she may wish to take a job and bring in extra money to help her husband support the family and would desire this all the more because of the realization that it could help take pressure off of her husband even though she knows he would never ask her to do this or blame her in any way if she chose not to.

"But what about preparing meals, washing cloths, buying furniture? There has to be a standard of right and wrong."

There absolutely is. The husband's job is to take care of everything that is his business and her job is to take care of everything that is her business. The selection of the bed he will sleep in is his business just as making it up or not is also his business. Keeping his clothes clean or dirty, washing the dishes he messes up after eating or leaving them alone, taking out the garbage and trash he accumulates or not taking this out will also be his business. In addition, knowing that it is not her duty to clean up his mess, he will dump his own garbage, wash his own plates, make his own bed, and see that she has enough money. Her business will be most of the same things plus caring for the children, preparing the meals, and taking care of what in the house is not his responsibility such as keeping the rest of the house clean, if she wants to. If they still are unsure as to who does what, they could make an agreement between them as to what each of their responsibilities should be around the house, knowing in advance that should they violate it there would be no blame, denying them any satisfaction in breaking it. Therefore, they must be very careful that the agreement is one they can live up to. But such an agreement is really not necessary unless it is desired. In our present world though, we are constantly blaming our partners because they didn't do what is expected of them. Let me clarify this. If the wife agrees to do the laundry, prepare the meals, and keep the house in order as part of her responsibility, and the very fact that her husband would never tell her it is her duty to wash the clothes, prepare the meals, keep the house in order, etc., as this is a judgment of what is right for her, she will want to do what she knows is her responsibility. Should luck have it that he has extra money and wishes to spend it on a housekeeper to save his wife some physical effort, he would desire this all the more because he knows she would never expect this luxury. Since he will prefer doing everything in his power to make her happy, he will desire to give her all that he possibly can; and she, in turn, will want to do the same. But she knows that if she wastes one penny burning electricity that is not needed, she is striking a first blow for which he would never blame her which makes it impossible for her to find satisfaction in being careless about these things. Bear in mind that this is something they will desire doing for each other, not because they are obligated to do so. No one will ever tell their partners what to do except to let them know when they are striking a first blow. The basic principle is always there to remind both husband and wife as to what is right and wrong.

Assuming the husband is the breadwinner (for purposes of discussion) he will take out all that he needs for the rent, gas and electric, telephone, water bill, and money for his own personal expenses while giving the rest to his wife for food, clothes, and whatever she wants to do with it. He will need to figure out very carefully his overall expenses because he has no one to blame if he overspends, knowing that his wife will never complain or ask for one cent more than what she has been given. In the new world she will never say a word to him about his income, never suggest that he change jobs, never tell him that he is not earning enough money or how to spend it, for these are judgments of what is right for him; but he, knowing that she will never ask for anything, never complain about the money he gives her is compelled, of his own free will, to do everything in his power to increase his income (God will help him here with mathematical wisdom). This is his money, his labor, and he is entitled to make all the decisions as to where the money goes, but no matter how it is disbursed he is compelled never to hurt his wife in the disbursement. In this world if he loses his paycheck at the casino dipping into money that was put aside for bills, and she complains, he gives her all kinds of excuses. This will be precluded by the realization that should he hurt his family this way he would not be blamed for this which will compel him to gamble only with the money he can afford to lose because he could not justify the possibility of losing otherwise. In other words, actions will speak louder than words and if he gambles away their money he would not be showing his love — which would control his behavior. Both spouses will be compelled to use only their disposable income for leisure activities since neither will desire to hurt the other when there will be no blame for this hurt. As for taxes, this will be paid every week, as described. All the husband does is enter the amount of his paycheck in his record book, less what he wants for himself, and hands the rest to his wife. He doesn't actually hand his wife anything, she just consults the books. Under these conditions there is no possibility that arguments over money can arise.

Assuming that she is in charge of the meals, he will never make a suggestion as to what she should prepare because what she makes will be up to her, and she, knowing that he would never criticize her even if the food she prepares is tasteless (which would be impossible for her to do as this reveals a lack of love) is compelled to make a study of cooking long before marriage. She will be motivated to learn which foods are his favorites and prepare meals that he enjoys because she knows he will never criticize her regardless of what she makes. In our present world she asks him what he would like for dinner which tacitly blames his desire for something she might not be able to prepare. When the meal is over he will tell her it was delicious even if he didn't enjoy it, again developing this undercurrent of dissatisfaction which is only offset by the sexual relation. After dinner he may express his views about Russia or China or something else, and when she cannot keep up with this learned discussion he feels like a genius and she believes he is one. Should she disagree at this early stage of marriage he cannot afford to get angry as this would disrupt the fun they are planning to have in their double bed so he will try, in a nice way, to show her where she is wrong. Just then he may say, "Honey, would you mind going upstairs and getting my pipe and slippers?" "Of course not, darling," she answers pleasantly, becoming more and more resentful.

As we have seen, more arguments arise because we are constantly judging what our partners should do, which starts a chain reaction of blame and retaliation. He will give her money to run the house or his entire income and before long she tells him it isn't enough. "You'll just have to make more money," she demands. Little by little as sexual desire begins to wane, these small requests that appear insignificant at first loom larger and larger until they explode into arguments, eventually destroying love. Then when he asks for his slippers she says, "Gee, honey, I've got something else to do this minute, would you mind getting them yourself this time?" And he does mind. Before long he finds it more and more difficult to get an erection, and by revealing her suspicion that she thinks he is playing around with another woman he justifies doing that of which he is accused. By making a couple conscious of this responsibility for which all the world excuses them, they are given no choice but to change. They can no longer justify their anger at those who refuse to do favors for them, therefore, they are compelled to think like never before to save themselves unnecessary physical effort. Because of their new understanding as to who has the right-of-way when there are conflicting desires, arguments resulting from this source must come to a permanent end. Consequently, the husband doesn't ask his wife for his pipe and slippers, for this he can do for himself, and even if she had said, "Sweetie, is there anything I can get you?" he would be compelled to reply, "Not a thing, dear." This knowledge compels a couple, of their own free will, when they realize that no more favors will ever be asked, to ask the other, "Is there anything I can do for you?" and the other, not wishing to take advantage of such a generous offer because to do so would be a sign of selfishness and would not reveal their love, replies in 99% of the cases, "No thank you" which means that this question will need never be asked. If either has something that cannot be done alone (excluding sex) they would simply request the assistance of the other who would never object because no advantage would ever be taken. Remember, the very fact that they will never ask favors of each other except in rare cases will compel them to ask each other if there is anything they can do, and neither will take advantage of this generous offer because to do so would reveal their selfishness not their love. Naturally, they will restrict their requests to those things they know their partners will take pleasure in doing for them. If the man asks if there is anything he can do for her, she may respond that she would enjoy going to dinner and a movie knowing that he would enjoy this also. As was mentioned throughout this chapter, all the fallacious standards that now exist which are responsible for innumerable arguments will be prevented, and how this will be accomplished by those who now find in them such satisfaction due to an unconscious feeling of superiority is marvelous to behold. At the dinner table the husband will not find it necessary to express his opinions about what is wrong with the world, will no longer desire to display his superiority because, for the very first time, he realizes that nothing is wrong with the world and that he is not in any way superior to his wife or anybody else. To clarify this even further, if there is no possibility for disagreement or discussion about two plus two equals four (because this accepted fact precludes any disagreement), how is there a chance for an argument to arise? This will be made clearer in the chapter on education. Let us now continue our analysis by moving on to another source of conflict.

Many couples find satisfaction in judging one another's personal tastes whether it's the way they dress, the way they act, or the way they spend their money. But in the new world no one will ever judge these things because no one will be judging them. For example, I might like a particular car but when no one is criticizing my choice, this will no longer be one of the motivating factors in making my selection.

Since the beginning of time there have always existed numerous standards for eating, dressing, color combinations, walking, talking, etc. It is mathematically impossible for someone to give up the desire to judge the rightness or wrongness of another's choices when it offers such enormous satisfaction, even though this judgment blames someone's desire to be different. Just as in the game of chess when they say checkmate, couples must relinquish all standards except those that are completely mathematical such as two plus two equals four, for two reasons. First, when they become conscious that they are hurting their spouse for which they will never be blamed, and second, when they realize how truly ignorant man has been because of them which then makes such a preference a motion in the direction of dissatisfaction. Just as long as they think the things they do and say reveal their superiority they are given no choice, but what happens when for the first time they discover, in an undeniable manner, that the very things they believed revealed their superiority was only a definite sign of their genuine ignorance? When she tells her husband to wear a different tie with his suit, she actually believes she is expressing her love for him and is telling him for his own good, but the truth is that she is ashamed to be seen with him because he is wearing a color combination that others will ridicule. Therefore, when the blame is removed she will discover that it doesn't make a bit of difference to her what he wears. When it comes time to pick out a tie, neither of them will be concerned about color combinations and any tie will do just as well, or no tie for that matter. What difference does it make what color it is or whether he wears a tie at all when nobody will criticize or talk about his clothes in front of him or behind his back. Unfortunately, because this blanket of blame exists, and because she does not like when her husband argues with her over these things which she judges are better for him, she needs to justify it by employing a fallacious standard that gives the appearance of being true. "Don't you agree certain colors go together better than others? And can't you see this with your very eyes?" Since it is impossible to judge what is right for someone else, all standards, customs, conventions are being removed but most important is the fact that once all mankind stops criticizing and ridiculing which must come about because this is a form of hurt, everything that came into existence to prevent this criticism and ridicule is completely displaced. This means that a person will be able to dress anyway he wants because nobody is being hurt except in this imaginary manner, this breaking with custom. Remember, there is no mathematical standard as to what is right and wrong in human conduct except this hurting of others, and once it is removed, once it becomes impossible to desire hurting another, then whatever value existed in asking for and giving advice has been permanently done away with.

In today's world decorating a home is designed to avoid criticism, or a way to receive compliments. When people visit someone's home, here is what they say, "How exquisite! How simply stunning! By the way, who did your decorating?" Another visitor takes it upon herself to criticize her friend's taste. "This picture in the hallway doesn't go with your new décor. It doesn't belong by the steps, and that table belongs on the other side. And what on earth were you thinking when you bought that chandelier? It's so gaudy looking! Well at least your colors are neutral and blend beautifully." In the new world there won't be any more opinions on these subjects for they blame a person for thinking differently. Consequently, I could never ask the person visiting, "What do you think of my house?" because I would be blaming her in advance if her opinion is not what I wanted to hear. Supposing she answered, "I think you could have done better." I certainly wouldn't like her answer. In response I would have asked, "What is it about my house you don't like?" Then we would have gotten into some kind of argument. The reason we were concerned about the opinions of others on various things was to try and conform so that we wouldn't be criticized or ridiculed. We learned to distrust our own taste and to hire someone with a 'flair' for these things to make our homes acceptable to others. Now let us watch what happens when these words are removed from our vocabulary, and the basic principle introduced.

When a visitor comes to our home she will never make comments about the way our house looks. The only thing she will be able to say is, "I really and truly love your arrangement." And since she knows that her hosts know that she can only pay a compliment, there is no need to say it. It only becomes a value when it is possible to criticize. In the free will environment each person was compelled to make

388

efforts to satisfy the likes and dislikes of others because of this criticism and ridicule, but when all forms of blame are removed which prevents you from hurting others with what you do to satisfy yourself, then you are only concerned with your own likes and dislikes. This is of extreme importance because so many people are criticized for personal preferences. There will be no standard that says one home is more beautiful than another which in this world would have created envy. When there is no criticism from the outside world, what pleases two people will be completely dependent on their own personal taste, nothing else. We have been dressing ourselves and decorating our homes a certain way to avoid criticism. Since how we dress and decorate our homes is our business that hurts nobody, and since criticism is a hurt and a first blow that will never be blamed, mankind will be completely free to dress and decorate their homes without the slightest fear of being criticized or ridiculed. All that you are now reading is just an extension of the principles that cannot be denied. Therefore all visitors will be compelled, of their own free will, to say nothing complimentary or critical because any criticism is a hurt for which they know there will be no blame. The value that existed in making it known to others that you also like what they like so you could get them to like you more has been removed because it is mathematically impossible for them to like you less even if you don't pay these compliments. There will always be admiration for specific differences but when all words that create external values are removed, there will no longer be any possibility of hurting others by placing them and the things they like in a position of inferior value. There is a big difference in saying, "Your home is lovely" and saying, "I like your home very much." The first implies that other homes are not lovely because they don't partake of this fallacious standard called 'lovely,' while the second is also done away with because there is absolutely no value in saying it, under the new conditions.

For the very first time newlyweds will not be concerned about what other people think since no one will be judging them, therefore they will make their homes comfortable for themselves and their families, no one else. They might like the interior of their home to be designed in a particular way, but this is also just a question of personal taste. Furniture will be arranged in a way that satisfies the individuals who live in that home, but if there is a conflict as to where something should be placed they would flip a coin because both would desire to yield to the other since there are no more standards as to what is a better arrangement, which obviates the need to ask the opinion of others. In the past the wife may have asked, "Honey, where shall we put the sofa (which shifts the responsibility to him); would you like it over here?" "Frankly, I think it looks better over there but you do what you think is best." In many cases the wife would not ask her husband for his opinion which he may unconsciously resent. If he is in the home decorating business he might not ask her at all and just take over because he feels that he knows much more than she does about decorating a house, which she might not resent because she believes he does. Even if there appears to be a final agreement, there is often an undercurrent of controlled resentment that can lead to problems later on especially if one partner feels that his opinion wasn't considered. In the new world, since the husband will no longer be concerned about the criticism of others he doesn't mind letting his wife fix up the house any way that pleases her; and she, knowing that he will never blame the way she arranges it will have no fears. What pleases him will no longer be influenced by what pleases other people who may come to his home. Therefore, when it comes time to buying furniture the husband would tell her how much he can afford and she will do all the rest, for this is her domain. He will only be interested in having his personal items such as his chair, his lamp, his desk, his computer, his bed, etc. arranged in such a way as to be comfortable for him. If a heavy piece of furniture needs to be moved she may say, "Honey, will you help me move this over here?" If he says, "I am sorry, not now" because he is too tired since he just came home from work, or for whatever reason, it must be remembered that he has the right-of-way. Still wanting to help he may decide to hire someone to do the job. He would never say a word about where anything should be placed because this would be a tacit judgment of what is right for her, and she would never ask him because she knows he would always respond, "It is up to you." Therefore, she is compelled to please him all the more and place everything in a position that she feels would suit his needs because, regardless of how she arranges things, she knows he would never criticize her decision.

This means that the need to compliment has seen its last days because it has no value unless there can be criticism, just as there can be nothing beautiful when there is nothing ugly. To criticize a person for anything that is not hurting others is a first blow, which means that to compliment someone for something that is not benefiting others is a criticism of those who desire not to do what has been complimented. We have been dealing in words only, not reality. But you must remember that in our present environment these choices were necessary because they gave greater satisfaction. When it is impossible for someone to be disrespected because of the way he prefers to decorate his house, and there is no possibility that anyone will comment or discuss its appearance in any way whatsoever, the services of an interior decorator will no longer be necessary because nobody will desire spending his money in this direction. The extra expense will not be worth it unless the taste of a decorator is preferred, but how you spend your money will be your business, no one else's. Just remember that regardless of what a couple chooses in the area of color and style, or how something is arranged, a man's home will be his castle in the true sense of the word.

At this juncture I would like to bring up an important point regarding the disrespect that is often shown to those visiting our home. In our effort to get our guests to conform to our expectations, homeowners have been showing the worst manners of all. We have been blaming people for wearing a hat in our home as a sign of disrespect not realizing that we were the ones who were disrespectful. To satisfy our desire it was necessary to tell our guest what to do, but for our guest to satisfy his desire he didn't have to tell us to do anything. Remember, if we ask someone to leave our home unless he removes his hat which is hurting no one, our realization that he would leave and not hold us responsible for striking this first blow prevents us from using this or any other fallacious standard that heretofore allowed us to judge what was right for him. On the other hand, if wearing a hat in a theater blocked our view of the screen, the person in front of us would want to remove it because this would be a first blow for which we would never blame him. If he should forget, he would want to be gently reminded because he could not get satisfaction in making us move to another seat upon realizing that he

391

was responsible for this inconvenience and for being unable to justify what he knows we must excuse. This is really not difficult to understand and needs no further clarification or elaboration.

The knowledge of what it means that man's will is not free draws an infallible line of demarcation between hurt that is real and hurt that exists only in the imagination. What each partner does with his own time will be his business. If a husband decides to play golf for the entire day it does not ask that his wife do anything for him, but yet his playing all day requires his use of their only car. For this reason he is imposing on her because she may desire to use the car for something she would like to do, which is a form of hurt. He would know this immediately and he would also know that his wife would never blame him even if he took the car and played golf all week. In fact, if he is the breadwinner he could stay out for fourteen nights in a row if he wanted to. Because he knows that she would never utter a word of criticism if he left her every night, he cannot find greater satisfaction taking more days for himself without considering his wife. This would be no advantage to him under the changed conditions which forces him, of his own free will, to stay home with the baby part of the time (if they are parents) and divide their spending money in an equal manner — so much for her and so much for him. He is compelled to think things through very carefully before he speaks and acts because he doesn't want to reveal anything that would display a lack of love since this would only encourage her to do the very things he doesn't want, and for which he cannot hold her responsible. Let me remind you that if a husband has a desire to play pool, softball with his buddies, or do any number of things while she desires to play tennis, bowl, garden, etc., they will not stand in each other's way because this would be telling them what they can and cannot do, and they have the right-of-way to do what they judge to be right for themselves. Although they are married, couples will be able to satisfy all their personal desires without being questioned or criticized, but they will be prevented from taking advantage not only because this would display a lack of love which would lessen the security and sexual satisfaction desired, but also because it would definitely hurt the other person who is in love. Realizing that this hurt would never be blamed makes it impossible to derive satisfaction from taking advantage for there would be no advantage under these conditions. This means that if his favorite sports program was on, the wife could prepare dinner earlier or else they could watch it together while eating dinner. The wife, who loves her husband and wishes to show this as often as possible, and her husband, who loves her in return and wishes to show her as often as possible, would both insist that the other watch their desired show which would give them no alternative but to flip a coin. If the husband wins he would want his wife to watch her program, and she would want the same for him if she won because they would be more interested in pleasing the other. All the little standards people assume make for harmony in a marriage will be completely removed because these very standards are the reason for the high rate of divorce and adultery. Besides, they permit a person an opportunity to justify injustice or, to phrase it differently, they permit an unconsciously selfish person to blame in another what exists only in himself. If it gives the husband satisfaction to watch basketball, is he hurting his wife in any way? Is he asking her to do something for him? If this was a genuine hurt he would not be able to do it because he would never think of doing something that was a true hurt knowing that she would never hold him responsible. Their marriage will reflect this change in attitude and as a result they will be happier than could ever be imagined. It should be understood that when the satisfaction of a husband's or wife's desire involves the other, there must be mutual agreement, and if there isn't, there can be no blame. The most one can do is extend an invitation. If the husband wants to take his wife out he could say, "Honey, would you like to go to the movies?" If she says no, not tonight, then he must postpone their date for another night. Should he decide to play cards with his buddies, she may decide to go to art class. This does not mean they will never desire to spend time together, but they will need to consider both desires which may require some advance planning. There will be many occasions when the husband and wife will want to partake of the same activities but only if they both agree without any obligation to do the same. The time spent with each other will be reserved for those occasions they both find pleasurable — so that being together is a joy rather than a burden. They will be controlled only by the desire that they might hurt their partner who will never blame them for this.

393

Furthermore, because opinions will no longer be offered as if they were absolute fact (God is teaching all of us to keep our opinions to ourselves), arguments stemming from this source will be entirely eliminated. This will make for a most harmonious marriage and when an invitation is extended nothing in this world could make them desire not to accept it. Sexual desire will remain at its peak because it will be mathematically impossible not to desire each other when nothing stands in the way. Remember, if it gives you satisfaction to stand on your head as a yogi, bump your head on a wall or do any number of things, this is definitely your business, but the moment you tell others that they should do as you do, then you are blaming in advance their desire to do as they want to do which means that you are minding their business, not your own. Of what value is holding your knife and fork a particular way, or tilting the bowl of soup one way instead of the other, if no one will ever criticize or ridicule the difference? It is obvious that if a husband spills soup on his clothes which he has to pay to have cleaned, he will figure out a way to prevent it. It is not your business if he spills the soup on his clothes unless you have to pay for the cleaning or clean them yourself. Under these conditions he would know that this is a hurt to you and since he also knows that you would never blame him for this extra workload because you know he cannot help himself — when he knows he can help himself if he wants to... It's the same story over and again.

When a boy and girl have sexual intercourse for the first time, they will fall more and more in love not only because this passionate thrill of orgasmic ecstasy is a new experience that has become associated with one particular person, but also because they will never do anything to make the other fall out of love. All couples marrying under the conditions described, even without being married as we know the word, will be compelled to fall more and more in love through the years as each constantly represents for the other the satisfaction of enormous passion, which prevents any thought of adultery or divorce. They will remain together until death do they part not because to leave would be a hurt for which there would be no blame, but only because they know who has the right-of-way when desires conflict and will never strike a first blow. In the final analysis, couples stay together because leaving under these conditions would be the worst possible choice. Is it humanly possible for either to desire giving up what is a tremendous source of happiness? The infinite wisdom that governs this universe of human relations through invariable laws can be seen when one realizes there is no law that can compel a man to live with and support a woman if he makes up his mind that anything else is better; but of what value is having this law when he, of his own free will, can never desire to leave under the changed conditions? However, it is important for a boy and girl to know what is and what is not a hurt. Think further about this immense wisdom (these invariable laws of God). At the very moment it is revealed what love actually is... nothing more than a strong desire for sexual satisfaction (as if we really didn't know), we are prevented from having more than one sexual partner all through life while being allowed to fall in love with a number of people who could satisfy this passion just by making us aware of what it means that our eyes are not a sense organ and that man's will is not free. It is difficult to envision such a world because it is vastly different from the world we live in, but it is only a matter of time before it becomes a reality as it is God's law which is bringing this wonderful change about.

When this book is released and understood, every husband and wife will be standing on this moment of time called here, making preparation, so to speak, to move to the next spot called there. If either spouse desires to get a divorce but in vain, it must be remembered that every individual will be completely free to do what he thinks is better for himself without any fear from the laws, which only make matters worse now that the truth is understood. This knowledge mathematically prevents any form of retaliation because it is impossible to strike back under the conditions described and gone over several times, while it also prevents the other from doing the very things that under our present circumstances occasioned this desire to strike back. When husbands and wives become citizens, the laws of their country will no longer play a role in their staying together which means that if either wants to leave after all first blows have been removed from their marriage, nothing will stop them but their own conscience. Should a husband walk out regardless and make no effort to support his family, it is equivalent to him dying as far as his wife is concerned and she would immediately come under the guarantee if she has no reserve cash, no job, and no possibility of a job. When she no longer blames him for what obviously is his responsibility, he cannot find greater satisfaction in leaving her if this can only be done at the taxpayer's expense. If he has enough money to support two families and can leave his wife because not to leave would make matters worse for himself (since he was already in love with another person when becoming a citizen), then he will be able to find greater satisfaction in leaving her. But when she begins to apply the principles of the examination, he could very well fall in love with her all over again and decide not to leave after all. The husband, knowing that his wife will never blame him should he desire to stop supporting the family, and that no one in the entire world will ever say a word of criticism, makes it impossible for him to derive any satisfaction or justification from doing so. Instead of giving a husband his freedom, it mathematically prevents him from hurting his family, of his own free will, by compelling him to continue an income far above what the laws require, and second by making the wife or husband realize that the power to keep the person desired has been given to them. Consequently, no wife need have any fear that her husband will hurt the family when he understands this knowledge, but it must constantly be borne in mind that the word hurt where money is concerned is a reality, whereas with sex it is only so when you are striking the first blow for which you wish to be excused.

When a young couple get married in the new world they are given no choice since they will understand all this, and will know that any word or act that judges or blames another reveals a selfish desire which destroys the very security and sexual satisfaction desired. This prevents them from ever taking each other for granted. Consequently, when marriage begins on a mutual basis of sincere love (equal passion) and the principles in this book are understood, the very things that contribute to adultery are mathematically precluded. All that is necessary is to show your partner in actions, not words, that you are truly in love. As for those of you who are not sexually satisfied because your partners are committing adultery or just not in the mood to have sex with you although they are not thinking about divorce — and since you can no longer blame them — then you must do everything in your power to arouse sexual desire without physical contact or obligation. When all the things that gave justification are removed, adultery is prevented, but this can only be accomplished if you want it to. Part of the excitement of adultery is in the deception (forbidden fruit is sweet) and in the higher degree of passion; but when a wife and husband know that the other will never blame anything, and when all arguments are removed because neither will ever tell the other what to do, they become somewhat like strangers where sex is concerned because no demands will be made. This in itself will arouse desire, but when they become extremely sexy because there is no other way to extend an invitation, and when they know they are completely free to have as many lovers as their conscience allows, you will see that even the atmosphere of the people already married when the transition begins will be forced in the direction of monogamy.

The expression 'for better or for worse' when interpreted properly is absolutely true in the new world because you are never going to blame, but in our present environment it allows us to strike a first blow making it worse for our partners and excuse it by saying, "You married me for better or for worse." We can let ourselves get out of that shape that originally attracted them and when their desire to make love diminishes because we are less appealing, we blame them for what is our responsibility. By doing things that reduce the desire for a sexual relation we are hurting our partner and demonstrating that we don't care which gives ample justification to commit adultery since a warm passionate sexual experience is the birthright of every individual. Therefore, we will be compelled to desire learning the secret of how to prevent this great hurt to each other because our own happiness is at stake. We can no longer be careless about our physical or sartorial appearance because we can no longer obligate our partner to remain under any conditions, but we will not want to be careless about anything because it will only deny us what we want. Knowing our partners will not blame us for letting ourselves get out of that shape that originally attracted them, we are forced to do everything we can to make their sexual life better because they will not hold us responsible for making it worse. Consequently, if a wife is in the mood for love she can no longer hold her husband responsible when it is within her power to get him hot enough to come to her. For the first time she becomes conscious that she is responsible for anything that is done to herself since she alone holds the secret that can keep their love alive. Realizing that this may require a complete transformation of herself, she also becomes conscious that this is not just for the benefit and happiness of the other partner but for her own happiness and satisfaction as well. By obeying God's will — Thou Shall Not blame — she is prevented from hurting herself by preventing others from hurting her. If she makes no effort to change her ways he will be completely free to leave her for another woman since it is only her love for him that can prevent this great hurt to her, otherwise, it would not be a hurt. If they decide to give their relationship another try, then they must never touch each other in any way until they have been aroused and offered an invitation. If their invitation is not accepted time and time again it becomes a first blow that conscience will not allow to continue when all criticism is removed. Sooner or later those committing adultery will have to make some kind of adjustment because it will be difficult for them to reject a partner who would not only not criticize them for this or anything else, but would not blame them no matter how much it hurts — even if adultery was committed right in view.

Couples can no longer turn to the laws, religion, or our experts in psychology and marriage counseling to try and get their partner to understand what should be done. They are given no choice in this matter when they see the happiness that lies ahead once they obey God's will, Thou Shall Not Blame, but it must be remembered that this only applies before a first blow is struck, not afterwards. Always keep in mind, there is no law that can compel a man to live with and support a woman if he makes up his mind that anything else is better. In the past when financial burdens increased along with a terrible feeling of insecurity, the slightest spark may have set off a tremendous explosion of arguments that gave ample justification to shirk one's responsibilities and transfer them to the government, friends, and relatives. The government does not come to an end because it is a form of blame, but only because it is a useless, costly appendage when the truth, which the world's philosophers have been searching for since time immemorial, is mathematically revealed. The service of a rabbi and priest during a marriage ceremony doesn't come to an end because it includes the inculcation of a couple's obligations to each other, which is a form of tacit blame, but only because the boy and girl are getting married in a superior manner which renders this service obsolete. Of what value is having a law that compels a man to pay alimony when he, of his own free will, will pay much more (providing this blanket of advance judgment; this blanket of tacit blame, is removed), or when he can never desire a divorce. As for widows and widowers, they too can fall in love and therefore will be compelled to search for a mate they do not want to hurt. In our present world the husband and wife blame each other because they were unconscious of who really was to blame. Always remember that everything developed just as it was meant to, otherwise, you will criticize and laugh at those who were that way before the transition gets officially launched. By revealing this knowledge that man's will is not free which releases the corollary that no person is to blame, we realize that everything that happened was part of a bigger plan. By removing all forms of advance blame — this judging in advance of what is right for others (habits that have developed over the years) which includes all forms of government and religion, man is mathematically prevented from doing those very things for which these institutions came into existence. The infinite wisdom that governs this universe is amazing when it is remembered that the laws and government are removed only because they are not needed at this stage of man's development. You will understand these principles much better when it is reviewed the second and even the third time.

In conclusion, just remember that to make a successful transition of marriage all that is necessary is for both husband and wife to realize that the greatest happiness imaginable is compelled to result from obeying God's will — Thou Shall Not Blame — before something is done. As a result, you are prevented from hurting yourselves by preventing your spouses from hurting you. If you want to hold onto your mate, if you want a passionate sexual relationship, if you want real happiness, just obey the mathematical law of God, and if you do not want these things (remember you are completely free to do what you want) just disobey this fantastic wisdom. God has given us the recipe for a wonderful life and it must come about once all mankind understands what it means that man's will is not free because it actually benefits everyone, without exception. Unfortunately, we cannot speed things up because we are moving at a mathematical rate which includes our efforts to speed things up. Now be perfectly honest, has God given us a choice? Show me how free is your will by doing what you know will drive the person whom you want for sexual satisfaction away from your arms. My friends, it is a mathematical impossibility. You must constantly bear in mind that all forms of tacit blame notwithstanding have an inverse relation to love; the more you judge how your partner should be, the less you are in love, which judgment only decreases passion by striking the first blow while justifying a retaliatory measure not desired, just as fear itself tacitly blames, encourages, and justifies what is feared.

It should not be necessary to analyze every minute detail of marriage as this slide rule is applicable at all times. It is necessary to remind you that both partners must understand these principles in order for them to work. If a wife and husband want their partner never to leave them for another sexual playmate, this is within their power, providing they show their love which only means the absolute giving up of judging what is right for the other. This demonstrates a complete respect for their partner's desires while it prevents any desire to hurt or take advantage of another. Remember, if the satisfaction of your desire requires your partner doing what she (or he, whatever the case may be) does not desire, then you are selfishly asking the sacrifice of her desire not to do what you want done, even though your partner is reluctantly willing. However, when she fully realizes that there are many things you need assistance with, and that you will never ask a favor, she will desire to do for you the things you cannot do for yourself. Under the new conditions, it will be impossible to desire to tell her what to do when there is no chance that she could do anything wrong.

In the new world you can no longer obligate anybody so if you want your partner to make love to you, don't be bashful, just extend a very warm invitation. If at the time of the transition you are in the process of divorce, the fact that your husband will know you will never blame him for not supporting his family even if he should stop giving you anything, will prevent him from desiring to hurt you and the children so your problem where marriage is concerned is only sex.

The very fact that we are prevented from taking our partners for granted and must arouse their desire to accept an invitation each and every time we are in the mood to make love will cause the greatest amount of passion imaginable. Couples will stay together not because to leave would be a hurt for which there would be no blame, but only because they are very much in love. The honeymoon will never be over because they will keep themselves fit as a fiddle and ready for love, and never do anything to sabotage the marital bond. In the next chapter it will be shown why we have never treated our children with respect, and here lies the cause of all parental problems. As we extend our basic principle we will see homes, once fraught with anger and rebellion, transformed into homes that are filled with peace, harmony, and the greatest familial love imaginable.

CHAPTER NINE

PARENTS AND CHILDREN

I will begin this chapter with a question, "Is there a way to bring up a child in the new world so the parents will never have a problem? We must first define the word problem as we did earlier because, in reality, there are no problems unless someone is being hurt in a concrete, not imaginary manner. As long as we believe that man's will is free and our only solution is blame and punishment, we will not be able to raise our children in the best possible environment. Nobody would think of blaming a baby for being born but shortly, thereafter, the parents and society will blame and punish this child for not acting as he should. Society judges what is right and wrong and then holds man responsible to these standards. Just as long as there is this safety valve of blame and punishment, society is permitted to strike the first blow of injustice with impunity.

Many years ago the philosopher Plato dreamed of Utopia, but the only manner in which he thought this could be accomplished was by removing the children from their parents at birth to prevent the passing along of ignorance from generation to generation. He began with a gigantic assumption that his men of Gold — he and others like him who received the necessary education and had the ability to pass through the necessary steps — had already possession of what the end result should be and only needed the means to this end, such as a system to develop these men of Gold, who would then remove the children from their parents for the purpose of controlling the environment, completely controlling what these little ones would experience. It never dawned on Plato and other philosophers that it was mathematically impossible for them to see the end result, for this included the removal of themselves and their ideas which were constantly judging what was right for others. But what made matters still worse (not in reality of course, since everything was necessary), what made matters more difficult to straighten out, was the fact these

403

men of Gold justified the veracity of their wisdom by calling themselves men of Gold.

At every turn I have observed individuals (perhaps you are one) who believe they are more qualified to teach what is right and wrong because of some fallacious standard which justifies the thought by its logic. The other day I happened to hear someone criticize a journalist for his ridiculous column on the rearing of children. To justify the criticism it was revealed that this writer never even had a college education. What this means is that the worst kind of ignorance imaginable, the kind that really doesn't know but thinks it does, is permitted to conceal itself in a logical relation which justifies its existence by assuming that the end result, as perceived by someone who has become a man of Gold, so to speak, is more valid. But the great humor lies in the fact that the end result where children are concerned has long been established in today's thinking and where it differs is not in what a child should become or develop into, but the best manner in which to accomplish this — which is exactly the thinking of Plato. In other words, you do not question the necessity of an education — but what is the best manner in which to get children to want it. You do not question the necessity of teaching your children the difference between right and wrong — but differ quite a bit on how to get children to obey what you think is right. What you know is better for your child is already taken for granted right from birth, which thoughts are contained in the words and air you breathe.

Don't smile and think of someone to whom this applies because everybody on earth, who is a parent, is innocently guilty. The only difference is that a teacher will justify what is taught by assuming that his knowledge is reliable, whereas the others will justify what they say by quoting the teacher, some writer, doctor, priest, etc. One mother in answer to my question as to what made her so certain she was teaching her children the right things replied, "A child psychologist told me, and he's a very brilliant man." Another answered — her minister knows the difference between right and wrong and gave her explicit instructions directly from God. In every case, even when nothing but your own common sense is employed, there are hidden standards that justify the thought although they are completely fallacious, yet they guide your every move. The rabbi was able to criticize the journalist because the standard he employed made him feel superior, but what would have happened if the same standard only revealed that he was misinformed; that he really didn't know; would he have desired to reveal this to his congregation? No child likes to have his toys taken away but if he is hurting others, then something must be done. Though they and others will be dissatisfied to learn the truth when it deprives them of such tremendous satisfaction, they are compelled to be silent because to utter any words in protest would only reveal their great ignorance which can give them absolutely no satisfaction — giving them no choice. However, just to announce that man's will is not free is not sufficient to make these experts — those who are constantly judging what is right for others — give up what they believe to be true. How was it possible for Plato to give up the notion that he was wrong when he saw that he was right? It always is this taking for granted that the end is true...that which you think is true. Even a person like the philosopher Will Durant takes for granted certain truths in bringing up a child, and what he considers wisdom makes no reference to any change in the end itself but only to certain techniques in the means to accomplish this end. He believes that certain foods are more wholesome than others, that a child of ten should be in bed at an early hour and consequently considers it wisdom if he can get his child to eat what he thinks is better, get her in bed at an hour which he thinks is better, play the kind of instrument and music he thinks is better, etc. A person like Durant does more harm to a child because of his successful means than a father who fails with his invectives and commands. Let us follow this philosopher for a while as a basis to demonstrate the source of this unconscious ignorance.

Rule number one with him is air. "Every night, whatever the season may be, open windows call in the wind to turn the cheeks of Ethel into roses and flame." He places great emphasis on rosy cheeks which teaches his daughter that 'opening the windows to call in the wind' is of great value. Now just supposing this child had a physical condition which became aggravated by this cold inhalation during sleep but which would never have developed into anything serious if she had been allowed to move in the direction that was better for herself. Her own nature would have made her uncomfortable during the night and she would have gotten up to close the windows even at the sacrifice of rosy cheeks. Being made to believe that her father is a genius who knows all the answers as to what is right and wrong, she would desire sacrificing her desire to keep warm in favor of her father's desire providing she did not develop an aversion to keeping the windows wide open in the middle of winter. If he conveyed the thought that he really didn't know what was better for her but he preferred for himself wide open windows, then at least she would have been in a position to be the judge as to what was more comfortable for herself. Following his suggestion she could have really gotten sick since he was judging what her body required which would then necessitate calling in a doctor who would literally guess at the trouble, prescribe some medicine to allay her fears and end up making matters altogether worse because his prescription might cause more harm than good.

Included in rule number one is the time he believes his daughter should be in bed. Will Durant believed a strict schedule was necessary for his young daughter. He writes — "Many a bribe of tender words, and dimpled arms about the neck, has been offered us for permission to 'stay up' beyond the year's decreed retiring time. But here we have been quietly and inconspicuously resolute; we will not condescend even to discuss so absurd a proposal; we turn it aside as a criminal idea, and send Ethel up to Morpheus every evening at her usual early hour. Now, though she is a great lady of almost ten years, she still disappears regularly at eight-fifteen, wishes us from the staircase 'tight sleep and pleasant dreams,' and is all tucked in and set by half-past eight. The law has been broken now and then, as when some genius of the piano was honoring our home; but for the most part it has been with us a sacred monastic rule, a trifle of surpassing moment in our philosophy."

He believes that the rules he has set up for his daughter to obey will prevent her from becoming spoiled, consequently, he has become 'quietly and inconspicuously resolute.' He turns aside her request to stay up as a criminal idea by 'not condescending even to discuss so absurd a proposal' because he believes this is the best way to raise his daughter. There is nothing wrong with his idea except one thing. He is not considering her desire but his. In this instance he shows absolutely no respect for his daughter's desire to stay up beyond a time that he judged was right for her, but this was necessary under the conditions that prevailed. Let us further test the knowledge of Durant and other parents who think this way or other ways, very simply.

By setting up a decreed retiring time, he blames his daughter in advance for her desire to stay up beyond that time. The important question here is not which means are being used toward a particular end, but the end itself, which has already been determined for the child. Therefore, the question is not asking about the ideal time a child should go to bed, but why this is important. He believed that there is an element of truth in the expression, 'Early to bed and early to rise...' and some truth in how many hours a child of a certain age requires. Besides, he wanted her to be rested for school so she would accomplish her work in a more healthful manner. If he didn't assume the responsibility of seeing that she gets enough sleep, she might not be alert enough the next day in school or, which is worse, she might be too tired to go at all. But how can it be possible for a doctor or philosopher to know what is better when there is no mathematical standard to determine this? He is constantly judging what is right for others, the very opposite of what God's mathematical corollary reveals to be undeniably true. He was compelled to believe in free will in order to justify his constant criticism and judging; how else could the Story and Mansions of Philosophy have been written?

His moral instructions are "First, use the word 'don't' sparingly"...not because this is an unconscious perception that no one can be blamed, but because he recognizes that this would only hinder the accomplishment of what every parent desires for his child. However, the reason he says parents should be restricted to a limited number of 'don'ts' is only because it is mathematically impossible, in the world of free will, to eliminate all of them. He says, "If a child misbehaves, apologize to it; for you have misfed or maltreated it. 'Don'ts' are necessary, but every parent should be restricted to a limited number of them, like a doctor with alcoholic prescriptions and perhaps, like the doctor, he should exhaust his annual allotment on January first and leave himself a clean slate for the rest of the year." This was his way of controlling his child's environment. Since it was impossible to get his daughter up to bed every night at the time he decreed without exercising the word 'don't,' he was permitted to use this alcoholic prescription which her dimpled arms about his neck could not change. But God states explicitly — Thou Shall Not Blame — and Durant definitely blamed the desire of his daughter to stay awake. However, this does not mean that Durant should not do everything in his power to get her in bed at that hour. God isn't stopping him from satisfying his desire, but he must do it without blaming her desire.

The entire problem of raising children in the best possible manner is easily solved the very moment we apply the mathematical slide rule, Thou Shall Not Blame, because then we are made conscious of the fact that only one road is open for travel. Since it is mathematically impossible to blame a child for being born and for the subsequent needs and desires that develop from his nature, it is obvious that we must prevent certain desires — the ones we consider harmful in some way — from arising. We are given no alternative but to prevent what we do not want. Because we are influenced even where the hurt is purely imaginary, our slide rule, or basic principle, sets up a mathematical standard to test all knowledge relating to children who must be guided by their parents until they can be taught what it means that man's will is not free, which would then allow them to assume responsibility for themselves. Consequently, from the very first day of birth it is important for parents to determine only what they feel would be a real, not imaginary, hurt to either their child or themselves for which the baby, now and all through life, cannot be held responsible. But if they are unable to prevent (take note of this mathematical wisdom) their child from desiring what they feel will be a hurt, or prevent their child from not wanting what they think will be for his benefit (both without any form of blame), it is rather obvious that what they like or dislike is something not in any way harmful to the child and exists only as an imaginary fear based upon false knowledge, otherwise, they would definitely have the power to prevent this harm without this blame.

If Durant perceived some great benefit to his daughter being in bed at eight-fifteen, then there is only one thing he can do in order not to blame her desire to stay up past that hour and that is to develop a habit whereby he retires at that exact time to show her how important this is. This means that he must shut off the television, stop whatever he is doing, turn off all the lights at a very early hour, and then get in bed. But what if he doesn't feel like going to bed that early to set the example since this kind of effort involves his desire in an extremely sacrificial way, especially if the entire family has to go to bed at the same time? He is obviously not ready to go to bed, therefore, he is compelled to blame her desire or else let her stay up. In other words, if it meant that he would have to give up hours on his books because of this imaginary harm, he would be given no choice — but God is giving him a choice — either leave the child alone to satisfy her own desire, or sacrifice his to develop this habit. If Ethel doesn't want to imitate in spite of her parents' efforts, this is her business, not theirs, and if she should desire to go downstairs after they are in bed and turn on the television to watch a later show, there is absolutely nothing they can do about it without blaming her desire. Consequently, they can never be assured that she may not desire to stay awake longer to read, watch television, or do something else. This proves that there is no harm whatsoever in a child not going to bed at a specific hour simply because the parents cannot prevent it without the use of blame.

Had Durant known man's will is not free and what this means he would never have been able to judge what the desire of his daughter should be, but believing he was correct in controlling her this way he was not concerned with her judgment about what was better for herself, only about his judgment which he felt was more important. He was not aware that every time he stifles her desire her entire body is unhappy which makes her vulnerable for sickness of some sort, even the kind that is feigned. In comparison to this father who says, "Ethel, get the hell upstairs to bed right now before I spank your little tail," Durant considers his means an expression of wisdom. But why should he make such an issue of her bedtime hour; what difference does it really make if the child is happier going to bed when completely exhausted from having fun? He takes for granted that the knowledge which guides his actions in raising his daughter is correct, and he never questions it. Isn't it obvious that she would have been much happier to stay downstairs? But he was not concerned with her happiness when it contravened principles which he held true. Yet though he was not doing what was healthier for her, he thought he was just by the fact that he considered himself a genius which justified the thought. If we wish our children to be in bed at a certain time, this is our business, but if we cannot justify punishing them for not going to bed because this is not a first blow, and the only way it might be possible to make them healthy, wealthy and wise is to sacrifice our desire to watch a television show so they will imitate us, we might soon be compelled to believe that early to bed and early to rise is not so vitally important. If we feel that staying up beyond a certain time might make them so tired the next day that they won't want to go to school, you are jumping to a premature conclusion because this is impossible just as long as staying home will give them less satisfaction. However, because being tired might make them enjoy school less, and because going to school will be such a fantastic pleasure under the changed conditions (as you will soon observe), they might prefer to go to bed early so they can enjoy school more by not being tired. Whatever they choose to do is their business, not ours, just as long as they are not hurting us with a first blow. "But," you might ask, "how is it possible not to criticize, judge, or blame some desires that children have?" This will be answered as we continue our analysis, so please have patience.

Rule number two in the philosophy of this individual is food. "We found that Ethel flourished on a vegetarian diet helped out with plenty of milk and whole wheat bread; she grew tall and strong, athletic and alert; and it seemed to us that she was getting every element needed for full development. But the vegetarians will be scandalized to hear that very soon in Ethel's history we added chicken to her menu once or twice a week. We call her a 'chicken vegetarian'; and on that queer unprincipled diet this little household has been prospering physically for a decade. Ethel's health-record is not perfect: she encountered German measles in her infancy, but recovered within a week; at four she caught whooping cough from a playmate, and beat it down with the help of the new serum; at eight she developed swollen tonsils. They were removed on the advice of a doctor." In actual reality, if man had something removed every time it became infected or swollen he wouldn't have much left. This does not mean that no tonsils

410

should ever be removed, but once again we must ask where is this mathematical line of demarcation when a doctor is dependent on this removal to earn a living? As we know, this operation is justified on the grounds that the tonsils are a vestigial organ which serves no purpose now, but are the doctors who remove them absolutely certain they do not serve a useful function? Durant continues to boast of Ethel's wonderful health record: "These are the blots on her 'escutcheon'; otherwise she is a stranger to doctors and disease." "How does it feel to have a stomach-ache?" she wants to know. Although it is true that she could not express a desire for a different kind of food when not given a choice, while being in good health Durant, once again, puts the cart before the horse by assuming that her physical condition was directly due to what she ate. Had this child been allowed to choose between various meats, poultry, fish, as well as a large variety of vegetables, or had her meals included this larger variety, she might have been a much happier person. By restricting her to whole wheat bread, milk and a chicken vegetarian diet, he once again assumed what her body required. Durant does not discuss the problems that some people have in trying to get their children to eat foods considered better and more wholesome. Most parents threaten their children with some form of punishment unless they eat the quantity and quality of food they mistakenly believe are necessary, but our philosopher never had this as a personal problem.

Rule number three is play, according to Durant, who judges constantly what is better for his daughter when he states, "and taking all these growing muscles, senses and limbs, teaches them coordination, precision, unity." The perfect parent (since he appears to know, he must be one) would have, as an element in his artistry, knowledge of just what toys to buy to encourage the development of every organ and every power. He is not interested to find out what the child prefers to develop; only what he thinks should be developed. He uses a similar strategy when trying to get his daughter to conform to his desire for her to play the piano. You see, in the world of free will parents were influenced by the criticism and ridicule of friends and relatives and if Durant belonged to a cultured group that looked down on rock and roll, etc., he would have preferred the piano and certain music to the risk of being looked down upon. It could be that Durant didn't believe he belonged to such a group because the way he got her to play what he wanted appeared that it was for her sake. He did this by methodically arousing her desire to play the piano without the use of force. He truly believed he was giving her a choice, but when she lost interest he once again employed a psychological technique not to satisfy her desire, but his own. It was the piano and classical music that he wanted his daughter to play, simplified selections from Beethoven, Mozart, Schumann, Schubert, Handel, Haydn and Bach; he was not interested in any other musical instrument or in rock and roll. He states on page 240 in Mansions of Philosophy, "But for weeks before putting the question we spoke of the glory of music, and of the high privilege of performing or composing it. Then we looked about for a teacher who would begin not with sleepy scales and terrifying finger-exercises, but with simple, ear catching melodies that would set the whole household humming them. We found the teacher, and soon our home rang with tunes played by a chubby finger laboriously. We older ones went about our work singing the melodies that Ethel evoked; she was pleased to note our delight, and felt herself already an artist; at the very outset the piano meant music to her, not noise and pain."

In certain instances Durant did very well. Look how expertly he handled the problem that agitates every home. Most people say, "Go practice the piano," which he says is a silly phrase, for it suggests, most unmistakably, "piano is a bore, practicing is torture; go and suffer; you deserve it." "We tried another plan with Ethel; we merely offered her the opportunity to learn the piano if she wished; we left it to her choice." You see, he believed he wasn't blaming her. To show you that he actually did blame his daughter for not wanting to learn, he says in the next paragraph — "Later a plateau in her progress came; she did not want to practice anymore; and we had to gird our loins and fight the demons of passion and custom that bade us command and compel. Instead, I sat down at the piano and practiced the lesson myself; it was within the measure of my ability. Then I invited Ethel to join me and make it a program for four hands. She came, and for a week I practiced with her; when she did not care to come I played her pieces alone. The teacher provided us with simple duets, and we learned them together. At this very moment she has called up to me, "Daddy, come down and practice with me!" Rapidly her pleasure in the piano returned. Soon she was playing simplified selections from Beethoven, Mozart, Schumann, Schubert, Handyn and Bach; we sang these famous strains with gusto, and made her know how grateful we were that she was filling our hearts with song. She came to feel that music was a great boon, worth all the trouble that it involved. "Now," she says, after playing the Adieu to the Piano, "I understand why you're so crazy about Beethoven." Although she stated how grateful she is now, gratitude is not in question but happiness. Durant is an example of a man who does not know the truth at all but thinks he knows (for which he cannot be blamed) because he, like the rest of us, is moving in the direction of satisfaction. The truth is, if it wasn't for his mistakes I would never have made my discovery. In reality, if Durant was sincerely interested in what was better for his daughter, he would have allowed her to hear every kind of musical instrument and every type of music for the sole purpose of letting her decide for herself which she preferred and what gave her the greatest satisfaction. But if he did that then she might select rock and roll in preference to Beethoven, and a set of drums to the piano. Consequently, he couldn't risk this possibility, so he limited her options. I, myself, cannot stand to listen to rock and roll. To me it sounds like the clanging together of pots and pans. But my three children enjoy it, and my little boy is in love with the Beatles. If I tried to influence them to like what I like, then I would be blaming them in advance for not liking it. There is a big difference between controlling the environment in order to protect a child from harm by restricting the play area so he can't get hurt, but also giving him complete freedom within those confines to play to his heart's content, and Durant's method of controlling his daughter's choices by not giving her the freedom of the musical world, only a part of it. He blames the other part of this world not because of any hurt it might do to his daughter, but because he doesn't like it, therefore he doesn't want her to have anything to do with it. He does not want her to become a drummer, bugler, saxophone player, so he arouses her interest to move in the direction he wants her to go by speaking of certain aspects of the music he desires until she feels like learning how to play, and when she doesn't practice he blames her very much for his

413

disappointment but in an inconspicuous way to make sure she will not go off again on another tangent. He then leaves it up to her choice which is no choice at all since she is obeying his will, not her own.

Durant's daughter might have preferred playing with dolls, toy trucks or doing any number of things, but he resented her not practicing so he set out methodically to force her to give up what was making her happy — not practicing — to do what made him happy. He was so successful in this regard that if his daughter could have ended up a happy lover of Elvis Presley, rock and roll, and the saxophone had he left her completely alone, his technique would have gotten her to sacrifice this happiness in favor of what made him happy. However, he had no choice to do otherwise. His friends and relatives looked up to a pianist and down on other instruments, up to parents who applied certain standards and down on those who did not, up to classical music and down on rock and roll, up to someone who completed college and down on those who never graduated high school, up to someone who had a big vocabulary and down on those who did not, up to one who became a good swimmer and down on those who did not, up to one who was taught etiquette and down on those who were not. Durant is not one ounce different than other fathers trying to impose their will except in the method he uses; the means to attain this end. In other homes this psychology was not applied and many fathers were not so subtle. Just as the father in the previous example demanded that his daughter go up to bed immediately or else get punished, most did not hesitate to punish their children severely which developed terrible guilt complexes because they were taught to honor their mother and father. When a child came home with poor grades the father would say — "This is unacceptable! Did mother see your report card yet? I warned you the last time, Billy, that if you fall short in arithmetic again you are really going to get it. Now just for that you cannot watch television for three whole weeks, you cannot go to the movies for three whole weeks, you cannot play sports after school for three whole weeks and...get the hell upstairs to your room this minute, and you'd better get that arithmetic correct or you'll really see what's coming." I am not criticizing Durant and these other fathers for bringing up their children the way they did because they couldn't help themselves under

414

the circumstances of not knowing what was truly better for everybody concerned. Their subconscious reasoning told them that this was the better choice. They may have been thinking on these lines, "Even though I don't like many things in the school system, if I don't adjust, my family could be hurt even more." These parents were constantly impelled by the desire to get a favorable reaction from the people around them. Each father wanted to hear the compliments of his friends and he certainly didn't want to be ridiculed by the comments of others about how poorly his children were turning out. In a situation like this I would not respond like Durant or the other fathers but instead I would tell my children what to expect from others if they don't act in a certain manner, and then I would leave it up to them. The difference between Durant and me even under the conditions of our present world is that he tries to protect his daughter by seeing, with his psychological persuasion, that she conforms to what society wants in a young lady. If my daughter came home with poor grades she would not expect punishment from me although I would let her know what society expects. I don't care whether my daughter conforms to what is expected of her but I want her to know what the reaction will be to a non-conformist. If she doesn't want to give in to them, this is her business. In this way, at least she could decide what she thinks is better for herself. This could possibly hurt her in later years, under the present conditions, but she would know this ahead of time so the decision would be hers to make. This you understand is only necessary in the world of free will because people hurt with their reaction. As soon as man learns the truth of his nature, this criticism and ridicule disappears and I would no longer have to teach my children how they can be hurt, only how they could hurt others — for which they would not be blamed. Remember, it takes two to tango, or it takes two people to understand these principles in order for them to be effective. Once again, there is nothing wrong with the way Durant aroused her interest in the world of free will. In fact it was commendable when compared with what other parents did, but we are not concerned with what is better, A or B, only with C which is the best. When compared with what God instructs through our mathematical revelation, it becomes obsolete. If he cannot prevent her from liking rock and roll instead of Beethoven (without any form of blame), it is obvious that the harm he perceives has existence only as a figment or improper relation of his mental development. When this blanket of blame, criticism, and ridicule is removed, when all words that describe nonexisting external values become obsolete, the only thing that could prevent a man like Durant from desiring that his daughter prefer the piano to the drums would be the pain of having to listen to that all day long. It would make no difference what his daughter preferred because nobody would negatively judge her choice. Durant would then have two possibilities. Either let his daughter select from among the various types of music and instruments while he lives elsewhere, just in case she chooses drums and bugles, or let her select from among the various types of music and instruments while he lives at home, regardless of what she chooses. If the music bothers him, one solution would be to set up a room with extra insulation to absorb the sound. In either case, he cannot blame her anymore for her desire to be different than what he wants her to be.

Many people believe that unless parents push their children in a certain direction it would be possible that they could end up doing something less satisfying than if they were psychologically guided, as Durant did with his daughter. For example, isn't it possible that she might have become interested in rock and roll at a very early age only to change later on in life and wish she had studied the piano instead of drums? Didn't she come to feel that classical music was a great boon, worth all the trouble that it involved; and didn't she find great enjoyment in understanding why her father was so crazy about Beethoven when she found herself feeling what he felt when playing the Adieu to the Piano? A father might direct his son to become a professional earning $50,000 a year, or a baseball player making twice as much. Supposing without this guidance the boy ends up a laborer earning $6000, don't you think if he had a choice he would have preferred his parents guide him in this other direction? This question assumes that without this guidance children could end up worse off, but this is completely erroneous as you will begin to understand. I shall once again take an excerpt from 'Mansions of Philosophy' to further analyze the psychological technique Durant used to get his daughter to do what he felt was best, but not what was best for her in her eyes. He writes, "Perhaps, too, we can substitute praise for blame in forming the character of the child," not realizing that whatever is praised to further his end is an inverted form of blame which justifies not doing what is desired when the praise is not forthcoming. In this instance he is only praising to avoid the necessity of blaming. He gives his daughter a monthly salary dependent upon her keeping her room tidy, making her own bed, getting up promptly, arriving at school on time and doing her lessons well which obviously blames her for not doing these things. Since this monthly salary is dependent on her doing certain things, and not to give it to her would certainly be a form of punishment which he doesn't approve of, he writes, "It is remarkable how well behaved a child can be without punishments and without commands," therefore he is compelled to resort to pride in addition to praise in order to prevent Ethel from desiring not to do that for which she is being paid so that he doesn't have to stop her salary, which would be a form of punishment. This is somewhat like a man who starts out by making a small investment in a new venture only to discover that he now has to invest more money to insure against losing the first. Before long he realizes that he bit off more than he can chew, and ends up getting deeper and deeper in the hole. "We suggest to Ethel that she is too proud to let anyone see her untidy or unclean; that she is too proud to run forward for gifts or preferment; too proud to let anyone surpass her considerably in her work." Each thing reveals the standards which govern his every thought and makes him a part and parcel of his time, except for the means. He writes, "Censure cramps the soul and makes the imperfect task forever hateful; praise expands every cell, energizes every organ, and makes even the most difficult undertaking an adventure and a victory. Egotism is the lever by which we can move the world to do the bidding of others without using force." He doesn't realize that this only changes the means, not the end. He continues, "Instead of pouncing upon work ill done and heaping up reproaches, we keep an eye alert for things done well and mark it with praise that shall linger sweet in the memory as a call to further accomplishment"…for the purpose of accomplishing what the parents want, not what the child desires. "If my daughter has to report she has fallen short in arithmetic, we show regret, but we have not the heart to reprove

417

her"…as if showing regret is not reproof when a child is being paid in praise that blames her for not doing what is expected, and demonstrates how easy it is for a philosopher to get confused with words. "But when she comes home with news of perfect marks we dance and celebrate, and exhaust our ingenuity to show new joy at each victory." This plainly tells us how powerful praise is as a means to an end because a child can be persuaded to do what is not liked, perhaps even hated, to earn the praise. In this case he blames certain desires and actions of his daughter by praising other desires, just as calling somebody beautiful is another way of calling someone ugly. In actual reality he employs the exact same psychology with his daughter as an expert male uses when winning the love of a girl, but neither show their own love. There is actually nothing wrong with praise if it does not blame the person praised for anything, or blame anybody else, but this is not what Durant is doing. Just supposing he is tired one day and doesn't feel like dancing, what then, when he is under this obligation to pay his debts? "When she has done something that especially delights us we have slipped a dollar into her bank"…just as a seal, for a good performance, is given extra fish. (This is equivalent to B. F. Skinner's behavioral modification which uses rewards as a means to an end). And what would he do if his daughter especially, especially, especially delighted him? Couldn't some fathers run out of cash or praise? It is quite obvious that she is performing to get paid whether with praise or cash, just like a man working at a job he doesn't like but stays because of the money he needs to support his family. The only difference between Durant and other fathers is that he resorts to praise, a monthly allowance, and pride, to get his daughter to do what he wants done while other fathers blame and threaten with punishment any failure to do what is expected. He punishes by not giving what is desired, while they punish by giving what is not desired. For example, Durant punishes his daughter by taking away the praise when he feels she hasn't earned it, as when she has fallen short in arithmetic. He punishes her by letting her see that he was disappointed and punishes her even more by implying that though she was responsible for this disappointment, he wouldn't reprove her, which makes her feel guilty and desire never to hurt her father again this way. He is using the worst form of punishment

418

imaginable although he is not conscious that it is the worst when he lets her see how her 'defection from honor has darkened the day for all.' He makes her conscious that she has committed a terrible crime which has hurt her father and mother very much who refuse to blame her despite this. This is cruelty personified because the parents were not hurt and it compels the sacrifice of a great part of her happiness to satisfy the selfish desires of her parents. It is equivalent to a father taking advantage of a child by asking her to go upstairs and get his slippers. If the child refuses because this service would entail interrupting something giving the child pleasure, the father, employing his psychological technique would then say, "That's all right, honey, you don't have to get it for daddy if you don't want to." In this case the child, being made to feel guilty, suddenly desires very strongly to do what was asked because she is conscious of hurting her father who is not blaming her for this. Durant was able to control his daughter because he reduced the amount of her unhappiness to a minimum in comparison to the average home by hiding his authority behind psychological tactics which he thought was wisdom and in this way was able to get her to love her daddy very much. There is no question how much Ethel loved her father as a little girl, but this love would have been much greater had he not been compelled by God's will to set up these fallacious standards of value. Everything Durant did was to satisfy his desire, not hers. It was psychological trickery that he found preferable and no matter how you look at this, it is pure and simple selfishness. It is true that Durant was showing a special kind of selfishness since he desired she give up certain preferences only because he wanted her to develop in a direction that he thought would make her ultimately more happy, and you certainly can't blame him for doing what he thought was better for his daughter and himself. But God is putting an end to all kinds of selfishness and is insisting that everybody henceforth — once the transition gets under way — mind their own business, which includes the kind that previously allowed parents to judge what they thought was better for their children when advance blame was involved.

By following Durant's reasoning we can clearly see that every standard of right blames someone in advance for doing what is judged wrong; but supposing this yardstick itself is wrong? Then it is accurate to say that the person who judges the conduct of another according to this measurement is permitted to strike the first blow of injustice with impunity while being permitted to blame any retaliation. A perfect example is when a parent tells his child that it is wrong to do certain things. The child, desiring to do what he said not to do, is blamed and punished while the parent justifies his own conduct by saying the child's actions were wrong since he didn't have to do what he did because he had the free will to act otherwise. For this reason it is imperative that we discover a way to prevent the child from desiring to do the very things for which blame and punishment were previously necessary, as the lesser of two evils. Are you beginning to see what takes place in our present world? If you know the difference between right and wrong, and you also know that a person cannot be blamed or punished for what he does because his will is not free, isn't it obvious that we are given only one alternative and that is to prevent the desire to do what is wrong from arising, which then makes it unnecessary to blame and punish? Just as long as man has this safety valve of blame and punishment, he doesn't have to find the solution to this doing of what is wrong. In the past, parents could be very careless and excuse themselves by blaming their children, but once it is discovered through mathematical reasoning that man's will is definitely not free, then it becomes impossible to blame a child for what he is compelled to do.

"In other words, your slide rule will demonstrate how to prevent a young child, before he knows what it means that man's will is not free, from ever doing those things for which blame and punishment are now necessary as the lesser of two evils."

"That is correct. But our slide rule, where these very young children are concerned, can only have application by our realization that when we blame them even before something is actually done, we are motivating and justifying in advance that for which they are being accused. To put it another way, since it is mathematically impossible to blame a child for being born or for the subsequent needs and desires that develop from his nature, in relation to those around him (because it is now a matter of undeniable knowledge that man's will is not free), we are given no alternative but to prevent what we cannot blame and punish any more. The first and most important thing to remember is that a child has his own desire, and under no conditions can his desire be criticized, blamed or punished for anything. Consequently, a mother cannot do anything to this baby or child unless she knows this is what the child wants, otherwise she is blaming his desire. You must understand that this slide rule is an invariable law that gives no one a free choice — once it is thoroughly understood. Do you realize what this means? For the first time parents are going to see how dishonest they have been compelled to be with themselves and their children. As we continue to extend our basic principle, Thou Shall Not Blame, we will eliminate many problems that had no solution until now. The problems facing parents with older children are dealt with differently than the ones confronting a couple with a brand new baby. Therefore, we shall first take care of the latter, then the former, and as we proceed we shall shed by the wayside a number of false beliefs or opinions with which you will be able to identify.

The first problem begins the moment a baby is born when a mother decides to preserve her breasts and feed her infant with the formula prescribed by the doctor even though there is no substitute for what the body developed naturally. Most babies will thrive in spite of, not because of, the kind of food given because the body is very tough and capable of adjusting to most conditions. This in itself is not a sufficient reason to feed them anything, but there is another reason which prevents us from doing so because it makes matters worse for ourselves. When a baby is born, his stomach has never had any food at all so it is possible that if mother's milk is not used since it developed with him (or even after he is weaned should we push into it what is not wanted) he could get all kinds of cramps, indigestion, colic, etc. If this should happen, the only way he can express his feelings is by screaming or crying. He could also be hungry, dirty, uncomfortable, or in pain. If the baby is already experiencing pain or discomfort, the parents may find it necessary to sooth the baby by either walking, bouncing, or rocking him to sleep, which is where the problem begins. In a short time the pain subsides and he falls asleep, but this wonderful feeling of being bounced around is remembered and he knows it occurs only when he screams at the top of his lungs. Soon he screams not because he is in pain, but only to get them to

421

give him that wonderful feeling again. This not only is an annoyance but right here is the origin of spoiling which is a habit, not good or bad in itself, that the parents allow to develop in the child who is then blamed for this annoyance. Before long he begins to annoy the parents by interrupting many moments of pleasurable activities and relaxation. Most of us have experienced this to a degree that was almost unbearable and at a time that was inconvenient. We were asleep for the night or making love. Therefore, the hurt I am primarily concerned with here is not to the baby but to the parents. If it is a source of annoyance to have to rock the baby to sleep, pace the floor at odd hours of the night, as the lesser of two evils, then you had better not develop this association. If he is making a demand, whether it is with screaming, crying or yelling (unless it is to eat, sleep, or be changed), you must never give in because this allows him to use you for the satisfaction of his desire, which does not satisfy you. However, if the baby is fed with the proper nourishment, the mother's natural formula (if you think otherwise, this is your business), given food that he prefers, kept clean, made comfortable so he is not in any discomfort, it appears that the chances of stomach pains are less likely to occur, and should he sleep soundly through the night then the conditions that compelled us to select the lesser of two evils, that is, this rocking and bouncing to stop the screaming, never occur. But if he is already spoiled and you know he is crying to make you do what you prefer not to do, just remember that you have the right-of-way because he needs you to satisfy his desire and you should let him scream, even if he becomes insistent, until he realizes that you cannot be controlled by his crying. In other words, once he sees that he cannot control you, he won't make the effort and will never become spoiled. Eventually he will find a way to entertain himself without the need for your attention, but you must allow him to find his satisfaction without you wherever possible. Remember, there are always two desires involved and spoiling is a habit that requires your desire to satisfy the baby. If you are in doubt as to the reason for his crying and it gives you greater satisfaction to comfort him by holding him in your arms, there is no one to tell you this is wrong. You have a perfect right to raise your child as you please, even spoil him if this is your preference, but should he become an intolerable monster who makes you yield as the lesser of two evils you have nobody to blame but yourself when he can no longer be blamed for what is your responsibility. Someone recently remarked, "I have a nephew who is so spoiled you wouldn't believe it. I remember when he was just an infant how his mother did those very things you mentioned and he has been spoiled ever since."

There may be some confusion here. This does not mean that a baby should never be picked up and played with, on the contrary, it could be done often but only when he is not crying and providing you do not want to develop this annoying habit. If by playing with him you receive satisfaction, this is fine, but should you decide to stop and he raises a fuss, you have three possibilities: Never to play with him at all, which is not satisfying to you. Continue to play with him, which is also not satisfying because you are choosing this only to put an end to his crying or screaming. Or you can just stop playing with him regardless of the fuss he makes. Since the last possibility can never spoil your baby and will make him realize that he cannot control you with his crying, you are given no choice as to what is better for yourself when the facts are understood. In our present world parents blame him for not stopping what they started, and when he continues, they spank him which starts a chain reaction of anger and retaliation. Since they cannot blame the baby anymore for a habit that they created, there is only one possibility open; they must try to prevent what they do not want to develop. In the new world it makes it absolutely impossible for a person to be careless anymore where children are concerned because the moment parents realize that they cannot judge what is right for their children — unless it is without any form of blame — they are compelled to think like never before in order to avoid starting a habit they have no way of stopping without blame, criticism, or punishment.

Very often visitors will pick up a crying baby without knowing that the parents are then left with the responsibility of breaking this habit. They will be prevented from doing this by the realization that they will never be blamed for this concrete hurt. Knowing that no one will take it upon themselves to pick up the baby without receiving permission, the mother might ask, "Dad, would you like to hold the baby?" If dad doesn't want to at that moment he will simply say, "No thank you."

If he does, he will take the baby in his arms. Once they are shown what is truly better for everyone, they are given no choice. For a moment, let us think back to when a baby is just beginning to explore the world. By following our basic principle, we can help the baby fulfill his desires without having to use blame in order to protect him. This demonstration is mathematically sound and cannot be denied.

When a baby first begins to crawl, if he should knock lamps over, scratch furniture or hurt himself in some manner, it is obvious that parents cannot blame the baby yet they will do just that by saying "don't," "no no," "mustn't do that," "don't touch," "stop," "come here," "bad boy," or they will just pick him up every time he is about to touch or climb on something that they would rather he stayed away from. No matter what words they use, no matter how they check his desire — they are still blaming him. Since our mathematical corollary reveals that man is not to blame, they are given only one possibility which is to prevent the desire of this child to climb on furniture from ever arising. In the world of free will a parent often became careless and when a child got hurt he was blamed for allowing the accident to happen. This blanket of blame justified the carelessness because he could always defend himself with an excuse or extenuating circumstance. But when the parent knows that whatever he carelessly does that hurts his child will never be blamed, even if the child should die, it is impossible for him to derive any satisfaction from being excused for what he knows he could have prevented had he not been careless. Consequently, a father will remove all his razor blades so that there is no possibility of a child getting hurt with them because he can think of nothing that offers greater dissatisfaction than that he should be directly responsible for hurting his child when there is no possible way he can excuse it. The mother, knowing that her husband would never blame her if the baby choked to death on a pin or a piece of glass, or hurt himself in any number of ways, is compelled to be extremely careful about everything she does because it cannot satisfy her to be excused for carelessness that can no longer be justified. This does not mean the mother doesn't already do everything she can to protect her baby, but knowing that she will not be blamed adds more weight, just as it does when the pediatrician is asked to offer his recommendations. This compels both husband and wife to think like they never thought before which prevents tragic mistakes from occurring.

A parent remarked, I can understand this but something confuses me regarding blame. When a baby begins to crawl or walk in the direction of furniture that could be broken, such as a lamp if he knocked it over, am I supposed to remove the lamp as I would a pin from the floor, stop him, or keep him out of the room altogether? I realize that to say 'naw naw, don't touch, stop', or just pick him up when about to knock over the lamp or put something in his mouth, is a form of blame, and since we can't blame him for anything, it is obvious that we must put him in a playpen, play yard or playroom so we can control the environment and prevent him from desiring to do those things for which it was necessary to blame. Is that correct?"

"No, that is not correct. What are we supposed to do when he gets older, put him in a playhouse, a play neighborhood, and then a play city? There is quite a difference between preventing him from breaking a lamp, which is a hurt to us, and preventing him from hurting himself. Let me explain this in another way.

The purpose of putting him in a playpen is to control the environment so he doesn't hurt himself. It is obvious that parents must control the environment in order to prevent the baby from desiring to do those things for which it then becomes necessary to blame. Under no circumstances can this child be blamed for anything because everything he does is in the direction of greater satisfaction, over which he has no control. When I put the baby in the playpen I am not blaming his desire for one type of toy in preference to another because there is nothing blocking his natural urge to explore; but by keeping him in an enclosed area he is prevented from getting hurt. During those times when the child is allowed out of the playpen, it is our responsibility to prevent him from doing anything to hurt himself even if we have to blame his desire by saying "naw naw, mustn't touch." We are also compelled to remove everything that might possibly hurt this baby because the knowledge that we would never be blamed for our carelessness, when we know it would definitely be our responsibility, gives us no satisfaction. Children must be guided by their parents until they are able to assume responsibility for themselves, and until that time we are guiding them so they do not hurt others or themselves. By the time children are allowed to enter the other living quarters they will have learned the difference, without being taught, between furniture and toys, living quarters and play quarters, and without ever being blamed for not knowing. They will never desire to play in the wrong part of the house without ever having to be told, which previously required this checking of their motion in the natural direction of greater satisfaction, or from here to there. Remember, all efforts must be made to allow children to fulfill their God given desires, as long as no one is being hurt by their actions.

Another example of how blaming in advance can cause harm is at the swimming pool. In any potentially dangerous situation parents must take extra precaution in order to protect their child from serious injury, but in most cases this can be done without any form of blame. The goal, therefore, is to create the conditions that keep a child safe but that allow him to have as much freedom as possible. As the child learns how to swim at his own pace, he will develop a healthy respect for water but under no circumstances must parents put their child into the water for this assumes that he desires this as well and blames him for not wanting what they want. This may cause him to develop a tremendous fear of the water — the very thing parents are trying to prevent. It may also cause extreme resentment toward those who are forcing him to do something he doesn't want to do. On the other hand, if a child is eager to go in the water the parent must provide a way for him to satisfy his desire but without there being a risk to himself. Since it is impossible to blame a child for his desires, and since a very young child might jump, slip, or fall in water that is over his head, he must be equipped with a life jacket wrapped around his body while he plays on the sand or grass. Should he then decide to go into the water, there will be nothing to check his desire because there is no chance of his head going under. Without this protection, a certain amount of advance blame is necessary. Obviously, a child should never be left unattended even if he is wearing a life jacket. There may also be times that he must listen to directions to stay out of the water. Having been given the freedom to play in an unrestrained fashion, the child will be much more inclined to follow directions when it is absolutely necessary. The problem arises when a child's desire is constantly being thwarted which may cause him to become rebellious. He may jump into the water even if it is over his head because he sees others swimming and resents anyone standing in his way. Each time you check a child's desire you strike a first blow, consequently, when your back is turned this child will desire to strike back at you whether it is as the swimming pool, at the grocery store, or when visiting friends. This is equivalent to the boy who went outside on a freezing day without a jacket and then ate an entire bag of candy because it gave him great satisfaction to do the very opposite of what his mother told him not to do. This is how it begins. His mother yells, "Don't climb on the furniture with your shoes on." As soon as she is not looking, he does just that. She then warns, "Be careful not to spill the milk on the kitchen floor!" He walks into the living room and deliberately spills it on the new carpeting. As she sits down to relax, she says, "You're blocking my view of the television." He stretches out his arms so she sees still less. As he is walking out the door she yells, "Put on your coat if you're going outside." He takes off his shirt and shoes. He then scans the neighborhood to see that nobody is looking and dashes out of the house half naked to hurt her, and ends up hurting himself. I told two kids to be careful about splashing mud on my new car and they said they would, but later when I went outside the fenders were literally coated with mud, and believe it or not they were just 4 and 5 years of age. One mother commented, "It seems to me that no matter what you teach them they desire to do the opposite; that's why I believe that if you stop a child by blaming his desire to knock the lamp over, he will do it the first chance he gets. Unfortunately, I've been compelled to punish my children, otherwise, I would have no control over them at all. How is it possible for me not to punish my son when he insists on doing what he was told over and over again not to do? Stopping him from breaking the lamp is teaching him that this is wrong, I grant that; but if he does it anyway, isn't it obvious that you have to punish him in some way? I thought that by controlling the environment the baby would not be placed in a position to break the lamp, which would prevent the need to blame him."

Sooner or later children have to be taught what is right and wrong (this hurt to others) which means that they must be blamed and punished if they should do something that hurts another, since they are still too young to understand the basic principle. This is the principle of 'an eye for an eye and a tooth for a tooth.' However (and this is the source of the problem), there is no way a child will not desire to strike back if this child has already been hurt. The hurt is often subtle, not the kind you see on the evening news, but has damaging effects nevertheless. For example, her parents compel her to eat what she doesn't want, go to bed when she isn't sleepy, and then they punish her if she doesn't do these things. They pull her hair when combing it, which hurts, and they frighten her when cutting it. To top everything, they show tremendous partiality by calling other children cute, adorable, precious, lovely, beautiful, a doll baby, etc. How long do you think it takes for her to know that she doesn't possess what these words signify? By the time she is old enough to understand what is being said she has become so belligerent, and has built up such a tremendous resentment towards her parents because they have hurt her so many times, that she can't wait for an opportunity to strike back. Then, when she is told not to do something the opportunity has arisen because she sees she has control over something they want and she will get tremendous satisfaction in opposing them, which starts a chain reaction of blame and punishment. This entire situation is prevented when we do nothing to hurt her, and this is accomplished when we remove every bit of advance blame, this judging of what is right for her after she has already expressed her desire, assuming that her desire is not to hurt us, herself, or others. In other words, if the mother decides to comb the hair of her daughter who starts to cry because it hurts, there is a conflict of desire, and if the mother ignores this cry and continues to comb, she is building up resentment in her daughter. It is obvious that the mother in this situation is wrong because in order to satisfy her desire which is to comb her daughter's hair, her daughter must sacrifice her own desire which is for her mother to leave her alone. Because she is judged by friends and relatives for allowing her child's hair to look so unkempt, she is given no choice but to choose the lesser of two evils. This proves conclusively that the reason she is willing to hurt her daughter is not because the condition of her child's hair is hurting anyone, but only because others are judging the mother by certain standards. When both parents know that this will not

428

occur, that their friends will never criticize or compliment their child's appearance no matter how long, short or twisted the strands of hair are, then they will get greater satisfaction in minding their own business, that is, in leaving the child alone because this is what she prefers and she is not hurting anybody with her preference. In reality, what difference does it make if they decide not to comb her hair or let it grow to the ground, just so nobody judges them as inferior because of this. By constantly interfering with the desires of our children and forcing them to do what they don't want with threats of punishment, they build up a tremendous amount of anger which may express itself in unhealthy ways, just like a pressure cooker will explode unless you release the pressure first. When this judging of what is right for them is removed — and it will be — then our children will not be hurt and will not desire to strike back when they are taught the true difference between right and wrong, that is, what is and what is not a hurt to others and themselves. By removing all forms of blame from the day a baby is born, and all through his life, he could never desire to do anything to hurt anyone, including himself.

There are certain problems confronting parents that cannot be handled in the usual manner this book has outlined and requires a deeper analysis because our children are still too young to understand the principles. This permits me to recall an experience that will adequately introduce the problem while revealing the great confusion by psychologists. One day a psychologist friend of mine visited my home with his little boy for the express purpose of telling me about a new principle being applied which stated: Nothing should be done to inhibit the desires of a child but especially — No punishment! As he was preparing to demonstrate his theory his little boy, getting restless, suddenly had an uncontrollable urge to use my brand new sofa for a trampoline. The father was somewhat embarrassed and tried his utmost to get the boy off without using any force. "Johnny, now you know this isn't the right thing to do, so please come off there right away." But Johnny was having too much fun and he appeared to be getting just as much satisfaction out of his father not being able to do anything about it, for he knew that dad wouldn't hit or punish him for anything. Finally dad just reached up and took the boy off, but even then Johnny jumped right back on. He at last told the boy that if he didn't go back on he would stop at a trampoline place and let him jump to his heart's content, and if one wasn't open he would give him something else to make up for it. Now the question arises, how is it humanly possible to get the boy off without blaming his desire? Actually my friend was right about not inhibiting the desire of a child in any way, providing this was applied while knowing that man's will is not free and what this means, otherwise, a tremendous amount of harm could be done to children as well as parents. Consequently, by applying the psychology just mentioned at the wrong time, these children were compelled to become little spoiled monsters who took advantage of their parents at every turn and this was the kind of situation that existed between Johnny and his father. I met a mother whose child was so spoiled rotten that it was absolutely miserable living with him, but the poor mother, having no way of knowing what was right and wrong except to follow what she was taught by the experts, was given no choice since she was made to believe that punishing her child was still worse. If Johnny were my son, I would take him off and tell him if he does that again I will have to punish him. I would need to resort to blame in this situation for the reason that children might have to live a little longer in the world of free will, but only until they can be taught the basic principle. If Johnny had known that jumping on someone's sofa was a form of hurt for which his father would definitely punish him, then before jumping on the sofa he would have thought twice. By preventing a child's desire from moving in the direction you don't want, he can never become spoiled. However, this cannot be used unless the behavior the child is displaying is a definite form of hurt to someone, not an imaginary hurt such as used by Durant.

"In other words, we know that Johnny was compelled to react in this manner because of his upbringing, and we can't blame him for his desire to jump on the sofa since, at that moment of time, this was beyond his control. However, even though we know he is not to blame, it would be necessary to prevent him from continuing to hurt somebody else. Therefore, the father needed to punish him as the lesser of two evils. Therefore the problem is to prevent his desire to jump on the sofa, and do similar things that hurt others, from ever arising, without any form of advance blame or threats of retaliation."

430

Bravo! When we extend the basic principle, the solution to this problem is very simple. The moment all parents understand what it means that man's will is not free, they are to distinguish very carefully between what is, and what is not, a real hurt. If a child can be made to understand that even though he should hurt someone in a real manner he will still not be blamed — which means that he can be taught the principles in this book — then of course nothing further has to be done with him because he would never desire to hurt someone under these conditions. But if the child is too young to understand, then you must tell him that if he continues hurting others in a concrete manner he will be punished in a specific manner, which leaves it up to his choice. Remember, a spoiled child is one who insists on doing what you do not want but still allow, as the lesser of two evils — not a child who is permitted to satisfy his desires to his heart's content. Inside of a very short while no child will desire to hurt another not so much because he knows he will be punished for this hurt, but because his parents have stopped standing in the way of his desires.

"But wouldn't allowing the child to satisfy his desires to his heart's content spoil him?"

"Not at all. How can a child be spoiled when he knows you don't want him to do certain things, which will never be done? It's true that a child in the new world will get his way, but when you and your child are not hurt, what difference does it make just as long as you also get your way? No one is stopping you from watching television, if not at home, elsewhere, so why should you judge that your child should not watch it, if he wants to?"

You must always keep in mind that there are two desires involved — yours and your child's — and it is not a form of blame in any way should you decide not to satisfy the desire of your child when your own desire is involved, unless you gave your child reason to believe that you would. By preventing his desire from moving in the direction you don't want, he can never become spoiled. But remember that by constantly telling him not to do this, don't do that, he will soon desire to do these all the more which necessitates punishment as a means of control, or spoiling. Which method of the three do you prefer, and have I given you a choice? Are you

431

beginning to recognize the difference between living in the one world and the other? Until these principles are taught, parents have a perfect right to refuse the satisfaction of any desires that involve their own. All other desires, however, are not their business just as long as no one is being hurt by their children. The mathematical standard I set up as a guide had only to do with preventing parents from hurting children. It is obvious that a child could never desire to jump on any sofa once he knows that this is a definite hurt for which there would be no punishment or blame of any kind. An important question was brought up that needs to be addressed: "What if a child wants to do something but he cannot do it for himself? For example, what if a six year old should ask, 'Daddy, will you run me over to grandma's house, I want to see her?' What if the father says 'no' because he is not in the mood to go at that moment. By turning the child down, isn't the father blaming his desire?"

In this situation the father is not blaming the child for wanting to go to grandma's house, but he must consider his desire as well. When walking in while his father is watching television because he wants to watch also, the child is not asking his father to do anything, but should he say, "Daddy, I don't like that show, will you please change it?"... then we have a different problem. Since the child has not yet learned what it means that his will is not free, we have a perfect right to refuse the satisfaction of a desire that involves or hurts us. If the child wants to go to grandma's house, the child's desire is to see grandma, not necessarily that daddy take him, therefore it may be possible to get him over there without sacrificing daddy's desire not to go. If, however, there is no other way to get him there and the father still doesn't want to go (the father has the right-of-way), then he must explain to the child that he does not mind him going if transportation can be provided. Should he insist that his father take him, under no conditions must he give in because this develops a spoiled child who will make all kinds of demands. It is necessary to point out the various ways children are hurt, and the ways in which children are made to hurt their parents who have been blaming them for what is their own responsibility. Consequently, since the parents do not like to disappoint a child who asks for things and favors which they cannot always give without annoying or hurting themselves in some way, they

432

are compelled to prevent, without blame, a child from ever asking for this or that just as if he knew what it means that will is not free.

As far as who gets to watch television, when it hasn't been turned on yet you just flip a coin, what else? Your desire because you're older is no more important than his. It is true that children do have some desires that definitely require the assistance of their parents for satisfaction. But dad, knowing this, and also knowing that his children will never take advantage of his generosity, will ask every now and then if there is anything he can do for them. Then little Johnny will answer, "Yes Daddy, there is something you could help me with. Would you mind taking me over to grandma's house?" In other words, once your children are taught what it means that man's will is not free, they will not desire to ask you for anything, but you, knowing this, will ask them if there is anything you can do for them, while they, knowing that you will never blame their suggestion, will be prevented from taking advantage of your generosity. My daughter knows that I would never ask her to get me a glass of water no matter how thirsty I might be, but seeing me perspire she of her own free will says, "Dad, can I get you a glass of ice water?" and I know she cannot have any other motive than to make me happy in this instance because to use this to impose an obligation would only tacitly blame me and justify my not doing what otherwise I would. My knowing that she cannot drive a car and that she would never ask me for any kind of favor compels me to ask her if I might drive her somewhere or ask if there is anything I might do to make her happy; and she, knowing that I would never blame her suggestion, regardless of what it was, is compelled not to take advantage of my generosity.

The next thing proven completely false even though it contravenes everything we have been taught to be true is the waking of a child for anything at all, since this obviously blames his desire to sleep. As we saw in Chapter Seven, when someone is asleep his body desires this and for him to be awakened by a doctor or anybody unless his sleeping is obviously harmful (such as a fire or an urgent medical condition which would reveal his desire to be awakened) you are imposing your desire and judging what is right for him. This offers conclusive evidence that any fears a doctor may impart regarding the necessity of waking a child to administer medicine (unless absolutely necessary),

433

or for a feeding, examination, or anything else you care to throw in, are completely unfounded and grounded in unconscious ignorance.

"But isn't it also obvious the child wants to be healthy, and to have this health it is necessary to wake him for a feeding and a regimen of medicine?"

Here again, it is important to understand the difference between an assumption and a fact. Do you put waking a child because the house is on fire in the same category as waking him to swallow some medicine (other than the kind that would be necessary to keep him alive, such as insulin if he was diabetic)? Isn't it possible that the sleep is of utmost importance, much more valuable than the medicine, but of no value in continuing to sleep when the house is on fire? This is that syllogistic reasoning doctors use when they want to make it appear that they know when they don't.

When a doctor advises these things it is only because you are asking for some advice which he takes advantage of to earn a living — for which he cannot be blamed. Therefore, it should be obvious that the only way you can get your children out of bed without blaming them for not wanting to get up at the desired time is to teach them how to use an alarm clock. Then it will be entirely up to them. If they desire to get up at a specific time; if they desire to go to school — they will — and if they desire to sleep, there is nothing you can do about it unless you blame them in some way. Furthermore, once the blanket of blame is removed, once you cannot prevent this desire to stay home from school without threats of punishment, then it is obvious that the harm you perceive in their not receiving this type of education is purely imaginary, but in today's world the value placed on going to school and the penalty the parents would receive if they honored their children's request to stay home compels them to make their children do what they may not find any value in. This may encourage them to think up a legitimate sounding excuse as to why they can't go to school. Do you see what is happening? We have been forcing our children to prefer lying as a solution to their problems; then we blame and punish them for what is not their responsibility as a solution to our problems. In other words, we strike the first blow by judging what is right for them and then when they strike back by disagreeing with our judgment, we blame and punish them for doing what they preferred under their set of circumstances which included the advance knowledge that they would be blamed. For example, how many times has a student been caught cutting classes he never wanted to take in the first place, and was then severely punished for this 'infraction' of the rules which hurt no one. The schools were able to shift responsibility and justify why the student was at fault, not their teaching methods. Having been forced to take courses he doesn't like he begins skipping classes on a regular basis, but the reason for this is never questioned. He is now labeled a truant by school authorities and the parents are asked to get involved by following through with an appropriate punishment. Not knowing what to do, and fearing they may be looked down upon in the eyes of the community, the parents continue where the school left off by taking away the one thing that gives him any pleasure — after school sports. When he reacts by running away or displaying extreme defiance, he is put in juvenile detention or punished for weeks on end. We now have a situation that has grown into a full blown crisis. By now the child has developed serious psychological problems because he is totally misunderstood and considered a serious behavior problem. His reputation as a troublemaker has spread among his peers and he finds himself in a downward spiral where it is difficult to pick himself back up. Let us fast forward the life of this child by 20 years to observe how he is doing. Sadly, but not surprisingly, he has ended up on the wrong side of the tracks which began in his early school years and he has never regained a sense of stability or direction. Although this analysis is far from complete it gives us an understanding of how easy it is for a child to get lost in the cracks of a broken system. It all begins when the school strikes the very first blow and then punishes the child for striking back in justifiable retaliation. This unfortunate chain of events is not an isolated occurrence and happens more often than anyone would like to admit.

It is easy to see why going to school has become very distasteful for children due to the fact that learning is often associated with fear, not pleasure. The majority of children will tell you they don't like school, and their attitude is one of quiet resignation. Can you see the disrespect we have been showing our children? In one breath we teach them to reach for the stars while in the next breath we express our displeasure when they don't live up to our expectations — and in the process we break their spirits. The very fact that there was mandatory attendance compelled parents to force their children to attend one way or another which increased the business of the doctors just from the feigning of illness these children preferred rather than be faced with the daily torture school represented. According to the Department of Mental Hygiene 3 million teens are facing clinical depression, 19% being high school students. In addition, 2 million teens contemplate suicide each year. Students are under extreme pressure to succeed academically and the competition has become fierce in recent years. This has caused some students to reach the breaking point. Put in a position where they must outrank their classmates in order to get into the best colleges, some may turn to cheating to keep up their grade point average knowing that their future hangs in the balance. Students who feel insecure when comparing themselves to others may resort to unhealthy ways of coping, such as perfectionism, in order to compensate for feelings of inadequacy. When they can't live up to the impossible standards they have set for themselves, they may turn their frustration inward which could lead to feelings of hopelessness. Underneath the veneer of confidence they are barely hanging on, yet they continue to raise the bar even higher to keep their competitive edge. Other students, unable to face the daily pressures of school, are at risk of becoming underachievers which is the opposite side of the coin. Having a difficult time meeting the demands of teachers, parents, and society in general, they may give up altogether. To make matters worse these students are often reprimanded for not trying hard enough. Soon they are labeled 'lazy, below average, discipline problems,' etc., and it doesn't take long before they develop a self-fulfilling prophesy of low performance and failure. This only adds to their lack of self-regard because they are now convinced these school-assigned labels are accurate — they are lazy, unmotivated, and below average.

At the same time social problems may begin to surface and a child who was once vibrant and full of energy has now become withdrawn. Alarmingly, this problem has reached epidemic proportions as younger and younger children are diagnosed with stress-related illnesses. Social pressures have taken a tremendous toll on the well-being of our children. According to recent surveys, approximately 8 million junior high school girls and 1 million boys have body-image and eating disorder problems. This obsession has reached children as young as 5 years old who tell their mothers they are too fat and shortly, thereafter, begin showing the first signs of stress ranging from generalized anxiety to bouts of uncontrollable crying. Some girls (boys are also at risk) may become anorexic while others may do just the opposite — eat to alleviate their emotional pain. The classic symptoms of depression — although manifested in various ways — can often be recognized by their telltale signs, but the key question remains: Why are so many of our children falling into such a state of despair that they may prefer death over life, as the lesser of two evils? They are taught in a world of obvious contradiction that what counts is on the inside, but the magazines and movies tell a very different story. The latest research indicates that 55,000 persuasive messages reach young audiences through the media every day. The need for economic security is the driving force behind commercialism. Unfortunately, in the effort to make a profit our children have become the target of an industry that knows how to capitalize on a booming market. Children younger than 8 years old have been shown to be cognitively and psychologically defenseless against advertising. They do not understand the notion of intent to sell and frequently accept advertising claims at face value. Our teenagers have become the latest casualties, being sacrificed on the altar of free enterprise and the almighty dollar. No matter how we try to convince our most impressionable what is truly important, it is often a futile effort because our children learn by what they see, and the popular culture wins out every time...but at whose expense? The disparity between these two realities has made the younger generation distrustful of themselves and others because they don't know who or what to believe. They are left adrift in a very confusing world with no lighthouse to guide them back to shore. Is it any wonder they are in such turmoil?

If you look at the current social milieu, it isn't difficult to see why girls (and to a lesser extent boys) have a difficult time accepting themselves. The first blow has already been struck by images that tell them they aren't pretty enough. Is it any wonder they struggle with self-acceptance when everything portrayed in the media convinces them that they don't measure up? This is confirmed by their lack of popularity in school which only reinforces their belief that they don't have what it takes. Even though these messages are not pointing directly at them, it isn't hard to fill in the blanks when they see that they can't compete with the other girls who are higher on the scale of physical perfection. The truth of the matter is that these feelings of inferiority among many of our teenagers are keeping the psychologists in business. Believing that beauty was a part of the real world, the most any psychologist could do was try and help these girls cope with the stigma of being judged "unattractive" (a polite term for "ugly," or interpreted as such) by present-day standards. Sadly, these young girls had no other choice but to accept their fate just as they would have to accept any other handicap, and learn to live with it. They were encouraged to appreciate other traits they possessed that were worthy of admiration. One psychologist stated, "What matters is not how you look on the outside, but who you are on the inside which is where real beauty comes from." He also stated that one's body-image does not necessarily determine one's self-image. He then went on to list all the other attributes this girl had in order to convince her of her good qualities — but to no avail. This advice, although well-intentioned, is difficult to accept given the number of commercials selling good looks as the answer to a happy life. In a society where 'beauty' is the ultimate prize because it wins the girl love, respect, and adoration from the opposite sex, all the pep talks in the world that try to tell her otherwise will do very little good. Furthermore, helping a girl to cope, although necessary in our present world, does not begin to address the underlying factors that are responsible for her lack of self-worth. It may take our daughters many years to erase the scars of an injustice that are the result of words, not reality.

Although this was the way it had to be in our years of development — all this is cleared up with one sweep of God's magic elixir when He commands that all words such as beautiful and ugly be removed. Eliminating these words will help solve our social problem because children will no longer be judged by a fallacious standard of beauty. The advertisers will no longer be able to use good looks as a selling point not only because these images are inaccurate representations, but because they are a definite hurt to so many girls who will never

438

blame them for this. Under the changed conditions they will be given no choice but to change their ways. As for academic achievement, when parents are compelled to withhold judgment as to what is right for their children which allows these boys and girls to stay home from school if they want to, the educational system will be forced to change in a drastic manner. Either the children will desire to go, of their own free will, or the schools as we know them will go out of business. Someone taken aback by this last statement commented, "Education is very important and many children thank their parents later in life for forcing them to get it. If my mother didn't get me out of bed every morning and literally chase me to school, I doubt if I would have finished elementary school. Besides, a person who has a certain amount of education gets a better job. The other day three of my friends were all turned down because they didn't have a high school education. At that moment I'll bet they wished their mother had seen to it that they had gotten an education."

Many parents assume that if a child is not pushed to get out of bed every morning he would never desire to go to school and, consequently, would not learn. They have set up a syllogistic equation from which to reason by assuming that what the mother wants her child to develop into is impossible without employing force, or perhaps I should say, advance blame. Furthermore, they are assuming that the mother knows what is better for her child to develop into — more so than the child."

"Do you mean that children will desire to go to school of their own free will?"

"It will not be of their own free will, naturally, but they will want to go only because they want to go, without anybody influencing or forcing them."

"If that's the case, then parents won't have to worry anymore about forcing their children."

"That's right, but remember, in order to get children to want what mother knows is truly better for them, it is first necessary to remove the forces that try to prevent the desire of these children from not becoming what mother and the school think is best. It is the same with government and religion, do you recall?"

"I can't think back that far."

439

"To render war and crime impossibilities, it is first necessary to remove the forces that try to prevent these evils through threats of retaliation, because this kind of effort unconsciously motivates and justifies the very things these forces are trying to prevent."

"Now I remember you saying that."

"As long as the school system and the parents are permitted to blame them, they are not compelled to change their ways. But when they are not permitted to blame, you will behold a fantastic transition as you will see in the chapter on education. Children will want to go to school only because they want to go, without anybody influencing or forcing them."

Just as a child will determine if he wants to go to school, in the new world a child will determine what time he wants to get up. If he has to meet someone at a certain place and time he will make a point to be there knowing that if he didn't show up this would be a hurt for which he would not be blamed; but if a child doesn't want to go to school, who is being hurt? How is your child hurting you by staying awake as long as he likes unless his presence annoys you in some way? What difference would it really have made to Durant if his daughter had stayed awake until she, herself, was ready to go to sleep? Think again of how happy children would be and how much conflict would be eliminated if there were no restrictions as to their bedtime. Many parents will say that the goal of parenthood is not to make their children happy at the cost of making them responsible human beings. But why does a child's happiness have to be sacrificed in order for him to learn the value of responsibility, and why do these two goals have to be mutually exclusive? In order to deconfuse your minds which may take some time since you have been trained to think a certain way, you must remember our slide rule, Thou Shall Not Blame, at all times. Most people, like Durant, have come to believe that children should be in bed at a certain time which only reveals their confusion when all the facts are understood. It is a fact that how much sleep a child requires is determined by his body. Some may desire to sleep ten hours, others eleven, and many more only seven or less. Moreover, sleep requirements change from day to day. One mother asked, "What if a child should go to bed at 3 in the morning and has to get up at 7 for school, isn't it obvious that he would be exhausted, and shouldn't responsible parents try to prevent this exhaustion? If Durant did not set up a 'decreed retiring time,' his daughter having a lot of fun with visitors might forget that she has to get up very early for school. Besides, I would like to have a dollar for the number of children that didn't go to school or were late just because they were exhausted the next day."

"It must be understood that in the new world ALL FORMS OF BLAME MUST BE REMOVED because man's will is not free. Durant blames his daughter by imposing standards of what he thinks is better for her."

"But shouldn't parents do what they think is better for their children?"

Definitely, but remember we are being guided by the mathematical standard that was just set up by our slide rule for the purpose of testing the accuracy of what parents think. From the very first day of birth it is important for the parents to determine only what they feel would be a real, not imaginary, hurt to their child and others for which the baby now, and all through life, cannot be held responsible. And if they are unable to prevent their child from desiring what they feel will be a hurt, either to himself or someone else, or unable to prevent him from not wanting what they think will be for his benefit, WITHOUT ANY FORM OF ADVANCE BLAME, it is rather obvious that what they like or dislike for him is something that is not in any way harmful to the child or others and exists only as an imaginary fear based upon false knowledge, otherwise, they would definitely have the power to prevent this harm without the use of blame.

When a child oversleeps, gets to school late, is punished by the teacher and parents, it is obvious that he made a mistake by sleeping late — just as it is obvious that he makes a mistake when not finishing high school or college since everybody judges him by certain standards — but when these standards are removed it can be seen that the fears of the parents and children were not directed toward the lack of an education, but to the judgment of their inferiority. You are in for a lot of surprises! Bear in mind that there is nothing wrong with wanting your child to get in bed at a specific time and if you can do it without blaming the desire of the child in any way, the more power to you, for no one will ever tell you what is right for yourself. The only thing that will make you prefer not blaming your child in any way is the realization that this will result in your complete happiness as a family. Every argument that exists between parents and children arises from ignorance, for which the parents are innocently responsible. By discovering that man's will is not free and what this means, we are compelled to remove all standards which allows the greatest happiness imaginable to exist in all homes in a manner far superior to what anybody now experiences.

Let us now turn to another difficult problem confronting parents which is how to distribute toys without causing envy. What often occurs is that one child sees what another child has and before long he wants the same thing. A mother asked, "How is it possible not to blame a child who grabs a toy from another? Shouldn't the child be reprimanded?"

Absolutely not, because you are then blaming the child for the fact that his desire has been aroused to want something that another child has. Let me clarify this. If you placed on the dinner table a pitcher of lemonade and a pitcher of milk, one child may prefer the former while the second selects the latter, but both were given an equal opportunity to satisfy their desire for either one, which does not in any way blame their desire. Could you possibly put on the table enough milk for one child and enough lemonade for two? Wouldn't this obviously blame the desire of one child should both desire the milk? "Mommy, Johnny got a glass of milk and I want some too." Isn't this just plain common sense, which we refer to as fairness? Children are very perceptive when it comes to noticing the slightest shade of discrimination, which parents are well aware of, and will resent their parents for taking something away from them which is what they do when they are not equitable. How many times have you heard a child say, "This isn't fair because you gave him more than me?" The truth of the matter is that it isn't fair if it blames another child's desire for wanting the same thing. Any type of discrimination, especially where young children are concerned, is a hurt. Let me show you the unconscious discrimination that actually goes on where toys are concerned.

One father could not understand why his fraternal twins, a boy and girl, were not satisfied, he with his toy soldier and she with her doll. Very young children often want what others have only because they see these differences and don't understand why they can't have the same thing. Soon they begin crying which may then develop into a full-blown tantrum. If you give a little boy a toy soldier and a girl a doll, what is this but an encouragement for them to quarrel? In reality, aren't you discriminating if you give a little boy a toy soldier and a little girl a doll? Why shouldn't the boy want to play with the doll and the girl with the soldier, and what if both should desire the doll at the same time, what then? All this can be prevented by realizing that every child must be given an equal opportunity to be happy, which is denied when parents set up fallacious standards of what is for a girl and what is for a boy. Let's observe the following dialogue.

Justin, this doll belongs to Suzie; dolls are for little girls, not for boys," says the father.

"But I wanna play widda dolly."

"Suzie, you're older than Justin, so you be a big girl (this blames him for not being big about it) and let Justin play with your doll just for a little while and you play with his soldier."

"No! Dolly mine; you get for Suzie, and you said dollies are for goils, Daddy, and Justin is a boy, not a goil."

So what's the solution? If it is a soldier you wish to give a boy, you must also give the same exact soldier to the girl; and if it is a doll you wish to give to the girl, you will give the same exact doll to the boy. When they discover that each has the same toy there can be no possessiveness, no jealousy, no envy, and what is much more important, no fighting to disturb your evenings. Wouldn't it be wonderful to get rid of all these things which cause such a disturbance and make your living so much less enjoyable? Are you given a choice? But, mind you, it is demonstrated that these things will take leave not because they are worse for the children but because they are definitely a source of dissatisfaction and unhappiness for the parents.

Birthday parties can also be a source of tension when the guests are too young to understand why they can't open presents too. A solution would be for the birthday boy or girl to open gifts after the children have gone home. During the party everyone would receive the

443

same toy or the parents would give nothing at all, and the toy would be identical in all details, including the color. For instance, if you give two little boys, one a blue truck and the other a red truck, this difference in color may encourage them to desire what the other has, and squabbling is bound to result. Obviously, we are talking about very young children who have no conception of equal value in abstract terms, nor do they have any conception of money or ownership at this age. There may still be times when one sibling cannot have what another sibling has (e.g., a gift that was given to one child for a special occasion, such as a birthday), and crying cannot be avoided. A toy that an older child has may not be age appropriate for a younger child, which also needs to be taken into consideration. As soon as children are old enough to understand what it means that man's will is not free, parents will not have to concern themselves with the various problems mentioned because they will not come up. Let me cite another example of how effective is this law in changing our conduct.

Two brothers, old enough to understand what it means that man's will is not free, are given one bike between them. They decide to take turns. They draw from a hat to see who goes first and Justin wins so he is allowed to use the bike from 1 to 3, while his brother Adam will use it from 3 to 5. In the world of free will Justin knows that if he keeps the bike out longer than his allotted time he will be blamed, criticized, condemned, even punished by his parents, so he is given unconscious justification to stay out longer if this should be his desire because he is prepared to pay the price of hurting his brother this way. Furthermore, knowing that he will be questioned as to why he is late, he is given an opportunity to prepare a reasonable excuse, or lie, which might mitigate the severity of the punishment. But when he knows as a matter of positive knowledge that his brother, though hurt should the bike be kept out longer, would never blame him, never criticize; and his father and mother would never think to question or punish him in any way for doing what he knows they must excuse since man's will is not free, he is given no alternative under these conditions but to refrain from hurting his brother since it is mathematically impossible to derive any satisfaction whatsoever from being excused for doing what he knows he doesn't have to do…if he doesn't want to. And he doesn't want to knowing that no one will say a word even if he uses up all of his brother's time. As a consequence, Justin would make every effort possible to be on time and if on the way home there was something unforeseen such as road construction, which delayed him, Adam would know immediately, without being told, that it was unavoidable. Regardless of who went first, neither could selfishly desire this bike without considering the other because they know this would never be blamed which compels them to discover an equitable manner to distribute the time. These are mathematical relations which all mankind can see when extended properly.

Going back to our previous example, children have an innate sense of fairness and will detect the slightest inequality. If they feel their parents are showing partiality in any way, they may act out by striking back in anger or by becoming withdrawn. Whining, fighting, and otherwise refusing to cooperate are often cries for attention. Parents can take an active role in clearing up any misunderstandings by allowing children to express their feelings, even if it means initiating the conversation. Remember, it is not always what children say that is important, but what they don't say. There will be no competition for a parent's love (which is a major source of jealousy) as long as children are appreciated in a way that makes them feel equally valued. One psychologist suggested that parents establish a separate 'love account' which is a special time devoted to each child. For example, parents might set up a plan where they take their child to dinner, bowling, or the park. Having unrushed one-on-one time allows parents to be emotionally available and creates an atmosphere of unconditional love and acceptance. It also conveys to the child that he is important to his parents, and that his feelings matter. If the family prefers staying home, they could have a special pizza night while playing board games, doing jigsaw puzzles, or baking homemade cookies. It really doesn't matter what the activity is, just so each child has time alone with his parents where he can express himself and be heard. By giving children undivided attention from their own account, so to speak, they will not have to compete with their siblings for the love they so desperately need. In the new world parents will never show the slightest hint of favoritism knowing that this is a concrete hurt to the child who is feeling this inequality; consequently, they will do everything in their power to give all of their children equal attention so that they will grow up feeling loved and secure.

There are many situations involving our children that cannot be foreseen, and it may be difficult to imagine certain times where a parent cannot control the child without blame. For example, manners (teaching children to say 'thank you' and 'you're welcome,' and how to speak and hold their knife and fork in a proper way), smoking, drinking, watching inappropriate T.V., and all the other things that adults do not want them to do. All these things are part of advance blame and the only thing that can make parents desire to change, even in this world, is the realization that forcing children to do anything only creates an unhealthy environment.

"Something doesn't seem to be kosher. If I teach a child to act in a certain way, this is advance blame, right?"

"That's right, you're blaming the child for desiring to act otherwise."

"But if by not teaching the child to act in a certain manner he gets hurt by being criticized or ridiculed... excuse me, for the moment I forgot that all criticism and ridicule are being removed. In other words, you're saying that there is no need to teach children anything anymore, and since the only hurt they could receive is from this criticism, it is prevented by removing this blanket of blame."

"I didn't say that children should not be taught."

"But the moment you teach them anything, aren't they being blamed for not doing it?"

"It depends on the manner in which they are taught and on what they are taught. If I teach a child that two plus two equal four, I am not blaming him for anything, am I?"

"I don't think you are."

"But if I teach a child that spinach is healthy I am expecting the child to eat spinach, which means that the child's desire is involved here."

"I see. The desire of the child is not involved in teaching him that two plus two equal four, unless he doesn't want to learn, but whenever his desire is involved in what is taught, then he is being blamed in advance."

446

"That is correct. The other things that parents try to force on their children (although they do not partake of advance blame) will be more easily corrected because this is only done as the result of people criticizing. When this stops — and it will — it will make no difference to parents what their children do."

Henceforth, there will be only one standard for children and parents, the happiness of each, but in an unconscious manner the happiness of parents up until now was the unhappiness of their children. Durant was happy when he got his daughter to go to bed, and was not moved even when she pleaded with her dimpled arms around his neck, but she was unhappy at that moment. She was happy when she didn't have to practice the piano, but he was unhappy at this which made him impose his will on her for his happiness, not hers. He was happy to see her drink plenty of milk and eat loads of whole wheat bread, but had she been left alone and given the opportunity to choose among other foods, she no doubt would have been much happier because taste plays an important role. This relationship between parents and children is so interwoven with resentment that in many cases the latter will refuse to eat what they might enjoy because the former will tell them they must try something, which gives them very little leeway to say no and blames the possibility that they won't.

Mother says, "Here is something real nice mommy just prepared, you will like it."

"I don't want it and I won't like it."

"How do you know when you haven't even tasted it yet?"

Once again, the child takes this opportunity to get unconscious satisfaction out of hurting mother because she has hurt him so many times by standing in the way of his desires, and just the knowledge that she wants him to eat it because it is good is sufficient proof in his mind that it is bad. Once a mother realizes that she can no longer blame her children for anything, regardless of what they do, she cannot punish them if they refuse to eat what is offered. The most she can do is make the food as enticing as possible so they will desire to eat what she wants them to have. In most cases she blames and yells at them not because they were hurting her or themselves in any way, but because she resents their disobedience. It will soon be discovered that this blame of the parents is that safety valve which I referred to previously that permitted them to shift their responsibility. When mom sees that she can no longer rush the children in the morning; that she can no longer blame them for not having their clothes ready, she is compelled to prepare everything well in advance or teach them, without blame, how to take care of themselves. Every bit of the hurt that exists between parents and children is occasioned by the former constantly trying to impose their will, nothing else.

A mother of a 6 year old needed clarification. "If you are guiding them, aren't you blaming them for the possibility of doing other than what you think they should? And didn't you say 'without any form of blame?' Where is the difference between what Durant did to arouse his daughter's desire to do what he thought was better for her in the long run, and your arousing a child's desire to do what you think is best? Aren't both forms of blame?"

On the contrary, they are not. Durant guided his daughter to the end he judged was better and blamed her inconspicuously for moving in a different direction than the one he picked. He could very easily arouse a child to eat more by putting less on the plate, which blames the possibility that enough might not be eaten. I put nothing on the plate and let the child decide how much. If Durant had been my father I would have developed in any direction he wanted me to go because his psychological techniques were pretty effective. Is it not difficult to get a child to eat more by putting such small portions on his plate that he is compelled to keep asking for more — or less, by using reverse psychology? It is the horse of another color when your child does not want to eat something because he doesn't like it, and you blame his desire by trying to persuade him. Likewise, if he wants to stay up beyond 'the years decreed retiring time,' you are blaming his desire if you tell him he must go to bed.

Another mother, not quite convinced that withholding blame was even possible, could not see where this principle could prevent all the problems that are bound to occur. She asked the following questions: "But what about the problem of eating too much candy, cake and ice cream? What about the development of talent? Supposing a very young child shows musical ability, shouldn't the parents influence him to desire what could lead to fame and fortune? Do you mean that parents can't mold him into what they think he would later be grateful for because this blames him in advance for not desiring at that moment what they want? And what about food; do you mean to tell me there is as much value in pickles and candy as in potatoes and meat? Isn't it fitting for a mother, who loves her children dearly, to lead them in the direction of what she thinks is better for them?"

The mathematical standard set up by our slide rule takes all this into consideration. Parents are supposed to do everything in their power to get their children to do what is thought to be better, but they must do it without blame in any form. To better illustrate what I mean, in order for a person to live in this world without blaming the children he has three possibilities: He must not allow desire to be aroused at all, must give up the things he likes but does not allow his children to imitate (drinking, smoking, staying up late, etc.), or he must allow children to choose what they want without giving up anything. Anytime you stand in the way of your child's desires, you hurt yourself. For example, if you are watching a television show you don't want your child to see, you can either turn the television off and watch these type shows elsewhere, or explain to the child that these programs are not real. The reason horror stories are so frightening in the world of free will is because they are related to ways of actually getting hurt, but when hurt becomes a mathematical impossibility these stories will be seen as fiction for the purpose of entertainment only. Similarly, until a child becomes conscious of sex, lovemaking will have no interest for him and he will prefer cartoons. Since there will be no censorship and no one will prohibit a child from viewing if he wants to, the desire to watch these movies will not interest him in the slightest. In the new world there will be absolutely no way pornography (the lovers on screen and television will by necessity have to be married to each other, which loses its derogating connotation) can hurt anybody when it will be so easy to have a sexual relation (get married) and impossible to get a divorce or commit adultery. In fact, television and motion pictures will be a teaching tool for those desiring to learn how to satisfy their partner since everything will be shown without the slightest fear that anything could go wrong. Don't misunderstand me, the hurt our moralists tried to prevent in the world of free will regarding sex and censorship was real, but when the possibility of hurt is removed, the need for moralizing censors has been obviated and God's wisdom is now made manifest.

"Even though I understand most of what you said, and I do agree, what about a preschool child desiring to stay up while a party is going on? Supposing I want privacy, and here comes my four year old wandering into the room at midnight. Do you mean I can't send her up to bed?"

"You can do anything you want to do, nobody is going to blame your actions. But if your friends see you do this they will know you are truly ignorant of the fact that man's will is not free and what this means. They would look at you with a certain amount of amazement, just as they would, should you ask one of them to do you a favor or tell them what to do. At the present time the opposite is true, they would look at you in amazement if you didn't send her up to bed."

Another fallacy which blames the child in advance is the belief that certain foods and beverages are for adults only. "No, dear, you can't have coffee, this is for grownups." When you constantly tell a child you can't have this, that, or something else because these things are not for children, then you have created in their mind a value that is now being denied. Consequently, they will drink and watch what they really don't enjoy only because they are trying to discover this unknown value. Children would never prefer tea, coffee, carbonated soda and alcoholic beverages to milk, providing you don't encourage their desire by denying them or telling them these are not for children. In our present world children see that certain foods and drinks are for adults only, which blames their desire to have the same. If you say they can't have a certain dessert, it doesn't take long before they will desire this dessert where and whenever it can be gotten, and they will also discover a yen to become more quickly an adult so they can do adult things. Many children do these things behind their parent's back and their satisfaction is not derived from any great pleasure in drinking and smoking until a habit is formed, but from the thrill of being a young grown up. Have you any conception of how many people eat and drink what they have acquired a taste for not because they liked it from the start but because they were determined to do what others, whom they admired, were doing? The very fact that children are told that coffee, cigarettes, liquor, are forbidden until they become adults places a fallacious value on becoming an adult and gives to these items a strong appeal. Some boys have gotten sick smoking cigars because they were determined to oppose the wishes of their parents, and girls have become promiscuous because they were constantly judged and blamed before anything was even done. "Don't do this and you can't have that" are challenges to children who resent authority.

In the new world children will never hear that certain things are for adults and other things for children. A young child at the dinner table will be given his choice of beverages. It is not necessary to remove what you like from the table, or for dad to drink his beer or highball, coffee and tea surreptitiously for fear a child will get hurt in any way, as his body will not permit the eating and drinking of what is preferred less providing — it is necessary to qualify — he is left completely alone. Every person at the table will be given an equal opportunity to have what the others have, without any psychological influences. Do you think it is possible when all these influences are removed, for a child to prefer these items? Children will not have to ask permission to try this or that. If you are worried that your little girl may become a drunkard or smoke cigars, then you had better remove everything that you like from the table which makes you happy because there is no way you can prevent this imaginative possibility without blame in some form. Durant prevented his daughter from staying downstairs, but he was compelled to blame her desire. The only alternative open to him was to go to sleep early himself which certainly could not make him happy, so is he given a choice when all blame is removed? If you have to give up everything you like for the happiness of your children you will soon be miserable, but you don't have to give up anything once the truth is understood. Let me show you why this is compelled to come about.

The very moment all fallacious values are removed which are frozen into the habitual use of words and expressions, children will eat, drink and do only what they really want to do of their own free will or desire. You couldn't make children do by force what they do not like, yet in our present world they are compelled to do what they really don't enjoy only because of some fallacious value that is

451

imposed in a negative or positive manner. As for alcoholic beverages, how is it possible for these to survive to any great degree when children will never be made to see any fallacious value in them? If a child should taste a beer he would spit it out, providing he hasn't already been conditioned, and once he tastes something he doesn't like he will always remember the experience and wonder how in the world people can actually drink that stuff.

"But wait until he learns that alcoholic beverages are taken not so much for the taste but for the effect, won't he desire to experiment, and if he likes the feeling, couldn't he become a customer?"

"Everything that gave rise to the desire to drink is being removed. Some people drink because they were hurt, and the liquor makes them mean so they can strike back. Others like to assume an uninhibited personality and drinking breaks down barriers otherwise impossible to bridge. Whatever caused the desire, each person will know that should he hurt someone while intoxicated he will never be blamed or punished, which means that all drinking and driving will come to an end because the risk is too great. How is it humanly possible to stand over someone you just killed and know that no one will ever blame or punish what you know he must excuse, and you cannot justify? This will never happen if you don't want it to happen — and how can you want it to happen? There are many factors that occasion this desire to drink in excess, but when I discuss education you will see how the final vestige of hurt is removed from our lives which means that in order to desire alcohol as a beverage in the new world it would be necessary to find pleasure in drinking it while isolated on an island.

If the parent feels like eating cake, candy, or ice cream after dinner or prefers a drink before, during, or after, along with a smoke, this is his business, but he must not judge what is right for his children by encouraging or discouraging these things, for this is advance blame. Remember, to tell them that drinking and smoking are for adults only arouses their desire to be like you, and the more they are blamed the more they will desire what you don't want them to have. If you are smoking, and your four year old son asks for a cigarette, you would be blaming his desire if you told him that this is for adults only. However, when all blame is removed, that is, when children are raised in the new world, parents will be surprised to learn

452

that drinking and smoking are distasteful to any young child whose desire has not been preconditioned with denial, and will prefer milk hands down; but when it has been preconditioned he will prefer staying up late even if he is exhausted, will eat candy and cake even when he's not hungry, and will go outside on a cold day without his jacket even though he shivers. If you are watching a television show that you think is too scary you can send your children to bed if you want to, but how is it possible to want to when blaming their desire to watch will only bring about a horrible relationship between you? If you say these things are bad for their health they will have a feeling you are lying and will want to find out why. This would compel them to continue with something absolutely distasteful in order to find out what it is you like. Soon they will feel like a big shot, like an adult. But if they are left completely alone they might desire to taste everything, and when they do, providing no comments are made, they will find certain things very distasteful. Try to make a baby smoke cigarettes and drink alcohol. This is equivalent to giving him Castor Oil. As a consequence of obeying God's will, Thou Shall Not Blame, within two generations the desire for alcoholic beverages and smoking will be reduced to an absolute minimum because when all psychological influences are removed, it is impossible to desire what one really does not like. The truth is that there is nothing wrong with children smoking cigarettes, cigars, chewing tobacco, drinking coffee, beer, liquor, highballs, and eating loads and loads of candy, cake, and ice cream providing they want to. However, the desire for these items is within your power to control without any form of blame, that is, unless you want your children to smoke cigars, drink beer, eat too many sweets, etc. When children are allowed to go in the direction they prefer, all these things will be virtually wiped from the face of the earth, in due time of course. Obviously advertising plays a great role in creating a desire for these things, but this will not influence children when there are no prohibitions. Advertisers in the new world will never want to be responsible for selling products to children that could harm them in any way, therefore they will be compelled to go in the direction of honesty.

Telling children what is right and wrong is the consequence of fallacious fears as well as real fears that will vanish with this blanket of blame. It is understandable that you should want your child to graduate high school because in our present environment this is judged valuable. Consequently, parents often push their children in the direction of this value, even if force is necessary. We saw that Durant was no different than these other fathers where the end result was concerned. The only difference was in the means. He exercised a psychological strategy which made his daughter desire this value so that force would not have to be used, as he did with the piano. When children are very young we rarely consider their desires at all, only what we believe is better for them. Therefore, if they push away certain foods, we blame them for not eating it. In our mind, there are certain beliefs that control our thinking. Carrots are good for the eyes while spinach will build muscle and make them strong like Popeye. If they do not eat enough (what we judge this to be) they will get underweight, undernourished, sick, and need a doctor. To prevent all this we push them to eat what they don't like the taste of. There is nothing wrong with thinking that certain foods have greater value, but until you have mathematical proof you cannot teach that these are better for a child's body, for this blames the possibility he might not like them. How do you know what his particular body might require? How do you know what foods are not best for him or what he may be allergic to? By assuming that you know what is better for his body you could very easily make him seriously ill and never know the cause. Then your fears will call in a doctor who will prescribe medicine that could possibly make matters much more serious. It is for this reason that God says — "Hands off, don't judge what is right for your child, don't blame him in advance by teaching the value of spinach, carrots, or any other food." If not eating a particular food is harmful to the child, then the mother will be compelled to discover a way to prepare it so that he can like it the very first time it is tasted, for persuasion in any form — which includes all efforts to arouse some desire in the direction of a particular end as Durant did with the piano, but especially after the desire of the child has already been expressed — can no more be used as it is a method of blame and an assumption of what is right for the child. Remember, my children, "One man's meat might be another man's poison." When she is not allowed to blame the children or her husband for not eating what she prepares,

454

or for filling up on what she prefers they did not eat, then she is given only one alternative and that is to make a complete study of cooking so that she can satisfy her own desire. This does not mean that a mother shouldn't prepare the type of food she feels would be better for her family providing she doesn't exclude other kinds from which they can choose, but if she remembers the rule she will have nothing to fear. When she knows that they cannot be blamed for disliking what food she thinks is for their benefit, or for liking what she believes is not for their welfare, she is compelled to prepare and combine their food in such a manner that they will not reject what she wants them to eat. Even if her children should eat absolutely nothing, she must leave them alone, for this is their business. There is nothing she can do except to find out what other foods they do like unless she prefers to force into their system what they do not want by making it the lesser of two evils, since the alternative is starvation. God is very emphatic when He commands that we are not to blame our children. The understanding of this law only demonstrates how we can at last accomplish the very things we have unsuccessfully been attempting to bring about. This means that all the values we have been using to guide our decisions, providing there is a conflict, must yield to their values. As a result, children will grow and develop like animals who are not forced to eat when not hungry and what is not liked.

If mother's domain is to prepare the meals (and in most cases it will be), her desire must be considered as well. She is not running a restaurant and cannot be expected to cook an entire menu each and every night, but at the same time she can no longer blame the children for not eating what she cooks, therefore, she is given no alternative but to prepare everything in such a tasty manner that her entire family looks forward to eating at every meal because she can blame no one anymore if they don't eat. Because it is impossible for her to judge that certain foods have greater value than others where another body is concerned unless science has established mathematical facts, she will be compelled to arrange a diversified variety over an entire week or two weeks so that her children and husband will look forward to eating certain meals on certain days. If the family likes spaghetti and meatballs which is served on Monday, that morning they will look forward to the evening when they will be served what they like. Tuesday morning, knowing that mother will have something else that evening, they will anticipate their evening meal just as they may look forward to a certain television show or something else. By setting up each day for a specific meal no one can ever get tired of eating the same thing, and when the week rolls around everybody will be looking forward to what is on the menu for that day. Holiday dinners that were reserved for one day of the year could be enjoyed more often. Looking forward to our meals is a form of pleasure, and eating is something we do all our lives.

"I understand why it's important for a mother to prepare the food so that her children will enjoy it the first time they taste it, but how can a mother have an influence on the healthy foods her children eat without blaming them for eating the wrong things such as too much candy and cake? It seems like this is an unsolvable problem."

In our present world mother serves so many meals the kids do not like, and she is constantly blaming them in advance for not eating what she thinks is for their welfare, that they're compelled to prefer filling up on cookies, ice cream and candy because they know this will irritate her which gives them compensating satisfaction. She never had to prepare the variety of foods that would make them prefer cookies and candy less because she could always blame them for not eating, even if they disliked the meal. They either ate what she cooked or they were punished for not doing as they were told. The unconscious belief in free will justified this blame and punishment, which relieved parents of their responsibility by making the cause of misbehavior lie in the willfulness of the child. Since they knew that children could act otherwise if they wanted to, because man has free will, there was no need to search for related factors; the child was the cause, and could justly be held responsible. Many children chose the punishment until extreme hunger compelled them to eat what they didn't like. Even a dog will eat what he likes less when what he likes better is not available. Another strategy mother used to get her children to eat their dinner was to offer them a treat later on. By constantly offering dessert as a bribe, they soon demanded it or else they wouldn't eat. Fearing for their health, the kids soon were allowed to live on cake and candy because this was the only way some of them would consider eating other foods. It is only by making children aware of a value which is then denied (I can't repeat this enough), that you stir up their desire to have it. In the new world if children prefer the sweetness of cake and candy to her vegetables, she can no longer blame them for what is her responsibility, consequently, she must do everything in her power to make the meals appealing unless it gives her satisfaction to see them eat what she doesn't want them to eat.

Another reason that dessert is valued so highly is the way in which it is served. When a child is made to believe that dessert is something special, he will not eat other things to make room for the dessert. Children discover very quickly that dessert is given at the end of a meal as a bonus if the rest of the food is eaten in sufficient quantity, which blames their desire not to eat. The very fact that pie, cake, and ice cream are called dessert places a greater value on these items and makes children look forward to them with every meal, and yet the concern parents have when their children eat too many sweets is understandable. Many children and adults overeat and get sick only because of this distinction between appetizer, the main course, and dessert, which makes them desire to eat this food even though they are filled to the brim. However, this habit can easily be broken without blaming the children and without removing these pleasures from the life of a family. All that is necessary is to include them not as a dessert but as part of the meal itself on certain days. Do you eat steak for every meal, or chicken, or spinach; why then should you have dessert, milk, and bread with every meal? A mother could very easily arrange a schedule so that all these desserts could be included as part of the main entre. Ice cream could be served during one meal, not as dessert, but as something else to be eaten that is enjoyed; and when the meal is over they will look forward to the next meal without expecting ice cream because this is served on another day, just as steak or chicken, bread and spinach. When this day rolls around they will look forward to the entire meal which includes the ice cream, cake or candy. By having the dessert and appetizer as part of the meal served as a whole at one time, children will be able to select what they want without any psychological impediments and as a result you will be amazed at how little of the cake, candy and ice cream will be eaten. Where are they going to put it? By including dessert as part of the meal on certain days children will gradually lose the desire to eat it in excess without ever being told what to do, and they will be happier as a result. Even if various desserts were placed on the table after dinner, as long as there were no comments they would never prefer this to meat, fish, vegetables, milk and fruit. In addition, they would no more think of eating ice cream and candy between meals than of eating vegetables and meat. If they are left completely alone to choose for themselves, and are not blamed with fallacious values, they can only go in one direction which is to fill up on what they prefer, not on what they don't prefer. Children are actually like animals and just as a dog would never prefer cake, candy and ice cream to meat and vegetables so neither will they unless preconditioned. To her surprise, a mother will soon discover that the food she has to throw out more and more is the cake, candy, and ice cream. Sweets will be reduced to such a minimum once mother realizes what it means that man's will is not free, in other words, once she realizes why it is better for herself when all forms of advance blame, this judging of what is right for someone else, is removed, that the candy and cake manufacturers will be virtually wiped out. Remember, there is no possibility of a child desiring to eat cake and candy in preference to other foods when there is only so much an individual can eat, unless he gets psychological satisfaction.

There may still be times when the mother cannot get her children to eat what she wants them to. If they still desire to fill up on cake, ice cream and candy, even though she has prepared a chicken dinner and has done everything in her power to get them to eat what she believes is healthy but can't unless she blames them, then whatever fears she has exists only in her imagination. Over and over we see that more arguments and punishment resulted when children dared to stand up to their parents who were constantly trying to force them to do what they did not want to do and all because mother and father mistakenly believed that they knew best, and in many cases even when they knew they were wrong they still persisted in exacting obedience solely for the satisfaction of putting the child in his place which started a chain reaction of mutual disrespect. Everything changes for the better when parents stop blaming their children. We will always have parties because they are a lot of fun, although we won't be having weddings in the Golden Age since the manner in which we now are married is coming to an end. Whether we will need alcohol and marihuana, ice cream and cake to have this fun depends on whether our children in the new world will like it. Those who believed the only answer was to deny their children these things will realize, for the very first time, that when the decision is left entirely up to the individual who will never be judged no matter what he does, he may decide to quench his thirst with lemonade, eat his meal without desert because he enjoyed the main course, and choose not to smoke because he is having too much fun living life — but whatever he does will be his business.

Therefore, the next hurt to be removed is that which we have been striking our children not because they violated a rule, regulation, commandment, standard or law that tries to prevent them from making matters worse for us, but only because they didn't agree with our judgment of what is better for them and we justified this first blow by calling it punishment. This occurs when we hurt people not because they did something to hurt us which is the retaliatory blow that when removed prevents the desire to strike a first blow, but only because they did not do what we judged they should, and we blame them for our disappointment or their disobedience. But when we become citizens of the new world and fully realize that they have the right-of-way to do anything that does not cause a first blow to us, we are forced to arouse their desire to move in the direction we prefer without us causing the very first blow (by forcing them to do what they have every right not to do) in order to accomplish our purpose. Just as non-citizens will continue to be punished should they be caught violating any laws (which we must enforce as the lesser of two evils until they pass their examination), so will children be punished as the lesser of two evils if breaking any rules makes matters worse for us. But when we are prevented from striking the first blow by imposing our will on our children by getting them to do what they don't want, and when our children are taught the basic principle which will not be difficult once they reach the stage where they can reason, they will never be able to find greater satisfaction in disobeying those regulations that represent first blows.

As far as good manners are concerned, anytime you expect children to act in a certain way you automatically blame them when they do not. Consequently, they must be taught only by what they see us do which, in the final analysis, is the best teacher. It is humorous to observe that when children receive a gift, the parents, feeling an unconscious twinge of obligation, will shift the responsibility of meeting it to their children rather than meet it themselves; but when the obligation is removed the desire to shift the responsibility disappears, the parents will be sincerely grateful without being under obligation, will express their thanks, and the children will imitate — all with one clean sweep of God's magic elixir. This, of course, can only take place when both parties to an action understand what this means. In our present world the child is making a scene of some sort because the mother is trying desperately to get him to say thank you, all in an effort to get this customary response for which the gift giver patiently waits. She is embarrassed and is wondering what this person is thinking about her training. But when the mother knows this person is not going to judge her or her child, not going to criticize or talk against them in any way because she knows she has not been hurt the slightest bit.

"Excuse me for the interruption, but hasn't this woman a right to expect appreciation for what she gives?"

"Of course not; how is it possible to expect a person to act in a certain way without blaming him for acting otherwise? What is the difference between telling your little girl to say thank you, and the woman to expect it?"

"But isn't it nicer when a child does say thank you?"

It is human nature to thank somebody for rendering a service or giving a gift, and any person would do this normally. When the obligation is removed because it is a form of blame, four things will occur; the desire to shift the responsibility disappears, the parents will be sincerely grateful without being under obligation, they will therefore desire to sincerely thank the person who gave the gift, and the children will very easily imitate. However, when someone expects something in return, then he is not a giver, he is a salesman, in other words, he wants to be paid. How many parents have given a child a gift and instead of a sincere 'thank you' there was disappointment, and how many ill feelings have arisen for this very reason? This often occurs when expectations are high, such as during the holiday season, which can quickly turn a wonderful time of year into a miserable time. Any person who expects something for what he gives is not being generous in the true sense of the word. As we all know, gift giving has become a serious problem in today's society. All this will change in due time, but it is important to remember that regardless of what form a gift takes it is meant to be given freely or it is not a gift at all. When you are given a gift for which you know absolutely and positively there is no obligation attached whatsoever — not even to say thank you — you will desire, of your own free will, to say thanks from the bottom of your heart. When a child sees and hears with the deepest sincerity his parents thank people for what is given generously, without expecting anything in return, he will soon imitate the very things they have been unsuccessfully trying to force. By removing the blame he expects nothing in return and gets paid with overwhelming appreciation. Children will learn this important lesson by observing and modeling the actions of their parents.

It is very difficult to see this new world in terms of the old without disagreeing, especially when there are so many variations of blame. This apparent difficulty is solved first by the very fact that the children born to parents who have married under the optimum conditions described will never hear an argument or raised voice, never hear a request for a favor, never hear one parent blame the other and, consequently, no words or expressions will develop with which to do these things. As we all know children learn by imitation, even your psychologists will confirm this, which is the reason why Russian children speak Russian, Chinese children speak Chinese, etc. If a child does not hear his parents telling each other what to do, how is it possible for him to imitate what never becomes part of his mental development? Asking favors of one another, or asking for anything that is not preceded with, "Is there anything I can do for you?" would have as much meaning for a child as this word BGHCA has for you. Besides, at a very early age children can be taught what it means that man's will is not free which will automatically prevent them from extending any word relations that tacitly blame another. Up until that time the manner in which children receive what parents and others have to give will play a vital role in teaching them who has the right-of-way when favors are asked. If your child does not know that

461

man's will is not free and should ask you to run her somewhere with the car, you have a perfect right to say 'no' because your desire is involved and if she nags you it is within your right to tell her that she is now upsetting you with her complaint for which she will be punished if it continues. But even this can be avoided by setting up some sort of reasonable schedule until children can be taught the principles. This is the heart of the problem — teaching everyone what it means that man's will is not free, and by the end of this book you will be on pins and needles to get this Great Transition under way. Remember, if there is anything you don't understand just take your time and read it over, and soon you will begin to grasp the relations.

As we begin to understand the various ways children are hurt, and the ways in which children are made to hurt their parents who have been blaming them for what is their own responsibility, we are able to prevent the conflicts that have disrupted family life. Since the parents do not like to disappoint a child who asks for things they want, or for favors which they cannot always give without annoying or hurting themselves in some way, they are compelled to prevent, without blame, a child from ever asking for this or that just as if he knew what it means that will is not free. As many parents can attest to, habits often develop under our noses and can be a source of frustration by encouraging undesirable behavior patterns which then have to be broken by blaming the child. Durant, by dancing for joy at his daughter's good marks is giving her a certain amount of entertainment which develops a habit that encourages her to study hard to get these real good marks in order to watch her father dance for joy; but supposing he doesn't feel like dancing, what then? The child is disappointed which blames her father and justifies not getting any more good marks. Just as Durant had to jump for joy over his daughter's progress in order to reward her, one father started out by giving a child a penny for this, a nickel for that, and a dollar when getting this and that together. Soon he was paying out more than he could afford, and how was it possible to stop without disappointing and blaming the child? What is given influences the child to do what is really not desired because of some intrinsic value to him, which makes him stop working when not paid. And what about the many things parents give that involve their desire, their having to do

462

something such as dancing for joy or taking a child somewhere in the car or getting down on their hands and knees to play with him even when they are not in the mood just because the child expects this, and the parents don't want to disappoint him although it is tiring them out. If you disappoint children, even with an explanation, they resent it which you can only compensate by renewing your promise for another time. Before long you are under a tremendous obligation to do many things you really don't want to do. However, this problem is very easily solved by giving children absolutely no gift directly and nothing in payment for something else, for the latter imposes an obligation while the former develops a habit of expectation which is often followed by disappointment. It also associates the giver with the gift which encourages partiality and makes a child possessive. This, in turn, engenders feelings of envy and jealousy. When a child expects what you cannot always give, you are compelled to blame him for being so annoyed with a situation that you created. If you prefer such annoying actions, this is your business, for which you will never be blamed, but how is it humanly possible to prefer what can only be a source of unhappiness where everyone is concerned since the children will always expect more than can be given. By the same reasoning, no praise or compliments are given to a child for anything at all because this places a fallacious value on what is being done since the motivation has shifted to something external. When we observe Durant's parenting style, everything he did was to place a fallacious value on what existed for his daughter. She did not go to school because she liked it but because he liked it for her, and he was willing to pay her a reasonable price to satisfy him just as an animal is fed something to eat for a performance. I know a child who literally hates school but I am willing to bet that he has his price. However, if you stop paying there may be nothing in school itself to make this child want to continue. Though Durant did what he thought was actually better for his daughter under the existing conditions, when the conditions change and he is permitted to see what is truly better for himself he is given no choice but to become a part of the change. Have you any idea how tough it is to break through this sound barrier of learned ignorance? Men like Durant are a real stumbling block. They don't know but what they don't know is taught from one end of

463

the earth to the other and this knowledge that isn't knowledge is used as a standard to test knowledge that is knowledge which permits them to tell me that I am wrong when I know that I am right. The man who believes the world is flat tells the man who knows it is round that he doesn't know what he's talking about. The man who believes that man's will is free tells the man who knows it is not free that he doesn't know what he's talking about. Can you see the difficulty in bringing this knowledge to light?

Another issue confronting our children revolves around clothing and has been responsible for much unhappiness. Parents have often asked, "Is there any blame involved when it comes to dressing children, and if there is, what can be done to avoid it?" Yes, blame is involved and there is a way to avoid it, but only because that for which this problem came into existence is prevented from arising. Let us start from the very beginning by pinpointing exactly where this problem originates and how it can be solved. A piece of clothing that a child wears belongs to him or her, just as his arm and leg, his toothbrush and bed, are his. Boys and girls learn quickly enough that they are different from one another and the clothing they wear reflects this difference. Therefore, jealousy over clothes is usually between children of the same sex. How does this jealousy begin? Clothing is used for three things; to keep warm, cool, and covered. Children do not think of what they wear as pleasurable until they get a reaction. The moment we use words like, "What an adorable dress!" then children begin to wear certain type clothes in order to get these compliments. This holds true with all words that praise or compliment another like cute, pretty, darling, beautiful, handsome, etc. which teach children to place a value on something about themselves or others which arouse these expressions, and when other children see that they do not evoke these expressions, and those compliments are not directed at them, they become jealous of their sisters, brothers, and others while unconsciously resenting their parents for this discrimination. When certain type clothes also bring forth a discriminating response, the child who was hurt will become envious, will blame, and will try to compensate in some way. For example, if a mother makes over one child's clothes by saying how great she looks and she doesn't compliment the other, the child who did not receive the compliment will place a value on this particular style and color of dress, a greater value on this type individual, etc., and be envious of her sister for having something she doesn't have which is a real, not imaginary hurt. Innocently complimenting one child's attire in front of another may cause an argument or arouse extreme envy. In fact, most arguments in the home are between children themselves, all because of jealousy. In the new world this will no longer be a source of contention, for without the compliment there can be no envy. When the parent's reaction is the same, when there is no reaction whatsoever, then children could never become envious over these differences. Due to this stratification of values, hundreds of businesses that add to the problem without recognizing the hurt they are causing, have come into existence for the purpose of helping others 'get more out of life.' What are we doing when we ingrain our children with the idea that there is a certain way to speak, walk, talk and act but to make them feel better than others when they do these things? You are going to be quite surprised as all these fallacious standards of value are compelled to take leave of our planet by mathematical necessity.

It is apparent that in our present world the way you dress your children and yourself entirely depends on what others think, for you don't like having your husband, yourself, or your children being ridiculed; but when you know, well in advance, that no one will ever again blame you or judge how you should dress, speak, walk, etc., what difference does it make to you what color dress your child wears, just so she likes it? Consequently, when this form of blame is removed it will be impossible to say a dress is cute because no one will ever judge or criticize its appearance. If the mother does not show any outward sign that she is pleased with one child's clothes over another, which criticizes the other child indirectly, it will not make one bit of difference to that child what she has on. Parents are often the first ones who make a fuss over clothes but this will discontinue in the new world because they will understand that what their children wear is no longer a reflection on them and this fuss is a criticism of those who do not wear the kind of clothes that get these complimentary remarks. Remember, once these fallacious words are removed, once the parents refrain from any outward sign that certain type clothing and physiognomies are of greater value because in reality they are not, then children will never desire to wear or have what their sisters, brothers and friends have only because these differences are not a source of importance to them until they see that others value these differences. What difference could it possibly make to a child what kind of dress you put on her if no one made any comments? And what difference would it make to a child what color and physiognomy she has if no one made any comments? There would be no difference.

Unfortunately, this is a societal problem which extends far beyond the home. In today's world there is tremendous pressure to keep up with the latest styles. Movie stars and athletes are often hired to market new lines of clothing which then become a status symbol for those who wear that particular label. Children are easy targets for this type of advertising because they, too, want to be identified with the powerful and glamorous. Wearing what their favorite celebrity is wearing makes them feel that they are part of the in-crowd. There are children who will do almost anything to boost their self-esteem even if it means stealing clothes right off of someone's back. We have all heard horror stories where a child was injured or killed over a jacket or a pair of sneakers. The jealousy over clothing is due to the belief that the latest designer jeans will get them the respect and admiration they are craving. It also shows the desperation many children feel to be accepted...to be somebody. The answer to this problem is to remove everything from the environment that makes one person feel superior or inferior over differences that are nothing but a projection of our realistic imagination. In other words, all words that project personal likes and dislikes onto the screen of undeniable substance, which then create a standard for everyone, must be removed in order for this problem to be solved. These words have become so ingrained in our culture that it is necessary for me to clarify, once again, why they are not a symbol of reality, and why they must become obsolete.

If a girl should design a dress, just as an artist paints a portrait, and you see that this dress stands out above all other dresses, this does not mean it is a wonderful or a beautiful dress. It is a dress that stands out for you. By using such words you make it appear that this girl has created something that partakes of a value called wonderful or beautiful, but in actual reality all that we know as a matter of mathematical knowledge is that you like what she is wearing. It is important to remember that there are no external values by themselves. Other differences, such as money and food, are not in the same category as the word beauty. Because they do exist externally, and because they are liked by all mankind, they have external value. But actually money and food though they exist externally have value for us only because we desire them. However, where the words beautiful and wonderful project our personal feelings about a particular thing, as if what we like exists that way in the external world for others, the words food and money do not. Our values do not exist as part of the external world, yet despite this, because our eyes are not a sense organ and because our brain is also a movie projector among other things, we are able to record these feelings on slides or words and then project them, through our eyes, onto the screen of the outside world. Then we photograph these feelings which we now see in relation to certain specific differences and thereafter when we project the word, we actually see with our eyes these values as existing outside of us. Were I to say at this moment — "Beautifully expressed," then I would be actually saying that your words are wonderful because other words are not wonderful. Since these differences that appeal more to me than another cannot be made into standards for others because this blames them for liking what I do not like, and since this also hurts them by criticizing their taste, the most I can say about anything I like...is that I like it. In the new world a girl will not even hear the comment, "I like your dress" or "I like it very much." When there is no possibility that others will criticize this girl's dress, why shouldn't I like it? As long as I know that she is happy wearing a particular dress, then I will like what she wears, and how is it possible for her not to be happy with what she wears when no one will ever criticize her taste? She will have no reason to ask for my opinion because she knows what my answer will be. The problem is to remove the desire to make any comments either up or down, either by praising or blaming these differences. In the new world children will never have any reason to criticize or compliment the clothes of another, and this pervasive jealously will disappear because the factors responsible will no longer play a role. People will be prevented from criticizing or ridiculing the way

467

someone dresses because they will know that this ridicule is a definite source of hurt, and the knowledge that they will never be blamed for striking this first blow because everyone must consider their desire as beyond their control — even by the one being ridiculed — makes it impossible for them to derive any satisfaction from being excused for what they cannot justify, and know they can prevent if they want to. When it is remembered that this is an inverted form of blame, as is pretty to ugliness, they will be compelled of their own free will to stop using all words and expressions that blame others, directly or indirectly, because this is a hurt for which there will be no blame. It's the same old story over and over again. This does not mean that all praise will be removed from our lives. This needs some clarification. First of all it is important to understand that all words of praise or compliment that describe a nonexistent value also blame a nonexistent value. In other words, the word beautiful praises something that is non-existent, therefore the word ugly blames something that is non-existent.

"But even if I don't use the word beautiful and just say to a child, "I like you very much," wouldn't this cause a child who is present to observe a difference in my reaction; so should I not say the same thing to him?"

"For what reason would you say this to one child and not to another? What if these differences that elicit a response make one child feel that you are more proud of his brother than of him, what then? If these differences are removed, then it would be mathematically impossible to be partial."

"Supposing one child sits down at the piano at the age of 3 and picks out a melody that I like very much, shouldn't I applaud him and say how much I liked it?"

"There is a big difference between saying, 'I liked that very much' and 'I like you very much,' although both expressions get displaced. Another child hearing me would become envious of his brother being able to do something that causes daddy to react differently. No matter how you slice it, there is a certain amount of discrimination because the one is being applauded and the other is not. It is a fact that if you just pick up one child, at that moment you have discriminated. Therefore, it is necessary to avoid all actions that

468

appear to show discrimination and partiality until children are old enough to be taught the basic principle."

"Do you mean that once they are old enough and are taught, then it is all right to show partiality?"

"Partiality itself is a form of hurt as is any kind of unjust discrimination. However, my realization that they would never blame me for this hurt prevents my desire to do it. But applauding my 3 year old for playing a piece on the piano is not showing unjust discrimination except for the fact that my other young children, who haven't yet been taught what it means that man's will is not free, will feel that I am showing partiality and may falsely conclude that I like this child better because of his ability to play the piano. Consequently, this is a real, not imaginary hurt to them. But once they are taught the principles they would know instantly that I couldn't possibly desire to hurt them under any conditions and would know that my applause is not a sign of partiality. However, applause itself will come to a virtual end except during paid performances."

"Well what about compliments and praise when other children are not around to be hurt?"

"Because it will be impossible for one child to desire teasing or hurting another, it would be perfectly all right providing your praise is not being used in a manner that blames the opposite for not being done. However, as with applause, the value in paying compliments is being removed. Because the desire to tease arises only from a feeling of envy and jealousy, anything that makes a child feel less important may also arouse envy. Children may show anger toward their brothers and sisters whom they wish to hurt in some manner, but when the envy and jealousy are removed this desire will never arise. It is true that specific differences will always be admired. However, this will be treated more thoroughly when we discuss education. When this mathematical standard has been thoroughly understood, you can very easily recognize false knowledge if it contravenes the blame being removed."

"According to what you wrote about parents and children, parents would have to become experts to raise their children properly, isn't that true?"

No, it is not. From the time of their birth until they are around

5 or 6 years of age, they will have no control over their desires and how they respond to the world around them, but as they reach school age they can be taught what it means that man's will is not free, they can be taught the two-sided equation, they can be taught everything it is necessary for them to know about the first blow and who has the right-of-way. Parents will assume complete responsibility for their children until they pass the examination and become full-fledged citizens. But this will not be a problem if parents give their children the right-of-way they're entitled to. In our present world most parents force their children to eat what they don't want to eat, to eat when not hungry, and to do many things they don't want to do and have the right-of-way not to do. Then they are struck a first blow which the parents call punishment for justification. But when the parents fully understand who has the right-of-way and what constitutes this form of first blow, and when children reach the age to understand the principles, parents will realize that most of the problems were caused by their hurting children for not obeying rules and regulations and standards that must come to an end. Remember, just as non-citizens will continue to be punished should they be caught violating any laws which is done as the lesser of two evils until they pass their examination, so will children if they know that breaking any rules will make matters worse for us. But when the injustice of this form of first blow is removed that forces them to do what they have the right-of-way not to do, and when they are taught the basic principle, they will never be able to find greater satisfaction in disobeying those regulations that represent first blows.

Let us now switch gears and go back in time to observe a young child who is just beginning to gain some independence. Many parents want to know how they can transfer responsibility to their children without blame. When it comes time to give the child some responsibility for his own care, the mother will teach her child not only by setting examples but by asking him if he wants to learn how to do specific things like tie his shoes and dress himself. He will have a natural desire to learn, but under no circumstances must mother ever blame the slowness of his learning nor compliment his success. It is obvious that up until he is able to do things for himself mother must do these for him, but if she wishes to lighten her load where he is concerned she must let him see what she is doing, and when she thinks he is capable of learning she will say, "Would you like Mommy to show you how to tie your shoe strings, brush your teeth, eat with a knife and fork, dress yourself, make your own bed, comb your hair...? Little by little, without any persuasion or blame, the child will develop the habit of making his bed every morning, putting his things away, etc., but under no conditions can she blame him if he doesn't want to learn, if he is slow in learning, if he stops while learning, or if he shows no interest in doing chores for her. Furthermore, if on some mornings the habit has not yet taken hold, mother will not blame him in any way but will continue helping him to develop in the direction he wants to go. No child will consider it a distasteful duty as long as mother doesn't communicate this idea, and mother will be prevented in the new world from ever thinking of it as such. Consequently, it will just be a matter of time before the habit will be successfully developed and the child will get great satisfaction in taking care of his own room just as a little baby learning to walk or learning to eat with a spoon gets great satisfaction in succeeding without assistance, but remember, no applause, no compliments, no praise, no nickels and dimes. The pleasure in keeping his room in order will come from the pleasure of keeping his room in order, and from nothing else. The pleasure he will experience in washing and brushing his teeth will come from the pleasure of feeling clean. On the other hand, mother would never try to get little Johnny to do his chores by asking him if he wants to learn how to carry out the garbage or wash the dishes. However, when he is older and knows that mother will never ask him to do any favors, he will desire to help her of his own free will. This is what you will hear in the new world.

Son: "Is there anything I can do for you, Mom?"
Mom: "Not right now honey, but thanks for asking."
Son: "Anytime."

It wouldn't matter how the offer to help was expressed, either in question form or a statement, since both convey the same intention. Here is another example:

471

Son: "That suitcase looks heavy; I'll help you to the car." Or, "Do you need help carrying that luggage to the car?"

Mom: "Thank you so much. That was such a big help."

Son: "No problem."

Here is one more example:

Son: "I can lend you a hand, Dad." Or, "Let me help you with that."

Dad: "I really could use the help. I tried to move the TV but it was heavier than I thought; would you mind helping me move it over there?"

Son: "Not at all."

Dad: "Thanks so much."

Son: "I am glad I could be of help."

What difference does it make how an offer of help is expressed when our slide rule works in either case.

"But what will the parents teach their children about good manners, how to hold one's knife and fork, etc?"

At the dinner table the child will be shown how to use a knife, fork and spoon, not because this is good manners but because he may find greater pleasure in eating with them. If, however, he should drop his fork and use his hands, he cannot be blamed. Even if he should lay the utensil down and prefer his hands, he cannot be corrected in any way as this blames him for doing something wrong, and he is not doing anything wrong. If he should pick up the fork that was dropped without wiping it off again, this cannot be corrected or criticized unless you can do this without blame of any kind. Likewise, if a child comes in to dinner after play and does not wash his hands, he cannot be corrected or criticized for he is not hurting anybody and for you to say, "Go wash your hands this instant" blames him for not washing them. This reveals that what harm a family perceived in this wiping away of germs existed only as a figment of their imagination.

"Wait a minute! Isn't it a mother's job to make sure her child stays healthy, and wouldn't it be irresponsible to let him come to the table with unwashed hands or to eat from a spoon that has fallen on a floor full of germs?"

Why must they be bad germs? Isn't it possible that children who are exposed to the 'run of the mill' germs that exist in nature develop stronger immune systems than children who are kept in a sterile, or controlled, environment? It has been observed that children who are raised in hyper sterile environments are more prone to developing asthma and allergies because their immune systems have not had the chance to encounter and conquer bacteria and viruses. Please don't misunderstand me. . . if you want your child to do certain things, you can do your best to get him to imitate you. If he drops a utensil and you wish to wash it off while he watches, this is your business, but it is not your business to blame him if he should not do this. If he decides to imitate you, this is his business, but if he doesn't, this is also his business. If you are worried and wish to spread a sterile sheet across the room every time he eats, this is your business because this makes no demands on his desire. If you don't like him coming to the dinner table without washing his hands, you can try to correct this in any manner you see fit just so you don't blame the child in any way, shape, or form. These habits of washing before dinner can easily be developed without blame. If you want to brush his teeth and wash his face because you feel this is better for him, this is your business, but if he complains, you must stop because this is his business. If you put him to bed, this is your business, but if he decides to get up, this is his business and you can't blame him for his desire because nobody is being hurt, not even himself. I'll guarantee he will go to sleep when he's tired enough. As for chores, you can assign him something to do, for this is your business, but if he decides not to do it, this is his business. He will desire to learn how to dress himself, make his bed, tie his shoes, thank others, simply because he will see you doing what is no way distasteful to imitate. If he doesn't imitate, what difference does it make to the parents when they are not going to be judged for this and when nobody is hurt? If mother wants to make his bed, this is her business. However, if she cannot solve this problem it shouldn't worry her because no one is going to criticize her for this and nothing is going to happen to the child other than becoming happier and happier at not being bossed around, for this

473

essentially is the whole problem. If we want our children to do chores without being paid in some way we must develop the habit so it becomes their responsibility because they have the right-of-way and are not striking a first blow by not doing what we want done, therefore we cannot justify punishment although we could strike this first blow to them if our conscience would allow it. Should we prefer to reward them for satisfying our desires remember that they have the right-of-way to stop doing what we want done should they prefer to sacrifice what we are paying them, or to ask for more if they feel we are not paying enough. If we don't accept their terms we must sacrifice whatever we were paying them to do, so we must be very careful about starting habits for which we can never blame them. As children develop the habit of doing their chores, it will become second nature. When they are old enough to understand that they are helping reduce our physical effort for which we would never blame them even if they stopped what has become their responsibility, and even if this meant we would have to work harder ourselves, they would soon prefer to continue helping us because not to would give them less satisfaction. The very things you don't like — other people telling you how to live your life — is the very thing you impose on your children. Good manners is showing respect for the other person and his desires, but in our present world the very people who have been trying to teach what they call good manners only reveal they are being disrespectful, insincere, selfish, and that they have the worst manners of anybody. Although this was discussed earlier, it is important to repeat because it also relates to our children.

"I know I shouldn't feel this way, but some people irritate the hell out of me, and I can't help blaming them for what they do, not so much for what they are."

"You will soon see how all the factors that gave rise to disrespect will be permanently removed, which will then prevent you from becoming irritated."

If someone was at your home for dinner and did not use his utensils correctly at the dinner table you would say he had no manners, and if he picked up the steak with his hands you would be positively convinced that he lived where there was no civilization. In reality, if this annoys you it only shows that you have no manners, not your guest, because how he consumes his food is his business which makes no imposition on your desire to eat any way you desire, but your desire that he eat with a knife and fork while removing his hat indicates that the sacrifice of his desire is what you require to be happy, and this is pure and simple selfishness, bad manners, and disrespect. Frankly I wouldn't care if he breaded the steak on the floor for himself, and covered it with ants, for this is his business, not mine, and if it makes him happy, more power to him. This is God's mathematical manner of revealing for the first time what is real and what is an imaginary hurt. The offense of my odor at your dinner table is real but my wearing a hat or eating with my hands is an imaginary offense which cannot exist once these fallacious standards are removed. Remember, if anything annoys you, regardless of what it is, you have a perfect right to try your utmost to correct it but this must be done without blaming another person because man's will is not free, and if this confuses you I suggest that you read this book over from the beginning. Your child knows that coming to the dinner table wearing blue jeans does not hurt you in any way, but if he came to dinner wearing dirty clothes that gave off an odor he knows that this might be offensive and the realization that you would never blame him for this annoyance which is real, not a figment of the imagination, makes him desire to come to dinner with a clean set of clothes. On the other hand, if your son was at a concert and was blocking someone's view, knowing that he would never get tapped on the shoulder with, "Hey pal, I can't see, you're standing in the way," compels him to desire to sit down because the thought that he would never get blamed for this real annoyance, which he knows is his responsibility, makes this motion in the direction of dissatisfaction wholly impossible. However, if he was unaware of someone behind him a gentle reminder from this person would be greatly appreciated, not resented. Good manners can be defined very simply; it is minding one's own business and minding one's own business is very simply never blaming another for anything he desires to do regardless of what this might be. Knowing that he will not be blamed for hurting someone only compels him to desire preventing the hurt which before was blamed and punished. This can only be applied when both parties involved in an action know what it means that man's will is not free.

475

We will have the best manners in the world when we have learned to mind our own business, and God is giving us no choice.

Asking favors of our children is an altogether different story and cannot be placed in the same category as chores, otherwise we could manipulate them by making them feel guilty by not blaming them for refusing to do what we have requested. The primary cause of all arguments between parents and children are parents blaming their children in advance for what they want to do. Keep in mind that the primary reason parents were compelled to do this was because they were blamed in advance by the priests, the doctors, the government, the school, their friends and relatives, the media, and everybody else. When all these forms of blame are removed, then mom and dad won't have to tell their children what to do. Another reason we often ask favors is because it allows others to do our work for us. This desire arises from a feeling of superiority toward the persons who are asked, and it assumes many subtle forms. In the case of our children, we justify our demands because we believe our children should do as they are told. When the transition gets officially launched, all forms of slavery will be done away with and the need for assistance will be volunteered. The big change here is that children will no more be the servants of their parents. "Johnny, do this, do that; bring me this, bring me that, or get me this and get me that," or a more polite way of saying the same thing, "Will you get me this or that?" is coming to an end, and with it all the headaches and arguments that parents have been unsuccessfully trying to remove. It is nice to have others work for you, especially when you don't have to pay them. Why would parents want to stop this when this denies them the satisfaction of doing less physical work? To bring this problem closer to home, below is a conversation between father and son to show the subtle way power is expressed in the parent-child relationship. Instead of telling his son to bring him the paper because this is an expression of authority which children often rebel against, he disguises his request in the form of a question. In the following dialogue the father tries to be polite but still ends up blaming his son when he doesn't do as he is told.

Father: "Timmy, would you mind bringing dad the paper?"

Timmy: "I'm too busy."

Father: "Look here, boy; it's right on the sofa; now bring it up here right away."

In this next dialogue a father uses a form of manipulation to get his daughter to do what he wants. This will be prevented in the new world.

Father: "Honey, would you mind running downstairs to get daddy the evening paper?"

Daughter: "Not now, Dad, I'm busy."

Father: "That's all right, sweetheart, you don't have to do it if you don't want to. I'll get it myself even though daddy is so tired."

His daughter, suddenly feeling responsible for the possibility of hurting her father answers reluctantly — "Never mind, Daddy, I'll get it for you." But when we know that they have the right-of-way to refuse what we have the right to ask, we can no longer justify making them feel guilty over not doing it, which forces us not to be careless about forgetting to do certain things that will make us work harder. In other words, we can no longer desire to hurt them or make them feel guilty for not doing what we should have done for ourselves, or for not desiring to do what we want them to do. Consequently, we are compelled to get into our own good habits because the constant asking of favors of our children would make them feel guilty, which we know is wrong and striking a first blow. Just as the girl volunteers getting her father a drink of water knowing he will resist asking her unless it is something he absolutely cannot do for himself, if a father broke his leg and was laid up in bed, his children would know that he is helpless and in this type of situation they would desire helping him in any way they could knowing he would never ask them unless absolutely necessary; and he, not wishing to take advantage of their generosity would sum up the things he needed so only very little effort would be required. A child being raised under the new conditions will bring about, out of absolute necessity, the greatest filial and parental love possible.

The hurt in human relations, minding other people's business, trying to force others to do what they don't want to do, criticizing their behavior, asking certain type favors and questions, and all the rest, comes to an end not because these things are wrong (we have the right to do anything we want, if we want to), not because of ethical or moral principles, the Ten Commandments, the laws of a nation, customs, conventions, tradition, etiquette, the teachings in the Bible, the belief in God, or anything else, but only because our conscience will not allow us to get greater satisfaction (the direction we are compelled to go because our will is not free) in continuing to do these things when we become citizens and understand the undeniable truth about our nature. You must remember that there are two sides to this equation and only when both sides understand the principles can we remove all the hurt and disrespect. Let me remind you that from the day of their birth children cannot be blamed for anything which means that you are compelled to prevent, without any form of tacit blame, what you do not want. Before this, children were pushed by the desires of others to accomplish their ends. To arouse their desire for an end you have determined for them such as classical music over jazz, or piano over saxophone is a definite form of advance blame, but to tell them that they can learn any instrument they wish after hearing them all, or that they can buy the genre of music they want after listening to all different types, is quite another thing. One method does not consider the innate tendencies of children which is the source of all arguments because you feel you know what is better, right, good, etc., while the other method does consider their desires which reveals respect for them and true parental love. It is understandable that you should want your child to accomplish certain things because in our present environment this is judged valuable. You had no choice until now because of the criticism and ridicule that influenced your decisions.

In concluding this chapter, I would like you to think about the way children will be raised in the new world, and the happiness that will abound. 'Early to bed and early to rise makes a man healthy, wealthy and wise' is adhered to by many families because they believe there is an element of truth in this saying, although it is very difficult to enforce without threats of punishment. Getting children to eat certain type foods because these are thought to be healthier does not consider their desire at all. All these things are part of advance blame and the only thing that can make parents desire to change, even in this world, is the realization that forcing children to do anything only creates an unhealthy environment. However, to ease your fears about what is right and wrong just remember this simple rule: If you are unable to prevent your children from desiring what you feel will be a hurt, or from not desiring what you think will be for their benefit (both without any form of blame), then it is rather obvious that what you like or dislike for them and cannot prevent without this blame is something not in any way harmful, existing only as an imaginary fear based upon false knowledge, otherwise you would definitely have the power to prevent this harm without blame in any form.

Should a certain amount of hurt still exist on the part of children to their parents and others because one-half of the equation is still too young to understand, then it is necessary to continue living for awhile longer in the world of free will even after the transition gets under way which means that mom and dad will still find it necessary to give their children a choice between hurting others and being punished, as we now do with our laws, and as I would have done had my son used a sofa for a trampoline. But remember, to punish children which still might be necessary even though both parents understand these principles, it is extremely important that the hurt you receive from your children be of a concrete nature, not one that exists only in the imagination. Durant was not hurt when his daughter showed him her marks in arithmetic but he made her think that he was and then punished her feeling of guilt by letting her know he would never blame or punish her for this. He didn't mean it to be that way but such an action is unconscious cruelty personified. I tell you this because it is so easy to abuse the knowledge you just learned when you don't understand it thoroughly. Henceforth, nobody is ever going to tell you, influence you, or do anything to try and make you do what you don't want to do. For the very first time, believe it or not, man's will is completely free to move in the direction of what he knows is truly better for himself.

Before I discuss the educational system in the new world and how

479

it will drastically change the way children learn, I shall reveal my final discovery which will absolutely shock all mankind. In fact, I consider it the most important discovery ever made on our planet, and it will make you very happy. It is not easy to follow the reasoning but take your time, and you will understand.

PART FOUR

MY THIRD AND FINAL DISCOVERY: THE EXTENSION
OF
A MATHEMATICAL RELATION INTO
THE WORLD BEYOND DEATH

CHAPTER TEN

OUR POSTERITY

E ven though the other two discoveries will bring about an entirely new world for the benefit of all mankind, the blueprint of which is demonstrated as I extend the principles into every area of human relation; the discovery which I am about to reveal in this chapter is my favorite. When thoroughly understood it might be yours too. Well, my friends, I have great news! Wouldn't it make you feel wonderful to know as a matter of undeniable knowledge, equivalent to two plus two equals four, that there is nothing to fear in death not only because it is impossible to regret it, but primarily because (don't jump to any hasty conclusion) you will always be here.

But there is an aspect of life that doesn't seem fair. There are people who have suffered and died to develop this world who will not be around when the fruits of their labor have ripened to maturity. "No matter how wonderful this Golden Age will be, how can God be a reality when there is no way perfect justice can prevail? Doesn't the thought occur to you that it is awfully cruel of God to make the man of the past pay a penalty and be made to suffer in order for the man of the future to reap the harvest of the Golden Age?"

"You will see shortly why perfect justice does prevail. But I don't want to get ahead of myself."

Although the basic principle has been an infallible guide and miraculous catalyst through the labyrinths of human relations, it cannot assist me here; but it did not help other scientists discover atomic energy, nor was it used to reveal itself. However, that of which it is composed, this perception of undeniable relations that escapes the average eye will take us by the hand and demonstrate, in a manner no one will be able to deny, that there is absolutely nothing to fear in death because we will be born again and again and again. This does not mean what you might think it means because the life you live and

483

are conscious of right now has no relation whatsoever to you and your consciousness in another life. Therefore, I am not speaking of reincarnation or a spiritual world of souls or any other theory, but of the flesh, of a mind and body alive and conscious of existence as you are this moment. Are you smiling? Can't you see, once again, Eric Johnson refusing to listen because he was so certain man's will is free, or Nageli not investigating Mendel's discovery because the very core was regarded as impossible? Didn't many of you smile when first hearing that man does not have five senses? I expect you to be skeptical, but please give me the benefit of the doubt and deny my discovery after you have studied the relations, not before. I would like to share a conversation I had with my friend regarding my final discovery in the hope of making these difficult principles easier to understand.

"Boy does that word 'death' give me the creeps! I can't stand the thought that one day I'll be gone from this earth; I won't see the sun, the moon, and the stars; I won't enjoy eating, sleeping, making love. What a horrible thought! And above all, I might not even be here when the Golden Age gets officially launched."

"Your thinking is typical of the majority of mankind."

"But a lot of religious people don't think that way. They believe that when they die they are going to heaven or some such happy hunting ground and consequently have no fear of death whatsoever."

Yes I know that. There are all kinds of explanations about the hereafter, this spiritual world of souls, but I am not interested in words, just the flesh. You are in for quite a pleasant surprise but because man's mind has been so filled with words such as afterlife, soul, spirit, metempsychosis, reincarnation, heaven, etc., which have been used to explain death, although they have absolutely no meaning whatsoever, we were unable to extract the pure unadulterated mathematical relations that existed when these words were removed. Theologians and other philosophers received intuitive incursions that man was truly immortal, but they had no way of communicating or translating their feelings into language that could not be denied simply because they were completely confused with words and beliefs. It will be proven, conclusively, that there is nothing to fear in death and when all the facts are in you will see that there is justice for those who have gone before us. You will gain a better understanding as you read and reread this chapter.

"This is quite confusing. You just said that I would be born again and again and again, and now you say there will be no connection between me now and me then."

"I realize that, but before I explain the proof I shall begin by asking you a very important question. Doesn't it seem strange that of all the millions of years the earth has been in existence (and what is a million years when the words through which you see this relation are clarified) you, of all people, should be born at this time to see the wonders of this world and the inception of the Golden Age? Why weren't you born back in the days of Socrates, or why did you have to be born at this time instead of a thousand years hence? Think again of this fantastic phenomenon with the earth perhaps billions and billions of years old, here we are alive at this infinitesimal fraction of time.

"I'm conscious now, and I know nothing of a consciousness in another life. I was born now, at this time, because my father met my mother, fell in love, got married and had four children; and I am the third. My grandparents gave birth to my parents, and so on. Furthermore, I have seen many people die and they never return as new babies or in any other form. Therefore since I, too, must die, why should I be an exception and return? The elderly who have lost many loved ones and know that their own death is near cannot help but think about what Durant referred to as the Great Enemy because you see and cannot deny that when someone gets buried in the ground he never rises again except in your imagination, as did Christ into heaven."

From a superficial observation this is all very true, but the reasoning as to what actually happens after your death is an inference based upon your observations during your life. This reasoning complicates even more the difficulty of understanding this phenomenon. While you are alive you know that many people die who never return. You also know that many babies are born who are in no way the people who died, therefore since you, too, must die and the babies born are not the people who died, you cannot be one of the babies born after your death. Another way of saying the same thing

485

is this: If you could remain alive for 200 years not one of the babies born during that time could possibly be you, so if you had died after 80 years why should one of the same babies born during the 120 years following your death be you when they were not you before? Can't you see how easy it is for reasoning to prove that we are not born again? But, to reiterate, your reasoning as to what actually happens after your death is an inference based upon your observations during your life. When you die you cannot possibly have any more observations. In other words, your reasoning doesn't reveal a deeper truth. Does matter itself reveal atomic energy? Do the individual planets, moon and sun reveal the solar system? Do individual people reveal the mankind system unless we observe certain undeniable laws? Does all of it together reveal the reality of God, unless certain mathematical relations are perceived? Certainly your grandparents gave birth to your parents who gave birth to four children, but this tells us nothing about the deeper law which is necessary to perceive in order to understand why there is nothing to fear in death and why we will be born again and again and again. At one time man was afraid of thunder and lightning thinking it was the wrath of God, but now we don't fear the thunder and try to protect ourselves as best we can against the lightning. Until man discovered the cause of an eclipse which required knowledge of the solar system, or to phrase it differently, knowledge of the laws that inhere in particular bodies in motion, he was afraid that something terrible was going to happen and it became an ominous sign that was blamed for whatever evil followed. Such is the reason it seems strange to be alive at this moment with all the millions of years behind you because you don't understand the truth. When it is thoroughly explained the strangeness disappears, but I must proceed with undeniable relations in order to prove why there is nothing to fear in death.

"But I see that death is a terrible thing."

"For the living only; the dead don't know it, right?"

"It's true that they don't know it, but I know that they don't know it and that's what disturbs me because one day I will also be in their position and I don't like to know that I won't know from nothing."

"I know this is a disturbing thought and one that science has not yet been able to solve — that is, how to get rid of this disturbance, but once the laws relating to death are thoroughly understood, then this disturbance will come to an end."

"The problem then is simply to discover and understand the various laws of this universe."

"But it isn't that simple. It took me two years to understand what it meant that man's will is not free and an additional three years to break through this sound barrier of words."

"Not ignorance anymore?"

"Just words; this is the source of the unconsciousness and the ignorance. However, without these words we could never have discovered the laws necessary for an adequate understanding of ourselves and the world we live in."

"How do words play a role in death? There is certainly a big difference between the theory of free will and the obvious evidence that when you're dead you're dead. What's that saying, "Ashes to ashes, dust to dust?"

"But when you use the words *you, I, him, she, he,* etc., you are making an assumption and not using mathematical language. The word orange circumscribes an undeniable bit of substance, but the word 'I', what word does that circumscribe?"

"It circumscribes me; little ol' me, from the tip of my toes to the top of my head."

"And you feel that when they lay you out in a coffin?"

"Do you have to use that word? It sends shivers up my spine."

"When they lay you out in a box, this body is still you? Is that the way you think?"

"I don't feel this way, I know for a fact that when I looked at my dead uncle it was my uncle, not anybody else."

"But if I can prove to you, beyond a shadow of doubt, that the word 'I' not only pertains to you as you are now existing but also to the sperm and ova that are still living in an unborn state, then you will know that when this part of you dies, the other still lives on."

"Is that supposed to satisfy me? To know that when I die I am part of a stream of ova and sperm that still continues to float around in a protoplasmic world?"

"Of course not; but it is supposed to reveal that when you say a certain word circumscribes you from the tip of your toes to the top of your head, this is an assumption because before you were born you were nothing but the union of a spermatozoa with an ovum and, according to you, if that particular spermatozoa had never united with that particular egg, you would never have been born, is that right?"

"That's exactly right."

The actual reason it is not strange that you are conscious now is because you, no one else (that is, not you as you are now, but you as someone else), will always be conscious as long as mankind exists (I shall prove this, remember?). It is you who will exist many years from now, not your posterity. The fact that your consciousness is the only consciousness that can exist does not mean that other people are not conscious of their existence also, only that they cannot be seen except through your consciousness. It would therefore make no difference when the question is asked, "Doesn't it seem strange..." because you, your consciousness, will always be present to answer. As you begin to understand what death actually is, your fear will be replaced by the certain knowledge that death is truly not the end.

Now to solve this apparently unsolvable problem, it is first necessary to establish certain undeniable facts. Therefore, let me begin by asking you if there is such a reality as the past? Does this word symbolize something that is a part of the real world?

"Of course...yesterday is the past, today is the present, and tomorrow is the future. And this is a mathematical relation."

It is true that yesterday was Thursday, and the day before was Wednesday, and there isn't any person alive who will disagree. But this does not prove whether the word past is an accurate symbol. Can you take it, like you can the words apple and pear, and hang it up on something so I can look through it at the real McCoy? When does the present become the past? I actually want you to demonstrate how the present slips into the past. That cannot be done by God Himself. The reason man cannot do what I asked is because there is no such thing as the past. The past is simply the perception of a relation between two points. As I move from here to there, the past is what I leave behind while in motion; it is my ability to remember something that happened. In actual reality you are not moving between two points, a beginning and an end, you are in motion in the present. I know that we were talking yesterday, and that I was talking a fraction of a second ago, and that I am still talking. The word 'past' is obviously the perception of a relation that appears undeniable because it has reference to the revolution of the earth on its axis in relation to the sun. You are conscious that it takes a certain length of time to do something, and because you are also conscious of space you perceive that as you traverse a point from <u>here</u> to <u>there</u> what is left behind as you travel is called the past, and your destination is the future. Here lies a great fallacy that was never completely understood, for how is it humanly possible for there to be such a thing as the past and future when in reality all we ever have is the present? Yet we have a word to describe something that has no existence in the real world. Socrates never lived in the past — he lived in the present, although our recollection of him allows us to think back to this time period. The reason we say that Socrates lived in the past is because this particular individual is no longer here. But is it possible for you to say that God existed in the past? Does anyone ever sleep in the past; does the sun ever shine in the past; is it possible for you to do anything in the past? If you were sitting up on a high cloud these last ten thousand years, never asleep, you would have watched Socrates in the present, just as you are watching me write this book in the present. In order for me to prove what seems impossible, it is absolutely necessary that I de-confuse the mind of man so we can communicate.

As we have learned in Chapter Four, our brain is divided into compartments, and in the memory section are innumerable word slides on which are recorded our experiences. A second ago, yesterday, last week, last month, two years ago, two thousand years ago, are slides in our brain projector through which we see the number of times, or what portion of one time, the earth revolves on its axis; but if we were not able to remember (store away these slides), the word past would never have come into existence because we are born, grow old, and die all in the present. In reality, everything that we can possibly do from the time we get up to the time we go to bed, and even our sleep, is done in the present, as is the shining of the sun.

"Are you saying that if man wasn't able to remember what he did, there would be no such thing as the past?"

If I said to you, "What did you do yesterday?" and you were

unable to understand my words, only the present would exist for you. The recollection of the various things we did in our life, or to put it another way, the recollection of our past is just as good as our memory, but if we were not able to remember (store away these word slides that contain every conceivable kind of relation), the word past would never have come into existence. Animals cannot think in terms of past and future because they don't have the ability to store away these word slides. We use words like beginning and end, apply this to the universe and think we perceive mathematical relations. We say God is the first cause, and we reason from here as if we are discussing reality. Yet there are innumerable relations which cannot be denied once they are understood. The actual reason it isn't strange to me that you are alive this moment and conscious of your existence with the earth as old as it is, is because there is no such thing as the past or future. Consciousness, like the sun, can only exist in the present and it is absolutely impossible for any consciousness to exist but your very own. By perceiving things that are born and die, and by not understanding the underlying substance, a fallacious relation develops which can easily be clarified once the word symbols are understood.

"I know that all we have is actually the present, so does everybody else, but what does that prove?"

"It is just fact number one; there is no such thing as the past or future simply because the only thing we can ever have is the present. Are we in agreement so far?"

"I can't disagree, so I guess I must agree."

"Therefore, the next fact to be established, and the most important, is that the only consciousness that can ever exist in the universe — is your consciousness, not hers or his, but only your consciousness. It is mathematically impossible to see this world through any consciousness but your own. It is true that others are conscious at the same time you are, but you observe this through your consciousness."

"Are you trying to tell me that I am the only one conscious?"

"You know that's not what I mean. Other people are conscious of what is going on in their lives, but their consciousness only exists as a relation to your consciousness. In other words, it is mathematically impossible to see this universe through anybody's

490

consciousness but your own, even though you are aware that others are conscious. Do you agree that it is mathematically impossible to see this universe through anybody's consciousness but your own?"

"Isn't it true that when I read a book I am looking at the world through the eyes of the author?"

"That may be true but no matter what people say, do, or write about, these things are perceived through your consciousness even though you are aware that others are conscious of these things also. I see the sun, and I also know that you see the sun, but I cannot see it through your consciousness, only through my own; do you understand?"

"Yes I do, and I agree."

"Then we have established fact number two. Now fact number three is that you are conscious of your existence at this exact moment of time; is that correct?"

"How can I deny what is undeniable?"

"Now let's put these three facts together so that we can look at them more closely. One, there is no such thing as the past, therefore all we have is the present. Two, it is mathematically impossible to see this universe through anybody's consciousness but our own. And three, we are all conscious of our existence at this moment of time."

"What are you getting at?"

"I want you to observe this mathematical reasoning which I will later prove in a different manner. Since there is no such thing as the past, only the present moment of time, and since we are conscious at this moment of our own existence, and since it is mathematically impossible for us to see this universe through any consciousness but our own, it becomes apparent that our consciousness of existence, not our body, must always be present during every lifetime."

"Are you trying to tell me that because I am conscious of my existence at this moment of time, I will always be conscious of my existence from now to eternity?"

"Didn't you just admit that it is mathematically impossible to see this universe through any consciousness but your own?"

"I did, and it's an undeniable fact."

"Then your consciousness must always be present at each moment of time because it is mathematically impossible to see this universe through any consciousness but your own. Remember, however, that the words 'your consciousness' applies to everybody who is presently conscious. If I lined everybody up and then said to each one — 'Is it mathematically possible to see this universe through any consciousness but your own?' they would all answer simultaneously, 'No, it is not possible.' Confusion arises when we think in terms of 'his' consciousness, but remember his consciousness can only have existence in relation to our consciousness. It is our eyes through which our brain looks out, not that of someone else. This is why we are conscious right at this moment, and why we will be conscious a hundred and a million years from now. As for being knocked unconscious we would then be only sleeping, not dead, and we are dealing with death not sleep."

"I'm still confused. Can't you explain this in an easier way?"

"Yes I can, but it was necessary to establish certain undeniable facts from which to do other reasoning. Are you ready, and do you have on your thinking cap?"

"Let's go, I'm as ready as I'll ever be."

Now pay close attention. Let us imagine that your mother and father, Adam and Eve, gave birth to ten children; you, me, Harold, Monroe, Ida, Roberta, Sue, Linda, Janis, and Madeline. Through the course of nature these children not knowing anything about incest got married; Ida with Harold, Madeline and I, Monroe with Roberta, and you and Janis. In the course of time these ten gave birth to 40 more children, and these 40 gave birth to another 150 until the earth's total population was all of two hundred and two. However, Adam by now is a very old man and about to die, but just before passing away he says to me, "Isn't it strange that with all the years the earth has been in existence I am conscious right now of this world? I am conscious of you, my wife, your brothers and sisters and all the rest in our family." When the last baby was born on my 100th birthday, I said to myself, "Wouldn't it be wonderful if that was me starting my life all over again so that I could enjoy the sun, the stars, and all the other things for another 100 years? But I know it couldn't be me because this is me, talking to you, and number 202 is a tiny infant while I am worn out with age. It would be wonderful, though, if people didn't have to die, not that I really mind because I've long forgotten what it's like to make love, but if I could be born again with a completely new body it would be heaven on earth and maybe in my new life there would be something made to cover my feet so they don't get all cut up from walking on small pieces of broken stone."

I have great news, Adam, because your wish is about to come true, but it is important to understand that just as long as you are living any person born cannot possibly be you. However, when you die, this you, this bubble of consciousness which burst with your death is gone, which makes it impossible for a new child to have any relation to you but only to those still living who refer to this baby as him or her when they have something to say. Now answer me very carefully. If you admit (remember, Adam, we have agreed on certain facts) that it is mathematically impossible to see this universe through any consciousness but your own, then when you die and are no longer here to see this world, who will possess this next bubble of consciousness?

"If it is a boy, he will possess it. If a girl, she will."

"But how is it possible for you to say this when you are no longer here to say it, for this expression must pass through your consciousness and you know it is not your consciousness because you have just died, so whose consciousness are we talking about? Since your body is no longer here when you die, who is the next child born?"

"I've seen a lot of babies born (it's true I haven't seen anyone die yet), but I cannot imagine how a child born after my death could be me."

To understand who this child is, let us turn back the clock to your birth. You grow, develop, and after a few years you are able to recognize your individuality and say — "I am alive, conscious of my existence," proof of which is the fact that you are reading this book. However, you know you will eventually die. Therefore, since every child born has the innate ability to recognize the genetic differences given to him by his parents, his individuality, in other words, and since it is absolutely impossible to say 'I' and be talking about someone else, one of the children born after your death can't possibly be him or her but must be you, someone who will grow, develop and recognize his individuality and say — "I am alive, conscious of my existence."

493

All through your life you say "he died, she died, they died; he was born, she was born, they were born," and you assume that these same observations that you make during your life will continue after your death. This relation is difficult to see because you must project what actually occurs after you are no longer here. You actually extend your reasoning beyond the grave, which is mathematically impossible to do. Remember, when you die you can no longer say "he is born" because this observation must pass through your consciousness, and your consciousness is no longer here since you died, so who is this child that is born? If it is mathematically impossible for you to say his or her consciousness regarding this infant that was conceived after your death and who was just delivered because this must have reference to your consciousness, and your consciousness is no longer here since you just died; and since the other 201 people in your family have their own consciousness, and since it is mathematically impossible for you to see this universe through any consciousness but your own (this was already established as an undeniable fact), then this new child must contain your consciousness, the consciousness of number 202; not the same individual, but someone who has just gone through nine months of gestation, who will be given a name, inherit what was passed on to him, grow, recognize his own individuality, see the world in relation to himself, see people die who will never return, and see babies born who cannot possibly be him because he is alive and conscious of his existence at this very moment. Another way of saying the same thing is this. When I say 'I', I must be talking about myself, and if everybody born must say 'I', the chain of consciousness is never broken so no matter how often I die, no matter when the question is asked, "Doesn't it seem strange..." I or you will always be here to answer. Let me clarify this in a different way.

From the time of your birth...hey wake up, are you sleeping?

"I agree. I think it's terrifically musical like Gibbon, but only you confuse me, and it was so nice dozing off."

As I was saying, from the time of your birth your body contains the consciousness of your existence and no matter how many live or die around you everything is seen in relation to your consciousness which makes it obvious that any child born after your birth cannot possibly be you while you are still living, for there is a mathematical

494

relation between your consciousness and the existence of others. But each individual consciousness that presently exists, represented by everybody alive, does not include those who have not yet been born, consequently YOU, number one, who just this second came into the world, will have a relation to all those alive and those yet to be born while you are living; but should you die at any time during your uterine journey at the age of one month, two years, 18, 67, or 100 years, you immediately lose your relation to the living, therefore any bit of consciousness that remains in the world cannot possibly be yours at that moment of time. In other words, since it is mathematically impossible to see this universe through any consciousness but your own, and since your consciousness is no longer here, the next person born is not his or her consciousness for this must be in relation to you and you are not here because you just died, but YOUR consciousness. It is YOU who was just born, not number one who just died, but YOU, whatever name you are given, whatever your sex, for you will now represent the consciousness of existence and your own individuality. Remember, as long as you are living as number one, two, etc., any person born cannot possibly be you.

"I thought your first discovery was tough to understand. Do you have this in your manuscript?"

"I do."

"I sure hope others understand it better than I do, and I sure want to thank you for clarifying it. What on earth would it have been like had you not made it so clear? Are you finished; can I go now?"

Not yet, I'm going to clarify this difficult relation a little more. The great confusion centers about the fact that man is not conscious that his consciousness, through which he perceives his own individuality, is not an individual characteristic. Your particular face and body are individual things perceived by our consciousness of differences, and these differences perish and die which cannot be denied. But your consciousness (and here's the key to the problem) never dies because it is the ability of the human brain to perceive relations which reveal the consciousness of individuality, and this consciousness, which is you at this moment of time, is passed along from generation to generation in the form of an unborn or potential mind. Let us go back to the time just before you were conceived. We

495

shall let A represent all the sperm pertaining to mankind, B all the ova, and the combination of one with the other will be designated C which is you, your potential consciousness of existence. Your parents have decided to create a child. This is you, but you don't know this yet, nor do they know whether you will be a boy or girl or what other characteristics you may have. You might be the first child, second, third, fourth, fifth, and so on. Now remember, you are not born yet so you cannot possibly be conscious of your existence, but you are a potential candidate for this consciousness. As luck would have it you die during your uterine journey when your mother has a miscarriage which means that the conditions are exactly as they were before. Consequently, you are not conscious of your existence because your body was never born to give you this and therefore the relation expressed in these words — he died, she died, or it died — would have no meaning where you are concerned (only those who are living), because you just died, and your existence is absolutely necessary for the relation. Now this potential mother and father still want their first baby — they want YOU — which word symbolizes human living substance, so they try again, but this time you are born only to die one month later of a heart problem. Still persistent and having a lot of fun they try again with viable success, but 18 years later you end up in a car accident where you die. Much older now but still capable of propagating, mom and dad are not satisfied to lose YOU so they try once more to bring YOU into existence. In actual reality, though heredity differences exist between the three C's, the word YOU is a designation only for the viable substance that comes into the world and is identified with a name to establish these differences which mom and dad grow to love. But what is the difference between the potential YOU who died during the uterine journey, the YOU who died one month after birth, or the YOU who died 18 years later? Because you are conscious of your existence and individuality during those years in the present, write a book, build a home, make a lot of friends who cry when you die, doesn't take away from the fact that you are a combination of A and B which continues in existence even while you are alive and regardless of what happens to C. Consequently, the consciousness of your individuality without understanding that you are not only C, which represents the hereditary differences that die, but the germinal substance A and B which never die because they are carried along from generation to generation and when united develop into your existence, makes you perceive an improper relation. Simply because the entelechy of A and B develops into the consciousness of C, which permits the recognition of individuality, does not negate the substance from which C is derived. Even if all the individual characteristics lie potential in the germinal substance, this still has nothing to do with consciousness which is not an individual characteristic like your face. The word 'I' or 'you' not only reveals this individual difference between yourself and others, but your consciousness of this. There is no actual difference between the potential YOU who died one month after birth, the YOU who will die in a relatively short period of time, or the YOU who lived for many years. If you had died a hundred thousand times in the uterus of somebody, eventually YOU, which is a word describing the consciousness of differences about yourself after your parents create you, would have been born.

In reality, the conditions are exactly the same before your birth as after your death. Since you cannot see this world through the consciousness of another, when you die what consciousness exists belongs to all those living. They are the ones who say him or her because this relation is seen through their consciousness, and they are still living. Since you are no longer conscious of your existence when dead, and since it is mathematically impossible to see this world through the consciousness of another, only through your own consciousness, and since everybody who is still alive has their own consciousness, it is obvious that the next person conceived and born after your death is not him or her, because this can only be in relation to your consciousness which is not here anymore once you died, but YOU, not the person who just died, but an individual who grows and develops and becomes conscious of his existence and individuality. Consequently, this allows us to make an undeniable observation. Because there is no such thing as the past, and consciousness can only be your consciousness (never that of another) which can only exist in the present, your consciousness, not your body, will always be here during every moment of time because it is not a personal characteristic like the shape of your nose, but that which applies to the

497

living substance of all mankind. This all pervasive consciousness can only be your consciousness because you are an individual expression of God's consciousness which pervades the universe and continues to exist in the potential of a protoplasmic state. Consequently each child born comes into the world with this I or ego which, since it is just an individual expression of the germinal or protoplasmic ego, continues to exist after the body dies; and the very moment after death his ego, the feel of himself as an individual existing which has never died because it exists as the potential of germinal substance from which all self consciousness is derived, is born into the viable substance of any A and B combination. Let me give another example to help you see the relation. Take your time with this and eventually you will understand.

Now that mom and dad have you they decide to have another child, and when it is born it is not you because you already exist. Soon mom gives birth to a total of ten. Then several years later you get married and give birth to two children, making a total of 14 in your family. Before long there are 50 family members in all. After reaching a ripe old age of 100 years you drop dead from heart failure, so this body, this bubble of consciousness is gone which makes it impossible for you to say that the next child born is him or her because this relation must pass through your consciousness which is no longer here. If you, the 50th member of your family said 'I' just before your death, and the remaining members of your family are still alive at the time that you died; and if it is impossible to be born and not say 'I' because everything must be seen through your consciousness, the next infant born cannot possibly be him or her, number 51, but YOU, number 50. In other words, since your family just lost YOU, which decreased the population to 49, and since these remaining 49 members are not you because they have their own consciousness, but they still want YOU, when you are born you will not be him or her, number 51, but you, number 50, who will grow, develop and become conscious of your existence. This 'I' or ego that you feel is definitely a reality for it is you, no one else, that tastes, sees, smells, touches and hears. But this consciousness is not only an individual thing like the various differences about yourself which we have considered C, but also A and B, the potential consciousness that

498

exists in the germinal substance. Since this substance is that from which your ego, the feel of yourself as an individual, is composed, and since this 'I' or ego is also the conscious expression of the germinal substance, both are one and the same. Consequently, the consciousness of all mankind is the ego or 'I' of the germinal substance which imparts individuality upon the birth of a child, as a tree does to a leaf in the spring of the year. But this all pervasive consciousness which exists always in the present (and here is the mathematical solution again) can only be your consciousness because it is impossible to see this universe through any body but your own. If you can see this universe through the consciousness of someone else you will be made king of all creation. You must be on the inside looking out because it is impossible to be on the outside of your body and look at this universe, which means that you must be able to say 'I'. It is our very own consciousness which is always here in the present that enables us to say, whether a million years ago or a million years hence, "Isn't it strange that I was born now to see the wonders of this amazing world?"

To draw up a comparison for a still better understanding, if we let A and B, that which is carried along from generation to generation equal a huge, live, headless body that never dies but from which human heads begin to grow, the first head will say, "I am the only human alive." When the second head appears he will say — "I am alive and I see you, my Siamese brother, and we are the only two humans alive." When the third head appears she says, "Our family consists of my two brothers and myself and I am alive, conscious of my existence." If God chopped off one of these heads, and like a hydra another one appeared instantly in its place, the new head would say — "I am alive, conscious of my existence, and there are only three heads in our family." This is exactly what happens when you die, your head is chopped off from the body of A and B which continues in existence from generation to generation, and when a boy and girl mate they create you, C, a body that grows and develops and says — "I am alive, conscious of my existence. I have brothers and sisters, a mother and father." But when you die your body and consciousness are gone only to be born again. If you examine all the facts you will find them undeniable.

499

When someone dies it is true that he is gone and will never return in our lifetime because these relations are also undeniable. I also know that my father and his father before him are derived from this protoplasmic substance that never dies and is handed along from generation to generation. It is very true that we have grown to love our fathers and mothers, husbands and wives, brothers and sisters, but their time of death and our relationship to them does not change reality. If my father had died during his uterine journey this does not mean that I would never have been born because the word 'I' is a symbol of any individual that is derived from this germinal world of potential consciousness, and is given to us upon being born. Our perception that we are derived from two specific people does not alter the fact that our consciousness of these relations is not derived from them but from the inherent ability of man's brain to perceive these differences in relation, which ability is carried along in the germinal world of potential consciousness and imparts individuality upon being born. It is impossible for me to have my consciousness and that of another, therefore the differences that are now me must die before the new differences, containing the same consciousness as the child that develops from birth during the present moment of time, can be born. If I should die this instant it only means that I, not the individual Seymour Lessans, but someone of two new parents, would start my life over again because this consciousness of individuality is given to each person at birth and has nothing to do with the individual characteristics themselves. Therefore, death is a mirage to those who die and a reality only to the living. It is our ability to recognize these deeper relations that give us our knowledge of personal immortality and our freedom from the fear of death, for then we know that even though God sweeps away our aging flesh, and our body and consciousness are gone, we will be born over and over again to see this miraculous world. This is an actual reality, not a figment of the imagination, and can easily be verified when you realize that with all the millions of years you, of all people, are born right now to see the universe. The truth is, you will also be born a million years hence because all we have is the present, and this universe can only be seen through your consciousness, not the consciousness of another.

Soon it will dawn on you, as you fully understand these relations,

500

that consciousness is the eternal window of God through which we, all mankind, look out upon this magnificent universe in all its glory and mathematical harmony. It should be further obvious that God can have absolutely no recognition for His existence and achievements unless through the consciousness of man who is an eternal attribute of God Himself. Once it is fully realized that we are the conscious expression of God who exists eternally because there is no such thing as the past or future, only the present which is eternal, we will become completely conscious of our own eternal life, otherwise, we will be eternal unconsciously.

"I liked that very much, and I'm beginning to understand it more clearly."

The perception of these relations make it obvious that the same general experiences we have gone through of being little boys and girls with a mother and father, growing up, getting married, raising a family in the new world and remarking about the time way back in the olden days when man used to believe the earth was flat, his will free, and his eyes a sense organ, will continue throughout eternity as long as man is able to reproduce himself because there is no such thing as a beginning and end since time, space, and consciousness are infinite and eternal attributes of the present. The full realization of what death actually is will destroy the desire to preserve corpses in cemeteries, for this is only a waste of land and the bodies of the deceased. Satisfaction in preserving this lifeless bit of matter can only be gotten when ignorance of the truth engenders the desire. No one will deny that it is sad to lose a loved companion, and it is also true that when someone dies he is gone and will never return in our lifetime because these relations are also undeniable; but through God's infinite wisdom, by revealing what it means that man's will is not free and what this means, it prevents in 90% of the cases any premature deaths by eliminating all war, crime, economic insecurity, jealousy, hate, and every other form of hurt that gave rise to a justifiable retaliation which was necessary up until now, while endowing man with the will, the freedom, and the ability to discover the remaining laws that will wipe away the other 10%.

"This news is so unbelievably wonderful that I can't praise God enough or thank Him enough for my existence. At the very time that

I have learned of this new world soon to unfold, which would make me sad to think that I might not be here to enjoy it, I have also learned that death is a realistic mirage and that this Golden Age will not only belong to our posterity, but also to ourselves. I only wish all the people who suffered and died would have had an opportunity to know this before they died."

"What difference does it make now, and are you forgetting so soon? Just before your birth you were among those individuals who were about to die. It might not have been you that got killed on the battlefield of World War I, but you were living during that period and died during that period."

"Do you mean that I lived through every period of history?"

"Yes you did, only, of course, you don't know who you were or whether you were a male or a female."

"This is just too fantastic. In other words, once it is understood that man's will is not free and what this means, our people, the Jews, cannot blame Hitler for slaughtering 6 million of us, nor can we feel sorry for the dead because we are not dead?"

You must remember that anybody living who lost a loved one in the Holocaust will never get over it. However, when he fully realizes that all evil came into existence because God needed it to develop mankind, and now that we are developed it will be forthwith removed, he won't ever again be able to blame another because there won't be anything left to blame. It might take 2000 years for this knowledge to come to light because it may blind those who have been looking for a different type solution, something in accordance with their own opinion. It was the same thing that gave Mendel posthumous recognition. In our Golden Age, the inception of which will take place just as soon as this discovery is confirmed valid by our world leaders, we will fall mutually in love, raise our families in complete health, security, wealth and happiness, live to a ripe old age without overpopulating the earth, and die only to be born for the same happiness again and again and again. Well, isn't this the most wonderful knowledge to behold? It reveals in an infallible manner the great wisdom that directs every aspect of this universe. Is God a reality and is He good? You bet your life He is, and we are in wonderful hands!"

"It is just too unbelievable, and I just feel like crying for sheer happiness."

"So will all mankind, once everything sinks in."

"It is like the unfolding of a drama."

"Only the players were unconscious of the role they played."

"Gosh, I certainly wish there was something I could do to get this Golden Age started in a hurry. After all, if this isn't explained carefully you know they'll call me a crackpot, right?"

"They will, so be careful. But remember, they will not call you anything once the principles are understood. Until that time, however, these are the risks I (you, too) have to take. My only hope is that no one will jump to conclusions until they read thoroughly what I have written; then I don't care how much they jump because they will be prevented providing — it must constantly be qualified — they understand mathematical relations. Now it is time to move on to my final chapter, but before I go I want you to remember this; no matter how long it takes for this new world to begin, YOU WILL BE THERE."

"You'll never know how much I appreciate what you've done."

"Always remember, don't thank me...thank God."

As we turn to the final chapter, The New Meaning of Education, we will learn how children have been struck a first blow time and time again, and then punished for not living up to the arbitrary standards the schools have forcefully imposed. Another serious problem which has added to the crisis facing our schools is bullying, which has become intolerable for those who have become the targets. The students who have been mistreated have reacted in various ways from withdrawing, to cutting class, to altercations with teachers and classmates, to dropping out, and in the most extreme form, to school shootings or suicides. Because there has been no immediate solution, society has focused its attention on quelling the symptoms but as we have witnessed in recent years anti-social behavior that is misunderstood is more likely to escalate from words to violence. The schools are a microcosm of what is going on in the world at large and what we are seeing is a reflection of the chaos children are experiencing in their homes and neighborhoods, but it is also a reflection of the school's methodologies and practices which have contributed to making the student's experience an unhappy one. The school system is failing to achieve its most valued objective which is to provide everyone with an education, because a significant number of students are losing their interest in learning. Unfortunately, we have been trying to fix a broken system whose very foundation is crumbling. We will begin to see how the new educational system, based on the knowledge of man's ultimate nature, creates a nurturing environment where all children are able to reach their maximum potential.

CHAPTER ELEVEN

THE NEW MEANING OF EDUCATION

The educational system in the Golden Age will far surpass what exists today because it will be based on the knowledge that man's will is not free. As we extend the basic principle it is quickly discovered that all the problems plaguing our schools are prevented once we leave behind the free will environment of blame and punishment and replace it with our new understanding of man's nature which commands us to obey the corollary, Thou Shall Not Blame. Due to a fundamental shift in ideology, as well as a complete restructuring of teaching practices, children will grow and blossom into happy, productive adults. Our schools will become vehicles for self-exploration and discovery where children not only will love attending, but will never have to be persuaded to learn. The remarkable changes reflected in the attitude and enthusiasm of our schoolchildren, from the elementary years all the way through high school and beyond, demonstrate that they do better when given the freedom to choose their own course of study. Based on this new educational model, which completely revolutionizes the way knowledge is acquired, children will never outgrow their intrinsic joy of learning because they will control the reins, and the direction, of their academic futures.

As early as kindergarten the very first thing children will learn is the basic principle, for this is the source of all the changes about to take place. Just as they will learn basic math facts, children will learn that man's will is not free along with a simple explanation. Each home will have commandments placed on the wall, as we have the Ten Commandments today, and these will say — Thou Shall Not Ask Favors... Thou Shall Not Tell Others What To Do ... Thou Shall Not Judge What Is Right For Someone Else, and so on. The parents will explain what this is to their children. Although it may take some children longer to understand the basic principle than others, this in itself has no real significance. Even if the principle is not completely understood (which it won't be, of course), children will at least know that no one will ever blame or punish them should they hurt others — and the reason for this. As they get older they will have a much greater understanding of what it means that man's will is not free. By the time children reach school age, parents will be permitted to do or say anything for the purpose of arousing their desire to enroll but the best method will be to show them what fun others are having and how learning certain things will help them achieve their goals. Parents have a perfect right to judge what they think their children should learn, but once they have expressed their desire — even if it does not agree with those of their parents — they must not be blamed because their will is not free and they are choosing what is best for themselves. Regardless of their age, children deserve equal respect as long as no one is being hurt by their actions.

If for any reason a child does not want to go to school, parents will not criticize him — unless they want to do what they know is wrong — because his decision not to go, for whatever reason, is in no way hurting anyone otherwise he couldn't do it. Consequently, the desire of the child, not a predetermined age, will be the deciding factor as to when he (or she) begins. As a consequence of being left alone to make his own decision, the child, without force or persuasion, will soon desire to attend school because there will be nothing distasteful about it, and nothing to engender rebellion. School will not be mandatory therefore if parents prefer teaching their child at home, this will be their business, but the reasons parents had for not sending their children to school will no longer be of concern. Regardless of how a child is taught, when he is not forced to do what he doesn't want to do he will find the greatest pleasure in learning and will be anxious to return to his studies day after day. If parents want their child to learn reading, writing and arithmetic, they must create an interest to move in this direction without blaming him if he chooses not to, but this is a very easy thing to do. When the parents feel this has been accomplished they will ask, "Would you like to go to school and learn how to read and write?" Children, without force or persuasion of any kind, will desire to learn these elementary subjects so they can do those things that depend on this basic knowledge, especially when they desire to imitate what their parents are able to do. But parents will never dictate what subjects should be studied for this blames the child if he chooses to take a different path. Remember, asking a child if he would like to learn how to tie his shoestrings is a means to greater comfort, as is learning how to eat with a knife and fork, but to ask if he would like to learn how to play the piano or listen to classical music is imposing the end you feel is better for him which you would not consider doing because this would be a selfish act. Once this difference is understood and children are allowed to move in the direction of greater happiness by choosing the subjects that interest them, there will be no conflict between parents and children in this regard. Furthermore, when children are not required by law to attend school there will be a major shift in the role of the educational system. In our present world boys and girls go to school with a certain amount of reluctance, just as boys going into the army. This is something they must do; there is no choice. But in the new world they will have a choice, and that choice will be respected. These changes are revolutionary but they will be for everyone's benefit, as you will soon observe.

Once enrolled, the child will receive a written schedule to remind him when class begins. He will know that it is important to be on time, otherwise this would be an inconvenience to the teacher (she wants to run an orderly class, not a madhouse) who is trying to do her work without any unnecessary interruptions. As a new student he will know in advance that if he disturbs the class there will be no punishment because everyone will know he couldn't help himself. If a child is too young to understand what it means that man's will is not free, and for one reason or another hurts other children or the teachers in any way, he will be given a simple choice — either to stop hurting others or to stay home from school, which will be a terrible form of punishment when he sees all the fun children are having once all tacit blame is removed. This method of punishment will only be necessary at the outset of the transition because these habits were developed over the years. However, the immediate change will prevent 99 percent of all possible hurt even here since the child will see that nobody wants to hurt him. He will soon learn — before he causes any disruption — that it is within his power to get there on time, and when it dawns on him that no one will blame him for this inconvenience, he finds no satisfaction walking in late and causing this kind of disturbance. In other words, since he knows that this annoyance will never be blamed by the teacher or students because they know his will is not free — but he knows that he doesn't have to be late if he doesn't want to — he is given no choice but to get there on time, that is, if he is interested in school. Furthermore, when he realizes that he will not be blamed for being unable to keep up with the other students, causing the teacher to work harder by the necessary questions he would have to ask in order to pass the test, he is compelled to desire being on time because he cannot get greater satisfaction in being excused for creating this unnecessary burden. In spite of the fact that authority and control are being removed as we know these, children can be controlled very easily. Parents and teachers will go out of their way to teach the basic principle because it is the key to this new world. Let us turn now to a constant source of conflict, the bedtime hour, where even here marvelous changes are about to take place.

When a child decides that he wants to go to school he will be given an alarm clock and be shown how to use it, for he will assume complete responsibility for himself even at this early age. This child will soon begin to understand that he cannot depend on his parents to wake him because this blames them should they not desire this — and because this is something he can do for himself. He also knows, absolutely and positively, that they will never insist he go to school unless he wants to since this blames him should he not desire this. Realizing that the responsibility of going or not going to school is entirely up to him, he will learn that if he wants to be rested each day it will be his job to regulate his own bedtime hour according to his physical needs. For this reason he would make sure his alarm clock was set to give him ample time. Then should someone visit his home, instead of being forced to go to bed as Durant did with his daughter, he might prefer excusing himself rather than staying up late and being exhausted the next day since the guest was more a friend to his parents than to him. If for any reason he doesn't get to school on time, this is also his business, but if his parents must now accommodate this change in schedule in order to get him to school on time, it becomes their business. If he is too young to understand the basic principle and is encroaching on their right-of-way, he should not get his way, even if it means that he miss a day of school. The worst thing parents can do is to give in to a child's demands because this teaches him to become spoiled.

"But supposing he does go to bed late and is tired the next day; what is to stop him from turning off the alarm and going back to sleep? When he awakens hours later, knowing that it would be an annoyance to the teachers to come late, who would never blame him for this, he decides to stay home for the entire day. How is he going to learn anything that way?"

There is an underlying assumption that a child will not learn what he wants to learn unless a parent pushes him. It also assumes there will be something about school that would make him prefer staying away. On the contrary children will make sure to schedule their time so nothing interferes. It is understandable that the reader is comparing the schools of today with those of tomorrow, but there is no basis for comparison. To understand why, you must bear in mind that no teacher will ever tell a child what or what not to do except where someone might get hurt. Children will be extremely anxious to go to school because they will love learning new things and there will be nothing not to like when all first blows are removed. Bear in mind that the problems which previously caused a child to resist what parents found of vital importance will not exist in the new world, consequently, he will desire to go to school every day with such eagerness (something rarely seen in today's world) that when the alarm goes off he will be anxious, not reluctant, to get there. Under these new conditions no one will have to pressure him to get out of bed. To appreciate the metamorphosis that will turn our educational system into a smorgasbord of enjoyable activities from which to choose, in the following passage we will observe a child going to school for the very first time.

When a child arrives on his first day he will be greeted by someone who will welcome him and ask if he would like to be taken on a tour. This will be his very own decision and he is not to be influenced, however, there will be no reason for him not to desire being shown around. The new schools will have huge playgrounds, swimming pools, and every conceivable kind of game, toy, and entertainment, as well as academic instruction. He will be asked if he would like to learn how to swim and do other physical things. At the same time the teacher will ask if he would like to learn how to read and write, add and subtract, not to influence him but to offer these subjects as part of the school program. Shortly thereafter he will be placed in the proper class based strictly on the subjects or activities that appeal to him. If the teacher prefers calling the student by his first or last name, this will be her business. By the same token this privilege will also be extended to the student because in the new world someone's age or stature will no longer demand more respect. No Miss or Mrs. or Master or Mister or Professor will be used (the reason will be explained in detail shortly). In addition, no teacher will ever remark about how studious, bright, scholarly, intelligent an individual is, for these words only develop fallacious slides through which a distorted version of reality is seen. Today the greatest disrespect in the world is shown by parents to children when they constantly criticize them, and by teachers to students and all those who consider themselves intellectually superior, more intelligent, more educated, to those who are judged inferior, less intelligent and less educated. We all have seen how children are scarred so deeply by the ignorance of adults who use these words because they obviously do not apply to the children who do not receive these compliments, that it is no wonder psychiatry came into existence. This proves conclusively that the expression in Chapter Four — 'Sticks and stones will break my bones but names will never hurt me' is completely fallacious and further reveals how unconscious man has been of his ignorance. As we continue to observe the truth of our nature, it becomes crystal clear that the famous expression of Shakespeare, 'To Thine Own Self Be True,' which has been alluded to throughout the book, is proven completely false, not only because it is mathematically impossible for man to be true to himself when looking through fallacious symbols but also because it is impossible not to be false to another when one recognizes in this dishonesty an advantage to oneself, for his motion is in the direction of greater satisfaction. Only when he sees there is no advantage or a still greater benefit by being truthful to others does he desire to mend his ways, but such a preference required knowledge that was not even available until now.

As we enter the Golden Age, all words that create external values will never be used or taught. Students will be given a list of words that are soon to become obsolete along with an explanation as to why they are being removed. Although there may be a number of books in circulation that still contain these words, children will understand that they were written long ago. When these words are permanently removed from our dictionaries, and a child is never made to feel the slightest bit inferior to any other child, the desire to learn will become insatiable. In a school setting such as the one described there can be no disrespect whatsoever and students who are given the utmost respect will learn to give respect to others. As these changes take effect the school's day to day operations will be noticeably different, as well as the relationship between teachers and students, because there will be an equality that was never before possible. Let us now take a closer look at how the school atmosphere is transformed from one of fear and intimidation to one of complete security by following our magic elixir, Thou Shall Not Blame.

From the day a child enrolls to the day he leaves absolutely no records will be kept as to his progress, for this imposes the fallacious standards of another's values. It is not the business of teachers to know anything about this child except his name, address, and phone number, just in case of an emergency. Just as the parents will not persuade their child what subjects to take, neither will the teacher, because this is an end the child has the right to decide for himself. The only thing that will be asked of him is if there is anything he would like to learn. Since children will be different ages when they start school depending on when they are ready, it is very possible that a five year old could be in the first grade with a seven year old, but because there will be no more bullying, and all instruction will be individualized, this will not be an important consideration.

As soon as the child has learned to read he will be shown the various books for his level of understanding without having any opinions expressed as to the superiority of one over another since this would be an indirect criticism if he should think otherwise. If a child desires to read what is being offered, or if he chooses another book that is more to his liking, this will be his decision. He may take a

511

couple of books home and within a week understand what the symbols mean. If not, the teacher will work with him until he achieves the necessary skills so that he can comfortably move on to the next level. Because children do not all learn in exactly the same way, teachers will make every effort to help students succeed according to their individual strengths so they can tackle these basic subjects. Some children may need visual reinforcement while others may need to hear the lesson more than once. Still others may need a hands-on approach in order to grasp and retain what is being taught. Finally, some will need a combination of many different modalities in order to fully integrate their newfound knowledge into a coherent whole. Computers will be of tremendous help in being able to match the child's individual learning style with the best tools available. Regardless of which teaching methods are used, a student who learns in an atmosphere of acceptance will flourish. The end result will be a child who feels good about himself and his abilities. No longer will a student be chastised for not doing his work correctly, nor will he be humiliated in other ways. Moreover, teachers will no longer be able to shift the blame to the student for failing to understand a concept when it was their responsibility to teach in a clear and understandable fashion. The buck stops here! In turn, teachers will no longer be pressured by the school administration to meet an artificial deadline which forces them to have the entire class understand the lesson at the same time. Every effort will be made so that each student can go at his or her own pace without any pressure to keep up. For example, it may take one student two weeks to learn the basic math facts while it may take another a month to learn the same lesson. Additionally, there will be no time limit as to when a student must stop what he is doing and move on to another subject, especially if a particular topic has captured his interest. How many children have been expected to stop what they were doing at the drop of a hat and switch to another subject when they were just getting started? A child may find a subject so interesting that he may desire to pursue it throughout the school year in order to learn all there is to know. Because teachers will no longer be able to judge what students should know, it will be up to the students themselves to decide what they want to learn and how much time they want to give to a particular topic. The development of magnet schools, which has recently gained popularity, is part of a growing national trend due to the realization that children have different aptitudes and predispositions, and educators are trying to respect those differences at an earlier age. For example, they now offer specialized programs emphasizing a consistent theme such as math-science or performing arts programs that cater to those who meet the criteria. The major difference between this innovative program and the program offered in the new world is that all students, not just a select few, will be able to expand their studies indefinitely and tailor a curriculum to fit their own academic interests and educational goals. This would have been unacceptable under the old educational paradigm until the student entered college or graduate school. Because the schools of yesteryear had to teach children according to a fixed curriculum, they were unable to give students the freedom to choose their own course of study for when it came time to take the competency assessment test — which was the Gold Standard of academic performance — they would have failed miserably. This would have reflected poorly on school administrators who would have been reprimanded by the Board of Education and warned that they must shape up and get their students back on track, or else. It never occurred to anyone to ask students what they wanted. Charles Nevi, a retired school administrator, has this to say about the failing of our educational system.

Low test scores, inevitable on many of the state tests that have been developed, result in blame. Fingers are pointed at teachers for inadequate preparation or for failing to teach the proper curriculum, at principals for losing control, at students for being unmotivated, at parents who don't care and at the state legislature for being unresponsive to local needs. Of course, the superintendent is rapped for not demonstrating leadership. The blame is followed by punishment. A teacher or principal is reassigned. A superintendent is fired. If individual blame is not possible, entire faculties are threatened with reassignment. If individuals or groups cannot be readily identified, then funding is withheld as an alternate form of punishment. Unfortunately, those closest to the site, especially the superintendent, usually receive the most punishment. Those equally responsible but more distant — notably legislators and state departments of education — seldom receive their deserved share of criticism for the state of educational performance.

Not frequently enough noted is the punishment of students who become the silent victims. The emphasis on high-stakes tests narrows the curriculum and places additional pressures on students. Schooling is not promoted as an experience of growing, developing and exploring interests. The purpose of schooling leans more and more to test preparation. Accountability is invariably linked to testing, usually a single test and preferably one for each grade level, based on high standards for all students and high stakes. As measures of accountability show improvement, dropout rates increase. Collateral damage may be too strong a term, but the concept is the same. The battle for accountability must be won at any cost. Unseen and unheard victims include the students. This throw-the bastards-out mentality offers little consideration to identifying what the actual problems may be and what can be done to correct them. The blame and punishment are in themselves a cleansing process, a ritual sacrifice to the gods of accountability that will magically result in an improved educational system. It should be obvious to any thoughtful observer that equating accountability with blame and punishment doesn't make good educational sense. The success of the educational process depends on too many people and too many variables for this blaming approach to be useful. Also, it frequently results in punishing the wrong people, the students being the best example, and allows others to shirk responsibility for failing to provide adequate resources.

We can see how teachers have been caught in the middle of a pecking order where those at the top are able to shift the blame and punish everyone down the line, forcing a no-win situation. Teachers and administrators have been operating out of fear that they may be the next ones held accountable for the failure of their students to make the necessary grades, when all along it was due to a fundamental flaw in the system. It is easy for those who set national and state policy to blame those not responsible because it eliminates the need to identify the root cause of the problem. Presently, the state has the authority to determine what is best for all students which is to attain a liberal arts education, and instructors have no leeway but to teach exactly what they are told. Based on this educational philosophy, policymakers believe that giving students too much flexibility would prevent them from becoming well-rounded individuals; in other words, they believe they know what is better for the students than the students themselves. But this is advance blame and can no longer be used to justify the forcing of students to take courses they don't want. Let us highlight the main points we have covered thus far.

Schools will be run like any other business offering students the kind of knowledge they want to buy. Teachers will engage students in activities that are a means to an end, not an end in itself, and they will teach only those subjects that their students want to learn about. All subjects will be selected by the students themselves, and it will be the students who have the final say as to what they desire to study. What interests them while in school will be their business, no one else's. They will go to school just as long as it serves their purpose...as long as they see some value to what they are learning. Therefore, they will be given an opportunity to engage in all types of activities, but under no circumstances will they ever be blamed or looked down upon if they find that a particular career track is not for them. As part of the course offerings, teachers will mention the various academic programs that are available but there will be no penalty if a student desires to take other classes such as art, physical education, or dance. A teacher will simply show these children the various things they can learn without trying to influence them which is a criticism should they desire what she does not desire for them. Parents, too, will present opportunities but not stand in judgment of a child whose desire is not what they prefer. With so many choices at their disposal, everyone will find something of interest. You may be thinking that if this liberal system was ever instituted, students would want to play all day and do no work. This is a false assumption which is predicated on our present educational system. When there is no distinction between required and elective courses, and students are absolutely free to choose what they want, you will be surprised how they will desire to study the subjects that will help them further their career goals, but remember that their choice of a profession will no longer be influenced by a political, educational, or corporate agenda. Students, for the very first time, will be intrinsically motivated to go in the direction they have chosen for themselves. They will achieve more than ever thought possible because their hopes, dreams, and aspirations will be their very own from the moment they enter the classroom. If students are interested in taking courses in a particular field, they will be guided by the standards set by that profession. The students will want to know before they leave school that they have met the highest standards possible because no one will be questioning their ability once they go out into the working world. At the very same time they will be prevented from hurting others with a first blow by the basic principle. Just as there are traffic regulations in the new world that tell us it is wrong to do certain things because someone might get injured, when they realize there will be no blame should someone get hurt by their actions, they will prefer obeying what might otherwise place them in a position where no satisfaction can be gotten. Consequently, the school system will set up rules that everyone will desire to follow. Once the basic principle is put into practice, and all of the distaste is taken out of learning, the behavioral problems that were once a constant source of disruption will be entirely eliminated. Let us continue to observe the beneficial changes that must come about as a result of our basic principle.

In the new world, just as it will be unimportant for teachers to concern themselves with a student's academic interests it will also be unimportant for them to concern themselves with a student's talents because this, too, will no longer be the business of anybody but that student. Someone may be drawn to a particular musical instrument but may prefer any number of instruments, or an altogether unrelated field. By asking if he would like to learn the piano it is possible that he could be slightly influenced and since this is not a means to an end but the end someone else may want for him, he must be left alone. What often occurs is that certain standards are set up by others and they unwittingly push the child in a direction that is not his own. Once again, it is perfectly all right for a teacher to ask a student if he would like to learn something just as long as she is not imposing her desire as to what she thinks is best for him or what might be better called the end, not a means to an end, she selects. If the student wants to learn anything at all, including how to swim, he will approach the teacher with his request. Many students will prefer competing in chess, checkers, swimming, boxing, mathematical games, etc., while others will prefer to read, write, dance, sing, act, do tricks and a host of other things. If ten children choose to be in track and field, they will desire to compete against each other. Contests will still exist as long as they have a mathematical standard by which the winner can be determined since this will help children identify whether they have genuine talent, although applause meters and judges will become obsolete because they do not employ a mathematical standard. There is no question that some people are naturally talented in music, athletics, or what have you. This is why every competition possible will be designed to test the mettle of each individual, for this is the only way a person can get to know himself. The ones who lose in sports will search for an activity in which they can succeed, and if they cannot find any then they will desist from competition. They will look for some other means of developing their innate abilities, but when no one blames them for losing even though everyone applauds the winner, they will be helped, not hurt, because they will get an accurate picture of themselves. Just because some people can do things better than others does not make them deserving of more respect, and when a child understands what it means that man's will is not free he will know instantly that the applause for another is in no way a discredit to himself. Sports can still be enjoyed when the competition is evenly matched even if the goal is not to play in the major leagues. Children who do not want to compete in organized sports will look for other avenues to express themselves. For example, a child may discover he has a talent for playing the guitar. If he has true musical ability — and he will find out soon enough — there will be nothing stopping him from developing in that direction with the dream of becoming famous. A genuinely talented individual will move in the direction of development especially if he recognizes the value to himself, without any form of advance blame being necessary. If an Einstein is among these children and is left alone he will be naturally drawn to science but this will be his business, not that of his parents or teachers. Regardless of the field that is chosen, no individual will be considered one ounce more valuable than another. This is a small sampling of the revolutionary changes about to take place the moment all forms of judgment and advance blame are removed. It is difficult not to compare the schools of today with those of tomorrow but, once again, there is no basis for comparison. You must remember that no teacher or parent will criticize a child's career path because what he does with his life is his business. God is determined to see that every baby born regardless of his race, color or sex is given an equal opportunity of finding happiness. All people have the same intrinsic value regardless of who they are, or the gifts with which they have been endowed.

Based on our new understanding of man's nature, there is a subtle form of disrespect that exists in our school system by the method of questioning teachers use. As we saw in the chapter on marriage, by asking a question you are actually asking someone to do you a favor. It is hidden behind an innocent request but can be equally destructive because it is an indirect way of telling someone what to do. By blaming those for not knowing an answer, as teachers do to students, are we not judging that this is something they should know? Asking these type questions (the answers of which are already known to the one asking) is a form of advance blame by judging what is right for someone else. When a teacher realizes that this is advance blame and a form of criticism, she is compelled to think like never before so as not to do those things that embarrass others and look foolish in her own eyes. Not only are the students hurt by these questions, but they have the right-of-way to refuse answering them because to satisfy the teacher's desire they must do something for her, whereas to satisfy their desire not to answer, she doesn't have to do anything for them. Since there is no way a student can be called upon without blaming him in advance for not knowing what she thinks he should know, the teacher is given no choice but to eliminate questions as a means of instruction. Let's put it another way.

We have already seen that the relationship between a teacher and a student becomes equivalent to that of a seller and a buyer. Teachers are there to sell what students want to learn, not what they want to teach. Although they will be completely free to teach what they want, students will have the right-of-way to learn whatever interests them which means that they can reject what the teacher might assign. Following this reasoning the only two questions allowed by the teacher that do not comprise a form of tacit blame will be, "Is there something you would like to learn?" and "Do you have any questions?" Because of this new method of imparting knowledge, the burden of the teacher's inadequacy cannot be shifted to the student, therefore when she asks, "Is there anything you do not understand," the student will reply, "I didn't understand so and so." Because the teacher cannot blame students in any way for not understanding the work, she will have to make everything crystal clear so that these questions will not come up. If she was not precise in her presentation she may be swamped with questions to reveal her own inadequacy, and since she cannot criticize them, as well as having to put forth a great deal of energy explaining the same lesson over and over again, she will begin to instruct in such a manner that there will rarely be any need for these questions or for further clarification.

It should be understood that when students ask questions of their teachers it is a horse of another color since it is the teacher's job to offer assistance to the students who desire it. Students will be permitted to ask any questions they wish once they have been taught the type that cannot be asked (questions that have nothing to do with the subject under discussion and impose an obligation on the person asked) because the students are the BUYERS and the teachers are the SELLERS. If the students don't understand something, they will approach the teacher for help. If they should give incorrect answers in any of the written tests it would be their right-of-way to question the teacher about anything they do not understand because this is what she was hired to do. Under no circumstance will teachers ever approach a student with a question unless it is to prevent a hurt of some kind or unless they are responding to a direct question. Students will do everything to find the answers they are looking for before coming to the teacher for help because they wouldn't want to take advantage of the fact that she is available to help them if they really need her. For example, if a student was reading Shakespeare and came to a passage that was confusing, he would be compelled to refer to another book for an explanation because it is impossible to desire asking favors, even of teachers, when one can find answers without the need to ask for help. Therefore, anything a student can do for himself, he will, and all other questions will be directed to the teacher who will be happy to offer assistance, if necessary. There may be times when the teacher doesn't know the answer to a question. Unless she knows that there is only one possible answer, an answer that is absolutely correct, she will not be of any help whatsoever because she would only be giving her opinion, and this would indirectly blame others for having a different point of view. In this situation the teacher would simply say, "I don't know for sure what he means." She may then direct the student to another source that could possibly help him in his search for the correct answer. This prevents her from acting as if she knows when she really doesn't and gives students the opportunity to express their own opinions on subjects that are open to interpretation. For example, students may offer their thoughts on how to use resources in the most efficient manner when funding a project. This may bring everyone's ideas together in order to come up with a practical solution. Often students are terrified to express their opinion or to let a teacher know they don't understand something because she blames them indirectly by a show of displeasure, and when others see this they will add to the student's humiliation by laughing and making hurtful remarks. But when there are no comments or subtle displays of disapproval, students will not hesitate to ask questions if something is unclear or to offer any suggestions that could add to the discussion. Now let us observe how a day's lesson is reinforced, and how students will monitor their very own progress.

When a lesson is given those who are interested in reviewing the material will be permitted to take the lesson home with them. Students who feel they have fallen behind and need extra help in understanding the work may also take home a book for review according to the suggestion of the teacher. She may suggest that they come to her after class for additional help if there is something they still don't understand. If that is the case, they will approach the teacher after hours and she will either tutor them directly or recommend other books that may help them with their studies. In the future, the role of the teacher will be that of facilitator, not enforcer of an arbitrary curriculum where children need to be constantly monitored. Presently, teachers use certain methods of testing to see if students are grasping the material, and the written exam has become an integral part of the evaluation process equivalent to other forms of testing which are used to determine the student's final grade. You will see why all testing that does not have a mathematical standard will be completely eliminated, although there will be many fields where the knowledge is not yet available for the school to set up any such standard. In addition, testing will only be done for the student's benefit, not the teacher's. For self-evaluation purposes only, the teacher may ask the students if they would like to see how they are progressing by providing a written test on one sheet of paper and the answers on another, or she may decide to return the test not only with how many answers they got right or wrong, but with specific corrections showing them exactly where they made mistakes so they can improve. In either case, the students will judge whether they are prepared to move to the next level. It will be strictly up to them to make this determination based on the results of their test. Should they discover that they did not do well, they will know their area of weakness so they can prepare for the next exam. The difference between the old system and the new is that everything the student does or doesn't do in regard to his education will be entirely up to him. Under no circumstances will students be placed under an obligation to do anything.

"Then how would it be possible for a teacher to give children something to do at home, when this blames them for not doing it? Isn't this the same as a teacher telling a child what time to be in school?"

"No it isn't. The time is the teacher's business, but what children do at home is their business. Homework, for the very first time, will not be something they have to do but will want to do because they will never accomplish their purpose otherwise. In our present system when a standard is set up by a teacher, students are criticized for falling short and praised for doing well which makes some feel inferior to others. Once all criticism has been removed, these standards will have absolutely no value because students will be driven by their own personal goals, nothing else. When there is no criticism, there will be no need for praise for the same reason. Now, once again, pay close attention to how our basic principle brings about marvelous changes.

The teacher will continue to design every conceivable kind of written test so the student can determine how he is progressing. In elementary school where the subject matter is a means to an end, the teacher will help the student recognize when he is ready to move to the next level of difficulty. She will also have the responsibility of helping students determine whether they have a thorough understanding of the subject matter and are ready to move on to a higher grade. When a student feels ready for grade number two, three, or four, or ready to change schools from grammar to junior high or junior high to high school, he will announce this to those who will help him register for the upcoming year. This does not mean that if a student fails the test he has the right-of-way to pass to the next grade — although he could enter if he wanted to. But just as a student will want to be on time for class so as not to be an extra burden to the teacher by the necessary questions he would have to ask, when he realizes that by moving to another grade he might not be able to keep up with the other students which would cause the teacher to work harder by having to explain things over and over again, he would rather pass the test before moving on so that he would not be a burden. Besides, of what advantage would there be to enter the next grade — which indicates a complete grasp of the material — when in the final examination before leaving school if he should not be satisfied with the results, he would never desire to accept a position doing what he knows he isn't completely qualified for when he also knows that his employer must excuse any mistakes he makes which he can never justify. Just as we will never pass judgment on whether people are sufficiently trained to drive a motor vehicle without hurting others because this is their business, not ours, so will we as teachers never pass judgment on whether our students are sufficiently trained to leave school and drive their profession or career, whatever you wish to call it, through the traffic of the economic world without hurting us because this is also their business. When it comes time for the exam teachers will recommend certain books and pages to be studied in preparation, but students will never have to prepare a paper or write a thesis to be evaluated in a subjective manner when this has no relationship whatsoever to the skills one must have in order to earn a living. From this time forward students will only be evaluated according to a mathematical standard, not a teacher's subjective point of view.

The final examination will be the most thorough and toughest ever given and may take several days or even weeks. Just as a teacher will no longer call on individual students as a method of instruction, she will no longer use verbal questions for testing purposes when the answer is already known to her since, once again, this can only be done to find out if students know what she thinks they should. This new method of teaching prevents students from being criticized by the uninvited questions of teachers who will no longer judge the rightness or wrongness of their present knowledge. Remember, what they know or don't know is no one's business unless the results of a test are being used to determine their qualifications for a particular job or unless they have not yet become citizens and are still too young to assume responsibility for themselves — but this does not take away from the fact that employers must assume responsibility for everybody they hire. The only thing that matters is what students desire to know for their own purposes, which is related to what they want to become. Therefore, the teacher will mark the exam and return it with the answers clearly visible so the students can judge for themselves whether they are ready to move to the next grade or leave school and enter the job market. They will get immediate feedback to see how well they did by comparing their test marks with the correct answers — just as they have done throughout the school year. The students will be shown the questions they got right and the ones they got wrong but will receive no letter grade because this would permit students to be satisfied with a certain percentage of wrong answers, and it may give them a false sense of what they actually know. This marking system has made it easy for students to gloss over their mistakes. In the new world students will be shown where they need improvement and will study until they are satisfied that they have a complete understanding of the subject matter, which may necessitate that they take the exam again (in this situation it won't matter how many times the exam is taken). Consequently, there will be no such thing as a passing or failing grade, just students moving on when they have mastered the material. How is it possible for them to desire cheating under these conditions? There will be no more grades, no report cards, no diplomas or titles because this would indicate that we have judged them qualified, whereas they will remain in school until they judge themselves qualified according to whatever standards the school

523

has available. Eliminating all grades also prevents students from being falsely identified as A students, B students, C students, etc. [Note: Getting all the answers correct does not make someone an A student, nor does getting three quarters of the answers wrong make someone a D student. The most anyone can say is that the student got this many correct and this many incorrect, which is a true statement]. This prevents students from defining themselves by an inaccurate label that they will carry with them all through life. This also allows the students to approach their teachers without the slightest fear because the teachers will no longer have the authority to determine who passes and who fails. The students, knowing that their job performance depends on the necessary skills they develop while in school, will hold themselves to a high standard of excellence. When it's time to leave school and start their careers, students will simply hand in their books. There will be no more class graduations since everyone will be leaving school at different times depending on when they successfully meet the requirements of their chosen field. Since there is no end point except in relation to each student's personal aspirations, graduations will no longer serve the same purpose they once did. This does not mean there won't be individual celebrations to recognize those who have reached a certain level of achievement, but they will not be used as a reward given to some students and not to others. All students are moving in the direction of greater satisfaction — and they will all leave school sooner or later. Consequently, there will be no more dropouts as such because every student will eventually drop out and the reason for their leaving will be nobody's business but their own. Furthermore, there will be no senior proms as they exist today. The students who are considered good looking are the ones who get the date and when prom night rolls around they feel on top of the world, while those who don't feel just the opposite. For these students, prom night symbolizes everything they don't possess and cannot have. Eligibility to become prom queen has excluded many young girls from the competition. How will this be justified in the new world knowing that the standards doing the judging are not only fallacious, but have caused so many young girls to be deeply wounded? As a consequence, prom night is going to come to an end out of absolute necessity. If there is a celebration to mark the end of a school year, these hurtful rituals will have long since become obsolete.

When a student is ready to leave for the working world — and he will know based on the results of his final exam — he will turn in a card with his name and address and will be notified where and when to report if he proves qualified for the job. The student, knowing that the employer would never blame him for making mistakes, is compelled to prepare himself so that if he is hired he will never do anything to jeopardize his profits. If two students are equally qualified the employer will flip a coin to give both students a fair chance. If one hundred apply for a position that calls for fifty, an equitable manner of selection will be devised. You may be wondering how it is possible for a student entering a career such as the medical profession that involves a great deal of study to know he is qualified without being thoroughly tested by professors before being turned loose. Wouldn't the universities be releasing a lot of ill-prepared doctors, and therefore wouldn't a diploma of graduation be necessary? Let me show you what harm a diploma can do by referring back to Chapter Seven: The Wisdom of Socrates.

In our present world a doctor is allowed to treat the sick, operate on them, administer drugs, etc. on the reasonable assumption that when he received his degree he automatically became qualified. But if he is not, that is, if the knowledge taught was inadequate despite all that he learned, then he is actually permitted by law to risk hurting his patients with impunity because he is not a quack, not an imposter, not someone who didn't study hard and pass all the necessary examinations, but a genuine healer, and to prove it we are constantly reminded not to consult those who are not doctors. How many times have you heard the expression, "He is not a doctor," or how about this one, "How would you know, you're not a doctor," or the expression, "This formula is recommended by doctors." Almost every day you hear some reference being made over television. When all tests used to determine his qualifications are withdrawn (in the new world, that is); when he is not granted this right by the university and state to practice on the bodies of live people, then he must determine for himself his qualifications which brings about a fantastic change. He knows that should anything happen to hurt his patients as a result of what was prescribed there is no way he can shift his responsibility because no one is holding him responsible. Everybody is admitting that he had no choice but to hurt them this way which compels him, of his own free will, or desire, to be absolutely certain (no opinions, no guessing, no assumption that the drug administered can't do any harm and may do some good if only to satisfy their fears) about everything he does. The great fear that they might get worse unless he prescribes something makes him deceive his patients about his great healing powers which allows him to be dishonest with himself; but when it becomes impossible to lie to them since they are not blaming or questioning his ability, he must be absolutely honest with himself and others. He realizes for the very first time that they could get worse because of, and better in spite of, his treatments. Because doctors are under a compulsion to earn a living like everybody else, it is suggested that we have a six month check up. He also recommends that the foreskin be removed along with the appendix and tonsils. The only proof that these things are of no value to the body is the fact that their removal is sanctioned by the medical profession which lays its arguments not so much on why it is better or healthier, but on who says it is. There are times when it is absolutely necessary to remove the appendix to save someone's life, just as there are times when a leg must be amputated, but how many times have tonsils and appendixes been removed not because there was any danger to the patient's life but only because these were considered vestigial organs. According to ancient religious custom there was a time when the entire body was sacrificed. The medical profession would never have absolved their conscience with the knowledge that circumcision was healthier, but when this meant millions of dollars in the pockets of doctors who now could justify getting all parents of infant boys to spend their money, not just Jewish parents, they were given no choice. However, it is important to emphasize that this is not a criticism of those who benefited from this opportunity because they, just like all of us, are constantly moving in the direction of greater satisfaction. It is only when these principles are thoroughly understood by all mankind that this Great Transition can come about by removing the factors that make someone desire to gain at someone else's expense because not to would make him a loser.

Every student knows that when he leaves school to earn a living, no one will ever blame him no matter how much he hurts others by his mistakes. Consequently, employers will not have to screen any applicant for a job because they will know he is completely qualified, otherwise he could not risk a position from which no satisfaction can be gotten unless a perfect job is done. Remember, a student can leave school at any time and pretend that he is adequately trained to do what he is being paid to do, but should he make mistakes that hurt his employer he will know that the employer will never blame him because the responsibility was his since he hired him which deprives the new employee of any satisfaction in being excused for pretending that he was adequately qualified when he knew he was not. This forces each student to learn all that school has to teach regarding the career selected so that if mistakes are made it would be through carelessness — which must also come to an end — or because there was not enough knowledge available to prevent what happened except by not taking on the risk, as was explained in relation to doctors. This places the full responsibility of when our students leave college not on whether they get a passing mark, for there will be no such thing, but strictly on whether they are satisfied with the results of their test. If a boy leaves before he has selected some kind of trade or profession because he finds studying too difficult and ends up taking a job as a laborer, no one will be comparing him to those who become brain surgeons. How many well-meaning parents pushed children into careers they believed were right...but for whom? As a consequence, children ended up miserable because they were not given permission to find their calling in life. God has purposely given everyone different abilities so that each person can fall into a particular group that enables the whole to function in a perfectly balanced mathematical equation — but this does not mean that one person is any better than another. I will show you that this laborer will not be respected less or the brain surgeon more; that his job will not be considered less important and he will be judged just as educated as anybody else. In previous chapters, you have seen that no one is beautiful or ugly, but who would believe that no one is educated, uneducated, intelligent or unintelligent. Although the word education is being defined, not beauty, the same principle applies.

"You can't be serious! Are you trying to tell me that this is simply

527

a word to describe certain other differences that do not exist, and that education is a word like beauty, or educated is like beautiful?"

That's exactly right, there is no difference between them; they are both words that project a nonexisting value. To explain the reason for this, we must go back to our earlier discussion regarding the eyes.

Take a look at the pictures of these two girls and tell me which one you consider more beautiful. I already explained the reason words like beautiful are going to become obsolete, therefore, you won't be able to tell me which one is more beautiful, but you can tell me which one appeals to you more. Although a person cannot help being born with particular features, and education can be acquired, the word educated is identical to the word beautiful. For any word to be symbolic of something real we must be able to see the reality through the symbol. We see cat, mouse, rat, dog, tree, apple, orange, sun, moon, book, male, female, etc. all through the symbols, but can you see a beautiful girl or an educated one through word symbols? You may respond that Elizabeth Taylor looks beautiful to you, but supposing someone else says she is not beautiful to him? Judges at a beauty contest don't all agree and in some parts of the world low hanging breasts, a huge rear end and big abdomens are considered the ideal. In other words, since a value is not contained in external substance, it cannot exist apart from the individual who gives that something its value. It could be that you like one girl better than another, but this is your personal preference, not an external reality. By saying a girl is beautiful, it implies by its opposite, that some girls are ugly. You are saying she contains a value that other girls do not have and you have placed other girls in a definite position of inferiority. There is a world of difference between saying, "This girl appeals to me because her nose is straight, her teeth together, her breasts pointed and firm, her skin smooth and soft" — and saying, "I like her because she is beautiful." Saying "this girl appeals to me" makes no one feel inferior because the expression does not create a standard for everyone. Even to qualify it by saying "she is beautiful to me" does not rectify the inaccuracy of the description because it is mathematically impossible for the word to describe anything externally real. The sun is not beautiful although on certain days I like it better than on others. It is simply a ball of fire. Many people resenting the word beautiful being applied to physical characteristics they did not possess, and yet wanting a share of this value would parry with beauty of the soul, not of the body. By defining it differently they derived a compensating satisfaction, as if definition determines what exists. Now if I draw a picture of a dog and put the word dog right next to it, no one will say the symbol is inaccurate because it is not, but try to do the same thing with the word education. Just as in the word beautiful, it is projected upon this screen of differences and then when you see these differences with your eyes it appears that this, too, exists as part of the external world because it is circumscribed with the word. This is why the word education is equally as inaccurate as the word beautiful in describing reality. However, before you jump to any conclusions, let me explain certain facts.

Supposing I draw a picture of an object and then call it X. If I point to the pictured object and say X, wouldn't you know I am talking about the object pictured? And if you have already experienced the object, wouldn't X then become related to the pictured object and the real object? Now if I drew a picture of the sun and then called it X, wouldn't this symbol suffice? What difference does it make what name is used when the difference between the sun and other objects can be seen through the symbol. The moon, sun, stars, sky, clouds, etc., as apple, orange, peach, plum and pear are words that accurately circumscribe specific differences that exist in the external world; they are actually pictures of these objects and when we see the words that symbolize them we then see in our mind a picture of these existing objects.

"Well that's certainly clear enough; but what are you driving at?"

"What I am driving at is this: If education was something externally real like the sun, the moon, an apple, orange, peach, etc., then any symbol would suffice to circumscribe this difference called education, but instead everybody and his brother define education according to what they think it is. The word education is assumed as symbolizing something externally real, whatever it may be, and then everybody employs syllogistic reasoning to confirm what they think this reality is. Our description of the sun may be inaccurate but we know this ball of fire exists. However, we assume education exists and we try to confirm its existence by giving an accurate description."

529

"But there is not a person living today who does not believe in the existence of education; it is considered an external reality."

"I know this, but if it were proven that there is no such thing as education, could we define the word?"

"Of course not. How is it possible to describe something that doesn't exist? But as far as I'm concerned, it does exist. I, for one, don't have a good education, and are you trying to tell me that I can't acquire this education by going back to school or reading more books on my own?"

I'm not denying that a person goes to school, graduates, reads many books, but what has this to do with the word education? In reality, the word education is no different than the word beautiful because it creates and then projects a non-existing value. In other words, when a word like education is used to describe certain differences, as when beautiful is applied to definite physical characteristics, these differences are real and a part of the external world, but the word contains a judgment of value and, consequently, can have no corresponding accuracy. If education was something actually real, then any symbol would suffice to separate it from other external differences, as the word sun distinguishes this bit of substance from the word moon. Again, let me clarify this.

We often notice two or more objects or patterns of behavior that are alike but have slight differences. Therefore, the shade of difference observed in this external substance is real and can be easily identified when given a separate name by means of a new word symbol. For example, many automobile manufacturers work to differentiate and distinguish their models from the standpoint of exterior and interior design. Giving each model a separate name allows the buyer to see the differences that set them apart. But all the words in the world such as mature, educated, intelligent, etc., are not going to better describe something that is not a part of the real world. It is this difference that either confused epistemology or those who tried to understand what the epistemologists themselves could not.

To understand what is actually going on with words in order to illustrate why the word education falls into the same category as the word beautiful, let us draw a picture of a girl, a picture of an apple, a picture of a boy and a picture of an orange. We now have four pictured objects. We shall call the first object number one, the second object number two, the third object number three, and the fourth object number four. If I ask you to identify each of these objects this would not be difficult to do. Now let us also draw a picture of exactly what you did in your life that makes you consider yourself educated. We will use Durant as an example. Suppose he has read 10,000 books. Next we shall estimate the number of grades he passed, and the diplomas and degrees he received. Let us say 100; okay so far? Let us imagine a picture is drawn of his entire life or better yet let us say a moving picture was taken of his life. To compare, we shall also take a moving picture of the life of this person to whom we referred to as illiterate. We shall call the first life, object number five and the other life, object number six. If I asked you to describe object number five you would say that this individual went to school, read 10,000 books, passed to the 100th grade and as a description of object number 6 you would say that this individual never went to school, never learned to read or write, worked hard on a farm, did this and did that. Now tell me...is it humanly possible for any person seeing these pictured differences to get confused as to which numbers they refer? Think carefully about this. If there is no chance of confusion by symbolizing them in this manner, why are two of these circumscribed differences symbolized in a manner that does confuse? In other words, aren't there differences of opinion as to which people are educated? I purposely drew a strong line between the two individuals pictured so there would be no disagreement. If it is possible to identify differences in such a manner that no opinions are necessary, wouldn't you say that this method of symbolism is mathematically accurate and preferable? I am not denying that a person goes to school, graduates, reads many books, etc., but what has this to do with the word education? "I grant that he can read various things, that he can pass various tests and that he can do any number of things, just as I'm sure there are people like Gibbon and Durant who read many more books than the average college professor and perhaps could surpass all of the requirements with accuracy and skill and graduate with honors, but what has this to do with the word education?"

Just as the word beautiful does not symbolize anything real, neither does the word education. This word also projects a value as existing externally as if the world is divided up into stratified layers of importance — but value is a personal relation between you and something else. I must reemphasize that when a word like education is used to describe certain differences, as is beautiful when applied to definite physical characteristics, these differences (brown hair, blond hair, reads 1000 books a week, reads no books) are real and a part of the external world but the words beautiful, handsome, educated that are used to describe these differences contain a judgment of value and, consequently, can have no corresponding accuracy. If two individuals are standing side by side and you have never met either but one is completely illiterate while the other has read everything written, you would desire, under the banner of free will, to give much greater respect to the latter. To be considered an educated person in the present world means that others will react to this knowledge of your education with greater admiration. People are also respected and given great admiration when they are considered beautiful or handsome because they possess values that other people admire. The reason people take such pride in possessing the values contained in these words is because there is so much disrespect shown to those who do not possess them. Consequently, to lose these values called beautiful, educated and handsome, you must also lose this reaction of others which offers such tremendous satisfaction. When respect levels off because there is no more criticism and ridicule, these differences will not be missed one iota nor will these differences be envied. However, in the new world it is mathematically impossible to give greater respect to these differences not only because man's will is not free which prevents the former from being blamed, but also because it is impossible to credit the other with a great education when the word education becomes obsolete. The slightest shade of disrespect is a hurt which will never be blamed in the new world, consequently, all words that show this disrespect such as beautiful, handsome, educated, brilliant plus all their synonyms and antonyms must be removed out of absolute necessity. No one wants to have something taken away which has been a source of satisfaction through the years. Do you think Elizabeth Taylor would like to hear that she is not beautiful? Would Gibbon and Durant like to hear that they are not educated? If I took an illiterate person and told you that you are no more educated than he is, wouldn't you resent it?

"Yes, I think I would."

And if I took several girls considered extremely homely, put them alongside Marilyn Monroe and then told the actress that she is not one whit more beautiful than these other girls, wouldn't she resent this and consider it somewhat of an insult? It is true though that Durant would not have liked the thought of losing this value called education, just as Paul Newman would not have liked losing this value called handsome. We have finally arrived at the heart of our problem and you can see the difficulty when you realize how the college students and professors would react to the news that they are not one bit more educated than anybody else. Our scientific world has not yet acknowledged that man does not have five senses, and religion has not yet received the news that man's will is not free. Once these various people understand that the truth will not hurt them but will only help remove the evil in the world, they will be grateful for what they have learned. The same thing applies here. Only in the very beginning does it hurt to think that you are no more educated than another — regardless of what this other person has done with his life — because it appears that something of value is being taken away from you, which is not the case at all as you will see. Today a great satisfaction is attained by having what others cannot get, but when others can acquire it without hurting you while allowing you to get more of what you like, can you object? Because of these words half the human race was treated with disrespect, but now for the very first time all of us deserve and will be treated with equal respect which heretofore has been denied.

At this juncture, however, and for the purpose of showing you again how words judge half the human race as uneducated, even those who graduate college, I shall breakdown and analyze thoroughly Will Durant's definition of education in order to show how confusing it has become to define a word that does not symbolize reality. Bear in mind that he knew nothing of a new world and had no idea that this word must come to an end because everybody acquires an education from the time of their birth. To define education would be equivalent to defining a human being. We are born human beings, each and every one of us. To say he is not a human being is to say that he is

533

not acquiring an education when everything learned, regardless of what it is, is an education. Nevertheless, let me show you again what happens with words. I will quote a passage by Durant and then analyze it as we proceed. Perhaps the reader will be able to understand more clearly what I am talking about.

He writes, "I believe that it is through reading rather than through high school and college that we at last acquire a liberal education." But if there isn't a way to define the word education, then his last statement is not symbolic of anything real. What if Durant had been shown the truth about man's relationship with the external world and the fact that the word education cannot be defined? Consequently, when someone listens to Durant's definition, most of you are not disagreeing about whether certain type reading material is better for one person than another — as one type food might be better for one person than another — you are disagreeing only because Durant did not qualify the type of reading necessary to acquire a liberal education. Durant, however, not understanding the difference between words and reality continues to give external value to something that has absolutely no existence, for he then goes on to say, "Mr. Everett Dean Martin has admirably described his book to those who wish to know what it is to be mature." In this context the word *mature* is a synonym for *liberal education*. And he uses the phrase *liberal education* instead of *education* as a means of categorizing a certain type of education so the universities are not up in arms. Therefore he avoids, in a subtle way, too much criticism by the school system because teachers, professors and educators in general like to believe that education belongs exclusively to them. According to Durant, these colleges do not produce an educated man and that is why he was disliked by a great many professors. The implication was that the schools and universities were actually preventing people from getting a *real education* which was a harsh criticism since the very purpose of going to college, or any school of higher learning, was to get a quality education. They resented his criticizing their method of acquiring what everybody agrees has actual existence. Are you beginning to recognize how an assumption for a major premise, and syllogistic reasoning to give it form, can make something appear realistic? No one is discussing whether education is or is not a reality, but only whether the school should have a monopoly on it. Similarly, no one is discussing whether man's will is free because its reality is taken for granted. The arguments are strictly over definition, as if definition confirms reality which it does not.

Will Durant, although he was not a university graduate, learned more from an informal education than he would have ever learned from a formal education. If diplomas were given for informal knowledge he not only would have received a Ph.D. for his efforts but he would have received a Ph-Ph-Ph-Ph.D. He had gone far beyond what the university could have taught him and he resented the preemption of the schools that there was only one way to become educated. He began to look down on them just as Edward Gibbon did. It irked him to such a degree because he considered education as something a definite part of the real world, that when Spencer defined it as 'the adjustment of the individual to the environment,' Durant opposed him by saying, "Today we think a man is educated if he can read the newspapers morning, noon and night; but though our colleges turn out graduates like so many standardized Fords every year there is a visible dearth of real culture in our life; we are a nation with a hundred thousand schools and hardly a dozen educated men." Considering this an external reality of great value and resenting the fact that millions of people imagine themselves educated because they completed high school and college, Durant resorts to a definition for the purpose of showing that the prevailing conception of education does not determine an educated man, and he points out why by relating other values which he judges are external to his own conception of education. According to his definition a person acquires a liberal education when he becomes intelligent and mature and since these college graduates do not develop into this they cannot be educated from his point of view. He is able to do this in a logical manner through the use of synonyms that also do not have any external value. At this point he qualifies the subjects necessary to acquire this liberal education, this maturity, and ridicules what the graduates of our colleges do with their learning, criticizing them still further for considering useless what he has found to be otherwise. Durant quotes Heine to support his view: "The Romans could not have had much time left to conquer the world if they first had to learn

Latin. But though the languages of Greece and Rome are necessary only to philologists, the literature of these nations is almost indispensable to education. A man can conceivably ignore Virgil and Horace, Lucretius and Cicero, Tacitus and Marcus Aurelius, and still become mature; but of all possible instruments of education that I know, none is so fine and sure as a study of Greek life in all the varied scope of its democracy and imperialism, its oratory and drama, its poetry and history, its architecture and sculpture, its science and philosophy. It is well that Latin and Greek are passing from our colleges for they consumed a hundred times more effort than they were worth. Let a student absorb the life and letters of the Periclean age, the Renaissance, and the Enlightenment, and he will have a better education than any college can give him. How dare these people consider themselves educated just because they graduated college." Is it any wonder he was so disliked by those he had excluded from this liberal education, namely the college graduates? Is it any wonder he became so popular among those who realized, for the very first time, that they didn't really have to go to school to acquire this great benefit called education? Durant then states, "No wonder that Mr. Wells and others have questioned the use of a college education." This is pessimism exaggerated to make a point. He apologizes to the schools by blaming Mr. Wells; "but it is well that someone should check us up in our notion that the multiplication of schools and graduates can make us into an intelligent people." He has now replaced the word 'intelligent' for *liberal education* and *mature*. Take note how he further separates the school system from this scarce value by saying that regardless of how many schools we have there is a visible dearth of real culture in our life. The term 'real culture' has now become for him a synonym like the word *mature* for obtaining this liberal education. According to Durant, because there are people in the world who have a certain amount of fallacious culture (again this syllogistic reasoning), he makes sure that you understand he is referring to 'real culture' which are still words without any substance. Again, Durant separates the values he has found preferable and projects them through his eyes upon differences that, although they are externally undeniable, are differences without any external value. It is true that his reasoning is logical, that is, it gives the appearance

536

of being true simply because he sees these external values with direct perception. Do you see what he's done? He has separated an educated man from a college graduate and the colleges would resent it because they, like the graduates, wanted to consider themselves educated. I am not criticizing him at all but showing how certain words can even confuse the mind of an individual who is supposed to be a profound thinker. My saying that there are people in the world who have a certain amount of fallacious culture is my way of showing the reader how easy it is for words to make something appear undeniably real.

Durant continues to defend his definition of education by trying to prove Spencer wrong. He writes, "This mechanical and practical education produces partial, not total men; it subordinates civilization to industry, biology to physics, taste and manners to wealth." In this passage he begins to multiply his synonyms of *liberal education, mature, real culture, intelligence,* by including 'total complete men,' as if this too were real just by changing the word. He tries to qualify what is required to possess this value as if it was obtainable in the real world. He goes on to say that Spencer's conception of education resulted in "the conquest of our schools by mechanical and theoretical science to the comparative exclusion of such useless subjects as literature, history, philosophy and art." He continues: "This formal schooling made its graduates into good office-boys, good clerks and good technicians who when their workday is over devour the pictorial press and crowd into theatres that show them forever the same love-scenes on the screen and the same anatomy on the stage." He expressed his disapproval of Spencer's definition when he writes: "It would have been better if Spencer never wrote on education." "Furthermore," he continues, "these mechanical, practical, scientific people will have different tastes. They will prefer physics to biology, money to taste and manners and consequently will be uncivilized individuals without knowing anything about beauty and wisdom." In this passage he implies that only a certain type of learning has value, and without it, you will be uncivilized and only half of a man. Durant, like all other normal people under the banner of free will, also resented Spencer simply because he did not understand him and consequently derived a certain amount of pleasure criticizing him, for this is one way of feeling superior. He states, "Our schools and graduates have suffered severely from Spencer's conception of education as the adjustment of the individual to his environment; it was a dead, mechanical definition, drawn from a mechanistic philosophy, and distasteful to every creative spirit." If you analyze Spencer's definition you will see that he has done away with further need for the word education, just as I am doing. How is it possible to have a word to describe a difference among mankind, when there isn't any? Isn't it obvious that everybody is compelled, by his very nature, to adjust to his environment? It is true that the environment is different for different people, but Spencer has defined education as 'the adjustment of each individual to his environment.' What he has said is mathematically undeniable; in other words, what is the need of having a symbol when every individual is included in the symbol? Are you beginning to understand what I mean by syllogistic reasoning? Durant's reasoning is logical, that is, it gives the appearance of being true simply because he thinks he sees with direct perception these external values which he has unconsciously projected, through his eyes, upon differences that in themselves are undeniable, all because of words that stratify personal values into what appear externally real. This projection of values onto real differences in substance has helped to give this projection credence, and the illusion of reality remains just that, an illusion.

Convinced that his view of education was correct, he continues to define what he believes makes an educated man: "Education should make a man complete; it should develop every creative power in him and open his mind to all the enjoyable and instructive aspects of the world." He qualifies a little more what is required to obtain this value; learning to appreciate the works of Beethoven or Corot or Hardy. "A man who is heavy with millions but to whom Beethoven or Corot or Hardy or the glow of the autumn woods in the setting sun is only sound and color signifying nothing is merely the raw material of a man; half the world is closed to the blurred windows of his spirit. An education that is purely scientific makes a mere tool of its product; it leaves him a stranger to beauty and gives him powers that are divorced from wisdom." He then arrives at the very heart of his definition. "Education does not mean that we have become certified experts in business or mining or botany or journalism or epistemology; it means that through the absorption of the moral, intellectual and aesthetic inheritances of our race we have come to understand and control ourselves as well as the external world; that we have chosen the best as our associates both in spirit and in the flesh; that we have learned to add courtesy to culture, wisdom to knowledge, and forgiveness to understanding. When will our colleges produce such men?" He tries, once again, to convince us that no matter what you study and become certified in you are not educated unless at the same time you are able to control and understand yourself as well as the external world, which cannot be done according to him unless you first absorb all the moral, intellectual, and aesthetic inheritance of our race. He doesn't understand that people could absorb all this and still have no control over the external world or themselves which would make them, by his definition, not educated. The word 'wisdom' in this context is no different than the word *education,* or other words that describe non-existing external values. As for forgiveness, how is it mathematically possible for me to forgive you for doing what I know you were compelled to do, which reveals that it exists only because man was lacking in his effort to understand. And then Durant really gets confused. In order to be educated you must choose the music, the books, and the cultured, refined, educated people as your associates. He blames those who do not consider Beethoven or Corot or Hardy of greater value than the newspaper, the love-scenes on the screen, the same anatomy on the stage by calling them 'merely the raw material of a man.' How is it possible to be more discourteous than to call people not educated because they don't like *his* music, *his* books, and *his* choice of friends? In his mind, if you don't acquire this liberal education found in reading, if you don't become cultured, if you don't open your mind to what he judges is instructive and enjoyable, you are not a complete but half a man. He is actually saying that through reading we can learn many more things than we can in high school and college. This, of course, depends on what books are read. Durant and Edward Gibbon, both tremendous readers found their teachers to have much less knowledge of the world at large and both criticized college as a means of acquiring this broad knowledge. Durant defines culture as the enlightenment and refinement of taste acquired by intellectual and aesthetic training which he excludes from our 100,000 schools and compares only to a dozen educated men, of which he is one. Because Durant found such pleasure in these things, which could never have come about without his vast reading, he believed that everybody should move in this direction if they truly wanted to become educated and cultured, which allowed him to look down upon as uncultured and uneducated even professors and Ph.D.s Is it any wonder they disliked him? According to Durant, you could be a billionaire, but if you don't like Beethoven, Corot or Hardy, let alone not know who they are, or if you don't like to watch the glow of the autumn woods in the setting sun, or if these things make no impression on you whatsoever, then 'half the world is closed to the blurred windows of your spirit.' Durant does not realize that the enjoyable and instructive aspects of the world are different for different people, and that the glow of the autumn woods in the setting sun has no value except to those who enjoy it. Not realizing what he is doing, and being no different than any other thinker in the world of free will, he arranges everything in stratified layers of external value and judges what he assumes is better for mankind by how close each person comes to these upper levels of stratification. This reveals conclusively how unconsciously ignorant Durant was compelled to be as he obeyed the law which made him move in the direction he did. He saw thousands of differences with his very eyes, and no one would have been able to convince him that what he referred to as direct perception was only a projection of words upon the outside world. He never understood himself or he would never have been able to write what he did, which indicates he had no real control over himself; he considers one person and one book better than another, although these are better for him. I read The Decline and Fall of The Roman Empire along with The Story of Civilization, and although I prefer the former this does not make it better. The kind of courtesy he has in mind permits criticism which is prevented in the new world; as for culture this obviously is only a judgment that certain people and certain pursuits have greater value than others, which is a wholly fallacious perception. And then because he doesn't have the ability to perceive mathematical relations, for which he cannot be blamed, he blames Spencer for a definition of education that was so accurate it completely does away with further need for the word since everybody, regardless of his motion from here to there, acquires an education from the day of his birth as he learns to adjust to his particular environment which included, in the world of free will, the criticism, judgment, blame and punishment of others. Are you beginning to understand what words have done? These words or slides have allowed man to be fooled by being able to project personal values onto substance that has existence in the real world. By eliminating from our vocabulary all words that judge half the human race as inferior productions (and we are given no choice in this matter) — and by knowing what it means that man's will is not free — we are able for the very first time to control the external world. Once it is understood that the word education is not a symbol for anything externally real but is a projection of what someone prefers for himself, projected onto a screen of specific differences which he then says are better for everybody because he can define why these are better since they partake of this value called education, then all words like *culture, mature, educated,* etc. become, along with their equivalents, completely displaced.

As we begin to understand our true relationship with the external world, God, in His perfect wisdom, is revealing to all mankind that NOBODY on this planet is more or less educated than anybody else. Since Durant's conception of education does not mean that we have become certified experts in business, or mining, or botany, or journalism, or epistemology, but describes other aspects, all that is necessary to solve this equation is to show him that there is no greater value between one thing a person prefers to do and another, that is, once the truth is known. Just as Spencer's definition of education is so accurate that it does away with further need for the word only because everybody is educated, so does the knowledge of what it means that man's will is not free do away with further need for the word wisdom, simply because everybody then becomes wise. I'm going to prove that everybody is equal in value, no better or worse, and the only reason we have never been able to see this equality is because of words like educated, cultured, good, etc. which projected stratified layers of value on word slides through our eyes into the external world. In reality, we are all acquiring an education all through our lives, which

541

renders that word as useful as the words human and mankind. We are all members of the human race and part of the mankind system, and we have all acquired an education. Don't be intimidated by this lack of understanding because even the most sophisticated thinkers have been fooled. You will see that when these word slides are removed, or when man stops using them, it becomes mathematically impossible to judge what is right for someone else regardless of what he does for a living, what he desires to study, or what pastimes he engages in because these activities do not hold greater value except for the person who partakes in them. How is it humanly possible for Durant to object at being denied the right to criticize when his very criticism, as well as the criticism of all others, is partly responsible for the very things he is criticizing? It is really no different from a preacher not objecting to doing away with his preaching against sin when he becomes aware that his preaching against sin is partly responsible for the sin.

Another reason Durant did not like Spencer was the fact that he disagreed with the belief that man's will is free. Since Spencer had proclaimed that man's will is not free, Durant employed fallacious reasoning to twist the meaning of his words into something of a 'mechanical nature' which then made it impossible, according to this philosopher, for man to be creative. This threatened Durant for he believed that if man's will is not free he could not take credit for the books he was writing and therefore would not be able to consider himself a genius. He believed that to feel one is a genius it was necessary to feel creative, and how was it possible for him to feel this way unless he could prove that man's will was free which would then allow him to receive credit for his accomplishments and creativity. But the word *genius* is a word like *beautiful, educated, cultured*, etc. which is designed to stratify certain differences by raising some people up, consequently, lowering others. Since he knew that it was impossible to prove this theory he resorted to the next best thing — criticizing those who thought otherwise, not realizing that it is mathematically impossible to prove something false when the opposite can never be proven true. Durant's chest swelled with pride over his masterpiece, The Story Of Civilization, and it annoyed him no end to have someone like Spencer tell him that he did not create what he spent years creating. He had already been bestowed the highest of honors for his great achievement by those in his field and was acclaimed the world over as a prolific writer. This is another reason why some people resent the thought that man's will is not free, for how is it humanly possible to be proud of anything they have done unless they believe consciously or unconsciously in freedom of the will? In actual reality no one is taking this achievement away from Durant, for this is certainly a worthwhile accomplishment. The only thing we are taking away is his pride that he did it of his own free will. For the first time he is made to realize that God pushed him in this direction, which is the truth.

Of course, words like *achievement* and *masterpiece* will no longer be used to describe anything that man does because these words imply that one person's efforts in a particular direction are better than another person's efforts in a different direction. It is a known fact that certain things have greater value for certain people, therefore, they will be drawn toward the values that make a difference to them. For example, if an accountant makes more money than a bookkeeper, and I desire more money, then this is a value that will attract me. If I see that a certain group of people prefer to associate with those who like to read particular books like Shakespeare, or listen to a certain kind of music like opera, then as long as I wish to belong to this group this type of reading and music will have a personal value. But this would not make you superior to someone who desires to associate with a group that likes rock and roll or comic books. There is no such thing as a good book, better music, a classic, a masterpiece, only what you like better. Although these words try to give external reality to personal taste and values, they are opinions that express personal preference only. I may like a painting by Rembrandt better than one by my daughter but this does not make it a masterpiece, nor does it become one because it is liked by the majority of mankind. If you say to yourself while visiting an art gallery, "I think this painting by Rembrandt is a masterpiece," then nobody can be hurt, but if you say this to the person next to you then you will automatically put him in a lower level of stratification the moment he disagrees with your opinion. This word is no different in that it projects a value as existing externally as if the world is divided up into stratified layers of importance — but (it must be reiterated) value is a personal relation between you and something else. Regardless of the definition used, the word *'masterpiece'* is a word just like *educated, cultured, or intelligent* that is projected onto real substance with no corresponding accuracy.

My efforts to write the book, Decline and Fall of All Evil, are of no greater importance than your efforts to play pool or do something else because we are all following our nature which dictates that we move in the direction of what is better for ourselves at any given moment in time.

"You have to be kidding. My pool playing isn't going to help get rid of any evil that exists in the world, but your knowledge will definitely do the job."

"But I can't take credit for removing the evil when my will is not free; there is a big difference you know."

"I'm beginning to lose you again."

Durant's Story of Civilization, his Mansions of Philosophy, and all the other books he wrote played just as important a role in this discovery. My understanding of what it meant that man's will is not free was the end result of the knowledge given by everyone who ever lived. Through the process of reading and studying I was privileged to acquire information that led me to this answer. All knowledge is a gigantic accumulation of what everybody does in his motion towards greater satisfaction. Just because I happen to be at the end of the line when everybody pushes me or sets the stage that induces me to find answers that were never before possible does not allow me to take the credit, nor is an individual to blame when everybody pushes him towards murder and war. I am only obeying a law that forces me to move in this direction because it gives me greater satisfaction. God deserves the credit, not me. Before long tears will be flowing in abundance, but happy tears, and the whole world will thank God for this wonderful new world. I am just a child of God, like everyone else. None of us are given a free choice.

Without doing any reading at all, those born in the new world will surpass in every way what Durant describes as a mature, liberally educated, really cultured, civilized, well mannered individual. Seeing these differences in relation to substance which could not be denied, and believing the eyes were a sense organ which allowed these

544

undeniable differences to strike the optic nerve for us to see them, we were given no choice but to say 'seeing is believing.' However, the very moment these fallacious words are removed a miracle is performed because then it becomes mathematically impossible to judge anybody as inferior in value, and we are given no choice because our magic elixir denies us the satisfaction necessary to continue judging others as ugly, uneducated, stupid, uncultured, unrefined, unintelligent or inferior in value when this is disrespect and a hurt for which there will be no blame. How is it possible for me to call myself more educated or more educated than you, the reader, without placing you in a position of inferiority? Later I will return to a quote by Durant to reveal, once again, how the truth has been hidden behind a facade of ostensible words, but to help me accomplish this let us find out what our basic principle has to say about disrespect because it appears that we are slightly confused as to who is showing this.

We have been born into a world that stratifies people according to what they do to earn a living, the amount of their wealth, their social position, their formal and informal education (remember, this word will soon be displaced), etc. Doctors, rabbis, priests, professors are entitled to a specific designation to reveal a difference that exacts greater respect to them than to others who are not entitled to these additional names. In our present world do you think a person would study for years and years if it weren't for the distinguishing titles bestowed upon him such as Sir, Doctor, Professor, etc.? He likes this respect, and he worked hard to get it. These differences also separate the professionals who want to keep a distance in order to keep the interaction respectful, from those who can afford to be friendly because everyone is on the same level. A doctor doesn't want just anybody calling him by his first name, nor does a professor. You have heard the expression, 'Familiarity breeds contempt.' What would happen if a student addressed his professor, "Hi Bill," or a child his father, "Hi Michael," or the President of the United States, "Hi George old boy!" Age often demands respect even if it is not heartfelt, therefore children are expected to call someone much older 'Sir' or 'Mister,' and the protocol of government is designed to show deference to someone's position, as in the Armed Services. Your Honor, Your Grace, Your Majesty — like all titles — are designed to separate a person or a group of distinguished individuals, from others. For example, when two men meet for the first time in the army, the person who has the kind of position in civilian life that puts him in a higher bracket of respect will generally desire to reveal this difference so he can get his share of respect, even here. "Say Brandon, what did you do in civilian life?" "I was a butcher." Already the classification has placed him in a category to be treated in a certain manner. "What school or university did you go to?" Again the effort is in trying to find out differences that can separate the two of them. "I never went to either high school or college." "Do you like to work out mathematical problems? If you do I have a couple of good ones." "And how about chess and checkers, do you play these games?" Every step of the way these type questions are designed to probe for the differences that can make him feel superior, and they are avoided when he knows that his position is so low on this scale that any difference can only make him feel inferior. "Do you like Shakespeare?" "Have you ever read the Critique of Pure Reason by Kant?" A steel worker is not anxious to ask, "Where did you work in civilian life?" because he knows he will be asked the same question, and having to answer is not a source of satisfaction knowing he can't compete. Should the answer to his question be, "I'm the Vice-President of a bank" then he is sorry he asked. Are you beginning to see how unjust we have been out of necessity?

In our present world it is obvious that our relationship to the person we are talking to plays an important role in how this person is addressed. We teach children to call us Dad, Mom, Uncle, and Aunt which we certainly have the right to do. But if they call us by our first name we criticize them when they have done absolutely nothing to hurt us. This does not mean it is wrong to develop the habit of having them call us by these terms, but if for any reason they should ever decide to address us by our first names, this is their right-of-way and not a sign of disrespect, whereas our criticism of them is not showing them respect. In the world of free will this would definitely be considered a sign, but in the new world it would not, and because it would not, a boy might prefer calling his male parent Dad because dad prefers it. If you do not like the name given to you upon your birth and wish to be called by another name, this is your prerogative.

However, you cannot demand to be called by that name because this is a judgment of what is right for others, but if the name doesn't create an atmosphere of disrespect there is no reason it would be distasteful. It is true that when we become accustomed to being addressed a certain way, or if a salutation is suddenly changed, it would feel strange in the beginning, but this does not make it disrespectful. Once again, this does not stop you from teaching your child to use 'Mommy' if you prefer. However, should he hear your first name being called and he copies this, to correct this blames him which is wrong. Similarly, if a father prefers to teach his child to call him Dad instead of Michael, there is nothing wrong with this just as long as he doesn't deny his son the right to call him Michael because he feels it is a sign of disrespect.

The reason these distinguishing names of respect came into existence was because there was so much disrespect unconsciously imposed by words. Away from home parents, uncles and aunts were abused, ridiculed, criticized and blamed for so many things that it was a source of satisfaction to be called Dad, Mom, Uncle and Aunt, for this meant that the children were looking up to them with at least this token of respect. One must remember that these things were a sign of disrespect and unwanted familiarity in our present world, just as keeping one's hat on in certain quarters is judged disrespectful. But I am talking about a new world and the reason these titles come to an end is very simple. First, by the fact that all questions which try to show someone more superior than another cannot be asked, and second, when the transition gets under way, just as we displaced all the material forms of money because this was advance blame, so likewise do we displace all names and titles except those to distinguish one person from another. If parents wish to use one, two, three, four or more names for a child, this is their business, just so the names are not designed to demand greater respect for one person than another. When dad returns from work in the new world and his son says, "Hi Michael" or "Hi Dad" there will be no disrespect whatsoever. This brings to mind how I changed from calling my uncle, "Uncle Dave" to just "Dave" when I got much older and felt this inequality. If it gives you satisfaction to call someone "Sir, Ma'am, Mommy, Daddy, Uncle, Aunt, Mr., Mrs., etc.," this is your business because nobody is being hurt, but by the same token if you prefer to call someone by his or her first, middle or last name, this is also your business, because this is not a concrete hurt. When all criticism is removed, and there is no salutation considered better than another, there would be no reason to feel disrespected regardless of how one is addressed.

This also revolutionizes how people will be addressed in the professions. For example, if a teacher desires his students to call him Professor, Mr. Smith, Instructor, or what have you, there is no reason for them to object unless he is trying to exact more respect than what he is prepared to give. If he said to his students, "I expect everyone to address me Sir,"and denied the young males in his class the same privilege when he addresses them, then an unbalanced equation of respect is created. This means that all titles of respect notwithstanding are disrespectful because they demand more respect than what they are willing to give, and judge what is right for others. Always bear in mind that anybody who judges what is right for someone else is wrong and the one who is showing disrespect. Since it is impossible to desire lowering others when you know this will be a concrete hurt for which there would be no blame, and since it is impossible to desire raising others when you know this is a hurt to yourself, you are given no choice but to remove all words that do this very thing, giving to all mankind a perfectly balanced equation of mutual respect. To show you how everything was motivated by this great need for respect, I would like to repeat an earlier passage.

Having gone far beyond these professors in his mental development Durant highly resented the preemption of education by the colleges, therefore, he defined it in a way to include those who did not finish school but continued to read and study on their own, which made the universities dislike him while the dropouts loved him. He found it necessary to criticize college graduates and professors for thinking they were educated because he learned more in his informal education than what these professors and college graduates could ever have hoped to attain through their formal education, and he began to look down on them just as Edward Gibbon did. To him education was a definite reality, something of great value. Awarding those who went to a university with more respect angered him because he felt he was the most deserving. He did not realize he was dealing only in empty words. He, as well as the professors, had no idea that no group has a monopoly on the word education, since everyone is educated in his own way and deserving of the same respect regardless of what school he goes to or how he lives his life. Consequently, whenever you use words that give to an individual greater respect than another, you automatically place yourself in a position of lesser respect. I am repeating this because it is the source of much of the injustice that exists today.

The truth of the matter is that everybody has been using fallacious standards to judge themselves because they were compelled to reach out in every conceivable direction for anything that could place them in this upper level of stratification. Keeping in mind that nothing of value can exist in the external world except in relation to the individual, the word education implies the existence of something that contains an intrinsic value and the more of it we acquire the more educated and valuable we become, which means that those who do not partake of it will be judged uneducated and of lesser intrinsic value. The very fact that the educational system passed everybody along from grade to grade and was responsible for innumerable fallacious standards that justified the existence of ignorance which passed for knowledge, it was assumed that when a certain grade was reached you were more educated than a person who didn't go as far as you. By accepting the belief that this external value called education was also a part of the real world you would hear one boy say, "I am more educated than both of you because I finished college." This formal system of learning allowed each child to measure his education, and when the top grade was reached he felt very proud of himself. It gave him a false notion of his superiority by implying that when he reached this level of education he was now the most educated and intelligent of all. As a consequence of this external value, everyone was treated with greater respect the more of it they acquired. Down the line this stratification went, making the student who only went to grade school feel very inferior to the intellectuals who finished college. But alas, when it comes to mathematical relations the average college student tries to remember a formula not realizing that the answer doesn't lie in the method, but in the ability to perceive the relations. A high school graduate recently told me that his best subject was algebra and that he was terrific at it because his teacher told him so. After finding that he was incapable of solving two problems I gave him he excused himself by saying, "I think that's college algebra." If someone drops out of high school he is not as educated as the individual who graduates nor is the high school graduate as educated as someone who completed college who is less educated than a professor who is less educated than a Ph.D. We all know that certain diplomas exact the title of doctor which requires that these Ph.D.s look down on us with less respect than is given to them; and someone who never learned to read or write is made to feel as if he is an absolute non-entity. It is difficult for him to hold up his head in the presence of these educated giants. These professors and Ph.D.s. were like gods among mankind and from their height of success they not only looked down with patronizing disdain but exacted from everybody a formal degree of respect by demanding that they be called 'Dr.' This word when analyzed means — "I have more knowledge than anybody who has not attained the same height as myself." From this source began the complete development of our unconscious ignorance because this misplaced pride in their achievement, which was necessary in the world of free will, permitted them to pass along from generation to generation theories and opinions that were accepted as facts only because they were the professors, the cream of the crop, which justified anything they wished to teach. It was considered a sign of disrespect to disagree with people of such high rank and education. The doctors of philosophy and those with additional titles say, "We are more educated than all of you put together." Many philosophers in trying to be educated have taken a simple truth which could have been explained in a very few words and then made a profound book out of it which nobody understood all because they judged the value of the book by the quantity of big words and how difficult of being grasped. How many poets, philosophers, psychiatrists and psychologists have been accorded fame because they imparted their own meaning and used this as a confirmation of wisdom. To agree with a famous person is an unconscious way of saying, "I am as smart as he is" only he got a lucky break or he is able to express himself better. Aristotle stopped the world from thinking for a while because everybody agreed with what he had to say — due to his world renown.

Can you imagine what he would say about this book? How many of you recognized in Durant's Mansions of Philosophy your own wisdom, which now turns out to be ignorance? Another way of building up one's own feeling of superiority is by disagreeing, but the great humor lies in the fact that the standards we used to judge another were equally fallacious. Because 6 is closer to the answer of the cow problem than 7 doesn't make it less wrong, nor does a book like Dianetics become more true because it is dedicated to Durant, or less true because it was not accepted by psychiatry.

This same stratification system allowed the professors and Ph.D.s who graduated from the most prestigious universities to be filled with pride and arrogance over absolutely nothing and they were resented by men like Edward Gibbon, Will Durant, and many others who discovered themselves superior by another fallacious standard. It is important to understand something Durant did not; that the words educated and intelligent develop a class of people who are considered superior when in reality they are not superior human beings, just different. When you consider one person more important not because of his value to you but only because you have judged the world in stratified layers of importance, then when an individual climbs to the top he feels he is the most important person alive. If it was you that had climbed to the very top and were now judged the champion of importance, would it be possible for you to say of another that he is as important as you? Consequently, when you use words that give some people a feeling of greater importance you automatically place yourself in a position of lesser importance, lesser respect.

As this demonstration clearly shows, the mistaken notion that some people are more important than others has caused half the population to be treated with utmost disrespect. You have probably asked yourself this many times: "What impels this desire to make someone feel inferior?" "The answer is very simple; the lack of respect for him." Do you show equal respect to the Blacks, the janitors, the garbage collectors, the street cleaners? Unfortunately, there are people who could never raise themselves beyond this adverse criticism, who were compelled to live out their lives while being falsely judged an inferior production of the human race, as many Whites consider the Blacks, and many Jews the Gentiles, and many Gentiles

551

the Jews, and many Catholics the Protestants, and the Protestants the Catholics, and so on. What makes the Catholics better than the Protestants, or vice versa, other than the projection of fallacious words? What makes a White man better than a Black? Now that we know the truth, the next thing demanded by our conscience is that we treat EVERY PERSON IN THE WORLD WITH EQUAL RESPECT which has been denied by words that make certain people (their physiognomies, pursuits and abilities) superior productions of the human race. To put down and ridicule an entire race is a hurt, and when those who hate anybody different from themselves (because they, too, have been hurt) fully realize that they will not be blamed or punished, criticized or ridiculed in return for this hurt, then they will lose their desire to do what they know others must excuse and they cannot justify. In the new world, if Black people walk into a restaurant and the owner refuses to serve them, which is certainly his business, they would simply walk out. But this restaurant owner knows that he definitely hurt these people by judging them not good enough to eat in his place, and when he fully realizes that this serious hurt to them would never be retaliated upon, never criticized or blamed because he knows that they must excuse this hurt since they know he cannot help himself (since it is a known fact that his will is not free), then he is given no alternative but to show no discrimination because he knows he does not have to hurt these people this way unless he wants to, and it is impossible for him to want to under these conditions. Let's go a step further.

The reason the restaurateur was discriminating in the first place when he certainly could use this increase in his business is because he believed that others who did not want Blacks in the restaurant where they ate would criticize him by not continuing to eat there. This is easily remedied when the owner knows that his guests will not criticize him because this is a hurt for which they know he will never blame them, consequently, they are given no alternative but to mind their own business, especially when the entire world is not blaming them. Prejudice came about out of God's will because we were in the early stages of our development, but it is not required anymore and God has commanded that it be removed. It is now time for God to prove to the world that not one person is better than anybody else and

552

therefore entitled to greater respect, but when these names are awarded to certain people there is a definite feeling of inequality. The menial services like a maid, butler, street cleaner, garbage collector, etc. will be brought up to a level of absolute equality. You can see the disrespect in the word 'menial' but the same principle applies regardless. Very soon all words that have the slightest nuance of disrespect will disappear. However, many services will come to an end, street cleaning for one. How is it possible for you to throw trash in the street which then makes it necessary to employ street cleaners, when you know this will be a hurt to the taxpayers who will never blame you for doing what you know they must excuse, and you cannot justify? Remember, this is God's will, proven mathematically when you fully understand what it means that your will is not free. Since it is impossible, once man understands his true nature, to judge what is right for others or to demand this respect, and since each person knows that to pay others compliments only lowers himself, he is given no choice but to relinquish every word, habit, custom, convention and motion from here to there that pushes another up which, out of mathematical necessity, must push someone down. You won't have to continue calling a person 'Dr.' once the transition begins (this must be qualified); he won't expect it, and you cannot ridicule him by saying, "Hey Doc ole buddy!" because this would be a hurt to him for which he would never blame you. If at first your habits and customs seem to conflict with this new way of life, it is only because people get a certain enjoyment out of telling others how to live and they derive great satisfaction in being able to talk about other people, to bring them down to a lower level of stratification which makes them feel superior. Consequently, the very moment you show respect to one and no respect to another you either place yourself in a position of inferiority or superiority depending on how you judge yourself according to these fallacious standards. If I call another person handsome, isn't this an admission that he has something I don't have? If I say he is quite an educated man, this is an admission that I am not quite what he is. To show you that this is completely mathematical, if you are the champion pool player of the world is it possible to point to another and say he is the best pool player in the world when talking about another player? Of course not, not if I am the champ. Well supposing you consider yourself a champion in the field of being educated like Durant, is it possible for you to say he has quite an education which would mean, in your eyes, that he is now the champ? Are you able to see how words alone have created a false reality? By raising others you lower yourself; by lowering others you raise yourself. In reality all of us are perfectly equal in intrinsic value and the knowledge of our true nature forces us, for the very first time, to treat each other as total equals, that is, not with greater or lesser respect. Everybody was judging by some standard that they felt was the truth, and all were entangled in words. For example, if one child says 'yes' and another says 'yeah,' there are those who actually believe that the tone of this one syllable word reveals some form of superiority. Think about this very carefully. In the new world, of what value is pronouncing yes instead of yeah when nobody will criticize or ridicule the latter if the thought is clearly expressed? Isn't the purpose of having rules of good English to enable people to communicate? What difference does it make what word is used to accomplish this end? There is no ambiguity when I say yeah instead of yes. Besides, how is it possible for anyone to blame me anymore for my not conforming when first, I am not hurting anyone and second, when it is known that man's will is not free and what this means? All this is changed when mankind finally knows the truth and everyone is compelled to keep his opinions to himself.

As for the word intelligent and all its antonyms, we set up certain tests to determine the I.Q. of our children and because some of them are unable to do as well we call them less intelligent. The only thing we really know when the word intelligent is removed is that some people can do certain things better than others, which is an undeniable fact. Let us analyze this in another way. Supposing we used the ability to play pool, golf, and chess as a test to determine the I.Q. of our professors and then graded them as to how well they did against the champions of the world in those fields. Would not most of them be considered very unintelligent if other beginners did much better? Can't you see now that the most we can say is that these professors cannot play these games as well, just as the champions of the world cannot do as well as the professors in their field? By removing the words *intelligent*, *educated*, and *beautiful* — which are not a part of reality but only a projected value onto the screen of undeniable differences — we are not showing any disrespect to the people these words were directed to, but by removing all the antonyms we raise those who were judged an inferior production to an absolute level of respect and equality except in their ability to do certain things. Now that we know the truth, everybody henceforth is exactly equal in value, as has been proven in a mathematical manner. As such, any words that criticize another for not being equal (or for being in this lower level of stratification) are a real hurt for which there will be no blame, consequently, no one will desire using them. They will become extinct out of absolute necessity. You can use these words if you want to, but should you say that a person is educated, cultured, mature, or intelligent you would be revealing your ignorance, not your knowledge. Since you cannot derive any satisfaction from being considered an ignorant individual, it is obvious that you will be forced to relinquish the use of these words because it won't give you satisfaction once the truth is known. Let me qualify, once again, what I mean by personal value.

It is absolutely true that someone who has learned certain things will prove more valuable to a corporation that requires this knowledge, just as certain features will prove more valuable to a movie studio looking for a particular type to fit a role, but this doesn't make him of any greater intrinsic value. When comparing someone who has gone to school for twenty years with someone who has been there for only three years, you may feel the one who went to school the longest would be more deserving of respect than the other, but when the truth is known you will have no desire to show any less respect to the one or more respect to the other. Just remember, there is no such thing any more as an education. If you wish to read 10,000 books, this is your business, but the only difference between you and those who only read 3, is 9997. If one man prefers to read 100 books and another 20 books and a third none at all, the only thing we can say without placing anyone in a position of inferiority, which is a hurt, is that some people like to read and study more than others. If he desires to read 10,000 books and go to school for 20 years, this is his business, but it does not make him any more educated than a particular physiognomy will make him handsome. He is actually different than

555

the person who never went to school, never read a book and instead fished for 20 years, but this does not entitle him to more respect which is what takes place when the word educated projects this fallacious value onto individuals whose existence cannot be denied. This description is absolutely accurate. There is no greater value in the person who reads a lot of books and the person who does not. Doesn't a man like Will Durant consider himself a genius because of his profound views on the entire world situation? It is true that I found great pleasure in reading the books he recommended but especially in studying his own Story of Civilization, and if it had not been for Will Durant this book would never have been written. But this did not make me mature, educated, cultured, a genius or anything else, although it helped me to accomplish my purpose by seeing things in better perspective. It did not give me a liberal or any other kind of education because there is no such thing, but when the very language I speak contains these words then it is possible to convince myself that the effort was worth it because I am now regarded as a highly educated individual, an intellectual. Durant spent a lifetime reading and learning which enabled him to earn a living by writing, but he was compelled to justify the expenditure of such great effort on the grounds that it made him into a better, finer, cultured person — only words. Gibbon became famous for "The Decline and Fall of the Roman Empire," but this did not entitle him to greater respect. It is a fact that there are big differences between these men and those who have never learned to read or write. Durant and Gibbon preferred reading a lot of books and studying so that one day they might write something and become famous, while the others preferred not going to school at all. It is also true that the two men recognized certain talents and went on to develop them while the others, not having these talents, were not motivated in that direction, but it was only because certain words came into existence that these others were made to feel inferior. It was this projection of value onto a screen of differences that created this feeling of superiority or inferiority.

Someone who was not quite clear as to why greater respect should not be shown to someone who has learned more asked this question: "If a person earning more money and working at a job that requires much more development of his mind, why wouldn't he get greater respect than, let us say, a laborer, even if the word education is done away with?" This question confuses someone's preference with the term respect. If someone discovers he is capable of earning the kind of money that would put him in a completely different tax bracket, thereby setting him apart, he is not entitled to more respect because this would be showing disrespect to others. What I think he meant by the question is if someone had a choice, wouldn't there be times he might prefer associating with one type of individual rather than another? The answer is yes, and there is nothing wrong with this because nobody is being hurt. For example, if you like to read Shakespeare, listen to Beethoven, and do the various things Durant judged to be preferable, this is your business, but if someone else likes to read comics, listen to hard rock, shoot pool or bet on the horses, this is his business, and there will be no lesser respect given to one over the other. If you become a brain surgeon and someone else works on construction, all anyone can say with accuracy is that the two of you have different abilities but it does not make the brain surgeon more deserving of respect even though he may be highly valued by those he has helped. Neither will be judged of greater or lesser value by words that stratify them.

In our present world people read to accumulate information, develop a large vocabulary which can be used in daily conversation so they will gain more respect, but when it is known that acquiring a large vocabulary or anything else that tries to distinguish one from another doesn't make them more superior but instead only reveals their ignorance, they are given no choice but to forgo any great effort to acquire knowledge unless there is an intrinsic pleasure in doing so, which in no way hurts another. Therefore, what good would it be if there was no way to show off what you know unless you were going to perform on some show? To give you a perfect analogy, how is it humanly possible for a person to desire spending years lifting heavy weights for the purpose of developing huge muscles so he can show off his physique, when he knows that he will be shipwrecked on an island where nobody will ever see the results of his efforts; and how could a person desire to memorize the encyclopedia if he was not granted an opportunity to display this mnemonic feat? Supposing on this shipwrecked island there was an individual who memorized every bit of knowledge in the entire world. He read every book, every encyclopedia, and could even recite The Decline and Fall of the Roman Empire while standing on his head. One day he sees a group of tumblers showing off for which everybody applauded, and he feels a great desire to show this group that he is the smartest man on all Earth, but how can he go about it? He begins by asking this one person what he did for a living, to which the reply is, "I'm a carpenter." But this carpenter doesn't return the question which leaves it again up to our genius to make the others aware of just who he is. "Say, do you know when the United States was founded?" "No, I don't." "Well, it was back in 1776." "My friend," says the carpenter, "if you already knew the answer what was your purpose in asking me the question?" "I was trying to reveal to everybody here that I am what people call the brain; there is no book I haven't read and absorbed, and no question I can't answer. I just wanted to entertain everybody as the tumblers are doing." "My friend," says the carpenter, "these tumblers don't bother us with foolish questions; they just start tumbling, and if we don't like the entertainment we can turn our backs and go to sleep without offending them in any way since we didn't ask them to start. However, we enjoy the tumbling and that is why we are applauding. Do you see that gentleman over there; well he can stand on one finger, and when he does that stunt everybody gets as close as possible to see how this amazing feat is accomplished; but if your entertainment involves us answering a lot of foolish questions I'm afraid you had better go back home because your desire makes an imposition on our desires. However, you certainly can parade up and down mumbling when America was founded without imposing on us, and you did say you can recite The Decline and Fall of the Roman Empire while standing on your head. You will get a lot of recognition for this feat, but of course that would require several months of your time standing on your head, and with this boat coming to rescue us I'm afraid we will have to postpone watching you, but perhaps one day we shall see you in a circus."

Are you beginning to see the immense humor and how much genuine ignorance passed for knowledge? Therefore I will repeat the question: How is it humanly possible to desire studying and memorizing certain things when it is impossible to use this knowledge? It would require a person to ask questions which wouldn't be likely as long as there are libraries and teachers available who are paid for this very purpose. Remember, to walk on a beach in swimming trunks so that people can see one's body type does not impose on anyone, nor does performing one's talent to an interested audience, but to show the world the differences inside of one's head, does impose.

As we honestly look at our motivation, every question was designed to lower someone in order to raise ourselves, or judge whether this person is worthy enough to associate with. As a consequence, we developed the habit of asking questions to see whether people knew the answer in order to justify learning all this empty knowledge. All unimportant questions, therefore, must come to an end out of necessity, as do statements. You will no longer hear, "Did you complete high school?" "What kind of degree did you get?" "How far did you go with your education?" "Can you work this problem?" "Do you know when Columbus discovered America?" "Can you name all the capitals and states in the Union?" "Do you read Shakespeare?" "Do you like opera, Beethoven, Corot or Hardy?" And how are you going to ask people the kind of questions that you would like to be asked when you already know the answer, which is only meant to show your superiority, when you would never be blamed for this? When this becomes mathematically impossible to do, then man is given no choice but to relinquish all those pursuits that had no other value.

As teachers are denied the satisfaction of trying to down others by asking questions the answers of which are already known, a great many subjects will not be pursued because these are imposed by the school only. Students are then obligated to choose between A and B of which they prefer neither. When they are compelled to wait for the students to express an interest in what they want to read, thousands of books will die a sudden death. The only reason many books continue in existence is because the teachers found keen satisfaction in raising their ego by imposing these 'deeper' meanings on students. You see, in the world of free will we were constantly faced with this stratification of values and it was a source of satisfaction to move in the direction of these upper levels. And this, my friends, makes it absolutely impossible to derive any satisfaction out of learning what can never reveal someone's superiority except where there is a competitive activity which uses a mathematical standard, unless the knowledge one gains is the source of income, or unless studying grammar, history, geography, literature, etc., is a source of pleasure in itself. If a student wants to study Algebra, Geometry, Trigonometry, and all the higher forms of mathematics, or Latin, Greek, the Periclean Age, the Renaissance, the Enlightenment and everything Durant recommended, this will be his business; and if someone else does not desire these things, this will also be his business. But how can we desire to exert tremendous effort in learning various things except for employment and personal gratification, when there is absolutely no value to this learning?

Can you see what is happening to our educational system? In the new world the desire for such knowledge will go by the wayside. Education as we know it is a real farce under these conditions because there is not the slightest bit of difference in value between you and others no matter what a person decides to study or do for a living. Why would anyone want to read books that are not in themselves enjoyable since there is no way this information can benefit the reader as much as one iota where others are concerned? There can be absolutely no pleasure in reading history unless you were planning to write a book or you have a motive in learning about the past; and what could possibly motivate what is not a pleasure in itself? Of what value is remembering dates, names, and events when you cannot use this information? If children want to learn about the past they can find much more enjoyment from stories and pictures than from reading the kind of material that requires great effort; and are they given a choice when it is mathematically impossible to use this knowledge or to ask a question of someone when the answer is already known? Any subject that has no personal appeal or relevance will fall by the wayside. Remember, no longer will children be going to school to get an education, to acquire culture, to become learned, mature, refined (these are all words that judge others as less important), to get a degree or to receive more respect, but for one reason only which is simply to learn what they want to, not what others think they should. Many students

560

were drawn to read Shakespeare not because they found any real enjoyment but because they knew that a certain type of cultured individual preferred this reading material, therefore to become cultured, they concluded, one must prefer the various things that are associated with culture — good manners, good breeding, good books, good music, good this and good that. You have been compelled to judge what is better for someone else the very moment you express an opinion as to what you think is good. Consequently, every definition unless it accurately describes reality is a judgment of what is right, which means that the dictionaries will be completely revised in accordance with undeniable terminology only. How is it possible to define culture, character, manners, etc. when these describe differences that do not exist? When these words are compelled to leave, when the slides through which you see these differences are removed, you will see only reality. It is exactly as with war and crime: by removing all tacit blame, which includes the removal of government and arms, war and crime are immediately prevented; and by removing the pretty colored glass through which you saw kaleidoscopic differences favorable to yourself, everybody becomes mathematically equal; but how was this possible unless it was known that man's will is not free and what this means?

Here is where a tremendous change occurs because it takes hard work to do what some students have been doing to get their degree. Once the diploma is removed along with everything else that was used to make students feel inferior, these subjects will hold no interest unless they find some intrinsic pleasure in them or unless their great effort to learn these subjects is for the purpose of earning a better living or becoming well-known for something that requires this knowledge. Students will study whatever they desire for the purpose of building a career and anything else they might have in mind, but not to make themselves more important and deserving of greater respect. They will no longer have to read or study unless they want to, and when it comes time to choose what they wish to do for a living they will look over the different careers that are available in order to match their skills and temperament with a profession they are most suited for. However, once they pick a career they will be constantly testing themselves to see if they are qualifying, and if they find they are not, they may decide to change their career track altogether, which will be entirely up to them. As we learned in the chapter on economics, many businesses that now exist will be displaced because they will no longer be needed. Of what value is there in studying to be a general, theologian, lawyer, salesman, office manager, accountant, criminal investigator, credit manager, manufacturer of security devices, etc., when these products and services will have absolutely no value? It should be obvious why the educational systems of the world will be changed when so many professions and occupations will be permanently displaced. To go to school and sell outdated information would be equivalent to desiring to expend this great effort on an island where there are so many other things you would be compelled to prefer doing with your time, although what you desire to learn will be up to you, no one else. Although no one will be telling children what subjects they must learn, they will have developed their mind much greater than high school graduates and even some college students due to the fact that they will learn to read early and will select from among the various subjects those that are most interesting to them. There will be no compulsion except what they put on themselves; the same with sports and physical activities in general. If they want to they can, if they don't want to they won't have to. Should they decide early what they want to be, the teacher will direct them to the books. You will discover that some children as young as 13-15 will be graduating high school and entering college. But the children who decide not to read or who do not desire to go to college will not be criticized, because this is their business. One will not be more intelligent or educated than the other, just different.

If parents do not have or do not wish to spend money for their children to go to college they will be able to borrow the amount needed, with very little interest, from the banks even before they have attained a standard of living. The students will benefit because the interest will be low enough to be affordable, and the banks will benefit because they will know the students will pay back the loans in a timely fashion, but no one will be checking to see whether they are paying it back under the terms of the agreement. Being able to borrow money for their tuition at such a low rate obviates the need to ask parents to do for them what they can do for themselves. The money they earn for a full year after leaving school will determine the amount that will be guaranteed. If they are able to improve their standard of living far beyond what it was during the first year of their career, the guarantee would only apply to the original figure if they should ever be forced to go back down.

This knowledge puts a permanent end to all traditions, customs, conventions, etc. unless an individual prefers continuing with those habits that do not judge others. You are given no choice as to whether you will be able to continue living as before because the knowledge that others (all mankind) will never blame or criticize you no matter how much you hurt them forces you to desire making a great change in your conduct because it can give you no satisfaction whatever in being excused for doing what can no more be justified by any living soul, including yourself. For the very first time in history we are going to be compelled to mind our own business for greater satisfaction which was denied by words like beautiful and educated since these were judgments by us of what was better for others to achieve. Removing all the synonyms and antonyms of the word educated does not mean that children will lose their desire to go to school because what they prefer to do with their time is conditioned by what they want to become, but it does mean that they will never again be shown less respect no matter what they look like or what they desire or do not desire to study. How is it humanly possible to define education when everyone born acquires an education from this time forward? Consequently, what choice will those intellectuals have but to treat everyone equally when it dawns on them that they will never be blamed by looking down on others who have not acquired the same knowledge that they now possess? This completely revolutionizes our educational system since the opinions of others, now removed once and for all, can no more be an influence when no one henceforth will ever desire to judge what is right for someone else. There will be no more college graduates, no more educated, uneducated, intelligent, unintelligent, beautiful or ugly individuals in the world, just people who will be doing something from day to day as they are compelled to move in the direction of greater satisfaction. In the new world each person will go to school for just as long as he wants and can afford, but if he remained there all his life he would still not be one iota more educated than anyone else. All the reading in the world can never make an individual courteous when he constantly ridicules, criticizes and judges by fallacious standards of value such as culture; nor can it give him wisdom without the knowledge of his own nature which no one has ever understood until now. When these words are removed, and they will be (God is giving us no choice), then what each man prefers to learn or do is his particular education; consequently, the word education loses all significance.

Most philosophers have spent a lifetime hovering directly over the meaning of wisdom and received a glimpse of this truth which allowed them to sniff this delightful aroma; but now everyone born can eat this delicious steak without having to go through a lifetime of tidbits. This is equivalent to a man who dreams of making passionate love, only to discover that when he gets married (in your present world) the passion disappears; but now everyone can have this passion all through their lives. It should be obvious that the books on philosophy have no further value because the knowledge revealed (by knowing what it means that man's will is not free) makes all such books a waste of time since they pertain to someone's opinions regarding human relations which has now become obsolete — unless a certain amount of pleasure is derived from this reading. Books like the Mansions and Story of Philosophy had great value in the world of free will, as did the Principles of Psychology by James, Freud's works, as well as many others, but their value did not lie in the truth being revealed. These men cannot be blamed for taking advantage of the ignorance that prevailed, including their own, in order to earn a reputation and a living. How else could religious leaders have been able to take advantage of those who were willing to believe that God sits up in heaven answering our prayers? But remember — and this is the greatest humor imaginable — everything came about out of God's will. The theologians reveal their ignorance for which they cannot be blamed by considering it blasphemous to show disrespect to a word like God which judges what is right for others and makes their thunder of blasphemy blasphemous since it is unconscious disobedience of God's will — Thou Shall Not Blame — which unconsciousness makes it not blasphemous. Hey, God, tell them, am I being disrespectful? Are you beginning to see the great humor of man's ignorance, or is it still difficult to smile? The following anecdote may give you a better understanding of what has been expressed throughout.

God felt awfully guilty through the years He made us develop ourselves because our development necessitated that we fight and kill each other, discriminate and hate each other. When Job cried out to him for understanding, God actually wept because there was no way He could communicate this knowledge. So he turned to the ministers of religion and said, "My dear cohorts, my wonderful assistants, through the years you have been kind enough to tell all the people of the world to have faith, to believe in me because I am a reality and one day in the very near future I shall reveal myself through a mathematical revelation." The truth is that we have all been sent here by God; I was, but so was Christ and so were you, and so was everybody else. We're all here at His bidding. Just because you do one thing for satisfaction and I do something else doesn't make me more His child and you less. And yet the very people involved in trying to accomplish what this revelation has brought about are actually not too happy over the news. My revealing this law is not done of my own free will because man's will is not free, nor is your reading this book done of your own free will. Remember, if you want to thank somebody for getting rid of all the evil, don't thank me because I had nothing to do with it. Thank God, He is the boss and orchestrates this wonderful thing called Life.

Everything takes a reverse turn because everything was built on the foundation of free will. I could go on and on and on in elaborating and extending the principles involved but this shouldn't be necessary if you understand the principles. If you have not, then I suggest you study the book several times. The wisdom here is so fantastic that it is no wonder men like Spinoza became God intoxicated, which has nothing to do with religion as you well know since he was excommunicated; but it is even more amazing when you realize that we ourselves are a part of God, and that we have been endowed with the ability to foresee what is truly better for ourselves when compelled to look ahead as a group, not as single, isolated individuals. Under these conditions of what value is prayer any more when our prayers are answered by obeying God's will — Thou Shall Not Blame? In other words, how is it humanly possible to desire hurting yourself when you are shown how to prevent it? The pride one now experiences because of his education, looks, clothes, wealth, ability, completely disappears, although one will derive great pleasure in making others happy because this is a tremendous source of satisfaction. The fact that we have been brought up a certain way makes us judge others in the light of our standards, and when they fall short we have something to criticize which to us reveals our superiority. Those who were seen as inferior were driven to try almost anything to gain recognition as human beings. Feeling the harsh sting of judgment compelled them to search for isolated groups that paid them the respect and acceptance they deserved. Our religious leaders have always preached about man's undeniable equality because of unconscious incursions of thought that revealed the truth, but because of the confusion with words man was never able to explain in scientific terms that this was an absolute fact. Now that God is removing all these fallacious standards, the person who before felt self-conscious in someone's presence is made to feel at home wherever he goes throughout earth. But there was a purpose to everything because, strange as this may seem, each and every individual that has ever lived has always been at the exact spot he was supposed to be each moment of his life, and this also holds true for every person who will ever live. All of us, no matter what we ever do, will always be cogs in the little wheel of this immense universe. In concluding this work and to show you what words can do in a more concrete fashion, I am going to quote Will Durant on education (which word, of course, must come to an end), and then paraphrase his thought. As we learn the truth, this word loses all meaning because all of us acquire an education from the time we are born to the time we die. Some of us acquire a school education while others acquire a self-planned book education; still others acquire an on the job training education. But the word education in the new world, unless qualified, has no significance. If you remember this important truth you will never feel inferior to another and you will walk with your head held high. This new meaning includes every human being in the definition, thereby giving equal respect to everyone on earth.

In the new world we are able to control and understand ourselves as well as the external world, not because we read the books Durant recommends as necessary for development, not because we have absorbed the moral, intellectual and aesthetic inheritance of our race, but only because we know what it means that our eyes are not a sense organ, that our will is not free, and why there is nothing to fear in death. We have chosen the best as our associates both in spirit and in the flesh, only because the knowledge that we will never be criticized or ridiculed allows us, for the very first time, to select what is truly best for ourselves even though we may prefer the Beatles to Beethoven, Zane Grey to Shakespeare, Elvis Presley to Caruso, the atmosphere of a pool hall to the glow of the autumn woods in the setting sun, or a garbage collector for a friend to an author, philosopher, historian or piano virtuoso. We have learned to add courtesy to culture and wisdom to knowledge only because we have really learned to mind our own business, learned what respect is, learned that all mankind are perfectly equal in intrinsic value and learned how unconsciously ignorant of the truth we have always been, which wisdom makes it impossible to be discourteous when there is no culture, no education, no beauty, and no other words to make us feel that we are an inferior production of the human race. We have added forgiveness to understanding only because we know at last that man is truly not to blame which gives us the understanding to prevent from coming back that for which forgiveness was previously necessary. When will our colleges produce such men? When we finally recognize the truth of our nature and become citizens of this new world. It is because we know that God asks absolutely nothing of mankind since He directs us with His invariable law of satisfaction which gives us no choice, that we are inclined to thank Him from the bottom of our hearts for granting peace, understanding, and brotherly love at last.

REVIEW

To become a citizen of this new world requires first that scientists, objective investigators capable of perceiving undeniable relations; not theorists, philosophers, professors, politicians, theologians, or anyone that uses his credentials or some title as a standard for rejection, thoroughly study the principles for the purpose of finding a flaw. When they are convinced that there is none, then they must break the sound barrier of learned ignorance that exists in the establishment by demonstrating the infallibility of these relations. When this has been done, when the schools and religious organizations begin to teach these principles, then the political leaders of the world will prepare and set a date for this great launching. The primary problem is that this knowledge does not immediately move our so-called scientific investigators who are the most part Ph.D.s and professors in the direction of greater satisfaction, because it cannot satisfy them to investigate what must reveal, if true, how learnedly ignorant they have always been. This can better be expressed by President Reagan who said, "Just imagine what I might have accomplished had I graduated college." In other words, if Reagan had never become a famous movie actor, never become President but had shown enormous talent as a young man, the professors would have said, "Just imagine what he might have accomplished had he graduated college," which presupposes that talent without a college education won't go too far. That is why Reagan's comment is so ironically humorous. Many famous movie actors were advised by their teacher when first breaking into this field to give up the thought of acting as a career because they would never make it which revealed that the teacher didn't have enough talent to recognize talent. And one professor failed a student who is now a multimillionaire, maybe a billionaire, because the ideas expressed in a thesis about how millions of dollars could be earned in a particular business seemed so far fetched to the intellectual capacity of the professor. Do you think our professors will be happy to learn that someone who never completed the 7th grade wrote this book? How dare I do this, or claim what I claim? Are you beginning to recognize that they must react with resentment just by reading the preface and introduction? This work in their eyes puts them down and they might discover that I didn't punctuate properly; that my sentences are too long, or that I contradicted myself when I wrote we must enter this world of our own free will. Another academic remarked to me that I admit man's will is free the very moment I demonstrate that nothing in this world can make us do anything against our will. Now if these people are our experts and do not have the intellectual capacity necessary to perceive these fairly difficult but undeniable relations, there is no telling how long it will take to bring about this new world. Fortunately, only some of these people are that way. There are many professors, many politicians, many theologians, and innumerable number of people who will understand the principles, but the question is how do we reach them? To help in this matter and to further help you understand this book, I will recapitulate salient points. Some of my clarification is in the form of a question and answer format, while other parts of my explanation are in general prose. At the end of this review, you will be able to test yourself to see if you understand the basic principles set forth. As I begin this discussion, I would like to make one thing perfectly clear. Turning the other cheek or not blaming people for what has been done to you is virtually impossible and not what this book is telling you to do. The principles can only become effective when the first blow is permanently removed which removes the justification to hurt others, and when you know, well in advance, that you will never be blamed again for anything you do. Until the political leaders of the world understand the principles and officially set a date for the great launching of this transition, we will be compelled to blame and punish just as we have always done.

Why is the will of man not free?

Because we are compelled to move in a direction of greater satisfaction from the day we are born to the day we die.

But if nothing in this world can compel us to do anything against our will, doesn't this mean our will is free? Isn't this a contradiction?

Of course not; nothing in this world that can compel us to do what we don't want to do because it gives us greater satisfaction not to do it, but we are under constant compulsion to prefer of available alternatives what gives us greater satisfaction. In this example, the one choice is for us to accept the alternative that is trying to compel us to do something against our will. But since nothing in this world can compel us to do something against our will, we don't have to do it if we don't want to because it gives us less, not greater satisfaction. Therefore, we were compelled to prefer not doing it because it gave us greater satisfaction. This was made perfectly clear in the first chapter and only your stubbornness, your dislike to give up the belief in free will, is giving you greater satisfaction to hold onto it as long as possible.

What are the implications that have kept free will in power since time immemorial?

Since theology could not blame God for the evil in the world man was given free will so we could assume responsibility, and were we given a choice? How was it possible to blame God for what Hitler did? Furthermore, can't you see the great humor and the great confusion in trying to understand these principles if Hitler was to say, "People of the world, I'm sorry about what I did but I couldn't help myself because my will is not free; God made me do it." Well, is it any wonder we were compelled to believe in freedom of the will? These are the implications that compelled Will Durant to reject determinism and Spinoza whom he loved dearly. But in reality God is responsible for everything in this world which includes this revelation of knowledge that now allows us to get rid of the evil permanently. This entire universe is controlled by mathematical laws over which we have absolutely no control. These invariable, eternal laws are God; but even though our destiny is predetermined by these laws, we can only go in one direction which proves that A. Cressy Morrison was right when he wrote his book, "Man Does Not Stand Alone." We have never been alone because God has always been with us. There have been some readers so completely confused as to my first discovery that when I asked them to explain what it was I had discovered they replied, "Your first discovery is that man's will is not free." To deconfuse any reader or listener who thinks that way please reread the last part of Chapter One.

This is an extremely crucial point because though it is true that will is not free, ABSOLUTELY NOTHING ON THIS EARTH CAN MAKE MAN DO ANYTHING AGAINST HIS WILL. He might not like what he did — but he wanted to do it because the alternative gave him no free or better choice. It is extremely important that you clear this up in your mind before proceeding.

This knowledge was not available before now, and what is revealed as each individual becomes conscious of his true nature is something fantastic to behold for it not only gives ample proof that evil is no accident, but it will also put an end to every conceivable kind of hurt that exists in human relations. There will take place a virtual miracle of transformation as each person consciously realizes WHAT IT MEANS that his will is not free, which has not yet been revealed. And now I shall demonstrate how these two undeniable laws or principles — that nothing can compel man to do anything against his will because over this his nature allows absolute control, and that his will is not free because his nature also compels him to prefer of available alternatives the one that offers greater satisfaction — will reveal a third invariable law — the discovery to which reference has been made.

What is the two-sided equation and what is the first discovery?

It is simply this. I must hold myself responsible for doing to you what I know you must excuse. My realization that you will never blame me for what I cannot excuse when all justification has been removed, raises my conscience now between 1 and 3 in a scale to 10 to its highest degree and prevents me from deriving greater satisfaction in being excused for what I know I don't have to do. My feeling of guilt will be so overwhelming that it would be impossible for me to desire striking a first blow under these changed conditions. You can site innumerable examples to prove this, but just study Chapter Two for further clarification. Therefore, my first discovery is the knowledge by which man's conscience can be raised to such a high degree that it becomes impossible for him to desire striking a first blow, and when all first blows are removed it becomes impossible to punish someone when he is not hurting you, impossible to retaliate against someone who has done nothing to hurt you, and impossible to turn the other cheek when your first cheek has never been struck. However, just as long as you are able to justify hurting someone then you are not striking a first blow, and how this justification is permanently removed is answered in Chapter Six. But Chapter Three demonstrates what happens in a human relation where there can be no justification to cause an automobile accident that hurts others.

Tell me, who has the right-of-way?

All motor vehicle operators will know who has the right-of-way in the new world because this is something they must know to clear themselves of responsibility should an accident occur. This simply means that anytime we enter territory belonging to other operators, they obviously have the right-of-way which plainly tells us that anytime we have an accident in their territory we are in the wrong. The truck driver knew that the territory at the intersection did not belong to him because the light was red, but such an accident is prevented in the new world along with all others because there is no way we can find greater satisfaction in speeding up to gain a few seconds when the alternative, the possibility of having an accident that hurts others who must excuse what we cannot justify gives us no choice whatsoever. In this world we can lie to others and to ourselves about what really happened because we don't want to be held responsible. But when we are prevented from lying because no one is blaming us; when it fully dawns on us that there is no escaping responsibility when it becomes impossible to shift it away from ourselves, the only avenue open to us for greater satisfaction is to do everything in our power to stay away from the risks and carelessness that could possibly place us in that kind of situation. This removal of risks and carelessness that could hurt others must come about in all human relations simply because we can find no satisfaction in knowing that we are responsible for hurting others who we know must excuse what we were not compelled to do. Furthermore, just think of the money we will save by not having to pay liability insurance, attorney fees, auto repairs, hospital and doctor costs and so forth, which will allow all of us to have money with which to improve our standard of living. Can anyone in his right mind prefer our present world to the new world? And think about this. Just the fact that people who take drugs and drink alcohol cannot blame the drugs and alcohol when they have an accident in the new world prevents them from driving under these conditions because they cannot find satisfaction in being excused for what they know could have been prevented. No matter how you study and extend these principles, they always come out the same. Well, do we need the Department of Motor Vehicles under the changed conditions? We only need tags during the transition. Once all of us are citizens and responsible for our children until they pass the examination, tags that identify us have absolutely no value because we are not going to do anything with our cars that would cause others to desire contacting us. Remember, no one is going to blame us. As for the examination, this will always continue because we must make absolutely certain that every person receives a guarantee and understands the principles. In time, however, after children are brought up in a home where all first blows have been permanently removed, it will be as difficult to find children and parents doing anything to hurt each other as it is difficult today to find people who still believe the earth is flat. It is humorous to observe at this point that someone I know got so confused over these principles that he thought how wonderful it would be to live in a world where he could satisfy his desires even if this meant hurting others for which he would never be blamed. "Wouldn't it be wonderful," he said, "to get rid of all the blame?" — not realizing that in our present world this would be impossible. I trust you are not confused about this. He placed the cart before the horse. It is the hurt we are getting rid of for which there won't be a need to blame.

What are the three forms of first blow that will be prevented?

The first form of first blow is the economic condition that makes us go below the net standard of living we have developed for ourselves, or that makes us go below a basic standard necessary for survival unless we do something to hurt others. Such an economic condition gives us

574

justification to do this, but when all mankind are guaranteed that their net standard of living will never go down, and that those who are poverty stricken will be raised to a basic standard, then the justification to hurt others to prevent ourselves from being worse off has been permanently removed. The second form of first blow is the hurt we do to others not to prevent ourselves from becoming losers but strictly to gain some advantage at the expense of others. The third form of first blow is the hurt we do to others who refuse to do what we judge they should do for us. In our present world, however, many of the things we judge they should do for us were to prevent them from hurting others, as with the speed limit. We punish them for going 40 m.p.h. in a 25 mile zone because we didn't know of any other method to slow them down. But when they know that there might be a danger of hurting others by exceeding the speed limit recommended for safe driving, for which there would be no blame, they would desire not to take any risks that might result in a hurt that never could be justified.

How is it possible to guarantee to all mankind what you just guaranteed when we might not have the money to do this?

But we will have the money. You will see the greatest boom in developing this planet by investors who will not be hindered by the laws of government. And they will not be hindered by the lack of available labor. Poverty will be completely wiped out not because of the guarantee which only starts the ball rolling, but because there will be jobs for everybody and they will desire to work because not to means they would be stealing money from the guarantee for which there would be no blame. Prices on everything will come down so low because we will be able to produce everything in such quantities that we will be compelled to work fewer hours to produce less. Just think, when everybody is employed our tax profit will be tremendous because nobody will be taking money from the guarantee which means it is to our advantage to spend instead of save. When we stop spending production slows down and the money we need for the guarantee increases. And are we given a choice as to what is better for ourselves under the changed conditions? In our present world we were afraid to let go of our reserve cash because we needed to save for a rainy day, but in the new world the guarantee prevents us from having a rainy day which forces us to put billions upon billions of dollars into constant circulation. However, this is not something you have to worry about. The economists know that this is true; so do our political leaders, but they didn't know how to bring it about. All Russia really wants is security for her people. Once the guarantee gives them this security without hurting anyone, it will give them as it will give us and the rest of the world the greatest pleasure to get rid of everything connected with war. Computers will be set up around the entire world to enable the immediate transference of funds to any nation who needs to receive money because they have fallen below their guarantee. For the very first time all nations of the world will be in friendly competition which gets better than ever because no one can be hurt. Communism and socialism and all forms of dictatorships will be wiped from the face of the earth because they violate the third form of first blow by telling others what must be done in order for these obsolescent methods of dealing with the world's economic problems to survive.

Taking for granted that the desire to strike this first blow can be permanently removed with the guarantee and the basic principle, Thou Shall Not Blame, how is it possible, seriously, to get this new world started?

The very first step is to get this knowledge confirmed by recognized leaders in the world of science. The next step is to get the political and military leaders of the world to thoroughly understand that they and their people will not be hurt one iota by launching this tremendous transition because of the guarantee. While this is going on all schools, colleges, universities, religious organizations will be teaching only the principles required to become a citizen of this new world. What a great day it will be when all political and military leaders have a meeting for the express purpose of signing the agreement that makes them the first citizens of this new world. When that has been done, everybody connected in any way with war will be permanently displaced the very moment they sign the agreement and become citizens. The police, however, although they too will become citizens immediately, will continue to apprehend for punishment any non-citizen who violates

576

the laws of his country. As the citizens increase in number, the police will decrease proportionately. The last group to become citizens will be all prisoners, but once they understand the principles, are treated with equal respect and know they will never be blamed for striking a first blow while receiving their guarantee, they will find it impossible to derive greater satisfaction in striking a first blow. This means that everybody in the world earning a living in any way connected with war and crime will be permanently displaced. As for religion, what can I say? It came into existence out of absolute necessity, but because God, not me, is delivering all mankind from evil at last, it will take leave of this earth also, out of absolute necessity. We are all God's children.

I don't completely understand how taxes will be paid to finance the guarantee and the remaining services of government we use.

The most equitable way is this. All of us will have a gross income. From that we will deduct the expenses necessary to earn the standard of living we will record as our guarantee. The amount left over is taxable. For example, if you earned $500 per week and your expenses to earn this is $50 per week while your guarantee is $250 per week, then your taxable income is $200 per week or $2600 for the quarter or 13 weeks. If it was estimated that 20% might meet the expenses of the guarantee on the first announcement, you would remit $520. If it did not, a second announcement would be made. There can be no more equitable manner to meet the guarantee. The first method suggested of keeping records of all the taxes paid and to pay a percent of taxes withheld when the announcement is made is really not necessary when there can be no more equitable manner then to pay taxes only on the amount left over to improve, not to maintain, your standard of living. I would like to recall an interesting experience that was partly responsible for one of my revisions. A group of teachers at Loyola College in Baltimore requested the privilege of studying my book titled, "Inception of the Golden Age." When they completed their study the leader of the group said to me, "Mr. Lessans, all my life I have believed man's will is free but now I know for an absolute fact that our will is not free. But even if your principles did put an end to all war and crime, and I see this could come about, it would only start

577

up all over again." It was this statement that made me realize the only way to prevent this from 'starting up all over again' was to have every person become a citizen of this new world, not just for a certain length of time but for always. Then the old world could never start up again. However, there seemed to be a certain amount of fear on the part of this leader to help in bringing this knowledge to light. I experienced this on more than one occasion. One professor told the student that gave him a copy of my book to study, "Everything that this author has written is truly undeniable, but I believe he is 2000 years ahead of his time." It never dawned on him that with his help the actual time could be 10 to 25 years, but these professors are afraid to confirm publicly something so far removed from the framework of modern thought. They would rather let this knowledge come to light without their help.

Let us now go back to Chapter Ten, Our Posterity. I am convinced that most of you have not understood this chapter on death, so I will attempt to clarify what might be impossible. Nevertheless, the first clue to our individual immortality comes from the fact that we are here, alive and conscious of our existence at this infinitesimal fraction of time with the earth perhaps billions upon billions of years old. This does seem rather strange at first. Now let's assume for the moment that immediately after your death, you, not the same genetic individual, but someone who recognizes his individuality and existence are born again, full grown. This would then explain why you are alive and conscious of your existence at this infinitesimal fraction of time with the earth perhaps billions of years old. But you are not born full grown and your experience with life shows that the babies born during your life cannot possibly be you so why should any one of them be you after your death? The next clue must come from the fact that consciousness is our ability to say 'I', which means that everyone born has the ability to say 'I', but here is where you get confused. I am saying 'I' but he says 'I' and she says 'I' and they are not me saying 'I', which is true. This simply means that as long as you can say 'I', no one born during that time can possibly be you because they are seen through your consciousness, but when you die your ability to say 'he' or 'she' is no longer possible, and the great confusion arises because you assume this relation in reasoning as to what happens after your death. You believe that because the people born during your life are not you, they cannot possibly be you after your death, which is 100% true if you are referring to their genetic characteristics. But if you bear in mind that every child born must say 'I', and if you also bear in mind that when you die you are no longer able to say 'I', one of the children born after your death must be you because you would then be saying 'I', which is not the same genetic individual you were, but someone who will recognize his own individuality and existence and say, "I am alive; conscious of my existence." This is the reason it is not strange that we are alive and conscious of our existence at this infinitesimal fraction of time with the earth as old as it is. This knowledge should make you very happy because it reveals that we not only have been developing this planet, but that we will be here to enjoy it. Well, what do you think of God now, these invariable laws that we are at last getting to understand? Study this chapter again and it may become clearer.

As for Chapter Four, Words, Not Reality, there is really not much clarification that can be done. You may ask me to explain again why words like beautiful must come to an end. If you bear in mind that nothing in the external world contains an intrinsic value because all values are in relation to you, and if you also bear in mind that all words projecting an intrinsic value into the external world cannot possibly be accurate symbols, then it should be obvious that we have been creating intrinsic values that have no existence in reality. It is true that gold has a greater value than silver, but this is not an intrinsic value, but a value in relation to someone. If I should say that she is like gold and someone else like silver, then I am projecting a greater value onto one than the other. This girl is of greater value to someone than other girls. By calling her beautiful, we make it appear that her physiognomic characteristics contain a greater intrinsic value than the other girls, which is completely false. She isn't beautiful, pretty, gorgeous, better looking, cute, adorable, etc. She is simply different than other girls. She may appeal to you more than girls with a different physiognomy, but that doesn't make them an inferior production of the human race which is what takes place when words make it appear that these intrinsic values exist externally. When children are brought up without ever hearing these words, they could find very appealing a girl with buck teeth, heavy legs, sagging breasts and a harelip, and they could fall very much in love. It was by realizing our scientists never fully understood the eyes are not a sense organ that I was able to open this hermetically sealed door and arrive at the truth. Many professors, however, will still find it difficult to accept this new knowledge because they were taught differently, and I only went to the 7th grade.

What are some of the questions on your mind regarding Chapter Five, Premarital Relations?

Most people in the world are already conditioned by these words like beautiful and handsome, so how is it possible for someone judged handsome to be attracted to a girl with a harelip, heavy legs, sagging breasts, and with a face considered ugly? She could very easily be attracted to him and he could take advantage of her if he wanted to, but he would never be attracted to such a girl, not as long as he has already been conditioned. However, under the changed conditions he is actually prevented from taking advantage because he knows that she would never blame him regardless of how much he broke her heart. This in itself will never get him to be attracted to someone who does not appeal to him, but it definitely prevents him from getting involved with a girl sexually unless he is absolutely certain he will never hurt her. If there exists the slightest possibility that she will fall in love with him but he will not fall in love with her because she is offering much less in physiognomic value than he is, then he is compelled for greater satisfaction to stay away from the possibility of breaking her heart because it can never give him greater satisfaction to do this when he knows she must excuse what he can never justify. This forces him to search only for the kind of girl who will have sex with him and that he doesn't want to hurt; and the same with her.

The question you may ask at this point is this: "Does this really mean that because they have sex they are married, as you wrote?"

They are not married in the traditional sense. There will be no more laws pertaining to marriage, no more priests or rabbis required to pronounce them husband and wife. They will be married only because they will desire to have sex with that individual, and will not want to do anything to hurt each other. They could leave each other at any time if that is their choice, but sex with someone where there is a mutual attraction is something that will make them fall more in love, not less, especially if it is their first love. In our present world first loves rarely work out, but in the new world there is nothing to prevent a first love from reaching fulfillment. The same thing applies to the many single people who already have had sexual experience. They will search for a person who is ready to have sex with them and one they won't want to hurt; and how is it possible to hurt their partner when all first blows are prevented from arising? When parents raise their children without ever using words that project non-existing values, when children are no longer conditioned by words, when all criticism of our choices for a mate is permanently removed, then you will see a boy and girl get married, that is, have sex (same difference) and live happily ever after.

Would you mind explaining to me why some people are not less educated, are not less intelligent? You yourself used the expression 'unconscious ignorance' in reference to certain people who you say don't have the intellectual capacity. Isn't this a criticism of them; aren't you judging them an inferior production of the human race?

You must bear in mind that I am still living in the old world, and what I have said is a reaction to their attitude towards me. I realize they are moving in the direction of what gives them satisfaction. But so is a burglar who enters my home with a gun. I wouldn't hesitate in defense of my family to put a bullet in his head and I don't hesitate now to criticize the professors who, whether it is because they don't have the intellectual capacity or are unconsciously ignorant of their capacity, are a stumbling block to my bringing this knowledge to light. However, there is a difference between the words intellectual capacity and intelligence. A professor may not have the intellectual capacity to beat Bobby Fischer in a chess game, but that does not mean he is not intelligent, just as Bobby Fischer may not have the intellectual capacity to solve some of the mathematical problems Einstein tackled, but this does not mean Fischer is not intelligent. All of us have different capacities but we are an intelligent race. We don't know everything which means we are ignorant of many things, but the words 'unconscious ignorance' only refers to those who don't know but think they do. As a result of believing that only certain people are intelligent, we have developed words like stupid, dumb, unintelligent and so forth, which words sit in judgment of half the human race as an inferior production. As for the word educated, remember, from the day of our birth we acquire an education. To believe that we are not educated unless we choose to move in a direction that gives others greater satisfaction, judges us to be inferior people. This is why a high school graduate puts down a high school dropout; why a college graduate considers that he has a superior education than one who never went to college; and why professors and Ph.D.s look down on everybody who, in their eyes, didn't accomplish scholastically what they did. But when the word educated is removed from our vocabulary because every human being acquires an education from the time of his birth, but only in a direction of his own choosing, then nobody is put down by what he chooses to do with his time. What he chooses to study or not to study will be his particular education. All mankind become perfectly equal in intrinsic value. God is giving us no choice but to move in this direction for greater satisfaction the very moment we know that to continue using these words is a hurt that not only cannot be justified but for which there will be no blame. Can't you see now why the leaders of the establishment must react against this work when they realize that they are not a superior production of the human race? Don't you think Miss America will find it difficult to believe that she is not more beautiful than the Wicked Witch? Can a professor believe that he is not more educated than someone who never completed the 7th grade? Can a professor believe that he is not more intelligent than someone who can't understand why 3 is to 6 what 4 is to 8? These people in our present world are judged superior human beings only because of words, nothing else. They are not and never have been superior human beings because all of us are perfectly equal in intrinsic value, although most of us have different physical and intellectual capacities. Because of these words, half the human race was treated with disrespect but now, for the very first time, all of us deserve and will be treated with respect which heretofore has been denied.

I am hoping that when I am no longer here, those who understand these principles will continue to carry the ball. It is important to understand that my prediction of 25 years or that this great change would take place in the 20th century was based on my conviction that there would be a thorough investigation and understanding of the principles involved, but as yet it has not been. In other words, if Gregor Mendel had predicted that his discovery about heredity would come to light approximately 30 years after his death, he would have been accurate, but he had no way of knowing when it would be confirmed by science. He knew it was coming, but could not know when. In my case, however, I was allowing 5-10 years for this knowledge to be understood by science and the political world, taking for granted that the intellectual capacity was available and would thoroughly investigate what could not be denied. I still believe the intellectual capacity to understand it exists today, but to quote Morrison again, "Now we encounter the stubborn resistance of the human mind which is reluctant to give up fixed ideas. The early Greeks knew the earth was a sphere but it took 2000 years to convince men that this fact is true. New ideas encounter opposition, ridicule and abuse, but truth survives and is verified." Can you see the problem I have with regard to my discovery? If it took 2 thousand years to get the shape of the earth scientifically confirmed so that all mankind would accept it, how long do you think it will take to get this knowledge in my book scientifically confirmed and accepted when 98% of mankind believe that man's will is free and when this belief hermetically seals a door behind which is the discovery that will bring about this Great Transition. However, two things are certain. This discovery must come to light sooner or later because God is giving us no choice in this matter. Until that time, however, every effort must be made to bring this knowledge to light in whatever way possible. With the public's help, there is every reason to believe that the dawning of the Golden Age will take place some time in the 21st century. And when it finally arrives, we will all be here to celebrate the inception of this wonderful new world.

AFTERWORD

This book was not meant to satisfy the connoisseur of style, grammar, punctuation, vocabulary and form in general (I'm quite sure this book has errors when measured by the standards of whether a certain word should have been capitalized, or a comma should have gone here instead of there), but was written primarily to reveal knowledge never before understood. I don't deny that others could have done a better job in explaining this discovery, and their services are still welcome if they can clarify it even more. My job was to make known this discovery, which I have done to the best of my ability. Because the knowledge herein is completely scientific and mathematical (undeniable), as with the simple equation given in the introduction, it should be obvious that if you find yourself in disagreement then there must be something you do not understand. It is for this reason that this work must be studied thoroughly, chapter by chapter, and also why it must be read more than once. When you have read it over at least two times, you will realize that all the problems of human relation have been unquestionably solved. Well, what are you waiting for? I did my part, now you do yours.

If you would like to see the transition get started as quickly as possible, then you will desire to help in disseminating this knowledge. If you will bear in mind that the end of all war must take place just as soon as the leaders of the world understand these principles, then you can help by writing a letter to the President to investigate the knowledge in this book. When he gets enough of these letters, just in case he hasn't already analyzed this knowledge, he will take the necessary steps to begin an investigation. If you cannot reach the President but you would still like to be of assistance, it will be necessary to select several people that you consider as qualified thinkers, with or without a title, so that they can also become part of the chain reaction. Before long it will spread like wildfire right across the entire globe. This knowledge will then become part of every school curriculum, and it won't be but a relatively short period of time that the Golden Age can be officially launched.

When man fully realizes that all evil came into existence out of necessity in his years of development, and out of necessity it will be removed as he comes of age, he will recognize the fantastic wisdom guiding this universe. No longer will man need to blame as a way to solve his problems because the actions that made blame and punishment necessary will be prevented from arising. Our prayers for peace on earth will be answered at long last. The next time you feel like expressing your appreciation or gratitude for this new world, don't thank me for pointing the way because my will is not free. Thank God, for it was His wisdom that has guided us to this Promised Land. And so, my friends, I bid you adieu. If God is willing, perhaps we shall all meet, one day, in the Golden Age.

POSTSCRIPT

As you know, the author passed away in 1991. Had he been alive today he would have done everything in his power to bring this discovery to light, although the odds were stacked against him because those in authority would not have liked such a world unless it came directly from their beliefs and teachings. He said many times that this knowledge belongs to the world. You can help in this effort by bringing this book to the attention of other interested readers who will, in turn, continue to spread the word. As the author expressed, it is only a matter of time before this discovery is understood and recognized for its invaluable contribution to humanity, but your efforts will certainly help speed up the process.

If you would like to become part of our grassroots movement, please feel free to join us at: http://www.facebook.com/DeterminismandConscience. To hear the author read and elaborate on the first chapter of his sixth book: Beyond the Framework of Modern Thought (a condensed version of the same discovery), you may go to our website at: http://www.declineandfallofallevil.com.

Before leaving would you take a few moments to give this book a positive review? The more 5 star ratings that are received, the greater the chances that this discovery will be formally investigated and brought to light.

Thank you.